Aquinas, Ethics, and Philosophy of Religion

INDIANA SERIES IN THE PHILOSOPHY OF RELIGION
MEROLD WESTPHAL, GENERAL EDITOR

Aquinas, Ethics, and Philosophy of Religion
Metaphysics and Practice

Thomas Hibbs

INDIANA UNIVERSITY PRESS
BLOOMINGTON AND INDIANAPOLIS

This book is a publication of

Indiana University Press
601 North Morton Street
Bloomington, IN 47404-3797 USA

http://iupress.indiana.edu

Telephone orders   800-842-6796
Fax orders   812-855-7931
Orders by e-mail   iuporder@indiana.edu

MANUFACTURED IN THE UNITED STATES OF AMERICA

Library of Congress Cataloging-in-Publication Data

Hibbs, Thomas S.
    Aquinas, ethics, and philosophy of religion : metaphysics and practice / Thomas Hibbs.
        p. cm. — (Indiana series in the philosophy of religion)
    Includes bibliographical references and index.
    ISBN 978-0-253-34881-4 (cloth : alk. paper) 1. Thomas, Aquinas, Saint, 1225?–1274. 2. Ethics.
3. Metaphysics. 4. Religion—Philosophy. 5. Virtue. I. Title.
    B765.T54H45 2007
    189′.4—dc22

                                                                    2006034519

1 2 3 4 5   12 11 10 09 08 07

FOR STACEY

In order to degrade the politics of Plato, Aristotle, or Saint Thomas to the rank of "values" among others, a conscientious scholar would first have to show that their claim to be science was unfounded. And that attempt is self-defeating. By the time the would-be critic has penetrated the meaning of metaphysics with sufficient thoroughness to make his criticism weighty, he will have become a metaphysician himself. The attack on metaphysics can be undertaken with a good conscience only from the safe distance of imperfect knowledge.

Eric Voegelin, *The New Science of Politics*

The proper use of techniques, in so far as it can be taught, remains abstract and devoid of necessary influence upon action; and, in so far as it entertains an infallible relation to action, it cannot be taught. The fully determinate and unmistakably effective knowledge of the right use is not science, but prudence; it is acquired, not principally by reading books and taking courses, but by practicing virtue. Whatever is scientific and teachable in the knowledge of use admits of being ignored at the time of action and of remaining without effect upon action. Moreover, the knowledge of the right use, even in so far as it is scientific and teachable, involves difficulties which render unlikely its uninterrupted maintenance and continuous progress. In this respect the science of the proper use of techniques—one function of ethics—resembles metaphysics rather than positive science. Like metaphysics, the science of ethics possesses, in history, the character of a rare and precarious achievement, more threatened by decadence and oblivion than blessed with promise of maintenance and progress.

Yves Simon, *Philosophy of Democratic Government*

Contents

PREFACE: METAPHYSICS AND PRACTICE

Informed by the thought of Thomas Aquinas and prompted by recent developments in Continental and Anglo-American philosophy, this book brings the texts of Aquinas into conversation with contemporary philosophy on the question of the relationship of metaphysics and practice. Why metaphysics and practice? Why not, as Aquinas would rather have put it, metaphysics and ethics? Or even theory and practice?

The particular conjunction of the title evinces the goal of bringing the metaphysical dimension of Aquinas's thought into dialogue with one of the most striking developments in contemporary philosophy, the revival of the primacy of practice in the fields of ethics and epistemology. The recovery of practice is intimately connected with the turn to virtue in both fields. In ethics and epistemology, virtue is an alternative to decision-procedure models of action and rationality. Decision-procedure models accentuate universality, impersonality, and pure rationality. These models have come under fire for being inappropriately theoretical and for conceiving of moral actions or acts of knowing as discrete entities or events abstracted from concrete conditions and isolated from ongoing commitments and habits in the human agent. By contrast, virtue ethics affirms the primacy of prudence, a non-rule-governed capacity of apprehension, articulation, discrimination, judgment, and action. Prudence supplies what a decision procedure cannot—a capacity to recognize and act in accord with what is salient in the concrete, singular conditions of human action. Similarly, in epistemology, a virtue approach focuses on the complex set of virtues, cognitive and affective, that are operative in the quest for knowledge in a variety of everyday contexts—from scientific experiments to the solving of murder mysteries. Instead of the maximization of discrete acts of knowledge without regard to what is known or how the knowledge is possessed by the inquirer, virtue epistemology makes qualitative distinctions among the objects of knowledge and attends to the way in which one holds the knowledge; for example, the extent to which the various parts of what one knows are integrated with one another. Furthermore, virtuous practice highlights the social conditions of knowledge and action in ways foreign to the decision-procedure models.

Recoiling from the abstract, the theoretical, the universal, and the procedural, the partisans of practice are often also in flight from metaphysics, which is seen, at best, as a distraction from the order of practice, and at worst, as an obstacle to its recovery, as a mode of thought afflicted with the same vices as those haunting decision-procedure models of rationality.

How ought one to respond to the dismissive scorn with which metaphysics is treated in contemporary philosophy? This is a particularly vexing question for those who have embraced and encouraged the contemporary revival of premodern philosophers such as Aristotle and Aquinas, often as contributors to the articulation of the primacy of practice in ethics. Both Aristotle and Aquinas distinguish between theory and practice, metaphysics and ethics; but the exclusive focus on practice and ethics cannot but give us a truncated and distorted picture of their thought. The most pointed rejoinder is to put into question the notion that virtue and practice can function adequately without any recourse whatsoever to abstraction, universality, or theory. Some of the flaws in virtue ethics—for example, its silence on matters of justice and, more broadly, on politics itself—may well be rooted in an excessive aversion to procedure and theory. Moreover, contemporary attempts to recover virtuous practice often find themselves unwittingly on the horizon of metaphysics, for example, in the implicit adoption of a normative philosophical anthropology of the virtues, or in the discrimination of better and worse objects of knowledge or more or less virtuous ways of engaging in inquiry. The inevitability of metaphysics, even in those most devoted to practice, confirms the Aristotelian and Thomistic suspicion that an authentic practical philosophy cannot postpone metaphysics indefinitely.

Not long ago, ancient and medieval philosophers were thought to have little or nothing to offer to the fields of ethics or epistemology. That is hardly the case today. The same philosophical myopia and impoverished historical imagination that led to the repudiation of nearly the entire history of philosophy now inform the dismissal of metaphysics. Greater erudition and more careful exegesis can enhance our understanding of metaphysics as they have already begun to improve our inquiries into ethics and epistemology. Indeed, the recent rehabilitation of the classical conception of philosophy as a way of life, anchored in the practice of moral and intellectual virtue, suggests that the contemporary penchant for seeing metaphysics as alien to, and as alienating agents from, ordinary practice is itself a contemporary dogma. How else could the ancient philosophical schools of antiquity, which embody the notion of philosophy as a way of life, have consistently regarded metaphysics as the culminating discourse of philosophy?

Contemporary approaches to metaphysics are typically vague and sweeping. They rarely take the time to specify precisely how the term is being used or to describe in any detail its subject matter, its scope, its methods, or its limits. A compelling case has been made in recent years that there is no single conception of the ethical or of human knowledge, but only multiple, divergent, and contending accounts. Aquinas, for example, inherits a specific conception of metaphysics from Aristotle. In this tradition, metaphysics is described variously as an inquiry into being insofar as it is being (*ens inquantum ens*), as first philosophy, and as theology. Of course, metaphysics involves abstraction; it could not be ranked among the speculative sciences if it did not. But the very grammar of *ens inquantum ens* indicates that it is a common investigation of what is true, not of abstractions, but of each concretely existing being (*ens*).

Although metaphysics itself is one mode of inquiry among others, it contains within its purview all that is. It thus exhibits an orientation to the whole and to the place of partial inquiries within the entire circuit of human knowledge. It is also first philosophy, but not in the temporal sense; in fact, it is the last science to be studied in the order of philosophical pedagogy. The order of learning is inversely related to the order of being. What we study first is what is most obvious to us, sensible substances, examined in physics; after the study of the soul, ethics, and politics comes metaphysics. Metaphysics is first, rather, in the order of being because it studies the principles underlying the other sciences and the first causes of all that exists. Since, for Aristotle, the first and most noble causes include the separate substances and God, metaphysics is also called theology. But this can be misleading, especially in contemporary Continental circles where onto-theology, the englobing of the divine within a common study of being, is a sort of heresy. But this accusation misses Aquinas's Aristotelian sense of the proper subject matter and goal of a science. In this case, God is not part of the subject matter of metaphysics; the divine enters into metaphysics only as cause of the subject matter, not as an object of inquiry in its own right.

If contemporary pictures of metaphysics lack historical and conceptual precision, they are also often narrow and positivistic. There is an instructive isomorphism here. Metaphysics as described by contemporary philosophers stands to the actual history of metaphysics in much the same relation as does metaphysics, as it is currently construed, to the concrete order of practice. What is lost, say, in the case of Aquinas's metaphysics, amid contemporary abstractions is the erotic appeal of metaphysics and its pervasive deployment of aesthetic language. Metaphysics is rooted in the natural human desire to know, the longing to behold and participate in the beautiful, to find one's place within, and to conceive all one's activities in relation to, the whole. Metaphysics is at once about being, truth, goodness, and beauty. Moreover, Aquinas distinguishes between metaphysics in its original sense, as a part of philosophy, and metaphysics as part of theology. In the latter sense, metaphysics is an ancillary discipline to theology; its principles at once aid in the articulation of theological claims and are also considerably deepened by the more penetrating insights into being provided by revealed truth. Theological teachings concerning the Trinity, creation as the bestowal of the gift of being, and the primacy of the virtue of charity cannot but transform our understanding of how metaphysics is related to practice.

In this way, Aquinas offers a distinctively theological contribution to a set of debates over the relationship of theory to practice, contemplation to action.

The central difficulty (*aporia*) in Aristotle's texts, a question addressed with great subtlety in *Ethics* and *Politics*, concerns the contest over the best way of life, the chief contenders for which are contemplation and action. If, in terms of the objects it investigates and its mode of operation, theory is higher than prudence, in another sense, prudence is regulative, since prudence determines how various activities, both theoretical and practical, are to be woven into a unified human life. The question of the best way of life is preeminently a question of practice, a question of how we ought to live. In this respect, one can speak of the primacy of practice. There is another way of framing the question of the relationship of metaphysics to practice. It concerns the construal of metaphysics as the fundamental inquiry of the theoretical life as a practice itself, as constituted by the activities of intellectual virtues. One of Aquinas's tasks is to tease out the various senses of theory and practice in Aristotle's texts.

Such considerations, both in philosophy and theology, have a direct bearing on the relationship of metaphysics to practice. The goal of the present study is not simply to render Aquinas acceptable to contemporary philosophy by illustrating how he might contribute to ongoing debates, as if the only reason to read Aquinas were because he might reinforce or extend or refine what we already think. In fact, contemporary questions and debates can help open up avenues to Aquinas that would otherwise remain unexplored. But such an inquiry should remain attentive to what Aquinas can teach us, not just concerning this or that current problem, but in the sense that he can help us to put our most basic philosophical assumptions into question. In the case of the nature of metaphysics and its relation to practice, he can do precisely this.

The topical or thematic approach adopted in this book cannot pretend to offer a comprehensive examination of all relevant issues or texts. The book makes no claim to cover all the relevant texts of Aquinas, or to supply an exhaustive treatment of the vast secondary literature on Aquinas, or to have included all the germane contemporary philosophical literature. In each case, primary and secondary texts, as well as contemporary philosophical debates and lines of investigation, have been selected with a view to the goal of the book: to articulate, by way of select contemporary debates, Aquinas's understanding of the relationship of metaphysics to practice.

ACKNOWLEDGMENTS

Some of the material in this book is revised and amplified from previous publications: "Aquinas, Virtue, and Recent Epistemology," *Review of Metaphysics* 52 (1999): 573–94; "Calvin and Hobbes: The Revival of Christian Philosophy" appeared in *The Weekly Standard*, December 24, 2001; "Kretzmann's Theism vs. Aquinas's Theism: Interpreting the *Summa contra Gentiles*," *The Thomist* 62 (1998): 603–22; "Portraits of the Artist: Joyce, Nietzsche, and Aquinas," in *Beauty, Art, and the Polis*, ed. Alice Ramos (Catholic University of America Press, 2000), 117–37; and "Review of *The Metaphysics of Creation: Aquinas's Natural Theology in Summa Contra Gentiles II*," in *The Thomist* 64 (2000): 309–13. I am grateful to these journals for allowing republication of revised material from these essays.

The remote origins of the thinking for this book date all the way back to my undergraduate days at the University of Dallas, where I was fortunate to study under such distinguished Thomists as Mark Jordan and Frederick Wilhelmsen. Less remote promptings came from conversations—both in person and through their published works—with Alasdair MacIntyre, Ralph McInerny, John O'Callaghan, and David Solomon.

While some of the material for this book was composed during my time in the philosophy department at Boston College, the idea for the book and the bulk of the writing occurred during my first two years as Dean of the Honors College at Baylor University. Those were turbulent years at Baylor but still remarkably productive, both in terms of the success we had in building a new Honors College and in terms of my own writing. I could not have succeeded in either arena were it not for the encouragement and example of two of the finest Christian scholars and administrators I have ever encountered: then president Robert Sloan, and then provost David Jeffrey. David, in particular, regularly encouraged the continuation of my scholarly work. Of course, behind every moderately sane administrator stands an indefatigable staff. I want to express particular gratitude to Paulette Edwards, the administrative assistant for the Honors College, whose organizational skills and devotion to the common good enable the Honors College to flourish and me the luxury of time for research and teaching.

The manuscript itself profited from the helpful comments of Matthew Levering and from the best of sympathetic yet critical readers for Indiana

University Press: Graham McAleer and Merold Westphal, the latter of whom is the general editor of the Indiana Series in the Philosophy of Religion. I am also grateful to Elizabeth Yoder for providing an astute eye in the stage of copyediting and to Miki Bird at Indiana University Press for assistance along the way. Dee Mortensen at Indiana University Press provided helpful comments as well as genial and good-spirited stewardship of the project at every stage.

The final word of thanks goes to my wife, Stacey, who in tough moments in our marriage has occasionally and only half in jest reminded me of the Rolling Stones song, "You Can't Always Get What You Want." Marriage, at times a harsh school, is about getting what you need and ultimately giving what is needed to spouse and children. Wendell Berry writes that fidelity is meant to preserve the "possibility of devotion against the distractions of novelty," to prepare for the return of moments when "what we have chosen and what we desire are the same." As we begin our twentieth year of marriage, I am grateful to say that those moments are, if not continuous, then nearly so, particularly when it comes to our common task of raising Lauren, Daniel, and Sara. Sanctification of the natural and the ordinary is, according to St. Thomas, what life is all about. In that task, we require, as instruments of grace, community, friendship, and examples. To our familial community and beyond, Stacey supplies all these.

To Stacey, who helps make possible and enjoyable things much more important than the writing of scholarly tomes, I dedicate whatever there is here of a book.

Aquinas, Ethics, and
Philosophy of Religion

one
Ethics as a Guide
into Metaphysics

James Joyce once quipped, "The difficulty about Aquinas is that what he says is so like what the man in the street says." And in response to a friend's derisive comment that Aquinas "has nothing to do with us," he stated, "It has everything to do with us."[1]

Joyce was schooled in the works of old Aquinas. As William T. Noon demonstrated some years ago in his *Joyce and Aquinas*, Thomistic themes pervade Joyce's corpus, particularly in *Portrait of the Artist as a Young Man* and *Ulysses*.[2] In the midst of the cascade of recent studies of Joyce, there has been a quiet resurgence of interest in the affinities between Joyce and premodern philosophy.[3] As we shall argue in some detail toward the end of this study, Joyce had a remarkably penetrating understanding of certain features of Aquinas's thought. The use and (deliberate?) misuse of Aquinas in Stephen Dedalus's discussions of beauty in *Portrait of the Artist* are well known. But Joyce also exhibits a sophisticated grasp of Aquinas's Trinitarian theology and its metaphysical and ethical implications, as is clear from *Ulysses*.[4] Conversely, in what he attacks, Joyce opens up the possibility of a recovery of certain strains of premodern thought: the criticisms of symbolist conceptions of art, the roman-

1

tic celebration of the autonomous creativity of the artist, the modern supposition of the transparency of the self to itself, and the voluntarism he encountered both in modern philosophy and in strains of Jesuit theology. All of these issues in Joyce—what he rejects and what he at least implicitly affirms—are allied to his affirmation of the primacy of myth, an affirmation that is most apparent in the use of the Homeric tale of Odysseus in *Ulysses*.

Now, Aquinas is no weaver of tales; indeed, some critics see him as a forerunner of modern rationalism. So, for example, Eric Voegelin objects to Aquinas's metaphysics precisely on the ground that it "ossifies it into a propositional science of principles, universals, and substances."[5] But this assessment, as we shall see in ample detail in the course of our study, involves a very selective reading of Aquinas's metaphysics.[6] It omits, for example, his notion of reason as participant in an order that encompasses it and exceeds its grasp; the prominent role of erotic and aesthetic discourse throughout his metaphysics; the intimate connection, in his theology, between the Trinity as exemplar of human action and the development of a social ontology of individuals-in-relation; and the construal of ethics itself as a mimetic practice. A number of these themes can be brought to the fore by a careful reading of the way Aquinas functions in Joyce's novels. None of this implies that Joyce embraces Aquinas's conclusions or, where he does embrace some, that he deploys them for the same ends as Aquinas. Just how far that takes us in the direction of Aquinas is certainly open to debate, and nothing in the exposition of Aquinas that follows hangs on an interpretation of Joyce as interpreter of Aquinas. Indeed, I will argue that Joyce's texts embody tensions, even debates, between rival conceptions of human agency, rationality, and narrative (dis)unity, only one of which can be traced to Aquinas. Whether Joyce can in any meaningful sense affirm the primacy of myth merely as a human construct, void of any metaphysical commitments, is itself a serious question.

One thing is clear. Joyce aims to capture a nonreductionist account of the ordinary. His famed biographer Richard Ellmann puts it succinctly: "The initial and determining act of judgment in his work is the justification of the commonplace. . . . Joyce's discovery . . . was that the ordinary is the extraordinary."[7] Ellmann's comments overlap nicely with Joyce's own sympathies toward Aquinas as expressed in the opening quotations. Of course, the recovery of the ordinary has been at the heart of an influential movement in philosophy at least since Wittgenstein. The problem with aligning Aquinas with this movement is its antipathy toward metaphysics. Stanley Cavell, a noted proponent of the return to the ordinary, contrasts metaphysics, understood as a "demand for the absolute," with the "ordinary or the everyday."[8]

Part of my thesis, following out the Joycean suggestion of Aquinas's fidelity to the "man in the street," is that Aquinas develops a metaphysics that provides the fertile backdrop to ethical practice, a metaphysics that demands only as much precision as the subject matter allows, to quote Aristotle, and that culminates, not in exhaustive certitude, but in a deepening sense of the mystery of things. Cavell identifies metaphysics as the "search for an order or a system or a language that would secure a human settlement with the world that goes beyond human sense and certainty."[9] In this description, Cavell's opposition of metaphysics to the ordinary shares something in common with Charles Taylor's worries over appeals to transcendent goods. The appeal to "hyper-goods," as Taylor calls them, can do damage to the rich complexity and contingency of the human good.[10] Aquinas, as we shall see, has a pretty sophisticated response to these concerns; indeed, he shares them.[11]

Aquinas would not allow himself to be put in the position of having to defend the introduction of alien metaphysical issues into our articulation of the ordinary. He would argue that the starting points of metaphysical discourse are already embedded within the ordinary. The perception of the extraordinary revealed in the ordinary draws the human person into an order that encompasses and transcends the human but without any claim to peremptory understanding or a comprehensive grasp. At least one contemporary author—both philosopher and novelist—has made this point rather forcefully. In her essay "Against Dryness" (published in 1961), Iris Murdoch urges, "Philosophy is not in fact at present able to offer us any . . . complete and powerful picture of the soul." In Anglo-American philosophy, the dominant conception of the person consists in "the joining of a materialistic behaviorism with a dramatic view of the individual as a solitary will." In French philosophy as well, there is a penchant for depicting the individual as "solitary and totally free. There is no transcendent reality, there are no degrees of freedom." At its noblest, contemporary moral philosophy celebrates the "brave naked will" of the moral agent, exalts choice at the expense of vision, substitutes a "facile idea of sincerity" for the "hard idea of truth," and leaves us with a desiccated "moral and political vocabulary."[12]

There are, of course, numerous questions to be raised about Murdoch's portrayal of modern philosophical positions, but there is no doubt that her dissection of moral philosophy's midcentury afflictions has proven remarkably prescient. The burgeoning field of virtue ethics rests largely on dissatisfaction with the accounts of human agency offered in twentieth-century Kantian and utilitarian ethics. In "Vision and Choice in Morality," Murdoch states that, in twentieth-century moral philosophy, "the moral life of the individual" is seen as "a series of overt choices which take place in a series of specifiable situations."[13] This view has its "charms." It "displays the moral agent as rational and responsible and also as free; he moves unhindered against a background of facts and can alter the descriptive meaning of his moral words at will." The rational freedom of the individual agent consists largely in the agent's disconnection, in the moment of choice, from passion or feeling, the nonrational components of human nature, from a community, and from previous or subsequent choices. The account of human agency is radically individualistic and atomistic. What seems a liberation is, according to Murdoch, a deprivation:

> What have we lost here? We have suffered a general loss of concepts, the loss of a moral and political vocabulary. We no longer use a spread-out substantial picture of the manifold virtues of man and society. We no longer see man against a background of values, of realities, which transcend him.[14]

The model of human agency operative here is at once abstract and theoretical. It is abstract in the sense that it separates the moment of choice from both the "background" of which Murdoch speaks and the foreground, the awareness of a rich context within which the singular object of choice is embedded. It is theoretical in that its model of practical rationality rests on paradigms of scientific or technical reasoning; it involves what the contemporary moral philosopher Joel Kupperman calls a "decision procedure."[15] What is missing is a sense of ethics as practice, involving virtues of perception, articulation, deliberation, and judgment.

In a number of ways, Murdoch anticipates the recovery of virtue and practice—indeed, of the practice of virtue—in a variety of fields in analytic philosophy, even as she echoes Continental worries about what Voegelin calls the "ossification" of understanding into mere propositional analysis. In ethics, there has in recent years been a turn from abstract decision-procedure models of practical reasoning to the concrete conditions of practice, in which non-rule-governed virtues of perception, articulation, deliberation, and judgment are prominent. A similar shift has occurred in epistemology, where virtue epistemology urges a retreat from the abstract and punctual analysis of isolated states of knowing and a movement toward the practice of a complex set of intellectual and moral virtues characteristic of the cognitive lives of those we admire for understanding or wisdom. The dominant twentieth-century models of epistemology stress isolated acts of knowledge, seek a quantitative maximization of true propositions through the following of reliable rules of belief formation, and focus more on avoiding blame in one's cognitive activities than on "achieving moral praiseworthiness." By contrast, contemporary virtue epistemology stresses the interconnectedness and continuity of our cognitive states, the importance of habits of inquiry; it focuses more on the quality of the things known than on the mere assembling of a set of true propositions; and it eschews the notion that knowledge or wisdom could be fully rule governed, and celebrates intellectual excellence.

As gratified as she might be by these developments, Murdoch would point us in the direction of a more complete recovery of ancient philosophy, at least in one respect, concerning the relationship of metaphysics to ethical practice, which remains an underappreciated issue in her project. In almost complete isolation from her contemporaries, Murdoch held that the aridity of ethical discourse, its impoverished conception of human agency, was due in part to the severing of the ties between ethics and metaphysics.[16] Contrary to the common philosophical assumption that metaphysics involves a retreat from common experience to a world of quasi-mathematical abstraction, Murdoch urges that the "elimination of metaphysics from ethics" is at odds with our ordinary experience of the world. Furthermore, its elimination deprives philosophers of the resources needed to offer a rich and nuanced account of human agency. She urges that contemporary philosophy presents us with a "stripped and empty scene." Morality is depicted "without any transcendent background. It is depicted simply in terms of exhortations and choices defended by reference to facts." One of the first to rail against the dogma of fact-value dichotomy, Murdoch asks, "[Why] can morality not be thought as attached to the substance of the world? Surely many people who are not philosophers and who cannot be accused of using faulty arguments since they use no arguments, do think of their morality in just this way?" On this alternative and historically dominant view—a view shared by "Thomists, Hegelians, and Marxists"—

> the individual is seen as held in a framework which transcends him, where what is important and valuable is the framework. . . .To discover what is morally good is to discover that reality, and to become good is to integrate himself with it. He is ruled by laws that he can only partly understand. He is not fully conscious of what he is. His freedom is not an open freedom of choice in a clear situation; it lies rather in an increasing knowledge of his own real being, and in the conduct which naturally springs from such knowledge.[17]

Although Murdoch gestures in the direction of metaphysics (recall the title of her Gifford lectures, Metaphysics as a Guide to Morals), she never develops a specific metaphysics.

One of the most noteworthy alterations in the landscape of Anglo-American philosophy is the flourishing of philosophy of religion, another development that Murdoch may well have applauded. One of the striking features of this development is how often philosophers of religion have come to the defense of the perspective of the ordinary human being. The common sense philosopher Thomas Reid figures prominently in these discussions, as, on occasion, does Aquinas. In this tradition of philosophy of religion, openness to the transcendent is woven into the fabric of ordinary human experience. The revival of philosophy of religion is not limited to analytic philosophy; it is now a burgeoning field within Continental philosophy as well.[18] As divergent as these two approaches are, they share a certain diffidence, in some cases hostility, toward metaphysics. Analytic thinkers generally suppose that ordinary language, without the intervention of metaphysics, has sufficient resources for philosophers to examine religion; whereas Continental philosophers, still under the influence of Heidegger and Derrida, continue their project of overcoming or deconstructing metaphysics as a kind of idol. It is perhaps not too much of a generalization to say that in both analytic and Continental circles, metaphysics is often set against practice, the practice of ordinary speech in analytic contexts and ethical or religious practice in Continental conversations.[19]

The present study is an attempt to reopen the question of the relationship of metaphysics and practice, although not always in a manner that would please Murdoch or contemporary philosophers of religion.[20] The focus is on the relationship of metaphysics to practice or on metaphysics itself as a form of practice and particularly on the articulation of that relationship in the writings of Thomas Aquinas.[21] In the opening half of the book, I examine the recovery of practice in ethics and epistemology and suggest ways in which contemporary conversations already border on metaphysics; indeed, a number of questions in ethics and epistemology point in the direction of what Elizabeth Anscombe calls "philosophical psychology" and thus toward metaphysics. Aquinas already figures in many of these conversations. I attempt to develop further the possible contributions of Aquinas to the contemporary recovery of virtue and practice. In the second half of the book, I consider metaphysics itself and how it might be seen as integrated into practice or as constituting a practice. Here it will be important to see the multiple ways in which metaphysics functions in Aquinas: first, as culminating inquiry of philosophical discourse, which begins and ends in wonder; and second, as a subordinate science within theology, where it provides a vocabulary that the theologian reworks in order to stress the journey of the human soul to God, a journey that must be especially wary of the various temptations to idolatry, particularly to forms of conceptual idolatry to which philosophers are especially prone.

If the opening section takes its bearings primarily, although certainly not exclusively, from contemporary debates in analytic philosophy, the subsequent section is informed largely by debates in contemporary Continental philosophy of religion, particularly those prompted by Jean-Luc Marion's writings on metaphysics, idolatry, and the divine.[22] At the center of Marion's writings is a highly suggestive, if controversial, argument for the overcoming of metaphysics by a certain sort of praxis, the praxis of praise, rooted in receptivity to the Gift.[23] Objections, some of which Aquinas would share, to Marion's project have focused on its ethical implications, on whether his elevation of "confused bedazzlement" does not undermine the possibility of ethical discourse. I propose a modified account of the relationship between metaphysics and ethics, wherein the metaphysics of the Gift is complemented by the practice of what Alasdair MacIntyre, following Aquinas, calls "just generosity" (*misericordia*).

As both Marion and MacIntyre note, Aquinas works out of an inherited tradition of philosophical and theological reflection, one that had much to say about metaphysics and practice. Although the influences on Aquinas's thought are numerous, there is no question that on the topic of the relationship of metaphysics to practice or even on the nature of practice itself, Thomas is preoccupied with a set of difficulties, knots, problems (*aporiae*) that he inherits from the texts of Aristotle. Before turning to contemporary debates and Aquinas's place within them, it might help to have a sense of these questions as Aquinas sees them in the texts of Aristotle.[24] The primacy of practice in Aristotle's early discussion of the good life in the *Ethics* is evident in his frequent claim that the virtues are inculcated in the same way as skills in crafts, that is, by repetitious action. It is, Aristotle insists, "by doing just acts that the just man is produced," not by taking "refuge in theory."[25] Practice, in the broad sense of engaging in a related and organized set of activities with the goal of inculcating appropriate skills or virtues, is pervasively operative in Aristotle and Aquinas, who repeatedly compare the development of ethical virtue to the way novices become skilled in various crafts. The contemporary philosopher most associated with practice as a framework for ethical life and theory is Alasdair MacIntyre. In *After Virtue,* he defines a "practice" as

> any coherent and complex form of socially established cooperative human activity through which goods internal to that form of activity are realized in the course of trying to achieve those standards of excellence which are appropriate to, and partially definitive of, that form of activity, with the result that human powers to achieve excellence, and human conceptions of the ends and goods involved, are systematically extended.[26]

In his reading of Aristotle and Aquinas, MacIntyre focuses on the pervasive use each thinker makes of craft analogies. He observes that "to become adept in a craft . . . , one has to learn how to apply" a distinction "between what as activity or product merely seems good to me and what really is good, a distinction always applied retrospectively as part of learning from one's earlier mistakes and surpassing one's earlier limitations."[27] The notion of craft pedagogy as moving the initiate from an imperfect and distorted understanding to greater understanding involves active engagement with the practices internal to the craft under the tutelage of a master of the craft. Yet the standards of excellence internal to the craft are "rarely fixed once and for all." A craft in good order would bear the history of the development of its practices to this point in time; it would be an "embodied tradition." The more complex the practice or set of practices in which one is engaged, the greater the need for a historical sense, "an ability to recognize in the past what is and what is not a guide to the future."[28] In the course of inquiring not just about the proper ordering of and participation in a single craft but in a number of crafts or practices or inquiries, each individual and community will encounter a series of questions about the integration and ordering of the practices. Individuals face questions regarding the unity of their lives, while communities face issues concerning the complex ways in which their practices embody the common good. According to MacIntyre, these questions will be both theoretical and practical: "There is . . . no form of philosophical enquiry . . . that is not practical in its implications, just as there is no practical enquiry that is not philosophical in its presuppositions."[29] We shall have occasion, as we proceed in our study, to tease out and examine critically MacIntyre's rather compressed assertions about virtue, practice, tradition, and the relationship between theory and practice. For now, it suffices to note their significance.

In his distance from metaphysics, MacIntyre is typical of contemporary philosophers, especially those committed to a revival of the primacy of practice.[30] Once again, we confront the supposition of a dichotomy between metaphysics or the life of *theoria* or *contemplatio* and *phronesis* or *prudentia*. Yet the relationship between these two might be said to constitute the central and unifying theme in Aristotle's philosophy. In his discussion in the *Politics* of the best regime, Aristotle returns to the central topic of the *Ethics*, the "most eligible way of life," and argues against those who dismiss contemplation. They do so on the assumption that "he who does nothing cannot do well." Aristotle concurs that we should not elevate "inactivity above action, for happiness is activity."[31] He proceeds to argue that contemplation is "practical" in the sense that it involves activities or practices.

Following Aristotle, Aquinas defines contemplation as an activity—indeed, as the highest type of activity. What is little noticed is that Aquinas's depiction of contemplation as an activity entails (a) that speculative activities must be conceived in terms of practices involving a set of virtues, and (b) that as one activity among many others in which human beings engage, speculative activities must be integrated by prudential judgment into other activities. Another way to put this is to say that the entirety of human life, each of the activities in which human beings engage, falls under the direction and command of prudence. Of course, prudence will be informed by, and in certain cases be ordered to, the teachings and practices of theory. But theory cannot directly determine action.

The similarities and tensions between theory and practice emerge even in Aristotle's various discussions of the sapiential task of ordering disciplines, inquiries, and activities. In the opening of the *Metaphysics*, Aristotle argues that first philosophy, or metaphysics, is the highest part of philosophy because it pursues knowledge of the highest principles and causes, knowledge to which all other inquiries are ordered.[32] In the opening of the *Ethics*, he describes politics as the architectonic art because it falls to politics to order all human activities to the end or good of the entire community.[33] While maintaining a distinction between theoretical and practical activities of the intellect, Aquinas frames his entire discussion of the good life in terms of the craft analogy, which highlights the communal pursuit of excellences embedded within practices. Among all arts and inquiries, wisdom is the one that orders other arts to the human good.[34] The prominence and preeminence of this way of framing the question of the human good means that practice, at least in one important sense, is more fundamental than theory. If theoretical contemplation is to be considered the highest activity, it will be so only in light of a conception of excellence internal to the notion of practice.

Of course, how we are to construe the relationship between metaphysics and practice depends crucially on how we understand practice and metaphysics. We have offered some introductory observations about practice, but what of metaphysics? As Stanley Rosen observes, any informed attempt to answer the question "What is metaphysics?" will quickly "dissolve into endless historical analyses" of the "many different types of metaphysics." We can "say nothing serious" about metaphysics "unless we engage in it" ourselves.[35] Or, as Voegelin puts it, "By the time the would-be critic [of metaphysics] has penetrated the meaning of metaphysics with sufficient thoroughness to make his criticism weighty, he will have become a metaphysician himself. The attack on metaphysics can be undertaken with a good conscience only from the safe distance of imperfect knowledge."[36] How does Aquinas understand and practice metaphysics?[37]

Metaphysics, for Aquinas, can be described in a number of ways, the initial formulations of which appear in Aristotle. First, metaphysics is the study of being, or more precisely, of *ens inquantum ens*, the common yet concrete inquiry to the attributes of everything that is, insofar as it is. Metaphysics is one science among many; it does not supplant the particular sciences such as physics, the study of the soul, or mathematics. But it does offer an inquiry, never directly pursued in any of the particular sciences, of what is common to, and presupposed in, the specific sciences. How do we know there is such a science beyond the others? That is a serious, contested question even within the text of Aristotle himself, who repeatedly speaks of the "science we are seeking." One foundational sign that there is such a science is that, in the midst of some other inquiries such as physics or the study of the principles of animate life, Aristotle proves the existence of activities, faculties, and beings whose natures are not reducible to matter. But the scope of the other sciences never exceeds material composites of matter and form. As Aristotle bluntly puts it in the *Metaphysics*, if there were no immaterial entities, physics would be first philosophy.[38] Since there are such entities, there is the possibility of another science of being, more universal than physics, which studies the attributes accruing to all things, material and nonmaterial, and their ultimate principles and causes. In this way, metaphysics is a comprehensive science. Yet it does not operate at a higher level of abstraction; indeed, mathematics and logic are more abstract than is metaphysics.

Second, metaphysics is called first philosophy, an ordering that indicates the priority of metaphysics to all the other sciences. But this is not a temporal priority. Instead, it signifies a priority in the order of being or the nature of things. According to the dialectical realism of Aquinas and Aristotle, what is first in the order of learning or discovery is last in the order of being. We move from effects to causes; we begin from what is most obvious to us and proceed to that which is first in the order of being. Although in specific sciences, say geometry or physics, we begin from principles that are first with respect to that science, we do not yet have in our possession the fundamental principles of all being. Metaphysics offers a dialectical examination of these principles; it cannot offer demonstrative proofs of those things underlying all proof. But it does move from these most common principles in search of the highest and most fundamental causes of all things.

Third, metaphysics is called divine science, or theology, because it reaches separate substances and ultimately the unmoved mover, called God, as principle and cause of the whole. Lest we think Aquinas or Aristotle guilty of ontotheology, the offense of idolatrously englobing God within metaphysics, of including God within the same scale of discourse as that of creatures, we should note immediately that God is not part of the subject matter of metaphysics. God enters into metaphysics only indirectly and in its culminating moment, not as part of its proper subject matter, but as cause or source of the subject matter. Although there are analogies between things in the universe and God, Aristotle stresses the gap between the two and repeatedly, in his reflection on the divine life, comments on how our attempt to think about that life inspires wonder in us. Metaphysics thus begins and ends in wonder, an avowal of human ignorance about the highest things. In that sense, the quest for foundations remains unfulfilled. In his engagement of philosophy, Aquinas highlights both the achievements and limitations of philosophical discourse about the highest things; in fact, the limitations are most evident and most deeply felt precisely at the moment of its greatest achievement, knowledge of God.

For Aquinas, this presents the possibility of a theological engagement of Aristotle, since philosophy is aware of that which exceeds its comprehension; indeed, the very *telos* of its inquiry escapes its grasp. Metaphysics, which embodies the natural longing (the human *eros*) for truth and beauty, can thus be brought into conversation with that which transcends it. Theology, in turn, can make use of metaphysics in its own inquiries, just as all higher sciences deploy resources from lower sciences in their investigations. There is an important distinction here. On the one hand, we have a theological moment within metaphysics—its final moment, which reaches God as unmoved mover and final cause of all motion in the universe. On the other, we have metaphysical theology, which operates not within metaphysics but within the ambit of revealed theology. For Aquinas, theology, which has under its purview all things in relation to God, is an even higher mode of inquiry than that of metaphysics. Its superiority is evident not just in the capaciousness of what it studies but also in its mode of operation in human beings. Unlike speculative metaphysics, which aims exclusively at knowledge, theology aims both at knowledge and action, since its goal is the perfection of the human agent in relation to the highest good, union with God.[39]

For Aquinas, then, ethics, the quest for the good life for human beings, is a guide into metaphysics; conversely, metaphysics, at least as it operates within theological practice, is itself a guide to ethics, since it involves a participation in the life of the exemplary cause of the whole.

The inclusion of practice as well as theory within the scope of theology has little to do with a new pragmatism or some sort of Christian utilitarianism; instead, it arises from the very nature of theological discourse as a participation in, and reflection of, God's own knowledge. "Sacred doctrine," Aquinas writes, "comprehends both" theory and practice, "just as God, in the same knowledge, knows both Himself and what He does." The implicit use of the Platonic language of divine exemplarity and participation becomes explicit and expansive in other parts of his theology.[40] Taking note of the presence of such language helps to correct a common misunderstanding of metaphysics as practiced by Aquinas. Such a misconception is present, for example, in the writings of Eric Voegelin, who accuses Aquinas of substituting an ossified set of categories and propositions (metaphysics) for the rich empirical experience of a participation in the mystery of being (myth).[41] At least as practiced by the believer, metaphysics is among a number of activities, including preaching and disputation, that arise from a surplus of contemplation, a surplus that always exceeds our ability to articulate it in speech. Theology thus reminds the philosopher of what she is always in danger of forgetting in her aspiration for intellectual self-sufficiency, namely, that the exercise of reason is itself a gift, a participation in an antecedent order of being whose source is a Being who creates from nothing.

The thorough integration of theory and practice, contemplation and action, can be seen in Aquinas's discussion of the role of teaching in the life of Christian wisdom. For Aquinas, teaching arises from a surplus of contemplation, as a fitting gift in response to the apprehension that knowledge itself is a gift. The motto of the Dominican Order, to which Thomas belonged, is *contemplata aliis tradere*, "to hand on to others things contemplated." The accent is less upon self-sufficiency than upon dependency, less upon vision than upon hearing, and less upon autonomous possession than upon receptive humility. Pedagogy once again comes to the fore. In his commentary on Aristotle's *Metaphysics*, Aquinas remarks that the animals who have hearing are "teachable." They can "accustom themselves to do or avoid something by the instruction of another: for such instruction takes place chiefly through hearing."[42] If for Aristotle the ability to teach is a sign of the presence of wisdom, for Aquinas the wise not only can but must teach, in an act of pious gratitude for what they received through hearing the Word of the divine teacher. Thus do the wise take on a public role of proclamation and instruction unknown to Aristotle.

This case is made in ample detail in one of Aquinas's earliest works, his *Inaugural Sermons* (1256), where he reaches back through Augustine to the Roman rhetorical tradition, according to which the gift of speech aims "to teach, to delight, and to change."[43] Aquinas advocates a public role for the teacher of wisdom, a Roman unity of *sapientia et eloquentia*. But both Roman and Greek models undergo decisive alteration in the context of Christian revelation. The human pursuit of wisdom, an aspiration for a kind of autonomous possession of wisdom that ascends in words and thoughts to the first cause and ultimate good, is subject to a dramatic reversal. The Word through whom the whole is made abides as Exemplar of the entire created universe, which is now understood as a series of signs and images pointing beyond itself to its source. Wisdom is not so much an achievement as a receptivity, not so much a property of the philosopher as a participation in that which exceeds all human fathoming. He proceeds to discuss the transforming and instructing power of the Word of God, whose ministers must themselves be transformed into the wisdom of Christ. Such a teacher must first ask for the gift of wisdom by speaking to God in prayer; only then can one teach others: "Illumined by the first beams of divine wisdom," the "holy teachers . . . receive the splendour."[44] This reception of wisdom is a gift that can be sustained only by continued participation in the life of the Giver: "The teachers do not communicate wisdom except as ministers. Hence the fruit . . . is not attributed to them but to the divine works."[45] In this way, the life of wisdom is a matter of consciously and freely becoming a work of divine art. The spiritual life involves mimetic practice, the participation in, and imitation of, the divine life. The "practice of theology," as Torrell describes it, is "an education in the spiritual life."[46]

two
Virtue and Practice

Over the last thirty years, perhaps the most striking alteration in the land-scape of Anglo-American philosophy has occurred in the field of ethics, where the ethics of virtue or character is now taken as seriously as Kantian and utilitarian ethics. Just as there are divisions and branches within those fields of ethics, so too there is an array of different versions in virtue ethics. Indeed, it is difficult to say exactly what virtue ethics is. The problem is not simply the wide variety of positions now located under the generic title *virtue ethics*; rather, it has to do with the way many of those who work on the topic of virtue gloss over the question of what precisely distinguishes virtue ethics from its rivals.

In one of the rare attempts to define virtue ethics, David Solomon suggests that there are two ways in which virtue surfaces in contemporary ethics.[1] First, moral philosophers have shifted some of their attention from abstract concepts like "right," "good," and "ought" to more concrete and descriptive terms, such as "courageous," "temperate," and "sensitive." Second, it is now generally agreed that any comprehensive ethical or political theory must include some account of virtue. But neither of these ways of discussing virtue poses much of a threat to the dominant twentieth-century theories of ethics, namely, Kantian and utilitarian theories. According to Solomon, virtue ethics becomes interesting only when it is construed as an independent and normative account of ethics. By contrast with its chief competitors, a normative virtue theory would treat the assessment of character and the virtues and vices constitutive of character as more fundamental than either the assessment of action and duty, which is basic in Kantian deontology, or the assessment of the value of the consequences of action, which is basic in utilitarianism. Thus understood, virtue ethics would have the task of developing and defending (a) some conception of the ideal person, (b) some list of the virtues necessary to become a person of that type, and (c) some view of how persons can come to possess the relevant virtues.

Solomon worries that without an articulation and defense of its distinctive features, virtue ethics will end up succumbing to its rivals. Thus, he is concerned to expose what he calls the "subordinating strategies" of Kantians and utilitarians who wish to embrace some of the insights of virtue ethics but subsume these within their own, allegedly more comprehensive, theories. Each of these attempts, Solomon holds, fails to give virtue its due.

But how we are to give virtue its due is a matter of tremendous debate, even among those in the virtue camp. Solomon's focus on what differentiates virtue ethics from its rivals suggests an avenue of entry into contemporary virtue ethics; indeed, widespread dissatisfaction with the two dominant ethical theories of the twentieth century precipitated the original turn to virtue in Anglo-American philosophy. To speak with introductory brevity, I would say that what virtue ethics principally objects to in twentieth-century ethics— indeed, in the most influential strains of ethics since the seventeenth century —is the forgetfulness of prudence, its necessity, its nature and scope, and its relationship to a host of other virtues. One of the early and enduring accomplishments of virtue ethics is to have rescued prudence from the clutches of Kantians and utilitarians, who see prudence merely as a clever, calculative skill for securing self-interest or maximizing desired ends.[2]

Instead of prudential assessment, decision procedures come to the fore in modern ethics. Two impulses motivate the aspiration for a system of morality characterized by impersonality, objectivity, and universality: first, a desire to construct a model of justice founded on notions of impartiality and equality; and second, a desire to mimic in morality and politics the rational methods of the sciences. What the decision-procedure model obscures from view are the concrete conditions of practice and the virtues of perception, articulation, and judgment necessary even to apply the decision procedure. In recent years, philosophical ethics has focused increasingly on the perspective of the virtuous agent. In recoiling from procedural accounts of justice and highlighting the limits of objective impartiality, virtue ethics leaves itself open to counterattack. Critics of virtue ethics counter the thesis of the limits of justice with their own accusation concerning the limits of virtue.[3]

Practice, Prudence, and Precepts

The central concerns, themes, and argumentative moves in late-twentieth-century virtue ethics often prompt a return to premodern authors such as Aristotle and Aquinas. In the mid-twentieth century and at the same time that Murdoch was blazing new paths in Anglo-American ethics, the German Thomist Josef Pieper began a series of investigations in the cardinal and theological virtues. His writings on the virtues, found in a variety of his works but especially in his collections entitled *The Four Cardinal Virtues* and *Faith, Hope, Love*, predate the Anglo-American rehabilitation of virtue and anticipate many of the central tenets of virtue ethics.[4] He too focuses on the need to rehabilitate prudence as a corrective. Echoing Garrigou-Lagrange's complaint that theologians had exercised a "quasi-suppression of the treatise on prudence," Pieper argues that a retrieval of prudence is necessary for an authentically Catholic understanding of the ethical life. The casuistical moral theology of the day, with its onerous list of prohibitions, had become a "science of sins instead of a doctrine of virtues, or of a theory of the Christian idea of man."[5] The corrective has especially to do with a reassertion of the primacy of prudence: "The first of the cardinal virtues is not only the quintessence of ethical maturity, but in so being is also the quintessence of moral freedom."[6]

Tracing the attraction of casuistry to the understandable but misplaced desire for "certainty and security," Pieper holds that to overvalue casuistry is to "confound model and reality" and to misunderstand the "meaning and rank of the virtue of prudence."[7] Casuistical guidelines can "never take hold of a real and whole 'here and now' for the reason that only a person really engaged in decision experiences (or least can experience) the concrete situation with its need for concrete action. . . . The guarantee of the goodness of concrete human action is given solely by the virtue of prudence."[8] The virtue of practical wisdom, prudence, is possessed only by the mature and experienced character who has the capacity to discern, deliberate, and judge of concrete singulars. A chief obstacle to recovering prudence is that we now tend to identify the prudent person with the "clever tactician" who devises stratagems to "shun danger" and "avoid commitment."[9] In fact, Aquinas would call this *astutia*, or cunning, the false prudence of the vicious. Since practical reasoning is either assisted or impeded by the passions that sensible singulars arouse in us, prudence requires the proper education and transformation of the passions by the moral virtues.

Thus does Pieper make a claim for the primacy of the virtues in Aquinas and for the recovery of virtue ethics as a salutary corrective to both academic and popular (mis)conceptions of morality. But Pieper's Aquinas offers more than this; it offers a corrective and supplement to contemporary virtue ethics itself, which has failed to be sufficiently ambitious, systematic, and comprehensive in its reflections on ethics. It still lacks what Elizabeth Anscombe called for in her famous essay, namely, an "adequate moral psychology." Parallel to this deficiency is an increasingly embarrassing gap on the question of justice as a virtue.[10] As we shall see in the course of our examination of the achievements of, and limitations to, contemporary virtue ethics, Aquinas's account of justice is capable not just of filling an egregious gap but also of providing a distinctive philosophical psychology.

Most discussions of the history of twentieth-century moral philosophy trace the return of virtue to Elizabeth Anscombe's essay from the late 1950s, "Modern Moral Philosophy."[11] In her apocalyptic attack on Kantian and utilitarian ethical theories, Anscombe criticized contemporary moral philosophy for its incoherent conceptions of obligation, its lack of terminological clarity, and the absence of an adequate philosophical psychology. Given the state of ethical discourse, she concluded that we should "banish ethics totally from our minds." She hinted, but only hinted, at the possibility that an adequate moral philosophy might be resurrected from Aristotle, a suggestion that was to be enthusiastically embraced by later proponents of virtue, most notably by Alasdair MacIntyre in his influential *After Virtue*.[12]

MacIntyre's name has become synonymous with virtue ethics. Yet in many ways his views are atypical of contemporary virtue ethics, since his advocacy of virtue is tied up with his wholesale rejection of modernity and with the thesis that the Enlightenment generates an emotivism that makes all too convincing Nietzsche's interpretation of moral language as the covert expression of the will to power. In the pivotal chapter in *After Virtue*, "Nietzsche or Aristotle?" MacIntyre argues that only something like Aristotle's conception of the virtues can withstand Nietzsche's critique. As idiosyncratic as MacIntyre's history of ethics may be, his dissatisfaction with the dominant modern ethical theories is widely shared by the most interesting and influential proponents of virtue ethics. Just what went wrong in twentieth-century ethics?

Joel Kupperman puts it this way in his book *Character*:

> A great deal of ethical philosophy of the last two hundred years looks both oversimple and overintellectualized . . . philosophers have treated morality as if each of us is a computer which needs a program for deciding moral questions. . . . Ethics . . . in this view is at work only at those discrete moments when an input is registered and the moral decision-procedure is applied.[13]

Kupperman addresses three problems with the decision-procedure model of ethics. First, the "decision-procedure is parasitic upon a classification scheme of features of the world that we are supposed to treat as salient." Input is never neutral or completely obvious; to know what is salient, relevant, significant in our experience requires capacities of perception and articulation that the decision procedure itself cannot provide. Kupperman appeals to the ineliminable role of the agent's sensitivity to the concrete situation. The ability to apply a decision procedure presupposes moral education and experience. This involves more than merely intellectual skills; it involves the cultivation of certain passions, not only that we might feel appropriate pleasure and pain in the face of virtue and vice, but also that we might be led by appropriate emotions to see actions and situations with greater sympathy and acumen. On this account, passions and emotions play an epistemological role in ethics. It also involves the formation and expansion of our imaginative capacities. Kupperman here provides his own version of Aristotle's warning at the outset of the *Ethics* that moral philosophy will profit only those who have already been well brought up and who already possess the starting points of ethics. Such an education inculcates an increasing realization of the inexhaustible richness of moral experience. "Where virtue is concerned," Murdoch writes, "we often apprehend more than we clearly understand and grow by looking."[14]

Second, even given such a classification scheme, the decision procedure is notoriously indeterminate in the results it yields. Consider, for example, the interminable debates over whether Kantian universalization does or does not rule out suicide, lying, or theft. In the case of utilitarianism, critics are fond of arguing that the maximization of happiness can be used to justify patently heinous acts like the murder or torture of the innocent. Of course, utilitarians offer clever rebuttals, arguing that the calculus need not result in the justification of such acts. The real problem is that the calculus seems to necessitate no specific course of action whatsoever. From the perspective of virtue ethics, the indeterminacy of Kantian and utilitarian decision procedures is instructive. It shows how misguided is the attempt to model practice on theory. The indeterminacy of applied ethical theories tells us something important about the nature of moral agency and the limits to ethical theory. As Amelie Rorty observes, "The more practical an ethical theory, the more it reflects the sorts of difficulties that virtuous agents have, and the more clearly it locates and explains our failures. Ethical theories designed to be practical and action-guiding cannot be expected to provide salvation where none is to be had."[15]

Third, the decision procedure is "oriented toward single decisions, viewed as disconnected from other decisions, in a way which ignores or slights the moral importance of continuity of commitment."[16] This objection touches upon the atomism of the decision-procedure model; sometimes this atomism is exhibited in a fascination with so-called moral dilemmas, as if morality were peripheral to ordinary life, coming into play only in unusual moments of conflict and confusion. Atomism also presupposes that acts and agents are intelligible in abstraction from contexts. To this, philosophers such as Murdoch oppose a notion of cultivated "attention," the ability to see what is salient in circumstances and act accordingly, an ability formed over time.

> If we see what the work of attention is like, how continuously it goes on, and how imperceptibly it builds up structures of value round about us, we shall not be surprised that at crucial moments of choice most of the business of

> choosing is already over. This does not imply that we are not free, certainly not. But it implies that the exercise of our freedom is a small piecemeal business which goes on all the time and not a grandiose leaping about unimpeded at important moments. The moral life, on this view, is something that goes on continually, not something that is switched off in between the occurrence of explicit moral choices.[17]

Here Murdoch calls to mind premodern conceptions of human agency, especially of human freedom. Aristotle and Aquinas, for example, depict human agents as already immersed in a world, as always already pursuing goods, as simultaneously influenced by and further articulating conceptions of the good.

As has often been noted, Aristotle has no term equivalent to our modern notion of freedom. Some medievals and many moderns locate our capacity for freedom in the will, but Aristotle has only the notion of desiring reason or reasoning desire. Freedom thus consists in a rational openness to goods, in the capacity to deliberate about means to ends. On this view, we are moved by objects, not cut off from them in a state of detached indifference. The predictable objection can be put thus: How does the movement of the will by reason's apprehension of the object avoid determinism? Aquinas responds, "If any good thing is found not to be good according to all the particulars in it, it will not necessarily move to the determination of the act. Someone will be able to will its opposite."[18] Only in the case where a single mean is the sole possible way of realizing the end must we choose that mean. But even here it is possible for us to reconsider the fittingness of the end in light of some more ultimate end. Thomas comments: "It happens that what is an end with respect to some things is itself ordered to another end, just as what is the principle in one demonstration is the conclusion from another. What is taken as an end in one investigation can be a means in another and thus there can be counsel about it."[19]

In an effort to make clear certain features of Aquinas's view of human freedom, John Jenkins distinguishes between synchronic and diachronic conceptions of free, voluntary choice. The synchronic view holds that "S voluntarily chooses A only if S could have done otherwise at t." Jenkins rightly notes that Aquinas, following Aristotle closely, rejects this view. "The Aristotelian view of free will is diachronic, for whether or not a choice is free depends not only on what is true of the subject at the moment of choice, but also on what was true in the past; it depends upon his past actions, which brought about his dispositions, which in turn brought about his present character."[20] The danger of this view is not just that it seems to despair of the possibility of moral change but also that it seems to defer the ground of moral responsibility into an ever-receding past, a sort of infinite regress of free choice. For at any moment, our actions generally and characteristically flow from the character we possess at that time. Both Aristotle and Aquinas want to hold that the formation of our current character is the result of an accumulation of past actions, actions for which we are responsible. Thus, we are somehow the causes of the way the good appears to us. But if we can run it backward in this way, we must also be able to run free choice forward, in the present and beyond. That is to say, Aquinas wants to avoid the notion that any given act is completely determined by antecedent character. Except in extreme cases, we do not lose complete control over our actions, although we cannot alter our character in the direction of virtue by a mere effort of will on one or two occasions. But this is not to say that the effort of will has no role to play. Here Aquinas may be more optimistic and less conservative than either Murdoch or Aristotle, since as a Christian he believes in the possibility of a source of moral transformation unknown to the pagans, namely, grace. But he is not a voluntarist even here. In cases where grace transforms the soul, it is not the case that this is the result of a merely human act of will, but of God altering the entire soul so that it comes, not just to will, but to behold and love the good in ways it hitherto could not.

Character accounts for the importance of continuity of commitment in ways that a decision procedure cannot, since it demands that we focus on agents over time and in a variety of settings.[21] A related problem with Kantian and utilitarian ethical theories is that even where they find an important role for virtue, say, in utilitarian benevolence or Kantian self-control, they seem to reduce the multiplicity of virtues operative in human life to one overriding virtue. This calls to mind Anscombe's charge against the impoverished vocabulary of "modern moral philosophy." Her modest proposal is that instead of identifying a bad act as "against the moral law or morally wrong," we should at least "name a genus," such as untruthful or unchaste. Again, we confront in the dominant modern ethical theories a penchant for reductionism, appropriate perhaps to the sciences but gravely misleading in ethical matters.[22]

According to virtue theorists, the basic flaw in an exclusively rule-based system is that it is too far removed from the concrete circumstance of action, from actual practice.[23] It relies too heavily on a deductive model of reason that begins and ends in universals. The deductive model disregards the distinctive object and term of practical reasoning: the concrete, singular action. Between universal and singular, the perception and judgment of the agent must intervene in decisive, non-rule-governed ways. The agent must be able to discern what is salient in the circumstance, and this involves not only measuring this experience against previous experiences (hence the crucial role of memory in prudence) but also an awareness of what is novel and of how to interpret that novelty. If rules are to be brought to bear on the singular, the agent must judge which rules are relevant and, if there are multiple rules, apparently in conflict, the agent must decide which rules apply and how. If we are to invoke further rules to cover the interpretation of ambiguous cases or cases where relevant rules seem to conflict, we invite an infinite regress of rules and moral paralysis. Moreover, the casuistical model replaces the virtues of perception, deliberation, and judgment (which can be possessed and exercised only by an individual agent) with an abstract decision procedure. All of this appears to make the agent superfluous and the irreducibly singular action merely an instantiation of a universal.[24]

Of course, Aquinas himself describes ethical reasoning—or at least an important portion of it—in deductive terms, for example, in his discussion of the derivation of human law from natural law (*ST*, I–II, 95, 2). As we shall soon see in our discussion of justice, Aquinas's integration of virtue with law or precept puts him in a position to respond to certain pressing objections to virtue ethics. What is needed now is to see how he introduces law into what is fundamentally an ethics of virtue; indeed, the very structure of Aquinas's greatest ethical work, the second part of the voluminous *Summa Theologiae*, indicates the primacy of virtue. Aquinas subdivides the second part into two sections, the first and shorter of which offers a general consideration of human action, while the second offers a detailed description of ethical matters. Only one segment of the first section focuses on law, while the entire structure of the second section is organized around the virtues.[25] Law, as Aquinas puts it, is an extrinsic principle of human action, whereas virtue is intrinsic. Borrowing a motif from Aristotle, Aquinas stresses the pedagogy of law, which is for the sake of virtue. Unlike later legal voluntarists, Aquinas accentuates the law's intelligibility. Law is a precept of reason, a rule or measure of human acts whose starting point is the ultimate end of human life, the good befitting rational animals.

Aquinas finds an Aristotelian basis for introducing law into the heart of ethical reasoning. He notes that "practical reasoning makes use of a kind of syllogism in determining a course of action." Thus, "there is something that stands in relation to actions as the proposition does to the conclusions in speculative reasoning."[26] The first principle in speculative reason is the principle of contradiction: the same thing cannot both be and not be at the same time and in the same respect. Assumed in all human discourse, the principle governs human reason and speech. Parallel to that speculative principle is the foundational precept of practice: "Good is to be done and pursued, and evil avoided."[27] Although he nowhere develops the point, Aquinas sometimes speaks of a hierarchy of precepts, with "do good, avoid evil" as the most common, with other intermediate precepts, such as prohibitions on murder or theft, falling beneath it. But except at the very top, where there is only one precept, it is never clear precisely which precepts reside at which levels or even how many levels there are, only that the various levels involve differing degrees of specificity. So, for example, when Aquinas speaks of the derivation of human laws from the natural, he describes the derivation of the prohibition against killing from the more general precept that one ought not to harm anyone (*ST*, I–II, 95, 2). It is also evident that there could be even more proximate precepts specifying certain types of action as falling under the more general prohibition of murder.

Although some commentators, such as John Finnis, speak of the missing intermediate precepts, there is no sense in Aquinas that we could fill in a deductive chain of reasoning from the most general precept all the way down to a particular action.[28] Indeed, it is hard to see how anything could be derived demonstratively from the most common precept. Even in the order of speculative inquiry, the principle of contradiction governs human discourse, not by providing a starting point for demonstrations but by indicating the framework of intelligibility itself. Similarly, in the case of "do good, avoid evil," other less universal precepts are not derived demonstratively from it. Headed in the other direction, that is, from the intermediates to the contingent singulars of action, Aquinas notes that the more particular conditions are introduced, the more likely it is that a common precept will fail (*ST*, I–II, 94, 4). He explains, "If in common matters there is a certain necessity, the more one descends to proper matters, the more a defect is found."[29] Here he underscores the crucial limitations to the analogy between speculative and practical reasoning.

If in one sense, we can speak of an activity of subsuming singulars under universals, say in the case of identifying this act as an act of murder, in another sense we can speak of the decisive activity of prudence as it is described in contemporary virtue ethics, that is, as a capacity of discernment, appraisal, and judgment of singulars in relation to proximate and more common precepts. For Aquinas, the inherent deficiencies in any deductive model of morality underscore the indispensable role for prudence even for natural law. The distinctive order of practice cannot be subsumed within that of theory. Although the law might aid our reasoning at various levels, it cannot itself provide observations or judgments of salience in the singular, nor can it tell us decisively which precepts apply in which cases. Even where there is the possibility of derivation of human laws from the natural law, Aquinas does not advocate anything like the abstract, context-free model of practical reasoning found in twentieth-century decision procedures. Instead, Aquinas insists that human laws must be framed according to the "various forms of government" and that the prudential legislator will tailor the laws to fit the customs of the society (*ST*, I–II, 95, 4). Custom, Aquinas writes, has the "force of law, abolishes law, and is the interpreter of law."[30] While not falling prey to legal relativism, Aquinas suggests that the way in which a people should be led to virtue will depend on antecedent customs, since "different things are expedient to different conditions."[31] Indeed, the manifestation or embodiment of the good will differ in different political regimes and according to the divergent configurations of custom within each society. Aquinas responds negatively to the question whether human law should repress all vice (*ST*, I–II, 96, 2). He argues that human law must forbid only the "most grievous vices," those that are most harmful to others. Through force and fear, it keeps the "audacity of the depraved in check" and thus "safeguards the innocent."[32] If it were to attempt to eradicate all vice, it may provoke greater, unanticipated evils. Even where it is concerned with promoting virtue, its focus is on those acts that are directly related to the preservation of the common good. While it may command acts of all the virtues, it does not command all the acts of any of the virtues (*ST*, I–II, 96, 3), let alone all the acts of all the virtues.

More strikingly, law cannot command that any act of virtue be performed as the virtuous person would perform it. And this points up an important implication for the relationship of law to virtue. Although law aims at inculcating virtue, it cannot enforce or make human beings virtuous. All it can do is to command the performance or avoidance of certain external acts. It cannot govern human intentions; nor can it insure that the act flows from a well-formed character. The truly virtuous choose the virtuous act for its own sake and from a fixed, virtuous character. The aim of the lawgiver, to make individuals virtuous, cannot itself fall under a precept. Hence, virtue itself exceeds the scope of law (*ST*, I–II, 96, 3).

If law aims to inculcate that which it cannot supply, namely virtue, it also depends on virtue for its efficacy. In response to the question whether the precepts of the natural law can be abolished from the human heart, Aquinas distinguishes among the most general precepts, the secondary precepts, and particular actions. In the singular act, passion can of course derail the application of a precept by distracting the agent from what should be done. Although the most general precepts cannot be obliterated, our recognition of secondary or intermediate precepts as fundamental as the one against theft can, Aquinas observes, be adversely affected by "depraved customs and corrupt habits."[33] Without virtue, the precepts will not effect what they command. Under the influence of vice, moreover, human beings lose their awareness of the precepts as an inhuman forgetfulness takes hold of the soul. Aquinas can hardly be faulted for naïve assumptions about legalistic ethics.

Another way to express the concern among virtue ethicists about the decision-procedure model is in terms of the contrast between ethical and technical reasoning, in Aristotle's terms between *phronesis* and *techne*. There are at least three issues here. First, for many, a legalistic ethic is too closely modeled on the practice of technical reasoning (*techne*) wherein an agent imposes an abstract form or plan upon raw matter. By contrast, practical reasoning concerned with action (*phronesis*) has more to do with discerning what ought to be done in given circumstances. As we have just noted in Aquinas's account of the role of the legislator, the art or *techne* of crafting laws is ultimately subservient to the judgment of prudence, which must cooperate with, rather than utterly transform, the customs of society. Second, a disparity between technical skills and ethical virtues emerges in Aristotle's and Aquinas's claim that intentional errors are culpable in the sphere of the ethical but not necessarily in that of the technical or even the artistic sphere. If a reputed pianist decides, on a whim, to sit at the piano and make noise, this does not make her any less of a musician. If, however, someone reputed for compassion decides, on a whim, not to rescue a toddler who wanders into traffic, we have serious reason to doubt her virtue. Ethical virtues differ from technical skills in that the former preclude the possibility of a gap between possession and exercise. Third, an important contrast between Aristotle and classical utilitarianism is evident in the consideration of means-to-end relationship. Both identify the end as happiness, but in addition to disagreeing about the meaning of happiness, they construe the means-to-end relationship differently. Utilitarianism has a technical or productive or merely instrumental understanding of the means-to-end relationship, the significance of which is captured by Alasdair MacIntyre:

> Each can be adequately characterized without reference to the other; and a number of quite different means may be employed to achieve one and the same end. But the exercise of the virtues is not in this sense a means to the end of the good for man . . . the exercise of the virtues is a necessary and central part of such a life, not a mere preparatory exercise to secure such a life. We thus cannot characterize the good for man adequately without already having made reference to the virtues.[34]

We can put this point in terms already familiar to us, in terms of the primacy of prudence. The virtue of practical wisdom concerns the choice of appropriate means to good ends, but prudence itself cannot be exercised in the absence of the moral virtues, the proper formation of character. Hence, neither end nor means can be construed or pursued apart from the good, apprehended and desired.

Justice and the Limits of Virtue Ethics

If contemporary virtue ethics has made impressive strides in the recovery of prudence and the revitalization of our understanding of practice, there still remains much work to be done in other areas of ethics. With the exception of prudence, analysis of specific virtues remains incomplete. The gap is especially noteworthy on the topic of justice. Now, the neglect of justice is perhaps a predictable result of the recoiling among virtue ethicists from the decision-procedure model of practical reasoning. Much of the discussion of justice in modern ethical thought is, after all, procedural. The great success of virtue ethics consists in its recovery of a richer conception of human agency. The dominant modern ethical theories, which are, by turns, rationalist and voluntarist, depict the human being as isolated, autonomous, and self-sufficient—a hollow self inhabiting a disenchanted moral universe. However decadent these accounts might be, there are good reasons that their ancestors prevailed in the first place. At the root of the Kantian and utilitarian revolution is not just the allure of the scientific model of theoretical reasoning or even the promotion of negative freedom, but a conception of justice. Both the Kantian and the utilitarian accounts of ethics rest upon determinate accounts of justice, duty, impartiality, and giving to others what is due. There are many shortcomings to an excessive attention to justice, especially in the forms in which it appears in modern ethical thought. Yet to ignore justice does equal damage, if in a different direction, and leaves virtue ethics vulnerable to attack.

Nowhere is this gap concerning justice more evident than in that segment of virtue ethics that overlaps with communitarian and feminist thought, whose criticisms of procedural liberalism and its conception of justice bear striking resemblances to Kupperman's critique of the decision-procedure model of moral reasoning. One thinks immediately in this context of Michael Sandel's first book, *Liberalism and the Limits of Justice*, which exposes the unencumbered self, the "person wholly without character, without moral depth" that Rawls's model of justice as fairness both presupposes and fosters.[35] To this, Sandel contrasts the "person with character" who is always already implicated in history and community. Now, Sandel's critique has had an enormous influence in ethical and political theory, even among the followers of Rawls. What Sandel lacks is a rival theory of justice. On this topic, Sandel has nothing positive to say; he simply accepts the liberal conception and displays its limits, the way it exacts costs and distorts our vision of self and others. At the end of *Liberalism and the Limits of Justice*, Sandel suggests replacing Rawlsian justice with the classical conception of friendship.[36] Sandel's apparent return to classical political philosophy, particularly to Aristotle, is deceptive. Although Aristotle's account of justice is unintelligible apart from his treatment of friendship, he nowhere reduces justice to friendship. Indeed, justice is not necessary for friends, but it is necessary in the political order, where not all can be friends. The political order encompasses a plurality of individuals and communities and a complexity of practices, over all of which justice rules.

Sandel's strategy is operative in Annette Baier's feminist critique of the hegemony of the ethics of obligation in modernity, which issues in an "abnormally coercive model" of human relationships as fundamentally contractual. Baier objects to this model as "symptomatic of the bad faith of liberal modernity."[37] Referring to Rawls's assumption that in a liberal society we suppose that parents will love their children and that in time children will love their parents, she urges that liberalism presumes a cultural deposit of character about which it is at best inarticulate.[38] Its focus on morality as a "game of mutual mutually corrective threats" leaves out of consideration the "conditions for the survival of the practices it endorses."[39] The liberal shift to a coercive model in cases of conflict among equals tends to suppress the question why we should entrust certain individuals and groups with the power to enforce obligations. "The whole question of when moral pressure of various sorts, formative, reformative, and punitive, ought to be brought to bear by whom is subsumed under the question of whom to trust when and with what, and for what good reasons."[40] So it is not just that coercive liberal politics rests on a deposit of character about which it is silent and which its procedures may over time erode, but also that its very foundations are morally precarious.

In another essay, entitled "The Need for More than Justice," Baier enlists the ethics of care as a challenge to Western individualism, to the "fairly entrenched belief in the possibility and desirability of each person pursuing his own good in his own way, constrained only by a minimal formal common good."[41] Liberal justice neglects not only concern for those at the margins of society but also "an education that will form persons to be capable of conforming to an ethics of care and responsibility." Even were we to grant these deficiencies in procedural conceptions of justice, it is unclear how either an Aristotelian model of friendship, something akin to which is operative in Sandel's rival communitarian conception of the self, or the notion of trust could replace justice in the political order. Aristotle does indeed say that where friendship is present, justice is superfluous, but he has a lot to say about justice precisely because true friendships are so rare. Baier may well be correct about the limits and distortions of liberal justice, but it does not follow that an ethics of care provides a viable, comprehensive alternative. As Elenore Stump puts it, "If the value of caring for others is the fundamental ethical value, then it isn't easy to explain why it is morally acceptable to withhold care for others in the interests of pursuing one's own projects." Without justice, the ethics of care alone can be too easily exploited.[42]

The opposition of care to justice is a contemporary one, and the sweeping indictment of *the* Western conception of justice will not withstand historical scrutiny. As MacIntyre has urged, there is not one doctrine of virtue but many. In specific accounts of the virtues as taught and lived, there is likely to be disagreement not only about the list of virtues, what is included and what excluded, but also about the rank and relative importance attached to particular virtues. Even where the same virtue is cited in two contexts, there need not be agreement about the nature and function of the virtue.[43] In an attempt to disabuse analytic moral philosophers of the assumption that there is something called *the* moral point of view or *the* standpoint of justice, MacIntyre argued in the sequel to *After Virtue*, entitled *Whose Justice? Which Rationality?* that there have been and are fundamentally different conceptions of justice. One need not adopt MacIntyre's specific brand of historicism to see that accounts of the virtues differ. Of course, no one aims to present an idiosyncratic picture of the virtues. Classical and many modern philosophers strive to depict the virtues proper to human nature or at least of a shared human condition. But they do not reach an account of the virtues proper to human beings by filtering out what is controversial to arrive at a human condition accessible to anyone, anywhere, regardless of education or training. Even where there is an attempt to reach something like a least common denominator, as in modern state of nature doctrines, the result is not consensus but strikingly different accounts of human nature and ethics, as is clear from a comparison of Hobbes and Rousseau. The goal is not to unveil the least common denominator in the human understanding of the good. Precisely because there are competing accounts of the virtues and because any generic account is misleadingly shallow, we must begin with a critique of misunderstandings of the virtue in question, misconceptions operative either within the current culture or within a rival philosophical school.

As a way of highlighting the distinctive features of Aquinas's account of justice, it will help to begin with a consideration of certain contemporary objections to virtue ethics. In his essay "On Some Vices of Virtue Ethics,"

Robert Louden argues that all contemporary schools of normative ethics are "mononomic"; each is incomplete, providing only a part of what is needed.[44] This is a version of the reductionist objection to which we referred earlier. Since this is precisely the sort of charge that virtue ethicists are fond of aiming at Kantian and utilitarian theories, they may be surprised to find Louden turning the objection against them. Nonetheless, he urges that the "strong agent orientation" of virtue ethics leads to an exclusive focus on agents over acts. Louden contends that the question "What sort of person ought I to be?" cannot substitute for the question "What ought I to do?" Louden's highlighting of the latter question has to do not just with the issue of how we become virtuous, with what sort of acts we need to perform in order to inculcate desirable habits. It also has to do with a different sort of question, "What must I never do?" That is, it concerns what Louden calls "intolerable acts . . . certain types of action which produce harms of such magnitude that they destroy the bonds of the community and render (at least temporarily) the achievement of moral goods impossible."[45] But justice, according to Aquinas, stipulates that any number of types of action must never be performed precisely because they are destructive of the good of the other.

Sometimes the objection against agent-centered ethics is formulated as an attack on *eudaimonism*, the thesis that all human action is motivated by the desire for the happiness of the agent, and hence, according to the critics, by self-interest. Even if Aristotle, the ancient progenitor of virtue ethics, does not neglect specific acts, the accusation of reductionism can be restated: even if acts are given their due, they are valuable only insofar as they are signs or manifestations of virtue, of the excellence of the agent.[46] But such a criticism misses the mark in two important ways. First, it misconceives happiness as subjective satisfaction. Second, and more importantly for our current concerns, it neglects what Aristotle and Aquinas have to say about the virtue of justice. Neither of these philosophers collapses the goodness of acts, at least acts of justice, into that of the goodness of the agent. Some acts are intolerable because of the harm they do to others and because they thwart the fundamental goods of political life. In fact, justice is distinguished from the other virtues in the nature of the mean. In contrast to the other moral virtues, where the mean is directly relative to the character of the agent, the "due" or mean of justice does not reside in the subjective disposition of the agent; it consists, rather, in the external act, in the harm or good done to the other. Unlike the moral virtues of temperance and fortitude that rightly order our passions, justice has to do with acts, not passions (*ST*, I–II, 58, 9). The mean is taken, not according to the standard of the virtuous person, but according to an objective mean, an arithmetical proportion between the "external thing and the external person."[47] He writes,

> It is proper to justice among all the virtues, to order man in those matters pertaining to his relation to others. For justice denotes a kind of equality . . .

and equality has to do with the relation of one man to another. The other virtues perfect man only in those things befitting him according to himself. What is right in the works of the other virtues, toward which the intention of the virtues bend as toward a proper object, has to do exclusively with a relation to the agent. What is right in the work of justice, beyond any reference to the agent, is constituted by a relation to others.[48]

The capaciousness of the virtue of justice is clear from Aristotle's claim that justice is "complete virtue in relation to another." The political dimension of justice is clear from Aquinas's quotation from Cicero's *De Officiis:* "The purpose of justice is the association of men with one another, and the maintenance of the life of the community."[49] Aquinas goes so far as to identify justice with the human good (*iustitita est humanum bonum*). Of the four cardinal virtues (fortitude, temperance, prudence, and justice), only the virtue of justice is essentially related to others; both Aristotle and Aquinas call it the good of the other (*bonum alterius*).

This is precisely where Aquinas's account of the common good must enter crucially into the discussion. As John Finnis nicely puts it, practical reason or prudence "directs one not only towards one's own fulfillment but also to a set of wider wholes of which my fulfillment is in each case a constituent part: the common good of human fulfillment as such, and the common good of every community, group, and friendship that can be integrated into human fulfillment."[50] Since prudence serves the end of bringing order into all human affairs, it serves a variety of orders of the common good, which extend from families and local associations through the republic and on to the entire community of mankind. Aquinas responds to the objection that the reach of prudence does not extend beyond the determination of one's own good (*bonum proprium*) by saying that reason "judges that the common good is better than the good of one."[51]

This is Aquinas's philosophical way of articulating the command to love one's neighbor as oneself. Neighbor points, in every instantiation, to a relevant affinity (*affinitas*), each of which ultimately reposes on a common human nature. We ought, Aquinas reasons, "to treat every human being as neighbor and brother."[52] From this decidedly communal perspective, Aquinas speaks of the entirety of virtue as serving our proper relations with others: "Each man is ordered, one to another, by all the acts of the virtues."[53] The virtue of justice, accordingly, is a "constant and perpetual will to render to each his due"; true justice involves a "will to observe what is due to others in all times and circumstances."[54]

But, someone might be wondering at this point, how did we move from the claim that justice consists in external acts rather than in a subjective disposition to the claim that it involves constancy of will? In another passage Aquinas puts the contrast thus: "Something is called just, having the rectitude of justice, when it is the outcome of an act of justice, without regard to the way in which the agent performs the act. By contrast, nothing is deemed to be right in the other virtues unless it is done by the agent in a certain way."[55] Now, to act in accord with a "constant and perpetual will" is certainly for the agent to do something "in a certain way." So does justice refer to the agent or not? In the longish passage just quoted, Aquinas states a "*thing* is said to be just." He refers to a "thing," not an "agent." The core meaning of justice is giving to another what she is due; its principal reference is to external acts, persons, and things, not to the agent. However, if we are to appraise an agent with regard to justice, we may say, if she performs just acts unwillingly and grudgingly, that she merely fulfills what is legally due to others. But we may hesitate to hold her up as a model of justice. By contrast, someone who with regularity and enthusiasm performs just acts may be seen as a paragon of the virtue of justice. Unlike prudence, which resides in reason, or temperance and courage, which perfect the passions, justice resides in and perfects the will itself. Also germane here is the distinction between political and personal justice or between general and special justice. Political or general justice, the whole of virtue, as Aquinas sometimes calls it, has to do with external acts for the common good. Personal or special justice is a particular virtue among the four cardinal virtues, which is, like the other cardinal virtues, perfective of the agent. We can discern in Aquinas's treatment of justice a parallel to the range of meanings or purposes that we saw operative in the account of the relationship of law to virtue. In its broadest and weakest sense, law is ordered to virtue only in that it forbids the most heinous vices; in a more narrow and stronger sense, law aims to aid in the inculcation of virtue.

Given that the recovery of the inherently social and communal character of human action has accompanied the revival of virtue, the neglect of the virtue of justice is surprising. Of course, this conception of justice as securing what is due to others cannot be fully codified in terms of abstract and ahistorical procedures. Instead, it involves attention to the range and hierarchy of the goods operative in the community and, in light of those goods, a prudential assessment of who merits what. Hence, any conception of purely procedural justice must on this view be woefully deficient. This is not, however, to say that procedures, rules, or laws are alien to justice; on the contrary, justice encompasses these as well and would be ineffective without them. Consider, for example, the analysis of theft and private property. Basing his argument on both *Politics* I.1 and the first chapter of Genesis, Aquinas holds that the "possession of external things is natural to human beings."[56] He offers three reasons that individuals should be lawfully permitted to "procure and dispose of external things." The individual possession of external things incites human beings to "greater diligence" in labor; such a manner of dispersing property is more orderly and less confusing than a situation where all is held in common; and finally, the private possession of property curbs the quarrels that arise when all belong to all (*ST* II–II, 66, 2). We should notice both how pragmatic are these arguments and how clearly they are subordinate to the common good. Following Aristotle, Aquinas holds that the common good of a political order is a union of an irreducible multiplicity of goods. In this case, the multiplication and dispersal of the private possession of property fosters the common good more efficaciously than would the common ownership of property. There is, it should also be observed, no absolute or unlimited right to private property—a point Aquinas drives home when he proceeds to argue that the private "use" of property is reasonably limited by the needs of others.

The rich, he writes, should be "ready to share." Although the prohibition against theft is a universal negative precept not admitting of exceptions, "in cases of necessity" it is permissible to take from the surplus of another. Is Aquinas here inconsistently allowing for exceptions on behalf of the poor? Not at all. His claim is much stronger than that. In cases of necessity, taking what one needs from another's surplus should not even be described as an act of theft, justifiable or otherwise. While the prohibition against theft is universal, the legitimate claim to private property is not. It is limited by reference to the common good. "According to the natural order established by divine providence,"Aquinas explains,

> inferior things should subserve the needs of men. . . . So whatever someone possesses in superabundance is by natural right owed to the poor for their sustenance. . . . Since many endure need and not all can receive assistance from the same source, the dispensing of his own property is entrusted to the discretion of each, so that out of it he may support the needy. If, however, there is a need so urgent and so palpable that it must be met instantly by means readily available . . . , anyone can lawfully supply his own need from the property of another by taking from it either openly or in secret. Nor would this act properly be described as theft or robbery.[57]

The best ways to encourage or require the more fortunate to aid the less fortunate would depend largely on the preexisting customs and legal traditions of a society. No abstract rule could be supplied in advance. The instructive implication of the method and content of Aquinas's teaching on property is that both the social engineering so popular on the left and the dogmatic appeal to a natural right to private property on the right rest on misleading abstractions.

Paradoxes of Justice: Ontological Generosity and the Illusion of Self-Sufficiency

If virtue ethicists were to devote greater attention to the virtue of justice, at least as Aquinas understands it, they would be in a better position to respond to other objections to virtue theory. It is sometimes argued, for example, that virtue theory is insufficiently social and other-oriented and that virtue theory is trapped in an idealized vision of self-sufficiency. Sometimes this objection takes aim at the eudaimonism of traditional virtue theory, a tradition that assumes the fundamental drive of human life is happiness and that the task of ethical theory is to determine which set of activities or character traits are constitutive of human happiness. At other times, the objection attacks the classical assumption that the good life is a self-sufficient life. Jerome Schneewind, for example, underscores the neediness and dependency of human beings and asserts that modern legal theories, in contrast to virtue theories, remind us of the "basic needs we share, and the difficulties, inherent in our nature, to overcoming them."[58]

We have already seen that, according to the basic precepts of justice, certain kinds of harm to others must always be avoided. To the most fundamental prohibitions on murder, theft, and adultery, Aquinas adds prohibitions on lying, since truthfulness is necessary for the preservation of society and is thus a precept of justice. To arrive at an adequate account of justice, we would also have to include a set of virtues, including gratitude, liberality, affability, and mercy, virtues that in some cases specify and in others supplement justice. Affability, for example, is the virtue of "behaving toward all," even strangers, "in a fitting way."[59] Affability fulfills neither a legal debt nor a debt from a favor received, the latter of which is fulfilled by the virtue of gratitude. Moreover, affability falls short of perfect friendship; hence, it does not exhibit the intimacy appropriate to perfect friendship. Still, because of our common humanity, we are "every man's friend," even strangers.[60]

Yet precisely because of its accentuation of friendship, Aquinas's entire conception of justice comes under fire for allegedly failing to appreciate the otherness or separateness of persons. This of course takes us back to tensions in Aristotle's conception of friendship. On the one hand, friendship is based in self-love, and the friend is described as another self, who enhances one's experience and one's happiness. On the other hand, the mark of true friendship is said to be the love of the friend for his or her own sake, not as an instrument of one's pleasure or utility. In fact, self-interested desire is antithetical, not just to friendship, but to the very practice of virtue, which requires, in the words of Pieper, an "informed and receptive silence of the subject before the truth of real things." This in turn demands "a youthful spirit of brave trust and . . . a reckless tossing away of anxious self-preservation. . . How utterly, therefore, the virtue of prudence is dependent upon the constant readiness to ignore the self, the limberness of real humility and objectivity?"[61]

Perhaps the best way to clarify the role of friendship in Aquinas's account of justice and its allied virtues is to make use of that most Thomistic of doctrines: analogy. In friendship, the self-other relationship is neither univocal nor equivocal, but analogous. If it were univocal, involving a redundant sameness, Aquinas would indeed be open to the charge of obscuring from view the distinction and separateness of persons. If it were equivocal—that is, if the other were regarded as radically other—then it is hard to see how an other could be at all intelligible to us, what would count as an appropriate response to the other, or even why an encounter with the other should be construed as significant. MacIntyre suggests that, while the more that obvious "limitations and blindnesses of merely self-interested desire" have received a great deal of attention, the more that subtle and more elusive cognitive and moral deficiencies of "blandly generalized benevolence" have received considerably less attention. He explains,

> What such benevolence presents us with is a generalized Other—one whose only relationship to us is to provide an occasion for the exercise of our benevolence, so can reassure ourselves about our own good will—in place of those particular others with whom we must learn to share common goods, and participate in ongoing relationships.[62]

MacIntyre's reading of Aquinas on self and other attends to the ways in which Aquinas's account of the human good involves a serious revision of Aristotle on self-sufficiency. Consider in this context the virtue of liberality, a mean between prodigality and covetousness, which concerns the proper stewardship of excess riches.[63] Aquinas takes this initial description of liberality from Aristotle but then goes well beyond Aristotle; in fact, Aquinas's account seems in an important respect at odds with that of Aristotle. Whereas Aristotle thinks of liberality as flowing from the clearly superior position of the generous person, Aquinas takes aim directly at the illusion of self-sufficiency. Indeed, he depicts prodigality, the vice most destructive of liberality, as eroding the virtue of justice. For prodigality is not just wastefulness but spending money on the flesh, which leads one to take no pleasure in virtue. In the treatment of covetousness, the inordinate love of possessing, Aquinas refers to its daughters, or offspring, which are treachery, fraud, falsehood, perjury, violence, restlessness, and insensibility to mercy. Nearly all the vices bred by covetousness assault justice. One of the daughters, insensibility to mercy, erodes our ability to see and respond appropriately to others in need. The root of this vice is a hardening of the heart such that we are not moved to assist the needy. Aquinas's explication of mercy takes direct aim at a certain conception of self-sufficiency. While conceding that a passion cannot be a virtue, Aquinas insists that the feeling of sorrow that is part of mercy is not a vice or defect.[64] In his statement that friendliness involves "consoling a friend,"[65] Aristotle provides a partial anticipation of Paul's injunction that we should "rejoice with the joyful and weep with the sorrowful." Aquinas contends further that "to repute oneself happy" and invulnerable to suffering is a result of the vice of pride, whose false sense of justice is actually a form of scorn.[66] By contrast, the wise who have fallen into misery are more merciful. The proudly self-sufficient disown any connection between themselves and those who suffer; yet this is an illusion, a failure to see themselves as at least always potentially in the very position of the needy and suffering other.

MacIntyre's rival account of justice rests on a renewed appreciation, derived from reflection on the thought of Aquinas, of the biological conditions of human action. In the Preface to *Dependent Rational Animals*, he admits that he was wrong to have repudiated Aristotle's "metaphysical biology." No account of the moral life "can be adequate that does not explain . . . how that form of life is possible for beings who are biologically constituted as we are, by providing us with an account of our development towards and into that form of life." Such development, of course, has "as its starting point our initial animal condition," but that initial condition perdures in many respects throughout the life of human beings. Attendant upon that embodied, animal condition is a set of vulnerabilities and disabilities, to which we are actually or potentially subject throughout the duration of our lives.[67]

Central to MacIntyre's appropriation of Aquinas's understanding of dependence is an account of "just generosity," MacIntyre's way of translating what Aquinas calls *misericordia*. The salient characteristics of relationships informed by just generosity are "communal relationships that engage our affections." They extend beyond the long-term relationships of the members of a community to include relationships of hospitality to strangers and exclude strict proportionality in giving and receiving. MacIntyre notes that for Aquinas, "extreme and urgent necessity on the part of another in itself provides a stronger reason for action than even claims based upon the closest of familial ties."[68] Out of these Thomistic theses, MacIntyre develops an account of the appropriate response to those at the margins of human society and human life, those who suffer from "afflictions of disfigurement and disability."[69] On this interpretation, the link between self and others, especially those others whom liberal society is increasingly tempted to exclude from the human community, is rooted in a conception of human dependence, a recognition of the many ways in which each of us has been, is, and will be dependent on others. A community organized around the virtues of acknowledged dependence will be not just a place where "children and the disabled are objects of care and attention." It will also be a community in which

> those who are no longer children recognize in children what they once were, that those who are not yet disabled by age recognize in the old what they are moving towards becoming, and that those who are not ill or injured recognize in the ill and injured what they often have been and will be and always may be. It matters also that these recognitions are not a source of fear. For such recognitions are a condition of adequate awareness of both the common needs and the common goods that are served by networks of giving and receiving and by the virtues, both of independence and of acknowledged dependence.[70]

Only in a community dedicated to the practice of these virtues can individuals learn "to assume the other's point of view."[71]

The nesting of justice within a host of other virtues evinces the precise scope and limits of justice. If Aquinas fails to reduce our needs to a short list, he does underscore our neediness in other, more pronounced ways. Moreover, the modern account described by Schneewind embodies its own conception of self-sufficiency, since it tends to view individuals as isolated from one another, lacking any common vision of their good, and primarily needing others in an instrumental fashion. The contractual model of justice presupposes a clean slate, where debits and credits emerge only after we have entered into the contract. On Aquinas's view, by contrast, many of our debts are incurred prior to and without our conscious consent. At the heart of the Thomistic account of justice is the paradox of debts that cannot be fully repaid. Pieper writes, "The just man, who . . . realizes that his very being is a gift, and that he is heavily indebted before God and man, is also the man willing to give where there is no strict obligation. He will be willing to give another man something no one can compel him to give."[72]

How different the Thomistic conception of justice is from its modern rivals is clear from its inclusion of the virtues of religion and piety, whose scope extends beyond debts to God to those owed to country and family, under its purview. This is an affront not only to our sense of the separation of religion from politics but also to the common supposition that an obligation is something that can be fully repaid. What is due to God, country, or family often cannot be repaid, however, at least not fully. Rather than neat procedures and a clear reckoning of debits and credits, at the heart of justice is the paradox of debts that cannot be repaid. Justice thus underscores its own limits. The Thomistic conception of justice points to the necessity of a host of allied virtues like gratitude, liberality, and hospitality, even as it eclipses contemporary divisions— divisions between proceduralism and communitarianism, universalism and particularism, and procedural justice and the ethics of care or friendship.[73]

Justice also presupposes that, and spells out the ways in which "morality is attached to the substance of the world," as Iris Murdoch puts it. The "elimination of metaphysics from ethics" is, for Murdoch, one of the chief causes of the deprivation of human agency in modern ethics. As she notes, this picture runs directly contrary to the ordinary beliefs of most human beings, who think of morality as "continuous with some sort of larger structure of reality, whether this be a religious structure, or a social or historical one."[74] This is the metaphysical background or foundation to MacIntyre's account of the philosophical anthropology exhibited in the practice of "just generosity." The metaphysics and the anthropology provide precisely what Murdoch calls for, namely, a fleshing out of the larger context within which a specific account of morality is intelligible. Borrowing from the title of one of MacIntyre's previous books, we might say that the questions to which he partially responds in *Dependent Rational Animals* and upon which we need to focus more extensively are Whose justice? and Which metaphysics?

Noting that one of his sources is Cicero, MacIntyre insists that Aquinas's teaching on *misericordia* is a properly philosophical teaching. But of course Aquinas takes up the philosophical understanding of that natural virtue and infuses it with a number of metaphysical and theological claims. Indeed, the guiding metaphysical assumption is what Norris Clarke calls "ontological generosity." He writes,

> The real beings in our universe go out of themselves in action for two reasons: one, because they are poor, in that as limited and imperfect they are seeking completion of themselves from other beings; two, because they are rich, in that they actually exist and so possess some degree of actual perfection and have an intrinsic tendency to share this in some way with others. Why this should, in fact, be so is, or should indeed be, a source of wonder for the metaphysician. Without it, of course, there would be no universe. But it seems the ultimate reason is that it is the very nature of God himself to be self-communicative love, and since all other real beings are in some way images, participating in the divine goodness, they all bear the mark within them, according to the nature of each, of this divine attribute.[75]

Behind the account of virtues of dependent animal rationality is a metaphysics of participation and a theological teaching on the internal life of God as self-communicative love. The same teaching, though much neglected, provides the foundation for Aquinas's account of the natural law, which he defines as "the participation of the rational creature in the eternal law."[76] Indeed, Aquinas locates the entire discussion of law under the purview of divine providence. The accent on participation is evident from the definition itself; the Trinitarian foundation is less palpable, until one asks in what sense the eternal law, which is identified as the divine reason itself, is a law. That is to say, how is it promulgated? Aquinas responds, "Promulgation occurs through word and writing; in both ways, the eternal law is promulgated, because the divine word is eternal and the writing of the Book of Life is eternal."[77]

three

Self-Implicating Knowledge

The Practice of Intellectual Virtue

In a teaching derived from Augustine, Aquinas identifies *curiositas* as a vice afflicting human cognitional activity. The vice consists in an inordinate or disordered desire for knowledge, particularly an obsession with information and minutiae that fails to nourish the intellectual and moral life of the individual. The countervailing virtue is *studiositas*, a rightly ordered application of the intellect to the search for knowledge. In the analysis of the vices and virtues of the intellect, we find a little-known point of intersection for Aquinas between ethics and epistemology. In developing the notion of an ethical monitoring of our cognitive activities, Aquinas draws mostly upon Christian rather than pagan sources and elevates the significance of virtues perfecting the will, which governs the "use" of our intellectual faculties. As he puts it, "A virtue that perfects the will such as justice or charity confers the good use of the speculative habits."[1] Aquinas thus opens up a rich avenue of inquiry concerning our practice of intellectual virtue.

The success of contemporary virtue ethics, its return to the concrete conditions of ethical practice, raises the question of the scope of virtuous practice. Can we conceive of the full range of our activities, including intellectual activities, as practices, involving a host of relevant virtues? Something like an affirmative response to this query has been advanced in recent years by virtue epistemologists. Indeed, recent debates in the field of epistemology are isomorphic to late-twentieth-century disputes in ethics. The dominant twentieth-century models of epistemology stress isolated acts of knowledge, seek a quantitative maximization of true propositions through the following of reliable rules of belief formation, and focus more on avoiding blame in one's cognitive activities than on "achieving moral praiseworthiness." By contrast, contemporary virtue epistemology stresses the interconnectedness and continuity of our cognitive states, the importance of habits of inquiry; it focuses more on the quality of the things known than on the mere assembling of a set of true propositions; and it eschews the notion that knowledge or understanding or wisdom could be fully rule-governed.

In place of using bizarre and barren examples to tease out skeptical issues, virtue epistemology would return us to the cognitive practices embedded within ordinary life and to the examples of cognitive excellence to which we find ourselves attracted in those who have a reputation for prudence or wisdom. It would also bring to the fore comprehensive and synthetic intellectual virtues such as understanding and wisdom. Of course, just as there is an irreducible plurality of the conceptions and ranking of virtues, so too with understanding and wisdom. Rich accounts of cognitive excellence would implicitly contain claims about what human nature is and what in the real order is more or less worthy of our intellectual effort and emotional investment.[2]

The parallels between discussions in virtue ethics and those in epistemology are most evident in the debates over externalism and internalism as accounts of the justification of acts of knowing. Virtue epistemology brings its distinctive contribution into that discussion just as it has in the debates in twentieth-century ethical theory. So we shall begin with the state of the question regarding externalism and internalism and with whether Aquinas's take on intellectual virtue can be neatly aligned with either camp. Second, we will consider to what extent the focus in virtue epistemology on the discovery of knowledge opens up neglected features of Aquinas's own account of knowledge. Third, we will examine what is perhaps the most fruitful point of contact between contemporary epistemology and Aquinas: the defense, in a certain influential strain of contemporary philosophy of religion, of realism and the reasonableness of faith. Here, we will examine the way in which virtue epistemology can help recover a sense of agency for acts of human knowing, of the way the pursuit of knowledge can be conceived as a practice, a practice that is peculiarly "self-implicating." Finally, we will consider whether certain moves in virtue epistemology entail an implicit metaphysical horizon.

Externalism, Internalism, and Aquinas

In the introduction to his study of contemporary epistemology, Alvin Plantinga asserts that the "ahistoricism" of analytic philosophy has proven an impediment to progress in epistemology; what we need, he urges, is "history and hermeneutics."[3] In its turning to history, epistemology is beginning to resemble recent ethical theory, which has readily availed itself of the history of philosophy as a means of enriching its discourse and circumventing seemingly insoluble debates. There are other similarities between contemporary epistemology and recent ethical theory. The standard division in contemporary epistemology pits internalism against externalism.[4] The former demands that individuals have cognitive access to (all) the justifying conditions of their belief and that the belief be formed in accord with appropriate rules.[5] The latter drops the requirement of internal access but demands that a belief be formed by a process that is reliably aimed at the production of truth. Internalism's accentuation of epistemic rights and duties calls to mind ethical deontology, while the externalist emphasis on the production of true beliefs is akin to moral consequentialism. Lately, virtue epistemology has emerged to counter the two dominant theories of knowledge, just as virtue ethics arose as an alternative to deontology and utilitarianism.[6]

There is little consensus, however, about where we should locate the most influential figures in the history of philosophy along the spectrum of contemporary positions.[7] Descartes, who thought all knowledge needed to be justified by reference to, and grounded in, clear and distinct ideas, is often cited as a paradigmatic internalist; while Thomas Reid, who thought such a project quixotic and instead grounded knowledge in the reliable operation of faculties, is often classified as an externalist. Beyond this, there is ample room for dispute, especially when one turns to premodern thinkers. The theory of knowledge of Thomas Aquinas, for example, has been called internalist, externalist, and, most recently, virtue theory. In what follows, I want to consider the strengths and weaknesses of each of these interpretations of Aquinas. Since any attempt to understand past thinkers in terms of current categories risks comic anachronism, we will have to spend some time clarifying each thesis in relationship to Aquinas. It turns out that none of the theories meshes neatly with Aquinas's position and that all are likely to overlook important features of his account.

Part of the problem is that the meanings of internalism and externalism are fluid. John Greco provides a useful catalogue of the most prominent senses. He first sets out the "standard" uses. Concerning the "accessibility of the criteria for justification or warrant to the consciousness of the believer," internalism requires that all criteria be accessible, while externalism denies this and holds that some are not.[8] A less standard distinction has internalism insisting that some of the criteria are accessible, and externalism holding that none are. The standard view contrasts a strong internalism with a weak externalism, while the less standard comparison is between a weak internalism and a strong externalism. In light of these criteria, where should we locate Aquinas? Given the complexity of Aquinas's position, it seems impossible that his account of knowledge should conform to an extreme version of either internalism or externalism. So according to the first, so-called standard use of the terms, Aquinas is an externalist, while on the second use, he is an internalist. This will have to suffice as an initial statement of my thesis.

Some recent work purporting to be Thomistic illustrates how strong the grip of the internalist model can be. I am thinking of Scott MacDonald's piece on Aquinas's "Theory of Knowledge," in *The Cambridge Companion to Aquinas*, wherein Thomas is simply conflated with Cartesian internalism.[9] MacDonald simplifies Thomas's entire theory of knowledge to the thesis that, to possess a *scientia*, one must have access to its starting points, the first principles of the *scientia*. While noting that Aquinas allows for the application of the term "knowledge" and its cognates to cognitive states, including states regarding sensible singulars, that fall short of the paradigm of *scientia*, MacDonald nonetheless insists that Aquinas is an epistemic internalist of the strong Cartesian sort.[10] He appeals to Aquinas's claim that human beings not only know but also know that they know, and to the depiction of *intellectus*, which supplies us with first principles, as a kind of seeing or insight into relevant data.

MacDonald seems to think that Aristotle's *Posterior Analytics*, which decisively informs Thomas's account of *scientia* and *intellectus*, is but an anticipation of Descartes's *Rules for the Direction of the Mind*.[11] The logic of Aristotle's *Analytics* does treat of the way of proceeding common to all the sciences—indeed, to all knowing. Even in that work, however, we do not find any attempt to restrict "knowledge" to a univocal set of criteria. Although it focuses on the most rigorous mode of knowing, to which we have our best access in the field of geometry, it allows for the sorts of demonstration found in physics, metaphysics, and ethics. The sciences are related only analogically; they have distinct subject matters, modes of defining and proceeding. The principles of the syllogisms appropriate to various sciences are not identical because the "genera of things are diverse."

As Thomas puts it in his commentary, "the common principles are received in the various demonstrative sciences according to analogy, that is, in so far as they are proportioned to that science."[12] Thomas follows Aristotle's teaching in the opening of the *De Anima*, where he notes that the question "What is it?" recurs in all fields of inquiry.[13] The same question is, however, answered in quite different ways in different subject matters. To desire the same kind of knowledge or the same degree of certitude in each discipline is to wish to distort the peculiar objects of knowledge and their appropriate spheres of inquiry: "The way of manifesting the truth in any science ought to be congruent to its subject matter." Moreover, "The same certitude is not able to be found nor is it required in all inquiries."[14] Aristotle does not, finally, conflate certitude with desirability: where there is a gap between these two, we prefer the more noble objects to the less noble even though we have less certitude in the former. Compare these qualifications with Descartes's assertions in the *Rules for the Direction of the Mind* that there is only one method and only one science and that the knowable is the certain.[15]

Since internalism is intimately connected with anxieties about skepticism, MacDonald must show that, contrary to appearances, Aquinas has arguments ready to hand to defeat the skeptic. One of Thomas's purported responses to the skeptic is to point "to cases in which we have certain and infallible cognition."[16] Of course, the sort of things Aquinas would point to are hardly likely to satisfy serious skeptics; the basic truths to which Aquinas might appeal are quite different from those to which Descartes turns in his foundationalist rejoinder to skepticism. Yet MacDonald presses the comparison with Descartes so far as to assert that Thomas's response to "global skepticism" is the same as Descartes's, namely, that we have been made by a good God.[17] That our knowledge of the existence of a good God presupposes the reliability of our faculties does not seem to trouble MacDonald; nor does the fact that, according to Aquinas's understanding of philosophy, God is reached last, as the culmination of inquiry, not first, as its justifying ground.

At the root of MacDonald's misreading of Aquinas are two difficulties: (a) a faulty supposition that Thomas's *scientia* can be rendered without loss into the contemporary analytic understanding of "knowledge," and (b) a failure to make explicit the precise meaning of the terms "externalism" and "internalism" in their application to Aquinas. The problem with the supposition of continuity between Aquinas and contemporary analytic philosophy is noted by John Greco, who observes that the chief characteristic of *scientia*, that of demonstrating conclusions from first principles, is completely foreign to "what we mean by knowledge today," which is, "very roughly, true belief that is both responsibly and reliably formed."[18] Another sort of anachronism arises from MacDonald's failure to entertain the thought that Aquinas's view might not mesh neatly with either a strong externalism or a strong internalism. MacDonald insists that "the reliabilist must hold not only that our belief-forming mechanisms are reliable but also that our justification for holding a given proposition consists in our belief's having been caused by a mechanism of that sort."[19] Even if we grant to MacDonald the identification of externalism and reliabilism (as we shall see shortly, Plantinga's externalism is distinct from reliabilism), his interpretation is still implausible. The description of externalism operative in the passage is that of the strong type, which allows for no internalist elements whatsoever. It makes sense to say that Aquinas's account of knowledge does not fit all the criteria of strong externalism, that it is not simply reducible to that view. It does not follow from this, however, that Aquinas is an internalist of the strong sort. Indeed, if we were to follow the standard division, we would have to call Aquinas an externalist.[20]

MacDonald's account thus leaves open the possibility that Aquinas is an externalist in a more modest sense. Perhaps the most powerful present-day version of externalism is that of Alvin Plantinga, who holds that a belief has warrant if it is "produced . . . by cognitive faculties that are working properly (functioning as they ought to, subject to no cognitive dysfunction) in a cognitive environment that is appropriate for my kinds of cognitive faculties."[21] This view is externalist in the sense that it grounds warrant in the proper functioning of the cognitive faculties of the agent. Plantinga traces the alternative, the internalist model, to the foundations of modern epistemology in Descartes and Locke and argues that the dominant premodern position was externalist. His two volumes on warrant attempt to resolve current debates in epistemology by reviving a notion of proper function from Aristotle, Aquinas, and Thomas Reid. The notion of proper function is reminiscent of Aristotle's conception of cognitive activity as perfective of the natural capacities of the human species. Plantinga's externalist position enables him to resolve or at least dissolve all sorts of modern skeptical worries. He defends a kind of common sense realism in response to skeptical worries over the external world and other minds. His decidedly anti-Cartesian approach to these issues is clearly closer to that of Aquinas and Aristotle than is the approach of MacDonald.

Throughout his study, Plantinga notes similarities between epistemological and ethical models. Yet his view does not fit our initial association of externalism with consequentialism. That association works fairly well for the dominant form of externalism, namely, reliabilism. Plantinga objects to reliabilism, however, precisely because one may reach true beliefs by processes that are only "accidentally reliable," and hence there will be no intrinsic link between the functioning of one's cognitive capacities and truth. The weakness of reliabilism resembles the problem with ethical consequentialism, which holds that the subjective condition of the character or intention of the agent is not directly relevant to the appraisal of an action as morally right; all that matters is that an action be productive of the most good. Plantinga's account of proper function requires more for warrant.

While concurring with Plantinga's reservations about the dominant contemporary models of knowing, Linda Zagzebski thinks that his theory does not go far enough in the direction of including motives and epistemic virtues as constitutive of warrant. She provides us with the most comprehensive and detailed account of how a theory of the virtues might be deployed in contemporary epistemology. Her definition of a virtue as "a deep and enduring acquired excellence of a person, involving a characteristic motivation to produce a certain desired end and reliable success in bringing about that end" fits neatly into neither an externalist nor an internalist position.[22] Placing virtue at the heart of a theory of knowledge entails combining the externalist feature of a reliable process with an internalist emphasis on "motives and governing virtues." On the one hand, the danger with externalism is that it risks reducing understanding to a merely superficial grasp. On the other hand, the internalist insistence on a univocal standard for appraising one's knowledge is reductionistic. According to a virtue epistemology, knowledge is subordinate to wisdom, a capacity to provide a non-rule-governed account of reality. Despite its similarities to internalism, the virtue approach allows for various motives and different standards, since its motives and standards are described as those that the virtuous person would adopt in a particular cognitive situation. In contrast, furthermore, to the tendencies in both contemporary epistemological camps to focus almost exclusively on the analysis of isolated propositions, virtue epistemology attends to the quality of the sorts of things one knows and to the range and integration of one's knowledge.

Knowing Virtuously: Discovery and Pedagogy

Perhaps the most eloquent statement of the role of intellectual virtue in our complex cognitive life is found in John Henry Newman's *Idea of a University*:

> We know, not by a direct and simple vision, not at a glance, but, as it were, by piecemeal and accumulation, by a mental process, by going round an object, by the comparison, the combination, the mutual correction, the continual adaptation, of many partial notions, by the employment, concentration, and joint action of many faculties and exercises of mind. Such a union and concert of the intellectual powers, such an enlargement and development, such a comprehensiveness, is necessarily a matter of training . . . of discipline and habit.[23]

Newman here encapsulates an entire tradition of thinking about thinking, a tradition that can be traced back to Plato, Aristotle, and Aquinas. The problem with bringing Aristotle and Aquinas into conversation with contemporary virtue epistemology is that these premodern philosophers have little to say thematically about the cognitive virtues governing the discovery of knowledge. Their focus is instead on organization and presentation of knowledge already discovered. Even here, however, one can sense a rhetorical concern with the conditions and nature of philosophical pedagogy. Although these philosophers highlight the importance of demonstrative reasoning, they also insist that demonstration presupposes dialectic, which is the path to the principles. And dialectic is not rule-governed. It involves the discrimination of what is salient in a variety of experiences, an ability to discern what sort of evidence is relevant and what is not, and a non-rule-governed sense of judgment about data and received opinions and theories. Moreover, wisdom involves a reflective apprehension of the interconnections among a variety of disciplines or inquiries. This is precisely one of the functions of metaphysics in the philosophical pedagogy of Aristotle and Aquinas.

Dialectical reasoning involves what Martin Warner calls philosophical *finesse*, a term he borrows from Pascal.[24] Warner shows that Pascal's approach echoes Aristotle's conception of dialectical inquiry, which sorts through received opinions (*endoxa*), paradigmatic examples, and reasoned theories in an effort to arrive at the most adequate account of the subject matter in question. What Pascal counsels about the interpretation of scripture is pertinent to all fields of intellectual endeavor:

> A good portrait can only be made by reconciling all our contradictory features, and it is not enough to follow through a series of mutually compatible qualities without reconciling their opposites; to understand an author's meaning all contradictory passages must be reconciled.[25]

Of the sort of principles apprehended by *finesse*, Pascal writes, "They are in ordinary usage and available for all to see," but they are "so delicate and so numerous that it takes a sense of great delicacy and precision to feel and judge correctly."[26]

The attempt to apprehend and account for complex and seemingly contradictory phenomena, which falls to Pascalian *finesse* and Aristotelian dialectic, is akin to what Gadamer calls the "art of questioning."[27] He explains,

> The art of questioning . . . is not an art in the sense that the Greeks speak of *techne*, not a craft that can be taught or by means of which we could master the discovery of truth. As the art of asking questions, dialectic proves its value because only the person who knows how to ask questions is able to persist in his questioning, which involves being able to preserve his orientation toward openness. The art of questioning is the art of questioning ever further, i.e., the art of thinking. It is called dialectic because it is the art of conducting a real dialogue.[28]

There is a certain lack of clarity in Gadamer's simultaneous denial that questioning is a *techne* or craft and his willingness to call it an art, since arts are crafts. What he seems to mean is that fruitful questioning is not a skill that can be purchased and deployed as a set of steps or rules leading to knowledge. Its artistry involves the transformation of the knower; it presupposes that one is already genuinely committed to the search for truth and that one is willing to enter into open-ended conversation with others. The art of questioning thus involves a host of virtues: the humble acknowledgment of what one does and does not understand; courage in the overcoming of obstacles to knowledge; temperance in the restraining of passions that can derail one's pursuit of knowledge; justice in a mutual accountability for what each interlocutor takes to be true; and an appreciation of the pursuit of knowledge as a common good shared by the interlocutors. As Gadamer puts it, "To reach an understanding in a dialogue is not merely a matter of putting oneself forward and successfully asserting one's own point of view, but being transformed into a communion in which we do not remain what we were."[29]

While the ethical implications—indeed, presuppositions—of this conception of dialogue are palpable, its metaphysical consequences may not be so clear. For now, it will suffice to point out the compatibility between Gadamer's dialogical ideal and a metaphysics of ontological generosity to which we alluded at the end of the previous chapter. Norris Clarke suggests that the most fruitful contemporary path into Aquinas's metaphysics is the experience of interpersonal dialogue, which involves conversation with "another real being . . . distinct from me" in a "common field of existence enveloping but transcending us both." Clarke explains, "This approach plunges us immediately into real being as a community of distinct but intercommunicating centers giving and receiving from each other across the bridge of self-expressive action. In a word, it reveals to us that to be is to be together, actively present to each other."[30]

As we shall see shortly, Aquinas explicitly affirms the ethical dimension to acts of knowing. Moreover, much of what Gadamer has to say about dialectic and dialogue is implicit in the very structure of Thomas's texts, in the dialectical pedagogy of his preferred mode of discourse, the disputed question. The literary genres of philosophical composition reflect the "forms of teaching" in the medieval university and are thus crucial to our understanding of the practice of intellectual virtue in Aquinas. In a discussion of "scholastic intellectual practices," Philipp Rosemann captures the significance of genre and forms of teaching: "The literary genre in which ideas are expressed is not an external garment, an element extrinsic to thought, but an important and intrinsic part of its formation. Our ideas are formed in their expression, and thus the mode and genre of this expression are essential to our understanding of thought."[31] As a number of commentators have observed, the disputed question—with a question followed by objections, a resolution of the question, and a response to the objections—has a dialectical structure to it. Indeed, it is a pale reflection, a snapshot, of the living practice of debate in the nascent universities of Thomas's day. For many of these disputes, a master teacher would stand before a crowd of scholars and students, field a question, and offer an implicit thesis, objections to which could be introduced by any member of the audience. In fact, in some such public debates the list of objections had no predetermined limit. The disputed question, then, stands to the practice of public debate in the universities much in the way a Platonic dialogue stands to actual conversations of Socrates.

In his commentary on the first book of Aristotle's *Physics*, Aquinas notes that Aristotle begins by sorting through the received opinions on the principles of natural things, how many and what they are. He eventually settles on matter, form, and privation as principles. Then Aristotle returns to a discussion of the inherited opinions, displaying what was true in them and what false, and, if they went astray, how and why they did so. Aquinas raises the question why, after having resolved the question, Aristotle returns to the now superseded opinions. Aquinas's response is that, even where there has been a demonstration of the truth, so long as questions endure, the intellect remains in suspense. The return to the inherited initiating opinions is essential to dialectical reasoning, which aims to show not just that some opinions are true and others false, that some arguments are valid and others invalid. It aims to include, wherever possible, the truth of rival positions. It also strives to inculcate intellectual virtues of discernment and judgment, a habit of perceiving where and why the intellect is most likely to go astray.

Dialectical reasoning and a variety of intellectual virtues are operative not just on the way to the principles of a variety of inquiries but even in the midst of the sciences, in the continuing refinement in our understanding of precisely how principles function, what their scope and extension is, where they apply and where they do not. Zagzebksi's more inclusive virtue epistemology thus comes closer than any other contemporary epistemology to capturing the complexities and nuances of Aquinas's theory of knowledge. For Aquinas too, knowledge is spoken of in many ways. If we take *scientia* to be the chief sense of knowledge, then the most natural way to spell out Aquinas's normative position on knowledge is in terms of the virtues. For *scientia* is the habit of demonstrating conclusions from first principles, principles apprehended by *intellectus*, the *habitus principiorum*: "Now a truth is subject to a twofold consideration—as known in itself and as known through another. What is known in itself is as a principle and is at once understood by the intellect." The habit that perfects the intellect in its apprehension of principles "is called understanding, which is the habit of principles. On the other hand, a truth known through another is understood by the intellect not at once but by means of the inquiry of reason."[32]

Even where Aquinas seems most internalist, as in his view that the starting points of the sciences are known in virtue of themselves, he is not a proto-Cartesian. The starting points of the various particular sciences do not provide presuppositionless and absolutely indubitable foundations for knowledge. Sciences cannot prove their own starting points, and Thomas sometimes speaks of these as being taken on trust and as being shown to be true in the discipline of metaphysics. Yet metaphysics is the last inquiry to be pursued by the philosopher: "What is last with respect to all human knowledge is known first and is chiefly knowable by nature." This is the basis of what Cornelio Fabro has called Aquinas's "dialectical realism," based on the inverse relationship between the orders of knowing and being.[33] Although wisdom involves giving an account of the various grounds of one's knowledge, such an account is not rule-governed or pellucid. The highest things, which are the principles of our knowledge, are simultaneously most knowable in themselves and least knowable to us. In metaphysics, we do not, then, reach a clear and distinct starting point for all of our knowledge. The culmination of metaphysics reaches God, the supreme ground of being and intelligibility. In contrast to Descartes's assertion that our notion of the divine infinity and perfection is positive, Aquinas holds that we know only that God is, not what he is.[34]

Although Thomas provides proofs for the existence of God, he nowhere supposes that a person without a proof is thereby unwarranted in holding that God exists. The truth of such a proof is attainable only by the few, after much effort, and even then with an admixture of error.[35] Many human beings have reasons for such a belief that are informal versions of one of the five ways; they suppose, for example, that because there is order in the universe there must be a principle of order. There are, of course, well-known objections to these sorts of arguments for the existence of God, and even for the ordinary believer doubts are likely to emerge. Yet what precisely one's responsibility is in these matters will vary from person to person and depend upon one's intellectual ability and the amount of time that one's state of life allows one to devote to such considerations.

The difficulty with classifying Thomas's position in contemporary analytic terms is not just that he never gives a response in anything like the terms contemporary philosophers would find satisfying, but that he never provides a systematic treatment of the wider and looser senses of knowledge. Surely he would think it important and possible to distinguish between reasonable and unreasonable belief; he would want to distinguish between the healthy operation of the powers of reason and cognitive dysfunction. Yet for ordinary folks this would not involve having internal access to all the justifying ground of their belief.

Aquinas's view of *scientia*, then, is not internalist in the strong sense, which requires that the believer have access to all of the justifying grounds of his belief. Aquinas's view resembles externalism in that it is largely dismissive of the sorts of skeptical worries at the heart of the internalist project. Anxieties over skeptical challenges tend to generate both the desire to have a strong refutation of the challenge and, consequently, a view of knowledge as that over which we have total control. Yet these worries never surface in Aquinas, and thus his response to skepticism is more externalist than internalist.[36] We might be tempted, then, to give an externalist interpretation to Aquinas's account of human knowing. Thus far, Aquinas's view seems compatible with that of Plantinga. Is it?

Common Sense Realism, Faith, and Self-Implicating Knowledge

This is an important question, not just for epistemology but also for philosophy of religion, where Plantinga occupies a position of great influence. Plantinga's "defense" of religious faith takes aim at the supposition that believers need to justify their faith before some neutral court of reason. Since his earliest work, Plantinga has adopted the following polemical strategy: Although there may be no universally persuasive argument on behalf of the truth of Christianity or even theism, there is no convincing refutation of it either. The belief in the existence of God stands on the same footing as many of our other beliefs, such as the existence of other minds, about which philosophers have not been able to reach a consensus.

Plantinga goes so far as to deny that religious belief is in need of any justification whatsoever. Like perceptual beliefs and memory beliefs, which ordinary folk accept without demanding proof, religious faith is a properly basic belief, not a belief that is arrived at through reasoning or inference. Now, critics see this as courting irrationalism and relativism. Cannot anyone declare any belief to be basic and thus remove it from rational scrutiny? According to Plantinga, basic beliefs are not immune to criticism and refutation. We typically take the reports of our senses and memory as basic and, quite reasonably, do not feel the need to justify them. But this does not mean that these beliefs are beyond revision or even repudiation. We may well encounter good reasons to question or reject them in a given case.

What is noteworthy about Plantinga's approach is the way it reverses the tendency in modern philosophy to suspend belief in what ordinary human beings take on trust. And this tilting of the balance away from doubt and back to trust involves a rethinking of the entire tradition of modern philosophy. In this, Plantinga is, as he notes, preceded by Thomas Reid, the eighteenth-century Scottish philosopher. One of the great dissenters from the mainstream of modern philosophy, Reid advocates a realism that puts him at odds with Descartes, Locke, Hume, and Berkeley. All of these philosophers are proponents of what Reid calls the "theory of ideas," the claim that the immediate object of the human mind is not a thing in the world but an idea in the mind. Given this starting point, the task for philosophy is to try to establish some sort of connection between the idea in me and the world out there. But all such attempts are futile and end either in Hume's skepticism or Berkeley's even more bizarre conclusion that matter does not exist, that there are only minds and ideas.

As Nicholas Wolterstorff shows in his recent book, *Thomas Reid and the Story of Epistemology*, Reid traces Berkeley's theory back to its roots, the theory of ideas, and begins to wonder what basis there is for this unproven assumption, shared by all modern philosophers.[37] When he finds none, he retreats to the naive assumption of the vulgar, namely, that we immediately perceive sensible things and that accompanying that perception is an immediate and irresistible belief in the existence of what we perceive. Reid observes that all human beings, whether they become philosophers or not, share these convictions. Reversing the trend in modern philosophy to hold all deliverances of common sense in abeyance until they have been vindicated by proof, Reid argues that in any contest between philosophy and common sense, the burden of proof is on philosophy. Of course, philosophy transcends common sense in its descriptive and explanatory tasks; it may even reach conclusions that contravene pre-philosophical beliefs. But it should do so only when driven by clear, unassailable arguments. The proponents of the theory of ideas have no such arguments.

Wolterstorff is careful to note that Reid does envision a positive reflective role for philosophy. Yet the philosopher needs to beware, lest her aspiration for certitude and unity lead her to flout the sheer variety of kinds of evidence that contribute to human knowledge. There is indeed the evidence of immediate consciousness, on which the philosophers have concentrated. But there is also the evidence of sense, memory, and testimony. Wolterstorff underscores Reid's prudent sense of the limitations to philosophical knowledge. The philosopher can note and describe the diverse criteria appropriate to the healthy functioning of our faculties. What she cannot do is reduce all the faculties to one formula.

The accent in Reid is on trust rather than doubt, and thus he stands athwart the dominant strain of modern philosophy. There is a telling passage in Descartes where he laments our ever having been children under the tutelage of others and without the full use of the critical powers of reason. His method of radical universal doubt is designed precisely to free us from such dependence on custom and authority, to free us from ever having been children. By contrast, Reid sees trust and testimony as constitutive of our nature and our intellectual activities: "It is the intention of nature, that we should be carried in arms before we are able to walk upon our legs; and . . . likewise that our belief should be guided by the authority and reason of others, before it can be guided by our own reason." Although we are not for long in this condition of utter dependence, "reason, even in her maturity, borrows aid from testimony. . . . For as we find good reason to reject testimony in some cases, so in others we find good reason to rely upon it with perfect security." Faculties are "innocent until proven guilty," and when doubts arise, as they inevitably do, they arise against a background of accepted knowledge and with respect to very particular questions. If doubt were to become global, there would be no remedy, at least no philosophical remedy.[38]

Aquinas would certainly welcome much of what Plantinga and Wolterstorff argue on behalf on the role of trust in knowledge, but he would also likely have reservations about the limitations to their project.[39] In this context, we can with profit consider an objection that Linda Zagzebski has raised against Plantinga's externalism. She thinks his position is unable to make sense of cases where unwarranted belief arises from a failure to exercise critical reflection. Zagzebski does, I think, underestimate Plantinga's willingness to admit a positive role for self-scrutiny and critical reflection. Nonetheless, her fundamental question remains a good one—is a defect in the exercise of one's critical capacities better understood in terms of dysfunctional faculties or intellectual vice? In the case of a failure to reflect critically, which is a sign of vice, it is not evident that there need be any malfunction of faculties. This is where subtle but crucial differences between a virtue theory and a theory of proper functioning begin to emerge. Sarah Broadie, in a passage that is crucial to Zagzebski's argument, glosses Aristotle's distinction between merely functioning well and functioning in accord with virtue. What we mean by the former is that an animal, for example, is "functioning healthily and effectively at this moment and can be reliably expected to do so at other moments." She explains,

> We may also imply . . . that its functioning well at all those moments is rooted in a single set of continuing empirical properties, which we may think of as constituting the relevant excellence. Yet this . . . may be misleading, for we should not be entitled to assert that at a given moment the animal's functioning is only fully good because it has and will continue to have the properties by which it functions well at this and other moments. These properties . . . make causally possible the functioning that is good, but their presence is not what makes it good functioning. By contrast, the human virtues . . . do not stand to human good functioning as a set of properties that make causally possible a functioning whose goodness can be explained as complete without reference to them.[40]

The view that the causally relevant set of properties could constitute proper functioning is clearly an externalist account, whereas the reference to virtue involves at least some internalist elements.[41]

A feature of internalism upon which Zagzebski rightly seizes has to do with the interconnection between the intellectual and the moral, with the way in which knowledge is "self-implicating." She urges that "knowing states" have a "particularly intimate relation to our sense of self." She expands: "Not only is it difficult to discuss knowledge without an awareness of its self-implicating aspect, but to do so would be to pervert its nature."[42] Given Aquinas's distinction between the theoretical and the practical operations of the intellect and his claim that we can possess the speculative intellectual virtues without the moral virtues, it might seem that he would have little to say on this issue. Yet this is decidedly not the case.[43]

Although Aquinas shows no tendency toward Enlightenment rigorism with regard to the governance of belief, he does not exempt ordinary thinkers from the responsibility to reflect critically. Since Thomas would classify under opinion or probable knowledge much of what Zagzebski and other contemporary analytical philosophers call knowledge, his discussion of the differences in assent in necessary and contingent matters is germane.[44] In necessary matters, where the intellect is moved by the object itself, the only relevant sort of habituation is that of the intellect itself. Thomas supplies the following example: "As long as the geometer demonstrates the truth, it does not matter how his appetitive part may be affected, whether he be joyful or angry, just as this does not matter in a craftsman."[45] As we shall see, Aquinas does not deny, and in fact affirms, the notion that our affections or passions can play a dispositive role in the discovery of all sorts of truths, even necessary truths; he resists the conflating of necessary theoretical truth with the dispositions of the knower. Ralph McInerny notes that, although rectified appetite may remove obstacles to seeing truths of the theoretical order, "the person is not thematic to the argument, not what the argument is about." The theoretical argument itself must be "appraised in terms of logic and of the truth of the propositions."[46] McInerny calls this the intrinsic appraisal of an argument, which he distinguishes from a moral appraisal of the existential circumstances in which an individual engages in argument—does he neglect other duties or fail to give credit to those whose ideas he has borrowed? The intrinsic and moral appraisals of the argument are incidental to one another. McInerny here puts his finger on one of the chief defects with attempting to reduce all knowledge to an appraisal of the subjective dispositions of knowers; instead of argument about the matter at hand, debate could degenerate into an unending critique of the flaws of the moral character of one's opponent.

The direct object of McInerny's censure is Newman, who, by means of what he calls the illative sense, attempts to extend Aristotelian *phronesis* beyond the practical order to encompass all relations of the intellect to truth. "We do not reason in one way in chemistry or law, and another in morals and religion; but in reasoning on any subject whatever, which is concrete, we proceed, as far indeed as we can, by the logic of the language, but we are obliged to supplement it by the more subtle and elastic logic of thought."[47] He concludes, "In no class of concrete reasonings, whether in experimental science, historical research, or theology, is there any ultimate test of truth and error in our inferences besides the trustworthiness of the Illative Sense that gives its sanction."[48] It seems that we have a straightforward refusal on Newman's part of the distinction that Aquinas, following Aristotle, makes between theoretical and practical truth, the former of which consists in the intellect's conformity to the way things are, while the latter involves the conformity of practical judgment to rectified appetite.

It is not clear, however, that Newman's position is as straightforward as it initially seems. It is difficult, for example, to fit this subsuming of the theoretical under the moral with Newman's persistent refrain in *The Idea of a University* that "knowledge is one thing, virtue another; good sense is not conscience, refinement is not humility, nor is largeness and justness of view faith. Philosophy, however enlightened, however profound, gives no command over the passions."[49] In this context, Newman aims to guard and preserve the notion of knowledge as an end in itself, to resist the clamors of religious pragmatism and commercial utility that knowledge is to be valued only if it serves practical ends. Extending a tradition that begins with Plato and runs through Aristotle and Aquinas, Newman proffers an eloquent defense of properly liberal education, of the nobility of wonder and contemplative aspirations as suitable to beings such as we are. Moreover, Newman repeatedly describes the illative sense, his version of *phronesis*, as having under its purview "all concrete matters." In this, there need be no disagreement with Aristotle or Aquinas, since, as I have argued, all sorts of virtues of perception and judgment can be involved in reasoning about contingent matters and even in the discovery of necessary truths. Indeed, we might here see Newman filling in a huge gap in Aristotle and Aquinas, who, while they say a great deal about the demonstration of truth already discovered, have precious little to say about the virtues of the discovery of knowledge, practical or theoretical, contingent or necessary.[50] Newman need only hold that the illative sense involves supple, nontechnical and non-rule-governed virtues of judgment in concrete matters; he need not hold that the illative sense entails or is identical to rightly ordered desire.[51] And that, as we have argued, is compatible with the view implicitly advanced in the texts of Aquinas.[52]

In contingent matters, Aquinas states, the intellect is moved through an act of choice by which it turns voluntarily to one side rather than to the other. Thomas brings out the crucial role of habit in the latter when he states that "just as by the habits of the virtues man sees what is fitting to him in respect of that habit, so by the habit of faith the human mind is directed to assent to such things as are fitting to a right faith."[53] This is but an amplification of the Aristotelian refrain that "as a man is, so does the good appear to him." Hence, in the vast majority of cases requiring assent, volition and habit play crucial roles.[54]

For Aquinas, the realm of opinion or belief is influenced by volition and habit and is subject to moral appraisal. We must be careful here: Aquinas offers no internalist program that would help us to monitor autonomously all of our thoughts. The discernment of responsibility in matters cognitive, as in matters more generally ethical, resists articulation in universal and univocal criteria.[55] Duties here will vary from person to person, depending on the state of life, and from circumstance to circumstance. Responsibility in matters cognitive is determined by prudential discretion rather than by a deontological appraisal of atomic acts in relation to abstract principles.[56]

On the question of the ethical dimensions to human knowing, Aquinas has a great deal to say, much more, in fact, than does Aristotle. In one respect at least, Thomas may be seen as drawing out a line of reasoning that is implicit in Aristotle. A succinct statement of it can be found in Thomas's discussion of the necessity of prudence: "Prudence is a virtue most necessary for human life, since a good life consists in good deeds. In order to do good deeds, it matters not only what a man does but also how he does it."[57] Moreover, since the human good is complex, a diverse set of human acts must be integrated in the achievement of our ultimate end. The teaching on the superiority of the theoretical to the practical virtues is itself a deliverance of theory. It remains at some distance from the immediate principles of human action. The determination of how the practice of the theoretical virtues fits into the whole of one's life is a matter for prudence.

For Thomas, then, even the intellectual virtues fall under the regulation of the moral virtues and prudence, not with respect to their objects or content but with respect to their exercise. He asserts that a "virtue that perfects the will such as justice or charity confers the good use of the speculative habits."[58] From Augustine, he derives the virtue of *studiositas*, a moral virtue that moderates and rightly orders our natural desire for knowledge. Having defined *studiositas* as a "vehement application of the mind," he puts to himself the objection that, since *studiositas* is cognitive, it is impossible that it be a moral virtue. Thomas responds that the acts of the intellect are commanded by the appetitive power, the will, and that these acts can be ordered variously "in one way or another and to this or that."[59] Precisely the ordering of these acts is subject to the moral virtue of *studiositas*, a part of temperance. Just as was the case in Aquinas's articulation of the primacy of justice among the moral virtues, so too with his treatment of virtues governing the acts of the intellect, we find Aquinas moving beyond Aristotle precisely through an expansion of his account of rational appetite, of the volitional conditions of thought and action.

Following Aristotle, Aquinas draws analogies between touching and knowing and claims that a greater cognitive power accompanies the better sense of touch.[60] Independently of Aristotle and in reliance on Augustine, Aquinas speaks of the vice of inordinate seeking after knowledge (*curiositas*) and the virtue of proper and ordered zeal in the pursuit of knowledge (*studiositas*). The symptoms of curiosity include a roaming unrest of the spirit (*evagatio mentis*), whose extreme form is "complete rootlessness."[61] "It may mean that man has lost his capacity for living with himself; that, in flight from himself, nauseated and bored by the void of an interior life gutted by despair, he is seeking with selfish anxiety and on a thousand futile paths."[62] Wisdom, as Nietzsche says, puts limits to knowledge.[63] Far from limiting the scope and function of temperance to the curbing of this or that sensitive impulse, Aquinas relates temperance "to the root of the whole sensual-intellectual life."[64]

The alternative to the vice of *curiositas* is *studiositas*, which is not just an absence of intellectual disorder but a positive and passionate commitment to knowledge, to truth, in a manner congruent with an individual's cognitive abilities and multiple duties. *Studiositas* thus entails a rich account of intellectual and moral virtue. Drawing out Aquinas's teaching on intellectual virtue and faith, Pieper focuses on the role of faith or trust in the exercise of natural reason. Aristotle's statement that "to learn one must believe" is the epigraph to his study of faith. In probing the theological virtue of faith, Pieper does not address properly theological issues such as the content or doctrine of faith or the operation of grace infusing virtue into the soul of the believer. Instead, he focuses on the nature of the act of believing and its problematic relationship to the nature of man. It is precisely in this context that we find material for a fruitful encounter with the positions of Plantinga and Wolterstorff.

The nature of faith raises the question of whether and why human beings should find themselves in such a state of dependence. Such questions cannot be answered by abstract analyses of the rationality of belief, but must be addressed by reference to the true nature of the human person.[65] Pieper concedes that an "intellect bent on critical autonomy will take such a course only with reluctance." And he warns believers against quickly branding such a person as arrogant; instead, he urges a deeper probing of the existential situation of man. Here Pieper appears more sympathetic than is Plantinga toward the dilemmas of the reflective unbeliever, particularly to her quest for greater evidence than that which would be required or appropriate in many other situations. In this, Pieper departs from Plantinga's simple alignment of faith in God with other supposedly properly basic beliefs. Pieper and Aquinas are less concerned with justifying religious belief or with turning back objections to the rationality of belief than with exhibiting the many ways in which faith enhances intellectual activity.

Although Aquinas would certainly affirm the attempt of Plantinga and Wolterstorff to recover the ineliminable role of trust in our cognitive and moral lives, he presents a picture of human life as having a greater positive impetus toward knowledge of the good and toward knowledge itself as a good. The virtue of *studiositas* helps to perfect our natural erotic longing for an apprehension of the true as good, a contemplation of the true as beautiful. The recovery of premodern philosophy and theology in Reid, Plantinga, and Wolterstorff is, it seems, but partial. The need for a virtue to temper and guide the acts of speculative reason evinces our tendency to be so captivated by the objects of knowledge that we are oblivious to other relevant goods and to the way any particular operation must fit into the whole of our life. No particular action or set of specific actions can constitute a good life. The opposed vice of *curiositas* consists precisely in an excessive attention to less noble inquiries or objects of knowledge; it sets up a partial and subordinate object of the mind as if it were the whole and highest object. The ethical appraisal of the intellectual virtues shifts our attention from the object or content of the acts of knowing to their nature as acts of a human being and even more broadly to the way these acts contribute to a way of life.

That way of life locates the pursuit of truth within a communal context of the practice of a host of virtues. There is, in fact, a moral virtue of truth and even a truth of life (*veritas vitae*). The moral virtue consists in speaking the truth when it is necessary and insofar as it is necessary.[66] We do not, of course, owe an avowal of all that we know to all persons; our duties in matters of truth-telling vary in both degree and kind, from person to person and circumstance to circumstance. While truthfulness refers primarily to speech, its scope is broader and includes deeds and signs, all of which must be disposed in a due order.[67] Truthfulness is a part of justice arising from our social nature, in light of which we owe to others all those things without which the constitutive goods of human society cannot be preserved.[68] One of these is the "manifestation of the truth." We do so in the broadest sense when we reveal ourselves in "life and speech to be such as we in fact are."[69]

There is perhaps no more apt or succinct formulation of Thomas's view of the good life than to say that it consists in the practice of the manifold virtue of truthfulness. From this perspective, there is no artificial gap between the moral and the theoretical, between the affective and the intellectual, or between the necessary and the contingent. Nor can the virtues of the mind be understood in an individualistic fashion. Here we should note an isomorphism between, on the one hand, the ethical account of the virtues, especially just generosity, befitting dependent rational animals and, on the other, the social role of truthfulness.

The Metaphysical Horizons of Virtue Epistemology

Thomas's analysis of the virtue of *studiositas* and the vice of *curiositas* establishes an interconnection between the intellectual and the moral, the way in which knowledge is "self-implicating." Yet there is an important disparity between Zagzebski's contemporary virtue theory and Aquinas's view. In her discussion of the changes in the lists of intellectual virtues, Zagzebski mentions that, while for us curiosity is a virtue, for the ancients it was a vice.[70] On one level this is merely a verbal difference, since we usually mean by curiosity an appetite for knowledge exhibited in persistent questioning, while Augustine and Aquinas mean by that term an inordinate desire for knowledge. The interesting question is whether our contemporary list of intellectual virtues and vices has room for anything like what the ancients called *curiositas*. Since curiosity is essentially a matter of paying excessive attention to less noble sorts of objects, it presupposes a hierarchy of beings. Might it be that absent a conception of human nature and of a hierarchy of goods appropriate to that nature, we can say little about the disordered desire for knowledge, except to counsel a kind of bland moderation, a balancing act in which we refuse to allow one desire to intrude too much upon other desires? So we should not pursue knowledge excessively because it might make us social bores or keep us from enjoying sports or other activities, from becoming all that we can be. Zagzebski herself concedes that criticism of an excessive desire to know is difficult apart from such an account of the harm that excess inflicts upon well-being or happiness.[71] The notion of well-being must at least broadly pertain to a species, to a particular natural kind.

The notion that, as Zagzebski puts it, one's doxastic structure could be at a higher level on account of the kind of truths one knows and the way in which one holds the knowledge is deeply compatible with Aquinas's account of the virtues of the human intellect.[72] Such a supposition underlies Aristotle's refusal to equate the desirable-to-be known with the certainty-attainable-by-us. Instead, as we have noted, he argues that the most noble objects of knowledge are least certain to us, yet the meager and tenuous knowledge we can have of them is more desirable than a sure and exhaustive knowledge of less noble objects. In the tradition of Aristotle, metaphysics is the highest and most desirable science, not because of its utility or its amenability to comprehensive certitude, but because it satisfies to some extent the natural human longing for wisdom.[73]

We might be able to bring Zagzebski and Aquinas closer together by attending to the way both depart from a true belief model of knowledge. Zagzebski herself has rather strong reservations about that model. In her criticisms of the dominant contemporary approaches to epistemology, she goes so far as to put into question the very depiction of knowledge as true belief. Late in the book, she substitutes the notion of "cognitive contact with reality" for that of true belief, because the former is holistic and refers to one's "entire doxastic structure," not just to isolated propositions.[74] On the true belief model, intellectual progress is the accumulation of more true propositions. This atomistic approach omits any consideration of the integration of knowledge or of the role of our habitual cognitive dispositions. While knowing fewer individual propositions, one's "doxastic structure" could be at a "higher level" because of the sorts of things one knows and the way one holds the knowledge. To establish distinctions among things known and among the ways of holding our knowledge of them presupposes some understanding of the larger framework within which human beings are ensconced and of the place of the intellect within it.[75] Thus we can see that a rich conception of practice, in this case the practice of virtues governing our cognitive activities, points us in the direction of some sort of metaphysics. We return yet again to the thesis of Murdoch, that rival accounts of ethics and inquiry will be predicated on divergent conceptions of human agency as "continuous with some sort of larger structure of reality."

Aquinas's version of knowledge as cognitive contact with reality and of wisdom as an habitual penetration of the parts or fields of human knowledge in relation to the whole and its ultimate cause has as its correlate a rich anthropology and metaphysics. The investigation in wonder of the common world of human inquiry allows for a reflective appropriation of the intellectual soul as a potency that is made actual through interaction with sensible substances. Wonder thus bespeaks the soul's kinship to the whole; the intellect is *potens omnia.* The human soul's peculiar receptivity of the whole indicates that the soul is not merely a part of the whole, but that part of the world in which, and through which, the whole is made manifest. Aquinas does not utterly reject the notion of interiority, but what sets his account of interiority apart from many modern conceptions is his insistence on reciprocity between the increased interiority of the human soul and its increased openness to the external world. As Josef Pieper puts it, "the higher a being stands in the order of reality, the wider and deeper its world. . . . The two together constitute spirit: not only the capacity to relate oneself to the whole of reality, to the whole world, but an unlimited capacity of living in oneself. . . . To have a world, to be related to the whole of reality, is only possible to a self, to a person, to a 'who' and not a 'what.' "[76]

four
Dependent Animal Rationality
Epistemology as Anthropology

The notion of substance as actualized and perfected through operations provides remote metaphysical underpinning for Aquinas's account of the human intellect as a potency actualized by interaction with sensible substances. Aquinas is not preoccupied with skeptical doubts about how a mind-in-here can make reliable contact with a world-out-there. The starting point for him is not a vacant mind trapped within itself and desperately seeking an exit into the world; rather, he observes an intellect already ensconced within a world about which it knows a great deal. The accent is not on doubt but on wonder. The result of the mind's awakening in wonder is not certitude but a heightened sense of mystery, a restfulness that is not to be confused with lethargy or mere inertness.

In the last two chapters, we focused on the recovery of the language of virtue and practice in contemporary philosophy, a recovery that emerges from dissatisfaction with decision-procedure models of knowing and acting. Attending to the ways in which Aquinas might contribute to debates within ethics and epistemology, we discerned implicit connections between ethics and epistemology, on the one hand, and anthropology and metaphysics, on the other.

Such a need was seen to be especially pointed in Zagzebski's defense of a virtue epistemology, to which notions of "cognitive contact with reality" and the qualitative assessment of what one knows and how one holds knowledge are central. Anthropological and metaphysical commitments were also seen to be operative in Aquinas's account of justice, especially in his conception of pious gratitude as the foundation of fulfilling what is due. The practices of gratitude and hospitality reflect and embody "ontological generosity."

These are the guiding assumptions of, the framework for, Aquinas's account of human knowing, of the place of the intellect within the real order. Yet not everyone has been convinced that Aquinas is entirely removed from, or innocent of, the modern epistemological project. His occasional habit of speaking of the concept as a mediator between the intellect and the object of its knowledge has led some to believe that he is an adherent of "mental representationalism," the thesis that what the mind principally knows is its own ideas, by means of which it comes to know external things. His teaching that the intellect knows by a process of abstracting intelligible species from sensible things also contributes to the suspicion that Aquinas is a precursor of the modern problematic.

As a way of addressing these issues in Aquinas and, more broadly, of highlighting his account of intellect and real being, it will prove useful to examine the most philosophically ambitious recent attempt to investigate the relationship between mind and world, John McDowell's influential *Mind and World*.[1] In a Wittgensteinian manner, McDowell wants to exorcise peculiarly modern anxieties over the relationship between the knowing subject and its objects of knowledge, anxieties that have beset philosophy since the rise of modern science. His qualified Kantian project treats receptivity and spontaneity, passivity and activity, and sensibility and understanding, as partners in human knowing. But McDowell goes beyond Kant in his attempt to integrate or reconcile the apparent antinomies in human knowing. Writing after Heidegger and Rorty, McDowell seeks to eliminate any vestige of "mental representationalism."

For a number of reasons, McDowell's book is relevant to our investigation. It pushes our investigation of virtue and knowledge forward to the frontiers of metaphysics. But it does so in a way that avoids grounding an account of mind and world in the private consciousness of the knowing subject. McDowell's project is in some ways similar to Aquinas's insistence on the darkness of the soul to itself and to his repudiation of the notion that the idea or concept is what is first and principally known. McDowell also relies heavily on accounts of first and second nature, human biology, and the space of socially inculcated reasons; this account makes for a nice comparison with Aquinas's discussions of the analogies between animal and human reasoning, to which we adverted above in our discussion of just generosity. Finally, McDowell's eschewal of "constructive philosophy," understood as the project of securing a theoretical ground or justification of knowledge and as alien from the concrete conditions of cognitive practice, also helps to sharpen the central issue of our investigation. McDowell's goal of giving philosophy peace, raises the question of whether there can be any positive role for philosophy.

Overcoming Mental Representationalism:
McDowell, Aristotle, and Aquinas

McDowell's forays into the history of philosophy have as their goal the resolution of contemporary problems. The two most important contemporary views of the relationship of mind to world are Wilfrid Sellars's myth of the Given and Donald Davidson's coherentism. For McDowell, the inadequacy of each of these positions generates its opposite. By confining reason within its own sphere, coherentism disavows the possibility that reason could bear on the world or the world on it. One might naturally recoil from this view and take refuge in the Given, in the supposition that the external world influences thought. But since the Given stands outside or beyond the realm of concepts, it is hard to see how it could exercise any normative control over thought. The inadequacy of the Given thus motivates the turn to coherentism. The apparent insolubility of the debate underscores how "difficult" it is "to have both rational constraint from the world and spontaneity all the way out." We seem to be saddled with the antinomy that "experience must and cannot stand in judgement" over thought.[2]

While coherentism entirely abandons the traditional notion of knowledge, recourse to the Given seems to generate the sort of skeptical doubts it was designed to answer. McDowell's alternative, put with introductory brevity, is that since we are, in the Gadamerian language McDowell deploys, "always already engaged with the world," the skeptical challenge is an illusion, engendered by the false supposition that we can see things "sideways-on," a perspective that purports to see the relationship of mind to world from a vantage point independent of our cognitive immersion in the world. Precisely this supposition is in need of exorcism.[3] "Understanding," according to McDowell, is "already implicated in sensibility."[4] Conversely, experience is an "openness to the layout of reality," which enables the latter to "exert a rational influence on what a subject thinks." The following passage is an early statement of his thesis about human knowledge:

> The relevant conceptual capacities are drawn in receptivity. . . . It is not that they are exercised on an extra-conceptual deliverance of receptivity. We should understand what Kant calls "intuition"—experiential intake—not as bare getting of an extra-conceptual Given, but as a kind of occurrence or state that already has conceptual content. In experience one takes in, for instance sees, that things are thus and so.[5]

There are, I think, three interrelated parts to McDowell's exorcism of the anxieties over mind and world. The first concerns the supposition, shared by both the skeptics and their opponents, that we can see the relationship of the mind to the world from a "sideways-on" perspective. The second involves a critique of abstraction, a critique based in Wittgenstein's attack on private language and in Peter Geach's repudiation of the notion that bare singulars could be the basis of conceptual knowledge. The third has to do with a positive alternative suggestion concerning the unboundedness of the conceptual. Since what is at stake in the first issue and how McDowell proposes to dissolve it will become clear as we proceed, it is best to begin with the critique of abstraction.

The dissatisfaction with abstraction is part of the assault on the adequacy of the Given. It is important to see that McDowell is not dismissive of the motive for turning to the Given. The turn is a result of the inability of coherentism to provide an account of how the world impinges upon thinking in anything more than a causal way. Coherentism "suggests images of confinement within the sphere of thinking, as opposed to being in touch with something outside it."[6] Although one may sympathize with the desire for something more than what coherentism offers, the turn to a pre-conceptual "bare presence" is equally inadequate. On that view, we "move from an impression, conceived as the bare reception of a bit of the Given, to a judgement justified by the impression."[7] This amounts to the construction of a private concept, arrived at through abstraction.[8] McDowell's critique of abstractionism rests on the work of Peter Geach, who defines "abstractionism" as the "doctrine that a concept is acquired by a process of singling out in attention some one feature given in direct experience—abstracting it—and ignoring the other features simultaneously given."[9] The problem with this position is obvious: selective attention presupposes some sort of abstraction already performed or at least some awareness on the intellect's part of that for which it should be looking. But this renders the account of knowledge superfluous, a point Plato makes in a number of contexts.

The reference to abstraction as the source of knowledge calls to mind Aquinas and indirectly Aristotle. But their account of how universal knowledge arises from sensible singulars is more complex than anything one finds in McDowell or Geach. For example, whatever one finally makes of the dialectically strained discussion of substance in *Metaphysics* VII, it is clear that the singular is no bare singular but a "this-such." Aristotle opens by pursuing the suggestion that substance is substratum and that the latter is to be identified with matter. The bare material substratum is reached, at least in a thought experiment, by stripping away all the qualitative features of things. However, once we reach our goal, bare matter, the underlying substratum, we no longer have a substance, for we no longer have a concrete "this." The process eliminates not only "thisness" but also "whatness." So both the "this" and the "such" are removed in the attempt to reach a bare singular.

The most theoretically intractable issue about substance, from which much of the dialectic arises, concerns its two inseparable features. The difficulty of moving away from the "such" has just been illustrated, but the movement away from the "this," which lacks one of the chief marks of substance, definability, also engenders difficulties. We seem to be moving not only away from the concrete whole, the compound of form and matter, but also in a Platonic direction, a direction that would eliminate matter from the formula or definition of substance. The conclusion here echoes the assertion at the opening of the *De Anima* that "unity has many senses (as many as "is" has) but the proper one is that of actuality"; the primary sense of unity is that of "an actuality to that of which it is the actuality."[10] Aquinas observes, "Form is essentially united to matter as its act; it is the same thing for matter to be united to form as for matter to be in act."[11] In *Metaphysics* VII, 15, in language that is broadly reminiscent of the distinction in the *Categories* between first and second substance, we are left with the assertion that substance is of two kinds and that there is neither definition nor demonstration of sensible substance. But for Aristotle, matter is a constitutive part of the sensible substance and thus in some sense figures in the formula. The upshot for knowledge is that sensible substances are manifest to us both as a "this" and a "such" and that the search for bare presences is unintelligible. In knowing existing things, we are aware both of a thing sensed and of some way in which the thing is known to exist, some formality under which we distinguish this sort of thing from that sort.

We are familiar with Aristotle's treatment in *Metaphysics* I,1 and *Posterior Analytics* II, 19 of how universal knowledge arises from sensible singulars. Along with the statement in the *De Anima* about the role of active *nous* in universalizing what is potentially present in the phantasms, these texts supply the basis for the traditional doctrine of abstraction. Even in the first two texts just mentioned, we find a much more nuanced presentation of how universal knowledge arises immediately from singulars than anything in Geach or McDowell. There is discrimination of similarities and dissimilarities and an inchoate apprehension that "things are thus and so" even at the level of sensation. But this is not the whole story. The depiction of universal knowledge as the result of an isolated individual encountering an isolated bare singular is highly artificial. It lacks the rich background that Aristotle presumes is operative in all our acts of knowing. How does Aristotle describe that background?

The basis of the familiar doctrine of abstraction is the assumption that, in coming to know existing things, we move from an apprehension of singulars through experience to a knowledge of the universal nature of those singulars. This is the basis of the familiar doctrine of abstraction: "Experience arises from a sorting of many singulars received in the memory. Collation of this kind is proper to man and pertains to the cognitive power, which is called particular reason."[12] By positing the operation of reason at the level of experience in the noting of likenesses among singulars, the passage comes close to affirming the conceptual character of experience. There are, however, stages in the movement from the apprehension of singulars to the abstraction of the universal from the phantasm. The operation of the particular reason in experience is a key intermediate stage in that ascent. As Gadamer puts it, "all aesthesis tends to the universal," since it involves not just mere reception but "seeing as."[13] Although Aristotle does not suppose that substances are inherently relational, he does think that we come to know any individual thing only by noting its similarities to and differences from other things. Yet, an objector might suggest, if we follow the analysis of the generation of the universal back to its ultimate source, do we not reach a bare singular or set of bare singulars?

If in one sense we move from sense to intellect, from singular to universal, in another and prior sense we move from a vague, general, and indistinct apprehension of those singulars to a more specific understanding of them. The authoritative passage is of course *Physics* I, 1, where Aristotle argues that the more common is in some sense prior in the order of our knowing. As John O'Callaghan notes, discussions of abstraction that deploy a "mechanistic image of a transfer of the form from one place to another" and the language of "selective attention" are incompatible with Aquinas's account.[14] Aquinas writes:

> Everything that proceeds from potency to act reaches, first, an incomplete act, which is between potency and act, and, then, a perfect act. The perfect act to which the intellect attains is complete knowledge, in which things are known distinctly and determinately. However, the incomplete act is imperfect knowledge in which things are known indistinctly and with a degree of confusion.[15]

We initially apprehend a particular by locating it within a remote or proximate genus and then try to discern what sets it apart from other natural kinds in that genus. Aquinas comments that at the level of sense, the "judgment of the more common precedes that of the proper . . . in reference to both place and time." He explains, "When a thing is seen from far off," for example, "it is seen to be a body before it is seen to be an animal, and an animal before a man, and a man before Plato or Socrates." A similar process can be seen in the order of time, in the development of a child's intelligence. A child "can distinguish man from not man before he distinguishes this man from that."[16] O'Callaghan writes that this is not a

> process of selective attention, but of developmental growth. We move from understanding the same thing generally and without distinction at first to understanding just as generally but now distinctly. If we push this initial generality without distinction back far enough (though not necessarily temporally), we would presumably conceive of things as "some stuff," or more technically, "some being."[17]

Of course, we need not make any of this explicit in our reasoning, but it is latent, able to be educed through analysis and questioning. The most basic generality is "being" or "a being"; this is the experiential ground for Aquinas's metaphysical principle that being is the first thing that falls into the intellect.

McDowell's alternative to the derivation of concepts from bare presences through abstraction is to depict "impressions themselves" as already possessing "conceptual contents."[18] He claims that "in experience one takes in, for instance sees, that things are thus and so." The rival account of sensation, as already thoroughly conceptual, initiates the transition to the third part of McDowell's argument, the thesis about the "unboundedness of the conceptual." For experience to exercise a rational constraint on our thinking, that is, for it to offer justifications and not merely exculpations, is for the conceptual to go all the way, for it to be coextensive with experience.

McDowell's insistence that the conceptual goes all the way out in our experience, that there is no bare presence that might act as a tribunal over our concepts, invites an idealist interpretation. When he states, for example, that although experience is passive, it "reflects conceptual capacities," we are led to wonder whether, contrary to his explicit intentions, he has not given priority to thought over world. McDowell contends that the content of our experience of the world is simultaneously conceptual content and "an aspect of the layout of the world: it is how things are."[19] He asserts that "the object of experience is integrated into a wider reality"; it is "held in place by its linkage into the wider reality." On this basis, we can make sense of the thought that "it would be so even if it were not being experienced to be so."[20] Since our present knowledge draws us into further inquiry about the as yet "unexperienced whole," we have but a partial knowledge of a world independent of our mind. Do not the limitations to our present knowledge of the world and the insistence that the world is independent of our knowledge undermine the contention of the unboundedness of the conceptual? To avoid this, McDowell avails himself of a distinction: How "things are is independent of one's thinking" but not of the thinkable.[21] The same sort of distinction figures crucially in another passage: "Justification can perfectly well include pointing out from the sphere of thinking, at features of the world" but "not through a boundary that encloses the sphere of thinkable content."[22]

The distinction sounds like Aristotle's distinction between things as actually known and as potentially knowable. For Aristotle, we may point beyond what we already actually know but it would be nonsensical to speak of pointing beyond what is potentially knowable. In fact, much of what McDowell has to say about the dual aspect of experience, as having conceptual content and as revealing features of the world, is reminiscent of Aristotle's assertion that, just as the sense in act is the sensible in act, so too the intellect in act is the intelligible in act. Aristotle presumes a certain connaturality between knower and known; the intellect is "potentially all things." As Aquinas notes in his commentary on the *Physics*, between mover and moved, agent and patient, there is one actuality.[23] In speaking of knowledge as a kind of receptivity or suffering of the world, Aristotle carefully crafts analogies to the receptivity proper to physical alteration and sensation. The original sense of receptivity entails a "certain corruption," which occurs in the destruction of one contrary by another, as, for example, when the white skin of a woman becomes tan. All natural substances undergo this sort of change, the replacement of one quality by its contrary. We may also speak of a passion or reception "commonly and less properly" insofar as it "involves a certain reception" (*importat quondam receptionem*), but without any destruction.[24] Aquinas expands on this peculiar case, "What is receptive of another is compared to it as potency to act. In this instance, however, act is the perfection of potency. Passion here refers not to the corruption of the receiver, but to the health and perfection of that which is in potency by that which is in act."[25]

In one sense, then, Aristotle might go so far as to agree with McDowell that we ought not to look for "a priority in either direction," that is, in the direction either of mind or of world. But in another sense, Aristotle clearly wants to assert a kind of priority to things. How is this so? Let's begin by making clear what this does *not* entail. It does not entail that the mind is purely passive with regard to things. Passivity and activity are cooperative even at the level of experience. Aristotle retains the grammatical and etymological significance of the Latin verb *experior*, a word that means "tried or proven." The verb is in the middle voice, which is passive in form but active in meaning. It thus depicts the subject of the verb, the agent of the action, as simultaneously active and acted upon. It is hard to imagine Aristotle objecting to McDowell's claim that "in humans, aesthesis immediately serves the capacity of selective attention to essential features."

For Aristotle, then, the intellect is both active and passive with respect to experience, and this is compatible with a weakened or clarified version of McDowell's thesis that the contribution of receptivity is "not even notionally separable" from its "co-operation with spontaneity."[26] But the intellect does not contribute content; rather, it actualizes the potentially intelligible content in the phantasm. The world informs the intellect, not the reverse, and we are always trying to catch up to the world, to articulate it in concepts. The underlying assumption here is that human beings, like other animals, have preconceptual experiences and that the task of human inquiry is to craft concepts to articulate those experiences. Precisely because of this ordering of the human intellect toward understanding that which is not in itself conceptual, it makes sense to wonder whether our concepts adequately capture our experience. McDowell's unwillingness to embrace this sort of position lends support to the worry that, despite his official repudiations, he has not escaped idealism.[27]

According to Aquinas, we know and encounter things not just by their presence but by their active presence; moreover, things act on us in determinate ways. As Norris Clarke notes, "action" involves "the self-revelation of being." To know other beings, the intellect "must be receptive and not creative of its objects." Basing himself on Aquinas's statements that "the operation of a thing manifests both its substance and its existence" and that the "operation of a thing shows forth its power, which in turn reveals its essence," Clarke amplifies the point in a helpful way:

> Since the action that flows out from a being is not simply an indeterminate surge of raw energy, but pours out from, and is self-expressive of, the whole unified inner being of the thing, . . . its action cannot help but be essence-structured action revealing to any potential receiver both the actual existence and essence of the being from which the action originates.[28]

Clarke concedes that we have no "direct unmediated intuition . . . of the agent as it abides in itself behind the actions, apart from and independently of these actions." But why do we think we need to know something other or more about the essences of these acting substances than that they are the "perduring centers of such-and-such characteristic actions" or as "this kind of actor on me"?[29] To suppose that we need to make an additional inference to conclude that the actions manifest the essence is already to have moved into the Lockean framework, which prepares the way for Kant's agnosticism about our knowledge of substances. But, as Aquinas and Reid would say, there is no good reason to make such a move. Action is "revelatory of its source."[30] Kant bifurcates (a) our knowledge, immune to skeptical doubts, that external things act upon us, from (b) our knowledge, defeated by skeptical worries, that the content or manner of acting manifests the nature of the thing. But the purported chasm looks like an arbitrary abstraction from the concrete conditions in which the human intellect is receptive of things. These idealist assumptions may infect not just Kant, but McDowell as well.

Another way to underscore the difference between McDowell and Aristotle concerns McDowell's anti-skeptical, and on the surface Aristotelian, claim that "no distance from the world" is implicit "in the very idea of thought."[31] McDowell's way of putting this is in terms of Hegel's statement that we are "free in thinking" because our thinking is "not in an other."[32] For McDowell, Hegel's statement captures the notion of the unboundedness of the conceptual. We have already noted the similarity between this view and Aristotle's claim that knowledge is an identity of knower and known. But Aristotle also conceives of knowing as knowing the other. The perfection of the intellect consists in its being informed by an-other. Aristotle and Aquinas underscore this point by insisting on the difference between the status of things as known in the mind and things as existing.

The postulation of such a difference has often been seen as the source of skeptical doubts about whether what is in the mind corresponds to what is out there in the world. Indeed, Aquinas's claim that the concept is a "mean between the intellect and the thing understood" seems to engender precisely the anxieties of which McDowell wishes to cure us.[33] It seems to invite precisely the picture-theory of knowing that Rorty's *Philosophy and the Mirror of Nature* has purged from philosophical discourse. Is this impression justified? I think not. Thomas quite clearly states that the intelligible species is that by which (*quo*) we know things, not what (*quid*) we know. The species is known, if at all, only indirectly by reflection upon our knowledge of sensible things. The species is not a foundationalist response to skeptical queries about the correspondence of mind to world; rather, it is a descriptive and secondary account of the way the world informs the mind.

The problem in the interpretation of what Thomas holds can be traced to a failure to overcome the imagination in thinking about acts of knowing. The attempt to capture the act of knowing in an image leads to a confusion of acts with things, a reification of an act. The species known thus becomes a thing standing between the mind and the existing thing.[34] The species thus becomes a representation, a copy, a stand-in for the existing thing, and the vexing and insuperable problem of getting from an isolated consciousness to the world arises. Another way to see this is to note the disparity between the modern use of the vocabulary of subject and object and Thomas's use. Whereas we have inherited the distinction between the conscious ego, or subject, and the object, or thing in the world, Thomas distinguishes between the thing known, that which is literally thrown up before the mind (*ob-iectum*), and that which exists in its own right (*sub-iectum*).

The primary orientation of the mind is always toward the world; the very being of knowledge is a being-in-relation. Following Aristotle, Thomas holds that the presence of a phantasm is necessary, not just as the remote and ultimate origin of our knowledge of things, but also as the basis for every subsequent act of knowing. Our intellect always operates with respect to images. This is necessary not only because of the intellect's weakness but also in order that the intellect be true. For example, the nature of a stone is not "completely and truly known unless it is known as existing in the particular."[35] As Frederick Wilhelmsen puts it, "The reflection is natural because there is no break between the intellect and the phantasm. The species is not illuminated by being cut away from the phantasm: The species is illuminated in the phantasm which presents it potentially."[36]

The emphasis on interaction with the world throughout the activity of knowing finds echoes in McDowell: "how things are is independent of one's thinking." We are "always already engaged with the world" and there is "no end to inquiry." Especially important is McDowell's argument that inner experience presupposes a world: "Inner experience cannot be a self-standing starting point."[37] Even from "within, the subjective take is situated in a wider context."[38] Aquinas would go further than this, however. As O'Callaghan nicely puts it, "At the risk of introducing a pictorial metaphor, St. Thomas is not interested in getting out of the soul to the world. On the contrary, beginning with a human being immersed by his or her acts in the world, he is interested in getting into the soul. The way in is by considering how the human being, a material being, acts in the world."[39]

The practice of knowing, the active engagement of the intellect with the world through the asking of questions about things, takes priority over any reflective analysis of the modes of human knowing. The illusion of skepticism is to think that doubts can arise in a global fashion with respect to the whole of our knowledge. But this is pure artifice. Doubts arise with respect to this or that alleged claim to knowledge and always against a background of things already known and assumed. If doubt were to become truly global, it would be fatal. Aquinas's technical way of putting this point is to say that the intellect, as a potency, cannot actualize itself; it must be actualized by objects external to it. Only once it is made actual in this way can it pose questions about how it knows. And the paltry progress it is capable of making in answering that question always presupposes first acts, acts of knowing things, upon which the intellect reflects, in order to understand how it knows.

McDowell wants philosophy to be cured of, to exorcise, the Cartesian model. Aquinas is in need of no such extreme medical or religious treatment. As Wilhelmsen's brilliant analysis of "The 'I' and Aquinas," demonstrates, Thomas does not hold that an already constituted ego intends objects. Indeed, there is no ego or self at all until there is thought.[40] The "ego is constituted in the act of becoming the other as other . . . self is simply nothing outside of an act of consciousness and to be conscious is to be conscious of an other."[41] The identity of knower and known in the act of understanding must be interpreted in light of the claim that the soul is a potency made actual by knowing objects, that it is nothing until it thinks the other as other. As Wilhelmsen puts it, "knowing in exercised act is the ego."[42] He spells out the distinction between signified and exercised act in this way: "Knowledge in signified act is the act of being-other-as-other, direct consciousness; knowledge in exercised act is the very doing of that knowing which doing . . . knows its own relation to the real."[43] The distinction between signified and exercised act, which is derived from Cajetan, involves two ways of describing one and the same act. In the very act of knowing the real, the intellect knows its own relation to the thing known.

In his discussion of human self-knowledge, Aquinas distinguishes between particular and universal. For particular self-knowledge, mere self-presence suffices, as when "Socrates perceives that he has an intellectual soul because he perceives that he understands."[44] Some sort of self-presence, at least of the indirect, reflective sort, is necessary for us to have a basis in experience to talk about the requisite activities and powers. But self-knowledge of the universal and philosophical kind requires a "diligent and subtle inquiry," precisely the oblique line of inquiry found in Aristotle's *De Anima*. The depiction of the self as existing only in its knowing of the other as other and its apprehension of itself only in reflection on that very act of knowing the other stands in marked contrast to McDowell's Hegelian conception of the identity of knower and known as a redundant sameness.

Given his debt to Gadamer's understanding of rationality as a social space of reasons, it is odd that McDowell never adverts to the phenomenon of interpersonal dialogue. As Clarke comments, "in the experience of an authentic successful interpersonal dialogue, it is impossible" for anyone "to believe sincerely that the other is not equally as real as his own self and equally interacting with him, to believe that he is somehow positing the other's reality and action from within himself."[45] More significantly, in a successful dialogue, or even for us to be aware that an attempt at dialogue has failed, it cannot be the case that form or structure comes from within or is imposed by the mind itself. Instead, the "whole point" of a dialogue is "that we do in fact succeed in taking in meaningful, intangible forms from without, preformed, prestructured by an active source other than ourselves."[46] Like all substances, persons are not just present to us but present to us in active and distinctive modes. Unlike other clearly nonrational substances, persons are, or at least can be, actively present to us in ways that demand that we interpret their actions in certain ways, or at least that we account for our rival interpretations of their actions. The dialogical other is not merely present to us, but actively present to us, actively confirming or actively resisting our interpretation of the content, meaning, and purpose of her speech and action.

Nature, Habit, and Animal Rationality

Were it not for interaction with others, inanimate and animate, we could not even know ourselves. Aristotle's entire method in the *De Anima*—the movement from object to act to power to essence—illustrates the indirect and oblique approach to human self-knowledge: "According to formula (*kata logon*), activities or actions are prior to powers." In marked contrast to modern approaches to mind, the study of the soul "pertains to natural philosophy from its mode of defining."[47] Nussbaum and Putnam comment,

> The mind-body problem . . . starts from a focus on the special nature of mental activity—therefore from just one part of the activity of some among living beings. . . . Aristotelian hylomorphism, by contrast, starts from a general interest in characterizing the relationship, in things of many kinds, between organization or structure and their material composition. . . . It asks two questions in particular . . . How do and should we explain or describe the changes we see taking place in the world? . . . What is it about individuals that makes them the very things that they are?[48]

McDowell himself appeals to Aristotle in his discussion of "second nature," but given the lingering Kantianism in his account, McDowell has real difficulty explaining the relationship between second and first nature. The relationship between first and second nature is far from clear. In some places, he states, "nature includes second nature."[49] In other places, the two remain rather bifurcated; second nature is the realm of meaning, while the realm of law is void of meaning. Another way of putting the difficulty is in terms of the project of reconciling Kant with Aristotle. McDowell's supposition is that either nature is neutral and law-like or it is enchanted; we thus seem not to have escaped the nineteenth-century division between science and romanticism, once again a Kantian dichotomy. McDowell traces the enchanted view of nature to the "common mediaeval outlook," wherein nature is seen as "filled with meaning" or as a "book of lessons."[50] The vain desire to re-enchant the universe risks a "return to mediaeval superstition."[51] But this is a less-than-helpful caricature of the use of functional or purposive language for animal behavior. McDowell's crude dismissal entails neglect of a sophisticated thesis that Alasdair MacIntyre advances with considerable empirical support and philosophical cogency:

> Adult human activity and belief are best understood as developing out of, and as still in some part dependent upon, modes of belief and activity that we share with some other species of intelligent animal, including dolphins. . . . [T]he activities and beliefs of members of those species need to be understood as in important respects approaching the condition of language-users.[52]

What MacIntyre point us toward is a rethinking of nature that might contribute to a reconsideration of freedom and of reason, or, in McDowell's terms, of the freedom of reason. McDowell provides no such account. At one point, he urges a rethinking of nature "to make room for spontaneity."[53] But he crudely reduces naturalism to what he pejoratively calls "bald naturalism," a position that subsumes the logical space of reasons under the logical space of nature.[54] Bald naturalism reduces the "space of reasons to something already unproblematically natural."[55] If there is an uneasy fit between the account of nature and that of second nature, then we seem not to have overcome the Kantian dichotomies but only to have produced more sophisticated versions of them. If we find this sort of dualism untenable, as McDowell purports to, then we can opt for bald naturalism or rethink our conception of nature. For the latter, we might turn to Aristotle, who locates the study of the soul as a part of natural philosophy, as an instance of the relationship of form and matter, soul and body, typical of animate life. In fact, McDowell often refers to second nature as "actualizing the potentialities of our nature." "Bildung," he writes, "actualizes natural potentialities."[56]

McDowell's view of the pervasiveness of the conceptual raises the question of how sub-human animals could have anything like an experience of the world. McDowell avails himself of Gadamer's distinction between animal environment and human world. The animal's interaction with its environment is driven by biological necessity. How are we not left with a dualism of the animal and the human, a dualism that would render otiose his appeals to construing our rationality and subjectivity as thoroughly articulated in terms of our animal nature? Since McDowell wants to avoid a Cartesian conception of animal life and behavior as thoroughly mechanistic, he attributes to animals a "proto-subjective sensitivity," an "analogue to subjectivity" in their "sensitivity to features of its environment."[57] As McDowell himself concedes, it is difficult to gain any clear sense of what this analogous sort of subjectivity could be, given that our experience is inherently conceptual, whereas an animal's cannot be. Whatever the nature of animal experience might be, there is a chasm between it and the human. It is hard to see McDowell's comparison of animal and human as analogous rather than equivocal.

Aquinas speaks of animal behavior and "reasoning" in much more differentiated terms. Clearly Thomas's account of animals is empirically inadequate from the perspective of contemporary science. Yet his approach, and especially that of his teacher, Albert the Great, does not involve deductions from metaphysical suppositions about the hierarchy of being. Instead, it is predicated on empirical observations about the physiological conditions for speech—a topic that should be of some interest to McDowell, given his own emphasis on second nature as a realm of rational discourse. Albert was concerned with the hierarchy of animals, and especially with their capacities to communicate through vocal sound.[58] His attention to differences among animal capacities does not "obscure . . . the significance of the continuity and resemblances between some aspects of the intelligent activities of nonhuman animals and the language-informed practical rationality of human beings."[59] Albert focuses especially on the physiological conditions necessary for voice (vox), for example, tongue, palate, larynx, and so forth. On this view, animals may indeed have experience, since they possess the middle powers of the soul such as memory and imagination requisite for receiving and retaining images and even for making limited inferences from them. Higher animals possess an estimative power similar to the human particular reason that allows for a comparison and contrast of singulars. Their experiential cognition is a shadow of reason. They have a kind of prudence that imitates human reasoning and are thus capable of receiving instruction. They cannot, however, be taught in the sense of receiving doctrine; for they are incapable of apprehending of the universal in the particular, of abstracting the universals that are the starting points of science. Of course, there will be differences even at the level of experience, since the intermediate powers in humans are not identical to those in animals. In us, the powers of memory and particular reason are accommodated to, and immediately serve, the higher powers of reason. Nonetheless, there are similarities in function between the intermediate powers in us and in animals.[60]

Albert and Aquinas deploy functional and purposive language in the description and explanation of animal behavior. But the use of such language need not exclude the use of more strictly physical or chemical descriptions. As Nussbaum and Putnam argue in their defense of Aristotle's account of the soul, Aristotle and Aquinas hold that all animal action has "necessary material conditions," and these conditions are capable of the sort of description typical of modern science. The question is whether such descriptions provide complete or adequate explanations. Indeed, the deeper question is whether the scientist can describe what she is explaining without the use of minimally teleological language. Even if it does not enter directly into all the types of explanation operative in science, it might nonetheless operate as an implicit background for identification and understanding. McDowell's conflation of meaning in natural science with medieval superstition implies that the introduction of any amount of teleological language leads inevitably to alchemy and magic.[61]

In his assertion of an unbridgeable gulf between the impoverished world of animals, wherein "sentience is in the service of a mode of life that is structured by immediate biological imperatives," and the "free, distanced attitude" of human beings toward the world, McDowell stands in the tradition of Gadamer and Heidegger, the latter of whom concentrates on the absence among animals of what he calls the "as-structure" of perception. MacIntyre notes that Heidegger's account works only for the less complex forms of animal life; it ignores or misunderstands the characteristic activities of "dogs, chimpanzees, gorillas, dolphins." These animals

> do not merely respond to features of their environment, they actively explore it; they devote perceptual attention to the objects that they encounter; they inspect them from different angles; they recognize the familiar, they identify and classify; they may on occasion treat one and the same object first as something to be played with and then as something to be eaten, and some of them recognize and even grieve for what is absent. Most important of all, they exhibit in their activity belief-presupposing and belief-guided intentions and they are able to understand and to respond to the intentions communicated by others.[62]

Thus does Aquinas note that some animals make "natural judgments" and exhibit a "semblance of reason" as "they share in . . . natural prudence." Animals do indeed lack a sense of the world as a whole, and they do not make judgments about their judgments, which Aquinas says "belongs only to reason."[63]

If Aquinas attends to the semblances of reason in animal behavior, he is also acutely aware of the bodily conditions of human knowing and acting. Responding to the query about whether God gave the human body an apt disposition, Aquinas focuses on the "upright stature" of human beings.[64] In animals, the senses reside primarily in the face; but these senses are disposed quite differently toward the external world in lower and higher primates. In us, the face is distant from the earth and turned toward what is above the ground. This befits the distinctive functions of our senses, which are not limited to fulfilling biological needs. Our senses provide avenues for higher-level interaction with nature and other human beings. Beyond meeting bodily needs, we take delight in the beauty of sensible things.[65] We are open to and receptive of the whole: "The more subtle sense of sight discloses the many differences of things . . . so that we can gather intelligible truth from all things, earthly and heavenly."[66] If our mouths and tongues resembled those of other animals, they would "obstruct speech, which is the proper work of reason."

Aquinas's attention to the apparently insignificant characteristics of the human tongue underscores the importance of the sense of touch for human intelligence. Contrary to the often-heard complaint that Western philosophy privileges exclusively the sense of sight and thus an abstract and detached model of objectivity, Aquinas highlights the role of touch.[67] By comparison with the bodies of other animals, the human body is feeble, that is, less immediately equipped with powers serving the maintenance of life. Instead of a "fixed" set of bodily powers, it has reason and the hand, the organ of organs, able to craft limitless tools. Moreover, the human body is capable of activities transcending those concerned with mere survival. For these activities of knowledge and communication, the human body is suited with an "equable complexion, a mean between contraries," which enable human beings to receive and discriminate an array of sensible qualities. Such a complexion is prominent in the sense of touch, especially in the hand, which actually grasps and takes on the form of the thing held. There is a striking analogy here between the hand's grasping of objects and the intellect's grasping of the forms of the things.[68]

The link between touch and intelligence, and the analogy between touch and thought, illustrate from yet another vantage point the remarkable union of soul and body. The intellectual soul is the first act of the entire body, animating and informing the whole. This has important ramifications for the subrational powers of the human soul. As was true for Aristotle, so too for Aquinas, the passions are not seen as powers inherently subversive of reason or as utterly alien to it. The participation of the lower, sensitive powers in reason is prominent in Aquinas's examination of the passions. Since the passions reside in the sensitive appetite, it might seem that they could not be subject to moral appraisal. Yet Aquinas's longest treatment of the passions occurs precisely in an ethical treatise, the opening of the second part of the *Summa Theologiae*, and not in his various investigations of human nature prior to ethics. The task of ethics is not to create a clear demarcation between reason and passion and then to have reason fend off the vagrant impulses of passion. The faulty assumption here is that of an unbridgeable gap between intellect and will, on the one hand, and the sensitive appetite, on the other. Aquinas counters with Aristotle's teaching that, while the lower appetites are not intrinsically rational, they are amenable to rational persuasion and thus may participate in reason.[69]

Aquinas divides the passions into concupiscible and irascible. The former (which includes love and hatred, joy and sorrow) pertains to sensible good and evil absolutely, while the latter (which encompasses hope and despair, daring and fear) has a more narrow scope: the arduous or difficult good or evil.[70] The restricted scope of the irascible passions indicates their auxiliary and subordinate role; they are called into action when we encounter arduous goods or onerous evils. Since they concern a restricted good, they pertain to movement alone, as in struggle or flight, not to repose. In contrast to an influential strain of modern philosophy, which sees human movement as motivated primarily by fear or flight from what is inconvenient or unpleasant, Aquinas sees this as a secondary motive, parasitic on the primary motivation of love for the good.

Thus the concupiscible powers are prior to the irascible; and among the concupiscible powers, the first is love, whose inclination to the good is the cause of all the passions.[71]

By contrast to Aquinas's account of the reciprocal suitability of intellect and body to one another, the approach of both McDowell and Gadamer leaves us with a dualism characteristic of the romantic, humanist attempt to safeguard the human from the scientific.[72] The question here is whether such a division allows for the possibility that science could teach us anything about the human. If so, and if we wish to avoid reductionistic naturalism, what McDowell calls bald naturalism, then the question is whether we can develop a naturalism sufficiently enriched to be a basis for the notion of second nature. A related sort of difficulty surfaces in McDowell's discussion of freedom. McDowell's own critique of Kantian interiority is implicitly a critique of the attempt to secure freedom by carving out a realm of autonomy uninfluenced by anything external to it. But what might an alternative account of freedom look like?

Modern attempts to ground knowledge in anthropology and metaphysics have typically led to two unwelcome stances: dualism or reductionistic naturalism. The latter obscures from view the peculiarly human capacities of engaging the world and others, while the former severs the human from the animal. There need not be so much of a gap between animals and humans if we can revive functional, that is to say, purposive, language for lower animals. Were we to discover not a sharp gap between animal environment and human world but a hierarchical and analogically differentiated set of relationships, then we would have to put into question the Kantian bifurcation of the realm of scientific law from that of human freedom.[73] It may well be that we would discover a sort of hierarchy of levels of interaction with the world and among members of particular species.

Here we might find Plantinga's recent work on proper function suggestive, if ultimately inadequate. Plantinga insists upon the way the language of function and purpose is pervasively operative in our discourse about natural and human substances. Can we distinguish Plantinga's naturalism from the reductionistic sort? Although he claims that his view is thoroughly naturalistic and provides the same sort of account as that typically put forth in the natural and human sciences, Plantinga does show signs of seeing the need for an enriched and enlarged naturalism.[74] He takes on directly the attempt in the sciences to rid themselves of all language of function and purpose, and he maintains that Quine's naturalism, based as it is in functional generalizations, needs and implicitly contains the normative notion of proper function.[75] He cautions, moreover, that proper function and its allied conceptions of normalcy and health are not to be understood merely statistically. Following Reid, he holds that sound understanding presupposes the proper development and training of the mind, not just the absence of dysfunction.[76] In contrast to the atomistic and individualistic analysis that standardly accompanies the true belief model of knowledge, he holds that while justification may be individualistic, warrant is not. Finally, Plantinga's rejection of the deontological "ought" and his suggestion of a different sort of normativity, a naturalistic "ought," is precisely the line of inquiry that needs to be pursued. Such an understanding of obligation evades the characteristic Kantian division of imperatives into hypothetical and categorical and thus has no need for extravagant Kantian notions of freedom and autonomy.

As we noted in the previous chapter, numerous aspects of proper function point us in the direction of a virtue epistemology. Plantinga's only explicit examination of nature and nurture is disappointing, however. In his discussion of the roles of nature and nurture in our perception of objects, Plantinga notes that although we are naturally endowed with the capacity to see and distinguish objects, speech about objects involves the to some extent socially inculcated ability to see an object as this or that. As he puts it, one must learn to perceive that a thing "looks thus and so." He comments that the proper functioning of faculties includes their modification in the way dictated by the design plan. This opens up the possibility of—indeed, seems to require—a substantive and rich account of virtue. What he states later about the need to combine in our conception of warrant the notion of proper cognitive function with a sense of "felt inclination," of a "perceived attractiveness" or "fittingness," would most naturally be spelled out in terms of a virtue theory.[77] Yet in the section on perception, Plantinga concludes his inquiry at precisely the juncture where it becomes interesting. Having implicitly raised a very interesting question about the role of second nature even in what appears to be most basic to our first nature, Plantinga ends his discussion with the unsatisfying remark that both nature and nurture contribute to perception.[78]

The lack of attention to nurture, to the role of habit and education in the development and proper functioning of our cognitive faculties, leaves Plantinga open to attack by Zagzebski, who hits upon the basic problem in Plantinga's proper function model, a problem that is the inverse of the difficulty generated by McDowell's account. The difficulty with Plantinga's position has to do with the focus on artifacts and machines as paradigmatic.[79] Zagzebski rightly counters that the proper functioning of machines is hardly an apt basis for understanding the excellences of the virtues. Even were Plantinga's naturalism not so mechanistic, it would still be inadequate, according to her. Given the intrinsic limitations of naturalism, she goes on to argue that we must overcome naturalism because of the difference between the natural scientist's "struggle with facts" and the moral scientist's emphasis on "what ought to be."[80] This reinstitution of the now-long-abandoned is/ought distinction is much too hasty. It is instructive to note that the attack on the is/ought distinction had to do with recovering functional and purposive language for human action. The goal then would seem to be to retain the language of function and purpose without taking machines and artifacts as normative. Indeed, Plantinga leaves himself open here to the charge that he has failed to take seriously the social conditions of proper function, the way particular practices inform our understanding of intellectual as well as moral excellence.

Freedom from Philosophy?

McDowell's attempted exorcism of skeptical worries and foundationalist projects involves a repudiation of what he calls "constructive philosophy." The realm of meaning or justification is that of second nature or *Bildung*; in our ethical training, we are "initiated into the space of reasons"; the "ethical is the domain of rational requirements."[81] In repudiating constructive philosophy, McDowell hopes to leave us with "no norms except specific ones," whose investigation is not especially philosophic.[82] He opposes modern anxieties over justification to Wittgensteinian therapy and sides with the latter, which desires to "give philosophy peace." There are two sorts of questions to be raised about McDowell's therapeutic cure for what ails philosophy.

The first sort are internal to McDowell's project in *Mind and World*. There are good reasons to think that McDowell's Wittgensteinian therapy is at odds with the epistemological internalism—with its accent on epistemic rights and duties, on the justification of knowledge—that he advocates, for example, in his reference to "rational requirements." A further echo of internalism can be found in McDowell's insistence that we reserve the notion of belief "for what is in one's control."[83] Even in cases where one simply finds oneself with a belief, "the question of one's entitlement to the belief can be raised." Are the strong ethical demands of reflection, demands of the rigorous internalist sort, compatible with his Wittgensteinian goal of giving philosophy rest? Given his calm dismissal of skeptical worries, the refutation of which figures prominently in internalism, McDowell's approach is at variance with classical internalism. What resurfaces here is "modern tension between knowledge as normative and as the result of an exercise of natural powers."[84]

The second kind of question has to do with whether McDowell's contrast between constructive philosophy and the therapy that gives rest exhausts the possibilities for philosophy. It is important to note that McDowell does not imagine that all meaningful questions will evaporate after the exorcism of constructive philosophy. But the remaining questions will be specific questions, not particularly philosophical. On this issue, McDowell leaves undeveloped his gestures in the direction of Gadamer, whose conception of philosophy as dialogical conversation between traditions of inquiry we have previously invoked. On this score, MacIntyre is much closer to Gadamer than is McDowell. McIntyre offers a detailed description of the rationality of practices or crafts and of narratives or traditions. Recall, for example, his statement that "to become adept in a craft . . . , one has to learn how to apply" a distinction "between what as activity or product merely seems good to me and what really is good, a distinction always applied retrospectively as part of learning from one's earlier mistakes and surpassing one's earlier limitations."[85]

MacIntyre thus points in the direction of standards of excellence internal to practices, standards embodied in the virtues germane to a particular practice and amenable to historical development through conversation about the aims and means of realizing the excellences proper to the practice. In this context and even more so in the context of questions about how any set of particular practices can be organized into a unified human life, theoretical questions will undoubtedly arise. As MacIntyre puts it, "There is . . . no form of philosophical enquiry . . . that is not practical in its implications, just as there is no practical enquiry that is not philosophical in its presuppositions."[86]

MacIntyre suggests a third way between the advocates of philosophy as a theoretical enterprise of establishing epistemological foundations and a flight from theory in its entirety. That, in some form, is the position we intend to develop on the basis of Aquinas's texts, a position most accessible through a consideration of Aquinas's reading of Aristotle. It turns out, as will be made clear in the next chapter, that Aquinas's reading of Aristotle highlights the aporetic or dialectical status of the questions regarding theory and practice. Aquinas's own attempt to move toward a more adequate set of responses to these questions involves, in part, an extension of certain positions latent in Aristotle and, in part, the deployment of Neoplatonic and Christian resources.

five
Metaphysics and/as Practice

One constructive response to the critique of "constructive philosophy," as found in McDowell and others, aims to recover the primordial sense of philosophy as a way of life. This sort of reading of Aristotle, indeed, of ancient philosophy, has gained a certain currency in recent years because of the work of Pierre Hadot. In his book, *What Is Ancient Philosophy?* Hadot notes in Aristotle "the intimate link between knowledge and affectivity."[1] He observes more broadly that entrance into the philosophical schools of antiquity involved the "choice of a certain way of life," an "existential option" requiring a "conversion of one's entire being, and ultimately a willingness to be and live in a certain way."[2] To readers of Gadamer or Wittgenstein, Hadot's remarks about the circularity of doctrine and practice of a way of life will sound quite familiar.

> This existential option implies . . . a certain vision of the world, and the task of philosophical discourse will therefore be to reveal and rationally justify this existential option. . . . Theoretical philosophical discourse is thus born from this initial existential option, and it leads back to it, insofar as—by means of its logical and persuasive force, and the action it tries to exert upon

the interlocutor—it incites both masters and disciples to live in genuine conformity with their initial choice.[3]

What remains somewhat suppressed in Hadot's account is the role of truth, propositional or otherwise, in the unfolding of this "existential option." The ancient philosophical genre of the protreptic, the discourse that seeks to initiate the beginner into a specific way of life, does not offer to the reader a series of demonstrative arguments; it is, rather, a rhetorical text aiming at rational persuasion and addressing the rational appetite for happiness. One cannot, as a precondition of adopting a way of life, test out each of the propositions or logical entailments of a particular philosophical school. But the conversion to a particular school is at least in part an invitation to begin probing its theses for their internal coherence and depth and for their superiority to the claims of other philosophical schools. There is also the question of whether a philosophical school can deliver on its promise to transform one's life. Thus it paves the way for the possibility that argument could lead one to adopt a different way of life as having a superior account of the good. Consider, for example, the way Socratic questioning makes Augustine intellectually dissatisfied with the teachings of the Manicheans, or the way, despite its rational superiority to Manicheanism, Augustine abandons Platonism for Christianity because only the latter could heal his soul and effectively turn him toward the good.

Aristotelian *Aporiae*

Like Augustine, Aquinas works out of an inherited tradition of philosophical and theological reflection, one that has had much to say about metaphysics and practice. Although the influences on Aquinas's thought are numerous, there is no question that on the topic of the relationship of metaphysics to practice, or even on the nature of practice itself, Thomas is preoccupied with a set of difficulties, knots, problems (*aporiae*) that he inherits from the texts of Aristotle.[4] Aquinas does his best to resolve these difficulties by internal appeal to parallel passages in Aristotle or by a development of what he takes to be the trajectory of Aristotle's thought on a variety of subject matters. But the dialectical engagement of Aristotle affords Aquinas the opportunity to find a place for authorities, texts, and arguments from rival traditions, particularly from the neo-Platonic tradition. It also affords him the opportunity to be quite explicit about the limitations to philosophical inquiry about the most significant questions, especially concerning God, creation, and the human good. This prepares the way for a dialectical encounter between philosophy and theology.

Very early in the *Ethics*, Aristotle affirms the primacy of practice in his examination of the good life for human beings. In the first book, Aristotle famously argues that the end of human life is happiness and then proceeds to try to delimit that activity or set of activities in which happiness consists. Although Aristotle will insist at great length later in the *Ethics* that the good life, or happiness, is the most pleasant life available to human beings, he begins by dismissing the life of pleasure as a candidate for the good life. Beyond his worry over the human propensity to identify happiness with the satisfaction of bodily appetites, he is concerned that the experience of pleasure is merely a passive and subjective state of contentment. Instead, Aristotle resolutely affirms that happiness is an *activity*, or rather that it is a set of coordinated activities involving the repetitious performance of acts of certain kinds. His succinct description is that happiness is "activity of soul in accord with complete excellence."[5] The good life is a way of being and acting in the world; habits—virtues or vices—determine one's character. They are inculcated by the repetitious performance of acts of certain types; once formed, habits reliably produce acts in harmony with the character from which they flow.

But all this talk about reliability, as we have seen previously, can be deeply misleading as a way of depicting virtue. Instead of a mechanistic picture, with connotations of mindless rote conformity, Aquinas's vision of virtue portrays the virtuous agent as capable of perceiving more, with greater subtlety, in concrete circumstances and thus as acting in accord with greater freedom.

The primacy of practice in Aristotle's *Ethics* is evident in his frequent claim that the virtues are inculcated in the same way as skills in crafts, that is, by repetitious action. It is, Aristotle insists, "by doing just acts that the just man is produced," not by taking "refuge in theory."[6] Some want to take Aristotle's worries about theory, in the sphere of practice, as opening up the possibility of subsuming *theoria* under *phronesis*. But this courts a reductionism of a different sort from the one so commonly discussed in twentieth-century philosophy. Instead of a reduction of prudential discrimination to theory, this move would reduce theory to prudence. Instead, what we find in the writings of Aristotle and Aquinas is an interplay between practice and theory, a complex set of analogies that presuppose fundamental distinctions. Of course, any such interaction must be seen in light of a set of fundamental distinctions.

In his discussion of types of virtuous activities, Aristotle distinguishes between theoretical and practical on the basis of whether the end pursued in the activity is for the sake of knowing (theoretical) or doing (practical). He further divides the practical into acting, in which the doing is an end in itself, and making, in which the goal is to produce something that flows from, but is extrinsic to, the activity itself. Aristotle rather hastily dismisses making (*techne*) as a possible candidate for the human good because its excellence is not principally in the human agent but in the product. By contrast, the goods sought in contemplation and in moral action inhere in the agent as perfective of her. As Aristotle puts it in the *Metaphysics*, there is a difference between immanent and transitive actualities, the former of which remain in the agent, whereas the latter pass into an extrinsic object. Despite the dismissal of *techne* as a candidate for the human good, neither Aristotle nor Aquinas underestimates the important role of arts and productive activities for the good life of human beings. A host of productive activities will enter directly into, and make possible human participation in, the good. Even here, Aristotle will insist that a good political order is not defined solely by its ability to be productive, but rather by the ways in which it fosters virtuous action on the part of citizens. But the lines are not as clearly drawn by Aristotle as they sometimes appear to be; for example, construction is involved in the sort of analogy-forming activities in which prudence (*phronesis*) regularly engages. Politics itself involves the cultivation, fostering, and ordering of a variety of productive practices.

The primacy of practice and the normative examples of practices or crafts for the good life render Aristotle's own explicit demotion of *techne* or craft somewhat misleading. On the one hand, the activity of a *techne*, since its perfection consists in external things and not in the agent herself, is not a candidate for the good life. On the other, crafts provide analogies for the inculcation of virtue since they involve the formation of an apprentice, under the guidance of a master practitioner, in the appropriate habits. Moreover, Aquinas's preoccupation with pedagogy, with the relationship of teacher to student, and with the integration of contemplation and action in the life of the teacher, whose ultimate model is Christ—all this underscores the importance of the craft or art of teaching. An even more striking elevation of *techne* or *ars* can be seen in the claim that the exemplar of all human endeavors, speculative or practical, is the divine art. Christ himself is called the "Art" of the Father. In this context, ethical practice itself is mimetic, an imitation of the divine life.

None of this, however, undermines the basic distinction between different types of activity or actuality; indeed, it is only from the perspective of these distinctions that we can begin to appreciate Aquinas's theological reworking of them. As Gadamer observes, *praxis* differs from *poesis* or *techne* precisely in that the product of the latter is separable from the one who produces it, while the former involves the "realization of the person himself." This has important consequences for teaching, the communication of knowledge and wisdom. What comes under the purview of *phronesis* cannot be taught in the way specialized techniques are; the sort of knowledge held by prudence is inseparable from the personal habits of discernment in concrete conditions. Thus, the knowledge is embedded within a specific set of practices and is not transferable as a set of abstract techniques. He broadens the point: "The ideal of objective theory, neutral in regard to all the interests at stake in any practical application of it, and consequently capable of any application one might wish to make, is neither Platonic nor Aristotelian."[7]

Underscoring the intimate connection between the discussion of actuality in *Metaphysics* IX and the discussion of the virtues in the *Ethics*, Aquinas quotes the *Metaphysics* in his commentary on the *Ethics*: "Action is an operation remaining in the agent himself, as to see, to understand, or to will. But making is an operation passing into exterior matter in order to form something as to build or to cut."[8] Conversely, in his commentary on the *Metaphysics*, he introduces the topic of value or perfection:

> When, beyond the act of a power, some work is constituted, that act perfects the work, not the agent of the work. . . . But when there is no other work produced beyond the operation of the power, then the action exists in the agent as its perfection and does not pass into some exterior thing. . . . Happiness consists in such an operation . . . because it is the good of the one who is happy.[9]

Aquinas here draws attention to connections between the *Ethics* and the *Metaphysics*. An old debate about the connection between moral philosophy and other disciplines in Aristotle's corpus has recently been revived, with partisans dividing up between, on the one hand, those who think that the arguments of ethics draw upon principles established elsewhere—say, in natural philosophy or metaphysics—and, on the other, those who insist on the autonomy of ethics whose principles are established dialectically by examining phenomena peculiar to moral inquiry. In her recent book, *Cognition of Value in Aristotle's Ethics*, Deborah Achtenberg argues for an alternative construal of the relation between metaphysics and ethics: metaphysics does not supply demonstrations for use in ethics but rather complements ethics by offering a fully worked out understanding of certain terms and theses.[10] This fits Aquinas's conception of metaphysics as a sapiential mode of discourse that investigates the principles or starting points of the particular sciences and orders the multiple sciences in relation to one another and in relation to the human good.

But Aquinas has even more precise distinctions to make regarding metaphysics. In addition to his commentary on the opening of Aristotle's *Metaphysics*, on the subject matter of metaphysics, also relevant is his extended reflection on the hierarchy of the sciences in his commentary on the *De Trinitate* of the neo-Platonist Boethius. In the hierarchy of sciences, metaphysics is preceded by physics, which treats of what exists in matter and motion, and mathematics, which treats of objects in abstraction from matter and motion. Of course, physics itself involves abstraction; it abstracts from what Aquinas calls "signate matter," the matter at which one can point—for example, this flesh and these bones. But in its study of the natures and universal attributes of physical things, it does not abstract entirely from matter; otherwise, natural things would be misconstrued. Definitions of animals must include reference to flesh and bones, but not to this particular flesh or these bones. One must include common matter, but not individualized matter. Mathematics is at a further remove from the sensible order. Its objects are neither in matter nor in motion. It might seem from the trend of consideration in these sciences that the last science in the hierarchy would be constituted by an even greater degree of abstraction. Metaphysics, however, does not study objects at a higher level of abstraction. Indeed, the order of the hierarchy can be misleading, since for Aristotle and Aquinas, and in marked contrast to Plato, mathematics does not provide a path into metaphysics. In the order of pedagogy that Aquinas inherits from Aristotle, mathematics and logic precede the properly philosophical disciplines of natural philosophy, the soul, ethics, and politics, and finally metaphysics. Not being tied to complex empirical conditions, logic and mathematics are more easily apprehended by inexperienced youth. A result of this departure from Plato's order of disciplines in the divided line, wherein mathematics is the bridge between the material and the immaterial, is that mathematics does not, for Aristotle or Aquinas, provide privileged access to being.

Instead of mathematics, physics, or natural philosophy, which includes the study of the soul, is the proper avenue into metaphysics. In each of these disciplines—in physics' conclusion with a proof for an unmoved mover or in the study of the soul's searching examination of the nonmateriality of the intellect and the prospects for its immortality—we encounter nonmaterial beings, powers, and activities that are not properly part of the subject matters of the disciplines antecedent to metaphysics. As was noted at the outset, Ralph McInerny provides a succinct description of the origins of metaphysics, its subject matter, and its goal, at least as Thomas construes these:

> In the study of natural things we are compelled to appeal to causes which are not themselves natural and we come thereby to see that not everything which is is material. This serves as the basis for seeking yet another science which will have as its subject, not being of a particular kind, but being as such. Proceeding horizontally so to speak this science will seek knowledge of what belongs *per se* to being after the fashion of properties of its subject. In what may be described as a vertical procedure, it will seek the cause of its subject, the efficient and, preeminently, the final cause of whatever is, of being as being.[11]

If the transition from physics to mathematics marks a retreat from the real order, the turn to metaphysics signals a movement in the direction of the real. Not abstraction but negative judgment (*separatio*) is the intellectual activity that Aquinas associates with metaphysical reasoning.[12] It involves the judgment that nonmaterial beings exist. If there were no objects capable of existing apart from matter, then physics would be first philosophy, the most comprehensive investigation of what is. Objects can be said to be independent of matter "either because they never are in matter, as is true of God and the other separate substances, or because they are not always in matter, as is true of substance, potency and act, and being itself."[13] So, the proper subject matter of metaphysics is *ens inquantum ens*. The very grammar of the phrase *ens inquantum ens*, being as being, with its use of the concretely signifying participle *ens*, indicates that the investigation is on the level of concrete beings; yet the mode of inquiry into these concretely existing beings concerns what is common to all (*inquantum*).

McInerny helpfully distinguishes between two ways of describing metaphysics: (a) as the study of being qua being, the horizontal path; and (b) as theology, the vertical path. Aristotle's third way of describing metaphysics, as first philosophy, involves a shift from the temporal order of the study of the disciplines to the order of being. What is first in the order of being is last in the order of learning or knowing. Metaphysics is first philosophy in the sense that it studies the principles, such as the principle of contradiction, assumed or taken for granted in the other specialized sciences. It also has within its purview the study of the first and highest causes.

The craft analogy figures prominently in Aristotle's various discussions of this sapiential task of ordering disciplines, inquiries, and activities. In the opening of the *Metaphysics*, Aristotle argues that first philosophy or metaphysics is the highest part of philosophy because it pursues knowledge of the highest principles and causes, knowledge to which all other inquiries are ordered.[14] In the opening of the *Ethics*, he describes politics as the architectonic art because it falls to politics to order all human activities to the end of the good of the entire community.[15] While maintaining a distinction between theoretical and practical activities of the intellect, Aquinas frames his entire discussion of the good life in terms of the craft analogy, which highlights the communal pursuit of excellences embedded within practices. Among all arts and inquiries, wisdom is the one that orders other arts to the human good.[16] The prominence and preeminence of this way of framing the question of the human good means that practice is more fundamental than theory. Aquinas puts it this way in the opening of his commentary on Aristotle's *Metaphysics*: "As the Philosopher teaches in his *Politics*, when several things are ordered to one, it is necessary that one be regulative and the others, regulated. . . . All sciences and arts are ordered to one end, namely to man's perfection, which is happiness."[17]

Aquinas situates the entire hierarchy of philosophical disciplines within the context of a way of life. There are similarities here to Stanley Rosen's depiction of Platonist metaphysics as the "attempt to think the whole in the sense of attempting to be at home in it; hence wisdom is more like *phronesis* or what comes to mean in Aristotle 'practical intelligence' than it is like dialectic."[18] In fact, metaphysics to some extent overlaps with ethics. The practice of metaphysics, motivated by the natural desire to know, involves a variety of goods of the rational appetite. If we are to speak of a contest for the best way of life, a contest in which the principal contestants are the active and the contemplative lives, then the practice of metaphysics marks the culmination of the contemplative life. In this sense, the practice of metaphysics as a partial fulfillment of the good life is subject to ethical appraisal; indeed, is itself an ethical ideal.

In Aristotle's texts, clarifications of the nature of the good life are especially prominent in the *Ethics* and the *Politics*. In the latter text, Aristotle returns to the central topic of the *Ethics*, the "most eligible way of life," and argues against those who dismiss contemplation. They do so on the assumption that "he who does nothing cannot do well." Aristotle concurs that we should not elevate "inactivity above action, for happiness is activity." He amplifies this point,

> Not that a life of action must necessarily have relation to others, as some persons think, nor are those ideas only to be regarded as practical which are pursued for the sake of practical results, but much more the thoughts and contemplations which are independent and complete in themselves, since acting well and therefore a certain kind of action is an end.[19]

Now, in the immediate context of this assertion, Aristotle is advancing and defending a position on the divine character of the life of contemplation. He holds that if perfect activity were limited to practical actions and productions, "God and the universe, who have no eternal actions apart from their own energies, would be far from perfection."[20] Or again, "God is a witness . . . , for he is happy and blessed, not by reason of any external good, but in himself and by reason of his own nature."[21] Indeed, contemplation fits rather neatly the criteria for happiness articulated in the opening of the *Ethics*. The good is desirable and pleasant precisely because it is congruent with the capacities of human nature. "It is," Aquinas notes, "of the very meaning of happiness that it be self-sufficient and lacking in nothing."[22] Happiness is "maximally continuous and permanent" (*felicitas est maxime continua et permanens*).[23] Aquinas himself entertains an objection to the very possibility of virtues being exclusively theoretical. Such activities seem not to be operative. Aquinas resists circumscribing activity or operation to the practical intellect; he states that the virtues of the speculative intellect are operative, ordered to the "interior act of the intellect, which is to consider truth."[24]

Intellectual Practice: Wonder, Work, and Truthfulness

In his remarkable little book, *Leisure, the Basis of Culture*, Josef Pieper provides an eloquent defense of the properly human dignity involved in the contemplative act of the intellect. He sees our age as afflicted by an absence of true leisure, by an immersion in work and a dismissive attitude toward activities that are other than productive or entertaining. In this way, the teleological ordering of human nature to the whole is denied, and humanity is understood in purely functional terms. Rooted in our capacity for wonder, true leisure and contemplation rupture the world of "total work."[25] Pieper is no doubt correct about much of what afflicts our age, and he provides a compelling defense of leisure as involving an openness to the transcendent; yet his hard opposition of leisure to work leaves us with no way to speak about work except in pejorative terms.

There is, of course, the important difference, evident not just in contrast between *techne* and *theoria* but also between *techne* and *praxis*. Neither *theoria* nor *praxis* realizes its end in external matter, but rather in the excellence of the agent. Still, there is a problem with insisting on too great a chasm between contemplation and crafts. The difficulty with Pieper's contrast between wonder or culture and work is that it establishes too sharp a dichotomy between the two arenas, as also between lower and higher, and body and soul. Responding to Pieper's strong contrast between leisure and work, the Thomist Yves Simon worries that stressing the dichotomy between culture and work may result in the reduction of culture to a realm of effete refinement, which itself courts a barbarism of reflection, as Vico called it. Simon counters, "We must insist that knowledge of truth, not possession of culture, be our regulating ideal. . . . The good worker and the lover of truth have much in common." Instead of a life of leisure, "the real basis of culture—its supporting structure and hard core—is to be found rather in activities in the performance of which a workmanlike disposition is indispensable."[26] This point is nicely expressed in Bernard Williams's recent account of "accuracy," the passion for getting things right, as a virtue of truthfulness. The sort of "workmanlike" dispositions commended by Simon are necessary because of the sheer difficulty of arriving at the truth on any subject, a task in which the investigator must confront both external and internal obstacles. Williams puts it this way:

> The external obstacles to truth-discovery are an example of the world's being resistant to our will. It is, of course, resistant to being changed in various ways, but equally it is resistant to being discovered, interpreted, unraveled. . . . The fact that there are external obstacles to the pursuit of truth is one foundation to our idea of objectivity, in the sense that our beliefs are answerable to an order of things that lies beyond our own determination. There is also another sense of "objectivity," in which it is a virtue of inquirers, and in this sense it is connected, rather, with internal obstacles to discovery and true belief. Self-conscious pursuit of truth requires resistance to such things as self-deception and wishful thinking, and one component of the virtue of Accuracy . . . lies in the skills and attitudes that resist the pleasure principle, in all its forms, from a gross need to believe the agreeable, to mere laziness in checking one's investigations.[27]

Aquinas, following Aristotle, keeps alive the analogy between virtue and work when he argues that the "virtue of a thing is what makes its work good."[28] Of course, the perfection of practical virtue, as of the contemplative intellectual virtues, is marked by the ease with which the acts are performed, but that is not to deny that habituation of character, a disciplining of will and intellect, is not a prequel to the achievement of virtue. Nor is it to deny that on occasion the exercise of practical or speculative virtue may involve effort and the overcoming of difficulties, as Williams nicely points out.[29]

As Yves Simon urges, the danger with Pieper's account is that it may set up too sharp a dichotomy within the life of the philosopher between contemplative leisure, on the one hand, and the intellectual work or effort of research and reasoning that takes up most of the philosopher's time and energy, on the other. Simon also worries that the oversimplified opposition of culture to work fosters a conception of culture as "frivolity" or as a decorative cover for idleness.[30] Simon sees a number of virtues in work, especially manual work. The worker must wrestle with conditions that are given; as an individual, the worker is always dependent for success on the help of others, on the division of labor, and on various forms of association. Simon writes that the "sociability of the worker" involves "activity proportioned to the balance of powers in man."

What is suggestive about Simon's approach to work is the way it counters the supposition that work or *techne* is rooted in a craftsman's model of *making*, a model that accentuates the independence of the human intellect from matter and tends toward a conception of the human intellect as autonomous "master and possessor of nature." Work, for Simon, is rooted in the concrete conditions of whatever craft is at issue and is dependent both upon the limitations of the antecedent material conditions and upon a community of workers. Here, *techne* does not so much lead us away from concrete conditions as it moves us toward them. Simon's thesis thus implies the possibility of a much greater integration of *techne* with *phronesis* than most Aristotelians or Thomists have acknowledged.

Of course, Simon is acutely aware of the contrasts between work and contemplation, and Pieper has no intention of fostering an effete, flowery culture.[31] If Simon, in this respect similar to McDowell, wishes to turn our attention to particular spheres of activity, to the concrete conditions of practices, he nonetheless shares Pieper's conviction that philosophy is not a specialized sphere of activity peculiarly focused on questions of epistemological justification. However much it might unsettle commonplace certitudes, wonder has its roots in a variety of everyday experiences: "the philosophical act, the religious act, the artistic act, and the special relationship with the world that comes into play with the existential disturbance of love or death."[32]

Although philosophy puts in question the "penultimate certitudes . . . of everyday reason," it is nonetheless oriented to an understanding of the shared human world and hence cannot be rooted in an individualistic conception of the mind. In fact, the pursuit of knowledge about our common world is a prime example of what the ancients meant by a common good, a good that is not diminished, but is instead increased, by being shared. Human persons dwell in the world, not in anxious skeptical doubt or in the comfortable certainty of a comprehensive vision, but in hope. The human world is the "whole reality, in the midst of which the human being lives, face to face with the entirety of existing things," an understanding of which is not given in the "perfection of total understanding, but only in expectation or hope."[33] What Pieper proposes, on the basis of a remarkably penetrating reading of Aquinas, is a metaphysics of hope, in which one may participate via a multitude of communal practices. To return to philosophy as hopeful wonder would be to recover Aquinas's alternative to constructive philosophy and the peace that gives philosophy rest.

The analogy between work and the intellectual life forces the social dimension back to the fore, since workers, as Simon notes, are permanently dependent on others, on a division of labor, and on associations of various sorts. Pieper himself, it should be said, draws heavily on pagan and Christian conceptions of leisure as rooted in the religious feast and in communal worship, not in flowery artistic expression. Moreover, the act of contemplation, although ordered to what is eternal and expressive of intimations of immortality, never fully transcends our finite, bodily condition of existence. To put it bluntly, it never transcends the condition of wonder, of ignorance on the way to knowledge. Hence, in the highest achievement of the human intellect, we sense the inherent limitations and the vulnerability of the human species.

> To wonder is to be on the way, *in via*. In the *Summa theologiae*, wonder is defined as the *desiderium sciendi*, the longing for knowledge, an active desire for knowledge. Although wonder means not to know, it does not mean that we are, in a kind of despair, resigned to ignorance. Out of wonder, Aristotle says, comes joy. . . . In its fusion of positive and negative, ignorance on the way to further knowledge, wonder reveals itself as having the same structure as hope, the same architecture as hope—the structure that characterizes philosophy—and, indeed, human existence itself.[34]

Following Aquinas, who repeatedly insists on our partial apprehension of the divine through philosophical discourse, Pieper introduces a temporal element into the very heart of the contemplative life and thereby links the practice of philosophy itself to the virtue of hope. The truth about philosophy thus becomes a truth, not just about a select few individuals, but also about the entire human race.

The social dimension of the intellectual life can be seen in a number of other ways. First, there is the ancient commitment to dialectical reasoning as beginning from received opinions, of the wise and the many. Although philosophy may, in its openness to the whole and in its critical attitude toward opinions, set itself at variance with the unreflective immersion in conventional life, it remains rooted in ordinary experience and in the language used in conventional life. In fact, Aristotle insists that a convincing philosophical argument must, even after it has demonstrated the truth, return to the originating opinions and save the phenomena, by accounting for what remains of value in them. Moreover, in the realm of philosophy itself, the sense of tradition is indispensable for progress. As Aquinas puts it in his commentary on the *Metaphysics*, "while each of the predecessors has discovered something of the truth (*aliquid de veritate*), all the truths brought together into one (*simul in unum collectum*) leads to a great knowledge of the truth."[35] Moreover, Aristotle's and Aquinas's defenses of the isolated act of contemplation against those who would reduce activity to productivity should not lead us to postulate a simple opposition of individual to community or of silence to speech. Instead, there is a fertile interplay of solitude and communion, silence and speech.

Second, Aristotle insists that through interaction with others we are "better able both to think and to act." As Paul Ricoeur has recently reminded us, the most fertile passages for sorting out the tensions and resources in Aristotle's account of the contemplative life and its social dimension occur in the discussion of friendship in the *Ethics*. Even the philosopher is naturally social. Others, friends, are crucial for self-knowledge. Ricoeur rightly focuses on the complementarity of metaphysics and ethics in this section of the *Ethics*. The human intellect, according to Aristotle's anthropology, is a potency that is made actual only by knowing things other than itself. It knows itself only indirectly by reflecting on its knowledge of other things. The order of knowing the soul is not through immediate self-possession or through cutting off connection to other things. Instead, we must follow an oblique route to self-knowledge, a route that illustrates the principle that the order of knowing is inversely related to the order of being. In the latter order, soul or nature comes first, then powers, then activities, then objects of activities. But we must reverse that path in coming to know our own intellects. What we are aware of first are the objects of our activities, from which we discern the activities and the powers engaged in those activities, from which in turn we can know something of our nature or essence. As Aristotle notes, this means that the activities of our friends will be better known to us than our own activities, or at least they will aid us in coming to an enriched understanding of ourselves. Ricoeur observes,

> A refined egotism, under the title of *philautia*, ends up, quite unexpectedly, propounding the idea that the happy man or woman needs friends (*EN* 9.9). Otherness, therefore, repossesses the rights that *philautia* appeared to eclipse. It is in connection with the notions of capacity and realization— that is, finally of power and act—that a place is made for lack and, through the mediation of lack, for otherness.[36]

Ricoeur's focus on capacity and realization, power and act is quite helpful. The ontology of substances contains an important distinction between first and second act, between the act of existing as a substance of a certain sort, in the case as a rational animal, and a variety of acts that the substance is capable of realizing because of the capacities peculiar to it. Neither Aristotle nor Aquinas treats the first act as involving relations to others. But, in the complex order of second acts, beings are inevitably related to others. Potencies are not self-actualizing. Moreover, their actualization aims at a kind of self-revelation or self-communication to other beings. Thus we can say that for Aquinas to be substance-in-action is "to be substance-in-relation."[37]

As I suggested at the outset, Aquinas's depiction of contemplation as an activity entails (a) that speculative activities must be conceived as a practice involving a set of virtues, and (b) that as one activity among many others in which human beings engage, speculative activities must be integrated by prudential judgment into other activities. Another way to put this is to say that the entirety of human life, each of the activities in which human beings engage, falls under the direction and command of prudence. No single activity or set of activities can constitute a good human life; indeed, Aristotle's own exalted criteria for happiness, the very criteria that point us inevitably in the direction of contemplation, also underscore the limits to the contemplative life as a model for the life of human excellence. These criteria underscore the permanence and continuity of happiness and thus turn our attention from isolated acts or activities to the whole of human life, to a "complete life." No single activity or set of activities can constitute a complete life. How any individual is to weave together her various activities, which ought to take precedence when, and for what duration, is not something that any deliverance of theory can determine; it is a matter of prudential discernment and judgment.

Of course, Aristotle and Aquinas hold that the objects studied in the speculative sciences are necessary; hence there is no need for counsel in the investigation of its objects.[38] What they have in mind here is best exemplified in a mathematical discipline such as geometry, where the truth of the Pythagorean theorem is not something that is subject to prudential appraisal. Nor, significantly, does the character of the geometer—whether she be temperate or intemperate, courageous or cowardly—affect her possession of the truth or her ability to demonstrate it before other students of geometry. Yet if we appraise an act of virtue, not so much in terms of its object, but "in relation to act," then the right ordering of the soul's powers to act is superior to the intellectual virtues. In this respect, and in regard to the exercise of the act, there is room and need for counsel to determine "how and in what order we must proceed in them" (sed quantum ad usum earum, utputa quomodo vel quo ordine sit in eis procedendum).[39] The point can be broadened. Counsel, a part of prudence, is necessary to determine when and in what ways we ought to engage in the acts of the speculative virtues. It would also fall to prudence to discern how the activities of the theoretical life are to be woven into the whole of one's life, what part they are to play in relation to other activities. The contemplative life cannot, strictly speaking, constitute a human life.[40]

Aquinas is more explicit than Aristotle about the inherent limitations to the achievements of the speculative life. In his discussion of Aristotle on contemplation in Book X of the *Ethics*, he observes that "the intellect is not simply something divine, but it is the most divine thing in us."[41] In this very context in the *Ethics*, Aristotle is responding to the urging of Simonides that we should be content with human things and not strive for things beyond us. Aristotle's poetic and hortatory response is:

> We must not follow those who advise us, being men, to think of human things, and, being mortal, of mortal things, but must, so far as we can, make ourselves immortal, and strain every nerve to live in accord with the best thing in us.[42]

Aquinas concurs with Aristotle's response to Simonides, a response that is spelled out more fully in the opening of the *Metaphysics*, where Aristotle notes the defective characterization of divinity with which Simonides operates, a characterization of God as hoarding knowledge, as capable of jealousy or sorrow at another's good fortune. But, as superabundant source of all perfection, God can in no way be diminished or adversely affected by others; nor can an increase in anyone else's good diminish his own. The condition for envy is not present.

As much as they may reject Simonides' despairing advice, Aristotle and Aquinas agree in part. Both insist that it is not insofar as we are merely human that such an activity is possible for us, but insofar as we have something divine in us. Whatever portion of wisdom we possess we hold as gift of the divine. In these and other ways, Aquinas stresses the inherent limitations to human knowledge of God, even as he introduces an element of temporality into the activity of contemplation itself. Of course, the normative conception of contemplation has to do with rest, not motion. Still, the contemplative life aspires to a knowledge of what escapes its grasp and what must be approached in multiple ways, beginning from the variety of perfections found in creatures. Thus, in the contemplative life, the intellect itself will make use of discursive reasoning and find no final resting place *in via*.

In a telling departure from Aristotle, Aquinas, in his commentary on the passage in question from the end of the *Ethics*, substitutes the term *intendere*, 'to reach out toward,' for Aristotle's *facere*, 'to make,' in Moerbeke's Latin translation. Whereas Aristotle seems here to identify the act of contemplation as an act that renders the intellect one with its divine object, Aquinas underscores the incomplete aspiration toward the divine, an aspiration that falls short, not just in its duration or intensity, but in its very mode. One might say that here Aquinas uses Aristotle against Aristotle to criticize an overly optimistic conception of the achievements of contemplation. He draws upon Aristotle's anti-Platonic teaching on human knowledge, a teaching that every act of knowing requires a phantasm, something that is neither possible nor desirable for the divine mode of knowing.

Aquinas finds further support for the limitations to contemplation in Aristotle's discussion of the life of God in *Metaphysics* XII: "The act of contemplation is what is most pleasant and best. If, then, God is always in that state in which we sometimes are, this compels our wonder; and if he has this life in a better way, then this compels it yet more."[43] Metaphysics begins and ends in wonder, a fact that leads Aristotle to compare the philosopher, the lover of wisdom (*amator sapientiae*), with the poet or maker of myths. There is a clear disparity here between the philosopher's avowal of ignorance concerning the highest things, the lack of possession, and what some fear about the dominance of self-sufficiency and controlled productivity associated with the craftsman analogy. Indeed, if Aristotle sometimes describes the contemplative life as self-sufficient and lacking in nothing, he also praises metaphysics for its uselessness and treats all knowledge of the divine as a gift only partially apprehended by the philosopher.

Metaphysics as Practice

What Aquinas lays bare in Aristotle is a series of *aporiae* or disputed questions about the contemplative life. Emerging from these investigations is both a sense of the importance of the kinds of questions and inquiries pursued in the theoretical disciplines and a sense of the inherent limitations of the speculative life as exhaustive of the good human life. This is one way, already described, of articulating the relationship between metaphysics and practice. Prudential discretion and judgment is involved in the determination of precisely how the practice of theoretical life, which culminates in metaphysics, is to be conducted and how it is to be woven into the manifold practices that constitute an individual human life and the life of a community. In this way, the notion that philosophical speculation, that is, metaphysical inquiry, is the highest good of human life is itself an abstract teaching; metaphysical inquiry is but one, even if in some cases the preeminent, part of the good life.

There are three ways in which one can consider the relationship between metaphysics and practice, or speculative philosophy and ethics. First, as we have just seen, the question can be formulated as a version of the question of the relationship of *theoria* to *phronesis* or of the contemplative to the active life. Second, one can ask about the status of *theoria* or speculative philosophical inquiry as an activity or practice, an *operatio*, involving a host of intellectual virtues. Third, one can inquire whether metaphysics as a practice or the practice of metaphysics involves phronetic reasoning. But there are serious objections to this last and most radical thesis. Prudence is about singulars, not universals; it is ordered to doing, not knowing; its judgments are informed not just by reason but by rightly ordered desire. Can any of this be said of the acts of *theoria* or *contemplatio*?

Certainly not, if we limit our consideration to this or that demonstration of a necessary truth, but such a punctual and atomistic conception is hardly the underlying focus or attraction of the contemplative life. Indeed, Aristotle and Aquinas commend it to us as a way of life, appealing to the rational appetite; that is, they present it as a good. Although subjective, affective dispositions may be irrelevant to the truth of the propositions in the speculative sciences; our discovery of those truths may indeed require the presence of certain virtues that rightly order our passions. There are other likenesses between metaphysical and ethical practice. Like ethics, and unlike mathematics, metaphysics is located toward the end of the disciplines to be studied in philosophy. Indeed, metaphysics comes after even ethics; like ethics, it presupposes much experience. Norman Dahl writes, "Content cannot be given to basic principles without a wide experience of particulars, and one cannot perceive particulars as falling under these principles without a wide variety of experience."[44] Dahl distinguishes between disciplines such as ethics, which presupposes experience in its students, and mathematics or logic, which does not. In fact, Aristotle makes the general case at the beginning of the *Metaphysics* that universal judgment arises from many insights (*ennoemata*) gained from experience. Metaphysics would seem to require an even broader range of experience than that requisite for ethical inquiry; it would also seem to demand a greater degree of reflective and critical appropriation of that experience, since metaphysics is the discipline, above all others, that investigates the "why," the ultimate principles and causes.

Support for this point can be garnered from the opening discussion of wisdom in the *Metaphysics*, where Aristotle lists the ability to teach as a sign of the presence of wisdom. The good teacher does not simply provide a set of pellucid first principles and then set off on deductions from the principles; at least outside of mathematics, this is not possible. The first principles themselves must arise from dialectical inquiry, which Aristotle describes as the "path to the principles." To teach by means of dialectic is to make a judicious selection from and ordering of examples and inherited opinions: "In the same way that the one teaching another leads her to the knowledge of what was unknown, so too by discovery someone may lead oneself to the knowledge of what was unknown."[45] Although Aristotle puts forth what he holds to be demonstrative arguments in the *Metaphysics*, the vast majority of the text consists of dialectical investigations of common principles, potency and act, and the relationship between singular and universal substance. Pedagogical wisdom in this case would involve discernment of which examples to adduce in which context. It would also presuppose numerous insights at the level of experience.

As much as it may deploy phronetic virtues, teaching remains an art; it is for Aquinas the supreme craft, for it involves not just the communication of truth from teacher to student but also the ordering of all knowledge in relation to the highest good. But teaching is not mere technique. Pedagogical *phronesis* or dialectical discernment is not to be confused with techniques easily communicable by teacher to student. On this distinction rests the central debate between Plato and the Sophists; indeed, this is the source of Socrates' apparent skepticism about whether virtue can be taught. As Gadamer notes, when it comes to the question of the good, "there is no body of knowledge at one's disposal"; "something else is required besides a technique."[46] Instead, what is needed is a *hexis*, a habit or disposition, which determines and reflects an entire way of being. Gadamer rightly adverts to the crucial role of the non-rule-governed activity of dialectic, "not demonstration or proof in the scientific sense of a proof (*apodeixis*), which cogently deduces things from presuppositions. On the contrary, the dialectical art of differentiation presupposes antecedent familiarity with the subject matter and a continuing preview of, and prospect toward, the thing under discussion. Aristotle was right."[47]

Gadamer argues that in their accounts of *phronesis* both Plato and Aristotle were "aiming at something common to both practical and theoretical knowing that transcends the distinction between them."[48] This is a fertile proposal, although it is not without a certain risk, namely, that of reducing everything to a kind of *phronesis*, so that the complex analogies between the *phronesis, techne,* and *theoria* are lost.[49] MacIntyre raises questions about Gadamer's exclusion of any role for *theoria* from hermeneutics and practical philosophy. The *phronemos* is not only someone habituated through practice but also someone who is "able on occasion, by reflection upon his own and others' activity, to arrive at some degree of theoretical understanding of the virtues, including, *phronesis,* and their relation to the human good. And the *phronemos* may then be able to bring this theoretical knowledge of practical concepts to bear upon his practice."[50] MacIntyre adverts here to Aristotle's suggestion in *Ethics* I that, like the target for an archer, the study of ethics will provide an account of the good at which human agents can aim. MacIntyre agrees with Gadamer that such an account is never sufficient to guide the archer, but that does not rule out the possibility that such theoretical knowledge may well be necessary to the human agent. To be a successful practical reasoner, MacIntyre urges, is to

> know how to bring to bear on the particularities of one's situation a concep-
> tion of the good that it is the task of the theoretical understanding to articu-
> late, and to which in their practice *phronemoi* may need to appeal, for
> example, when doing the work of legislators. . . . The concept of *phronesis*
> cannot after all be detached from the theoretical framework of which it is an
> integral part, as Gadamer detaches it, and put to uses that do not presuppose
> some of Aristotle's theoretical and indeed metaphysical commitments.[51]

Despite Gadamer's overly zealous attempt to subsume theory within prac-
tice, he does provide a basis for conceiving Platonic and Aristotelian texts (as well as Thomistic texts, I will argue) as fields for the teacher's exercise of pedagogical *phronesis* and the student's practice of dialectical discernment. Metaphysics is no exception; indeed, its heavy reliance on a wide range of experience and its thoroughly dialectical mode of inquiry exacerbates, rather than diminishes, the need for such discernment.[52]

Some role for phronetic discrimination would seem to be required in Aquinas's more detailed discussion of the divine names, particularly in the lengthy investigation of the divine goodness or perfection, an investigation of the resources of human language to speak about God—all of which have a decidedly neo-Platonic pedigree. Directly pertinent to our argument is the issue of how we begin to understand the meaning, function, and scope of the divine names. Aquinas thinks the resources of the names of God derive from the ways in which created things, to which our naming is tied, reflect the divine. "The same things are similar and dissimilar to God. They are similar in so far as they imitate as much as they can him who is not perfectly imitable . . . ; they are dissimilar as things caused fall short of their causes."[53] As David Burrell convincingly argues, something like the practice of phronetic judgment is necessary to be able to discern the proper "use" of analogous terms, especially in the case of God. We must "assess the way in which a term is being

used in relation to its primary analogate. Yet such an assessment demands . . . that we identify the primary analogate as well as grasp how the use in question relates to it, and each of these apperceptions belongs to judgment."[54] Although analogous usage is not to be identified with metaphor, each requires "deftness of judgment." In practice, this comes down to "adducing appropriate examples." But this capacity to adduce the right example cannot be separated from a sense of how particulars function within the whole way of life into which the teacher is attempting to initiate the student.

The pedagogical task is complicated by the fact that there can be no simple ascent to the divine that would leave creatures behind; instead, we gain greater insight into, and a greater affinity for perceiving, the reflections of the divine in things by an ever-greater penetration of the created order. In this sense, the highest realms of metaphysics would seem to require a great deal of experience, a familiarity with created things and with the manifold ways in which the glimmers of the divine can be glancingly apprehended in them.

The teaching on the divine names is a grammatical or logical doctrine that brings together neo-Platonic sources with Aristotle's account of how things are named analogously. Although Aristotle clearly indicates that God is the ultimate cause, the final cause that moves as an object of desire and thus as good, he focuses on attributes such as simplicity, eternity, and intelligence, rather than on moral perfection. Following Scripture and neo-Platonic authorities such as Augustine and Dionysius, Aquinas develops a lengthy treatment of names falling under the rubric of perfection. Our knowledge of these attributes, which is rooted in our experience of the natural and the human world, is decidedly ethical. Thus does metaphysical reasoning, especially in its culminating investigation of God as first, uncaused cause, involve an exercise of judgment that presupposes wide experience and a reflective appropriation of one's experience. One can, of course, develop an ability to rattle off premises in support of God's existence or in support of a variety of divine names: God is good, God is wise, and so forth. But the depth of understanding of these assertions will vary greatly, depending on how penetrating is one's understanding of each of the predicates in question. What does one understand when one states, "God is good"?

Before answering this question, we need to face another question, one arising from Aristotle's relative silence about the goodness of God. What basis is there in Aristotle for calling God good? There is a rather straightforward Aristotelian way of affirming the goodness of God. The good, as Aristotle depicts it in the opening of the *Ethics*, is what all desire. Yet Aristotle reaches the unmoved mover, or God, as the final cause of motion in the universe, an object of motion that moves other beings as an object of their desire. God would seem to be that which all things desire above any other desires that they have. God is thus not just good, but the supreme good. As Aquinas puts it in his commentary, Aristotle shows "how the first mover is good and desirable" (*qualiter primum movens sit bonum et appetibile*).[55] A possible objection to this line of reasoning can be found in Aristotle's repudiation in *Ethics* I of the Platonic idea of the Good. Thomas is careful to circumscribe the scope of the critique: "Aristotle does not intend to disprove Plato's opinion that there is one good separate from the whole universe, on which all goods depend."[56] If Aristotle treats God principally as a final cause of motion, neo-Platonic authors treat God primarily as the exemplary cause of finite creatures.

Aquinas's teaching on the divine names, which rests on the crucial notion of God as exemplar, is largely derived from Dionysius, who has, as Aquinas puts it in the prologue to his commentary, a "Platonic way of speaking." Aquinas, as Jan Aertsen notes, is at pains to rework and combine two accounts of goodness of things: the nature approach, found in Aristotle, and the creation or participation approach, found in a variety of neo-Platonic authors. Aertsen describes the task in these ways,

> If transcendentals are, on the one hand, common names, and, on the other, divine names, that is, names that are proper to God, then the question arises of how these two kinds of naming are related to each other. How is the transcendental character of the good that goes through all the categories related to the transcendence of the Good who surpasses all categories? Or, to put it in a more historical manner, is the approach inspired by Aristotle compatible with the neo-Platonic approach?[57]

Developing an Aristotelian metaphysics of actuality, Aquinas holds that all things are good insofar as they exist. To call a creature "good" is not a veiled way of saying "caused by good." The ultimate source of their goodness is of course God, but this does not erase the goodness they possess as beings in their own right; rather, it is a condition of it.[58] This is Aquinas's Aristotelian corrective to the Platonic penchant for identifying what is real, knowable, and good in finite, sensible beings, not with the beings themselves, but with their ideal transcendent Forms. Aristotle here functions in defense of the integrity and intelligibility of created nature. But so long as we do not posit separately existing Forms between created things and the uncreated cause of all things, Aquinas wants very much to hold onto the Platonic notion of exemplary causality. Precisely because every being comes from a transcendent cause, God is the "first exemplar, efficient, and final cause of all goodness."[59] Aquinas is equally opposed to the hasty reduction of things to the divine, as he is to the reduction of assertions about divine goodness to God's causal role in creating good things. Of course, that causal role is the basis for our attributing goodness to God, but precisely because of exemplary causality, we are able to reach conclusions about God, not just about God as cause.[60]

Commenting on the role of images in Plato, John Sallis writes: "The 'seeing' of an image always involves a tension, an instability," which drives us "beyond the image to the original."[61] If the tension and instability is not to degenerate into aimless wandering, there must remain some way to trace a path from image to exemplar; otherwise, we could have no confidence precisely in what or whose direction we were headed. The discussion of the divine names puts us on the cusp of theology. Indeed, it is in his theological texts that we find his most expansive treatments of the names. It is also the context in which he stresses the gap between what we aspire to in the way of knowledge about God and what we can grasp; another goal is to exacerbate the student's erotic appetite for God. This, too, is a prominent neo-Platonic theme and strategy. Precisely because we ascend through likenesses to a source that escapes our vision, we have nowhere to rest.

Eros, Metaphysics, and Theological Mimesis

In an early commentary on Boethius, Aquinas puts to himself the question whether it is licit to treat the divine by way of investigation. His response pairs a quotation from Scripture ("Be ready always with an answer to everyone who asks a reason for the hope that is in you") with Aristotle's rejoinder to Simonides. Yet the bulk of the article is devoted to the ways in which we can err in this matter by assuming that we can comprehend divine things; by supposing that, in the arena of faith, reason should be given primacy; or by scrutinizing matters beyond one's individual ability. The sixth objection develops a line of reasoning from Dionysius's *Celestial Hierarchy* that we ought to honor "the secret that is above us with silence." Aquinas's measured response runs thus: "God is honored by silence, not because nothing is said or asked about him, but because we understand that whatever we say or ask about him fails to comprehend him."[62] Aquinas thus underscores the interplay of presence and absence in our speech about God. Earlier in the same commentary, Aquinas poses the question whether the human mind can attain knowledge of God. After citing the affirmation in Romans that the invisible things of God can be known from the things that are made, Aquinas stresses the limitations to our knowledge of God. From his effects, we can know only that he exists, not what he is. Aquinas ends the body of the article with a quotation from Gregory's gloss on Genesis 32.30, "I have seen God face to face": "The sight of the soul when it turns to God vibrates with the trembling of his immensity."[63]

One of the most striking features of metaphysical discourse in Aquinas is his pervasive use of aesthetic and erotic language. In contrast to the confidence in the human mind's ability to make itself divine through a process of natural knowledge, erotic language always appeals to a lack, an as-yet-unsatisfied desire or longing. We need to deploy not just a name but multiple names, indicating the endless number of possible starting points for an ascent from creatures to Creator; multiple names of God affirmed, denied, and then affirmed again, as tracing a trajectory of desire beyond discourse. A passage on the importance of the study of creatures for progress in faith puts the point eloquently: "If the goodness, beauty, and allurement of creatures thus entices human souls, then the divine fount of goodness, compared to the small streams of goodness discovered in particular creatures, will draw totally to himself the aroused souls of human beings."[64]

In a theological context, the names serve a rhetorical and pedagogical function of moving the believer beyond philosophy to theology, Scripture, and the practice of the Christian life. In the intimate connection between contemplation and charity, knowing and loving, Christianity offers human persons an interior act higher than any known to the philosophers. As we have already noted, the hierarchy of philosophical activities moves from the arts, which terminate in external, physical objects; to the moral virtues, which involve bodily activities but are properly perfections of the soul; to contemplative activities, which are "interior acts." Christian contemplation, by contrast, gives rise to—indeed, is rooted in—a corresponding set of practices, internal and external, spiritual and en-mattered. As the Scripture scholar N. T. Wright observes, in announcing that the "time of return and renewal was now dawning," Jesus indicated that the "kingdom-story he told would be designed to produce *both* the inward state *and* the outward praxis, which would be appropriate for that renewal."[65]

With his many references to Dionysius, to sacred silence, and to a kind of holy terror in our experience of the divine, the passages just quoted call to mind the writings of the contemporary Continental philosopher of religion Jean-Luc Marion, who begins his discussion of the divine names in Dionysius by noting that there is no simple dialectical opposition of affirmation and negation. There is, Marion notes, a third way beyond affirmation and negation, the way Aquinas calls "super-eminence." Aquinas describes the three ways as proceeding from an attribution of some perfection—say, goodness or wisdom—to God, followed by a negation—for example, God is good but not in the limited way creatures are good—which itself gives way a higher affirmation, God is good in a way that infinitely exceeds every created instance of goodness. Marion asserts that the third way "transgresses the first two." Marion calls this the realm of prayer or praise, the "function" of which is no longer "predicative but pragmatic." As we shall see, Marion opens up neglected issues in Aquinas, especially that of idolatry and of the way metaphysics fittingly gives way, in theological discourse, to a *praxis* of praise.[66] The practice of theology involves a purgation of idolatry. As Torrell puts it, "Like every believer," the theologian

> must abandon idols and turn toward the living God (Acts 14:14). He must also renounce the constructions of his own mind, personal idols that have no less a hold. In his way, Thomas invites us to this when he distinguishes the contemplation of the philosophers from Christian contemplation. The former is always tempted to stop with the pleasure of knowledge in itself and, in the end, proceeds from self-love. The latter, the contemplation of the saints, completely inspired by love for the divine Truth, ends in the object itself.[67]

Still, against Marion, if not against Torrell, Aquinas would insist that negations themselves will be aimless and utterly uninformative without presupposing some sort of affirmation, however imperfect: "Understanding of negation rests upon a certain affirmation. Unless the human intellect were to know something affirmatively of God, it would not be able to deny anything either."[68]

Metaphysics, Theology, and the Practice of Naming God

As we saw in the last chapter, Pierre Hadot has been a leading proponent of the re-appropriation of the ancient notion of philosophy as a way of life grounded in the practice of "spiritual exercises" and involving the communal practice of a host of moral and intellectual virtues. Yet according to Hadot, in the medieval period philosophy is no longer a way of life but rather a "purely theoretical and abstract activity."[1] The practice of philosophy becomes reduced to the detached examination of a set of propositions. We have previously raised questions about Hadot's bifurcation of philosophy into a way of life and an analysis of propositions. We now want to propose that he is wrong to hold that the pursuit of wisdom as a way of life disappears in the medieval period. Aquinas's metaphysical doctrine, for example, is of a piece with his account of the practice of the best way of life, the pursuit of wisdom.

Aquinas sees his work as a contribution to, and an enactment of, a way of life, the pursuit of wisdom shaped by a specific set of practices that determine the horizon within which all activities are pursued. The connection between text and way of life is most apparent in a still-neglected work of Aquinas, the *Summa contra Gentiles*, to whose consideration we shall devote ourselves in the next two chapters. Building on the opening chapters of Aristotle's *Ethics* and *Metaphysics*, Aquinas begins the prologue to his *Summa contra Gentiles* by addressing the office of the wise, the one who orders parts in relation to the whole and teaches the authoritative truth about the good life for human beings. Aquinas develops his entire argument on the basis of a sustained comparison of the life of wisdom with the practices of crafts. He highlights the pursuit of goods internal to practice—goods identified, ranked, and achieved only through the guidance of master artisans. He writes,

> Of all things ordered to an end, the rule of their governance and order is taken from the end. A thing is best disposed when it is suitably ordered to its end, for the end is the good of the thing. Thus we see in the arts that the one to whom the securing of the end pertains is governor and ruler of others. . . . Arts that rule other arts are called architectonic. . . . The artisans of these arts claim for themselves the name of the wise.[2]

Aquinas here rehearses Aristotle's teaching about master practitioners of crafts and about the inscribing of one craft within another, for example, shipbuilding within military, and both of these within the craft of politics. He restates Aristotle's claim that wisdom has to do with knowledge and order, and that the wisest of all will be the one who has the knowledge to order the lower practices to the higher and achieve the ends of that practice in light of which others are pursued. This is of course the political corollary to Aristotle's ethical thesis that the human good is that which is pursued for its own sake and which is last in the interlocking chain of means-to-ends relationships. Aquinas proceeds to introduce the teaching from *Metaphysics* I concerning wisdom, namely, that it is the highest activity available to human beings, since only it orders all knowledge in relation to the ultimate aspiration of human nature itself: contemplation of the first principles and highest causes. Aquinas concludes by making a claim that Aristotle never explicitly states, namely, that it falls to the one who contemplates the highest causes to order all human activities in relation to this end.

The appeal to practices and the use of the craft analogy could not be more prominent. Yet Aquinas seems to have quietly settled an unresolved difficulty or tension in Aristotle's texts. In the opening of the *Ethics*, Aristotle defends politics as the architectonic discipline since it identifies and secures the goods of multiform practices that constitute communal life; later in the same work, he claims that it would absurd for contemplation to be subordinate to the practical life, because the former activity is intrinsically superior. Although Aquinas does not belabor the point, it is important to see that his bestowing upon the wise the public and comprehensive role of ordering human activities in relation to the highest good rests on doctrines of creation and providence. He notes, for example, that the end of the universe is also its beginning, and that end is "intended by its first author." Hence, Aquinas's Christian reworking of pagan metaphysics informs the practice of wisdom.

In previous chapters, we have seen a number of ways in which contemporary philosophical discussions, especially in ethics and epistemology, revive a notion of practice, of the primacy of prudence in the order of human action, and of the broadly ethical dimensions to human cognitive activity. We have also seen the way in which contemporary conversations in ethics and epistemology point us in the direction of anthropology and metaphysics. The latter point can be seen (a) in the need for a rich philosophical psychology or anthropology as a complement to an account of the virtues of human excellence, and (b) in the way different accounts of the virtues, even of a particular virtue such as justice, rest on a concrete and detailed conception of the human person. A turn to metaphysics may also be provoked by debates in contemporary epistemology, particularly by virtue epistemology. Like virtue ethics, virtue epistemology brings to the fore the complexities of our cognitive activities and intellectual practices. Precisely because of its emphasis on practice, virtue epistemology opens a path for asking questions on the border of metaphysics, questions concerning the basis for discriminating between better and worse objects of knowledge, and between better and worse ways of holding and acting upon what we know.

Aquinas is also a well-known proponent of metaphysics as the culminating science of philosophical inquiry. What is less known is that Aquinas frames the entire discussion of metaphysics in broadly ethical terms: metaphysics arises from the human desire (*eros*) for knowledge. The motive for the inquiry is erotic, the cognitive passion to know, evident in our persistent wondering about the world in which we are immersed. By comparison with Platonic eros, Aristotelian eros seems at times a rather pedestrian matter. Such cannot be said of Aquinas. In decidedly erotic language, which could have been lifted straight from Dionysius or Bonaventure, he writes,

> If the goodness, beauty, and allurement of creatures so entices human souls, then the divine fount of goodness, compared to the small streams of goodness discovered in particular creatures, will draw totally to himself the aroused souls of men. Whence it is said in the Psalms: They will become intoxicated from the abundance of your dwelling . . . and you will give them to drink from the torrent of your delight.[3]

Metaphysics itself culminates, or fails to culminate, not in the cessation of desire through comforting certitudes, but in the exacerbation of desire, of wonder inflamed at the gap between what we long for in the way of contemplation and what we can achieve by the powers of our own reason. The peak of philosophical inquiry is simultaneously an avowal of ignorance. As Maritain once commented, "for us the intellectual life concludes with an avowal of poverty."[4]

Aquinas's *Summa contra Gentiles* contains his most important reflections on the issues that preoccupy contemporary philosophers, issues regarding the source, nature, and limits of metaphysics; the role of *eros* and the good in metaphysics; and the relationship between metaphysics and practice. The abiding themes of this work dovetail nicely with debates in contemporary philosophy of religion in both Continental and analytic circles. The most influential voice in Continental philosophy of religion, Jean-Luc Marion, has devoted sustained attention to Aquinas.[5] Before turning to Marion's position and his interpretation of Aquinas, we shall consider the robust defense of Aquinas's metaphysics put forward by the late Norman Kretzmann, perhaps the premier analytic philosopher of medieval thought in the last half of the twentieth century. The consideration of Kretzmann's interpretation will afford us a number of opportunities. First, as the most sustained exegetical encounter with Aquinas available in contemporary analytic philosophy, it will enable us to consider the strengths and weaknesses of a representative approach to Aquinas. Second, and more specifically, it will provide an occasion for pointing up the limitations to one standard approach to God in analytic philosophy of religion, an approach known as perfect-being theism. Third, it will supply a basis for a fruitful comparison between the approach of an analytic commentator on Aquinas and that of a Continental figure such as Marion.

Perfect-Being Theism?

For many years the *Summa contra Gentiles* has been read as a high-powered manual of apologetics intended to reach a God common to philosophers as well as to Christians, Jews, and especially Muslims. Yet the historical, manuscript, and exegetical evidence no longer supports the traditional view. There are a number of reasons for the waning of the traditional interpretation. First, except for a few excerpts, the *Summa contra Gentiles* was never used in missionary work. Second, in making no reference to the religious texts of the Muslims, the work does not follow the common practice of the Dominican order, which was always to argue from the sources of one's opponent. Third, as is clear from the prologue, where Thomas famously speaks of the "twofold mode of truth in what we confess about divine things," Thomas has a Christian audience in mind. The reference to the twofold mode of truth, with which Thomas distinguishes the subject matter of the first three books from that of the fourth, gives the impression that the first three books treat of philosophy while the last book is properly theological. There is something to this, especially since in the first three books Aquinas avoids premises derived from revealed principles or sources, just as he postpones until the fourth book topics such as the Trinity, the incarnation, and the sacraments that can in no way be known by reason. Yet this extended philosophical, even metaphysical, investigation is inscribed within an overarching theological structure. Thomas distinguishes philosophy from theology, not just on the basis of differing subject matters, but also by the order of proceeding proper to each. Philosophy begins with what is most evident to us and ends with what is least evident to us although absolutely prior in nature, namely God. And God enters into philosophy only as ultimate cause, never as a direct object of inquiry. By beginning from God and treating of God himself, the *Summa contra Gentiles* manifests its theological character. Yet it is a theology that contains within itself a sustained investigation of a host of philosophical topics.

Any reader of the *Summa contra Gentiles* must come to terms with a set of *aporiae* that arise from its peculiar structure. In the prologue, Thomas introduces the "twofold mode of truth concerning divine things."[6] The first mode, to which Books I–III are devoted, treats of that portion of divine things amenable to rational investigation; while the second mode, to which Book IV is devoted, considers teachings like the Trinity and the incarnation that utterly exceed rational demonstration. Is the first mode then philosophy? Thomas clearly seeks to avoid the deployment of premises from revelation in the first three books. But the issue is not so simple. Unlike the more purely philosophical project of the commentaries on Aristotle, wherein Thomas follows Aristotle's dicta concerning the proper order of philosophy—beginning with the study of nature and culminating in metaphysics—the *Summa contra Gentiles* begins from God and descends to creatures.[7] By beginning with what is first in the order of being rather than what is first in the order of learning, the work follows an order that Thomas typically calls theological rather than philosophical. Finally, the consideration of God does indeed enter into the discipline that Aristotle calls metaphysics, and for this reason metaphysics is sometimes called theology. However, God enters into that science as cause or principle of *ens commune*, not as part of the proper subject matter of metaphysics. By contrast, theology proper treats of God in himself. Now, the first book of the *Summa contra Gentiles* is devoted to God in himself.[8]

In his *Metaphysics of Theism: Aquinas's Natural Theology in Summa contra Gentiles I*—the first of a three-volume study of *Summa contra Gentiles* I–III—Norman Kretzmann sets out to confront the first book on its own terms and in detail.[9] His project is philosophically ambitious, an attempt to reconstruct and clarify some of the key arguments in the first book. Indeed, his approach has the advantage of treating the *Summa contra Gentiles* as having a distinctive aim, not one that is merely a stage in the development of Thomas's theological writings. It thus circumvents one of the chief obstacles to uncovering the intention of the *Summa contra Gentiles*: the tendency to read it as an imperfect realization of what is achieved in the later and more famous *Summa Theologiae*, as perhaps the penultimate stage in what Michelle Corbin calls the *chemin* of Thomas's thought.[10]

The Metaphysics of Theism offers more than a commentary on *Summa contra Gentiles* I; it also provides an intriguing, if finally unpersuasive, claim about Aquinas's intention and strategy in composing the entire work. To state Kretzmann's thesis with introductory brevity, he holds that the work was intended for atheists, to instruct them in generic "perfect-being theism." As we shall see, the problem with this approach is not just the anachronistic supposition about the audience, which Kretzmann readily concedes did not exist in Thomas's own time. The deeper problem has to do with the imposition of a contemporary conception of perfect-being theism upon Thomas's own distinctive theism in *Summa contra Gentiles* I. For all its clarity and sophistication, Kretzmann's interpretation leaves Aquinas vulnerable to the charges of an idolatrous metaphysics. His reading rests on an inadequate grasp of the nature and function of analogy in Aquinas, which requires that in its ascent to divine things, human thinking must turn upside down if it is to avoid lapsing into the conceptual idolatries of the philosophers. At the same time, Kretzmann's interpretation also blocks from view Aquinas's pervasive use of erotic and aesthetic language in his discourse about God.

One problem with Kretzmann's way of describing the relationship between philosophy and theology is that it invites a conception of metaphysical inquiry as operating at the highest level of abstraction possible to the human intellect. Reasonably enough, Kretzmann asserts that both philosophy and theology treat the "first principles and most fundamental aspects of reality." But then he moves quickly to the opaque conclusion that either theology is part of philosophy or both are parts of the "same genus," which he calls the "Grandest Unified Theory."[11] This amounts to a conflation of philosophy and theology. Charles de Koninck puts his finger on the difficulty with this approach:

> Those who define metaphysics by nothing more than generality would find this generality superseded by a far greater one; for what could prevent us from saying "let A stand for the subject of every such science including that of metaphysics," or "let B stand for what is impossible as well as for its opposite." The art that does not name anything . . . would be queen. . . . That a degree of generality does not carry with it more actual intelligibility can be seen from the fact that, in knowing man only as an animal, we do not know him distinctly as man, for the elephant too is an animal. The general here is more potential and confused, whereas the perfection of knowledge lies not in the direction of the more general but rather in the direction of something less general which must include nonetheless the more general, in the way man includes animal.[12]

Misconceptions of the nature of metaphysical inquiry have infected certain strains of Thomism for many centuries. There is, for example, a tradition of reading Aquinas's articulation of a hierarchy of sciences—physics, mathematics, and metaphysics—as indicating a ranking in accord with degrees of abstraction. But Aquinas says no such thing. What we noted above bears repeating here. The movement from physics, which treats of what exists in matter and motion, to mathematics, which treats of objects in abstraction from matter and motion, does indeed involve increased abstraction. Metaphysics, however, does not study objects at a higher level of abstraction. Some of the confusion results from the listing of metaphysics after mathematics, but this does not mean for Aquinas that mathematics is a path into metaphysics. Instead, Aquinas follows Aristotle's ordering of the disciplines of philosophical pedagogy, in which physics is the proper avenue into metaphysics. Along with logic, whose level of abstraction is akin to that found in the quantitative disciplines, mathematics is a preparatory study, to be pursued prior to the initiation into properly philosophical disciplines. Indeed, what distinguishes metaphysics from mathematics is that while the latter does mark a retreat from the real order, the former signals a movement in the direction of the real. Not abstraction but negative judgment (*separatio*) is the intellectual activity that Aquinas associates with metaphysical reasoning. It involves the judgment that nonmaterial beings exist. If there were no objects capable of existing apart from matter, then physics would be first philosophy, the most comprehensive investigation of what is. Objects can be said to be independent of matter "either because they never are in matter, as is true of God and the other separate substances, or because they are not in matter universally, as is true of substance, potency and act, and being itself."[13] The movement from physics to metaphysics does not involve unmediated access to a translucent realm of Cartesian ideas. Instead, metaphysics investigates objects absent from our direct vision. Mark Jordan warns against the "reifying of *ens inquantum ens.*" He argues, "*Ens* is not a subsisting replacement for the inaccessible separate substances. It is not a thing to be seized in any intuition, whether intellectual or sensible. . . . *Ens commune* is an analogical consideration of substances with very different structures and very different conditions." Jordan observes that the limited, oblique, and opaque knowledge had in metaphysics is, for Aquinas, completely in keeping with the *status viae*, the condition of human knowledge on its journey to a blessedness that can be had only after this life.[14]

Aristotle's remaining way of describing metaphysics, as first philosophy, has also puzzled commentators. The initial question concerns the priority indicated by the term "first." Clearly, this is not a temporal priority, since metaphysics is pursued last among all the arts and sciences. On the complexity and distinctiveness of the sciences, Aquinas states that "there are diverse sciences corresponding to the diverse orders that reason considers" in things.[15] The intellectual virtues of *intellectus*, the apprehension of the principles proper to each science, and *scientia*, the habit of demonstrating conclusions from principles, are operative in each of the sciences. The various sciences discover their principles in different ways, have distinct modes of proceeding, and achieve different degrees of certitude. In contrast to the practical order, wherein the moral virtues are interconnected and directly reliant upon the master intellectual virtue of prudence, in the speculative order the virtues appropriate to each science are "about different matters having no relation to one another."[16] But there is a comprehensive speculative virtue: *sapientia*, which Aquinas describes as a "certain virtue of all the sciences" (*sapientia est virtus quaedam omnium scientiarum*).[17] If the activities of the speculative intellect are not inherently connected with one another in the way ethical activities are, then how can metaphysics or the intellectual virtue of wisdom supply such a unity?

It does so in numerous ways. First, since no science proves its own principles, metaphysics investigates the foundations of the particular sciences and offers proofs of the principles assumed commonly in all the sciences. Of course, one must use the term "proof" carefully with respect to principles, which unlike conclusions derived from them cannot be demonstrated from anything prior. These common principles would include the principle of contradiction; notions of causality, potency, and act; and so forth. This is one way in which metaphysics is first philosophy in that it studies principles presumed in and thus prior to the investigations of the particular sciences. The unifying sapiential function of metaphysics can also be seen in its role of organizing, comparing, and ordering the various arts and sciences, speculative and practical, into a unified philosophical pedagogy. To the extent that the human intellect is capable of it, metaphysics provides a panoramic or synoptic vision of the whole of human inquiry.

The close affiliation between metaphysics and the various particular sciences makes one wonder whether there is a distinct science or inquiry called metaphysics. A related question has to do with whether physics might not be the comprehensive discipline. Doubts such as these, combined with the indirect character of metaphysical reasoning grounded not in abstraction but in negative judgment, account for the thoroughly dialectic tenor of Aristotle's writing in the *Metaphysics*. It is not surprising that, instead of simply embarking upon the science, he speaks repeatedly of the "science we are seeking." Of course, Aristotle does eventually describe a subject matter proper to metaphysics, *ens inquantum ens*. Under its purview also falls the question of ultimate principles and causes of the subject matter, the final cause of all that is. God enters into that subject matter, not as part of its proper object of inquiry, but as the ultimate cause of being. Hence, in metaphysics God is studied only as source or cause, or as what is. Indeed, Aquinas takes the turn to the study of God in himself, and of other things in relation to God, as a sign that we have moved from philosophy to theology.

As the title of Kretzmann's volume indicates, the focus of his interpretation of the *Summa contra Gentiles* is on metaphysics, the last of the disciplines to be studied within Aristotle's philosophical curriculum. Although Thomas has little to say about the disciplines ancillary to metaphysics, he reasonably presupposes many of its principles and conclusions. The ideal audience of the work is not the philosophical novice, but one who has already been trained in the lower Aristotelian sciences. Philosophical pedagogy begins with logic and mathematics, and proceeds through the study of nature to the intermediate inquiries into the soul and the human good. Metaphysics, or first philosophy, is actually the last discipline to be studied. The structure of the *Summa contra Gentiles*, which is sometimes said to mirror the Neoplatonic vision of the cosmos as a going forth (*exitus*) followed by a return (*reditus*), reverses the natural, philosophical order of learning. Thomas typically describes the *exitus-reditus* order as proper to theological inquiry. This is where Kretzmann's appeal to the structural advantage of the text's beginning at the real beginning can be misleading.[18]

Admittedly, Aquinas's procedure in the *Summa contra Gentiles* is a bit puzzling. He postpones until the fourth book an investigation of theological doctrines, such as the Trinity and the incarnation, that wholly eclipse reason's power of investigation; furthermore, he does not typically appeal to Scripture as a basis of the arguments in the first three books. But by beginning with God in himself and proceeding to consider creatures as they relate to God, Aquinas adopts in the first three books a theological order of presentation. The questions that interest him most in the first three books are those that touch directly or indirectly upon properly theological doctrines concerning divine creation and providence. It is also the case that the consideration of God in the first three books, although it develops numerous arguments from Aristotle's *Metaphysics*, offers a much ampler consideration of God and the names of God.

Book XII of the *Metaphysics*, which was the final book in the Latin translation Aquinas used, contains Aristotle's discussion of the unmoved mover, whom he identifies as God and whose life involves the pure activity of thinking on thinking. The brevity of Aristotle's discussion, according to Aquinas, befits the status of God in metaphysics, into which God enters, not as part of the proper subject matter, but only as ultimate cause and first principle of being. From Aquinas's perspective, it is striking that Aristotle, who speaks of the divine life as provoking human wonder, underscores the limits to human knowledge about God. The culminating inquiry of Aristotle's science of metaphysics indicates that the philosopher is never more than a lover of wisdom (*amator sapientiae*).[19] Aquinas's more ample treatment of the divine names clearly has theological motives, even if it does not deploy premises from revelation. Aquinas underscores both the complexity in our approach to the divine and the erotic character of that pursuit, the sense in which human desire for God exceeds the bounds of philosophical metaphysics. In this way, metaphysics becomes a propaedeutic to theology, and, within theology, a subordinate science supplying principles for use in the architectonic science of the human good.

Kretzmann notes that Aquinas makes a "special, restricted use of revelation" in his citation of scriptural passages at the end of each chapter. Given his emphasis on the properly philosophical character of these investigations, one might expect Kretzmann to treat the scriptural passages as no more than a nod in the direction of revelation, a momentary advertence that shows the compatibility of what reason has proven with faith. While the theism of the work turns out to be Christian in the fourth book, Kretzmann states that there is "nothing distinctively Christian about I–III."[20] In fact, these books teach only "generic theism," and their appropriate audience is "non-Christian." Since it is not a missionary work, or a work of revealed theology or of apologetics, it is unclear what the audience or intent of the work is. In this, Kretzmann departs from the more accommodating view of the work adopted by Anthony Kenny, who states, "The *Summa Contra Gentiles* is meant as a philosophical work; it is directed to people who are not Christians, who may be Muslims or Jews or atheists. It aims to present them with reasons—reasons that any human being of good will can see to be good reasons—for believing that there is a God, that the soul is immortal and so on."[21]

Kenny's view of the audience is too broad for Kretzmann. Reiterating his rejection of the missionary thesis, he asserts that the Muslims, for whom many have thought that the work was composed, do not "need an education in perfect-being theism."[22] Kretzmann further circumscribes the audience of the work: it is intended not for non-Christians as a whole but for only a small segment of them, namely, intelligent atheists. Given the decidedly theistic context in which Thomas is writing, whom could Thomas have had in mind as his audience? Kretzmann is driven to ask: "Why would a 13th century philosopher-theologian undertake this?"[23] Indeed. Kretzmann's astonishing response, or lack thereof, is that, when it was composed, the work had "no discernible practical purpose."[24] Having begun promisingly by setting aside implausible theses about the intention and audience of the text, Kretzmann proceeds to render the intention of the work more conceivable to us than it was to its author.

Practices of Wisdom

Kretzmann's error here is instructive, especially since his apparent innocence regarding the significance of the life of reason within the life of faith is shared by those of a philosophical persuasion, namely, deconstructive postmodernism, that is deeply at odds with his own. It is as if some of the most prominent strains in contemporary analytic and Continental philosophy of religion can see in Aquinas's descent from faith to reason only an apologetic strategy. But, as Chenu puts it,

> Revelation provided more than an external corrective to mistakes in philosophical speculation; it inspired men of faith to produce a frame of reference which served them in their rational constructions no less than in their art or culture. Neither the essential disparity between philosophy and religion nor the transcendence theology assigned to faith limited the possibilities of a Christian exercise of reason, without faith in any way supplanting reason or perverting the workings of the rational process.[25]

Revelation, then, points believers back to a recovery of nature, to an appreciation of the twofold mode of truth, the dual way in which God communicates to his creatures, through nature and grace, reason and faith. In Aquinas's appeal to Aristotelian nature, "he was giving supreme expression to that Christianity in which a return to the gospel had secured for the believer a presence in the world, for the theologian a mature awareness of nature, and for the apostle an effective appreciation of man."[26]

The embrace of natural reason is not as an apologetic weapon to be deployed against secular rationalists or skeptics. Instead, it involves a recovery of the natural, created conditions of human knowledge and action. Far from being any sort of threat to faith, philosophy is made possible by the first gift of

God in creation. Aquinas describes both supernatural and natural principles as "contained by the divine wisdom" (*haec ergo principia etiam divina sapientia continet*). He speaks in thoroughly pedagogical terms: "The knowledge of the teacher contains what is brought forth into the soul of the student by the teacher. . . . The cognition of principles naturally known is divinely given to us, since God himself is the author of our nature."[27]

Instead of trying to make instant capital out of Aquinas for contemporary analytic discussions, we would do well to pause a little longer over his prologue. Its most striking feature concerns claims about wisdom and the office of the wise, whom Thomas describes as ordering parts in relation to the whole and as teaching the authoritative truth about the ultimate end of the universe. Since wisdom is common to both philosophy and Christian theology, the work promises to do more than fulfill the passing needs of the Spanish mission. It promises to consider the relationship between pagan and Christian wisdom. Far from being historically pointless, as Kretzmann would have us believe, the work addresses the fundamental question of antiquity and the Middle Ages. Among all of Thomas's works, only the *Summa contra Gentiles* focuses extensively on the great debate of antiquity over the best way of life and over who teaches authoritatively concerning the highest good, precisely the question Hadot insists was at the heart of ancient philosophy.

The comprehensive consideration of wisdom, which can be seen only if one reads the work as a whole (that is, books I–IV, not just I–III), has properly theological motives, since the pursuit of wisdom is integral to the Christian life. What could be more timely than a project devoted to appraising, correcting, and extending pagan wisdom in order to show how it is comprehended by Christian wisdom? Although Thomas never deploys the objectionable phrase "Christian philosophy," there can be no objection—textual, historical, or substantive—to the notion of Christian wisdom.[28] Why not see the distinction between the two modes of truth, in accordance with which Thomas separates the first three books from the fourth, as an attempt to distinguish in order to unite the rival traditions of wisdom? Whatever indirect audience Thomas may have had in mind, he clearly composed the book for a Christian audience. Indeed, the distinction between two modes of truth arises from within what "we confess about divine things." The use of the first person plural and the presupposition of an underlying unity to truth provides at least prima facie evidence that the intended audience is Christian. This does not, of course, preclude Thomas's vigorous engagement of a variety of philosophical and theological traditions; it simply means that he does so from within a particular community of practice and inquiry.

This line of interpretation in no way diminishes the importance of philosophy for the work. It is precisely the intention of addressing the questions of the best life and its authoritative teaching and practice that explains the extended engagement with philosophy. The book persistently underscores both the achievements of and the limits to philosophical inquiry about the highest things. Thomas's understanding of Christian wisdom, furthermore, is a salutary corrective to any sort of Christian anti-intellectualism, since it requires at least some believers to appropriate philosophical teaching and cultivate the intellectual virtues.[29] The advantage of the method and structure of the *Summa contra Gentiles* is that it displays the achievements of and limitations to pagan wisdom, that is, of philosophical metaphysics, in relationship to Christian wisdom. Thus it articulates fully the terms of the debate over the best way of life.

The "principle of economy" in the work, as Mark Jordan notes, dictates that greatest attention be given to topics that "have a direct bearing on persuasion to the highest good."[30] Jordan's protreptic interpretation entails that the reading of the text is itself a kind of practice involving a host of intellectual virtues. In the very first chapter of the work, Aquinas indicates the primacy of a certain kind of practice, as ordering parts in relation to the whole. Here we might recall with profit our previous discussion of virtue epistemology and the role of wisdom as a non-rule-governed intellectual virtue, a virtue that enables its possessor to apprehend the relations among parts, particular disciplines, in relation to the whole. In the opening of the *Summa contra Gentiles* and its interrogation of the best life, *theoria*, or contemplation, is conceived as the partial enactment of an overarching practice of wisdom; similarly, truth, which Aquinas boldly identifies as the "end of the universe," is understand as a good. In this way, Aquinas offers countervailing evidence to Pierre Hadot's claim that in the Middle Ages philosophy as understood in antiquity vanishes. There is a limited, if pedestrian, truth to Hadot's claim. Although Aquinas contributes to philosophical conversation, he cannot be called a philosopher in the classical sense, that is, one who takes philosophical discourse to be the highest discourse and to constitute the most authoritative way of life. That is now theology, not philosophy. Still, the pursuit of wisdom endures in theology.

The plethora of references to the Wisdom literature of the Old Testament in the opening books of the *Summa contra Gentiles* illustrates the centrality of wisdom and inscribes the discourse of the book within a tradition of religious practice, a practice at once exegetical and meditative, a practice that issues in the exercise of virtues such as wisdom, prudence, justice, and liberality— virtues God possesses as exemplars of ours, virtues that in God are indistinguishable one from another.[31] Kretzmann returns a number of times to the status and function of scriptural passages in *Summa contra Gentiles*, but nowhere more revealingly than in his discussion of the "metaphysics of Exodus."[32] In chapter 22 of the first book, after Aquinas argues for the identity of essence and existence in God, he quotes the famous passage from Exodus 3:13–14, where God tells Moses that his name is "I am Who Am." Kretzmann thinks this marks the first place in the work at which we "might be said to have some warrant to begin replacing the noncommittal designation 'Alpha' with the name 'God.'"[33] When Aquinas refers to the denial of the *esse-essentia* distinction in God as "this sublime truth," Kretzmann describes him as stepping "outside the confines of natural theology." This makes it sound as if this were an unusual practice, but, as Kretzmann notes, Aquinas "steps outside" natural theology to adduce scriptural passages in nearly every chapter. This passing from the philosophical to the theological, from reason to revelation, is the very telos of the entire work and anticipates the inscribing of the first three books within the fourth. As Mark Jordan observes, "complete persuasion to wisdom is accomplished when the reader sees that the intelligibility of argument leads into the intelligibility of scripture."[34]

The office of the wise, as described in the prologue, lies ambiguously between an Aristotelian and a Christian understanding. Although Thomas develops analogies between the two, the latter is more comprehensive and more fundamental to the *Summa contra Gentiles*. Kretzmann ends his discussion of the intention, method, and structure of the work by quoting Thomas on wisdom: "Among all human pursuits, the pursuit of wisdom is the most excellent, the loftiest, the most beneficial, and the pleasantest."[35] In addition to being intrinsically desirable in the ways that Plato and Aristotle described it, contemplative wisdom is practical in the sense that it issues in numerous desirable results. But this is not to instrumentalize the life of contemplation, since in the context of faith the contemplation of God *in via* is a beginning of eternal life. In his explication of these attributes of wisdom, Thomas associates the nobility or loftiness of wisdom with its uniting human persons to God in friendship and its utility or its beneficial consequences with its leading to immortality. What other evidence for the primacy of Christian wisdom do we need? Consider, moreover, the significance of the quotation from Hilary in the opening chapter: "I am aware that I owe this to God as the chief duty of my life, that my every word and sense may speak of Him." For Aristotle, teaching is a sign of wisdom; for Aquinas, it is a duty, undertaken out of gratitude. One way to put this point is to say that *theoria* or contemplative wisdom naturally overflows into the activity of charity; another and perhaps more accurate way of speaking is to say that the practice of theological metaphysics is but one part of a more comprehensive set of activities or practices that have as their source and goal the very life of God.

Lest we be misled by all the talk about revelation comprehending philosophy, leading us into a greater intelligibility, Aquinas accentuates the darkness of human inquiry into the highest things. Indeed, he advocates what Josef Pieper nicely calls a *"philosophia negativa,"* a conception of philosophy as longing for that which exceeds its grasp. Although revelation teaches with greater authority than does philosophy, it deepens rather than erases our sense of mystery and our sense that whatever we possess, we possess as a gift. Thomas speaks, accordingly, of philosophy leaving "the human race in the blackest shadows of ignorance." In this context, revelation is an act of mercy (*clementia*) that directs human beings to a "higher good than human fragility is able to experience in the present life." In the most prolix description of the office of the wise, Thomas quotes the Christian author Hilary:

> By believing these things, begin, press on, and persist. Even though I know that you will not reach an end, I will congratulate your progress. He who piously pursues the infinite, although he will not ever achieve it, will nonetheless make progress by proceeding. But do not intrude into that secret, and presuming to comprehend the summit of understanding, plunge into the mystery of endless truth. Instead, understand that these matters are incomprehensible.[36]

More so than human reason, revelation acts as a corrective to the intellectual vice of "presumption." We apprehend a mixture of presence and absence; whatever we receive is a gift that cannot be covetously held as a private possession but instead invites us to a greater participation in the mystery of things.

That the nature of things is fundamentally and ultimately mysterious does not mean that argument has no place. This reading is congruent with other features of the prologue. First, the goal, as we learn in the opening chapter, is to teach the truth and refute the opposed errors. Second, in the chapter on the book's mode of proceeding, Thomas five times uses a variant of the phrase "to convince an adversary" (*adversarius convinci possit* [ScG I, c. 9]). Some see these two passages as supporting the apologetic thesis.[37] However, the work of Gauthier on the term *convincere* renders that supposition dubious. *Convincere* does not mean to persuade, but rather to destroy totally. It is thus not part of an apologetic project of persuading unbelievers, but is integral to Thomas's depiction of the office of the wise. Gauthier writes,

> The necessity of the double office of the sage is thus founded not on the need to persuade an adversary, but on a requirement internal to the manifestation of truth itself: in order to be in the complete possession of truth, it does not suffice to have accomplished the first task of the sage; to express the truth, it is also necessary to be acquitted of the second task—to show the cause of the opposed error.[38]

Thomas's fulfilling of the dual role of the sage does not suit the violent etymology of *convincere* stressed by Gauthier, namely, the extirpation of opposed views. Instead, Thomas seeks to show where and why opposed views go wrong and how the partial truths contained in fallacious opinions can be salvaged by a more comprehensive account. His practice reflects Aristotle's conception of dialectical reasoning; as Aristotle puts it in *Topics* 1.2, the raising of searching difficulties on both sides assists in the detection of truth and falsity. The engagement of conflicting views and the refutation of adversaries are characteristics of dialectical inquiry. For this type of inquiry there are no clear rules, and the result is not pellucid deductions; instead, dialectic involves a kind of phronetic practice, what David Burrell calls "deftness of judgment" and Newman calls "the illative sense."

Naming God as Spiritual Practice

Frequently, a naive assumption about the power of language to attain the divine accompanies an excessive emphasis on demonstration to the denigration of dialectical discrimination. This does not seem to be the case in Kretzmann's reading of *Summa contra Gentiles* I, since he rightly stresses Thomas's repeated statements about the limitations to our speech about God. In fact, in the conclusions of the arguments for God's existence, we reach not the very being of God but only the being true of the proposition "God exists." Immediately after the discussion of God's existence, Thomas insists that we must use the way of remotion in trying to reach what God is. As Kretzmann aptly notes, the discussion of God's perfection marks a transition from the "eliminative method" to saying something more positive about God, but the transition is attended by greater dangers:

> The results of the eliminative method . . . are hardly liable to any kind of misinterpretation. But questions of interpretation arise as soon as God is called perfect. For we can, and sometimes do, correctly use the word "perfect" in talking about daisies or memorizations, having learned the word in such ordinary usage, and the cumulative effect of the eliminative method has been to show us how deeply different God is from any ordinary thing · that we talk about.[39]

As Kretzmann notes, Thomas describes the divine perfection in intensive terms having to do with its purity and distinction from all things, and in extensive terms having to do with its containing the perfections evident in every genus of being.[40] The consequence is instructive:

> The multiplication of attributes for a simple God is motivated practically by natural theology's need to construct an a posteriori, analogical, piecemeal account of the being whose simple essence couldn't be known to us as such. . . . The complexity of natural theology's theory of a simple God is expressly linked with the extensive aspect of universal perfection.[41]

He then refers to Aquinas's claim that, as a result of our cognitive limitations, "it is necessary for God to be given many names. For, we are not able to know him naturally except by reaching him from effects. Thus, it is necessary that the names by which we signify his perfection be diverse, just as the perfections found in things are various."[42]

Not only must we multiply the names of God, but we must also consider each positive name in stages. Having identified a perfection in the natural order, it "must be stripped of any ordinary implications that cannot be associated with God."[43] Next, the term "must be subjected to an incompletely specified extension beyond experience," since God exemplifies each perfection in a more eminent way. The stages in the consideration of the names of God are "designed to filter out imperfections." Kretzmann's account is correct, even if his use of physical language, which in this case can be no more than meta-phoric, may be misleading. References to "stripping away" or "filtering out" might lead one to think that we could actually produce a purified concept in the way we produce a desired physical object by removing its defects. All that we can do at the level of thought and language, however, is multiply acts of reasoning to correct the limitations of one by the other. The trajectory of desire-informed discourse cannot rest in any one affirmation or set of affirmations.

Kretzmann's articulation of Thomas's account of naming by remotion may have a welcome effect on the residual tendency among analytic philoso-phers of religion to construe religious language in univocal terms.[44] But the use of analogous naming in reference to God requires more than a sense of the limits to human discourse. At the heart of Aquinas's doctrine of analogy is a sense of the reversal of discourse necessitated in the ascent to God. Reason must turn upside down.

In his definitive study of analogy in Aquinas, Ralph McInerny focuses on Aquinas's overcoming of Platonism; as interpreted by Aquinas, Plato conflates the logical and real orders. He confuses the order of knowing with the order of being. Denying that the famous doctrine of analogical predication mirrors the real order of being, McInerny asserts, "We are aware that what we last name is what is ontologically first." He explains,

> If the "analogy of being" refers to real relations, so that what is first is the cause of what is secondary, and if "analogous names" involve an ordered plurality of meanings of a common name in which the first, controlling meaning, the *ratio propria*, is not the cause of the rest, the difference is as important as the difference between the logical and real orders. Thomas Aquinas took this difference between the order of our knowledge and the order of being to be decisive as between Plato and Aristotle. He accuses Plato of confusing these two orders and assuming that what is first in the order of knowing is first in being. Any confusion of the logical and real orders comes under the same criticism. A correct understanding of Thomas on analogy saves him from the grievous mistake he attributed to Plato.[45]

As McInerny further notes, Aquinas never speaks of "analogous concepts," but rather of "terms used analogously." Prompted by McInerny's reflections, David Burrell suggests that something like the practice of phronetic judgment is necessary to be able to discern the proper "use" of analogous terms.[46] Al-though analogous usage is not to be identified with metaphor, each requires "deftness of judgment." This calls to mind Gadamer's description of *phronesis* as coming into play in cases where the practical task of differentiation faces "confusion" that is "especially threatening" to understanding and action.[47]

Burrell goes on to contrast the use of the term "order" in the context of a parent trying to keep order in a household, with the use of "order" as applied to God. Although in the former case we may have a fairly clear sense of the primary analogate, in the latter case it escapes our intellect. Are we then bereft of orientation? Burrell responds by invoking Pierre Hadot's notion of the practice of "spiritual exercises" informed by a way of life. Burrell argues that the Christian way of life, its pattern of practicing the intellectual and moral virtues, is decisively informed by the revealed doctrine of creation *ex nihilo*. He explains,

> Properly analogous use . . . demands an awareness that we are functioning as creatures ourselves in a created order whose principles remain unknown to us, yet whose lineaments can be glimpsed from time to time. . . . As the cause of being, the creator is not an extrinsic cause of creatures, since their very to-be is to-be-in-relation to the creator.[48]

Burrell's description of the practice of metaphysics is quite similar to Stanley Rosen's depiction of Platonist metaphysics as "the attempt to think the whole in the sense of attempting to be at home in it; hence wisdom is more like *phronesis* or what comes to mean in Aristotle 'practical intelligence' than it is like dialectic."[49] Aquinas's sense of metaphysics as oriented to the whole is clear in numerous places, for example, when he writes: "We judge those to be completely wise . . . in respect of every genus of beings and not according to a part." Participated being, which defines our existence as creatures, is the basis for analogous naming, what keeps our language from lapsing into sheer equivocity. At the same time, participation is what forestalls the possibility of univocal language, since creator and created, exemplary source and participated image, cannot be located on the same plane or encompassed within some neutral, independent language of being or perfection. Burrell's tersely articulated thesis finds ample support in Aquinas's discussion of divine perfection in the *Summa contra Gentiles*, a discussion that rests on a peculiarly Christian understanding of God's relationship to the world, an understanding that entails a repudiation of the idolatries of the philosophers, whose contemplative aspirations, according to Aquinas, are always vulnerable to the vice of self-love.

Of course, the demonstration of the existence of a supreme being on whom everything depends can in itself engender a sense of dependence of even the philosopher on a principle that exceeds her grasp. Jacques Maritain follows this line of reasoning when he argues,

> To demonstrate the existence of God is neither to subject Him to our grasp, nor to define Him, nor to seize Him, nor to manipulate anything except ideas which are inadequate to such an object, nor to judge anything except our own proper and radical dependence. The procedure by which reason demonstrates that God exists, puts reason itself in an attitude of natural adoration and of intellectual admiration.[50]

We have already noted that such admiration is on display in Aristotle's culminating discourse about God in the *Metaphysics*, in which wonder bordering on awe is the dominant response to God's existence.

The extent to which the philosophical model of knowledge and wisdom must be undone in the ascent to God is most evident in Aquinas's examination of God's knowledge of singulars and lowly things. By far the longest section of the first book, embracing chapters 45–72, treats divine knowledge. Although Thomas is not especially exercised by the issue to which Kretzmann bends his analytical and reconstructive efforts, namely, that God is intelligent, he is worried about God's knowledge of things other than himself. So he takes up objections both to the compatibility of divine simplicity with God's knowing a multitude of objects and to God's knowledge of singulars.[51] The latter issue is particularly contentious among Aristotle's commentators, for the variety in conceptions of divine knowledge arises from differences in the understanding of divine perfection. Thomas makes explicit the link between conceptions of divine perfection and knowledge when he notes that "certain persons try to take away the knowledge of singulars from the perfection of the divine knowledge."[52] Contrary to what Kretzmann supposes, there is no such thing as "generic theism," unless that be limited to the minimal, incipient theism we reach in the initial chapters of the *Summa contra Gentiles*. His naive assumption of the possibility of generic theism rests on his equally dubious belief in the existence of generic "perfect-being theism."

Kretzmann does devote considerable space to the argument establishing that God has knowledge, but he overlooks entirely the most lengthy dialectical segment of the first book, which is devoted to a consideration of received opinions among Aristotle's commentators, opinions that would circumscribe God's knowledge of the world and hence severely compromise his providence. Kretzmann moves quickly from God's knowledge, through his will, to his possession of moral virtues, which fully bring out God's "personhood."[53] What this obscures is the crucial intermediate step of showing that God not only is intelligent but also is cognizant of singulars and lowly things. The capacity to love and to exercise the moral virtues entails an apprehension of ultimate particulars. But pagan as well as some Arabic philosophers tend to view the divine perfection as solely contemplative and to model it on the life of the philosopher. Crucial objections in *Summa contra Gentiles* I, c. 63 to God's knowledge of singulars cite (a) the natural, human ascent in knowledge away from sensible singulars to immaterial universals, and (b) the ignobility of lowly singulars. Thomas's response hinges on a twofold remotion. First, the knowledge of lowly singulars is ignoble only when concentration on lower beings distracts from knowledge of higher things, as is the case with us.[54] But God knows all things through one simple, timeless act of understanding. Thomas quotes Dionysius: "Knowing itself, the divine wisdom knows all things, material things immaterially, divisible things indivisibly, and many unitedly."[55] Second, not only is God's knowledge simultaneously comprehensive and specific, but it is also related to things in a way that is fundamentally different from our intellect's relation to things. Our knowledge is dependent on and secondary to things, and it operates by abstracting universals from singulars. God's knowledge, by contrast, is prior to and causative of things. God thus has a practical knowledge of things; his knowledge is akin to the knowledge appropriate to the practical, intellectual virtue of art.[56]

The central teaching here is the doctrine of God as truth, who has a practical knowledge of created things as objects of his creative art.[57] In this notion of divine practical truth concerning ultimate singulars, we can uncover the basis of Aquinas's very rich rethinking of *techne* as allied to a type of practical wisdom or prudential discretion. If at one level Aquinas shares Aristotle's sense of the subordinate status of *techne* by comparison to *theoria* or *phronesis*, on another level he elevates *techne* as a model for thinking about divine creation. Of course, this is but an analogy, and there are rather striking disparities between human art and divine art, the most notable of which is that God's act of creation presupposes absolutely nothing, whereas human making is always parasitic, dependent on antecedent material conditions. Only by an extension from its original meaning in our experience can God be said to "make" at all; conversely, it is inappropriate to attribute "creation" to any finite created being. Once corrected, however, divine artistry provides a fertile model for rethinking art and its relationship to prudence and truthfulness.

Throughout the discussion of God's knowledge of things, Thomas's conclusions bring him into apparent conflict with Aristotle and into explicit conflict with his commentators. Thomas must combat the theses that composition and division are essential to truth, that knowledge of lowly singulars is unworthy of the divine, that the infinite and future contingents are unknowable. He does so by insisting on the proper scope and meaning of terms and by noting their equivocal uses. Thus, he uses a number of dialectical strategies from Aristotle's *Topics* 1.

Thomas's dialectical resolution of inherited philosophical problems issues in a more adequate understanding of nobility, perfection, and excellence. The perfection of finite intellectual creatures, to whom the etymology of "perfection" ("thoroughly made") literally applies, is to move from singulars to universals, from the material to the immaterial. God needs no such process to achieve "perfection." Thomas's response effectively accuses Aristotle's Arab interpreters of an anthropomorphic conception of God, which is a natural result of an insufficient use of remotion in moving from human to divine perfection. This is the crucial and pivotal discussion in the first book of the *Summa contra Gentiles*, the one that paves the way for a provident Christian God who is active in history. Kretzmann is simply too taken by the contemporary assumption of generic perfect-being theism to identify the crucial debates and strategies in the theism of Aquinas's *Summa contra Gentiles*. What this also obscures from view is Aquinas's transformed understanding of the practices constitutive of the life of wisdom, a way of life that is a participation in, and a dim reflection of, the divine life. No longer conceived as a straightforward ascent from singulars to universals, the good life is, on the basis of

Aquinas's metaphysics of creation, a matter of investigating and negotiating the concrete singulars in which being is actualized, the divine is indirectly manifest, and the working of divine providence is realized.

The implications of these themes in Aquinas's theological engagement of philosophy, themes that escape the notice of Kretzmann's interpretation, will be developed in the next chapter, where we will encounter the most significant Continental interpretation of Aquinas, that of Jean-Luc Marion.

The Presence of a Hidden God

Idolatry, Metaphysics, and Forms of Life

In their introduction to a volume of essays entitled *God, the Gift, and Postmodernism*, John Caputo and Michael Scanlon note the upturn of interest in religion and theology among contemporary Continental philosophers. The deconstructionist fascination with what the Enlightenment had "declared off limits" has finally opened up the possibility of reflection about religion. "This was not," Caputo and Scanlon explain, "the way it was supposed to turn out . . . on the point of religion," at least not according to "deconstruction's more secularizing . . . admirers," who "expected not the loosening up of the Enlightenment but the fulfillment and completion . . . of Enlightenment secularism. They expected Derrida . . . to administer the lethal dose . . . to a still gasping deity."[1] Now, how things will turn out regarding God and religion in contemporary Continental thought is not at all clear. In flight from the metaphysical idols of presence, the religious faith of Derrida awaits a messiah, a wholly-other messiah, a messiah who by definition will never arrive. Waiting for this always-beckoning, always-receding messiah prompts tears and a longing for justice in the form of hospitality toward the stranger as radically other. The religion of deconstruction has no particular content; instead, it replicates the general structure of religion and its form of hope.[2]

Unlike discussions in analytic philosophy, which focus on questions of arguments for the existence of God and the coherence and philosophical viability of specific religious doctrines regarding, say, the incarnation or the atonement, Continental philosophy continues to be preoccupied with issues of the death of God and the critique of metaphysics found in authors such as Nietzsche and Heidegger. Jean-Luc Marion, for example, shares postmodern worries about the way the conceptual idolatries of metaphysics generate their own demise, a process analyzed trenchantly in Nietzsche's *Twilight of the Idols* and *The Gay Science*. Marion thinks that Nietzsche provides a much-deserved burial and wake for the God of modern philosophy, yet the God of Scripture, of the church fathers, and of the majority of medieval Christian thinkers is not susceptible to this critique. Among the latter group of thinkers, Dionysius is Marion's chief authority. In treating Dionysius as his primary interlocutor, Marion restores to Dionysius some measure of the authority and importance he held among the philosophers and theologians of the Middle Ages, not least for Thomas Aquinas, who composed a lengthy commentary on Dionysius's *The Divine Names* and who appeals to Dionysius in key arguments throughout his corpus.

Now, Aquinas's interpretation of Dionysius is controversial. In his influential *God Without Being*, Marion depicts Thomas's commentary as a betrayal of the fundamental doctrine and intention of Dionysius. The decisive shift, what Marion calls the "rupture," occurs in Thomas's granting priority to Being over Goodness in the order of the names of God.[3] Much has already been written on the primacy of being in Aquinas and on the adequacy of Marion's locating God beyond being.[4] Indeed, Marion has himself moderated his criticisms of Aquinas and acquitted him of the charge of falling prey to onto-theology.

What has yet to be noticed is how prominently worries over idolatry— especially conceptual, philosophical idolatry—figure in Aquinas's teaching on God. The so-called metaphysics of Exodus, which has been attributed to Aquinas by friends and foes alike, is less a way of identifying God with the concept of "being" than a way of protecting the name of God from idolatrous appropriation. Moreover, before Marion, Aquinas appropriates the chief pedagogical strategy of Dionysius's doctrine of the divine names, the strategy of deploying names as a means of arousing human *eros*, of beckoning human inquirers to pursue that which exceeds the grasp of thought and language. In his teaching on God, Aquinas leads us through philosophical descriptions of God to a God who is Lord of history, in relation to whom not only redemption but creation itself must be conceived as a gift freely and contingently dispensed. Just as was the case in the last chapter, in our discussion of Norman Kretzmann's analytic reconstruction of Aquinas's theological metaphysics, so too here in the discussion of Marion, critical engagement will allow us to bring to the fore neglected features of Aquinas's thought, particularly concerning the so-called metaphysics of Exodus, the dual idolatries of same and other, and the role of beauty and mimetic practice. Before turning to these themes, it will help to have before us a brief account of Marion's project.

Marion's Aquinas

Marion's essay "In the Name," the lead essay in the volume *God, the Gift, and Postmodernism*, is in large part a response to Derrida's objections to so-called "negative theology." As far back as *The Idol and Distance*, Marion had repudiated the notion of negative theology, noting, for example, that the phrase does not appear in Dionysius. Here Marion begins by noting that Dionysius's discussion of the names of God contains not two but three elements. It does not simply oppose affirmation and negation in some sort of dialectic of the predicates but subordinates both of these to a third way, which "transgresses the first two." The third way, the way of supereminence, as it has come to be called, rather than reasserting affirmation actually "deepens the unknowing."[5] It "aims at what remains above every affirmation and negation" and marks not so much a resting in a proposition as a trajectory of desire beyond discourse. Marion calls this the realm of prayer or praise, the "function" of which is no longer "predicative but pragmatic," a matter not of "naming or attributing something to something but of aiming in the direction of . . . , of relating to . . . , of comporting oneself towards."[6] In direct contrast to any idolatrous attempt to "attain God" conceptually and maintain his presence "under our gaze," in the speech of prayer beyond predication we are "exposed to the point of receiving from this non-object determinations that are so radical and new that they determine and shape me far more than they teach and inform me."[7] We are now involved in a "new praxis," a liturgical and eucharistic practice that "operates in the very horizon of God."[8] In this reversal of discourse, we no longer comprehend or grasp God but are instead comprehended and grasped by God. As Marion puts it, "The Name is not said, it calls." The call of the Name allows us to "acknowledge it as goodness, thus to love it."[9] This, for Marion, is the significance of Dionysius's postulation of the good rather than being as the first and most proper name of God. It underscores the erotic dimension in the human relationship to the divine, the need for us to move toward what calls us but always exceeds our grasp. In more philosophical language, Marion speaks of the saturated phenomenon that "exceeds what the concept can receive, expose, and comprehend."[10] More dramatically, he speaks of an unbearable excess in the intuition of the divine, an excess that (in the words of Dionysius and Chrysostom) "conquers the human power of language" and incites in us a "holy terror," in the presence of which the soul "shudders and becomes afraid."[11]

Whatever might be the merits of Marion's attempt to rescue Christian theology from the idolatries of metaphysics, the position is open to important criticisms. The sort of reservations we have in mind come neither from the defenders of traditional metaphysics, who think Marion cedes too much to postmodernism, nor from the radical deconstructionist critics of metaphysics, who deem Marion too traditional. Instead, we have in mind the objections raised by Richard Kearney, who is sympathetic with Marion's project of over-coming onto-theology, the "attempt to capture God" in conceptual categories. But he worries that the ethical dimension of the divine will be lost if God is "entirely removed from being."[12] The absolute alterity of the divine leaves us with no ground to distinguish God from a "sublime monster," the love of God from madness, true from false revelations, or holy from unholy ghosts.[13] Tak-ing his cue from God's appearance to Moses in the burning bush, where God both calls Moses and orders him to remove his sandals out of reverence, Kearney argues that we need to think about God as neither too familiar nor too distant and as enjoining upon us the eschatological responsibilities of justice and charity. If, for Kearney, "God's relation with mortals is less one of concep-tuality than of covenant," this does not mean that God is encountered only in the unknowing stupor and terror of the "saturated phenomena." Such an experience of "confused bedazzlement," Kearney worries, would lead less to "praxis than paralysis." He explains, "If the saturated phenomenon is really as bedazzling as Marion suggests, how can we tell the difference between the divine and its opposite? How are we to distinguish between enabling and disabling revelations?" As Kearney puts it in his book *Strangers, Gods and Monsters*, the fascination with the Other risks a regression to a pre-Hebraic sublime, to mythic monsters beyond good and evil. If the "Other surpasses all our categories of interpretation and representation, we are left with a problem —the problem of discernment. How can we tell the difference between benign and malign others?" We need, he urges, a "critical hermeneutic capable of addressing the dialectic of others."[14] Marion's approach would seem to deprive us of the very practices necessary for the inculcation of habits of discernment in our naming of God, what Burrell calls deftness of judgment. For Kearney, God is known as he makes himself known in and through history, in the narrative of salvation. Thus, he opts for a narrative theology over both what he takes to be the traditional metaphysics of God and the wholly other God of deconstruction.

Although Kearney does not develop it here, the attractions of narrative theology are clear. First, instead of emphasizing what philosophers can accom-plish autonomously by the use of their own reason, through the conceptual analysis of abstract propositions, narrative theology situates all propositions within the concrete and contingent events of a narrative. Second, although we are participants in the narrative of divine providence, we are not its author; thus, the entire drama and our understanding of it are entirely dependent on divine initiative, on gifts freely bestowed by the author of the whole. Given that the narrative is not over until the end of time (when there shall be a new heavens and a new earth), the outcome from the perspective of each individ-ual is radically contingent and as yet undetermined. Whatever knowledge, experience, or certainty through grace that we have concerning God can never be a complete presence but only a presence mixed with absence. Third, appreciation of the narrative cannot be had from the perspective of the impartial spectator but only by participation in the story, a participation that encompasses and unites thought and praxis, the cognitive and the affective. Thus, narrative avoids the pitfalls associated with an idolatrous metaphysics even as it allows us to distinguish God from a sublime demonic monster. Being is present, but not in a complete or peremptory way; being is absent, but not to such an extent that we are utterly bereft of proper orientation. As we noted in the opening chapter, Aquinas thinks that negations are pointlessly uninformative unless they be preceded or accompanied by some sort of affirmation, however imperfect.

Metaphysics of Exodus?

In the teaching on God in the first book of Aquinas's *Summa contra Gentiles*, and especially in the use Aquinas makes of the teachings of Dionysius, we can uncover Aquinas's profound interest in many of the issues that preoccupy Marion and Kearney. As Thomas notes in the prologue, his goal is to speak of the truth concerning God and to combat errors: "My mouth shall meditate truth and my lips shall hate impiety" (Prov. 8:7).[15] Idolatrous conceptions of God, especially prominent among the *gentiles*, are the chief target of his attacks in Book I. The *Summa contra Gentiles* lacks the formal structure of the disputed question, wherein objections, stated at the outset, are resolved after the body of each article. Instead, in each chapter Thomas marshals a vast array of arguments on behalf of the thesis he wants to defend, arguments pitched at various levels of complexity and often with different authorities in mind. At the end of most chapters, Thomas identifies the authoritative sources of the errors refuted in the body of the chapter. It is in these concluding comments that we find him adverting to the *gentiles*, about which there has been so much debate in the literature on the intent of the *Summa contra Gentiles*. In these passages, the term *gentiles* refers exclusively to the pagans, not to Muslims or Jews. The phrase *contra gentiles* indicates Thomas's intention to correct the idolatrous conceptions of God among the *gentiles*.

The focus on purging idolatry helps to explain some odd structural features of the first book. For example, one of the longest chapters of the first book (*ScG* I. 20) repudiates the thesis that God is a body. Since Thomas has already demonstrated that God is not matter or potency or composite, the denial of a body to God would seem to be a topic easily dispatched. As he intimates in his cataloguing of those who have succumbed to this error, the tendency to limit God to the imaginable is at the root of idolatry. His prolix examination of the question whether God is bodily reflects the intention of the work; an opinion that has been the source of the most pervasive form of idolatry in the human race merits careful scrutiny.

Aquinas ends this chapter by observing that those who have fallen prey to the error of supposing God to be bodily have been led astray by their imagination. He goes on to counsel that it is necessary to relinquish the imagination in the investigation of incorporeal things. Of course, Aquinas does not suggest that we can think our way clear to God by replacing images with pristine concepts. He has not abandoned the Aristotelian thesis that human beings require phantasms in order to think. Instead, we must engage in a complex chain of reasoning wherein negation figures prominently. The entire discussion of God begins with Thomas insisting, in Dionysian fashion, that "the way of remotion is especially to be used in the consideration of the divine substance, since by its immensity it exceeds every form that our intellect attains."[16] We will need to apply negations not just to images but to concepts as well.

As the first book progresses, the worry over the pagan tendency to identify God with sensible images gives way to a protracted attack on the idolatry of the philosophers, who risk conflating God with ideas or concepts. The less tied to concrete images an idea is, the more likely we are to be deceived into thinking that we have reached or comprehended God. This is why in some contexts Dionysius expresses a preference for the concrete images of Scripture, what he calls unlike likenesses, to abstract perfections. Once we have escaped the crude idolatry of equating God with what we can sense or imagine, we are less likely to think that in calling God fire, for example, the image actually comprehends God. If Aquinas counsels us to transcend the imagination, he is acutely aware that our very success in this endeavor can be perilous. He is especially worried about the identification of God with *ens commune*, an identification that would conflate God and the common being of created things. God's pure being is not to be identified with the mere fact of existence, indifferently said of all existing things. Indeed, *ens commune* does not exist on its own, but only as the act of existence of finite beings. Thomas explains the contrast between this common yet derived sort of being and divine being in this way:

> Divine being is without addition not only in thought but also in the nature of things; not only without addition, but even without any receptivity to addition. God is thus proper not common being; for his being is distinguished from all others in that nothing can be added to it.[17]

Not *ens commune* but *esse subsistens* provides the best description of God. For some, the appearance of *esse* denotes Thomas's capitulation to onto-theology and the metaphysics of presence. For others, like Marion, even if it does not vitiate Aquinas's project in this way, it does risk making "being" rather than "good" the primary name of God. We shall see shortly that Aquinas finds in Exodus not just the name of God as subsistent being but also a complex divine pedagogy, wherein the notion of God as nothing other than being gives way to an experience of God as manifesting the good in and through temporal moments. For now we need to attend to the grammatical character of *esse subsistens,* which combines two modes of signifying, the abstract *esse* and the concrete *subsistens.* The abstract mode of the infinitive points to the limitless existence of God. The concrete mode of the participle *subsistens* points to a concretely existing being. The somewhat jarring juxtaposition of these two modes of signifying precludes two possibilities: first, that of lumping God together with other beings, of treating him merely as one being among many, even as the highest member of a hierarchy; and second, that of confusing God with any abstract concept, no matter how elevated or informative. It simply will not do to accuse Aquinas of associating God with an order of abstractions or concepts, or—what is worse—to suppose that Thomas associates God's being with the category of substance. We can assert, indeed, reason con-clusively to, the truth of God as *esse subsistens,* but we can provide no image or single idea of what we know to be the case about God. The grammatical lessons of *esse subsistens* frame the entire discussion of divine perfection.

Aquinas emphatically rejects the suggestion that we can define God in any strict sense. Definition requires that we locate the thing to be defined within a genus and then determine its specific difference, what distinguishes it from all other members of the genus. God is not in a genus; he transcends all genera. Were we to leave it at this, however, we would not have said anything very helpful. Aquinas argues that we can arrive at some knowledge of God by the multiplication of negative differences, which contract the divine essence and set it apart from all other things. Thus, Aquinas will say that we are coming to a knowledge of God as distinct from all other things. But, as we noted in the discussion of Thomas's preferred name for God, *ipsum esse subsistens,* there is no possibility here of resting in a conceptual vision of God. Each step in the contracting of the divine essence, each multiplication of negative difference, only serves to underscore the distance of God from us, from our language—indeed, from the whole of created being. As Marion puts it, "Being does not erect an idol before God, but saves his distance."[18]

In this way, Aquinas is not an exception to Marion's claim that "the requirement neither to know nor name God in terms of presence traverses the entirety of Christian theology." In the course of enumerating orthodox authori-ties who testify to God's transcendence of discourse, Marion mentions Thomas Aquinas, "for whom . . . it is necessary that man know how to unknow," since what God is remains hidden and unknown. He cites with approval Aquinas's gloss of Dionysius: "What the substance of God is remains in excess of our intellect and therefore it is unknown to us; on account of this, the highest human knowledge of God is to know that one does not know God."[19] From our perspective, none of this entails that we cannot reject certain claims about God as false or that we are cannot know anything positive about God. Indeed, as we have stressed throughout, Aquinas insists that the activity of negation rests on affirmation of some sort. Marion himself attempts to capture this in the precise significance he bestows on the term "distance." It indicates not merely separation or otherness but a "separation that unites" or a "communing gap" (*l'ecart communiant*).[20] Distance thus signifies at once transcendence and immanence, absence and presence.[21]

Aquinas himself speaks of our knowledge of God as shrouded in the shadow of ignorance (*in tenebra ignorantiae*).[22] Whatever positive knowledge we have will fail to comprehend the divine essence. The sense of mystery about the divine is nowhere more operative than in the discussion of God as an eternal being. Eternity, we should immediately note, is a negative term, indicating the absence of time or change in God. But the negation does not put us in a very good position to apprehend anything positive about eternity; nor does recourse to the bare present, experience of which eliminates memory and anticipation, the two requirements for any sort of intelligible human experience of the world. Yet we also have, to borrow a phrase from Wordsworth, intimations of immortality or eternity. Insights about eternity are perhaps best—that is to say, least misleadingly—expressed in terms of a poetic coincidence of opposites.[23] The claim that the identification of God with *esse* involves conceiving of eternity purely in terms of a frozen temporal present moment is not just a woefully misleading caricature; in fact, it exhibits the sort of inordinate confidence in the ability of human language to capture the divine that Thomas is constantly at pains to undermine. It also runs counter to Thomas's supple interpretation of Exodus, which he reads as teaching us our ignorance of the "sublime knowledge" of God, when it says of Moses that "he approached the dark cloud in which God dwells" (Exod. 20:21).

If we were to associate Aquinas with an alleged metaphysics of Exodus, we should at least have to see how expansive this discussion is. We should need especially to see that, although Thomas does not write narrative theology, his own teaching on God in the first book of the *Summa contra Gentiles* reflects in some measure the narrative order of God's revelation to the Jews. Just as God's self-revelation to Moses does not cease, but only begins, with "I am who am," so too, Thomas does not think that *ipsum esse* exhausts the God of Exodus. In fact, in the very chapter where he argues on behalf of divine perfection, Thomas first provides an argument that bridges the earlier discussion of *esse* to the present topic. He argues that whatever is highest in a certain order is the measure of all that falls under that order, possessing whatever perfection is included in that order. God, who is "his own being," is the measure of all beings; consequently, no "perfection appropriate to this or that thing is lacking to Him." He then adds the following striking argument: "This is why, when Moses asked to see the divine countenance, or glory, he received this reply from the Lord: 'I will show thee all good,' as it is written in Exodus (33:18, 19)."[24]

Thomas's procedure in *Summa contra Gentiles* I reflects, in an understated and indirect manner, the narrative development of God's self-revelation to Moses in Exodus. God's revelation of himself as "I am who am" underscores the divine simplicity and transcendence of all that can be experienced and grasped by humans. This name functions to separate God from all else that is and thus serves to combat any attempt to conjure God by an idolatrous name or magical incantation. Yet this is preparatory to a further and more intimate self-disclosure of God to Moses, which occurs as Moses is being taught the Ten Commandments and the proper worship of the divine. In this context God speaks of his friendship with Moses. There is no question, then, that goodness, rather than being, is the richer, more informative name of God. The future tense of the verb in the statement, "I will show thee all good," also highlights the future-oriented tenor of God's revelation, his promise to continue to communicate himself to his chosen people in history.

God thus reveals a code of conduct, a way of living righteously or justly. Aquinas describes the precepts of the natural law, which overlap with the teachings of the Decalogue, as exhibiting the dictates of justice. The law also promises aid, for it invites human beings to live more fully in accord with that code precisely by living in greater fidelity to God and others. As Kearney describes it, "future-oriented praxis" runs counter to all "fatalist archeologies of evil" because it resists acquiescence "in the fate of an origin that precedes us."[25] Here again we confront the paralyzing vices of philosophies or theologies that celebrate the Other as utterly alien, which forces us dangerously close to the position of "abandoning ethical praxis."[26] Without some notion of intelligible and continuous selfhood over time, there is no determinate other with whom I can keep faith and "no self to be faithful"; accountability and the practice of its allied virtues would dissolve.[27]

Idolatries of Same and Other

Accountability does not necessarily entail equality or perfect reciprocity. As MacIntyre's account of the role of accountability in intellectual and moral pedagogy makes clear, beginners in any inquiry or discipline are dependent upon the authority and example of their teachers. Philosophy itself remains rooted in the received authorities of its principal teachers and their texts; to assert the autonomous independence of philosophy, its grounding in pure reason, is to deprive the philosopher of the sources of knowledge and progress. From this vantage point, we can appreciate not only the tragic character of any philosophic attempt to start out from a beginning free of all presuppositions (Aristotle said, "To learn one must believe"). We can also appreciate that the discussion of the act of religious faith will have important implications, not just for theology, but for philosophy as well.

According to Josef Pieper, faith has two dimensions: a belief about something and a belief in someone, the witness or possessor of knowledge.[28] In the case of religious faith, these two dimensions coalesce: God is both the one trusted and the one about whom we believe something. Faith is a type of personal knowledge, the goal of which is "communion with the eye witness," a "participation in the knowledge of the knower."[29] Since faith is technically defined as thinking with assent, it involves mental investigation and probing.

Instead of giving us rest, it incites us to greater intellectual activity. Faith is not just a path toward understanding, but it also involves some apprehension of truth in its very act. Pieper quotes Aquinas: "Man could not believingly assent to any proposition if he did not in some way understand it."[30] If God were, as some would have it, "absolutely other," the involvement of the intellect at all in the act of faith would be rendered otiose. One of the chief analogies between human and divine on which Christian theologians have insisted concerns the scriptural and creedal claim that God is a personal being. Thus, although faith is a matter of accepting a number of propositions on trust, it is fundamentally and ultimately about sharing in the life of a personal God. The key question concerning the nature and possibility of divine revelation is "How do you perceive a person?" Pieper remarks pointedly, "If God is conceived as a personal Being, as a Someone rather than a something, and a Someone who can speak, then there is no safety from—revelation."[31]

In the pivotal sections of the discussion of God in the first book of the *Summa contra Gentiles*, Aquinas subtly underscores the sort of point made by Pieper, namely, that if God is a transcendent personal being, there is no safety from revelation, no safety in the primitive idolatry of the worship of things and images, and no safety in the conceptual categories of the philosophers. In this section of the book, Thomas makes explicit and sustained use of Dionysius, the thinker to whom Marion repeatedly turns. The discussion of naming is provoked by the question of whether God can be called perfect; the problem of divine perfection might be said to constitute the chief and culminating dialectical battle of the first book of the *Summa contra Gentiles*, a contest which is absolutely crucial to the structure and plan of the entire work and in which Thomas finds himself at odds with the imposing figures of Averroes and Avicenna and their interpretations of Aristotle. Although he does not take Marion's path, Thomas does combat the dangers of philosophical idolatry by underscoring the distance that separates us—our language and thought—from God and by accentuating the erotic character of discourse about God.

The three elements in the Dionysian way of speaking about God are operative here in Aquinas. When we refer to an order of affirmation, negation or remotion, and affirmation by supereminence, we should not think that at the third stage we have reached a purified concept. It is not as if negation peels away the imperfect crust of human language to arrive at an intelligible core; indeed, this would be to think of this process in physical terms. Instead, the limitations of the original concept remain; the corrective consists in multiplying acts of reasoning. The causal likeness of creatures to God at once justifies our use of analogous perfections and underscores the distance that separates our modes of knowing and speaking from the prime analogate.

Marion himself now notes that the analogy of naming does not locate God and creatures on the same plane. In a pertinent passage from *Summa contra Gentiles* I, 12, which Marion quotes, Aquinas denies that there is any composition in God and adds: "The to be (*esse*) in which God subsists in himself is unknown to us, just as his essence is." Correlatively, as Marion notes, Aquinas rejects the claim that God is part of the subject of metaphysics, as would be required by onto-theology.[32] Instead, God enters metaphysics, not as part of the subject of the science of metaphysics, but as a principle or cause of the subject. God is never the direct object of metaphysical inquiry.

Still, this acknowledgment of the transcendence of God does not utterly annul the language we use to speak of God. Thomas's conclusion is less volatile than Marion's:

> Because we arrive at a knowledge of God from other things, the reality in the names said of God and other things belongs by priority in God according to his mode of being, but the meaning of the name belongs to God by posteriority. And so he is said to be named from his effects.[33]

In this sense, Marion's broad assertion that the sole point of the divine names is to undermine all language about God is unfounded. On this view it would be hard to make sense of Dionysius's patient analysis of the differences and ordered relationships among the various names. What is the rationale for this specific set of names? Aquinas's emphasis on the access that we have to God through nature does not set up a comprehensive and self-satisfied philosophy of God; instead, it is an acknowledgment of the first gift of creation. Thomas explicates the "twofold mode of truth" in pedagogical terms, as two ways in which God instructs, one through creation and another through revelation.

The supremacy of theology need not exclude philosophical or metaphysical investigations; indeed, the first three books of the *Summa contra Gentiles* should be seen as a sustained philosophical moment within a remarkably complex theological pedagogy, as a recovery of the created order for the purpose of a greater penetration of the divine. Pertinent here is Aquinas's statement, "To take away from the perfection of created things is to detract from the perfection of divine power."[34] This involves a robust conception of reason and a welcoming attitude toward reason on the part of faith. It also involves careful and simultaneous attention to both the capacities and the limitations of reason. Such a supple and divided appraisal of reason has been rare in the history of philosophy and theology, especially in the modern period, where rationalism competes with skepticism and fideism. The contemporary danger, as Turner describes it, is that the negative or apophatic element in speculative theology is "recast as lying in the simple deficiency of reason" and as an unlearned ignorance (*ignorantia indocta*) rather than a "learned ignorance" (*docta ignoranita*). The "delicately constructed tension" between the positive and negative "within both reason and faith" would thus become "a polarity between the negative possibilities of reason and the positive possibilities of faith."[35] The theologian cannot, of course, leave it at this, with spelling out the achievements and limits of reason.[36] As Turner describes it, theology's defense of reason and philosophy has to do with a "necessary condition of faith's own self-articulation through the exercise of reason within faith, that is to say, with what reason must be capable of in its own terms if it is to serve its purpose within faith's self-exploration as *quaerens intellectum.*"[37]

Perhaps we should see Thomas as curbing certain tendencies in Dionysius. In a striking anticipation of contemporary concerns about Marion, Umberto Eco voices the following reservations about Dionysius: "In a Dionysian universe, coruscating with beauty, mankind risked losing its place, of being blinded and then annulled."[38] But one also wonders whether there are not the resources in Dionysius himself for a corrective to Marion's reading. Hans Urs von Balthasar, the contemporary theologian to whom Marion is perhaps most indebted, underscores the need to balance Dionysius as the defender of the God beyond all limits, even that of being, with Dionysius as the theologian of creation as the establishment of limits.[39] Balthasar cites Dionysius's pervasive use of terms for order, measure, arrangement, hierarchy, and limit. Dionysius carefully works out a logic of whole and part that describes the whole as containing particulars without "endangering their individuality."[40] For Balthasar's Dionysius, divine love draws all things into an "unconfused union."[41] Dionysius is the great articulator of creation as a hierarchical system, wherein creation and divine providence "preserve and operate in accord with the nature of each being."[42] Precisely these principles inform Thomas's description of creation in the second book of the *Summa contra Gentiles.* Thomas quotes Dionysius approvingly: "Divine wisdom links the ends of higher creatures with beginnings of lower creatures."[43]

Without the intelligibility of images and judgments, the orientation of human persons toward God—whether in philosophy, theology, or liturgy, in what Marion calls the pragmatics of the language of worship—would seem to be derailed. The vertigo induced by the saturated phenomena would render us aimless, a condition more akin to the pagan Dionysiac rites celebrated by Nietzsche in *The Birth of Tragedy* than to the liturgical practices recommended by the Catholic Dionysius.[44] Von Balthasar rightly sees Dionysius as an enormously rich source for his own theological aesthetics, but his reading of Dionysius underscores the proportion or harmony between revelation and the human capacity for receiving the revelation. As John Milbank puts it, "To convert the given into the gift, to receive love, one must admit the mediation of appearing and revelation."[45] This is a theme that Aquinas develops in his discussions of the fittingness of God being worshipped under sensible signs and images; a parallel line of reasoning figures in the discussion of the appropriateness of the incarnation. As he puts it in the *Summa contra Gentiles,* the sacraments mirror the logic of the incarnation. Quoting the Mass of the Nativity, Thomas writes: "While we know God visibly, we are seized by a love of things invisible."[46]

Aquinas does not go as far as Marion in stressing the "radical otherness" of God to sinful humanity, the alterity of agape and grace to human nature. The worry about Marion's so removing God from being that we entirely lose our bearings and are unable to distinguish God from a sublime monster surface once again. Thomas would put the objection this way: If grace were so opposed to human nature that its operation constituted, not a reparation or elevation of nature, but a destruction and reconstruction of human nature, then nature would rightly resist grace. Every nature is naturally opposed to what is inimical to its own being. However weakened, disordered, and darkened is human nature by the stain of sin, nature never loses its inherent goodness, its *telos* toward the good.

As Kearney astutely notes, in its flight from the idolatry of being and goodness, the "postmodern sublime" courts a "new idolatry: that of the immemorial, ineffable Other."[47] In this, "the upwardly transcendent finds its mirror image in the downwardly monstrous. Both extremes are so marked by the experience of radical alterity that they transgress the limits of representation" and "revert to a primordial indistinction" that "negates any notion of the ethical."[48]

By contrast, Aquinas always keeps in view the human orientation to the good, even as he underscores the various ways in which through vice we may become blind to its presence and deaf to its call. Throughout the second and third books of *Summa contra Gentiles* on creation and providence, Thomas urges upon believers the importance of the study of creatures, since this inquiry destroys idolatrous errors about God, promotes proper understanding of God's wisdom and power, and incites souls to a love of divine goodness. In decidedly erotic language, Aquinas describes the "aroused souls of men" becoming "intoxicated" in the presence of God and drinking from the "torrent" of divine delights.[49]

Not precisely what Marion calls holy terror, but something not entirely dissimilar either, can be found in Thomas's description of the human ascent to God. In the culminating chapters of the first book, but especially in the treatment of creatures in the second, Thomas makes pervasive use of the language of beauty. Just as in the discussion of the divine names, so too in the discussion of creatures, Thomas simultaneously underscores the status of creatures as reflections of the divine and the distance that separates creatures from their source. In both cases, the discourse is erotic. The goal is to inflame rather than satiate human desire for God. This is the profound lesson of Thomas's common and overlooked practice of ending each chapter of the *Summa contra Gentiles* with passages from Scripture. Far from being an afterthought, they illustrate the inscribing of philosophical investigation into the narrative of Scripture, the passage of discursive reason into the language of prayer and praise as proper responses to the revealed gifts of beauty and goodness.

The experience of beauty has an ecstatic dimension for Aquinas. It involves being borne out of oneself and into the object of delight. Such a vision of the relationship of the human person to goodness and beauty is incompatible with voluntarism, with a conception of the human person as standing aloof from the world, indifferently related to good and evil, choosing her own set of values. Here again there is a convergence between Aquinas and Murdoch, who regularly insisted on the good and the true as attractive powers, drawing us onward and shaping our freedom. "Life," Murdoch writes, is a "spiritual pilgrimage inspired by the disturbing magnetism of truth, involving ipso facto a purification of energy and desire in the light of a vision of what is good."[50] The interpretation of contemplation as ecstatic love is also deeply incompatible with the craftsman model of self-sufficiency and autonomous control that some have detected in the ancient philosophic adulation of contemplation.

If Murdoch insists on the primacy of the Good, she is equally emphatic about our need to "keep constantly in view the distance between good and evil, and the potential extremity of evil." Indeed, the ubiquitous experience of "moral failure," whose presence pervades Murdoch's novels, underscores the transcendent nature of the good. The "purely good," she writes, is "essentially beyond us."[51] By comparison, Aquinas might seem to neglect or downplay "the potential extremity of evil" in his account of human nature. In spite of his rich depiction of human agency, he might be said to anticipate the naïve optimism of modern liberalism. Do we find evidence in Aquinas of an appreciation that we are, in Murdoch's words, "benighted creatures sunk in a reality whose nature we are constantly and overwhelmingly tempted to deform by fantasy"?[52] We can, I think, find ample evidence for Aquinas's appreciation of human evil. For example, in his discussion of the universal knowability of the natural law, he asserts that sin can erode precepts as basic as the one against theft.[53] In his description of the vices, he highlights the way intemperance hardens the heart, rendering us indifferent to the needs of others, and the way pride creates in us the illusion of self-sufficiency that exhibits itself in a blindness to the needs of others less fortunate than ourselves. More generally and most dramatically, Aquinas insists that there is no limit to our progress in evil. He makes such a claim on the basis of the primacy of the good and an understanding of evil as a privation. Since evil presupposes the good and cannot exist except in a subject whose being retains its goodness, there is no limit to the erosion of the good by evil. Such examples and analyses of evil in Aquinas could be multiplied.

Of course, Aquinas thinks that we cannot gain an adequate handle—theoretical or practical—on evil apart from revelation. Although he thinks that we can discern "probable signs" of original sin in our experience, we could never reason from these to the doctrine of original sin.[54] But Aquinas's account of sin embodies Paul's assertion that where sin abounds, grace abounds all the more. And it is in the discussion of grace that the perception of the good as beautiful resurfaces. The beautiful plays an important role in Thomas's understanding of the nature and efficacy of divine pedagogy. For example, grace closes the gap, introduced by sin, between the precepts of the natural law, which concern goods appropriate to human nature, and the apprehension of the suitability of the law to human nature. Grace restores beauty to the human soul and makes possible an appreciation of the good as beautiful.[55] It re-establishes the connaturality of the good, which is a precondition of love.[56] Grace restores the ability to perceive, take delight in, and appropriate the *claritas*, or radiant beauty, of the good, which is embodied in the virtues.

Vita Apostolica as Mimetic Practice

But precisely how do grace and revelation transform our understanding of human nature and its good? The alteration is evident in many ways. Given our previous discussion, it might be best to focus on the topic of contemplation. We have already seen Aquinas accentuate the enduring role of wonder in the philosopher's contemplative yearning to know the ultimate good. In his discussion of Christian contemplation, he highlights not only its erotic and aesthetic character but also the integration of contemplation with action in the life of the believer. Moreover, the distinctively Christian understanding of beauty is modeled on Christ's incarnation and his sacrificial offering of himself to the Father.

The contemplative life has its roots in the affections: "From the love of God we are inflamed to behold his beauty" (*ex dilectione Dei aliquis inardescit ad eius pulchritudinem conspiciendam*).[57] Beauty encircles the contemplative life. The perception of the beautiful initiates desire; contemplation of spiritual beauty or goodness is the beginning of spiritual love.[58] Conversely, the experience of beauty is a consequence of contemplation. In Christ, we see the beauty of the divine life, and our desire to participate in that life is thus inflamed.[59] Torrell suggests that in Aquinas's theology, Christ is understood as the "Art of the Father."[60] The action of Christ, Aquinas writes, was "for our instruction" (*Christi actio fuit nostra instructio*).[61] The ceremonial portion of the law, which determines the proper manner of divine worship, mirrors the descent of God to us and the manifestation of the eternal in time, of the spiritual in the sensible. It renders the divine truth proportionate to our embodied, temporal condition and enables the "ray of divine light to shine upon us under the form of certain sensible figures."[62] Through divine worship, the likenesses of divine things are "expressed in words" and "proffered to the senses."[63] The ceremonial precepts are a synecdoche for revelation itself; they evince the capacity of Scripture to encompass, divide, and order the whole of time. As Thomas puts it, "The external worship of the old law prefigures not only the future truth to be manifested in the fatherland, but also Christ, who is the way leading to the truth of the fatherland."[64] As the incarnate Word and the Word according to which the world is created, Christ is simultaneously means and end, sign and signified. In his emphasis on Christ's beauty, Aquinas does not gloss over the horrific suffering that Christ endured. In his commentary on the *Epistle to the Hebrews*, he writes, "Christ through his blood has opened up for us a new path. . . . Just as the high priest enters through the Veil into the Holy of Holies, so if we want to enter the sanctuary of glory, we must pass through the flesh of Christ, which was the veil of his divinity: 'You are truly a hidden God.' (Isa. 45:15)."[65]

The model of the life of the Christ informs Aquinas's transformation of the pagan understanding of the relationship of contemplation and action. Thomas states that the contemplative life is intrinsically superior to the active life, yet the life devoted solely to contemplation is inferior to one given to both contemplation and instruction or preaching. In his articulation of this teaching, Aquinas simultaneously brings to bear the full resources and central claims of a metaphysical theology and a social account of the good. Such a life imitates the very structure of being, the pattern established in God's going out from himself to communicate his goodness with creatures. It also supplies what was commonly known in the medieval period as a scale or ladder of perfection that diverges sharply from the dominant model, which culminated in activities geared to personal perfection, rather than a "social orientation."[66] The religious life is a "certain kind of exercise where one aims by practice at the perfection of charity."[67] The apostolic life is a participation in the activity whereby the superabundant beauty of the Creator is manifested to creatures and whereby one angel communicates to another. As Guy Bedouelle, O.P., puts it, the Dominican purpose was to restore the "bond between the Word received and the Word given, and thus to incarnate it in a significant way of life."[68]

The life of teaching and preaching is superior to the merely contemplative life only when the former derives from an abundance of contemplation (*ex plenitudine contemplationis derivatur*). The notion of an abundance or plenitude of contemplation overflowing into the activity of teaching or preaching recalls Thomas's remarks about *claritas* as an irradiation of superabundant beauty and as a manifestation of splendor. The basic argument on behalf of the mixed life runs thus: "The contemplative life is simply better than the active life concerned with bodily acts. But the active life of preaching and teaching, wherein one hands on to others things contemplated, is more perfect than an exclusively contemplative life because the former presupposes an abundance of contemplation. Thus Christ chose such a life."[69] A complicated pattern of ascent and descent, rather than a simple ascent from the things of the world to the transcendent good, characterizes the Christian understanding of the good life. In this context, the practice of virtue is intimately tied to theological metaphysics; it involves a mimesis of the very life and activity of God, whose essence is indistinguishable from his being.

Now, Aquinas's account of God as identical to goodness and of Christ as truth and beauty incarnate runs counter to Murdoch's insistence that to identify any singular being or particular example of goodness with goodness itself is to construct an idol. Good, she holds, is "real as an Idea, and is also incarnate in knowledge and work and love. This is the true idea of incarnation, and is not something obscure."[70] The "indefinability of Good," she continues, "is connected with the unsystematic and inexhaustible variety of the world and the pointlessness of virtue. . . . A genuine sense of mortality enables us to see virtue as the only thing of worth; and it is impossible to foresee the ways in which it will be required of us. That we cannot dominate the world may be put in a more positive way. Good is mysterious because of human frailty, because of the immense distance which is involved."[71]

Aquinas can concur with Murdoch, although not for precisely the same reasons, on the inexhaustibility of the good, on the pointlessness of virtue, and on the fragility of the human possession of goodness. He would have reservations, however, about Murdoch's continued reference to the Idea of the Good. Of course, Murdoch is careful not to lapse into problematic assertions about the ontological status of the Ideas. Yet Murdoch seems to move beyond the dialectic between the Idea of the Good and its concrete instantiations precisely in her attempt to retain the divine, without recourse to God or revealed religion. In words that unintentionally expose the weakest point in Murdoch's philosophy of the good, she concludes her most ambitious philosophical book, *Metaphysics as a Guide to Morals*, with words from Psalm 139:

> Whither shall I go from thy spirit, whither shall I flee from thy presence? If I ascend into heaven, thou art there, if I make my bed in hell, behold, thou art there. If I take the wings of the morning and dwell in the uttermost parts of the sea, even there shall thy hand lead me, and thy right hand shall hold me.

The preponderance of "thys" and "thous" in the words of the psalm bespeaks a personal presence that haunts, thwarts, cajoles, entices, guides, and comforts us. But, as Murdoch herself was well aware, the Good cannot pursue, but can only be pursued. By contrast, the God of the Psalms manifests goodness as a personal presence.

On the topic of *eros*, Aquinas is much closer to Dionysius than Marion is. Marion's understanding of *eros* is derived at least in part from Heidegger's conception of the utter alienation of *Dasein* and, through Heidegger, from Luther's view of human nature as totally depraved by original sin. These are odd and uncongenial authorities through which to mediate Dionysius's understanding of *eros*. While acknowledging the debilitating effects of sin, both original and actual, on human nature, Aquinas nowhere posits a violent opposition between the fallen creature and its transformation through grace. Such a severe denigration of created nature diminishes God's first communication of himself to human beings in the act of creation. This is the first gift, preceding the gift of grace.

The sharp opposition of *eros* to *agape*, of human to divine love, entails a dichotomy between nature and grace, rendering one the enemy of the other. The greatest evisceration of *eros* occurs in the post-Freudian understanding of *eros* as sexual stimulation or as a need that leads us toward others only so that we might devour their separateness and subordinate their existence to our wants. Pieper attempts to restore a proper understanding of *eros* as a "desire for full existence, for existential exaltation, for happiness and bliss." His defense of *eros*, properly understood, recurs to the integrity and goodness of creation. The denigration of *eros* risks reducing the creature, the very one to whom the commandment of love is issued, to nothing. Is *eros*, he asks, "strange and foreign" to *agape*? Or is it not the ground within which supernatural grace takes root and blossoms?[72] As Aquinas is fond of noting, we are commanded to love our neighbors *as* we love ourselves. "If love (*amor*) were not good in itself, charity (*caritas*) would not perfect it."[73]

Dare we speak, as Aquinas does, of the perfection of *eros* by *agape*? "Perfection always includes transformation. And transformation necessarily means parting from what must be overcome and abandoned precisely for the sake of preserving identity in change."[74] Such a transformation occurs in and through the sacrifice of praise. Charity and its allied virtues inform the Christian way or form of life as Aquinas understands it and practices it. Marion himself quotes the famous phrase "form of life" from Wittgenstein's *Investigations*: "The language of praise utilizes unverifiable significations but, through the intention and 'form of life,' delivers an intelligible and in fact understood meaning: the usage of linguistic praise is not founded in an absurd empirical verification of the Requisite, but in the quasi-liturgical 'form of life' that establishes it in distance, for a request, in the manner of a requestant."[75] But questions about the intelligibility of our comportment toward a God utterly beyond being persist. What is the intelligibility of this "form of life"? For Aquinas, at least, the form of life that comports us toward God consists in the communal and ecclesial practice of the virtues, intellectual and moral, natural and infused. As Chenu has splendidly argued, the twelfth- and thirteenth-century recovery of nature and reason is hardly a movement in the direction of idolatry. It is instead a direct result of the rejuvenated evangelical impulse: "The return to the primitive life of the church, to the life of the apostles, the *vita apostolica* . . . inspired a new awareness of the ways that grace could take root in nature."[76]

As much as it may capture a certain and enduring experience in the religious life, Marion's "confused bedazzlement" must give way to, or at least be understood within the context of, a set of virtuous practices. The practice of virtue is a participation in the "form of life" proper to the gospel, which is itself a revelation of the fullness of being as beautiful and lovable. Of course, as Marion is at pains to remind us, these practices and the dispositions they seek to foster in us can never be reduced to habits in the Aristotelian sense. They never become attributes possessed autonomously by human agents. They are rather gifts whose sustaining center is God. In this context, it would not be misleading to describe charity, which Aquinas identifies as the form of the virtues, as a "communing gap," that is, in Marion's terms, as "distance."

eight
Portraits of the Artist
Eros, Metaphysics, and Beauty

In *The Idol and Distance*, Jean-Luc Marion argues that Nietzsche's critique of the Christian concept of God maintains its pertinence only as long as it attends to a clearly identifiable " 'God,' an idol that it sees."[1] Marion quotes Heidegger's assertion that "God" is the "name for ideas and ideals."[2] In what devotees of Nietzsche would doubtless see as a heretical reading, Marion suggests that Nietzsche lays the groundwork for conceiving of atheism itself as idolatrous, as presupposing that it has an adequate conceptual starting point for thinking "God" and then moving on to repudiate that concept. Nietzsche associates the twilight of the idols with nihilism, the time in which transcendent values devalue themselves. Nihilism, as Nietzsche writes in *The Will to Power*, means that the whole no longer speaks through human beings, that the aim is lacking, that the human being is forlorn and left to the devices of her own wishes.[3] Nihilism is the natural result of the heavy-handed moralization of reality in the great religious and philosophical traditions; it fosters *ressentiment* toward what is, in favor of a separate world of ideas and ideals.

For Aquinas, God is clearly not a name for "ideas and ideals." As we saw in the last chapter, the language of perfection must be turned upside down to apply to God at all. Aquinas offers an alternative to the conceptual idolatries of the metaphysics of presence and the anarchic wallowing in Dionysian otherness. Creation itself—the concrete actualization of singular beings—is a gift from, and participation in, a personal being whose mode of existence escapes conceptual expression. Our approach to the Giver of every good and perfect gift involves not so much logical deductions as the exercise of phronetic discrimination, a capacity for discernment inculcated and honed by involvement in a way of life. What Pierre Hadot has demonstrated concerning the ancient philosophical schools is true of Aquinas's pedagogy. Indeed, his pedagogy seeks to arouse and engage the natural human longing for the beautiful, for a way of life that pursues an ever deeper penetration of the manifestations of beauty in the created order and an ever more complete appropriation of the virtues constitutive of the good life. Thus, Aquinas's language regarding God and creation is thoroughly aesthetic.

Although Marion does not develop or even note them, there are numerous points of convergence between Aquinas and Nietzsche on aesthetics, metaphysics, and the role and limitations of reason. The prominence of the language of eros and the beautiful in both authors has much to do with the sense of reason as enveloped within a larger context in which it participates as an incomplete part. Erotic language always appeals to a lack, an as-yet-unsatisfied desire or longing. And eros is not merely aimless desire or the sense of lack; it is not "negative excitation" or a "projection outward" from the intellect or will; rather, it is, as Stanley Rosen describes it, a "force from above and outside the soul that comes down into it and raises it to the heavens."[4] An instructive consequence of this conception of eros is a certain downgrading, at least from a post-Romantic perspective, of the status of the artist: there can be no autonomous artistic creation, since the artist herself is but a participant in a larger order.[5] Nietzsche's corrective to naïve romantic assertions of ethical autonomy and artistic self-expression is to construe the artist as a participant in, or even as an artifact of, a primordial source.

Neither Nietzsche nor Aquinas limits art and the beautiful to the specialized sphere of the aesthetic, as it has come to be called in the last two centuries.[6] As we shall see, Nietzsche conceives of tragic art as an expression of the very nature of the human condition and as having salutary social and political lessons. Aquinas's metaphysics of participated actuality renders every creature artistic to some degree. Norris Clarke writes,

> If every being turns out to include a natural dynamism toward self-communication through action, we can say truly, in more than a metaphorical sense, that every being is naturally a self-symbolizer, an icon or image-maker, in some analogous way like an artist, expressing itself symbolically, whether consciously or unconsciously. . . . The self-symbolizing tendency in all the finite beings we know turns out to be an imperfect participation or imitation of the inner being of God himself, revealed to be supremely and

perfectly self-symbolizing in its eternal interior procession of the Son from the Father and the Holy Spirit from both.[7]

Of course, this is an account that Nietzsche repudiates, often with great vehemence. He thinks that Christianity is hostile to eros: "[It] gave eros poison to drink; he did not die of it but degenerated into a vice."[8] But the different starting points, orientations, and conclusions of Nietzsche and Aquinas only make more striking the parallel set of concerns each author investigates. Both authors must face questions concerning the nature and role of artistic creation, the sources of aesthetic experience, and the relationship between making and knowing.

Precisely such an encounter, on precisely these issues, between Nietzsche and Aquinas is woven into the very fabric of James Joyce's *Portrait of the Artist* and *Ulysses*. Although Joyce is not a philosopher, his fiction embodies a number of strategies for undermining strains of Enlightenment modernity and of Romanticism, modernity's reactionary mirror image. In the midst of the cascade of recent studies of Joyce, there has been a quiet resurgence of interest in the affinities between Joyce and premodern philosophy, especially Aristotle. Weldon Thornton's interpretation of *Portrait* presupposes something like the Aristotelian metaphysical teaching on potency and act—a teaching Hugh Kenner once identified as the "sharpest exegetical instrument we can bring to the work of Joyce."[9] Even more than Kenner, Thornton demonstrates the exegetical fecundity of the doctrine of potency and act, which is to suggest unrealized possibilities toward which the action of the novel points but which remain frustrated by particular defects in the characters.

Thornton makes a convincing case for the presence of Aristotelian notions of human agency and narrative rationality in Joyce, especially in *Portrait of the Artist*. He does not, however, investigate the interplay of elements from Thomistic metaphysics, theology, and aesthetics in *Portrait* and *Ulysses*.[10] Although Joyce does not embrace Aquinas's original formulation, he understands the affinity between Aquinas's Trinitarian metaphysics and his conception of ethical practice in a human community. Joyce also sees that these theological and ethical teachings have implications for questions concerning the unity or disunity of narratives of human action and the relationships of self to other.

Nietzsche and Joyce:
Enlightenment Demise, Romantic Dissolution

Among the many fascinating aspects of Joyce's deployment of philosophical currents is the way Thomistic themes figure alongside Nietzschean themes in his stories. In *Portrait of the Artist* this is particularly the case when it comes to the issue with which Stephen Dedalus is most occupied, namely, aesthetic creation. The germane text from Nietzsche is *The Birth of Tragedy*. In this early and seminal text, Nietzsche depicts the history of the West as a struggle between two gods, two models of art, and two experiences of the relationship of the individual to the whole of society and nature.[11] The hidden source of Greek society and hence of the West is Dionysius, the primordial will, the surging force of chaos at the root of all human activity and thought. Dionysius is prior to the distinctions between good and evil and among objects. Dionysius, who is the primal suffering and source of wisdom and creativity of all things, is the spirit of music and is prior to language. Since it eliminates the possibility of individuation, it is void of conscious awareness and hence cannot know its own wisdom. By contrast, Apollo, as the *principium individuationis*, is responsible for the introduction of distinctions between good and evil and among objects. It is embodied in the plastic arts. It thus makes rational comprehension and articulation possible.

Given its dependence on Dionysius, the triumph of Apollo is always tenuous and unstable. If Apollo seeks to dominate Dionysius, it becomes effete, rationalistic, and static. The "entire existence" of Apollo depends "on a hidden substratum of suffering and knowledge revealed to him by Dionysius." Nietzsche writes:

> And now let us imagine how into this world, built on mere appearance and moderation and artificially damned up, there penetrated, in tones ever more bewitching and alluring, the ecstatic sound of the Dionysian festival; how in these strains all of nature's excess in pleasure, grief, and knowledge became audible, even in piercing shrieks; and let us ask ourselves what the psalmodizing artist of Apollo, with his phantom harp-sound, could mean in the face of this demonic folk-song.[12]

For a brief but remarkably fertile period, the period of Greek tragedy, the Dionysian and the Apollonian existed in a kind of harmony. The Apollonian elements in tragedy, the role of speech and individual characters, make possible our indirect apprehension of the primal will, whose confrontation we cannot endure directly. Apollo, who is the source of the maxims "Know thyself" and "Nothing in excess," individuates and allows for conscious apprehension and expression.

The history of the West is the story of the increasing dominance of Apollo, the crucial stage of which is the Socratic turning away from poetry and music toward the good, the true, and the beautiful. Socratic rationalism is developed further in Christianity, and especially in modern science. The following out of the trajectory of rationalism undermines itself: "Science, spurred by its powerful illusion, speeds irresistibly toward its limits, where its optimism, concealed in the essence of logic, suffers shipwreck." The "limits of theory" engender a "turn to art." Logic "bites its own tail" and gives rise to a "tragic insight." Socratic culture suffers from "the delusion of limitless power."[13] Another way to express science's undermining of itself is in terms of the search for truth, which Judaism and Christianity introduced into the world and which is carried forward most forcefully by science. That very pursuit leads inevitably to the acknowledgment that all these systems are but lies, concealing the chaotic abyss at the root of all things.

By contrast, tragic culture exalts "wisdom over science," seeks a "comprehensive view," and embraces "with sympathetic feelings of love, the eternal suffering."[14] Tragic art serves life and restores health and wisdom to the human soul. Nietzsche urges that we consider science in light of art, and art in light of life. This does not entail the rejection of reason, but rather its relocation. It can no longer stand apart from the rest of nature as its tribunal; instead, it is but a part, subordinate to, and nourished by, an extra-rational order of instinct. Its ideal is the Socrates who practices music. Where does this view leave the artist?

In some ways, Nietzsche's theory is compatible with a romantic understanding of the artist. He exalts art over science, instinctive wisdom over discursive reason, and myth over inquiry. In other and more important ways, however, his theory is surprisingly critical of the standard romantic view of the artist. As Peter Berkowitz observes, it deprives the artist of self-consciousness, autonomy, and creativity.[15] As a participant in the Dionysian primordial unity, according to Nietzsche, he is "no longer an artist"; instead, he has "become a work of art."[16] Nietzsche goes so far as to say that the "individual with egoistic ends" is the "antagonist of art."[17] He also repudiates the romantic, and for Nietzsche residually Christian, view of nature. He comments that "this harmony . . . this oneness of man with nature . . . is by no means a simple condition that comes into being naturally. . . . It is not a condition that, like a terrestrial paradise, must necessarily be found at the gate of every culture. Only a romantic age could believe this."[18] This view of nature, which is an Apollonian myth, culminates with the thoroughly modern image of the "sentimental, flute-playing, tender shepherd."[19]

How would a Nietzschean reading of *Portrait of the Artist* proceed? The very structure of the *Portrait* mirrors that of the progression toward a recovery of pagan art in *The Birth of Tragedy*. The Christian religion occupies the third and middle chapter in *Portrait*; it has the same intermediate status in the novel that it does in Nietzsche's history. The description of the religious life is reminiscent of the dominant themes in Nietzsche's own account. It is founded in fear; the entire focus of the third chapter of *Portrait* is the part of the Ignatian retreat that treats of the last things: death, judgment, heaven, and hell. Yet heaven is not touched upon at all. Fear of the unknown or of the certainty of eternal punishment for the unrepentant drives a wedge between the rational system of final judgment and the passions and instincts. Indeed, the notion of the self is atomistic, isolated into discrete moments, and to be subject to the control of isolated acts of will. The narrator describes Stephen's life immediately after his conversion as being "laid out in devotional areas."[20] As he begins to be tempted again by the "insistent voices of the flesh," he experiences an "intense sense of power to know that he could by a single act of consent, in a moment of thought, undo all that he had done." But then, "almost at the verge of sinful consent," he would be "saved by a sudden act of will" (165).

To emphasize exclusively the negative elements in the Christian religion is to obscure Nietzsche's view of it, for he detects in the religious impulse an inchoate and unconscious artistic impulse. We are awed by the interplay of opposites in the saint, by his project of self-overcoming, of transforming the self into a work of art. Similarly, Stephen Dedalus inclines toward an aesthetic view of the religious life. He speaks of how "beautiful" it would be to love God. To the mortification of the senses, especially touch, "he brought the most assiduous ingenuity of inventiveness" (163). The kinship between art and grace is clear from its power to create an entirely new world, "The world for all its solid substance and complexity no longer existed for his soul save as a theorem of divine power and love and universality" (162). In fact, certain elements of the purported life of grace as Stephen experiences them resemble the vices of the romantic artist. Stephen's scrupulous vanity is akin to artistic self-absorption (166). Both grace and art sever his ties with the ordinary lives of others. He was unable to "merge his life in the common tide of other lives" (164).

As in *The Birth of Tragedy*, so too in *Portrait*, the opposition of the pagan and the Christian is prominent. The contrast is present in the name of the novel's protagonist, Stephen Dedalus, who has both the name of the first Christian martyr and that of the famous artificer of Greek myth. At the crucial transitional section of the novel, Stephen rejects the possibility of a vocation to the priesthood and realizes his artistic call. In his meeting with the Jesuit who suggests that he pursue the path of a religious calling, he is counseled: "And let you, Stephen, make a novena to your holy patron saint, the first martyr" (173). Later in that chapter, precisely when Stephen realizes his artistic vocation, he is called Stephanos by his friends. The Hellenization of the Christian part of his name signifies the transition from the modern Christian world to the premodern pagan world. It thus reflects Nietzsche's rebirth of tragedy, wherein the limits to the Christian worldview open up the possibility of a recovery of the primacy of pagan culture.

In spite of these similarities between the development of Stephen's realization of his artistic vocation and Nietzsche's history, there are crucial differences, differences that might lead us to appraise Stephen's character as falling short of the Nietzschean vision of the artist. As we noted above, Nietzsche does not celebrate the crude romantic depiction of the artist as an isolated individual, cut off from others, who creates from autonomous sources. Precisely this vision of the artist entraps Stephen. Many commentators have expressed a sense of disappointment at the final chapter of the *Portrait*. Instead of a further development of Stephen's character, we find a kind of stasis and an inability to create anything substantial. His lone piece of writing is a short villanelle that critics have described as narcissistic and as Joyce's parody of symbolism. Stephen thinks it crucial to his artistic achievement that he "fly" past the nets of nation, language, and religion. His goal is "to discover the mode of life or art whereby" his "spirit could express itself in unfettered freedom" (267). Stephen's assertions of independence are undermined throughout the novel, but nowhere more explicitly than in his growing awareness of and identification with the myth of Dedalus. The primacy of that myth is evident in the epigraph to the entire work from Ovid: "Et ignotas animum dimittit in artes." The primacy of myth indicates that, although there is a gap between Nietzsche's self-understanding and Stephen's, that gap may be bridged by the perspective of the narrator.

Stephen is repeatedly described as yearning for and answering a call: first in his desire to sate his lust with the prostitute, then in his repentance of his lust and his flirtation with a religious vocation, and finally in his realization of his artistic mission. In all these cases, he is moved by things outside him or by passions that are within him yet beyond his control. In fact, the entire work begins with Stephen's father telling the children's story of the meeting between a moocow and baby tuckoo, in which Stephen is identified with the "nicens little boy baby tuckoo." The location of an individual within a myth, story, or tradition can be given various interpretations. One plausible interpretation is that of Nietzsche. Consider, for example, Stephen's earliest nonreligious experience of self-transformation, which occurs as he performs his part in a school play, where he sheds his normal timidity and self-consciousness: "Another nature seemed to have been lent him. . . . It surprised him to see that the play which he had known at rehearsal for a disjointed lifeless thing had suddenly assumed a life of its own. It seemed now to play itself, he and his fellow actors aiding it with their parts" (90). The passage is strikingly reminiscent of Nietzsche's description of the tragic chorus: "The tragic chorus is the dramatic proto-phenomenon: to see oneself transformed before one's own eyes and to begin to act as if one had actually entered into another, another character. . . . Here we have a surrender of individuality and a way of entering into another character."[21]

Consider, furthermore, that the rebirth of tragedy arises out of the spirit of music. Stephen is frequently described as hearing and being moved by music. "The vast cycle of starry life bore his weary mind outward to its verge and inward to its center, a distant music accompanying him outward and inward." (110). Music breaks the artificial divisions, characteristic of Apollo, between inner and outer. As he begins to escape from family into the university, Stephen anticipates a "new adventure." He hears "notes of fitful music leaping upwards a tone and downwards a diminished fourth . . . It was an elfin prelude, endless and formless; and as it grew wilder and faster, the flames leaping out of time, he seemed to hear from under the boughs and grasses wild creatures racing, their feet pattering like rain upon the leaves" (147). The passage comes remarkably close to Nietzsche's depiction of the Dionysian.

For all the apparent approaches toward the Dionysian, Stephen falls short of the achievement Nietzsche lauds. Stephen's lack of creativity mirrors his moral and psychological solipsism. He is detached from and indifferent to all others and thus suffers from an inability to communicate or to love. In a telling exchange with Cranly, he is asked whether he loves his mother and responds that he doesn't know what the words mean. Cranly persists, "Have you ever felt love toward anyone or anything?" "Staring gloomily at the footpath," he responds, "I tried to love God . . . It seems to me now I failed. It is very difficult. I tried to unite my will with the will of God instant by instant. In that I did not always fail. I could perhaps do that still . . ." (261). The most persistent themes in the final fragmentary sections of the novel have to do with women. He is troubled by his inability to love or even remember his mother in any detail and is confused and angered over his complicated feelings toward the woman he cannot love and yet cannot free himself from. His adolescent self-consciousness is evident in one meeting with her: "Talked rapidly of myself and my plans. In the midst of it unluckily I made a sudden gesture of a revolutionary nature. I must have looked like a fellow throwing a handful of peas into the air" (275). Stephen's pathologies and vices are summed up in his repeated use of the phrase "*non serviam.*" His life is a kind of comic *imitatio diaboli.* How are we to appraise Stephen's multiform lack of fecundity?

Given what we have argued above about the parallels between the novel and Nietzsche's theories, it might make sense to understand Stephen's impotence as a failure to break through the Apollonian to the Dionysian. Does not Stephen embody precisely that antagonism to art that Nietzsche detects in the individual with egoistic ends? Stephen's romanticism is the antithesis of, and an enduring impediment to, true art. For the Nietzsche of *The Birth of Tragedy* and *The Advantage and Disadvantage of History for Life,* creation is possible only through a kind of historical rootedness and, at least in *Birth,* through a radical subordination of the individual self to the primordial will by becoming its instrument. The modern notion of progress, with its abandonment of tradition and memory, eliminates the conditions for the possibility of creativity. Yet Nietzsche himself often depicts creation as an act of violence and destruction, as an evisceration of the past and present for the sake of an unknown future. Perhaps on account of his growing realization that Germany would not provide creative cultural soil, Nietzsche moves in the direction of the life-affirming individual who sets himself against a decadent culture to become a creator of values. This is but one of many unresolved tensions in Nietzsche's thought.

In *Portrait,* Stephen embodies this tension in Nietzsche's account of creativity. In Stephen's mind, the contrast is embodied in the distinction between the feminine cultivation of memory and the voluntarist, masculine orientation toward the future. One pertinent passage runs thus: "Certainly she remembers the past. Lynch says all women do. Then she remembers the time of her childhood—and mine if I was ever a child. The past is consumed in the present and the present is living only because it brings forth the future" (273). The emphasis on creativity and novelty entails not only overcoming the past but also emptying the present—the only moment of time that we actually experience—of any except instrumental significance. Stephen's conscious attempt to repudiate the past is rooted in his voluntarist conception of Christian conversion, evident in his momentary belief that the past was now behind him. Stephen would seem here to be the embodiment of that peculiarly modern type from which Iris Murdoch recoils, the type of humanity as reduced to brave, naked, solitary will. The project of gaining an autonomous, conscious control over all of one's powers alienates one from the past and from the penumbral elements of one's conscious awareness. Such a project is doomed to failure: As Stephen attempts to forget the object of his affection, "on all sides distorted reflections of her image started from his memory. . . . she was a figure of the womanhood of her country, a batlike soul waking to the consciousness of itself in darkens and secrecy and loneliness" (239–40).

If there are numerous connections between Joyce's *Portrait* and Nietzsche, there are also disparities. Nietzsche's typology of tragedy and comedy does not fit neatly with Joyce's writing. Nietzsche contrasts the universal typology of the tragic hero with the treatment of the individual as an individual in the comic.[22] He attributes the decline of tragedy to the "victory of the phenomenon over the universal, and the delight in a unique, almost anatomical preparation." In place of tragedy's "eternal type," we find the "prevalence of character representation and psychological refinement."[23]

The ending of *Portrait* anticipates a tragic fall. Stephen's calling upon Dedalus in the words "Old father, old artificer, stand me now and ever in good stead," clearly portends Stephen's own failure, as it identifies Stephen with Icarus, whose ambitious flight ended in a fall. The deeper incongruity between Joyce and Nietzsche has to do with the latter's celebration of aristocratic tragedy, which is virulently antidemocratic, perhaps even antipolitical. Joyce's approach, by contrast, is democratic and more comic than tragic. In the only passages in which Stephen seems heroic, he also appears foolish. In the penultimate fragment, Stephen writes of his mother, "She prays now, she says, that I may learn in my own life and away from home and friends what the heart is and what it feels" (275). Her answer to Stephen's dilemma is that he should identify himself more fully with ordinary folk. This seems to be the attitude the narrator wishes to induce in the reader as well. Stephen is young; we feel sympathy for him that we feel for a precocious but inexperienced child. We also pity his foolishness.

Such a perspective presupposes that the narrator's point of view is not simply to be identified with that of Stephen. It also suggests that the simplistic account of Joyce's style as first person stream of consciousness must be abandoned. The individual consciousness gives way to a more comprehensive third person point of view. As Thornton persuasively argues, the narrator does not seek to reflect the flow of conscious activity in the protagonist, but to capture the more complex flow of his entire psychic environment, much of which Stephen is unaware. The narrator does, as Stephen suggests he should, disappear behind or beyond his work, but it is not at all clear that he adopts a position of neutrality or indifference toward his main character. As both

Thornton and Stanley Sultan show, Joyce's use of irony frequently serves to enrich rather than merely subvert a character's self-understanding.[24] Irony does not undermine the individual quest for meaning, but rather locates it within a more comprehensive account; it urges compassion toward human weakness, and its laughter presupposes some measure of identification with ordinary human beings. Ellmann captures this nicely: "The initial and determining act of judgment in his work is the justification of the commonplace. . . . Joyce's discovery . . . was that the ordinary is the extraordinary."[25]

The prominence of ordinary human beings sounds less like Aristotelian tragedy than comedy, wherein there is a certain proportion between characters in a drama and the audience. Comedy contains persons at our own level or slightly lower. The narrator in Joyce's novels treats these ordinary folks as objects neither of romantic celebration nor of cynical dismissal. He may share some of Nietzsche's reservations about the deleterious effects of religion on the human psyche, but he shares none of his virulent criticisms of slave morality or devotion to noble ethics.[26]

If this interpretation is correct, then there is a disparity between Stephen's account of the relationship between author and work and that operative in the novel. At the end of his development of his aesthetic theory in Part V of *Portrait*, Stephen traces the transition from the lyrical through the epical to the dramatic, wherein the author progressively distances himself from his work: "The personality of the artist . . . finally refines itself out of existence, impersonalizes itself. . . . The mystery of esthetic like that of material creation is accomplished. The artist, like the God of the creation, remains within or behind or beyond or above his handiwork, invisible, refined out of existence, indifferent, paring his fingernails" (233). Of course, the assertion is in part a denunciation of the conception of art as principally a matter of self-expression. But there is something to Lynch's retort, "Trying to refine them also out of existence," an aptly sardonic comment indicating that the creator's indifference is actually an antipathy. Aquinas, to whom Stephen has been appealing as his authority in things aesthetic, pervasively deploys analogies between human and divine artistry, but he does not take them as literally as Stephen does, nor does he depict the creator of the universe as indifferent to his creation. Joyce does not cynically mock the all-too-human foibles of his characters, nor does the narrator imply that he is indifferent or that the reader should be.

The ambivalence we feel toward Stephen at the end of the book allows for multiple interpretations. As some critics have argued, the vices that impede Stephen's growth as a human being and as an artist are precisely those decried in the sermon on hell that stands at the center of the story. Consider, for example, the echoes of Satan's "*non serviam*" in Stephen's proud refusal to identify himself with the lot of others and his self-absorbed attempt to create *ex nihilo*. The painful isolation of Stephen at the end of the book recalls St. Thomas's teaching—cited by the priest—that the greatest spiritual punishment of hell is the pain of loss, the isolation from the greatest good and hence from all other goods.

As critics have remarked, Joyce may have lost his faith, but he retains many of its philosophical categories. In part, what the novel seems to retain is a Thomistic moral and philosophical critique of the exaltation of the creative will. The final section of *Portrait* draws out the untoward consequences of radical voluntarism, a voluntarism that emerges in the sermon on hell, a sermon replete with a thoroughly modern and typically Jesuit conception of the Christian life. As Stephen's pagan roots begin to eclipse his Jesuit education, the voluntarism continues to surface. The echoes of the Satanic refusal to serve reveal the envy and pride at the root of Stephen's willfulness. The self thus supplants the divine and becomes a sort of self-creating divinity.

Nietzsche himself is not entirely clear on this point. As we have seen in *Birth of Tragedy*, he repudiates the autonomous creativity of the artist who, in order to create, must become an artifact, a participant in the Dionysian source of all creativity. Yet elsewhere, particularly in his late investigations, he celebrates the value-creating capacities of the great-souled. Nihilism itself is "ambiguous." If nihilism is the "unwelcome guest," it is also an opportunity, clearing a path for "increased power of the spirit."[27] In contrast to the despairing herd mentality of the passive nihilists, active nihilists see the decline of traditional moral and religious systems as an occasion for the thoroughgoing destruction of desiccated ways of life and for the creation of a new order of values. Active nihilists, the philosopher-artists of the future, will engage in the "transvaluation of values." They stand beyond good and evil and engage in aesthetic self-creation, a project that is an affront to society's religious and democratic conventions. The problem is that Nietzsche consistently repudiates the very possibility of any sort of natural or metaphysical standard in light of which aesthetic self-creation might be appraised. In the end, Dionysian chaos engulfs all. Yet he simultaneously holds that the philosophers of the future will engage in a new rank ordering of human values.

Nietzsche's remedy for the nihilistic epoch, his path beyond nihilism, promotes a particularly virulent form of aristocracy. As he puts it frankly in the chapter "What is Noble?" from *Beyond Good and Evil*:

> Every enhancement of the type "man" has so far been the work of an aristocratic society—and so it will be again and again—a society that believes in the long ladder of an order of rank and differences in value between man and man, and that needs slavery in some sense or another. Without that pathos of distance that grows out of the ingrained difference between strata . . . keeping down and keeping at a distance, that other, more mysterious pathos could not have grown up either—the craving for an ever new widening of distances within the soul itself, the development of ever higher, rare, more remote, further-stretching, more comprehensive states . . . the continual "self-overcoming of man."[28]

For all of the positive reflections of Nietzsche in the novel, there is in the critique of voluntarism a crucial departure from certain tendencies in his thought, tendencies encapsulated in the notion of the primacy of willing. According to the perceptive analysis of Berkowitz, the fundamental tension in Nietzsche is this: Although he wished to base right making on right knowing, to ground a proper evaluation of levels of creative power on a rank order of character, his complete repudiation of any sort of natural, civil, or religious standard puts his entire project into question. As Berkowitz puts it, Nietzsche "pursues the antagonism between knowing and making to its breaking point."[29] The primacy of the will stultifies the understanding and ends up paralyzing the will itself, since there is nothing in light of which the will might deliberate and act. Nietzsche's project of incessant self-overcoming would seem to lead to precisely the sort of nihilism that he detests. As Stanley Rosen puts it, "Chaos empties rank-ordering of its significance."[30]

Beauty, Romantic Isolation, and Human Communion

In his exposition of Aquinas's conception of the relationship between reason and faith, natural theology and revelation, Denys Turner turns to music as one way to encounter the limits of reason. Turner argues that Aquinas shares with post-Nietzschean thought the belief that "reason points to an otherness that it cannot know." For Aquinas, however, the otherness is not complete, nor is the unknowability intrinsic to what is other by way of an excess of intelligibility. In the Derridean celebration of the difference of difference, Turner sees no prospect of rescue from nihilism, from the sense that beyond reason there is nothing but a "vacuous, empty nothingness, an endless prolongation of postponements." If, however, it were possible to name the otherness as God, then we might have some recourse. Indeed, the meaningfulness of our speech rests precisely on such an affirmation, as Nietzsche negatively indicates when he states that we have not rid ourselves of God because we have not rid ourselves of grammar.[31]

Joyce would not seem to share what Turner identifies as Nietzsche's logophobia. Even if he does not clearly affirm a Thomistic alternative, he presents a powerful version of that alternative in his two most influential works, *Portrait* and *Ulysses*. Combined with Stephen's penchant for Thomistic aesthetics, the subtle departures from Nietzsche in *Portrait* suggest the possibility of an alternative reading grounded in the thought of Aristotle and Aquinas. Aquinas appears as an authority late in the book, after Stephen has acknowledged his artistic vocation, when he elucidates his aesthetic theory. But this is precisely the point at which we begin to realize that Stephen's progress as an artist and a human being is far from complete. If art is sometimes conceived as an inappropriate escape from life, then Stephen's taking refuge in aesthetic theory rather than immersing himself in the artistic process might be seen as a further retreat from life. Stephen would thus embody an antithesis to Nietzsche's subordination of science or theory to art, and of both of these to life. Furthermore, Stephen's emphasis on the stages in the rational apprehension of objects in aesthetic perception lies clearly on the side of the Apollonian, not the Dionysian. All this is true, but it fails to capture the complexity of Stephen's character as revealed in his theory. One of the problems with appraising the use of Aquinas is that there are so many errors of interpretation interspersed with the insights that it is difficult to know what to attribute to whom.

That we should take the theory somewhat seriously is, I think, evident from its usefulness in accounting for Stephen's ecstatic aesthetic vision of the girl on the beach, a vision that marks the realization of Stephen's call and the high point of the novel. The vision illustrates not only the stages of apprehension but also the claim that aesthetic perception is void of desire and loathing—indeed, of kinesis itself. The vision is an example of static aesthetic experience.

The theory, which Stephen explicitly claims to have borrowed from Aquinas, explicates the famous statement that "the beautiful is that which pleases when seen" in light of the three marks of the beautiful: wholeness, harmony, and radiance. The first stage is the observation of an object as distinct from all others, as "selfbounded and selfcontained" (230). So, on the beach, Stephen first sees a "girl . . . before him in midstream, alone and still" (285). In the second stage, there is an apprehension of the fitting relationships among the parts of the object and of each part to the whole. So, he proceeds to observe her bodily parts—her legs, her thighs, her waist, her bosom, her hair, and finally her face. Stephen compares the first stage to the second as the "synthesis of immediate perception" to the "analysis of apprehension." The third stage is also described as a synthesis, in which the "supreme quality of beauty, the clear radiance of the esthetic image, is apprehended luminously by the mind which has been arrested by its wholeness and fascinated by its harmony" (231). So Stephen sees in the girl's face, to which her bodily parts have gradually led his gaze, the "wonder of mortal beauty" (186).

There are a number of problems with Stephen's purported fidelity to Aquinas, not the least of which is his couching the theory in distinctively modern, epistemological terms. Indeed, the very notion of an aesthetic *theory* is alien to Aquinas.[32] Although aesthetic themes surface throughout Aquinas's writings, they are not subject to sustained theoretical analysis. Not just in his penchant for theory, but also in the particular content of his account, Stephen's views are in some measure incongruous with those of Aquinas. Stephen's theory embodies a set of dualisms. The split between soul and body, intellect and sensation, reason and desire runs through the entire discussion. True art, according to Stephen, is static rather than kinetic because the latter is associated with passions that are "[nothing] more than physical." At one point, Stephen revealingly comments to Cranly that, although we are animals, we are just now in a mental world. While in his examples of aesthetic perception he focuses on the concrete apprehension of sensible objects, he also speaks of the senses as "prison gates of the soul." None of these oppositions is characteristic of Aquinas.

Aquinas shares Nietzsche's concern with the limits to human reason and with the need for an integration of the ecstatic and the rational in human art and life. Reason is circumscribed in mystery; at the peak of human inquiry, the human intellect dwells in the shadow of ignorance (*in tenebra ignoratiae*). But the surplus that encompasses and overwhelms reason is not, in Aquinas, a chaotic Dionysian abyss surging with irrational and amoral violence. For Aquinas, the ecstasy of erotic love is the human correlate to the divine being as source of every good and perfect gift. Gratitude, rather than resentment, is the proper response to the divine initiative.

One way to clarify Aquinas's teaching on the limits to reason and reason's natural longing for an ecstasy in which it transcends itself by participation in an order not its own devising is to consider the role of beauty in his theology. There are, Aquinas says, three marks of beauty: *integritas, claritas,* and *proportio,* the latter two of which are most prominent in his analyses.[33] In his discussions of *claritas,* Thomas adduces the examples of light and color. Yet the scope of *claritas* extends beyond the sensible realm to that of intellect or spirit, according to which *claritas* is said to be an "illumination," "manifestation," or "splendor." Thomas follows Dionysius in seeing *claritas* as an overflowing of an abundance of divine beauty. *Proportio* or *consonantia* has to do with a coming together of things necessary for an end; these terms surface in the explication of hierarchical ordering. Thomas often speaks of a diverse and fitting order of goods or beings. The third, less prominent mark of the beautiful is *integritas,* which is translated as completeness or wholeness. The term *integritas* refers to the realization of a thing's proper perfection; it involves the judgment that something is what it ought to be. For Aquinas, the beautiful is closely allied to the good; identical in subject, the two are distinct in notion. While the good refers primarily to the will or the appetite, the beautiful has, in addition, a reference to the cognitive power, to perception. The connection between the beautiful and cognition underlies another of Thomas's most well-known remarks about beauty: The beautiful is that which pleases when seen.

Thomas writes that "for the appetite to terminate at the good, the peaceful and the beautiful is not for it to terminate at diverse things. By the very fact that someone desires the good, he also desires the beautiful and the peaceful."[34] Or again, "the object moving the appetite is a good apprehended; whatever in the apprehension itself appears beautiful is taken as fitting and good."[35] These passages suggest that the beautiful should be understood as the way the good manifests itself to the rational creature. We have already noted that Thomas associates the term *claritas* with radiance and brilliance and that one of the principal examples of *claritas* is intellectual light, the manifestation of intelligibility. The entire created order is of course an example of *claritas,* since it manifests the splendor of divine understanding. Yet human beings provide a particularly instructive instance of *claritas.* Human beings are not simply parts of the created order; rather, they have a capacity to grasp that order, to understand and take delight in it. They have the ability to provide demonstrations, intelligible connections, and arrangements to themselves and to one another. The operation of human intelligence made sensible through speech is a manifestation of divine intelligence in the corporeal order.

Aquinas's account of beauty does not reduce the Dionysian to the Apollonian; instead, just as God exceeds every affirmation and every negation, so does the transcendent source of beauty escape the dichotomy between Dionysius and Apollo.

Instead of seeing the limits to reason and reason's self-transcendence through the encounter with beauty as a virtue of Aquinas's account, Umberto Eco, who has written the best treatment of Aquinas's aesthetics, argues that it constitutes the "central *aporia*" in Thomas's aesthetics. "Aesthetic *visio*," Eco asserts, requires "a deep and exhaustive knowledge of the object," the kind of knowledge available only to the creator of natural forms.[36] Hence, aesthetic *visio* is possible only for God, not human beings. Eco's is an instructive error, the clarification of which is twofold. First, unlike some modern philosophers, Aquinas does not create a chasm between apodictic knowledge and utter ignorance; nor does he depict partial knowledge as a source of anxiety. Responding to the objection that wonder presupposes ignorance and is thus unpleasant, Thomas asserts that wonder is pleasant insofar as it inspires the desire and the hope of gaining knowledge.[37] Pleasure engenders thirst or desire, especially when one possesses a perfect thing yet not perfectly, but obtains that possession little by little.[38] We can detect here the importance of hope as a virtue constitutive of the cognitive life of human beings.

Second, delight in beauty is ecstatic. Thomas speaks of the good as the cause of love, as that which draws desire to itself; the Greek term *kalos* is derived from the verb *kaleo*, "to call or summon." The effect of pleasure is expansion or dilation.[39] For rational animals, the call of beauty reminds us that we are artifacts, not autonomous creators. The effect of delight can be seen with respect to both the apprehensive and the affective powers of the soul. With regard to the apprehensive power, the soul is said to be enlarged or dilated (*animus hominis dicitur magnificari seu dilatari*); and with regard to the affective powers, they are said to hand themselves over to continue within the object of delight (*sic dilatatur affectus hominis per delectationem, quasi se tradens ad continendum interius rem delectantem*).[40] Although Aquinas does not wallow in Dionysian otherness, neither does he reduce beauty to the human desire for rational order, as embodied in Apollo. Rather, as Turner points out, he names the otherness as God, as a superabundant source of goodness, wisdom, and beauty, but as a source that utterly escapes our rational and linguistic grasp. In his fine study of ecstasy in Aquinas, G. J. McAleer observes, "The appetite for self-conservation which reduces all objects to itself is reversed in the appetite for the *visio dei*: a natural centeredness on self is constantly being absorbed and transformed by an ecstatic other-centeredness."[41]

To contemporary readers, Aquinas's account of beauty seems, on the one hand, laden with metaphysical and ethical baggage, and, on the other, lacking in ambitious theoretical foundations. In addition to criticizing the theory-laden approach to beauty in modern philosophy, Jean-Marie Schaefer, in *Art of the Modern Age: Philosophy of Art from Kant to Heidegger*, argues against two modern tendencies: (a) the "reduction of art to its creative aspect," a reduction that isolates art from the broader field of human works and misleads us into thinking of art as the only or only important human work, and (b) the cutting off of the work of art from its "hedonic dimension"—gratification or pleasure—as a result of an "exacerbated Puritanism." By contrast, Joyce and Aquinas share a conception of beauty as manifest in sensible images, as naturally fostering pleasure, and as drawing the beholder into participation in an order greater than the isolated self. Although Joyce gives no evidence of embracing the metaphysics or theology of Aquinas, the two would certainly share reservations about modern, romantic conceptions of art and the artist. They would also find comical the twentieth-century tendency to reduce art to aesthetic theory and to detach it from the ordinary and pleasurable experience of beautiful objects. Indeed, we should avoid identifying Joyce's own view of Aquinas with Stephen's misinterpretation of Aquinas along idealist and inordinately intellectualist lines. Stephen's errors here mirror and reflect the defects in his own character, both ethical and artistic. Moreover, as we shall see shortly, Joyce makes especially impressive use of Aquinas's theological doctrine of the Trinity as a corrective to a faulty conception of human community and artistic creation.

To see more clearly the way in which Aristotelian and Thomistic categories function in Joyce, we need but advert to the structure of *Portrait*, which exhibits the problem of individual creativity by juxtaposing, and thus putting into question, diametrically opposed conceptions of the relationship between the individual and the community.[42] The first four chapters alternate between corresponding sets of opposites: the social vs. the individual, outer vs. inner, and male vs. female. The family and the cliques at school dominate the first chapter; in these social contexts, where men are dominant, Stephen struggles to decode the language and to find his place within the community. The discovery of the interior impulses to sensuality pervades the second chapter; these impulses set Stephen apart from others and lead up to his encounter with the prostitute. The third chapter focuses on the Jesuit teaching of religious doctrine, in light of which he strives to interpret his own experience. Finally, in the fourth chapter, Stephen, in isolation from all others, experiences the vision of the girl on the beach, and the accent is on his internal sense of ecstasy. The alternation between these opposites is not so neat as it might appear. Two examples will suffice. Stephen supposes that his lust is somehow peculiar to him, yet he comes to see it as common to all men. Conversely, he thinks that he can willfully separate himself from the institutional church, yet its teachings are deeply constitutive of who he is. These superficially clear oppositions, upon which the novel plays and which are endemic to modern thought, are characteristics of the immature Stephen, of the sorts of conflicts he must overcome to reach maturity. The novel works toward, without ever reaching, their reconciliation. In fact, Stephen's retreat into quasi-solipsism in the last chapter serves to re-entrench the dichotomies. What has thwarted the progress is precisely the exaltation of the creative individual will in Stephen's self-understanding.

Another way to bring out the problem of aesthetic self-creation is to attend to the novel's persistent contrast between art and life, and the way the former can be used as a refuge from and falsification of the latter. At the very end of Part IV, Stephen experiences his aesthetic ecstasy, which is described variously as a "profane joy," as an ecstasy, and as a rapture (186–87). At the very beginning of the next chapter, he is at home with his family the following morning: "He drained his third cup of watery tea to the dregs and set to chewing the crusts of fried bread that were scattered near him, staring into the dark pool of the jar" (188). As he leaves the house and walks through the squalid neighborhood, his mind takes refuge in books. The "splendor" of his thoughts allows the world to "perish about his feet as if it had been fireconsumed." (191). Art is ambivalent; it provides for a transforming experience of the world, even as it tempts the artist to an evasion of life. Of course, the artistry of the narrator of the novel captures all of this, and so his art is not subject to the same criticisms as is that of Stephen. How are we to understand the art of the narrator?

An Aristotelian interpretation of the comedy of *Portrait* is possible. A congruence can be seen in *Portrait*'s conception of art and life. On Aristotle's view, art partly imitates and partly completes nature, by aiding in the realization of possibilities to which nature points but rarely achieves. Do not the first four chapters point to an overcoming of a set of peculiarly modern oppositions? Given the parallel and related failures of Stephen as artist and human being, would not this anticipated reconciliation mark the way toward a healthy human life and a fecund artistry? If Stephen thwarts the realization of this *telos*, the art of the narrator gives us more than a glimmer of it.

Might the dichotomies permeating Joyce's text point us in the direction of a more unified and more adequate account of aesthetic experience, the rudiments of which can be found in Aquinas? On these matters, Aquinas resides on the other side of the great rift, described by the modernist poet T. S. Eliot as a "dissociation of sensibility." Eliot argues that in the seventeenth century there arose a separation of thought from sense and imagination, prior to which, poets offered a "direct sensuous apprehension of thought, or a recreation of thought into feeling."[43] Joyce would seem to share Eliot's critique and, at least in this, his project of reuniting thought and sensation, imagination and intellect. Joyce's critique of Romanticism and of the Symbolist movement calls to mind Iris Murdoch's negative judgment that the "pure, clean, self-contained 'symbol,' the exemplar incidentally of what Kant, ancestor of both Liberalism and Romanticism, required art to be, is the analogue of the lonely self-contained individual."[44] In Joyce, the reservations about Romanticism and Symbolism can be seen in the life of Stephen, whose failure as an artist parallels his narcissistic character. If only by indirection and negative example, Joyce's *Portrait* can aid us in the task Murdoch thinks essential to our recovery from the ill effects of Romanticism in both aesthetics and ethics. "We need," Murdoch urges,

> to return from the self-centred concept of sincerity to the other-centred concept of truth. We are not isolated free choosers, monarchs of all we survey, but benighted creatures sunk in a reality whose nature we are constantly and overwhelmingly tempted to deform by fantasy. Our current picture of freedom encourages a dream-like facility; whereas what we require is a renewed sense of the difficulty and complexity of the moral life and the opacity of persons.[45]

A number of scenes in *Portrait* and *Ulysses* invite us to put Murdoch's thesis to the test. Take, for example, Stephen's aesthetic vision on the beach, of which we have already provided an initial analysis. If there is a compatibility between the narrator's description of Stephen's aesthetic vision and Stephen's own aesthetic theory, then perhaps the weaknesses of the latter can also be seen in the former. In the exultant, "Yes. Yes. Yes. He would create . . . as the great artificer," there is an important affirmation of the beauty of the girl, of his place in the cosmos, and of his own vocation. Yet the affirmation may be constrained by the limits of Stephen's own character. It does mark a progress over his previous interactions with women; he is no longer the son in need of coddling, nor the immature devotee of Mary, nor the adolescent succumbing to a woman merely as an object to satisfy his lust. Between him and the girl on the beach there is a sort of communion, even a kind of reverent acknowledgment of one another. And yet in the detached vision, "no word had broken the holy silence of his ecstasy" (186). Is it wrong to see in this an anticipation of the multiple failures of speech in the final chapter, failures that both illustrate Stephen's defective character, his isolation from others, and have a mysterious connection to his inability to create? Language is the vehicle of communication between persons. It is the instrument through which we have access to the traditions and myths in light of which we understand ourselves in relationship to others. By contrast, Stephen's aesthetic vision, to which we have access only because of the language of the narrator, is a sort of Rousseauian attempt to bypass language in the attempt to establish a prelinguistic harmony.

Immediately preceding the vision, Stephen speaks softly to himself: "A day of dappled seaborne clouds." The narrator comments, "The phrase and the day and the scene harmonised in a chord." As Stephen begins to contemplate the words, he seems to retreat from the harmony of word and world into language itself. The question is then asked, "Was it that . . . he drew less pleasure from the reflection of the glowing sensible world through the prism of language manycoloured and richly storied than from the contemplation of an

inner world of individual emotions mirrored perfectly in a lucid supple peri-
odic prose?" (180–81). The collapse of language upon itself is symptomatic of
Stephen's artistic failure. He fails to mediate his ideal, timeless vision of beauty
to others through language.

If we continue the line of interpretation we have been pursuing in our
reading of the *Portrait*, we can see in Stephen's failure, not just a foreshorten-
ing of his artistic vocation but also a stultifying of his humanity. We have
already noted Aquinas's metaphysics of actuality, simultaneously an account
of being and goodness, according to which the perfection of every agent involves self-communication: "It is the nature of any act whatsoever to communicate itself insofar as it is able. Every agent acts according as it is in act. To act
is nothing other than to communicate that through which is in act, insofar as it
is able."[46] The production of some other being as expressive of an individual's
being and goodness is itself an example of the general metaphysical principle
that the "good is diffusive of itself." Of course, Stephen's failure to produce, to
manifest himself to others, has its roots further back, in his narcissistic isolation
of himself from others. The dialogical principle of communication as involving a receptive openness to others is minimally operative in Stephen's life.

Failures of communication, sometimes under the guise of illusory experiences of unity, are comically present throughout Joyce's work, but never more
effectively than the famous "Nausika" chapter in *Ulysses*, wherein Bloom's
contemplation from afar of the young Gerty culminates with his act of autoeroticism. Only vision links them, yet Bloom comments that there was a kind
of language between them. The irony of the assertion is lost on Bloom but not
on the reader. The absence of speech, the safe distance of sight, enables Bloom
and Gerty to idealize one another in their imaginations. When Bloom realizes
that Gerty is lame, the falsity of his idealized vision is revealed, and he is
disappointed. Conversely, the masturbatory culmination of Bloom's watching
of Gerty underscores his own isolation and impotence.

Identity and Difference: Trinitarian Themes and
Thomistic Sexual Ethics in *Ulysses*

Aquinas's emphasis on the unity of understanding, speech, and will in
communication, and on friendship as essential to the human community,
provides Stephen with the theoretical and implicitly practical material to
overcome the voluntarism and atomism endemic to modern philosophy. In
Ulysses, Joyce makes especially effective use of Aquinas's teachings on the
Trinity. As always in Joyce, there is a penchant for the odd, entertaining, and
instructive juxtaposition of the lower and the higher, the most routine and
squalid of bodily activities with the most refined of intellectual pursuits. So, for
example, in *Ulysses* we find Joyce not just deploying Aquinas's Trinitarian
doctrines but also adverting to Aquinas's teachings on incest and masturbation.

The comic effect is palpable. Less obvious, but nonetheless operative, is Joyce's continued philosophical and theological critique of certain conceptions of art and the artist. The Trinitarian and sexual ethics themes both function to undermine Stephen's artistic narcissism and his naïve romantic conception of art.

In the opening chapter of *Ulysses*, Buck Mulligan, Stephen's nemesis, jokes to another fellow that Stephen has a theory about Hamlet: "He proves by algebra that Hamlet's grandson is Shakespeare's grandfather and that he himself is the ghost of his own father."[47] Later in the same chapter, Stephen reflects to himself about the earlier Trinitarian heresies, among which the error of Sabellius, who held that the "Father was Himself His own Son," figures prominently (18). The same pairing of Stephen's Hamlet theory and Trinitarian doctrine is central to Stephen's lengthy theoretical diatribe later in the book. He refers to the "bulldog of Aquin, with whom no word shall be impossible," as refuting Sabellius (171). Yet Stephen's theory of artistic creation is itself a version of the Sabellian heresy. He asserts not only a special relationship between Shakespeare and Hamlet, but also an identity of Shakespeare with every character in the plays. "He is the ghost and the prince. He is all in all. . . . In Cymbeline, in Othello he is bawd and cuckold. He acts and is acted on" (174). Stephen then generalizes from art to life: "He found in the world without as actual what was in his world within as possible. . . . Every life is many days, day after day. We walk through ourselves, meeting robbers, ghosts, giants, old men, young men, wives, widows, brothers-in-love, but always meeting ourselves" (175). It is not surprising that this theory, which entirely denies the reality of otherness and is thus a variant on Sabellianism, leads Stephen to conclude by echoing Hamlet's prohibition of future marriages. There are no independent others left to be united in matrimony and no new beings to be brought forth into the world. Both procreation and artistic creation have been rendered otiose.

In marked contrast to this aesthetic narcissism stands Aquinas's Trinitarian account of divine creation:

> God is the cause of things, through his intelligence and will, as an artisan is of things made. Now, the artisan works through the word, conceived in his intellect, and the love of his will toward his work. Thus God the Father has produced the creation through his Word, who is the Son, and through his Love, which is the Holy Spirit.[48]

In the Trinity itself there is difference within unity, a distinction of persons united through knowledge and love. The trinity of persons creates human persons who participate by their very being in the life of the divine; further participation is not forced or compelled but is a matter of a free and loving response in gratitude toward her creator. Aquinas rejects the claim of certain Arab philosophers that the divine causal power usurps the efficacy of all secondary created agents, not principally because it abolishes the dignity of creatures, but because it diminishes the power of the Creator: "God communicates his goodness to creatures in such a way that, what is received, can be transmitted to others. To refuse to creatures their own proper action would thus be to detract from the divine goodness."[49] Creatures are "co-workers" with God. Of course, what Aquinas says about the Divine Artist could hardly be true of human artisans, who make nothing from nothing and whose source of creativity is not autonomous but is rather a dispensation from the Divine Artist.

In Stephen Dedalus's interconnected failures in love and art, we may detect something like Murdoch's theses about art and ethics. Murdoch asserts, "The good artist in relation to his art, is brave, truthful, patient, humble." Stephen lacks these and other virtues. His failure in art involves a kind of narcissism revealed most clearly in his failure in love, which Murdoch describes as the "painful realization that someone other than myself exists." But Stephen is not entirely lost, either as a human being or as an artist. Authentic aesthetic experience occasionally pulls him out of himself, as Aquinas would suggest it should and would. Yet these very experiences can mislead, by suggesting that art and love are found exclusively in unusual peak experiences, not in the midst of the ordinary experiences of life. We might call that the romantic temptation. Here the contrast between Stephen as character and Joyce as author is palpable. Joyce embraces the ordinary and helps us to see it as extraordinary. His art involves the "transfiguration of everyday life," the perception in the ordinary of what Charles Taylor calls "epiphanies of modernism." Conversely, as Murdoch notes, "art transcends selfish and obsessive limitations of personality and can enlarge the sensibility of its consumer."[50] This is not far from Aquinas's thesis that the encounter with beauty dilates the soul of the beholder.

Three Thomistic teachings are mentioned during the discourse in *Ulysses*. First, there is Thomas's refutation of the heresy of Sabellius, to which we have referred. Thomas's orthodox position depicts the divine life as a union of thought, speech, and love among three distinct persons. Second, Stephen quotes Aquinas on the necessity for society of there being friendship among many: "In societate humana hoc est in maxime necessarium ut sit amicitia inter multos" (169). Friendship presupposes distinction between the persons united through common activities and traits of character. The friend may be described as another self, but it is a distinct self, whose association with me expands and enlarges my experience and my knowledge. What distinguishes true friendship from its simulacra is that only in the former is the friend loved as an end in herself, not as a means to my achievement of some extrinsic good. For Aristotle and Aquinas, friendship is the centerpiece of their view of human nature as inherently social. The unity of civil society presupposes distinct individuals who complement one another in the pursuit and enjoyment of common goods, chief among which is the good of friendship itself. By contrast to the Aristotelian-Thomist understanding of friendship, Stephen's account of the unity of characters and persons negates all difference.

It is no coincidence that in the midst of Stephen's diatribe reference is made to both incest and masturbation. In his discussion of incest, we find the third use of Aquinas. In his "gorbellied works," Stephen says, Aquinas writes of "incest from a standpoint different from that of the new Viennese school" and "likens it to an avarice of the emotions. He means that the love so given to one near in blood is covetously withheld from some stranger who, it may be, hungers for it." Incest thus shortcuts an affection whose natural *telos* is to communicate with an-other. Thus, experience and creation utterly lack novelty or difference; they are but redundant expressions of the self. In the order of sexual sins, the logical term of this failure to open oneself to the offer and reception of love is autoeroticism. Stephen's theory, which he concedes even he does not believe, involves a similar sin on the level of intellect. After the speech, Mulligan mockingly announces a play. The title, "Everyman his own Wife or a Honeymoon in the Hand," captures the upshot of Stephen's theory. We are thus invited to compare Stephen's form of intellectual masturbation with Bloom's physical act of autoeroticism in Part XIII. In both cases, impotence or sterility is the theme, yet Bloom at least receives a kind of bodily relief from his act. As he departs the library, Stephen senses with apprehension the presence of Mulligan behind him and stands aside to let him pass. "Part. The moment is now. . . . My will: his will that fronts me. Seas between" (178). In life, if not in theory, Stephen confronts otherness. He thus alternates between indulging in a theory that consumes otherness in the self and living a life of evasion of others, whom he sees as threats to his autonomous will. Creation itself lacks difference or novelty; it is but the redundant expression of the self.

In ways not often noticed by commentators, Joyce intertwines the topics of artistic creativity with Aquinas's orthodox teaching on the Trinity and his doctrines in the area of sexual ethics. On our reading, these teachings provide an ongoing critique of Stephen's romantic narcissism and his philosophical idealism. A very different take on sexual ethics in Joyce can be found in the writings of Martha Nussbaum, who focuses on Joyce's depiction of Molly. In her recent commentary on *Ulysses*, Nussbaum divides the critical appraisal of Molly into two categories, sentimentalist and moralist. An early representative of the former interpretation, Joyce himself praised Molly for her "acknowledgment of the universe." By contrast, the moralists "minimize Molly's infidelities and stress her reunion and planned fidelity to Bloom."[51] Both groups want a "happy ending." But this is to falsify and constrain "the infidelity of the sexual imagination . . . the surprising heterogeneity of life" that Molly embodies.[52] We know not where Molly's sexual imagination, her fantasies, will lead her.

Nussbaum reads Molly's soliloquy and the encounter at a distance through the fantasy of Bloom and Gerty as illustrations of Joyce's sympathy toward the sexual fantasies of real bodies. Indeed, in the long tradition of philosophical, theological, and literary reflections on human love, Joyce stands alone. Only in his writings, she writes, "does love wear a real-life body with its hungers and thirsts and fantasies, its all-too-human combination of generosity with forgetfulness."[53] In contrast to Plato, Dante, and even modern writers on love, Joyce depicts a "world where the stars that guide people's lives are not united . . . and where individuals in chaos do both un-Platonic and un-Christian not to mention un-American things."[54] Although Nussbaum is careful to show that Joyce undercuts a naïve belief in "perfect authentic sexuality," she does place an enormous redemptive burden on fantasy, which she sees as a key to ethical and political liberation: "In the text's tenderness toward its protagonists, across the barriers of fantasy that divide and also join them, there passes a kind of love and sympathy." The "energy of fantasy" enlivens the moral imagination that enables us to appreciate "another's good and ill that the novel shows to be a central fact in the moral life."[55]

From her depiction of fantasy as central to the moral imagination, Nussbaum moves to the assertion that Joyce's

> focus on the body's universal needs is an essential step on the way to the repudiation of localism, therefore of ethnic hatred. The root of hatred is not erotic need, as much of the ascent tradition repeatedly argues. It is, rather, a refusal to accept erotic neediness and unpredictability as a fact of human life. Saying yes to sexuality is saying yes to all in life that defies control—to passivity and surprise, to being one part of a very chancy world.[56]

There are numerous reasons to doubt this interpretation. Among all the characters in *Ulysses*, Molly certainly comes the closest to embodying the heterogeneity of sexual fantasy. It is not clear, however, that she is the book's best representative of sympathetic imagination or that the book affirms an indissoluble link between the sympathetic imagination and sexual fantasy. In fact, Bloom would seem to be the book's principal example of sympathetic imagination. Recall the introduction of Bloom as he fixes breakfast and ponders what the world looks like from the vantage point of his cat: "Wonder what I look like to her. Height of a tower? No, she can jump me" (45). Despite, and even in the midst of, his vagrant sexual fantasies, Bloom wants to remain faithful to Molly. A case can be made that the comic failures of Bloom's sexual fantasies, for example in the scene with Gerty, foster in him a deeper sense of moral imagination, of sympathetic identification with others. But these specific points of literary interpretation raise a more fundamental philosophical issue, the relationship between fantasy and imagination. By contrast with Nussbaum's position, consider the words of Wendell Berry:

> In sex, as in other things, we have liberated fantasy but killed imagination, and so have sealed ourselves in selfishness and loneliness. Fantasy is of the solitary self, and it cannot lead us away from ourselves. It is by imagination that we cross over the differences between ourselves and other beings and thus learn compassion, forbearance, mercy, forgiveness, sympathy, and love.[57]

Taking aim at liberal politics and conservative economics, Berry argues that the two opposed camps conspire together to turn the "body" itself into a sort of "product, made delectably consumable."[58] The consequence for our understanding of sex is predictable. What is left is a "dispirited description of the working of a sort of anatomical machinery—and this is a sexuality that is neither erotic nor social nor sacramental but rather a cold-blooded, abstract procedure."[59] So, Berry is critical of the very tendencies toward sexual fantasy in contemporary culture that Nussbaum lauds.

But Nussbaum's account also runs afoul of those who advocate a recovery of Dionysian erotics. Nussbaum may well concur with Camille Paglia's suspicion that a "perfectly humane eroticism may be impossible," that the "search for freedom through sex is doomed to failure."[60] But Paglia goes further than Nussbaum in her frank, Sade-inspired embrace of the violence inextricably intertwined with sexual liberation. Whereas Nussbaum thinks sexual heterogeneity, surprise, and passivity can be combined with generous, sympathetic imagination, Paglia takes a darker view, asserting that "wherever sexual freedom is sought or achieved, sadomasochism will not be far behind. Romanticism always turns into decadence."[61] She argues that "sex is power and all power is inherently aggressive"; mainstream liberal sexual liberation "misses the blood-lust in rape, the joy of violation and destruction. An aesthetics and erotics of profanation—of evil for the sake of evil, the sharpening of the senses by cruelty and torture."[62] On the connection between sexual liberation and violent degradation, Berry and Paglia are closer to one another (and to Aquinas) than either is to Nussbaum.[63]

Nussbaum's celebration of chance raises other difficulties for her interpretation. She writes, "Saying yes to sexuality is saying yes to all in life that defies control—to passivity and surprise, to being one part of a very chancy world." But in *Ulysses*, the principal example of a female "saying yes to all in life that defies control . . . to being one part of a very chancy world" involves sexual activity that is open to, and results in, pregnancy and giving birth. A woman in labor's "throes now full three days" inspires "wonder" at "women's woe." In chapter 14, Stephen proclaims, "all Malthusiasts go hang" and repudiates "copulation without population." In contrast to Molly's attempt to eliminate the chance of pregnancy from her sexual activities through the artifice of birth control, Joyce focuses on the risk and chance involved in pregnancy, childbirth, the death of children, and the thousand natural shocks that familial dependency creates in an individual human life. From this perspective, Nussbaum's focus looks misdirected and a trifle parochial.

Oneself as Another: Friendship, Otherness, and Narrative Continuity

Implicit in Stephen's theory of artistic creation is a series of oppositions that pervade the whole of *Ulysses*. Perhaps the most important oppositions are those between the same and the other, and between newness and repetition. Both can be found in Bloom's reflections in the Nausika chapter. Just as his idealized view of Gerty is corrected by her movement, so too he comes to see that what he had at dusk taken as clouds on the horizon were actually trees. Gaining a new perspective thus allows one to correct the limitations of one's previous point of view. Bloom observes to himself in this context that it is good "to see oneself as others do" (307–8). He ponders the fact that "history repeats itself" and that "there is nothing new under the sun." The conclusion is that you "think you're escaping and run into yourself" (309). A short time later, Bloom wonders to himself what it is women love in men and responds hypothetically, "Another themselves?" Yet at the end of the same paragraph, he recalls posing the question to Molly of why she chose him. Her answer: "Because you were so foreign from the others" (311). These oppositions are, I think, related to the sets of contraries that Thornton has identified in *Portrait*, and they may well perform similar functions. Neither of the mutually exclusive alternatives is adequate, and the story points toward but never exhibits their reconciliation. In Thomistic language, the reconciliation would involve seeing the self-other relation as neither univocal nor equivocal but analogical.

The principal alternative to the quasi-Thomistic exegesis we have been developing is the so-called deconstructive reading, which celebrates the "drama of the alternatives." On this view, the oppositions we have described perdure. There is no sense of potentiality, realized or unrealized, but only the dynamic interplay of opposites without hope of resolution. The sense of sameness and continuity is exploded by the jarring encounter with otherness and with utterly unanticipated novelty. While the jarring experience of strangeness can certainly have pedagogical value in the expansion of our sense of the range of human possibility, it cannot by itself constitute an ethic. Commenting on Derrida's phrase "Every other is wholly other" (*tout autre est tout autre*), Denys Turner objects that the

> otherness of another person . . . cannot be an absolute heterogeneity; an incorrigible and incommunicable "thisness" which is not a this something or other; it cannot be an inaccessible singularity, not unless some ethic of the other is to be founded upon the otherness of the other as some blank, anonymous reference point of a semantically empty demonstrative pronoun.[64]

On this issue, we might turn with profit to Aquinas's metaphysics, particularly the detailed discussion in the *De Veritate* of the transcendentals, "modes which accompany every being. Every being, in so far as it exists, is a *res*, a thing with an essence specifying it as this or that sort of thing. Every being is also *unum*, a singular thing, a unity of diverse parts or organs." Turning from the transcendental modes of every being in itself to its relations to others, Aquinas writes,

> According to the division of one from another, and this is what the noun *aliquid* expresses: for *aliquid* is spoken of as "another what" (*aliud quid*), just as being is called one (unum) insofar as it is undivided (*indivisum*) in itself, so it is called *aliquid* insofar as it is divided from others.[65]

It is interesting that Aquinas should include, not just *res* and *unum*, but also *aliquid* understood as *aliud quid*, in the list of transcendentals. (He immediately adds *bonum* and *verum*.) The inclusion of *aliquid* indicates that every being is understood in relation to other beings. Aquinas does not, however, develop a dialectic of sameness and otherness; instead, as both Clarke and Phillip Rosemann have argued, he develops a metaphysics of actuality in which "to be is to be substance in relation."[66] Such a position does not entail that substance is itself a relation, but only that substances exist for the sake of operation, and operation involves actualization of potencies by means of interaction with other substances. Thus, every being is involved in a process of (a) going out to others in order to make itself fully actual and to manifest or communicate its own goodness, and (b) returning to itself (*reditio ad essentiam suam*). Rosemann comments, "By returning to itself through the mediation of the other, it not only leaves its own stamp upon the other, but also takes the other into itself, as it were, so that its own identity comes to be affected by the otherness of the other."[67]

This is one possible way of resolving the dialectic of self and other in Joyce's novels. In our reading of Joyce, at least two issues remain at stake, neither of which is easily resolvable. First, there is the question of the self-other relationship, especially of friendship. Stanley Sultan has argued that the overlappings of, and resemblances between, the life stories of the various characters in *Ulysses* represent more than mere coincidence. They hint at the substantive likenesses between characters and at subtle interconnections in their destinies. He develops a compelling case for seeing Buck Mulligan and Bloom as representing the fundamental options for Stephen. The latter's movement from Mulligan to Bloom would thus be a sign of progress in the development of his character.[68]

A second and related issue concerns the question of teleology in the novel, of whether there is a potency, a direction to the action it describes.[69] Many critics adopt the view that the characters of *Ulysses* are incapable of growth, insight, or development. A Nietzschean interpretation of the lack of development suggests itself: eternal return. The circular shape of Bloom's travels, which dimly mirror those of Odysseus, fails to reconcile opposites or to reveal any progress. There is instead only the affirmation of the interplay of differences, the resounding "Yes" of Molly's soliloquy. If, however, Molly's affirmation indicates a kind of progress in her domestic relationship with Bloom, then it may be seen as a sign of development in the action of the novel.[70] This raises the crucial question concerning the role of chance in the entire story: Is the narrative to be understood in terms of mere chance, or does it have a discernible shape?

The question of the divine is intimately connected to the question of directedness. The link between the two is, as Sultan has noted, providence. Ample use of coincidence by an author leads inevitably to the question of who is orchestrating events and thus to the question of providence, the third relevant issue. Although Stephen mocks God as old Nobodaddy, Molly pauses in the midst of her musings to slight the atheists, who "might as well try to stop the sun from rising" as to uproot belief in God from the human heart (643). Her conception of God as a just judge is blandly traditional. But the structure of *Ulysses* pivots on the chance meetings of Stephen and Bloom, an appreciation of the significance of which has been prepared by the Telemachus-Ulysses theme, rich symbolic and philosophical allusions to paternity, and the references of the characters themselves to fathers and sons. So the work itself provides multiple starting points that converge on the chance meeting of Stephen and Bloom.

Whatever we might make of the dramatic unity and implicitly providential structure of Joyce's great novel, we have certainly detected a rich deposit of classical philosophical and theological themes. For all his modernist tendencies and his embrace of modern pluralism and secularism, Joyce's style remains in many ways antimodern, if not premodern. He repudiates the symbolist and romantic mentalities and seeks to unite what modernity severs or lets fall apart. Thus, he fuses contemporary events and persons with classical myth and alternates between the concrete and the general, the individual and the whole. Whereas a variety of tendencies in modernity, as Murdoch observes, push in the direction of isolated individualism, Joyce shows in ample detail the multiple dependencies to which human thought and agency are liable. But Joyce does not fall into the opposite error of submerging or dissolving the individual in the totalizing power structures of modernity. Instead, he seeks to reestablish something of the premodern dialectic between particular and universal, concrete and general. From *Dubliners* onward, Joyce's writings give us characters and stories inseparable from their times and places but with import that carries beyond those times and places. Nowhere more Aristotelian than in this, Joyce's epiphanies of modernism train the reader to perceive the universal in the particular.

For all the points of convergence between Aquinas and Joyce, and for all the ways reading one brings out unanticipated insights into the other, a gap remains precisely on the issue of epiphanies and aesthetics. As is the case for Iris Murdoch, so too for Aquinas and Joyce, symbols, analogies, and a host of literary devices serve to underscore the participation of individuals in orders larger than themselves, orders that rational investigation can never fully exhaust. This does not entail, as we have been at pains to point out, that the realm of metaphor or symbol is the realm of feeling or even merely of the imagination. This realm calls for intellectual probing, for a distinctive sort of intellectual activity closely allied to the imagination and always including appropriate emotional response. But of course Aquinas reads this symbolism, not just as revealing a dimension of depth latent within our ordinary experience, but as pointing upwards, beyond themselves, to a divine source, the exemplar of all created things.

"Symbolism," as de Bruyne puts it in his famous study of medieval aesthetics, is "the aesthetic expression of ontological participation."[71] With this, Joyce might well agree. But it is not clear that he would see this ontological participation in the way Aquinas does. As M. D. Chenu puts it, "the mental operation proper to symbolism" is a "*translatio,* a transference or elevation from the visible sphere to the invisible."[72] Aquinas explicitly embraces such a Dionysian understanding when he describes our indirect access to the divine as involving a "translation of likenesses from sensible things to immaterial substances" (*similtudines rerum sensibilium ad substantias immateriales translatas*).[73] Thus does Aquinas link his account of the logic of poetic discourse to an ontology of participated being.

nine
Metaphysics of Contingency, Divine Artistry of Hope

The created universe, the whole of things, is, in words from Joyce's *Ulysses*, "predicated on the void." Wanting to avoid any hint of an antecedent "something" out of which God creates, Aquinas insists that all that is, apart from God, is predicated on nothing. Creation is not so much a making as it is a "transcendental appearing," as Fabro once called it. What Robert Sokolowski has called "the distinction" between God and creatures frames Aquinas's theological understanding of the radical contingency of the entire order of the universe.[1] This has important and cascading ramifications for our understanding of being, which is now understood as a gift, as the first grace offered in creation. As Kenneth Schmitz eloquently puts it, "the term gift is rooted in a domain of significance that is charged with discontinuity and contingency, with risk, vulnerability, and surprise. Moreover, the gift points beyond itself to its source, to a more or less definitely apprehended giver."[2]

Of course, Aquinas detects an appreciation of contingency in Aristotle's thought; he notes, for example, that Aristotle goes out of his way in the logical treatise *On Interpretation* to defend the notion of future contingents, in order "to save the roots of contingency" (*ad salvandum radices contingentiae*).[3] But

163

none of this reaches Aquinas's theological understanding of the radical contingency of created being, for which to be is to exist in a relation of unilateral dependency on a source that transcends the entire order of creation. Creation is the very dependency of created being upon its source (*ipsa dependentia esse creati ad principium* [ScG II, 18]).

This raises certain questions about metaphysics and creation. In such a context, what could be left of metaphysics as an inquiry into the universal and necessary properties of whatever exists insofar as it exists? As we should by now not be surprised to learn, Aquinas's response is a sort of prudential mean between those who argue for necessity all the way up to God, and those who hold that contingency means unintelligibility. A reconsideration of these matters will also help us to see the way Aquinas anticipates another objection. This one concerns the supposition that the very appeal to transcendent goods—"hyper-goods," as Charles Taylor calls them—can do damage to the rich complexity and contingency of the human good. Far from neglecting contingent singulars, Aquinas inscribes metaphysics, even in its mode as divine science, within a comprehensive narrative of creation and redemption, the centerpiece of which is a series of historical events unknown to, and unknowable by, philosophy. Divine artistry thus gives birth to a hope at once more audacious, and more suitable to the human condition, than anything the philosophers dared dream.

Creation, Contingency, and Metaphysics

Few philosophers have been bold enough to trace the contingency of the created order all the way down. The obstacles to coming to terms with this account of creation, contingency, and providential history are evident from the way minds as powerful and penetrating as Kretzmann fail to see its point.[4] In his discussion of divine creation in *The Metaphysics of Creation*, Kretzmann follows Aquinas's line of argument fairly closely. He denies, for example, that God's perfection unduly circumscribes his creative options. He rejects the notion that God must create the best possible world if what we mean by "best possible world" is a world none better than that which can be conceived.[5] Indeed, a best possible finite world would seem to be inconceivable since we could always imagine that any given proposed best world could be improved by the addition of a little more of this or a little more of that. While Kretzmann agrees that God is not necessitated concerning what he creates, he departs from Aquinas on the question of whether God *must* create. The latter necessity is not a requirement of justice but of God's goodness, following from the principle of the diffusiveness of the good. Kretzmann's position is not reducible to the necessitarian view of Avicenna, whom Aquinas is at pains to combat in the *Summa contra Gentiles*. Avicenna's necessitarianism is that of natural necessity, wherein the cause is determined to one effect; it is what Kretzmann calls "single-effect causation." Kretzmann's position is that the necessity of creating is compatible with freedom concerning what to create. But what is his argument that God must create? There is an "inconsistency in the notion of goodness that is forever unmanifested, never shared by the perfectly good, omnipotent agent." This follows from Aquinas's principle that "the sharing of being and goodness proceeds from goodness" as "its defining characteristic." Kretzmann elaborates: "A being that is good . . . simply is a being productive of good things external to it."[6]

Of course, he is adding to Aquinas's position the term "external," since Aquinas holds that God's communication of his own goodness is completely shared only within himself. In fact, it would seem that the Trinity is God's complete self-diffusion. In a footnote, Kretzmann anticipates this line of argument and notes that Aquinas himself argues this way in the *Sentences*. His response is twofold: first, such arguments can have no place in natural theology; second, it is "God, not some one divine Person, whom Aquinas identifies as 'goodness itself. . . .' Consequently . . . the essential self-diffusiveness of goodness as an aspect of the essence of God remains in force, necessitating external, volitional diffusion."[7] The latter rejoinder is wide of the mark, since the basis of the Trinity is not a single person, which would create an inappropriate inequality among the divine persons, but rather, the divine essence itself. The crucial question concerns the necessity of external manifestation. Such a requirement rests on too strict an analogy between natural and human productivity, on the one hand, and divine artistry, on the other. Kretzmann can, of course, recur to his claim that such arguments are out of place in natural theology, but then we have to insist, as Aquinas so often does in *Summa contra Gentiles*, on the limits to natural reason. In this case, reason can assert only that God's self-knowledge and self-love are limitless and involve complete self-communication, without being able to hazard anything more than feeble guesses as to how this self-communication occurs. The attempt of philosophy to do more than this leads to the variety of neo-Platonic emanationist schemes that Aquinas repudiates; it also flirts with philosophical idolatry. As Laura Garcia puts it,

> The hesitation to affirm that there is such a best possible world is in part due
> to the fact that we have so little to go on in determining what God's purposes
> are. Further, on Aquinas's picture of things, God's purposes cannot con-
> strain him to create anything at all, much less to create any particular
> universe, since the only purposes he has necessarily are already fulfilled by
> his own existing.[8]

How apt reason is to be led astray in its musings about creation is clear from Aquinas's insistence that *creatio ex nihilo* with a beginning in time cannot be proved by reason and must "be held by faith."[9] Aquinas depicts the revealed doctrine of the Trinity as offering instruction in the "proper way of thinking about the creation of things." That "God made all things by His Word excludes the error of saying that God produced things by a necessity of nature. When we say that in Him there is a procession of love, we show that God produces creatures not because of some need, nor because of any other extrinsic cause, but because of the love of His own goodness."[10] Just as was the case with the ultimate foundations of natural law in the eternal law, which is promulgated in the very procession of the Word from the Father, so too here the Trinitarian doctrine of Aquinas proves crucial in negotiating an impasse into which philosophical theology, absent revelation, is likely to fall. In his discussion of the fittingness of the world not having existed eternally, Aquinas argues that creation in time manifests the transcendence of God over creatures. Through the revealed teaching on creation, "we are able to avoid the assorted errors of the gentile philosophers, some of whom posited an eternal world; some, an eternal matter of the world, out of which at some time the world began to be generated, either by chance, or by some intellect, or even by love or strife."[11]

But is Aquinas caught here between an Aristotelian appreciation of natural order and metaphysics, on the one hand, and a Christian teaching on the contingency of all things, on the other? Does his theological resolution of philosophical *aporiae* undermine his metaphysical starting points? And, to repeat a question issued at the outset, does he thereby risk emptying this world of significance?

As for the first question, concerning the status and intelligibility of metaphysics in a created, contingent universe, Aquinas deploys the doctrine of creation itself as a means of salvaging not just contingency but also intelligibility. To put it more precisely, we can say that Aquinas wants to combat two errors, that of imposing necessity on God, and that of reducing creation to mere chance. In his account of creation in the *Summa contra Gentiles*, Aquinas writes, "Thus can we proceed in assigning the reason of the divine will. God wills man to have reason that man might exist; he wills man to be for the completion of the universe; he wills the existence of the universe because it befits his goodness."[12] Thomas uses an aesthetic term here, *decet*, to describe the fittingness of God's creating. Elsewhere, he uses versions of the term *conveniens*. The striking deployment of aesthetic language of appropriateness or suitability is Aquinas's way of getting around the extremes of necessity and arbitrariness. For us, the apprehension of fittingness is always retrospective; we learn about God's wisdom and beauty from what he has already created. Conditional necessity arises from the "naturally prior in relation to the naturally posterior" (*ScG* II, 28–29). Each creature is due "parts, properties, and accidents" that it needs in order to be what it is.[13] In creating, God acts according to his wisdom, to which we have no independent access except through the order of creation itself. Divine art is exhibited principally in the order of the parts of the universe to one another (*in ordine partium advicem, ScG* II, 24).

Divine Art: Foolishness Wiser than Philosophy

Aquinas's specifically Christian account of creation counteracts the pagan tendency to think of the real as the universal. As we have noted, Aquinas attends, in the *Summa contra Gentiles*, to the various sources of idolatry, one of which is the philosophical tendency to impose the conditions accompanying the pinnacle of philosophical knowledge onto the nature of divine knowledge. The philosophical neglect of the need for reversal, the failure to exercise appropriate negations in movement from creature to Creator, underlies the faulty conceptions of God among some Aristotelian commentators. In the culminating chapters of Book I of the *Summa contra Gentiles*, he is concerned with an especially subtle and pernicious kind of idolatry. The precise error, which Thomas finds in the writings of Averroes and Avicenna, consists in denying that God has knowledge of and care for singulars and lowly things. The entire debate over these issues hinges on the meaning of divine perfection; those who deny God's knowledge of singulars and lowly things do so because they think it unworthy of God. They quote Aristotle's statement from the *Metaphysics* that "vile things are better ignored than known."[14] The pure intellect would avert its attention from vile things; indeed, the perfection of the intellect consists, not just in shunning base things, but in ascending from singulars to universals—or so some of the philosophers would have us believe. Moreover, in the life of *theoria*, the highest and most divine life available to human beings, the concentration on lowly singulars is an indication of intellectual incapacity or moral weakness. In the philosophical ascent from what is first in our experience to what is first in the order of being, lower things can be distractions from, impediments to, the goal. Thus can the supreme "hyper-good" of pagan philosophy—contemplation of the highest being, immaterial goodness—engender a repudiation of all lower goods. What has gone wrong here?

As Thomas sees it, the problem is not just that, in moving from intellectual creatures to God, some philosophers have failed to strip away the lingering imperfections accruing to the philosophic life. Rather, in projecting onto God modes of understanding more appropriate to human beings, they have failed to see that God's knowledge of things is the exact inverse of that of human knowing. The human mind is measured by things, whereas the divine mind is the measure *of* things. The reversal is palpable in the following passage:

> Through its knowledge, the divine intellect is the cause of things. Its knowledge is the measure of things, as art is the measure of artifacts, each one of which is perfect insofar as it is consonant with art. The comparison of the divine intellect to things resembles that of things to the human intellect.[15]

The discussion of truth echoes the prologue of the first book of the *Summa contra Gentiles*, where truth is identified as the end of the entire universe, and the philosopher as the pursuer of truth. Now, it is not the life of the philosopher that is normative, but rather the life of God, who is truth in person. We now see the philosophical ascent as derivative of a prior descent, and philosophical activity as the reception of a gift of truth manifest in creation, the first mode of divine instruction. As the exemplary cause of all created things, God knows and cares for all things, the lowly and the high alike, effortlessly and in the same way. Thomas quotes repeatedly, in this debate, variants on the following passage from Dionysius: "Knowing itself, the divine wisdom knows all things, material things immaterially, divisible things indivisibly, and many unitedly."[16]

Such knowledge, at once comprehensive and detailed, is characteristic of the divine wisdom, according to Aquinas.[17] This is the upshot of Aquinas's critical response to the Arabic commentators on Aristotle. Indeed, the way critics such as Jean-Luc Marion frame the debate between Dionysius and Aquinas over the order of the names of God, over whether priority should be given to being or goodness, blocks from view Aquinas's systematic attention to divine wisdom. Just as was the case with the discussion of truth, so too in the discussion of wisdom, Thomas speaks of God as the exemplary source of wisdom, both the foundation and summit of the highest human activity. The philosophical pursuit of wisdom is a reflection of, and a participation in, the exemplary cause of the whole, a sharing in the life of the being whose life is wisdom.

In his attempt to bring revealed theology into conversation with philosophy, Aquinas speaks, not of Christian philosophy, but of the two modes or ways in which divine wisdom is made manifest to us. Wisdom is the predominant theme of the prologue of *Summa contra Gentiles*. By far the largest number (somewhere in the neighborhood of 80%) of scriptural quotations in the first three books come from the Wisdom literature of the Old Testament. If Thomas engages philosophy in terms of its quest for wisdom, its contemplative yearning to behold the first principle and highest cause, the partial overlap between philosophy and theology does not allow for seamless continuity. If theology can be said to fulfill the philosophical aspiration for wisdom, it does so in ways that are likely to surprise the philosopher. It does so through an unexpected reversal of, and an internal disruption to, the philosophical ascent to God. This is hinted at in the prologue itself, when Aquinas defends the fittingness of assenting to truths that exceed the grasp of reason.[18] He cites the Christian religion's inspiration of "idiots" to perform heroic deeds and give wise speeches.

Aquinas provides a metaphysical account of being that accords rather nicely with a narrative conception of the good, access to which can be had only through participation in practices that cultivate certain virtues. Indeed, we have good reason to construe even the mundane and seemingly rationalistic project of natural theology in precisely these terms. As Ralph McInerny puts it,

> How could any character in the human drama fail to search in some way for his author? We are to God as characters to their author. . . . For us it is all but inevitable that, however momentarily, we feel ourselves to be part of a vast cosmic drama and our thoughts turn to the author, not merely of our roles, but of our existence. Natural theology is one version of that quest.[19]

Although Aquinas does not write narrative theology, he inscribes all discourse, ethical and metaphysical, within the narrative of redemption, whose history pivots on the Word becoming flesh and embracing the death of an outcast. A careful reading of Aquinas's texts, especially the *Summa contra Gentiles*, evinces his quiet preoccupation with (a) removing impediments to the concept of creation as having a temporal beginning and end, and (b) turning back objections to the possibility of God's intervening in time.

The articulation of God as utterly transcendent and yet knowing and loving singulars sets aside obstacles to conceiving of God as Lord of history. Beyond mere time, narrative requires an order, a plot—at a bare minimum, a beginning and an end. So, in the opening of Book II, Aquinas argues that the question of the eternity of the world is a "dialectical problem" (as defined in Aristotle's *Topics*), an issue about which plausible arguments can be adduced both for and against. The limitation of human reason on this topic allows for the possibility of conceiving of creation in narrative terms as having a beginning. Conversely, in *Summa contra Gentiles* IV, 97, Aquinas argues against the creation of an infinity of souls on the ground that infinity is contrary to the very notion of an end. In the treatment of creation, Aquinas not only underscores the unilateral dependency of the creation on the Creator (creation is the very dependency of created being upon its source [SCG, II, 18] *ipsa dependentia esse creati ad principium*), but also the notion of creation as *narratio*, that is, a "setting forth, an exposition, a telling or relating." The examination of God as creator introduces a reversal of discourse that marks the transition from philosophical to theological discourse about God. Aquinas puts the contrast this way: whereas the philosopher examines natural things in themselves, the believer studies them as "effects and signs of God."[20] God himself is the transcendent and exemplary source of all that is. Creation, as we noted above, is not so much a making as it is "transcendental appearing."

A distinctive unity emerges from parallel investigations of Aquinas's metaphysics, ethics, and theology, at the center of which is the twin teaching on creation and incarnation. Based on an utterly gratuitous act, creation itself is the first gift, the framework and foundation for the entirety of his metaphysics and ethics. The consequences, which we noted previously, for our understanding and practice of justice and the other virtues are palpable. Equally conspicuous are the implications for metaphysics, which must operate in a universe constructed not simply in terms of universal principles such as potency and act but also as a set of signs, pointing beyond themselves to a source that eludes capture in images or concepts. The first gift of creation is complemented and elevated by the unanticipated and unmerited second gift, grace or redemption, made available to us through a dramatic reversal in human history, a reversal that pivots on the author of the whole entering his own drama and embracing sin, despair, and death. The most elaborate and most compelling expression of dependent rationality and just generosity is the iconic image of the crucified God.

The creator God differs from the demiurge not only in the nature of the initial act of creation but also in its enduring, pedagogical relationship to the created artifact. In defending the fittingness of miracles—that is, of God intervening in creation—Thomas appeals to the image of God as artist:

> It is not . . . opposed to the nature of an artifact that the artist should work in a different way on his product even after he has given it its first form. Nor therefore is it against nature that God should work otherwise in natural things than as the customary course of nature operates.[21]

The radical contingency of creation simultaneously underscores the unilateral dependence of creation on the Creator and the openness of creation to continued divine intervention. God intervenes in order to instruct. Miracles have the pedagogical goal of intensifying our sense of reverence, awe, and wonder. "We marvel at something when, while seeing the effect, we do not know its cause."[22] In the experience of miracles we encounter the presence of a hidden God. The philosophical analogy of God and the artist anticipates the scriptural image (St. Paul's image) of God as potter who has power over the clay "to make one vessel unto glory and another unto disgrace" (Rom. 9:21; SCG III, 161). If Aquinas insists that the ultimate plan of divine providence is hidden from us, he is nonetheless careful in nearly every major battle in the *Summa contra Gentiles* to repudiate philosophical arguments that would foreclose the possibility of envisioning God, in whom there is no composition of essence with act of existence, as active in history. We return here to the twofold self-revelation of God to Moses: the first, "I am who am," cancels all possible sources of idolatrous naming and conjuring of the divine; while the second, "I will show thee all good," underscores the future-oriented character of divine revelation and locates human beings in a position of communal dependency on God throughout the moments of time.

Hopeful Practices

The rethinking of being as gift underscores the primacy of the virtue of trust, of receptivity to the givenness of our existence and nature. It also elevates hearing over vision and points to the significance of another virtue, hope. The gap between faith and vision underscores the future-oriented character of the Christian life. We are wanderers or wayfarers: this is the "core of our creaturely existence," as Josef Pieper observes.[23] The general object of hope is a difficult future good (*bonum arduum futurum*). The need for hope signifies both our "absence of fulfillment," our "proximity to nothingness," and our "orientation to fulfillment."[24] As a virtue, hope stands between the twin vices of despair and presumption.[25] It is thus related to the virtues of magnanimity, which urges us to pursue difficult goods, and humility, which counsels us not to claim as our autonomous possession goods that exceed our capacity or merit.

Pieper's consideration of hope as a virtue that speaks to the character of our temporal existence evinces the link between hope and all the virtues. Since the ultimate good is hidden, we are, as practitioners of the virtues, ordered in a certain direction, pursuing a *telos*, but not yet in possession of it. We are situated between presumption and despair. Although presumption is a "false similitude of hope" and involves a "perverse security," despair is the greater vice. The former, while dangerous, retains a simulacrum of the virtue of hope, whereas the latter abandons the power of divine grace altogether. The consequence of the loss of hope is an atrophying of the soul. Aquinas notes that "natural hope" accompanies youth, for whom "the future is long and the past is short."[26] Supernatural hope gives eternal youth, "that strong-hearted freshness, that resilient joy, that steady perseverance in trust that so distinguish the young and make them lovable."[27] God, as Augustine says, is "younger than all else."

From this perspective, philosophy can be conceived once again as the quest for wisdom, a quest undertaken out of wonder and abiding in hope. Pieper writes,

> Out of wonder, Aristotle says, comes joy. . . . In its fusion of positive and negative, ignorance on the way to further knowledge, wonder reveals itself as having the same structure as hope, the same architecture as hope—the structure that characterizes philosophy and, indeed, human existence itself.[28]

The theme of hope also surfaces in the discussion of history, especially in Pieper's dissection of modern claims concerning historical progress. In his book *Hope and History*, Pieper highlights the intimate connection in modern thought between history and hope. Kant, for example, includes "What can I hope for?" among the most basic questions.[29] Pieper concurs on the question's importance but denies that history itself gives us any rational ground for belief in the inevitability of human progress.

Here Pieper's work dovetails nicely with that of the early MacIntyre. If neither Aquinas nor Pieper would embrace MacIntyre's hasty and wholesale dismissal of modernity or liberalism, they would share his concern over certain tendencies in liberalism—toward radical individualism, toward the complete privatization of the good, and toward the invasion of market forces into all areas of human life.[30] Aquinas would also want to defend the centrality of the virtue of hope for human life, a virtue that will have a different ranking, role, and purpose, in different conceptions of the human good. In *Marxism and Christianity*, MacIntyre makes the bold assertion that "liberalism . . . simply abandons the virtue of hope. For liberals the future has become the present enlarged."[31] Of course, its orientation toward the future gives the impression that liberalism is about nothing but hope. For MacIntyre, however, this judgment only serves to demonstrate how successful liberalism has been at shrinking our sense of the viable possibilities for human life. Like Murdoch, MacIntyre aligns Marxism with Christianity as alternatives to a regnant liberalism: "Both Marxism and Christianity rescue individual lives from the insignificance of finitude . . . by showing the individual that he has or can have some role in a world-historical drama."[32] The grand narratives of Marxism and Christianity constitute comprehensive accounts of the place of human beings in history and in the cosmos, analyses of the current disorders and resources of the human condition, and proclamations of the grounds for hope in a transformed future. MacIntyre contends,

> Secularization has not resulted . . . in the working class—or indeed any other group as a social group—acquiring a new and more rational set of beliefs about the nature of man and the world. Rather, men have been deprived of any over-all view and to this extent have been deprived of one possible source of understanding and of action. The conditions which are inimical to religion seem to be inimical to Marxism too.[33]

As we have seen in our previous discussions of *Dependent Rational Animals*, MacIntyre now expresses the deprivations of liberalism less in terms of the desuetude of grand narratives, and more in terms of a deficit of self-knowledge, an erosion of the conditions that make possible education about the common good in and through communal practices.

Modernity's dislocation of thought and practice from the vitality of traditions entails deep confusion about hope. MacIntyre's dissection of the decline of hope as a virtue resembles the interpretation of hope in Sheldon Wolin's reading of Tocqueville, according to which modernity, in contrast to the premodern elevation of the past, "fetishizes the future."[34] "Instead of development or fulfillment of potential," we experience in modernity the "exhaustion of time in the conquest of space by beings in a hurry." Wolin describes it thus: "Culture is end-less process, the formalized method by which artifacts are produced continuously."[35] MacIntyre deploys what Wolin identifies as one of the chief strategies for combating liberalism: "to enlarge modernity's understanding of progress to include the experience of loss."[36] Otherwise, we have not hope but empty, anxious longing for what we do not yet possess.

To bring MacIntyre closer to Aquinas's position, we would need to unite his late emphasis on practices of the common good with his early accentuation of world-historical dramas. Yet even here, he does not quite reach Aquinas's sense of creation as ordered by and toward that which transcends creation and time. Pieper is more accurate. He patiently examines, and finds wanting, a number of arguments on behalf of historical progress, construed as the complete realization of a universal society of just relations among persons.[37] Pieper concludes, "If earthly existence is pervasively structured toward what is 'not yet in being,' and if a man, as a *viator*, is truly 'on the way to' something right up to the moment of death, then this hope, which is identical with our very being itself, either is plainly absurd or finds its ultimate fulfillment on the other side of death."[38]

Modernity's failure to fulfill the hopes that modernity itself has fostered in humanity generates forms and degrees of despair peculiar to modernity. Pieper's response is not so much to deny the hope for universal justice but to insist that hope can be a real and vigorous virtue only if it is grounded in eternity, not merely in the flow of time. But does the turn to eternity not risk a denigration of limited, temporal goods? Pieper responds: "It is this identical, created reality here and now present before our eyes, whose fulfillment, in direct overcoming of death and catastrophe, we hope for as salvation."[39]

The wisdom of revelation operates through contingent historical events unknown to the philosopher; it embraces and focuses on death and catastrophe, precisely those features of ancient tragedy that philosophy supplanted in its account of the good life.[40] The vehicle of revelation is a historical narrative, the narrative of salvation history. The source of Christian wisdom is the singular, contingent event of the incarnation, upon which the whole of history pivots and in which time and eternity cross. "If anyone should consider diligently and piously the mystery of the Incarnation," says Thomas, "he will find such a profundity of wisdom that it exceeds all human knowing. As the Apostle states: The wisdom of men is foolishness before God."[41] Aquinas does not speak in Marion's terms of a holy terror, but he does describe an excess, a surplus, a saturation of wisdom in the incarnation that is apt to disorient and confuse human minds in their initial encounter with it. This is why Christ taught, healed, and established a church with sacraments and a priesthood. The dialectic of presence and absence continues in salvation history, in the church and the sacraments. After performing wondrous deeds, Christ withdraws, so that "by his absence" we might be prepared for spiritual gifts.[42]

The wisdom of Christ is most emphatically and most paradoxically present in the very moment when God seems most distant, in the moment of death on the cross. Marion's most audacious interpretive move is to suggest that in his increasing preoccupation with the Crucified One, Nietzsche himself comes close to seeing in Christ's final "Amen," his willingness to embrace all that life offers without complaint or repudiation, as an affirmation of all that is—the antithesis to *ressentiment* and nihilism. For our present purposes, we need not tarry over the adequacy of Marion's exegesis of Nietzsche; what matters is that Marion's way of articulating the incarnation, cross, and resurrection operates as a dual corrective—against idolatry and against the temptation to repudiate the significance of contingent temporal events. Christ's cross indicates that the "world is not only acceptable and bearable, but credible and faithful."[43] Christ "expresses the great awaited Amen of a Dionysian breakthrough"; "in his own way he bears the unbearable within the innocence of an affirmation."[44] Marion asks pointedly,

> Would abandon become the condition of relation to God as a person and not as an idol? But then one would have to admit that abandon offers one of the faces of communion—perhaps the highest. . . . the conjunction of the persons in the unique danger of their mutual abandon, or even the conjunction of the gift and abandon in the play of persons—there is the mystery that Nietzsche just touches upon only then to avoid it.[45]

The significance of abandonment is not lost on Aquinas. We have already noted his statement, "Christ's Passion suffices to instruct us fully about our life." He continues, "Whoever wants to live perfectly has nothing more to do than spurn what Christ spurned on the Cross and desire what he desired." He who possesses all the treasures of wisdom in his very person "appears naked on the Cross, an object of mockery, spit upon, beaten, crowned with thorns, offered gall and vinegar, and put to death. No example of virtue is absent from the Cross."[46] The encounter with Christ crucified continues in the life of the church, whose sacraments "receive their specific power from Christ's Passion. . . . The water and blood flowing from the side of Christ hanging on the cross are signs of this truth—one of baptism, the other of the Eucharist."[47]

For Aquinas, then, the Good is not just, as Murdoch sees it, "a magnetic centre to which we are drawn"; it is also a gift, or rather, it is the source of and beyond every gift we receive, the Giver of every good and perfect gift. It is also the Gift made manifest to us in the flesh, in the person of Christ and in the sacramental presence even unto the present day. We have already noted the way Murdoch moves back and forth between a Platonic notion of the Good as an impersonal power of attraction, and a more Augustinian and psalmist conception of God as a personal voice that beckons alluringly. But Murdoch resists the identification of the Good with God. Her version of Anselm's so-called ontological argument entails that "no existing thing could be what we have meant by God. Any existing God would be less than God. An existent God would be an idol or demon."[48] The point here seems to be that no singular being can, by the very fact of its singularity, embody all that we mean by perfection; conversely, our judgment that "this being is God" would seem to presuppose the independence and transcendence of a notion of perfection in light of which we appraise this particular being as divine. Aside from reflecting a crude notion of God as a singular being in the midst of other singular beings, Murdoch's account instructively inverts Aquinas's understanding of the relationship between God and perfection, the latter of which is especially susceptible to idolatrous misunderstanding and abuse. As we noted above, the identification of the divine with a set of perfections constitutes a more sophisticated, and therefore more dangerous, form of idolatry than that found in the confusion of the divine with sensible objects and images.

Murdoch is of course aware of the vices of idolatry. Thus, she insists that we experience "both the reality of perfection and its distance away, and this leads us to place our idea of it outside the world of existent being as something of a different unique and special sort."[49] The latter claim does not entail for

Murdoch that there is some point to the universe independent of it, some transcendent *telos* that would give meaning to finite, contingent acts and lives. Instead, she acknowledges the sheer pointlessness of virtue.

By contrast with this view, Stanley Hauerwas urges that the Christian task is to "see the contingent as 'gift' whose purpose is to praise the creator. Such a task does not mean the otherness of the contingent is obliterated by its place in a larger purpose, but that its contingency can be enjoyed because God so enjoys God's creation."[50] In Genesis, God comments on, and takes delight in, each stage in his creation. At its most profound level, Aquinas's metaphysical practice is precisely a training of embodied souls to take delight in the being of creatures, both in themselves and as hopeful signs of the fulfillment of divine promises. This, Hauerwas continues, is a

> telos of hope that gives us the confidence to believe that we are not fated by our collective or individual pasts. We know that we cannot avoid being creatures of history, but that way of putting the matter presumes we should desire, if possible, an alternative. Such a desire cannot help but appear to the Christian as a sinful attempt to escape our creatureliness. Our only alternative is not a salvation that mystically frees us from history, from our past, but rather an alternative history made possible by a community of people across time who maintain a memory of God's hope for us and for the world.[51]

NOTES

1. Ethics as a Guide into Metaphysics

1. Related in Richard Ellmann's *James Joyce* (Oxford: Oxford University Press, 1983), a revision of the original 1959 edition, on p. 63.

2. William T. Noon, *Joyce and Aquinas* (New Haven, Conn.: Yale University Press, 1957). The book is still regularly cited in studies of Joyce, even if its suggestions of Joyce's affinities with premodern philosophy have been less well received in the trendy attempts to deploy Joyce as an authority for a host of postmodern "isms."

3. Weldon Thornton's *The Antimodernism of Joyce's Portrait* (Syracuse, N.Y.: Syracuse University Press, 1994) is a case in point. Thornton makes a convincing case for the presence of Aristotelian notions of human agency and narrative rationality in Joyce, especially in *Portrait of the Artist*. He does not, however, investigate the interplay of elements from Thomistic metaphysics, theology, and aesthetics in *Portrait of the Artist* and *Ulysses*.

4. The most important link to Aquinas can be found in Stephen Dedalus's lecture in the National Library of Dublin in *Ulysses*, whose theoretical content has been too often dismissed by commentators. A notable exception can be found in Rene Girard's discussion of Joyce in *A Theater of Envy: William Shakespeare* (Oxford: Oxford University Press, 1991; reprint South Bend, Ind.: St. Augustine's Press, 2004), 256–70. Preoccupied with Joyce's relation to Shakespeare, Girard does not comment on the way Aquinas figures in the conversation. By contrast, Noon's book regularly recurs to this chapter as a basis for examining Joyce's relationship to Aquinas.

5. Eric Voegelin, *Anamnesis: On the Theory of History and Politics*, in *The Collected Works of Eric Voegelin*, trans. M. L. Hanak, ed. David Walsh (Columbia: University of Missouri Press, 2002), 392.

6. A similar sort of selectivity afflicts many contemporary interpretations of Aquinas's account of human knowledge. We shall address these problems in later chapters.

7. Ellmann, *James Joyce*, 5.

8. Stanley Cavell, *Cities of Words* (Cambridge, Mass.: Harvard University Press, 2005), 4.

9. Ibid., 4.

10. Charles Taylor, *Sources of the Self: The Making of the Modern Identity* (Cambridge, Mass.: Harvard University Press, 1992), 63–73, 100–106.

11. In his recent book, *Faith, Reason and the Existence of God* (Cambridge: Cambridge University Press, 2005) Denys Turner brings Aquinas into conversation with the post-Nietzschean critique of metaphysics. Aquinas concurs with one of the assumptions of the critique, namely, that reason points to an otherness that it cannot

know. Turner, who wants to defend the theological significance of Aquinas's arguments for the natural knowability of God, observes that in the contemporary context, there is nothing to guarantee that "beyond reason there is anything but a vacuous, empty nothingness, an endless prolongation of postponements." The only way out of this nihilism is for reason to be able to name the otherness, to justify the existence of God as that to which it points. Interestingly, Turner turns to music as marking the limits of reason, a point made extensively in Joyce's writings, especially in *Portrait of the Artist*, where Nietzschean and Thomist interpretations of the limits of reason and the significance of music are in contention with one another. See Turner, *Faith, Reason and the Existence of God*, 118 and 108–16.

12. Iris Murdoch, *Existentialists and Mystics: Writings on Philosophy and Literature*, ed. Peter Conradi (New York: Penguin Books, 1998), 287-89.

13. Ibid., 77.

14. Ibid., 290.

15. Joel Kupperman, *Character* (Oxford: Oxford University Press, 1991).

16. Murdoch advanced this argument in a number of places, most notably in her Gifford Lectures, published as *Metaphysics as a Guide to Morals* (New York: Penguin, 1992). In this she was not entirely alone, since Elizabeth Anscombe contended that ethics was in dire need of a "philosophical psychology." See her influential, "Modern Moral Philosophy," which first appeared in *Ethics* 33 (1958); its most recent reprint is in *Virtue Ethics*, ed. Crisp and Slote (Oxford: Oxford University Press, 1997), 26–44. In current philosophy, Charles Taylor, who makes the case that reflection on the inescapable moral horizons of ordinary human agents provides access to moral ontology, continues the project of Murdoch. See Taylor, *Sources of the Self*. In *Dependent Rational Animals* (Chicago: Open Court, 2001), Alasdair MacIntyre defends a conception of human animality and dependency that echoes certain features of Murdoch's thought; while Stanley Rosen advances a version, which shares much with Murdoch, of Platonic metaphysics as arising from the experience of the good in ordinary human experience. For Rosen, see especially *The Question of Being: A Reversal of Heidegger* (South Bend, Ind.: St. Augustine's Press, 2002) and *Metaphysics in Ordinary Language* (South Bend, Ind.: St. Augustine's Press, 2004).

17. Murdoch, *Existentialists and Mystics*, 292.

18. Analytic philosophy of religion flourishes in America in part because of the Society of Christian Philosophers and its journal *Faith and Philosophy*. Books in philosophy of religion from both analytic and Continental perspectives are published with regularity by all the major academic presses. Both Fordham University Press and Indiana University Press publish series in philosophy of religion from a Continental vantage point.

19. Of course, there are serious questions, which we will raise later, as to whether the flight from metaphysics does not itself risk undermining practice. Denys Turner comments on Derrida's insistence that "every other is wholly other": "The otherness of another person is not and cannot be an absolute heterogeneity, . . . an absolutely inaccessible singularity, not unless some ethic is to be founded upon the otherness of the other as some blank, anonymous reference point of a semantically empty demonstrative pronoun" (*Faith, Reason and the Existence of God*, 267).

20. Murdoch's commitment to metaphysics was hardly deep or consistent. She writes at one point, "We need more concepts than our philosophies have furnished us with. We need to be enabled to think in terms of degrees of freedom, and to picture, in a

non-metaphysical, non-totalitarian and non-religious sense, the transcendence of real-ity" (*Sovereignty of the Good* [New York: Schocken Books, 1971], 95).

21. Waxing and waning in popularity, Thomism has a long and varied history. Popularity, of course, does not guarantee, and sometimes actually inhibits, understand-ing. After the surge of interest in Thomas among Catholics in the late nineteenth and first half of the twentieth century, the study of Aquinas went into steady decline. Recent years have witnessed a resurgence of interest in Aquinas in both theological and philo-sophical circles, and not always by Catholics. Analytic philosophers in particular have exhibited interest. See, for example, *The Monist* 80 (1997) devoted to *Analytic Tho-mism*, edited by John Haldane. For a critical response to analytic Thomism, see Brian Shanley's review discussion in *The Thomist* 63 (1999): 125–37. See also Aidan Nichols, *Discovering Aquinas* (London: Darton, Longman and Todd, 2002); Jean-Pierre Torrell, *Saint Thomas Aquinas*, Vol. 1: *The Person and His Work* (Washington, D.C.: Catholic University of America Press, 1996), and Vol. 2: *Spiritual Master* (Washington, D.C.: Catholic University of America Press, 2003); and Fergus Kerr, *After Aquinas, Versions of Thomism* (Malden, Mass.: Blackwell, 2002). For the history of Thomism, see Gerald McCool, *From Unity to Pluralism: The Internal Evolution of Thomism* (New York: Fordham University Press, 1992); and Romanus Cessario, *A Short History of Thomism* (Washington, D.C.: Catholic University of America of Press, 1995).

22. Long before analytic philosophers had any sense that something was deeply awry in ethical discourse, the recovery of Aristotelian *phronesis* was already well under-way in the writings of John Henry Newman (*The Grammar of Assent*); at the time of the developments in analytic philosophy, Hans Georg Gadamer was working out an ac-count of hermeneutics grounded in a reading of Aristotelian prudence (*Truth and Method* and *The Idea of the Good in Platonic-Aristotelian Philosophy*). For the non-analytic resources on the question of praxis, see Joseph Dunne, *Back to the Rough Ground: Phronesis and Techne in Modern Philosophy and in Aristotle* (Notre Dame, Ind.: University of Notre Dame Press, 1993). As we shall see, just about the time Murdoch and Anscombe were issuing their pleas for a philosophical psychology of the virtues, the German Thomist Josef Pieper was completing his remarkable studies of the cardinal and theological virtues in language at once traditional and contemporary.

23. The seriousness with which Marion takes Aquinas has reopened a debate that closed prematurely in Continental circles with the publication of John Caputo's *Hei-degger and Aquinas: An Essay on Overcoming Metaphysics* (New York: Fordham Uni-versity Press, 1982).

24. Aquinas's relationship to Aristotle has of course been vigorously and hotly debated since Aquinas's own time. For the case of fundamental incompatibility, see, for example, Harry Jaffa, *Thomism and Aristotelianism: A Study of the Commentary by Thomas Aquinas on the Nichomachean Ethics* (Chicago: University of Chicago Press, 1952); R. A. Gauthier, *La morale d'Aristote* (Paris: Presses Universitaires de France, 1958); and Mark Jordan, *The Alleged Aristotelianism of Thomas Aquinas*, Gilson Lec-ture, no. 15 (Toronto: PIMS, 1992). For a defense of Aquinas as an Aristotelian, see Ralph McInerny, *Aquinas Against the Averroists: On There Being Only One Intellect* (West Lafayette, Ind.: Purdue University Press, 1993), and *The Question of Christian Ethics* (Washington, D.C.: Catholic University of America Press, 1998). Also of interest are Leo Elders, "Saint Thomas d'Aquin et Aristote," *Revue Thomiste* 88 (1988): 357–76; Joseph Owens, "Aquinas as Aristotelian Commentator," in *St. Thomas Aquinas 1274–1974, Commemorative Studies*, Vol. 1, 213–38 (Toronto: PIMS, 1974); and John

Jenkins, "Expositions of the Text: Aquinas's Aristotelian Commentaries," *Medieval Philosophy and Theology* 5 (1996): 36–62.

25. *Ethics*, 1105b10–15. All references to, and translations of, Aristotle's texts are from *The Complete Works of Aristotle: The Revised Oxford Translation*, Vols. 1 and 2, ed. Jonathan Barnes (Princeton, N.J.: Princeton University Press, 1984).

26. Alasdair MacIntyre, *After Virtue* (Notre Dame, Ind.: University of Notre Dame Press, 1981), 187.

27. Alasdair MacIntyre, *Three Rival Versions of Moral Enquiry* (Notre Dame, Ind.: University of Notre Dame Press, 1991), 127.

28. Ibid., 128.

29. Ibid.

30. It is instructive, however, that, since the famous repudiation of "metaphysical biology" in *After Virtue*, MacIntyre has moved steadily in the direction of affirming the need for metaphysical commitments. So, for example, in *Dependent Rational Animals*, he offers an anthropology of the virtues, and in his recently published book, *Edith Stein: A Philosophical Prologue, 1913–1922* (Lanham, Md.: Rowman & Littlefield, 2006), he speaks positively of Stein's movement toward a "Thomist ontology."

31. *Politics* VII, 3, 1325a19–32.

32. *Metaphysics*, 981b25–982a1.

33. *Ethics*, 1094a28–1094b11.

34. Aquinas, *Summa contra Gentiles* (Turin, 1961), hereafter *ScG*. See *ScG* I, 1: Inter alia quae homines de sapiente concipiunt, a philosopho ponitur quod *sapientis est ordinare*. Omnium autem ordinatorum ad finem, gubernationis et ordinis regulam ex fine sumi necesse est: tunc enim unaquaeque res optime disponitur cum ad suum finem convenienter ordinatur; finis enim est bonum uniuscuiusque. Unde videmus in artibus unam alterius esse gubernativam et quasi principem, ad quam pertinet eius finis: sicut medicinalis ars pigmentariae principatur et eam ordinat, propter hoc quod sanitas, circa quam medicinalis versatur, finis est omnium pigmentorum, quae arte pigmentaria conficiuntur. Et simile apparet in arte gubernatoria respectu navifactivae; et in militari respectu equestris et omnis bellici apparatus. Quae quidem artes aliis principantes architectonicae nominantur, quasi principales artes: unde et earum artifices, qui architectores vocantur, nomen sibi vindicant sapientum.

35. Rosen, *The Question of Being*, 30.

36. One might wonder whether Voegelin took this lesson to heart in his own readings of Aquinas's metaphysics. See Eric Voegelin, *The New Science of Politics: The Collected Works of Eric Voegelin*, vol. 5, ed. Manfred Henningsen (Columbia: University of Missouri Press, 2000), 103.

37. Among the most important studies of Aquinas's metaphysics are the following: Etienne Gilson, *Being and Some Philosophers* (Toronto: PIMS, 1949); Jacques Maritain, *A Preface to Metaphysics: Seven Lectures on Being* (New York: Sheed & Ward, 1946); Cornelio Fabro, *Participation et causalité selon S. Thomas d'Aquin*: Préface de L. De Raeymaeker (Louvain: Publications universitaires de Louvain, 1961); Louis Geiger, *La participation dans la philosophie de S. Thomas d'Aquin* (Paris: Vrin, 1942); Rudi T. Velde, *Participation and Substantiality in Thomas Aquinas* (Leiden: E. J. Brill, 1995); Fran O'Rourke, *Pseudo-Dionysius and the Metaphysics of Aquinas* (Leiden: E. J. Brill, 1992); Jan Aertsen, *Medieval Philosophy and the Transcendentals* (Leiden: E. J. Brill, 1996); Norris Clarke, *The One and the Many* (Notre Dame, Ind.: University of Notre Dame Press, 2001); David Burrell, *Knowing the Unknowable God: Ibn-Sina, Mai-*

monides, *Aquinas* (Notre Dame, Ind.: University of Notre Dame Press, 1986); John Wippel, *The Metaphysical Thought of Thomas Aquinas* (Catholic University of America Press, 2000); James Doig, *Aquinas on Metaphysics: A Historico-Doctrinal Study of the Commentary on the Metaphysics* (The Hague: Nijhoff, 1972); Matthew Levering, *Scripture and Metaphysics: Aquinas and the Renewal of Trinitarian Theology* (Malden, Mass.: Blackwell, 2004); Brian Davies, *The Thought of Thomas Aquinas* (Oxford: Clarendon, 1992); and Wayne J. Hankey, *God in Himself: Aquinas's Doctrine of God as Expounded in the Summa Theologiae* (Oxford: Oxford University Press, 1987).

38. There is a heated debate over this issue in Thomistic circles; references to the relevant literature will be made in a subsequent chapter.

39. *Summa Theologiae* (Turin, 1948), hereafter *ST*. See *ST* I, 1, 4: Sacra doctrina, ut dictum est, una existens, se extendit ad ea quae pertinent ad diversas scientias philosophicas, propter rationem formalem quam in diversis attendit, scilicet prout sunt divino lumine cognoscibilia. Unde licet in scientiis philosophicis alia sit speculativa et alia practica, sacra tamen doctrina comprehendit sub se utramque; sicut et Deus eadem scientia se cognoscit, et ea quae facit. Magis tamen est speculativa quam practica, quia principalius agit de rebus divinis quam de actibus humanis; de quibus agit secundum quod per eos ordinatur homo ad perfectam Dei cognitionem, in qua aeterna beatitudo consistit.

40. For elements of Platonism in Aquinas's metaphysics, see Fabro, *Participation et causalité selon S. Thomas d'Aquin*; Geiger, *La participation dans la philosophie de S. Thomas d'Aquin*; Velde, *Participation and Substantiality in Thomas Aquinas*; O'Rourke, *Pesudo-Dionysius and the Metaphysics of Aquinas*; Aertsen, *Medieval Philosophy and the Transcendentals*; Clarke, *The One and the Many*.

41. See Voegelin, *Anamnesis*.

42. Aquinas, *Sententia libri Metaphysicorum* (Turin, 1950), hereafter, *In Met.* See *In Met.* I, lc. 1: Inter ea vero, quae memoriam habent, quaedam habent auditum et quaedam non. Quaecumque autem auditum non habent, ut apes, vel si quod aliud huiusmodi animal est, licet prudentiam habere possint, non tamen sunt disciplinabilia, ut scilicet per alterius instructionem possint assuescere ad aliquid faciendum vel vitandum: huiusmodi enim instructio praecipue recipitur per auditum: unde dicitur in libro de sensu et sensato, quod auditus est sensus disciplinae.

43. *Inaugural Sermons* is available in a translation by Ralph McInerny in *Thomas Aquinas: Selected Writings* (New York: Penguin Classics, 1998).

44. *Principium Rigans montes*, 2 (Turin, 1954): Primo enim montes radiis illustrantur. Et similiter sacri doctores mentium splendorem primo recipiunt. Sicut montes enim doctores primitus radiis divinae sapientiae illuminantur, Psal.: *illuminans tu mirabiliter a montibus aeternis turbati sunt omnes insipientes corde*; id est a doctoribus qui sunt in participatione aeternitatis, Philipp. II: *inter quos lucetis sicut luminaria in mundo*.

45. *Principium Rigans montes*, 4: Sed doctores sapientiam non communicant nisi per ministerium. Unde fructus montium non ipsis, sed divinis operibus tribuitur.

46. Torrell, *Saint Thomas Aquinas*, Vol. 2: *Spiritual Master*, 34.

2. Virtue and Practice

1. David Solomon, "Internal Objections to Virtue Ethics," in *Ethical Theory: Character and Virtue*, Midwest Studies in Philosophy 13, 428–41 (Notre Dame, Ind.:

Notre Dame University Press, 1988). Other attempts at definition include Michael Slote, *From Morality to Virtue* (Oxford: Oxford University Press, 1992); G. V. Trianosky, "What Is Virtue Ethics All About?" *American Philosophical Quarterly* 27 (1990): 335–44; Rosalind Hursthouse, *On Virtue Ethics* (Oxford: Oxford University Press, 2002); and Daniel Statman, "Introduction to Virtue Ethics," in *Virtue Ethics* (Cambridge: Edinburgh University Press, 1997), 2–41.

2. Although we will concentrate on contemporary Anglo-American debates, the revival of prudence is not limited to that context. In fact, renewed attention to prudence came to Anglo-American philosophy long after it had resurfaced in Continental and Catholic philosophy. To see that this is so, one need only mention the names of Arendt, Pieper, and Gadamer, all of whom resuscitate the classical virtue of *phronesis* as central parts of their projects. For discussions of Arendt and Gadamer on *phronesis*, see Joseph Dunne, *Back to the Rough Ground*, 88–167. Dunne includes a discussion of Newman on pp. 31–54.

3. Indeed, virtue ethics has had difficulty generating much in the way of a virtue politics. The problem is not a dearth of available material on politics and virtue. See, for example, William Galston, *Liberal Purposes: Goods, Virtues, and Diversity in the Liberal State* (Cambridge: Cambridge University Press, 1991); Quentin Skinner, "The Republican Ideal of Political Liberty," in *Machiavelli and Republicanism*, ed. G. Bock, Q. Skinner, and M. Viroli (Cambridge: Cambridge University Press, 1990); Amy Gutmann, *Democratic Education* (Princeton, N.J.: Princeton University Press, 1987); Richard Sinopli, *The Foundation of American Citizenship: Liberalism, the Constitution, and Civic Virtue* (Oxford: Oxford University Press, 1997); Richard Dagger, *Civic Virtues: Rights, Citizenship, and Republican Liberalism* (Oxford: Oxford University Press, 1997). But none of these accounts arises from recent developments proper to virtue ethics.

4. English versions of these works are available as *The Four Cardinal Virtues* (Notre Dame, Ind.: University of Notre Dame Press, 1966) and *Faith Hope Love* (San Francisco: Ignatius Press, 1997). In British philosophy, Philippa Foot's work was heavily influenced by Aquinas. See *Virtues and Vices and Other Essays in Moral Philosophy* (Oxford: Oxford University Press, 2003); the book contains essays written between 1957 and 1977. For a sample of the literature on virtue in Aquinas, see Daniel Mark Nelson's *The Priority of Prudence* (University Park: Penn State University Press, 1992) for an attempt to eliminate law in favor of virtue. Correctives to Nelson's imbalanced position can be had in Daniel Westberg's *Right Practical Reason: Aristotle, Action, and Prudence in Aquinas* (Oxford: Oxford University Press, 1994); Pamela Hall, *Narrative and the Natural law* (Notre Dame, Ind.: University of Notre Dame Press, 1999); Russell Hittinger, *A Critique of the New Natural Law Theory* (Notre Dame, Ind.: University of Notre Dame Press, 1987); and especially Ralph McInerny, *Ethica Thomistica* (Washington, D.C.: Catholic University of America Press, 1997). In moral theology, see Stanley Hauerwas, *Vision and Virtue* (Notre Dame, Ind.: University of Notre Dame Press, 1981); Thomas O'Meara, "Virtues in the Theology of Thomas Aquinas," *Theological Studies* 58 (1997): 256–87; and the magisterial treatment by Servais Pinckaers, *The Sources of Christian Ethics*, trans. St. Mary Thomas Noble (Washington, D.C.: Catholic University of America Press, 1995).

5. Pieper, *Four Cardinal Virtues*, 30.

6. Ibid., 31.

7. Ibid., 26–27.

8. Ibid., 28.

9. Ibid., 4–5.

10. Rosalind Hursthouse observes this lacuna in *On Virtue Ethics*, 5.

11. Anscombe, "Modern Moral Philosophy," 26–44.

12. MacIntyre, *After Virtue* (Notre Dame, Ind.: University of Notre Dame Press, 1981).

13. Kupperman, *Character*, 71–72.

14. Murdoch, *Existentialists and Mystics*, 324.

15. Amelie Rorty, "Virtues and their Vicissitudes," in *Essays on Aristotle's Ethics*, ed. Amelie Rorty (Berkeley: University of California Press, 1981), 147. For a more extended defense of this point, see Bernard Williams, *Ethics and the Limits of Philosophy* (Cambridge, Mass.: Harvard University Press, 1985).

16. Kupperman, *Character*, 74.

17. Murdoch, *Existentialists and Mystics*, 329.

18. Aquinas, *Quaestiones Disputatae De Malo* (Turin, 1953), hereafter *De Malo*. See *De Malo*, 6, 1: Si autem sit tale bonum quod non inveniatur esse bonum secundum omnia particularia quae considerari possunt, non ex necessitate movebit etiam quantum ad determinationem actus; poterit enim aliquis velle eius oppositum, etiam de eo cogitans, quia forte est bonum vel conveniens secundum aliquod aliud particulare consideratum, sicut quod est bonum sanitati, non est bonum delectationi, et sic de aliis.

19. *ST* I–II, 14, 2: Principium autem non cadit sub quaestione, sed principia oportet supponere in omni inquisitione. Unde cum consilium sit quaestio, de fine non est consilium, sed solum de his quae sunt ad finem. Tamen contingit id quod est finis respectu quorundam, ordinari ad alium finem, sicut etiam id quod est principium unius demonstrationis, est conclusio alterius. Et ideo id quod accipitur ut finis in una inquisitione, potest accipi ut ad finem in alia inquisitione. Et sic de eo erit consilium.

20. John Jenkins, *Knowledge and Faith in Thomas Aquinas* (Cambridge: Cambridge University Press, 1997), 206.

21. A virtuous character is constituted by habits that amount, in Kupperman's language, to a set of commitments. Indeed, virtues circumscribe the types of acts a virtuous agent is willing to undertake or even consider. Yet utilitarianism, as Bernard Williams has argued, requires that the only commitment we are to have continuously is the commitment to maximization. For a good utilitarian, commitments imposed on us by certain virtues would always have to be tentative and conditional; that is, we would always have to be willing to act against a virtue if acting in accord with virtue would bring about a less than optimum set of consequences. And while Kant advocates purity of will in a habitual willingness to do one's duty, it is not clear that doing one's duty in Kantian terms is always compatible with actions flowing from virtue. At least one influential essay ponders the contrast between visiting a sick friend because of friendship or because of a universal impersonal duty. See William Stocker, "The Schizophrenia of Modern Ethical Theories," *Journal of Philosophy* 14 (1976): 453–66. For a response to Stocker and others who suppose Kant's conception of agency and moral motivation are antithetical to Aristotle's, see the chapter on Aristotle and Kant in Hursthouse's *On Virtue Ethics*.

22. Of course, Kantians and utilitarians are not without resources to respond to the attacks from virtue ethicists. Nancy Shermann, in *Making a Necessity of Virtue: Aristotle and Kant on Virtue* (Cambridge: Cambridge University Press, 1997), has shown that there is much room in Kant to develop a richer conception of agency and the role

of judgment. The best assessment of how far Kant can be taken in this direction is Robert Pippen's "Hegel, Ethical Reasons, Kantian Rejoinders," in *Idealism as Modernism* (Cambridge: Cambridge University Press, 1997), 92–128, especially 111–24. And even consequentialists, such as Samuel Scheffler in *The Rejection of Consequentialism* (Oxford: Clarendon, 1994), have argued that they can carve out a space for agency and character. Furthermore, in its flight from acts and consequences, virtue ethics is vulnerable to Kantian and utilitarians countercharges that virtue ethics is itself reductionistic. Later in the chapter, we shall consider a specific version of this argument.

23. As is now commonly known, the first step in this broadening rests on Wittgenstein's account of what it means to "follow a rule." Joseph Dunne's study of *phronesis* in *Back to the Rough Ground* is partly inspired by this famous line of reasoning in Wittgenstein.

24. Once again, Pieper anticipates later developments. He traces the attraction of casuistry to the understandable but misplaced desire for "certainty and security." Pieper holds that to overvalue casuistry is to "confound model and reality" and to misunderstand the "meaning and rank of the virtue of prudence" (*The Four Cardinal Virtues*, 26–27).

25. I have tried to say more about the moral pedagogy in the *Summa Theologiae* and particularly about the relationship of law to virtue in Thomas Hibbs, *Virtue's Splendor: Wisdom, Prudence, and the Human Good* (New York: Fordham University Press, 2001). The literature on natural law is vast. For a sampling of new and old, see John Finnis, *Aquinas: Moral, Political, and Legal Theory* (Oxford: Oxford University Press, 1998); Ernest Fortin, "St. Thomas Aquinas," *History of Political Philosophy*, ed. Leo Strauss and Joseph Cropsey (Chicago: Rand-McNally, 2nd and 3rd editions); John Finnis, *Natural Law and Natural Rights* (Oxford: Oxford University Press, 1980); Ernest L. Fortin, "The New Rights Theory and the Natural Law," *Review of Politics* 44 (1982); Robert P. George, ed., *Natural Law Theory: Contemporary Essays* (Oxford: Oxford University Press, 1994); Pamela Hall, *Narrative and the Natural Law* (1999); Russell Hittinger, *A Critique of the New Natural Law Theory* (1987); Ralph McInerny, *Ethica Thomistica* (1997); E. A. Goerner, "On Thomistic Natural Law: The Bad Man's View of Thomistic Natural Right," *Political Theory* 7 (1979); idem, "Thomistic Natural Right: The Good Man's View of Thomistic Natural Law," *Political Theory* 11 (1983); Jacques Maritain, *The Rights of Man and Natural Law* (San Francisco: Ignatius Press, 1986).

26. *ST* I–II, 90. 1, ad 2: Et quia ratio etiam practica utitur quodam syllogismo in operabilibus, ut supra habitum est, secundum quod philosophus docet in VII Ethic.; ideo est invenire aliquid in ratione practica quod ita se habeat ad operationes, sicut se habet propositio in ratione speculativa ad conclusiones.

27. *ST* I–II, 94, 2: In his autem quae in apprehensione omnium cadunt, quidam ordo invenitur. Nam illud quod primo cadit in apprehensione, est ens, cuius intellectus includitur in omnibus quaecumque quis apprehendit. Et ideo primum principium indemonstrabile est quod non est simul affirmare et negare, quod fundatur supra rationem entis et non entis, et super hoc principio omnia alia fundantur, ut dicitur in IV Metaphys. Sicut autem ens est primum quod cadit in apprehensione simpliciter, ita bonum est primum quod cadit in apprehensione practicae rationis, quae ordinatur ad opus, omne enim agens agit propter finem, qui habet rationem boni. Et ideo primum principium in ratione practica est quod fundatur supra rationem boni, quae est, bonum est quod omnia appetunt. Hoc est ergo primum praeceptum legis, quod bonum est faciendum et prosequendum, et malum vitandum.

28. See Finnis, *Natural Law and Natural Rights*, 51.

29. *ST* I–II, 94, 4: Aliter tamen circa hoc se habet ratio speculativa, et aliter ratio practica. Quia enim ratio speculativa praecipue negotiatur circa necessaria, quae impossibile est aliter se habere, absque aliquo defectu invenitur veritas in conclusionibus propriis, sicut et in principiis communibus. Sed ratio practica negotiatur circa contingentia, in quibus sunt operationes humanae, et ideo, etsi in communibus sit aliqua necessitas, quanto magis ad propria descenditur, tanto magis invenitur defectus. Sic igitur in speculativis est eadem veritas apud omnes tam in principiis quam in conclusionibus, licet veritas non apud omnes cognoscatur in conclusionibus, sed solum in principiis, quae dicuntur communes conceptiones. In operativis autem non est eadem veritas vel rectitudo practica apud omnes quantum ad propria, sed solum quantum ad communia, et apud illos apud quos est eadem rectitudo in propriis, non est aequaliter omnibus nota. Sic igitur patet quod, quantum ad communia principia rationis sive speculativae sive practicae, est eadem veritas seu rectitudo apud omnes, et aequaliter nota. Quantum vero ad proprias conclusiones rationis speculativae, est eadem veritas apud omnes, non tamen aequaliter omnibus nota, apud omnes enim verum est quod triangulus habet tres angulos aequales duobus rectis, quamvis hoc non sit omnibus notum. Sed quantum ad proprias conclusiones rationis practicae, nec est eadem veritas seu rectitudo apud omnes; nec etiam apud quos est eadem, est aequaliter nota.

30. *ST* I–II, 97, 3: Et secundum hoc, consuetudo et habet vim legis, et legem abolet, et est legum interpretatrix.

31. *ST* I–II, 97, 1: Lex recte mutari potest propter mutationem conditionum hominum, quibus secundum diversas eorum conditiones diversa expediunt.

32. *ST* I–II, 96, 2: Lex autem humana ponitur multitudini hominum, in qua maior pars est hominum non perfectorum virtute. Et ideo lege humana non prohibentur omnia vitia, a quibus virtuosi abstinent; sed solum graviora, a quibus possibile est maiorem partem multitudinis abstinere; et praecipue quae sunt in nocumentum aliorum, sine quorum prohibitione societas humana conservari non posset, sicut prohibentur lege humana homicidia et furta et huiusmodi.

33. *ST* I–II, 94, 6: Quantum vero ad alia praecepta secundaria, potest lex naturalis deleri de cordibus hominum, vel propter malas persuasiones, eo modo quo etiam in speculativis errores contingunt circa conclusiones necessarias; vel etiam propter pravas consuetudines et habitus corruptos; sicut apud quosdam non reputabantur latrocinia peccata, vel etiam vitia contra naturam, ut etiam apostolus dicit, ad Rom. I.

34. MacIntyre, *After Virtue*, 139–40.

35. Michael Sandel, *Liberalism and the Limits of Justice* (Cambridge: Cambridge University Press, 1982), 179.

36. In *Democracy's Discontent* (Cambridge, Mass.: Belknap Press, 1998), Sandel details how in twentieth-century America the mechanisms of the procedural republic have supplanted the formative project of civic republicanism. Excessive reliance on such procedures serves to further fragment society and dislocate individuals, thus fomenting conflict and increasing our dependence on procedures. *Democracy's Discontent* has the virtue of putting constitutional and legal matters at the forefront of the discussion of justice and in this way suggesting that character cannot do the political work so neglected in some circles of virtue ethics. Alas, this book has been much less influential than *Liberalism and the Limits of Justice*.

37. Annette Baier, "What Do Women Want in a Moral Theory?" in *Virtue Ethics*, ed. Crisp and Slote (Oxford: Oxford University Press, 1997), 270.

38. Ibid., 267.

39. Ibid., 272.

40. Ibid., 274.

41. Annette Baier, "The Need for More than Justice," in *Justice and Care: Essential Readings in Feminist Ethics*, ed. Virginia Held (Boulder, Colo.: Westview Press, 1995), 48, 52, and 55.

42. Eleonore Stump, "Aquinas on Justice," in *PACPA* 71 (1997): 61–78. Perhaps Baier is not open to this charge, since she is careful to state that the notion of trust, for example, must be balanced by a notion of appropriate distrust (see "What Do Women Want in a Moral Theory?"). Still, the silence on justice is striking.

43. In one essay, MacIntyre singles out an unlikely virtue for comparative analysis, *sophrosyne*, or temperance. See "Sophrosune: How a Virtue Can Become Socially Disruptive," in *Midwest Studies in Philosophy*, Vol. 13, *Ethical Theory: Character and Virtue* (Notre Dame, Ind.: University of Notre Dame Press, 1988), 1–11.

44. Robert Louden, "On Some Vices of Virtue Ethics" in *Virtue Ethics*, 204.

45. Ibid., 207. Attentive readers will hear in this passage echoes of (the pre-Thomistic) MacIntyre's insistence that a list of virtues needs to be paired with a list of actions never admitting of a mean (*After Virtue*). But Louden fails to articulate the complementarity of virtues and rules in MacIntyre's Aristotelian language; instead, Louden appeals to Frankena's thesis that "the Greeks held that being virtuous entails not just having good motives or intentions but also doing the right thing." Since the Greeks do not have a lot to say about motives or intentions, at least not in the modern senses of these terms, Frankena's claim needs to be reformulated in less historically objectionable language. Indeed, what is most problematic is his imputation of a good/ right split to Greek ethics. We might more accurately say that for Aristotle an act is good only if it is good in every respect. More broadly, for Aristotle being virtuous is a matter of having a certain kind of character, spelled out in terms of possessing a set of virtues. A virtue is a habit standing midway between potency and act, or more precisely, a potency that is oriented in a determinate way. But such a habit exists in order that it may be actualized. This accords with Aristotle's doctrine of *energeia*, wherein capacities are ordered to activities (cf. *Metaphysics* VII).

46. Obviously a host of difficulties need to be addressed here. The same act can at least superficially be performed by a virtuous and a non-virtuous agent. A virtuous person can retain a noble character even when she is impeded from realizing virtuous actions. I suspect, although I cannot demonstrate it, that one of the reasons virtue ethicists resist an act-oriented approach to virtue is that this seems to give too much ground to rival contemporary theories. It might also appear that we are shifting the accent from being to doing in the sense of producing effects in the external world. But this fails to distinguish between doing as acting and doing as making, the former of which is an immanent perfection or actuality, while the perfection of the latter is transitive, passing into the thing made.

47. *ST* II–II, 58, 10: Aliae virtutes morales consistunt principaliter circa passiones, quarum rectificatio non attenditur nisi secundum comparationem ad ipsum hominem cuius sunt passiones, secundum scilicet quod irascitur et concupiscit prout debet secundum diversas circumstantias. Et ideo medium talium virtutum non accipitur secundum proportionem unius rei ad alteram, sed solum secundum comparationem ad ipsum virtuosum. Et propter hoc in ipsis est medium solum secundum rationem quoad nos. Sed materia iustitiae est exterior operatio secundum quod ipsa, vel res cuius est

usus, debitam proportionem habet ad aliam personam. Et ideo medium iustitiae consistit in quadam proportionis aequalitate rei exterioris ad personam exteriorem.

48. *ST* II–II, 57, 1: Iustitiae proprium est inter alias virtutes ut ordinet hominem in his quae sunt ad alterum. Importat enim aequalitatem quandam, ut ipsum nomen demonstrat, dicuntur enim vulgariter ea quae adaequantur iustari. Aequalitas autem ad alterum est. Aliae autem virtutes perficiunt hominem solum in his quae ei conveniunt secundum seipsum. Sic igitur illud quod est rectum in operibus aliarum virtutum, ad quod tendit intentio virtutis quasi in proprium obiectum, non accipitur nisi per comparationem ad agentem. Rectum vero quod est in opere iustitiae, etiam praeter comparationem ad agentem, constituitur per comparationem ad alium.

49. *ST* II–II, 58, 2: Sed contra est quod Tullius dicit, in I de Offic., quod *iustitiae ea ratio est qua societas hominum inter ipsos, et vitae communitas continetur.* Sed hoc importat respectum ad alterum. Ergo iustitia est solum circa ea quae sunt ad alterum.

50. Finnis, *Aquinas: Moral, Political, and Legal Theory,* 118.

51. *ST* II–II, 47, 10: Sicut philosophus dicit, in VI Ethic., quidam posuerunt quod prudentia non se extendit ad bonum commune, sed solum ad bonum proprium. Et hoc ideo quia existimabant quod non oportet hominem quaerere nisi bonum proprium. Sed haec aestimatio repugnat caritati, quae non quaerit quae sua sunt, ut dicitur I ad Cor. XIII. Unde et apostolus de seipso dicit, I ad Cor. X, *non quaerens quod mihi utile sit, sed quod multis, ut salvi fiant* . Repugnat etiam rationi rectae, quae hoc iudicat, quod bonum commune sit melius quam bonum unius. Quia igitur ad prudentiam pertinet recte consiliari, iudicare et praecipere de his per quae pervenitur ad debitum finem, manifestum est quod prudentia non solum se habet ad bonum privatum unius hominis, sed etiam ad bonum commune multitudinis.

52. *ST* II–II, 78, 1, ad 2: Omnem hominem habere quasi proximum et fratrem.

53. *Super I Epistolam B. Pauli ad Timotheum lectura* (Turin, 1953). In *I Tim.* I, 2: per omnes actus virtutum ordinatur homo unus ad alium.

54. *ST* II–II, 58, 1: Iustitia est constans et perpetua voluntas ius suum unicuique tribuens.

55. *ST* II–II, 57, 1: Sic igitur iustum dicitur aliquid, quasi habens rectitudinem iustitiae, ad quod terminatur actio iustitiae, etiam non considerato qualiter ab agente fiat. Sed in aliis virtutibus non determinatur aliquid rectum nisi secundum quod aliqualiter fit ab agente.

56. *ST* II–II, 66, 1: Respondeo dicendum quod res exterior potest dupliciter considerari. Uno modo, quantum ad eius naturam, quae non subiacet humanae potestati, sed solum divinae, cui omnia ad nutum obediunt. Alio modo, quantum ad usum ipsius rei. Et sic habet homo naturale dominium exteriorum rerum, quia per rationem et voluntatem potest uti rebus exterioribus ad suam utilitatem, quasi propter se factis; semper enim imperfectiora sunt propter perfectiora, ut supra habitum est. Et ex hac ratione philosophus probat, in I Polit., quod possessio rerum exteriorum est homini naturalis. Hoc autem naturale dominium super ceteras creaturas, quod competit homini secundum rationem, in qua imago Dei consistit, manifestatur in ipsa hominis creatione, Gen. I, ubi dicitur, faciamus hominem ad similitudinem et imaginem nostram, et praesit piscibus maris, et cetera.

57. *ST* II–II, 66, 7: Secundum autem naturalem ordinem ex divina providentia institutum, res inferiores sunt ordinatae ad hoc quod ex his subveniatur hominum necessitati. Et ideo per rerum divisionem et appropriationem, de iure humano procedentem, non impeditur quin hominis necessitati sit subveniendum ex huiusmodi

rebus. Et ideo res quas aliqui superabundanter habent, ex naturali iure debentur pauperum sustentationi. Unde Ambrosius dicit, et habetur in decretis, dist. XLVII, *esurientium panis est quem tu detines; nudorum indumentum est quod tu recludis; miserorum redemptio et absolutio est pecunia quam tu in terram defodis* . Sed quia multi sunt necessitatem patientes, et non potest ex eadem re omnibus subveniri, committitur arbitrio uniuscuiusque dispensatio propriarum rerum, ut ex eis subveniat necessitatem patientibus. Si tamen adeo sit urgens et evidens necessitas ut manifestum sit instanti necessitati de rebus occurrentibus esse subveniendum, puta cum imminet personae periculum et aliter subveniri non potest; tunc licite potest aliquis ex rebus alienis suae necessitati subvenire, sive manifeste sive occulte sublatis. Nec hoc proprie habet rationem furti vel rapinae.

58. Jerome Schneewind, "The Misfortunes of Virtue," in *Virtue Ethics*, 200.

59. *ST* II–II, 114, 2, ad 3.

60. *ST* II–II, 114, 1, ad 2.

61. Pieper, *Four Cardinal Virtues*, 21.

62. MacIntyre, *Dependent Rational Animals*, 119. For an account of self and other that avoids MacIntyre's objections, see Paul Ricoeur, *Oneself as Another*, trans. Kathleen Blamey (Chicago: University of Chicago Press, 1992).

63. *ST* II–II, 117, 1.

64. *ST* II–II, 30, 3.

65. *ST* II–II, 30, 2: Quia enim amans reputat amicum tanquam seipsum, malum ipsius reputat tanquam suum malum, et ideo dolet de malo amici sicut de suo. Et inde est quod philosophus, in IX Ethic., inter alia amicabilia ponit hoc quod est condolere amico. Et apostolus dicit, ad Rom. XII, *gaudere cum gaudentibus, flere cum flentibus.*

66. *ST* II–II, 30, 2, ad 3: Superbi non miserentur, qui contemnunt alios et reputant eos malos. Unde reputant quod digne patiantur quidquid patiuntur. Unde et Gregorius dicit quod falsa iustitia, scilicet superborum, non habet compassionem, sed dedignationem.

67. MacIntyre, *Dependent Rational Animals*, x.

68. Ibid., 125.

69. Ibid., 138.

70. Ibid., 146.

71. Ibid., 150.

72. Pieper, *Four Cardinal Virtues*, 111.

73. Aquinas's ethical thought transcends not only these divisions but also contemporary divisions between law and virtue. Indeed, in the current philosophical climate, to call Aquinas a virtue ethicist is likely to be as misleading as calling him a theorist of law.

74. Murdoch, *Existentialists and Mystics*, 65.

75. Clarke, *The One and the Many*, 33.

76. *ST* I–II, 91, 2: Lex naturalis nihil aliud est quam participatio legis aeternae in rationali creatura.

77. *ST* I–II, 91, 1, ad 2: Promulgatio fit et verbo et scripto; et utroque modo lex aeterna habet promulgationem ex parte Dei promulgantis, quia et verbum divinum est aeternum, et Scriptura libri vitae est aeterna. Sed ex parte creaturae audientis aut inspicientis, non potest esse promulgatio aeterna.

3. SELF-IMPLICATING KNOWLEDGE

1. *ST* I–II, q. 57, a. 1: Quod utatur scientia habita, hoc est movente voluntate: et ideo virtus quae perficit voluntatem, ut charitas vel justitia, facit etiam bene uti huiusmodi speculativis habitibus.

2. On the virtue epistemology view, our cognitive life is intimately informed, both for good and for ill, by our emotions and passions, by the presence or absence of moral virtue. In the virtues of intellectual inquiry, it is impossible to sever the moral from the cognitive, the intellectual from the bodily or the passionate. In the most detailed contemporary discussion of virtue epistemology, *Virtues of the Mind: An Inquiry into the Nature of Virtue and the Ethical Foundations of Knowledge* (Cambridge: Cambridge University Press, 1996), Linda Zagzebski draws upon Aristotelian *phronesis*, but she might as well have drawn upon Pascal's account of *finesse*, a capacity that involves a discriminating vision of complex, concrete circumstances, of a host of data, organized not according to a deductive, rule-governed model, but seen "at a glance." As Martin Warner has shown in *Philosophical Finesee: Studies in the Art of Rational Persuasion* (Oxford: Oxford University Press, 1989), Pascal's account of *finesse* as complementary to, but more fundamental than, geometrical reasoning, invokes the dominant premodern account of human knowing.

3. Alvin Plantinga, *Warrant: The Current Debate* (Oxford: Oxford University Press: 1993), 11.

4. The terminology is of relatively recent origin. See William Alston, "Internalism and Externalism in Epistemology," *Philosophical Topics* 15 (1986): 179–221; and Alvin Goldman, "The Internalist Conception of Justification," *Midwest Studies in Philosophy* 5 (1980): 27–73.

5. There are stronger and weaker versions of both internalism and externalism. For a discussion of these variations, see John Greco, "Catholics vs. Calvinists on Religious Knowledge," *American Catholic Philosophical Quarterly* 71 (1997): 13–34.

6. For a comparison of contemporary ethical and epistemological theories and a defense of virtue epistemology, see Zagzebski, *Virtues of the Mind.*

7. What we lack are detailed historical studies. For a conspicuous and instructive exception, see Nicholas Wolterstorff, *John Locke and the Ethics of Belief* (Cambridge: Cambridge University Press, 1996).

8. Greco, "Catholics vs. Calvinists," 15.

9. Scott MacDonald, "Theory of Knowledge," in *The Cambridge Companion to Aquinas* (Cambridge: Cambridge University Press, 1993), 160–95.

10. Ibid., 174–78 and 185–88.

11. MacDonald does not cite the very fruitful literature on the relationship between the *Analytics* and the treatises, or on the supple and variegated meanings of *nous* in Aristotle's corpus. The work of Jonathan Barnes has of course been hugely influential; see especially "Aristotle's Theory of Demonstration," *Phronesis* 14 (1969): 123–52; and "Proof and Syllogism," in *Aristotle on Science: The Posterior Analytics* (Padua: Editrice Antenore, 1981), 17–59. One should also consult James Lesher, "The Meaning of NOUS in the Posterior Analytics," *Phronesis* 18 (1973): 44–68; and William Wians, "Aristotle, Demonstration, and Teaching," *Ancient Philosophy* 9 (1989): 245–53.

12. Aquinas, *Expositio libri Perhermeneias* (Turin, 1955), hereafter *In Peri Hermeneias.* See *In Peri Hermeneias*, 1.1.18.154: Communia principia accipiuntur in un-

aquaque scientia demonstrativa secundum analogiam, id est secundum quod sunt propotionata illi scientiae.

13. Aristotle, *De Anima* 1.1.402a10–25.

14. Aquinas, *Sententia Libri Ethicorum Leoninum* (Rome, 1969), hereafter *In Eth.* See *In Eth.* 1.1.3.62: Modus manifestandi veritatem in qualibet scientia, debet esse conveniens ei quod subiicitur sicut materia in ilia scientia . . . certitudo non potest inveniri, nec est requirenda similiter in omnibus sermonibus.

15. Descartes, *Rules for the Direction of the Mind*. See Rules 1 and 2 and throughout. The same aspiration and standard can be found in parts 1 and 2 of the *Discourse on Method*. Both works can be found in *Descartes: Philosophical Essays*, trans. Laurence Lafleur (Indianapolis: Bobbs-Merrill, 1964). On the shift from an analogical conception of language to an univocal one and from a plurality of methods to homogeneity, see Amos Funkenstein, *Theology and the Scientific Imagination* (Princeton, N.J.: Princeton University Press, 1986), 50–72.

16. MacDonald, "Theory of Knowledge," 187.

17. Ibid., 185–88.

18. Greco, "Catholics vs. Calvinists on Religious Knowledge," 33.

19. MacDonald, "Theory of Knowledge," 186–87.

20. For a response to MacDonald and a reading of Aquinas as an externalist, see Jenkins, *Knowledge and Faith in Thomas Aquinas*.

21. Since proper function is not to be equated with a statistical conception of what happens most of the time, but with a normative conception, we shall need an understanding of the design plan for our cognitive activities. But it seems reasonable to suppose that a design plan will aim at all sorts of things, not just at the production of truth; hence, we must specify that the "segment of the design plan governing the production of that belief is aimed at the production of truth" (Plantinga, *Warrant and Proper Function*, 46–47).

22. Zagzebski, *Virtues of the Mind*, 13.

23. John Henry Newman, *The Idea of a University* (Notre Dame, Ind.: University of Notre Dame Press, 1982), 114–15.

24. See Warner, *Philosophical Finesse: Studies in the Art of Rational Persuasion*.

25. Blaise Pascal, *Pensées*, trans. A. J. Krailsheimer (London: Penguin Books, 1966), fragment #257.

26. Pascal, *Pensées*, #512.

27. Hans Georg Gadamer, *Truth and Method*, trans. Garrett Barden and John Cumming (New York: Seabury Press, 1975), 367.

28. Ibid., 367.

29. Ibid., 379.

30. Clarke, *The One and the Many*, 39–40.

31. Philipp Rosemann, *Understanding Scholastic Thought with Foucault* (New York: St. Martin's Press, 1999), 85.

32. *ST* I–IIae, q. 57, a. 2: Virtus intellectualis speculativa est per quam intellectus speculativus perficitur ad considerandum verum, hoc enim est bonum opus eius. Verum autem est dupliciter considerabile, uno modo, sicut per se notum; alio modo, sicut per aliud notum. Quod autem est per se notum, se habet ut principium; et percipitur statim ab intellectu. Et ideo habitus perficiens intellectum ad huiusmodi veri considerationem, vocatur intellectus, qui est habitus principiorum. Verum autem

quod est per aliud notum, non statim percipitur ab intellectu, sed per inquisitionem rationis, et se habet in ratione termini.

33. Cornelio Fabro, "The Transcendality of Ens-Esse and the Ground of Meta-physics," *International Philosophical Quarterly* 6 (1966): 389–427.

34. For Descartes, see *Meditation* III, trans. Donald Cress (Indianapolis: Hackett Publishing, 1993); for Aquinas, see *ST* I, q. 2, a. 1. This is the basis of his repudiation of the claim that the existence of God is self-evident to us: Dico ergo quod haec propositio, Deus est, quantum in se est, per se nota est, quia praedicatum est idem cum subiecto; Deus enim est suum esse, ut infra patebit. Sed quia nos non scimus de Deo quid est, non est nobis per se nota, sed indiget demonstrari per ea quae sunt magis nota quoad nos, et minus nota quoad naturam, scilicet per effectus.

35. *ST* I q. 1, a. 1: Quia veritas de Deo, per rationem investigata, a paucis, et per longum tempus, et cum admixtione multorum errorum, homini proveniret, a cuius tamen veritatis cognitione dependet tota hominis salus, quae in Deo est. Ut igitur salus hominibus et convenientius et certius proveniat, necessarium fuit quod de divinis per divinam revelationem instruantur. Necessarium igitur fuit, praeter philosophicas disci-plinas, quae per rationem investigantur, sacram doctrinam per revelationem haberi.

36. As we shall see in the next chapter, Aquinas's dismissal is akin to John McDow-ell's recent argument that the skeptical challenge presupposes an impossible point of view, a "sideways-on view" of the world and its relationship to our minds, a view that falsely supposes that we could prescind from our immersion in the world. See McDow-ell, *Mind and World* (Cambridge, Mass.: Harvard University Press, 1994), 34. From a Thomistic standpoint, McDowell's attempt to dissolve the dichotomy between the conceptual and the real fails to escape idealism. Of course, the rejoinder is that Thomas and Aristotle are part of an antiquated and misleading epistemological project. They are often identified as sources of "mental representationalism," the view that the immedi-ate objects of knowledge are internal entities. For a recent attempt to pin this tag on Aquinas, see Robert Pasnau, *Theories of Cognition in the Later Middle Ages* (Cam-bridge: Cambridge University Press, 1997), 11–27, 195–219, and 256–70. A corrective to such contemporary readings of Aristotle and Aquinas can be had in John P. O'Callaghan, "The Problem of Language and Mental Representation in Aristotle and St. Thomas," *Review of Metaphysics* 50 (1997): 499–541.

37. Nicholas Wolterstorff, *Thomas Reid and the Story of Epistemology* (Cam-bridge: Cambridge University Press, 2004).

38. Reid, as quoted in Wolterstorff, 180.

39. On this issue, see Ralph McInerny, "Thomas Reid and Common Sense," in an *American Catholic Philosophical Quarterly* volume devoted to Thomas Reid and edited by John Haldane, volume 74 (2000). Also see John Haldane, "Reid, Scholasticism and Current Philosophy of Mind," in *The Philosophy of Thomas Reid*, ed. M. Dalgarno and E. Matthews (Dordrecht: Kluwer, 1989). One sign that Plantinga's approach has missed something in the tradition of Aquinas is that, at the end of two volumes on the proper functioning of human cognition, he seeks to deploy the link between function-ing and design to argue that epistemological naturalism is most at home in the context of metaphysical supernaturalism. That is, we cannot explain proper function without reference to design and, in turn, to the author of that design. By way of conclusion, he cites Thomas's fifth way of proving the existence of God. Yet the fifth way refers exclu-sively to the purposive action of subrational creatures, creatures whose directedness cannot be explained by conscious self-direction.

40. Sarah Broadie, *Ethics with Aristotle* (New York: Oxford University Press, 1991), 84; quoted in Zagzebski, *Virtues of the Mind*, 321–22.

41. Although Plantinga does not develop his own theory in terms of the virtues, his moderate or weak externalism does not rule out the presence of internalist elements and thus could be developed in the direction taken by Zagzebski. To see that this is possible, it might help to consider Plantinga's position on cognitive voluntarism. Given the internalist emphasis on the careful monitoring of the grounds of one's beliefs, there is often a close connection between it and voluntarism with respect to belief. Externalism, by contrast, tends to eschew the possibility of our having complete control over our beliefs. While Plantinga thinks that we very often simply find ourselves having beliefs over which we have little or no control, he admits that we have some control, at least of an indirect sort, over our beliefs: "It is within my power to adopt policies that influence and modify my propensities to believe. I can adopt such policies as paying careful attention to the evidence, avoiding wishful thinking, being aware of such sources of belief as jealousy, lust, contrariety, excessive optimism, loyalty, and the like."

42. Zagzebski, *Virtues of the Mind*, 333.

43. See *ST* I–IIae, q. 58, a. 5.

44. *ST* II–IIae, q. 1, a. 4: Fides importat assensum intellectus ad id quod creditur. Assentit autem alicui intellectus dupliciter. Uno modo, quia ad hoc movetur ab ipso obiecto, quod est vel per seipsum cognitum, sicut patet in principiis primis, quorum est intellectus; vel est per aliud cognitum, sicut patet de conclusionibus, quarum est scientia. Alio modo intellectus assentit alicui non quia sufficienter moveatur ab obiecto proprio, sed per quandam electionem voluntarie declinans in unam partem magis quam in aliam. Et si quidem hoc fit cum dubitatione et formidine alterius partis, erit opinio, si autem fit cum certitudine absque tali formidine, erit fides.

45. *ST* I–IIae, q. 57, a. 3: Dummodo enim verum geometra demonstret, non refert qualiter se habeat secundum appetitivam pattern, utrum sit laetus vel flatus, sicut nec in artifice refert.

46. Ralph McInerny, *Characters in Search of Their Author: The Gifford Lectures Glasgow 1999–2000* (South Bend, Ind.: University of Notre Dame Press, 2003), 106.

47. John Henry Newman, *An Essay in Aid of a Grammar of Assent* (Notre Dame, Ind.: University of Notre Dame Press, 1979), 281.

48. Ibid.

49. Newman, *The Idea of a University*, 91.

50. Attention to *The Idea of a University* would aid McInerny's attempt to find common ground between Newman and Aquinas (*Characters in Search of Their Author*, 100–108), even as it would complicate Joseph Dunne's attempt to align Newman with Thomas Kuhn (*Back to the Rough Ground*, 31–54). But what about McInerny's claim that Newman has confused the truth of what is with truth that corresponds to virtuous appetite? Newman does not clearly argue in *Grammar of Assent* for the expansion of *phronesis as understand by Aristotle*. As McInerny notes, Aristotle thinks that practical wisdom is impossible apart from rightly ordered desire, which occurs through the moral virtues; prudence and the moral virtues are inseparable. Now, Newman explicitly rejects the unity of the virtues thesis; with respect to the moral virtues, this dissociation of one virtue from another is clearly at odds with Aristotle and Aquinas. With respect to the speculative intellectual virtues, however, Aquinas notes that, because the subject matters of different disciplines are diverse in their modes of procedure, one can excel in one without excelling in another. Newman observes that an individual may "possess it

in one department of thought, for instance, history and not in another, for instance, philosophy." For anyone who has spent any time among academics from a variety of disciplines, this claim will seem unimpeachable. This is not to say, however, that Newman opts for narrow specialization. This is another way in which attention to *The Idea of a University* provides a more complex and richer picture of Newman's position, since in that book he argues for a kind of intellectual virtue, the fruit of truly liberal education, that affords a vision of the interconnections among the various fields of inquiry.

51. This quick discussion of Newman is not intended to resolve all points of disagreement with Aristotle and Aquinas; indeed, Newman repudiates Aristotle's thesis concerning the unity of the moral virtues. The point, rather, is to suggest that Newman is an important resource for the development of the notion of intellectual virtue, particularly concerning the virtues involved in the discovery of knowledge

52. Thomas's position does not exclude the role of what Yves Simon calls intellectual inclination in the discovery of knowledge. See Simon, *The Tradition of Natural Law* (New York: Fordham University Press, 1992), 130. Nor does it deny that character traits like temperance and courage may play a dispositive role in the pursuit of knowledge.

53. *ST* II–IIa, q. 1, a. 4, ad 3: Sicut enim per alios habitus virtutum homo videt illud quod est sibi conveniens secundum habitum ilium; it etiam per habitum fidei inclinatur mens hominis ad assentiendum his quae conveniunt rectae fidei.

54. The kind of perception and the sorts of intellectual inquiry operative in these cases would, as Zagzebski urges, be hard to classify as exclusively practical or exclusively theoretical. We could do so only by determining the final end intended for a specific set of actions or investigations.

55. The revival of virtue is intimately allied to an attack on Kantian conceptions of obligation and an attempt to find alternative conceptions. For an early attack, see Elizabeth Anscombe's "Modern Moral Philosophy." Some philosophers have wanted to construe obligations in terms of hypothetical imperatives; see, for example, Philippa Foot, "Morality as a System of Hypothetical Imperatives," in *Virtues and Vices*; and Bernard Williams, "Internal and External Reasons for Action," in *Moral Luck* (Cambridge: Cambridge University Press, 1981), 101–13. For worries about whether Williams's distinction between internal and external reasons is adequate, see Alasdair MacIntyre, "The Magic in the Pronoun 'My,'" *Ethics* 94 (1983): 113–25. MacIntyre points us in the direction of an "ought" that reduces neither to the categorical nor to the hypothetical imperative of Kant. For a more recent attempt to derive obligations from an aretaic or virtue-based theory, see Michael Slote, *From Morality to Virtue*. By far the best discussion of freedom as understood in the tradition of Aristotle and Aquinas is Yves Simon's *Freedom of Choice* (New York: Fordham University Press, 1969).

56. On this, Plantinga would seem to concur. He writes, "No brief and simple, semialgorithmic account of warrant carries much by way of illumination. Our epistemic establishment of noetic faculties or powers is complex and highly articulated; it is detailed and many-sided. There is knowledge of . . . an astonishingly wide variety of topics. . . . These faculties work with exquisite subtlety and discrimination, producing beliefs . . . that vary all the way from the merest suspicion to absolute dead certainty. And once we see the enormous extent of this articulation and subtlety, we can also see that warrant has different requirements in different divisions . . . of that establishment; perhaps in some of these areas internalist constraints are indeed necessary for warrant" (*Warrant: The Current Debate*, 184).

The complexity of our noetic activity means that we cannot have a univocal conception of knowledge or warrant. Plantinga cites Aristotle's counsel that we should "not expect more clarity than the subject permits" and argues that the topic of warrant is not best handled by "producing a set of severally necessary and jointly sufficient conditions." Instead, we have "paradigm" cases of knowledge to which other cases are "related by way of analogy and similarity," 212–13. This approach defends proper function against the typical analytic assault by counterexample, since we shall now have to determine whether the counterexample applies to the central or to the penumbral cases.

57. *ST* I–II, q. 57, a. 5: Prudentia est virtus maxime necessaria ad vitam humanam. Bene enim vivere consistit in bene operari. Ad hoc autem quod aliquis bene operetur, non solum requiritur quid faciat, sed etiam quomodo faciat.

58. *ST* I–II, q. 57, a. 1: Quod utatur scientia habita, hoc est movente voluntate: et ideo virtus quae perficit voluntatem, ut charitas vel justitia, facit etiam bene uti huiusmodi speculativis habitibus.

59. *ST* II–IIae, q. 166, a. 2, ad 2: Actus cognoscitivae virtutis imperatur a vi appetitiva, quae est motiva omnium virium, ut supra habitum est. Et ideo circa cognitionem duplex bonum potest attendi. Unum quidem, quantum ad ipsum actum cognitionis. Et tale bonum pertinet ad virtutes intellectuales, ut scilicet homo circa singula aestimet verum. Aliud autem est bonum quod pertinet ad actum appetitivae virtutis, ut scilicet homo habeat appetitum rectum applicandi vim cognoscitivam sic vel aliter, ad hoc vel ad illud. Et hoc pertinet ad virtutem studiositatis. Unde computatur inter virtutes morales.

60. Pieper, *Four Cardinal Virtues*, 186.

61. Ibid., 200–201.

62. Ibid., 201.

63. Ibid., 198.

64. Ibid., 187.

65. Pieper, *Faith Hope Love*, 59–60.

66. *ST* II–IIae, q. 109, a. 1 ad 2: Ex parte autem actus medium tenet, inquantum verum dicit quando oportet, et secundum quod oportet. In the body of the article, Aquinas explains, Alio modo potest dici veritas qua aliquis verum dicit, secundum quod per eam aliquis dicitur verax. Et talis veritas, sive veracitas, necesse est quod sit virtus, quia hoc ipsum quod est dicere verum est bonus actus; virtus autem est quae bonum facit habentem, et opus eius bonum reddit.

67. *ST* II–IIae, q. 109, a. 2.

68. *ST* II–II, q. 109, a. 3, ad 1: Quia homo est animal sociale, naturaliter unus homo debet alteri id sine quo societas humana servari non posset. Non autem possent homines ad invicem crederent, tamquam sibi invicem vertitatem manifestantibus.

69. *ST* II–IIae, q. 109, a. 3, ad 3: Veritas qua aliquis et vita et sermone talem se demonstrat, qualis est.

70. Zagzebski, *Virtues of the Mind*, 148.

71. Ibid., 197.

72. The view of the theoretical virtues as ordered to knowing necessary and universal truths sees the mind as informed and determined by the object, indeed, by a hierarchy of objects of knowledge. This does not mean that the mind contributes nothing to the object, since the intellectual power of abstracting universal natures contributes universality to the object of knowledge, but the intellect does not contribute

content. See Aquinas, *Expostitio super librum Boethii De Trinitate* (Leiden, 1955), hereafter *Super De Trinitate*. See *Super De Trinitate*, qq. 5 and 6. The apprehension of the universal is always an apprehension of the nature of sensible singulars. See *ST* I, q. 84, aa. 6–7 and q. 85, a. 2.

73. Aquinas, *In Met.*, proemium.

74. Zagzebski, *Virtues of the Mind*, 316.

75. In a footnote, Plantinga notes the "intimate connection between epistemology and metaphysics." What "you take to be properly basic will depend, in part, upon what sort of creatures you think human beings are" (*Warrant and Proper Function*, 183 n. 9).

76. Josef Pieper, *Leisure, the Basis of Culture*, trans. Alexander Dru (New York: Pantheon Books, 1964), 110, 118.

4. Dependent Animal Rationality

1. John McDowell, *Mind and World* (Cambridge, Mass.: Harvard University Press, 1996). For a variety of responses to McDowell's book, see *Reading Mind and World*, ed. Nicholas Smith (Routledge, 2002).

2. McDowell, *Mind and World*, 8.

3. Ibid., 34.

4. Ibid., 46.

5. Ibid., 9.

6. Ibid., 15.

7. Ibid., 9.

8. Ibid., 19.

9. Peter Geach, *Mental Acts* (London: Routledge and Kegan Paul, 1957), 18.

10. Aristotle, *De Anima*, 412b8–9.

11. Aquinas, *Sentencia Libri De anima* (Turin, 1959), hereafter *In De Anima*. See *In De Anima* II, lc. 1, note 234: Forma per se unitur materiae, sicut actus eius; et idem est materiam uniri formae, quod materiam esse in actu.

12. Aquinas, *In Met.*, I, lc. 1, 15: Experimentum enim est ex collatione plurium singularium in memoria receptorum. Huiusmodi autem collatio est homini propria, et pertinet ad vim cogitativam, quae ratio particularis dicitur: quae est collativa intentionum individualium, sicut ratio universalis intentionum universalium.

13. Gadamer, *Truth and Method*, 90.

14. John O'Callaghan, *Thomistic Realism and the Linguistic Turn: Toward a More Perfect Form of Existence* (Notre Dame, Ind.: University of Notre Dame Press, 2003), 221.

15. *ST*, I, 85, 3: Omne autem quod procedit de potentia in actum, prius pervenit ad actum incompletum, qui est medius inter potentiam et actum, quam ad actum perfectum. Actus autem perfectus ad quem pervenit intellectus, est scientia completa, per quam distincte et determinate res cognoscuntur. Actus autem incompletus est scientia imperfecta, per quam sciuntur res indistincte sub quadam confusione, quod enim sic cognoscitur, secundum quid cognoscitur in actu, et quodammodo in potentia. Unde philosophus dicit, in I Physic., quod *sunt primo nobis manifesta et certa confusa magis; posterius autem cognoscimus distinguendo distincte principia et elementa*.

16. *ST*, I, 85, 3.

17. O'Callaghan, *Thomistic Realism*, 222.

18. McDowell, *Mind and World*, 9.

19. Ibid., 26.

20. Ibid., 32.

21. Ibid., 25 and 28.

22. Ibid., 39.

23. Aquinas, *Commentaria in octo libros Physicorum* (Turin, 1954), hereafter *In Phys*. See *In Phys*, III, lc. 5.

24. *In De Anima*, II, lc. 11: Alio modo passio communiter dicitur et minus proprie, secundum scilicet quod importat quamdam receptionem. Et quia quod est receptivum alterius, comparatur ad ipsum sicut potentia ad actum: actus autem est perfectio potentiae; et ideo hoc modo dicitur passio, non secundum quod fit quaedam corruptio patientis, sed magis secundum quod fit quaedam salus et perfectio eius quod est in potentia, ab eo quod est in actu. Quod enim est in potentia, non perficitur nisi per id quod est in actu. Quod autem in actu est, non est contrarium ei quod est in potentia, inquantum huiusmodi, sed magis simile: nam potentia nihil aliud est quam quidam ordo ad actum. Nisi autem esset aliqua similitudo inter potentiam et actum, non esset necessarium quod proprius actus fieret in propria potentia. Potentia igitur sic dicta, non est a contrario, sicut potentia primo modo dicta; sed est a simili, eo modo quo potentia se habet secundum similitudinem ad actum.

25. *In De Anima*, II, lc. 11.

26. McDowell, *Mind and World*, 41.

27. Thomas was aware of something like this position in the Averroistic account of knowing, some version of which was adopted by Albert the Great. In "St. Thomas, St. Albert, and Knowledge," *ACPQ* 70 (1996): 121–25, Lawrence Dewan contrasts Thomas and Albert in this way: "The thing-oriented nature of knowledge, and the way this raises the issue of the mode of our knowing, is paramount for St. Thomas. Albert, in contrast, takes as the focal-point of discussion the union of knower and known. The result seems to be to attribute to intellect itself a 'visibility' of a sort it never acquires in St. Thomas" (135).

28. Norris Clarke, *Explorations in Metaphysics* (Notre Dame, Ind.: University of Notre Dame Press, 1995), 11 and 55.

29. Ibid., 11 and 55.

30. Ibid., 59.

31. McDowell, *Mind and World*, 27.

32. Ibid., 44.

33. Aquinas, *Quaestiones disputatae de veritate* (Roma, 1970), hereafter *De veritate*. See *De veritate* I, 4, 2, ad 3: Conceptio intellectus est media inter intellectum et rem intellectam, quia ea mediante operatio intellectus pertingit ad rem. Et ideo conceptio intellectus non solum est id quod intellectum est, sed etiam id quo res intelligitur; ut sic id quod intelligitur, possit dici et res ipsa, et conceptio intellectus; et similiter id quod dicitur, potest dici et res quae dicitur per verbum, et verbum ipsum; ut etiam in verbo exteriori patet; quia et ipsum nomen dicitur, et res significata per nomen dicitur ipso nomine.

34. On this, see Robert Sokolowski, "Exorcising Concepts," *Review of Metaphysics* 40 (1987). For a view that the history of philosophy, from Aristotle on, is in the grips of mental representationalism, see Hilary Putnam, *Representation and Reality* (Cambridge, Mass.: MIT Press, 1988), 19.

35. *ST* I, 84, 7: Unde natura lapidis, vel cuiuscumque materialis rei, cognosci non potest complete et vere, nisi secundum quod cognoscitur ut in particulari existens. Particulare autem apprehendimus per sensum et imaginationem. Et ideo necesse est ad

hoc quod intellectus actu intelligat suum obiectum proprium, quod convertat se ad phantasmata, ut speculetur naturam universalem in particulari existentem. Si autem proprium obiectum intellectus nostri esset forma separata; vel si naturae rerum sensibilium subsisterent non in particularibus, secundum Platonicos; non oporteret quod intellectus noster semper intelligendo converteret se ad phantasmata.

36. Frederick Wilhelmsen, *Man's Knowledge of Reality* (Englewood Cliffs, N.J.: Prentice-Hall, 1960), 127.

37. McDowell, *Mind and World*, 25, 34, 31.

38. Ibid., 101–102.

39. O'Callaghan, *Thomistic Realism and the Linguistic Turn*, 227.

40. Frederick Wilhelmsen, "The 'I' and Aquinas," *PACPA* (1977): 47–55.

41. Ibid., 50.

42. Wilhelmsen adds later that one's sense of ego in the larger sense of myself, or "mineness" has to do with one's history and my relationships to others. For a development of this conception of the self, see Alasdair MacIntyre, "The Intelligibility of Action," in *Rationality, Relativism, and the Human Sciences*, ed. Margolis, Krausz, and Burian (Dordrecht: Martinus Nijhoff, 1986).

43. Willhelmsen, "The 'I' and Aquinas," 55, n. 23.

44. *ST* I, 87, 1: Quia connaturale est intellectui nostro, secundum statum praesentis vitae, quod ad materialia et sensibilia respiciat, sicut supra dictum est; consequens est ut sic seipsum intelligat intellectus noster, secundum quod fit actu per species a sensibilibus abstractas per lumen intellectus agentis, quod est actus ipsorum intelligibilium, et eis mediantibus intellectus possibilis. Non ergo per essentiam suam, sed per actum suum se cognoscit intellectus noster. Et hoc dupliciter. Uno quidem modo, particulariter, secundum quod Socrates vel Plato percipit se habere animam intellectivam, ex hoc quod percipit se intelligere. Alio modo, in universali, secundum quod naturam humanae mentis ex actu intellectus consideramus. Sed verum est quod iudicium et efficacia huius cognitionis per quam naturam animae cognoscimus, competit nobis secundum derivationem luminis intellectus nostri a veritate divina, in qua rationes omnium rerum continentur, sicut supra dictum est.

45. Clarke, *Explorations in Metaphysics*, 36.

46. Ibid., 37.

47. *In De Anima* I, lc. 2: Quod consideratio de anima pertinet ad naturalem. Et hoc ex modo definiendi concludit.

48. Martha Nussbam and Hilary Putnam, "Changing Aristotle's Mind," in *Essays on Aristotle's De Anima*, ed. A. Rorty and M. Nussbaum (Oxford: Clarendon, 1992), 28–29.

49. McDowell, *Mind and World*, xx.

50. Ibid., 71.

51. Ibid., 109.

52. MacIntyre, *Dependent Rational Animals*, 41.

53. McDowell, *Mind and World*, 77.

54. Ibid., xviii.

55. Ibid., 73.

56. Ibid., 87.

57. Ibid., 119 and 116.

58. On Albert, see an exposition of Albert's *De Animalibus* by Irven Resnik and Kenneth Kitchell, "Albert the Great on the 'Language' of Animals," *ACPQ* 70 (1996): 41–61.

59. MacIntyre, *Dependent Rational Animals*, 50. Also see Judith Barad, *Aquinas on the Nature and Treatment of Animals* (San Francisco: International Scholars Publication, 1995).

60. *ST* I, 78, 4: Oportet ergo quod animal per animam sensitivam non solum recipiat species sensibilium, cum praesentialiter immutatur ab eis; sed etiam eas retineat et conservet. Recipere autem et retinere reducuntur in corporalibus ad diversa principia, nam humida bene recipiunt, et male retinent; e contrario autem est de siccis. Unde, cum potentia sensitiva sit actus organi corporalis, oportet esse aliam potentiam quae recipiat species sensibilium, et quae conservet. Rursus considerandum est quod, si animal moveretur solum propter delectabile et contristabile secundum sensum, non esset necessarium ponere in animali nisi apprehensionem formarum quas percipit sensus, in quibus delectatur aut horret. Sed necessarium est animali ut quaerat aliqua vel fugiat, non solum quia sunt convenientia vel non convenientia ad sentiendum, sed etiam propter aliquas alias commoditates et utilitates, sive nocumenta, sicut ovis videns lupum venientem fugit, non propter indecentiam coloris vel figurae, sed quasi inimicum naturae; et similiter avis colligit paleam, non quia delectet sensum, sed quia est utilis ad nidificandum.

61. Consider, by contrast, Alvin Plantinga's defense of the pervasiveness of the language of proper function in natural science, "We think a hawk's heart that beats only twenty-five times a minute is not functioning properly, that AIDS damages the immune system and makes it function poorly, that multiple sclerosis causes the immune system to malfunction. . . . The notions of proper function, disease, and damage apply here and in a thousand other contexts; thinking in these terms is natural and apparently unavoidable for human beings" (*Warrant and Proper Function*, 196).

62. MacIntyre, *Dependent Rational Animals*, 46.

63. Ibid., 54.

64. *ST* I, 91, 3.

65. *ST* I, 91, 3, ad 3: *Solus homo delectatur in ipsa pulchritudine sensibilium secundum seipsam.*

66. *ST* I, 91, 3, ad 3: Quia sensus praecipue vigent in facie, alia animalia habent faciem pronam ad terram, quasi ad cibum quaerendum et providendum sibi de victu, homo vero habet faciem erectam, ut per sensus, et praecipue per visum, qui est subtilior et plures differentias rerum ostendit, libere possit ex omni parte sensibilia cognoscere, et caelestia et terrena, ut ex omnibus intelligibilem colligat veritatem.

67. *ST* I, 76, 5: Ad organum autem tactus requiritur quod sit medium inter contraria, quae sunt calidum et frigidum, humidum et siccum, et similia, quorum est tactus apprehensivus, sic enim est in potentia ad contraria, et potest ea sentire. Unde quanto organum tactus fuerit magis reductum ad aequalitatem complexionis, tanto perceptibilior erit tactus. Anima autem intellectiva habet completissime virtutem sensitivam, quia quod est inferioris praeexistit perfectius in superiori ut dicit Dionysius in libro de Div. Nom. Unde oportuit corpus cui unitur anima intellectiva, esse corpus mixtum, inter omnia alia magis reductum ad aequalitatem complexionis.

68. See Stanley Rosen, "Thought and Touch: A Note on Aristotle's *De Anima*," *Phronesis* 6 (1961): 127–37.

69. *ST* I–II, 24, 1, ad 2: Etiam inferiores vires appetitivae dicuntur rationales, secundum quod participant aliqualiter rationem, ut dicitur in I Ethic. It is striking that McDowell has nothing to say about the intermediate status of passions between the purely rational and the purely sub-rational.

70. *ST* I–II, 23, 1: Ad cognoscendum ergo quae passiones sint in irascibili, et quae in concupiscibili, oportet assumere obiectum utriusque potentiae. Dictum est autem in primo quod obiectum potentiae concupiscibilis est bonum vel malum sensibile simpliciter acceptum, quod est delectabile vel dolorosum. Sed quia necesse est quod interdum anima difficultatem vel pugnam patiatur in adipiscendo aliquod huiusmodi bonum, vel fugiendo aliquod huiusmodi malum, inquantum hoc est quodammodo elevatum supra facilem potestatem animalis; ideo ipsum bonum vel malum, secundum quod habet rationem ardui vel difficilis, est obiectum irascibilis. Quaecumque ergo passiones respiciunt absolute bonum vel malum, pertinent ad concupiscibilem; ut gaudium, tristitia, amor, odium, et similia. Quaecumque vero passiones respiciunt bonum vel malum sub ratione ardui, prout est aliquid adipiscibile vel fugibile cum aliqua difficultate, pertinent ad irascibilem; ut audacia, timor, spes, et huiusmodi.

71. *ST* I–II, 25, 2: Respondeo dicendum quod obiectum concupiscibilis sunt bonum et malum. Naturaliter autem est prius bonum malo, eo quod malum est privatio boni. Unde et omnes passiones quarum obiectum est bonum, naturaliter sunt priores passionibus quarum obiectum est malum, unaquaeque scilicet sua opposita, quia enim bonum quaeritur, ideo refutatur oppositum malum. Bonum autem habet rationem finis, qui quidem est prior in intentione, sed est posterior in consecutione. Potest ergo ordo passionum concupiscibilis attendi vel secundum intentionem, vel secundum consecutionem. Secundum quidem consecutionem, illud est prius quod primo fit in eo quod tendit ad finem. Manifestum est autem quod omne quod tendit ad finem aliquem, primo quidem habet aptitudinem seu proportionem ad finem, nihil enim tendit in finem non proportionatum; secundo, movetur ad finem; tertio, quiescit in fine post eius consecutionem. Ipsa autem aptitudo sive proportio appetitus ad bonum est amor, qui nihil aliud est quam complacentia boni; motus autem ad bonum est desiderium vel concupiscentia; quies autem in bono est gaudium vel delectatio. Et ideo secundum hunc ordinem, amor praecedit desiderium, et desiderium praecedit delectationem. Sed secundum ordinem intentionis, est e converso, nam delectatio intenta causat desiderium et amorem. Delectatio enim est fruitio boni, quae quodammodo est finis sicut et ipsum bonum, ut supra dictum est.

72. In fact, Gadamer's account is much more satisfying. Developing further the relationship between first and second nature might help to temper the quasi-religious language of conversion that McDowell uses to describe second nature. He speaks repeatedly of "having one's eyes opened." The contrast with Gadamer, who focues on receiving, interpreting, and articulating, and thus on hearing, is sharp. McDowell's language invites comparison with a kind of magical illumination, whereas Gadamer underscores the dialogical giving of an account about a shared world (*Truth and Method*, 462). McDowell's reconciliation never allows Aristotle's conception of nature to enter the debate; rather, it simply supplements Kant's account of freedom with a notion of second nature derived from Aristotle and Gadamer. But Gadamer does not leave the realm of natural law intact and autonomous in the way McDowell does. He does concede to it its own immanent normativity of laws of success, but he argues for the priority of ordinary language to scientific language. Gadamer's hermeneutics "corrects modern science" by focusing on what its mode of knowing through "making and producing" presupposes, namely, the "truth of remembrance." What we pursue in science and why we pursue it cannot be explained by recourse to the language of mathematical physics. We are always in the hermeneutic circle of whole and part, and philosophy is precisely that discourse which seeks to speak about the whole. The

"certitude and dominance of science" results from its techniques of governing a particular domain (*Truth and Method*, 450–51). Modern science is thus always in danger of becoming anti-philosophical, of reducing itself to tyrannical, unreflective technique.

Other than an unwillingness to offend scientific sensibilities, McDowell provides no reason for thinking that second nature could not encompass science as well. At times he comes close to a sort of integration or at least overlap of the two. He asserts that "conceptual capacities are in one sense natural" (*Mind and World*, 87), and he wants first nature to exercise some sort of limiting function with respect to second. Conversely, while the realm of law is devoid of meaning, "understanding—the very capacity we bring to bear on texts—is involved" even in our cognition of this realm (97). Can one separate science as natural law from science as a tradition of inquiry into which one is initiated by the inculcation of certain habits? Instead of investigating these matters, McDowell leaves us with a set of antinomies between first and second nature.

73. On this topic, see Richard Bernstein's criticisms of McDowell in his Romanell Lecture, "Whatever Happened to Naturalism?" in *PAPA* 69 (1995): 57–76.

74. Plantinga, *Warrant and Proper Function*, 194.

75. Ibid., 46–47.

76. Ibid., 164.

77. Ibid., 192.

78. Ibid., 99–101.

79. Ibid., 136 and 196.

80. Zagzebski, *Virtues of the Mind*, 336.

81. McDowell, *Mind and World*, 82.

82. Ibid., 95.

83. Ibid., 60.

84. Ibid., 80, n. 12. On the salient features of internalism, see Plantinga's *Warrant: The Current Debate*, 3–29.

85. MacIntyre, *Three Rival Versions*, 127.

86. Ibid., 128.

5. METAPHYSICS AND/AS PRACTICE

1. *What Is Ancient Philosophy?* (Cambridge, Mass.: Harvard University Press, 2002), 85.

2. Ibid., 3.

3. Ibid.

4. Aquinas's relationship to Aristotle has of course been vigorously and hotly debated since Aquinas's own time. For the case of fundamental incompatibility, see, for example, Harry Jaffa, *Thomism and Aristotelianism*; R. A. Gauthier, *La morale d'Aristote*; and Mark Jordan, *Alleged Aristotelianism of Thomas Aquinas*. For a defense of Aquinas as an Aristotelian, see Ralph McInerny, *Aquinas Against the Averroists* and *The Question of Christian Ethics*. For a balanced assessment, see John Jenkins, "Expositions of the Text: Aquinas's Aristotelian Commentaries."

5. Aristotle, *Ethics*, 1102a5.

6. Ibid., 1105b10–15.

7. Hans Georg Gadamer, *The Idea of the Good in Platonic-Aristotelian Philosophy*, trans. by P. Christopher Smith (New Haven, Conn.: Yale University Press, 1986), 161.

8. *In Eth.* VI, lc. 3, note 1151. Aquinas refers to *Metaphysicae* IX and explains: ibi

enim ostensa est differentia inter actionem et factionem. Nam actio dicitur operatio manens in ipso agente, sicut videre, intelligere et velle, factio autem dicitur operatio transiens in exteriorem materiam ad aliquid formandum ex ea, sicut aedificare, urere et secare.

9. *In Met.* IX, lc. 8: Talis autem differentia inter praedictas potentias est considerenda, quod quando praeter actum ipsum potentiae, qui est actio, sit aliquod operatum, actio talium potentiarum est in facto, et actus facti, ut aedificatio in aedificato, et contextio in contexto, et universaliter motus in moto. Et hoc ideo, quia quando per actionem potentiae constituitur aliquod operatum, illa actio perficit operatum, et non operantem. Unde est in operato sicut actio et perfectio eius, non autem in operante. Sed, quando non est aliquod opus operatum praeter actionem potentiae, tunc actio existit in agente et ut perfectio eius, et non transit in aliquid exterius perficiendum; sicut visio est in vidente ut perfectio eius, et speculatio in speculante, et vita in anima, ut per vitam intelligamus opera vitae. Unde manifestum est, quod etiam felicitas in tali operatione consistit, quae est in operante, non quae transit in rem exteriorem, cum felicitas sit bonum felicis, et perfectio eius. Est enim aliqua vita felicis, scilicet vita perfecta eius. Unde sicut vita est in vivente, ita felicitas in felice. Et sic patet quod felicitas non consistit nec in aedificando, nec in aliqua huiusmodi actione, quae in exterius transeat, sed in intelligendo et volendo.

10. Deborah Achtenberg, *Cognition of Value in Aristotle's Ethics: Promise of Enrichment, Threat of Destruction* (Albany: State University of New York Press, 2002), 61–96.

11. Ralph McInery, "Ontology and Theology in Aristotle's Metaphysics," in *Being and Predication* (Washington, D.C.: Catholic University of America Press, 1986), 66.

12. The debate over whether, and if so how, *separatio* marks the foundation of metaphysics is at the heart of the debate over whether metaphysics is dependent on conclusions reached in natural philosophy concerning the existence of immaterial beings or capacities such as the intellectual soul, the separate substances, and God. See John Wippel, "Metaphysics and Separatio according to Thomas Aquinas," *Review of Metaphysics* 31 (1978), pp. 431–470. This essay and related essays can be found in Wippel, *Metaphysical Themes in Thomas Aquinas* (1995). For a rejoinder to Wippel's claim that metaphysics is independent of physics, see Mark Jordan, *Ordering Wisdom: The Hierarchy of Philosophical Discourses in Aquinas* (Notre Dame, Ind.: University of Notre Dame Press, 1986), 156–63. See also the crucial manuscript study by Louis Geiger, "Abstraction et separation d'apres S. Thomas," *Revue des Sciences Philosophiques et Théologiques* 31 (1947): 3–40. See also Mark Johnson, "Immateriality and the Domain of Thomistic Natural Philosophy," *Modern Schoolman* 67 (1990): 285–304.

13. *In Phys.* I, lc. 1: Quaedam vero sunt quae non dependent a materia nec secundum esse nec secundum rationem; vel quia nunquam sunt in materia, ut Deus et aliae substantiae separatae; vel quia non universaliter sunt in materia, ut substantia, potentia et actus, et ipsum ens.

14. *Metaphysics*, 981b25–982a1.

15. *Ethics*, 1094a28–1094b11.

16. *ScG* I, 1.

17. *In Met.*, Proemium: Sicut docet philosophus in politicis suis, quando aliqua plura ordinantur ad unum, oportet unum eorum esse regulans, sive regens, et alia regulata, sive recta. Quod quidem patet in unione animae et corporis; nam anima naturaliter imperat, et corpus obedit. Similiter etiam inter animae vires: irascibilis enim et concupiscibilis naturali ordine per rationem reguntur. Omnes autem scientiae et

artes ordinantur in unum, scilicet ad hominis perfectionem, quae est eius beatitudo. Unde necesse est, quod una earum sit aliarum omnium rectrix, quae nomen sapientiae recte vindicat. Nam sapientis est alios ordinare.

18. Rosen, *The Question of Being*, 132.

19. *Politics*, VII, 3, 1325a19–32.

20. *Politics*, VII, 3, 1325b14–32.

21. *Politics*, VII, 1, 1323b21–25.

22. *In Eth.*, X, lc. 9.

23. Ibid.

24. *ST* I–II, 57, 1, ad 1.

25. Pieper, *Leisure, the Basis of Culture*, 24–37.

26. Yves Simon, *Work, Society, and Culture* (New York: Fordham University Press, 1971), 185–87.

27. Bernard Williams, *Truth and Truthfulness* (Princeton, N.J.: Princeton University Press, 2002), 125.

28. *ST* I–II, 55, 2.

29. For a fully developed argument along these lines, see John Bowlin, *Contingency and Fortune in Aquinas's Ethics* (Cambridge: Cambridge University Press, 1999).

30. Simon, *Work, Society, and Culture*, 182.

31. Ibid., 10–17. Pieper's entire account of leisure is predicated not on ornamental romanticism but on the practice of divine worship.

32. Pieper, *Leisure, the Basis of Culture*, 68.

33. Ibid., 92.

34. Ibid., 103–104.

35. In duodecim libros Metaphysicorum Aristotelis expositio, 2, 1, 287. quia, sicut dictum est, dum unusquisque praecedentium aliquid de veritate invenit, simul in unum collectum, posterioris introducit ad magnam veritatis cognitionem.

36. Ricouer, *Oneself as Another*, 182.

37. See Norris Clarke's essay by this title in *Explorations in Metaphysics*, 102–22.

38. *In libros Eth.* VI, lc. 6.

39. *In libros Eth.* III, lc. 7.

40. As Walter Thompson puts it, "If . . . practice is concerned with ultimate particulars, then a theoretical teaching on human nature and the human good cannot be determinative of action; it cannot simply be enacted." See Walter Jay Thompson, "Aristotle: Philosophy and Politics, Theory and Practice," *PACPA* 68 (1994): 109–24.

41. *In Eth.* X, 10 and 11: Alii vero intellectum partem animae posuerunt, sicut Aristoteles. Et secundum hoc intellectus non est simpliciter quiddam divinum, sed est divinissimum inter omnia quae in nobis, propter maiorem convenientiam quam habet cum substantiis separatis, secundum quod eius operatio est sine organo corporeo.

42. *Ethics*, 1177b30–1178a1. See Thomas's commentary on Book X, lectio 11: Deinde cum dicit: oportet autem etc., excludit quorumdam errorem, qui suadebant, quod homo debeat intendere ad sapiendum humana et mortalis ad sapiendum mortalia. Et fuit hoc dictum Simonidis poetae, ut patet in principio metaphysicae. Quod quidem philosophus dicit esse falsum, quia homo debet tendere ad immortalitatem quantum potest, et secundum totum posse suum facere ad hoc quod vivat secundum intellectum, qui est optimum eorum quae sunt in homine, qui quidem est immortalis et divinus. Quamvis enim hoc optimum sit parvum mole, quia est incorporeum et

simplicissimum, et per consequens caret magnitudine molis, tamen quantitate virtutis et pretiositatis multum excedit omnia quae in homine sunt. . . . Nec hoc est contra id quod supra dictum est, quod non est secundum hominem, sed supra hominem: non est enim secundum hominem quantum ad naturam compositam, est autem propriissime secundum hominem quantum ad id quod est principalissimum in homine: quod quidem perfectissime invenitur in substantiis superioribus, in homine autem imperfecte et quasi participative. Et tamen istud parvum est maius omnibus aliis quae in homine sunt. Sic ergo patet, quod iste qui vacat speculationi veritatis est maxime felix, quantum homo in hac vita felix esse potest.

43. *Metaphysics*, 1072b23–27.

44. Norman Dahl, *Practical Reason, Aristotle, and Weakness of Will* (Minneapolis: University of Minnesota Press, 1984), 235.

45. *De veritate*, XI, 1: Contingit in scientiae acquisitione, quod eodem modo docens alium ad scientiam ignotorum deducit sicuti aliquis inveniendo deducit seipsum in cognitionem ignoti.

46. Gadamer, *The Idea of the Good*, 41.

47. Ibid., 43.

48. Ibid., 38.

49. See Ricoeur, *Oneself as Another*. The best study of the complex relations among *techne* and *phronesis* in Aristotle and in contemporary philosophy remains Joseph Dunne's *Back to the Rough Ground*.

50. Alasdair MacIntyre, "On Not Having the Last Word: Thoughts on Our Debts to Gadamer," in *Gadamer's Century*, ed. Malpas, Arnswald, and Kertscher (Cambridge: MIT Press, 2002), 168

51. Ibid., 168–69.

52. Such virtues are operative even in the most abstract of sciences, say, in geometry. In *The Ethics of Geometry: A Genealogy of Modernity* (New York: Routledge, 1989), David Lachterman supplies a book-length comparison of the geometry of Euclid with that of Descartes. His thesis concerns the "disparate ways (*mores*) and styles in which the Euclidean and the Cartesian do geometry" and "comport themselves as mathematicians both toward their students and toward the very nature of those learnable items (*ta mathemata*) from which their disciplined deeds take their name. Hence, the difference in the source of intelligibility is itself an expression of this ethical difference" (p. xi). Lachterman focuses on the differing roles of, and emphases on, construction and problem-solving techniques in the two geometries. Following Proclus's famous study of Euclid's *Elements*, in which he refers to its "dialectical methods," Lachterman argues that the "context in which Euclidean phronesis is put to work is shaped by the dialogue between teacher and student. . . . The prudential rhetoric suited to this dialogue must resist, as far as that is possible, the seductive blandishments of any technique unharnessed from the directing control of that shared pre-understanding" of student and teacher (122).

53. *ScG* I, 29. Huic autem rationi Dionysius concordat, qui in IX cap. de Div. Nom. dicit: *eadem similia sunt Deo et dissimilia*: similia quidem, secundum imitationem eius qui non est perfecte imitabilis, qualem in eis contingit esse; dissimilia autem, secundum quod causata habent minus suis causis.

54. David Burrell, "From Analogy of 'Being' to the Analogy of Being," in *Recovering Nature* (Notre Dame, Ind.: University of Notre Dame Press, 1999), 260.

55. *In Met.* XII, lc. 12.

56. *In Eth.* I, lc. 6: Circa primum considerandum est, quod Aristoteles non intendit improbare opinionem Platonis quantum ad hoc quod ponebat unum bonum separatum, a quo dependerent omnia bona, nam et ipse Aristotiles in XII metaphysicae ponit quoddam bonum separatum a toto universo, ad quod totum universum ordinatur, sicut exercitus ad bonum ducis. Improbat autem opinionem Platonis quantum ad hoc quod ponebat illud bonum separatum esse quamdam ideam communem omnium bonorum.

57. Jan Aertsen, "Good as Transcendental," in *Being and Goodness,* ed. Scott MacDonald (Ithaca, N.Y.: Cornell University Press, 1991), 58. See also the other essays in this volume.

58. *ST* I, 6, 4. Omnia sunt bona inquantum sunt. Sed non discuntur omnia entia per esse divinum, sed per esse proprium. Ergo non omnia sunt bona bonitate divina, sed bonitate propria.

59. *ST* I, 6, 4. Sic ergo unumquodque dicitur bonum bonitate divina, sicut primo principio exemplari, effectivo et finali totius bonitatis.

60. *ST* I, 13, 2. Cum igitur dicitur Deus est bonus vel sapiens, non solum significatur quod ipse est causa sapientis vel bonitatis, sed quod haec in eo eminentius praeexistunt. Unde, secundum hoc, dicendum est quod secundum rem significatam per nomen, per prius dicuntur de Deo quam de creaturis: quia a Deo huiusmodi perfectiones in creaturas manant. Sed quantum ad impositionem nominis, per prius imponuntur creaturis, quas prius cognoscimus.

61. John Sallis, *Being and Logos: The Way of the Platonic Dialogue* (Bloomington: Indiana University Press, 1996), 422.

62. *Super De Trinitate,* 2, ar. 1, ad 6: Deus honoratur silentio, non quod nihil de ipso dicatur vel inquiratur, sed quia quidquid de ipso dicamus vel inquiramus, intelligimus nos ab eius comprehensione defecisse, unde dicitur Eccli. 43: *glorificantes dominum quantumcumque potueritis, supervalebit adhuc.*

63. *Super De Trinitate,* 1, ar. 2: In hoc autem profectu cognitionis maxime iuvatur mens humana, cum lumen eius naturale nova illustratione confortatur; sicut est lumen fidei et doni sapientiae et intellectus, per quod mens in contemplatione supra se elevari dicitur, in quantum cognoscit Deum esse supra omne id, quod naturaliter comprehendit. Sed quia ad eius essentiam videndam penetrare non sufficit, dicitur in se ipsam quodammodo ab excellenti lumine reflecti, et hoc est quod dicitur Gen. 32 super illud: *vidi dominum facie ad faciem,* in Glossa Gregorii: *visus animae, cum in Deum intenditur, immensitatis coruscatione reverberatur.*

64. *ScG* II, 2: Haec consideratio animas hominum in amorem divinae bonitatis accendit. Quicquid enim bonitatis et perfectionis in diversis creaturis particulariter distributum est, totum in ipso universaliter est adunatum, sicut in fonte totius bonitatis, ut in primo libro ostensum est. Si igitur creaturarum bonitas, pulchritudo et suavitas sic animos hominum allicit, ipsius Dei fontana bonitas, rivulis bonitatum in singulis creaturis repertis diligenter comparata, animas hominum inflammatas totaliter ad se trahet. Unde in Psalmo dicitur: *delectasti me, domine, in factura tua, et in operibus manuum tuarum exsultabo.* Et alibi de filiis hominum dicitur: *inebriabuntur ab ubertate domus tuae,* quasi totius creaturae, *et sicut torrente voluptatis tuae potabis eos: quoniam apud te est fons vitae.* Et Sap. 13–1, dicitur contra quosdam: *ex his quae videntur bona,* scilicet creaturis, quae sunt bona per quandam participationem, *non potuerunt intelligere eum qui est,* scilicet vere bonus, immo ipsa bonitas, ut in primo ostensum est.

65. N. T. Wright, *Jesus and the Victory of God* (Minneapolis: Fortress Press, 1996), 283.

66. Jean-Luc Marion, "In the Name: How to Avoid Speaking of 'Negative Theology,'" in *God, the Gift, and Postmodernism*, ed. John Caputo and Michael Scanlon (Bloomington: Indiana University Press, 1999), 34.

67. Torrell, *Saint Thomas Aquinas*, Vol. 2: *Spiritual Master*, 34. Torrell cites a passage from the *Sentences* commentary (*In III Sent*. d. 35, q. 1, a. 2), in which Thomas compares the differing role of affectivity in the contemplative lives of philosophers and the saints.

68. *De Potentia*, q. 7, ar. 5: Intellectus negationis semper fundatur in aliqua affirmatione: quod ex hoc patet quia omnis negativa per affirmativam probatur; unde nisi intellectus humanus aliquid de Deo affirmative cognosceret, nihil de Deo posset negare. Non autem cognosceret, si nihil quod de Deo dicit, de eo verificaretur affirmative. Et ideo, secundum sententiam Dionysii, dicendum est, quod huiusmodi nomina significant divinam substantiam, quamvis deficienter et imperfecte: quod sic patet.

6. Metaphysics, Theology, and the Practice of Naming God

1. Pierre Hadot, *Philosophy as a Way of Life* (Malden, Mass.: Blackwell, 1995), 270.

2. *ScG* I, 1: Omnium autem ordinatorum ad finem, gubernationis et ordinis regulam ex fine sumi necesse est: tunc enim unaquaeque res optime disponitur cum ad suum finem convenienter ordinatur; finis enim est bonum uniuscuiusque. Unde videmus in artibus unam alterius esse gubernativam et quasi principem, ad quam pertinet eius finis: sicut medicinalis ars pigmentariae principatur et eam ordinat, propter hoc quod sanitas, circa quam medicinalis versatur, finis est omnium pigmentorum, quae arte pigmentaria conficiuntur. Et simile apparet in arte gubernatoria respectu navifactivae; et in militari respectu equestris et omnis bellici apparatus. Quae quidem artes aliis principantes architectonicae nominantur, quasi principales artes: unde et earum artifices, qui architectores vocantur, nomen sibi vindicant sapientum.

3. *ScG* II, 2: Haec consideratio animas hominum in amorem divinae bonitatis accendit. Quicquid enim bonitatis et perfectionis in diversis creaturis particulariter distributum est, totum in ipso universaliter est adunatum, sicut in fonte totius bonitatis, ut in primo libro ostensum est. Si igitur creaturarum bonitas, pulchritudo et suavitas sic animos hominum allicit, ipsius Dei fontana bonitas, rivulis bonitatum in singulis creaturis repertis diligenter comparata, animas hominum inflammatas totaliter ad se trahet. Unde in Psalmo dicitur: delectasti me, domine, in factura tua, et in operibus manuum tuarum exsultabo. Et alibi de filiis hominum dicitur: inebriabuntur ab ubertate domus tuae, quasi totius creaturae, et sicut torrente voluptatis tuae potabis eos: quoniam apud te est fons vitae. Et Sap. 13–1, dicitur contra quosdam: ex his quae videntur bona, scilicet creaturis, quae sunt bona per quandam participationem, non potuerunt intelligere eum qui est, scilicet vere bonus, immo ipsa bonitas, ut in primo ostensum est.

4. Jacques Maritain, *Distinguish to Unite, or, The Three Degrees of Knowledge*, trans. under the supervision of Gerald Phelan (Notre Dame, Ind.: University of Notre Dame Press, 1995), 15.

5. An early, pejorative verdict on Aquinas's metaphysics as falling prey to an idolatry of being eventually gave way to an acquittal on the charge of practicing the forbidden art of onto-theology. See, first, Jean-Luc Marion, *God Without Being*, trans. Thomas Carlson (Chicago: University of Chicago Press, 1991), esp. xxiii; then "Saint Thomas d'Aquin et l'onto-théo-logie," *Revue Thomiste* 95 (1995): 31–66.

6. *ScG* I, c. 3: Est autem in his quae de Deo confitemur duplex veritatis modus. Quaedam namque vera sunt de Deo quae omnem facultatem humanae rationis excedunt, ut Deum esse trinum et unum. Quaedam vero sunt ad quae etiam ratio naturalis pertingere potest, sicut est Deum esse, Deum esse unum, et alia huiusmodi; quae etiam philosophi demonstrative de Deo probaverunt, ducti naturalis lumine rationis.

7. James Collins made a convincing case for the proper order of philosophical pedagogy in "Toward a Philosophically Ordered Thomism," *New Scholasticism* 32 (1958): 301–26.

8. *ScG* I, 9: Intendentibus igitur nobis per viam rationis prosequi ea quae de Deo ratio humana investigare potest, primo, occurrit consideratio de his quae Deo secundum seipsum conveniunt; secundo, vero, de processu creaturarum ab ipso; tertio, autem, de ordine creaturarum in ipsum sicut in finem.

9. Norman Kretzmann, *Metaphysics of Theism: Aquinas's Natural Theology in Summa contra Gentiles I* (Oxford: Oxford University Press, 1997).

10. See Michelle Corbin, *Le chemin de la théologie chez Thomas d'Aquin* (Paris: Beauchesne, 1972). The traditional assessment of the *ScG* as a missionary work has made it a relatively neglected text in Aquinas's corpus. Kretzmann follows recent scholarship on the *ScG* that simultaneously puts into serious question the traditional interpretation and elevates its philosophical and theological significance in Aquinas's corpus. See R. A. Gauthier, *Introduction historique au tome I de l'edition bilingue de la Summa contra Gentiles* (Paris: P. Lethielleux, 1961), 7–123; idem, "Introduction" to *Somme Contre les Gentiles* (Paris: Editions Universitaires, 1993); Mark Jordan, "The Protreptic Structure of the *Summa contra Gentiles*," *The Thomist* 50 (1986): 173–209; Thomas Hibbs, *Dialectic and Narrative in Aquinas: An Interpretation of the Summa contra Gentiles* (Notre Dame, Ind.: University of Notre Dame Press, 1995). For a summary of the interpretations of the *Summa contra Gentiles*, see Torrell, *Saint Thomas Aquinas*, Vol. 1: *The Person and his Work*, 91–116. Kretzmann rejects not only the missionary thesis but a broadly apologetic one as well. The problem with the latter is that Aquinas is "not answering objections to the faith"; his approach is not "reactive" (46–47).

11. Kretzmann, *Metaphysics of Theism*, 22.

12. Charles de Koninck, "Abstraction from Matter II," *Laval théologique et philosophique* 16 (1960).

13. *In Phys.* I, lc. 1: Quaedam vero sunt quae non dependent a materia nec secundum esse nec secundum rationem; vel quia nunquam sunt in materia, ut Deus et aliae substantiae separatae; vel quia non universaliter sunt in materia, ut substantia, potentia et actus, et ipsum ens. De huiusmodi igitur est metaphysica: de his vero quae dependent a materia sensibili secundum esse sed non secundum rationem, est mathematica: de his vero quae dependent a materia non solum secundum esse sed etiam secundum rationem, est naturalis, quae physica dicitur. Et quia omne quod habet materiam mobile est, consequens est quod ens mobile sit subiectum naturalis philosophiae.

14. Mark Jordan, *Ordering Wisdom*, 153.

15. *In Eth.* I, lc. 1: Et quia consideratio rationis per habitum scientiae perficitur, secundum hos diversos ordines quos proprie ratio considerat, sunt diversae scientiae.

16. *ST* II–II, 65, 1, ad 3: Virtutes intellectuales sunt circa diversas materias ad invicem non ordinatas, sicut patet in diversis scientiis et artibus. Et ideo non invenitur in eis connexio quae invenitur in virtutibus moralibus existentibus circa passiones et

operationes, quae manifeste habent ordinem ad invicem. Nam omnes passiones, a quibusdam primis procedentes, scilicet amore et odio, ad quasdam alias terminantur, scilicet delectationem et tristitiam. Et similiter omnes operationes quae sunt virtutis moralis materia, habent ordinem ad invicem, et etiam ad passiones. Et ideo tota materia moralium virtutum sub una ratione prudentiae cadit.

17. *In Eth.* VI, lc. 6.

18. Kretzmann might have been better off adopting Kenny's broader conception of the intended audience (see Anthony Kenny, *Aquinas on Mind* [London: Routledge, 1993]), even if that conception is fraught with problems of its own. In a footnote, he relates Kenny's response to his objection that the first three books would be wasted on Muslims or Jews: "I don't think Books I–III are wasted even if the whole thing is meant for Jews and Muslims. They can be regarded as a softening-up exercise, designed to show how much the great monotheistic religions have in common. 'You're with me so far? Now let me show you the little extra step you have to take in order to be saved'" (quoted in *Metaphysics of Theism*, 50, n. 37). Set aside the dubious suggestion that Jews or Muslims would regard the acceptance of the doctrines of Book IV as a "little extra step"; the problem with Kenny's thesis is internal to the *Summa contra Gentiles*. Thomas begins the fourth book by insisting that probable arguments on behalf of revelation should not be put forth to non-Christians, since they would be led to suppose that faith rests on such flimsy rational foundations (*ScG* IV, c. 1).

19. *In Met.* I, lc. 3, note 56.

20. Kretzmann, *Metaphysics of Theism*, 48.

21. Kenny, *Aquinas on Mind*, 13.

22. Kretzmann, *Metaphysics of Theism*, 50.

23. Ibid., 43.

24. Ibid., 51.

25. Marie Dominique Chenu, *Nature, Man, and Society in the Twelfth Century*, ed. and trans. Jerome Taylor and Lester K. Little (Chicago: University of Chicago, 1968), 234.

26. Ibid., 238.

27. *ScG* I, 7: Illud idem quod inducitur in animam discipuli a docente, doctoris scientia continet: nisi doceat ficte, quod de Deo nefas est dicere. Principiorum autem naturaliter notorum cognitio nobis divinitus est indita: cum ipse Deus sit nostrae auctor naturae. Haec ergo principia etiam divina sapientia continet. Quicquid igitur principiis huiusmodi contrarium est, divinae sapientiae contrariatur. Non igitur a Deo esse potest. Ea igitur quae ex revelatione divina per fidem tenentur, non possunt naturali cognitioni esse contraria.

28. Kretzmann seems to like the notion of Christian philosophy, but he appears to be innocent of the detailed debates over that notion and its applicability to Aquinas's thought among Thomists earlier in the twentieth century. For a rehearsal of some of the arguments, see John Wippel, "Thomas Aquinas and the Problem of Christian Philosophy," in *Metaphysical Themes in Thomas Aquinas*, 1–33.

29. More attention to this aspect of Thomas's project might assist Kretzmann's attempt to engage Christian critics of natural theology like Plantinga. Even once one has answered the objections to the practice of natural theology, as Kretzmann has, there remains the question of why a believer should adopt as positive a stance toward philosophy as Thomas does.

30. Jordan, "The Protreptic Structure," 182.

31. *ScG* I, 90–96.

32. Kretzmann, *Metaphysics of Theism*, 128–29.

33. Ibid. "Alpha" is the name Kretzmann gives to the being reached by the proofs in chapter 13, since he thinks that the proofs do not reach God as a personal being.

34. Jordan, "The Protreptic Structure," 192.

35. *ScG* I, 2: Inter omnia vero hominum studia sapientiae studium est perfectius, sublimius, utilius et iucundius. Perfectius quidem, quia inquantum homo sapientiae studium dat, intantum verae beatitudinis iam aliquam partem habet unde sapiens dicit, beatus vir qui in sapientia morabitur, Eccli. 14–22. Sublimius autem est quia per ipsum homo praecipue ad divinam similitudinem accedit, quae omnia in sapientia fecit: unde, quia similitudo causa est dilectionis, sapientiae studium praecipue Deo per amicitiam coniungit; propter quod Sap. 7–14 dicitur quod sapientia infinitus thesaurus est hominibus, quo qui usi sunt, facti sunt participes amicitiae Dei. Utilius autem est quia per ipsam sapientiam ad immortalitatis regnum pervenitur: concupiscentia enim sapientiae deducet ad regnum perpetuum, Sap. 6–21. Iucundius autem est quia non habet amaritudinem conversatio illius nec taedium convictus illius, sed laetitiam et gaudium, Sap. 8–16.

36. *ScG*, I, 8: Cui quidem sententiae auctoritas Hilarii concordat, qui sic dicit in libro de Trin., loquens de huiusmodi veritate: haec credendo incipe, procurre, persiste: etsi non perventurum sciam, gratulabor tamen profecturum. Qui enim pie infinita prosequitur, etsi non contingat aliquando, semper tamen proficiet prodeundo. Sed ne te inferas in illud secretum, et arcano interminabilis nativitatis non te immergas, summam intelligentiae comprehendere praesumens: sed intellige incomprehensibilia esse.

37. See Michelle Corbin, *Le chemin*. Corbin resolves the apparent tension between "a theological project ad intra" and "an apologetic project ad extra" in the following way: "The errors are neither epiphenomena exterior to a disinterested contemplation nor a unique object of attack, no longer in need of inquiry after truth. The response to the question of truth is identically the response to the problem posed by the errors that he knows, the response for him [ad intra] is identically the response for the others [ad extra]" (516).

38. R. A. Gauthier, Préface to *Sententia libri de anima*, Leonine edition (Paris: J. Vrin, 1984), 289–94. See also Gauthier's Introduction to *Somme contre les Gentiles* (1993), 147–56.

39. Kretzmann, *Metaphysics of Theism*, 143.

40. Ibid., 141.

41. Ibid., 170.

42. *ScG* I, 31: Ex quo patet necessitas plura nomina Deo dandi. Quia enim eum non possumus cognoscere naturaliter nisi ex effectibus deveniendo in ipsum, oportet quod nomina quibus perfectionem ipsius significamus, diversa sint, sicut et perfectiones in rebus inveniuntur diversae. Si autem ipsam essentiam prout est possemus intelligere et ei nomen proprium adaptare, uno nomine tantum eam exprimeremus. Quod promittitur his qui eum per essentiam videbunt, Zach. ult.: in die illa erit dominus unus et nomen eius unum.

43. Kretzmann, *Metaphysics of Theism*, 176.

44. In "Eternity, Awareness, and Action," *Faith and Philosophy* 9 (1992): 463–82, Kretzmann and Eleonore Stump attack simplistic attempts to render the notion of eternity incoherent. See also Brian Shanley, "Eternal Knowledge of the Temporal in Aquinas," *ACPQ* 71 (1997): 197–224; Eleonore Stump and Norman Kretzmann,

"Eternity and God's Knowledge: A Reply to Shanley," *ACPQ* 72 (1998): 439–445; and Brian Shanley, "Aquinas on God's Causal Knowledge: A Reply to Stump and Kretzmann," *ACPQ* 72 (1998): 447–57. Also see Brian Davies, "Classical Theism and the Doctrine of Divine Simplicity," in *Language, Meaning, and God*, ed. Brian Davis (London: Geoffrey Chapman, 1987).

45. Ralph McInery, *Aquinas and Analogy* (Washington D.C.: Catholic University of America Press; reprint, 1998), 162–63.

46. Burrell, "From Analogy of 'Being' to the Analogy of Being," 260.

47. Gadamer, *The Idea of the Good*, 42.

48. Burrell, "From Analogy of 'Being' to the Analogy of Being," 259.

49. Rosen, *The Question of Being*, 132.

50. Maritain, *Distinguish to Unite, or, The Three Degrees of Knowledge*, 239.

51. *ScG* I, cc. 51–52 and 63.

52. *ScG* I, c. 63: Sunt autem quidam qui perfectioni divinae cognitionis singularium notitiam subtrahere nituntur.

53. Kretzmann, *Metaphysics of Theism*, 238 and 250.

54. *ScG* I, cc. 65 and 70.

55. *ScG* I, c. 58: Dionysius etiam dicit, VII cap. de Div. Nom.: igitur divina sapientia, seipsam cognoscens, cognoscit omnia, et materialia immaterialiter et indivisibiliter divisibilia et multa unitive.

56. *ScG* I, c. 65: Deus cognoscit alia inquantum est causa eis. Effectus autem Dei sunt res singulares. Hoc enim modo Deus causat res, inquantum facit eas esse in actu: universalia autem non sunt res subsistentes, sed habent esse solum in singularibus, ut probatur in VII metaphysicae. Deus igitur cognoscit res alias a se non solum in universali, sed etiam in singulari. See Eleonore Stump's discussion of problems with certain ways of construing God's knowledge as causative. Stump's resolution hinges on shifting from efficient to formal causality in the articulation of the way God's knowledge is said to be causative (*Aquinas* [New York: Routledge, 2003], 159–66 and 178–820).

57. *ScG* I, cc. 59–63.

7. THE PRESENCE OF A HIDDEN GOD

1. John Caputo and Michael Scanlon, Introduction to *God, the Gift, and Postmodernism*, ed. Caputo and Scanlon (Bloomington: Indiana University Press, 1999), 4–5.

2. There is an irony here. No, I don't have in mind the sort of irony Derrida himself happily and playfully embraces, namely, that of renouncing all claims to knowledge even as one goes on speaking, arguing, and interpreting. Instead, I have in mind the irony involved in deconstruction's escape from the alleged conceptual abstractions of metaphysics only to find itself advocating a set of religious abstractions and formalisms derived, but quite distant from, concrete traditions of faith.

3. See Marion's preface to the English edition of *God Without Being*, xxiii.

4. For the response in France, see Marion's references in the preface to the English edition of *God Without Being*, 199–200, n. 5. Perhaps the best piece written in English by a Thomist is a response, not to *God Without Being*, but to the reading of Dionysius in *The Idol and Distance*; see Mark Jordan, "The Names of God and the Being of Names," in *The Existence and Nature of God*, ed. Alfred Freddoso (Notre Dame, Ind.: University of Notre Dame Press, 1983), 161–90. See also Derek Morrow, "Aquinas, Marion, Analogy, and *Esse*: A Phenomenology of the Divine Names?" *International Philosophi-*

cal Quarterly 46 (2006): 25–42; Kenneth Schmitz, "The God of Love," *The Thomist* 57 (1993): 495–608; and Michael B. Ewbank, "Of Idols, Icons, and Aquinas's *Esse:* Reflections on Jean-Luc Marion," *International Philosophical Quarterly* 42/2 (2002): 161–75.

5. Jean-Luc Marion, *The Idol and Distance*, trans. Thomas Carlson (New York: Fordham University Press, 2001), 145–48.

6. Jean-Luc Marion, "In the Name: How to Avoid Speaking of 'Negative Theology,'" in *God, the Gift, and Postmodernism*, ed. John Caputo and Michael Scanlon (Bloomington: Indiana University Press, 1999), 20–42.

7. Ibid., 34.

8. Ibid., 38.

9. Ibid., 32.

10. Ibid., 39.

11. Ibid., 40–41.

12. Richard Kearney, "Desire of God," in *God, the Gift, and Postmodernism*, ed. John Caputo and Michael Scanlon (Bloomington: Indiana University Press, 1999), 120. A related objection to Marion's project can be found in John Milbank's essay, "Only Theology Overcomes Metaphysics," in *The Word Made Strange* (Cambridge, Mass.: Blackwell, 1997), 42–43, where Milbank argues that Marion eliminates the possibility of an intelligible manifestation of a divine gift or, conversely, of any intelligible response.

13. Richard Kearney, *The God Who May Be: A Hermeneutics of Religion* (Bloomington: Indiana University Press, 2001), 145.

14. Richard Kearney, *Strangers, Gods, and Monsters: Ideas of Otherness* (New York: Routledge, 2002), 67.

15. ScG I, 1: *Veritatem meditabitur guttur meum, et labia mea detestabuntur impium.* Prov. 8:7.

16. ScG I, 14: Est autem via remotionis utendum praecipue in consideratione divinae substantiae. Nam divina substantia omnem formam quam intellectus noster attingit, sua immensitate excedit: et sic ipsam apprehendere non possumus cognoscendo quid est. Sed aliqualem eius habemus notitiam cognoscendo quid non est. Tantoque eius notitiae magis appropinquamus, quanto plura per intellectum nostrum ab eo poterimus removere.

17. ScG I, 26: Divinum autem esse est absque additione non solum in cogitatione, sed etiam in rerum natura: nec solum absque additione, sed etiam absque receptibilitate additionis. Unde ex hoc ipso quod additionem, non recipit nec recipere potest, magis concludi potest quod Deus non sit esse commune, sed proprium: etiam ex hoc ipso suum esse ab omnibus aliis distinguitur quod nihil ei addi potest.

18. Jean-Luc Marion, "Saint Thomas d'Aquin et l'onto-théo-logie," *Revue Thomiste* 95 (1995): 45.

19. Ibid.

20. See Marion, *The Idol and Distance*, 199.

21. I am grateful to Derek Morrow for making this point clear to me.

22. *Scriptum super Sententiis* (Parma, 1856), hereafter *In Sent.* See *In I Sent.*, dist. 8, q. 1, a. 1, ad 4: Unde quando in Deum procedimus per viam remotionis, primo negamus ab eo corporalia; et secundo etiam intellectualia, secundum quod inveniuntur in creaturis, ut bonitas et sapientia; et tunc remanet tantum in intellectu nostro, quia est, et nihil amplius: unde est sicut in quadam confusione. Ad ultimum autem etiam hoc ipsum esse, secundum quod est in creaturis, ab ipso removemus; et tunc

remanet in quadam tenebra ignorantiae, secundum quam ignorantiam, quantum ad statum viae pertinet, optime Deo conjungimur, ut dicit Dionysius, et haec est quaedam caligo, in qua Deus habitare dicitur.

23. This is not to say that the notion of divine eternity is incoherent or riddled with contradictions. For a response to criticisms of Aquinas's account of divine simplicity and eternity, see Stump, *Aquinas*, 92–158; and especially Matthew Lamb, "Eternity and Time," in *Gladly to Learn and Gladly to Teach: Essays on Religion and Political Philosophy in Honor of Ernest L. Fortin, A.A.*, ed. Michael Foley and Douglas Kries (New York: Lexington Books, 2002), 195–214.

24. ScG I, 40: Hinc est quod dominus, suam visionem Moysi promittens, dicit, Exodi 33:19: *Ego ostendam tibi omne bonum.* Et Sap. 8, dicitur de divina sapientia: *venerunt mihi omnia bona pariter cum illa.*

25. Kearney, *Strangers, Gods, and Monsters*, 101.

26. Ibid., 99.

27. See especially, MacIntyre, *Three Rival Versions of Moral Enquiry* (Notre Dame, Ind.: University of Notre Dame Press, 1991). Also pertinent is Ricoeur, *Oneself as Another.*

28. Pieper, *Faith Hope Love*, 29–31.

29. Ibid., 42.

30. Ibid., 25.

31. Ibid., 61.

32. See Marion, "Saint Thomas d'Aquin et l'onto-théo-logie." See also the reaction of Brian Shanley, "St. Thomas, Onto-Theology, and Marion," *The Thomist* 60 (1996): 617–25.

33. ScG I, 34: Quia ex rebus aliis in Dei cognitionem pervenimus, res nominum de Deo et rebus aliis dictorum per prius est in Deo secundum suum modum, sed ratio nominis per posterius. Unde et nominari dicitur a suis causatis.

34. ScG III, 69: Perfectio effectus demonstrat perfectionem causae: maior enim virtus perfectiorem effectum inducit. Deus autem est perfectissimum agens. Oportet igitur quod res ab ipso creatae perfectionem ab ipso consequantur. Detrahere ergo perfectioni creaturarum est detrahere perfectioni divinae virtutis. Sed si nulla creatura habet aliquam actionem ad aliquem effectum producendum, multum detrahitur perfectioni creaturae: ex abundantia enim perfectionis est quod perfectionem quam aliquid habet, possit alteri communicare. Detrahit igitur haec positio divinae virtuti.

35. Turner, *Faith, Reason and the Existence of God*, 79.

36. Ibid., 75. The theologian must also investigate "how reason, in the exercise of its own native powers, in some way 'replicates' or 'anticipates' the shape of faith," in its "sacramental" and "mystical structure." Thomas does this in part by reconsidering in the fourth, explicitly theological book, many of the topics of the first three books and by inscribing the opening discussions within revelation.

37. Ibid., 5.

38. Umberto Eco, *The Aesthetics of Thomas Aquinas* (Cambridge, Mass.: Harvard University Press, 1988), 48.

39. In *The Idol and Distance*, Marion acknowledges Balthasar's influence on his own understanding of distance in Dionysius. Following Balthasar, Marion speaks of "the areopagitic feeling of distance, a distance which preserves" (155, n. 32).

40. Hans Urs von Balthasar, *The Glory of the Lord: A Theological Aesthetics*, Vol. II: *Studies in Theological Style: Clerical Styles* (San Francisco: Ignatius Press, 1984), 166–

71. Also see the study by Gilbert Narcisse, *Les raisons de Dieu: Argument de convenance et esthétique théologique selon saint Thomas d'Aquin et Hans Urs von Balthasar* (Fribourg, Suisse: Editions Universitaires, 1997).

41. Balthasar, *The Glory of the Lord*, 191.

42. Ibid., 195.

43. *ScG* II, 86.

44. In addition to the obvious differences between Nietzsche and Aquinas, there are some suggestive parallels that we will investigate in the next chapter on James Joyce.

45. Milbank, "Only Theology Overcomes Metaphysics," 49.

44. *ScG*, IV, 54: Cum amicitia in quadam aequalitate consistat, ea quae multum inaequalia sunt, in amicitia copulari non posse videntur. Ad hoc igitur quod familiarior amicitia esset inter hominem et Deum, expediens fuit homini quod Deus fieret homo, quia etiam naturaliter homo homini amicus est: ut sic, dum visibiliter Deum cognoscimus, in invisibilium amorem rapiamur.

47. Kearney, *Strangers, Gods, and Monsters*, 229.

48. Ibid., 88.

49. SCG II, 2.

50. Murdoch, *Metaphysics as a Guide to Morals*, 14.

51. Ibid., 509.

52. Ibid., 293.

53. *ST* I–II, 94, 6.

54. In this, Aquinas anticipates Stanley Hauerwas's point that original sin is not a self-evident fact of the human condition. We must be taught what it means to be a sinner.

55. *ST* I–II, 109, 7: Cum enim decor gratiae proveniat ex illustratione divini luminis, non potest talis decor in anima reparari, nisi Deo denuo illustrante, unde requiritur habituale donum, quod est gratiae lumen. S; and III, 87, 2, ad 3: Ita etiam in anima inducitur macula uno modo per privationem decoris gratiae per peccatum mortale, alio modo per inclinationem inordinatam affectus ad aliquid temporale; et hoc fit per peccatum veniale.

56. *ST* I–II, 27, 1: Amoris autem proprium obiectum est bonum, quia, ut dictum est, amor importat quandam connaturalitatem vel complacentiam amantis ad amatum; unicuique autem est bonum id quod est sibi connaturale et proportionatum. Unde relinquitur quod bonum sit propria causa amoris.

57. *ST* I–II, 180, 1: Movet autem vis appetitiva ad aliquid inspiciendum, vel sensibiliter vel intelligibiliter, quandoque quidem propter amorem rei visae, quia, ut dicitur Matth. VI, ubi est thesaurus tuus, ibi est et cor tuum, quandoque autem propter amorem ipsius cognitionis quam quis ex inspectione consequitur. Et propter hoc Gregorius constituit vitam contemplativam in caritate Dei, inquantum scilicet aliquis ex dilectione Dei inardescit ad eius pulchritudinem conspiciendam. Et quia unusquisque delectatur cum adeptus fuerit id quod amat, ideo vita contemplativa terminatur ad delectationem, quae est in affectu, ex qua etiam amor intenditur.

58. *ST* I–II, 27, 2: Amor requirit aliquam apprehensionem boni quod amatur. Et propter hoc philosophus dicit, IX Ethic., quod visio corporalis est principium amoris sensitivi. Et similiter contemplatio spiritualis pulchritudinis vel bonitatis, est principium amoris spiritualis. Sic igitur cognitio est causa amoris, ea ratione qua et bonum, quod non potest amari nisi cognitum.

59. *ST* III, 1, 2.

60. Torrell, *Saint Thomas Aquinas*, Vol. 2: *Spiritual Master*, 116.

61. *ST* III, 40, 1, ad 3.

62. *ST* I–II, 101, 2: In statu autem praesentis vitae, non possumus divinam veritatem in seipsa intueri, sed oportet quod radius divinae veritatis nobis illucescat sub aliquibus sensibilibus figuris, sicut Dionysius dicit, I cap. Cael. Hier., diversimode tamen, secundum diversum statum cognitionis humanae.

63. *ST* I–II, 99, 3, ad 3: sicut Dionysius dicit, I cap. Cael. Hier., divina hominibus manifestari non possunt nisi sub aliquibus similitudinibus sensibilibus. Ipsae autem similitudines magis movent animum quando non solum verbo exprimuntur, sed etiam sensui offeruntur. Et ideo divina traduntur in Scripturis non solum per similitudines verbo expressas, sicut patet in metaphoricis locutionibus; sed etiam per similitudines rerum quae visui proponuntur, quod pertinet ad praecepta caeremonialia.

64. *ST* I–II, 101, 2: Et ideo oportebat exteriorem cultum veteris legis non solum esse figurativum futurae veritatis manifestandae in patria; sed etiam esse figurativum Christi, qui est via ducens ad illam patriae veritatem.

65. *Super Epistolam B. Pauli ad Hebraeos lectura* (Turin, 1953), hereafter *In ad Heb*. See *In ad Heb*. X, lect. 2: Christus per suum sanguinem *initiavit*, id est inchoavit, *novam viam nobis* . Mich. II, 13: *ascendit pandens iter ante eos*. Io. XIV, 3: *si abiero et praeparavero vobis locum*, et cetera. Is. XXXV, 8: *sancta via vocabitur, et pollutus non transibit per illam*. Haec est ergo via eundi in caelum. Et est nova quia ante Christum nullus invenit eam, quia *nemo ascendit in caelum nisi qui descendit de caelo*, Io. III, 13. Et ideo qui vult ascendere, debet ipsi tamquam membrum capiti suo adhaerere. Apoc. II, 7: *vincenti dabo edere de ligno vitae, quod est in Paradiso Dei mei* . Et c. III, 12: *et scribam super eum nomen novum, et nomen civitatis novae Ierusalem*, quia scilicet de novo introducuntur. *Viventem*, id est, semper perseverantem, in quo apparuit virtus deitatis, quia semper vivit. Sed quae sit ista via ostendit subdens *per velamen, id est, carnem suam*. Sicut enim sacerdos per velum intrabat in sancta sanctorum, ita si volumus intrare sancta gloriae, oportet intrare per carnem Christi, qui fuit velamen deitatis. Is. XLV, 15: *vere tu es Deus absconditus*.

66. See Chenu, *Nature, Man, and Society*, 246–54. Chenu notes that the evangelical awakening of the twelfth century gave rise to "masters," teachers or apostolic leaders who "had to accomplish three operations in order to bring the world of God into full exercise: *legere, disputare, praedicare*" (252).

67. *ST* II–II, 188, 1: Status religionis est quoddam exercitium quo aliquis exercetur ad perfectionem caritatis.

68. Guy Bedouelle, *Saint Dominic: The Grace of the Word* (San Francisco: Ignatius Press, 1987), 245.

69. *ST* III, 40, 1, ad 2: Vita contemplativa simpliciter est melior quam activa quae occupatur circa corporales actus, sed vita activa secundum quam aliquis praedicando et docendo contemplata aliis tradit, est perfectior quam vita quae solum contemplatur, quia talis vita praesupponit abundantiam contemplationis. Et ideo Christus talem vitam elegit.

70. Murdoch, *Metaphysics as a Guide to Morals*, 508.

71. Ibid., 381.

72. Pieper, *Faith Hope Love*, 216.

73. Ibid., 260.

74. Ibid., 280.

75. Marion, *The Idol and Distance*, 192.

76. Chenu, *Nature, Man, and Society*, 203.

8. PORTRAITS OF THE ARTIST

1. Marion, *The Idol and Distance*, 30.

2. Ibid., 34.

3. Friedrich Nietzsche, *Will to Power*, trans. Walter Kaufmann (Vintage, 1968): "European Nihilism," #2.

4. Rosen, *The Question of Being*, 159.

5. In *Faith, Reason and the Existence of God*, Denys Turner compares Nietzsche and Aquinas on the limits to reason (108–16).

6. For a corrective to the modern temptation to reduce all artistic activity to aesthetic theory, see Jean-Marie Schaefer's *Art of the Modern Age: Philosophy of Art from Kant to Heidegger* (Princeton, N.J.: Princeton University Press, 1992). Schaefer argues against two modern tendencies: (a) the "reduction of art to its creative aspect," a reduction that isolates art from the broader field of human works and misleads us into thinking of art as the only or only important human work; and (b) the cutting off of the work of art from its "hedonic dimension," gratification or pleasure, a result of an "exacerbated Puritanism" (274).

7. Clarke, *Explorations in Metaphysics*, 52.

8. Friedrich Nietzsche, *Beyond Good and Evil*, trans. Walter Kaufmann (Vintage Books, 1966) #168.

9. See Thornton, *The Antimodernism of Joyce's Portrait*, 39–63; and Hugh Kenner, "The Cubist Portrait," in *Approaches to Joyce's Portrait*, ed. Staley and Benstock (Pittsburgh, Pa.: University of Pittsburg Press, 1976), 179.

10. A minor classic in the vast literature of Joyce criticism, William T. Noon's *Joyce and Aquinas* (New Haven, Conn.: Yale University Press, 1957) traces the Thomistic themes pervading Joyce's corpus. The book is still regularly cited in studies of Joyce, even if its suggestions of Joyce's affinities with premodern philosophy have been less well received in the trendy attempts to deploy Joyce as an authority for a host of postmodern "isms."

11. Friedrich Nietzsche, *The Birth of Tragedy*, trans. Walter Kaufmann (New York: Random House, 1967).

12. Ibid., 46.

13. Ibid., 97, 96, 98, 111.

14. Ibid., 112.

15. Peter Berkowitz, *Nietzsche: The Ethics of an Immoralist* (Cambridge, Mass.: Harvard University Press, 1996), 45.

16. Nietzsche, *The Birth of Tragedy*, 37.

17. Ibid., 52.

18. Ibid., 43.

19. Ibid., 61.

20. James Joyce, *Portrait of the Artist as a Young Man* (New York: Penguin Books, 1992), 159. Subsequent page numbers in the text are from this edition.

21. Nietzsche, *Birth of Tragedy*, 64.

22. Ibid., 73.

23. Ibid., 108.

24. See Thornton, *Antimodernism*, 79; and Stanley Sultan, *Eliot, Joyce, and Company* (Oxford: Oxford University Press, 1990), 63 and 76.

25. Ellman, *James Joyce*, 5.

26. The references to Zarathustra are thoroughly comic and sardonic; indeed, in *Ulysses* they are spoken by the cruelly mocking Buck Mulligan, the least admirable character in the novel (see chap. 1, p. 19, ll 727–28). When Nietzsche associates his laughter with the project of making himself into a god, a result of which would be superhuman laughter, he is at variance with Joyce, whose laughter is closer to that appropriate to Aristotelian comedy.

27. Nietzsche, *Will to Power*, #22.

28. Nietzsche, *Beyond Good and Evil*, #257.

29. Berkowitz, *Nietzsche*, 269.

30. Rosen, *The Question of Being*, 249. For Rosen's view of the "central problems" in Nietzsche, see also pp. 132, 151, 158–59, 220.

31. See Turner, *Faith, Reason and the Existence of God*, 118.

32. On this, see Jean-Marie Schaefer's *Art of the Modern Age*.

33. On the theme of beauty in Aquinas, see Mark D. Jordan, "The Evidence of the Transcendentals and the Place of Beauty in Thomas Aquinas," *International Philosophical Quarterly* 29 (1989): 393–406; and Armand Maurer, *About Beauty* (Houston, Tex.: Center for Thomistic Studies, 1983).

34. *De veritate*, 22, 1 ad 12: Appetitum terminari ad bonum et pacem et pulchrum, non est eum terminari in diversa. Ex hoc enim ipso quod aliquid appetit bonum, appetit simul et pulchrum et pacem: pulchrum quidem, in quantum est in seipso modificatum et specificatum, quod in ratione boni includitur; sed bonum addit ordinem perfectivi ad alia. Unde quicumque appetit bonum, appetit hoc ipso pulchrum. Pax autem importat remotionem perturbantium et impedientium adeptionem boni. Ex hoc autem ipso quod aliquid desideratur, desideratur etiam remotio impedimentorum ipsius. Unde simul et eodem appetitu appetitur bonum, pulchrum et pax.

35. *ST* II–II, 145, 2, ad 1: Obiectum movens appetitum est bonum apprehensum. Quod autem in ipsa apprehensione apparet decorum, accipitur ut conveniens et bonum, et ideo dicit Dionysius, IV cap. de Div. Nom., quod *omnibus est pulchrum et bonum amabile* . Unde et ipsum honestum, secundum quod habet spiritualem decorem, appetibile redditur. Unde et Tullius dicit, in I de Offic., *formam ipsam, et tanquam faciem honesti vides, quae si oculis cerneretur, mirabiles amores, ut ait Plato, excitaret sapientiae.*

36. Eco, *The Aesthetics of Thomas Aquinas*, 48.

37. *ST* I–II, 32, 8: Est autem admiratio desiderium quoddam sciendi, quod in homine contingit ex hoc quod videt effectum et ignorat causam, vel ex hoc quod causa talis effectus excedit cognitionem aut facultatem ipsius. Et ideo admiratio est causa delectationis inquantum habet adiunctam spem consequendi cognitionem eius quod scire desiderat. Et propter hoc omnia mirabilia sunt delectabilia, sicut quae sunt rara, et omnes repraesentationes rerum, etiam quae in se non sunt delectabiles; gaudet enim anima in collatione unius ad alterum, quia conferre unum alteri est proprius et connaturalis actus rationis, ut philosophus dicit in sua poetica.

38. *ST* I–II, 33, 2.

39. *ST* I–II, 33, 1.

40. *ST* I–II, 33, 1.

41. G. J. McAleer, *Ecstatic Morality and Sexual Politics* (New York: Fordham University Press, 2005), 24.

42. See the masterful explication by Thornton in *Antimodernism*, 85–107.

43. T. S. Eliot, *Selected Prose* (New York: Farrar, Straus and Giroux, 1975), 63.

44. Murdoch, *Existentialists and Mystics*, 292.

45. Ibid., 293.

46. *Quaestiones disputatae de potentia* (Turin, 1953), hereafter *De Potentia. See De Potentia*, 2, 1: Natura cuiuslibet actus est, quod seipsum communicet quantum possibile est. Unde unumquodque agens agit secundum quod in actu est. Agere vero nihil aliud est quam communicare illud per quod agens est actu, secundum quod est possibile. Natura autem divina maxime et purissime actus est. Unde et ipsa seipsam communicat quantum possibile est. Communicat autem se ipsam per solam similitudinem creaturis, quod omnibus patet; nam quaelibet creatura est ens secundum similitudinem ad ipsam.

47. James Joyce, *Ulysses* (Gabler edition; New York: Random House, 1986), 15. Subsequent quotations from *Ulysses* are from this edition. For an interpretation of *Ulysses*, see Weldon Thornton, *Voices and Values in Joyce's Ulysses* (Gainesville: University Press of Florida, 2000).

48. *ST* I, 45, 6: Deus est causa rerum per suum intellectum et voluntatem, sicut artifex rerum artificiatarum. Artifex autem per verbum in intellectu conceptum, et per amorem suae voluntatis ad aliquid relatum, operatur. Unde et Deus pater operatus est creaturam per suum verbum, quod est filius; et per suum amorem, qui est spiritus sanctus. Et secundum hoc processiones personarum sunt rationes productionis creaturarum, inquantum includunt essentialia attributa, quae sunt scientia et voluntas.

49. *ScG* III, 69.

50. Murdoch, *Existentialists and Mystics*, 370–71.

51. Martha Nussbaum, *Upheavals of Thought: The Intelligence of Emotions*, (Cambridge: Cambridge University Press, 2003), 703

52. Ibid., 706–707.

53. Ibid., 682.

54. Ibid., 686.

55. Ibid., 696.

56. Ibid., 709.

57. Wendell Berry, *Sex, Economy, Freedom, and Community* (New York: Pantheon, 1993), 143.

58. Ibid., 135–36.

59. Ibid., 122.

60. Camille Paglia, *Sexual Personae: Art and Decadence from Nefertiti to Emily Dickinson* (New York: Vintage, 1991), 4.

61. Ibid., 3.

62. Ibid., 29.

63. On this and related topics, see McAleer, *Ecstatic Morality and Sexual Politics*.

64. Turner, *Faith, Reason and the Existence of God*, 167. For an attempt to reason about ethics from such a radical conception of otherness, see John Caputo's revealingly titled *Against Ethics* (Bloomington: Indiana University Press, 1993). Caputo regularly deploys Joyce's phrase that "greekjew is jewgreek."

65. *De veritate*, I, 1: Si autem modus entis accipiatur secundo modo, scilicet

secundum ordinem unius ad alterum, hoc potest esse dupliciter. Uno modo secundum divisionem unius ab altero; et hoc exprimit hoc nomen aliquid: dicitur enim aliquid quasi aliud quid; unde sicut ens dicitur unum, in quantum est indivisum in se, ita dicitur aliquid, in quantum est ab aliis divisum.

66. This is the title of a Norris Clarke essay. See *Explorations in Metaphysics*, 102–22.

67. Rosemann, *Understanding Scholastic Thought with Foucault*, 140.

68. See Sultan, *Eliot, Joyce, and Company*, 49–87.

69. Given the way we have framed the issue, the key question is whether we can see the Stephen-Bloom relationship as a kind of friendship, and if so, of what sort. On this issue, see Marilyn French's *The Book as World* (Cambridge, Mass.: Harvard University Press, 1976), 85, in which she argues that Bloom embodies *caritas*.

70. For a summary of recent interpretations and a reading of the soliloquy as an "auto-debate" in which Molly resolves her attitude to Bloom and reaffirms her fidelity, see Sultan, *Joyce, Eliot, and Company*, 289–98.

71. Edgar de Bruyne, *L'esthétique du Moyen Âge* (Louvain, 1947), trans. Eileen B. Hennessy as *The Esthetics of the Middle Ages* (New York: F. Ungar, 1969).

72. Chenu, *Nature, Man, and Society in the Twelfth Century*, 138.

73. *Super De Trinitate*, VI, 3.

9. Metaphysics of Contingency, Divine Artistry of Hope

1. See Fabro, "Transcendality of Ens-Esse," 418; Robert Sokolowski, *The God of Faith and Reason: Foundations of Christian Theology* (Washington, D.C.: Catholic University of America Press, 1995).

2. Kenneth Schmitz, *The Gift: Creation*, the Aquinas Lecture (Milwaukee, Wis.: Marquette University Press, 1982), , 44.

3. *In Peri Hermeneias* I, lectio 14: Et haec quidem dicta sunt ad salvandum radices contingentiae, quas hic Aristoteles ponit, quamvis videantur logici negotii modum excedere.

4. Norris Clarke also inclines toward the view that God must create. For his position, see "Person, Being, and St. Thomas," in his *Explorations in Metaphysics: Being, God, Person*, 211–27. For the ensuing debate, see the fall 1993 and spring 1994 issues of *Communio*.

5. Norman Kretzmann, *The Metaphysics of Creation: Aquinas's Natural Theology in Summa Contra Gentiles II* (Oxford: Oxford University Press, 1999), 224–26.

6. Ibid., 136.

7. Ibid., 135.

8. Laura Garcia, "Divine Freedom and Creation," *Philosophical Quarterly* 42 (1992): 191–213. In his article, "Aquinas and Kretzmann on Creation," Lawrence Dewan argues that at the root of Kretzmann's misreading is a failure to understand "unqualifiedly infinite being, perfection, goodness." Kretzmann erroneously locates God "within an order . . . of creatures." In other words, Kretzmann succumbs to onto-theology. See *Nova et Vetera* 4 (2006): 495–514.

9. *ST* I, 46, 2: Fidei articuli demonstrative probari non possunt, *quia fides de non apparentibus est*, ut dicitur ad Hebr. XI. Sed Deum esse creatorem mundi, sic quod mundus incoeperit esse, est articulus fidei, dicimus enim, credo in unum Deum et cetera. Et iterum, Gregorius dicit, in Homil. I in Ezech., quod Moyses prophetizavit de

praeterito, dicens in principio creavit Deus caelum et terram; in quo novitas mundi traditur. Ergo novitas mundi habetur tantum per revelationem. Et ideo non potest probari demonstrative.

10. *ST* I.32.1.ad 3: Cognitio divinarum personarum fuit necessaria nobis dupliciter. Uno modo, ad recte sentiendum de creatione rerum. Per hoc enim quod dicimus Deum omnia fecisse verbo suo, excluditur error ponentium Deum produxisse res ex necessitate naturae. Per hoc autem quod ponimus in eo processionem amoris, ostenditur quod Deus non propter aliquam indigentiam creaturas produxit, neque propter aliquam aliam causam extrinsecam; sed propter amorem suae bonitatis. Unde et Moyses, postquam dixerat, in principio creavit Deus caelum et terram, subdit, dixit Deus, fiat lux, ad manifestationem divini verbi; et postea dixit, vidit Deus lucem, quod esset bona, ad ostendendum approbationem divini amoris; et similiter in aliis operibus. Alio modo, et principalius, ad recte sentiendum de salute generis humani, quae perficitur per filium incarnatum, et per donum spiritus sancti.

11. *ScG* II, 38: Ex his autem quae praedicta sunt, vitare possumus diversos errores gentilium philosophorum. Quorum quidam posuerunt mundum aeternum. Quidam materiam mundi aeternam, ex qua ex aliquo tempore mundus coepit generari: vel a casu; vel ab aliquo intellectu; aut etiam amore aut lite. Ab omnibus enim his ponitur aliquid praeter Deum aeternum. Quod fidei Catholicae repugnat..

12. *ScG* I, 86: Sic igitur procedere possumus in assignando divinae voluntatis rationem: Deus vult hominem habere rationem ad hoc quod homo sit; vult autem hominem esse ad hoc quod completio universi sit; vult autem bonum universi esse quia decet bonitatem ipsius Non tamen praedicta triplex ratio secundum eandem habitudinem procedit. Nam bonitas divina neque dependet a perfectione universi, neque ex ea aliquid sibi accrescit. Perfectio autem universi, licet ex aliquibus particularibus bonis ex necessitate dependeat, quae sunt essentiales partes universi, ex quibusdam tamen non dependet ex necessitate, sed tamen ex eis aliqua bonitas vel decor accrescit universo: sicut ex his quae sunt solum ad munimentum vel decorem aliarum partium universi. Particulare autem bonum dependet ex necessitate ex his quae ad ipsum absolute requiruntur: licet et hoc etiam habeat quaedam quae sunt propter melius ipsius. Aliquando igitur ratio divinae voluntatis continet solum decentiam; aliquando utilitatem; aliquando autem necessitatem quae est ex suppositione; necessitatem vero absolutam, solum cum vult seipsum.

13. *ScG* II, 28: Necessitas autem quae est a posteriori in esse licet sit prius natura, non est absoluta necessitas, sed conditionalis: ut, si hoc debeat fieri, necesse est hoc prius esse. Secundum igitur hanc necessitatem in creaturarum productione debitum invenitur tripliciter. Primo, ut sumatur conditionatum debitum a tota rerum universitate ad quamlibet eius partem quae ad perfectionem requiritur universi. Si enim tale universum fieri Deus voluit, debitum fuit ut solem et lunam faceret, et huiusmodi sine quibus universum esse non potest. Secundo, ut sumatur conditionis debitum ex una creatura ad aliam: ut, si animalia et plantas Deus esse voluit, debitum fuit ut caelestia corpora faceret, ex quibus conservantur; et si hominem esse voluit, oportuit facere plantas et animalia, et alia huiusmodi quibus homo indiget ad esse perfectum; quamvis et haec et illa ex mera Deus fecerit voluntate. Tertio, ut in unaquaque creatura sumatur conditionale debitum ex suis partibus et proprietatibus et accidentibus, ex quibus dependet creatura quantum ad esse vel quantum ad aliquam sui perfectionem: sicut, supposito quod Deus hominem facere vellet, debitum ex hac suppositione fuit ut animam et corpus in eo coniungeret, et sensus, et alia huiusmodi adiumenta, tam

intrinseca quam extrinseca, ei praeberet. In quibus omnibus, si recte attenditur, Deus creaturae debitor non dicitur, sed suae dispositioni implendae.

14. *ScG* I, 70: Patet etiam quod haec veritas non repugnat dictis philosophi in XI metaphysicae. Nam ibi intendit ostendere quod divinus intellectus non cognoscit aliud a se quod sit sui intellectus perfectio quasi principale cognitum. Et secundum hunc modum dicit quod *vilia melius ignorantur quam cognoscuntur:* quando scilicet est alia cognitio vilium et nobilium, et vilium consideratio considerationem nobilium impedit.

15. *ScG* I, 61: Intellectus autem divinus per suam scientiam est causa rerum. Unde oportet quod scientia eius sit mensura rerum: sicut ars est mensura artificiatorum, quorum unumquodque in tantum perfectum est inquantum arti concordat. Talis igitur est comparatio intellectus divini ad res qualis rerum ad intellectum humanum.

16. *ScG* I, 58. Dionysius etiam dicit, VII cap. de Div. Nom.: *igitur divina sapientia, seipsam cognoscens, cognoscit omnia, et materialia immaterialiter et indivisibiliter divisibilia et multa unitive.*

17. Novelists often aspire to such knowledge. While explicitly conceding an inability to approximate divine knowledge, which is at once comprehensive and detailed, Joyce aspires in *Ulysses* to be both general or comprehensive and specific or detailed. We have already mentioned the way Joyce attempts to re-wed the singular and the universal, to recover the Aristotelian epistemological assumption that the universal can be perceived in the singular. Consider the way Joyce attempts to reduplicate the history of English prose style in chapter 14 of *Ulysses* or the way he seeks to incorporate in his narrative allusions to all the major myths in Western civilization. The Homeric structure embodies a journey outward from home followed by a return, a journey that encompasses many minds and cultures, the most important and most ordinary of which, it seems, can be found in Dublin. Another example of the aspiration for comprehensive vision with detailed apprehension is evident in chapter 6, in the scene at the cemetery during Dignam's funeral, when Bloom ponders the innumerable dead:

> How many! All these here once walked round Dublin. Faithful departed. As you are now so once were we. Besides how could you remember everybody? Eyes, walk, voice. Well, the voice, yes: gramophone. Have a gramophone in every grave or keep it in the house. . . . Remind you of the voice like the photograph reminds you of the face.

Throughout this scene, Bloom attempts to gain a handle on the whole without sacrificing specificity. As if to underscore the elusiveness of such intelligibility, Joyce in this very chapter locates a great, if apparently insignificant mystery of the novel: "Who is Macintosh?"—a man who is apparently at the funeral but whose identity is never clarified at any point in the novel. Comprehensive knowledge is elusive in this detail, as in so many others.

18. *ScG* I, 6.

19. McInerny, *Characters in Search of Their Author,* 4.

20. *ScG* II, 4.

21. *ScG* III, 100: Omnes creaturae comparantur ad Deum sicut artificiata ad artificem, ut ex praemissis patet. Unde tota natura est sicut quoddam artificiatum divinae artis. Non est autem contra rationem artificii si artifex aliter aliquid operetur in suo artificio, etiam postquam ei primam formam dedit. Neque ergo est contra naturam si Deus in rebus naturalibus aliquid operetur aliter quam consuetus cursus naturae habet.

22. *ScG* III, 101: Haec autem quae praeter ordinem communiter in rebus statutum quandoque divinitus fiunt, miracula dici solent: admiramur enim aliquid cum, effectum videntes, causam ignoramus.

23. Pieper, *Faith Hope Love*, 93.

24. Ibid., 93.

25. Ibid., 113.

26. Aquinas as quoted in Pieper, 110.

27. Ibid., 111.

28. Pieper, *Leisure, the Basis of Culture*, 103–4.

29. Pieper, *Hope and History*, five Salzburg lectures, trans. David Kipp (San Francisco: Ignatius Press, 1994), 18.

30. For my objections to certain features of MacIntyre's deployment of Aquinas in his dismissal of modern politics, see Thomas Hibbs, "MacIntyre, Aquinas, and Politics," *Review of Politics* 66 (2004): 357–83.

31. Alasdair MacIntyre, *Marxism and Christianity* (New York: Schocken Books, 1968), 115.

32. Ibid., 112.

33. Ibid., 111.

34. Sheldon Wolin, *Tocqueville Between Two Worlds* (Princeton, N.J.: Princeton University Press, 2001), 566.

35. Ibid., 568.

36. Ibid., 566.

37. We must be careful here not to conflate the views of Pieper or Aquinas with those who would despair of all earthly politics or repudiate the practice of justice here and now in favor of eschatological prophecy. Aquinas certainly thought that we could make informed, prudential judgments about politics and that we had obligations, both natural and supernatural, to perform just deeds and promote a just political order. Perhaps the best modern Thomistic attempt at thinking about the foundations of the political order can be had in Yves Simon's *Philosophy of Democratic Government* (Chicago: University of Chicago Press, 1951).

38. Pieper, *Hope and History*, 107–11.

39. Ibid., 109.

40. Aristotle is commonly believed to have softened the Platonic critique of tragedy, but it is striking how little Aristotle has to say in the *Poetics* about those features of tragedy to which Plato was most resistant: the gods, fate, and religious prophecy.

41. *ScG* IV, 54: Si quis autem diligenter et pie incarnationis mysteria consideret, inveniet tantam sapientiae profunditatem quod humanam cognitionem excedat: secundum illud apostoli: *quod stultum est Dei, sapientius est hominibus.* Unde fit ut pie consideranti semper magis ac magis admirabiles rationes huius mysterii manifestantur.

42. *ScG* IV, 55.

43. Marion, *The Idol and Distance*, 58.

44. Ibid., 63.

45. Ibid., 66.

46. *Expositio in Symbolum Apostolorum* (Turin, 1954), 4, nn. 919–924: Nam, sicut dicit beatus Augustinus, passio Christi sufficit ad informandum totaliter vitam nostram. Quicumque enim vult perfecte vivere, nihil aliud faciat nisi quod contemnat quae Christus in cruce contempsit, et appetat quae Christus appetiit. Nullum enim exemplum virtutis abest a cruce. Si enim quaeras exemplum caritatis, *maiorem car-*

itatem nemo habet ut animam suam ponat quis pro amicis suis, Ioan. XV, 13. Et hoc in cruce fecit Christus. Et ideo si pro nobis animam suam dedit, non debet nobis esse grave quaecumque mala sustinere pro ipso. Psal. CXV, 12: *quid retribuam domino pro omnibus quae retribuit mihi?* Si quaeris exemplum patientiae, excellentissima in cruce invenitur. Patientia enim ex duobus magna ostenditur: aut cum quis magna patienter suffert, aut cum ea suffert quae vitare posset, et non vitat. Christus autem magna in cruce pertulit. Thren. I, 12: *o vos omnes qui transitis per viam, attendite, et videte si est dolor sicut dolor meus*; et patienter, quia, *cum pateretur, non comminabatur*, I Petr. II, 23; et Isai. LIII, 7: *sicut ovis ad occisionem ducetur, et quasi agnus coram tondente se obmutescet.* Item vitare potuit, et non vitavit. Matth. XXVI, 53: *an putas quia non possum rogare patrem meum, et exhibebit mihi modo plusquam duodecim legiones Angelorum?* Magna est ergo Christi patientia in cruce. Hebr. XII, 1–2: *per patientiam curramus ad propositum nobis certamen, aspicientes in auctorem fidei et consummatorem Iesum, qui, proposito sibi gaudio sustinuit crucem confusione contempta.* Si quaeris exemplum humilitatis, respice crucifixum: nam Deus iudicari voluit sub Pontio Pilato, et mori. Iob XXXVI, 17: *causa tua quasi impii iudicata est* . Vere impii: quia, *morte turpissima condemnemus eum*, Sap. II, 20. Dominus pro servo, et vita Angelorum pro homine mori voluit. Philip. II, 8: *factus est obediens usque ad mortem.* Si quaeris exemplum obedientiae, sequere eum qui factus est obediens patri usque ad mortem. Rom. V, 19: *sicut per inobedientiam unius hominis peccatores constituti sunt multi: ita per unius obedientiam, iusti constituentur multi.* Si quaeris exemplum contemnendi terrena, sequere eum qui est rex regum et dominus dominantium, in quo sunt thesauri sapientiae; in cruce tamen nudatum, illusum, consputum, caesum, spinis coronatum, et felle et aceto potatum, et mortuum. Igitur non afficiaris ad vestes, et ad divitias: quia *diviserunt sibi vestimenta mea*, Psal. XXI, 19; non ad honores, quia ego ludibria et verbera expertus sum; non ad dignitates, quia plectentes coronam de spinis imposuerunt capiti meo; non ad delicias, quia *in siti mea potaverunt me aceto*, Psal. LXVIII, 22. Augustinus super illud Hebr. XII: *qui proposito sibi gaudio sustinuit crucem, confusione contempta, dicit: omnia bona terrena contempsit homo Christus Iesus ut contemnenda monstraret.*

47. ST III, 62, 5: Unde manifestum est quod sacramenta Ecclesiae specialiter habent virtutem ex passione Christi, cuius virtus quodammodo nobis copulatur per susceptionem sacramentorum. In cuius signum, de latere Christi pendentis in cruce fluxerunt aqua et sanguis, quorum unum pertinet ad Baptismum, aliud ad Eucharistiam, quae sunt potissima sacramenta.

48. Murdoch, *Metaphysics as a Guide to Morals*, 508.

49. Ibid.

50. Stanley Hauerwas, "Murdochian Muddles: Can We Get Through Them If God Does Not Exist?" in *Iris Murdoch and the Search for Human Goodness*, ed. Maria Antonaccio and William Schweiker (Chicago: University of Chicago Press, 1996), 204–205.

51. Ibid., 206.

BIBLIOGRAPHY

Achtenberg, Deborah. *Cognition of Value in Aristotle's Ethics: Promise of Enrichment, Threat of Destruction.* Albany: State University of New York Press, 2002.

Aertsen, Jan. "Good as Transcendental." In *Being and Goodness*, ed. Scott MacDonald. Ithaca, N.Y.: Cornell University Press, 1991.

——. *Medieval Philosophy and the Transcendentals.* Leiden: E. J. Brill, 1996.

Alston, William. "Internalism and Externalism in Epistemology." In *Philosophical Topics* 15 (1986): 179–221.

Anscombe, Elizabeth. "Modern Moral Philosophy." In *Virtue Ethics*, ed. Crisp and Slote, 26–44. Oxford: Oxford University Press, 1997. First appeared in *Ethics* 33 (1958).

Aristotle. *The Complete Works of Aristotle: The Revised Oxford Translation*, Vols. 1 and 2. Edited by Jonathan Barnes. Princeton, N.J.: Princeton University Press, 1984.

Baier, Annette. "What Do Women Want?" In *Virtue Ethics*, ed. Crisp and Slote, 263–77. Oxford: Oxford University Press, 1997.

——. "The Need for More than Justice." In *Justice and Care: Essential Readings in Feminist Ethics*, ed. Virginia Held, 47-60. Boulder, Colo.: Westview Press, 1995.

Balthasar, Hans Urs von. *The Glory of the Lord: A Theological Aesthetics*, Vol. 2, *Studies in Theological Styles: Clerical Styles.* San Francisco: Ignatius, 1984.

Barad, Judith. *Aquinas on the Nature and Treatment of Animals.* San Francisco: International Scholars Publication, 1995.

Barnes, Jonathan. "Aristotle's Theory of Demonstration." *Phronesis* 14 (1969): 123–52.

——. "Proof and Syllogism." In *Aristotle on Science: The Posterior Analytics*, 17–59. Padua: Editrice Antenore, 1981.

Bedouelle, Guy. *Saint Dominic: The Grace of the Word.* San Francisco: Ignatius, 1987.

Berkowitz, Peter. *Nietzsche: The Ethics of an Immoralist.* Cambridge, Mass.: Harvard University Press, 1996.

Bernstein, Richard. "Whatever Happened to Naturalism?" In *Proceedings of the American Philosophical Association* 69 (1995): 57–76.

Berry, Wendell. *Sex, Economy, Freedom, and Community.* New York: Pantheon Books, 1993.

Bowlin, John. *Contingency and Fortune in Aquinas's Ethics.* Cambridge: Cambridge University Press, 1999.

Broadie, Sarah. *Ethics with Aristotle.* Oxford: Oxford University Press, 1991.

Bruyne, Edgar de. *The Esthetics of the Middle Ages.* New York: F. Ungar, 1969.

Burrell, David. "From Analogy of 'Being' to the Analogy of Being." In *Recovering Nature.* Notre Dame, Ind.: University of Notre Dame Press, 1999.

——. *Knowing the Unknowable God: Ibn-Sina, Maimonides, Aquinas.* Notre Dame, Ind.: University of Notre Dame Press, 1986.

Caputo, John. *Against Ethics.* Bloomington: Indiana University Press, 1993.

——. *Heidegger and Aquinas: An Essay on Overcoming Metaphysics.* New York: Fordham University Press, 1982.

Caputo, John, and Michael Scanlan, eds. *God, the Gift, and Postmodernism.* Bloomington: Indiana University Press, 1999.

Cavell, Stanley. *Cities of Words.* Cambridge, Mass.: Harvard University Press, 2005.

Cessario, Romanus. *A Short History of Thomism.* Washington, D.C.: Catholic University of America Press, 1995.

Chenu, Marie Dominique. *Nature, Man, and Society in the Twelfth Century.* Ed. and trans. Jerome Taylor and Lester K. Little. Chicago: University of Chicago Press, 1968.

Clarke, Norris. *Explorations in Metaphysics.* Notre Dame, Ind.: University of Notre Dame Press, 1995.

——. *The One and the Many: A Contemporary Thomistic Metaphysics.* Notre Dame, Ind.: University of Notre Dame Press, 2001.

Collins, James. "Toward a Philosophically Ordered Thomism." *The New Scholasticism* 32 (1958): 301–26.

Corbin, Michelle. *Le chemin de la théologie chez Thomas d'Aquin.* Paris: Beauchesne, 1972.

Dagger, Richard. *Civic Virtues: Rights, Citizenship, and Republican Liberalism.* Oxford: Oxford University Press, 1997.

Dahl, Norman. *Practical Reason, Aristotle, and Weakness of Will.* Minneapolis: University of Minnesota Press, 1984.

Davies, Brian. "Classical Theism and the Doctrine of Divine Simplicity." In *Language, Meaning, and God,* ed. Brian Davis. London: Geoffrey Chapman, 1987.

——. *The Thought of Thomas Aquinas.* Oxford: Clarendon, 1992.

Descartes, René. *Philosophical Essays.* Translated by Laurence Lafleur. Indianapolis: Bobbs-Merrill, 1964.

Dewan, Lawrence. "Aquinas and Kretzmann on Creation," *Nova et Vetera* 4 (2006): 495–514.

——. "St. Thomas, St. Albert, and Knowledge." *ACPQ* LXX (1996): 121–25.

Doig, James. *Aquinas on Metaphysics: A Historico-Doctrinal Study of the Commentary on the Metaphysics.* The Hague: Nijhoff, 1972.

Dunne, Joseph. *Back to the Rough Ground: Phronesis and Techne in Modern Philosophy and in Aristotle.* Notre Dame, Ind.: University of Notre Dame Press, 1993.

Eco, Umberto. *The Aesthetics of Thomas Aquinas.* Cambridge, Mass.: Harvard University Press, 1988.

Elders, Leo. "Saint Thomas d'Aquin et Aristote." *Revue Thomiste* 88 (1988): 357–76.

Eliot, T. S. *Selected Prose.* New York: Farrar, Straus and Giroux, 1975.

Ellmann, Richard. *James Joyce.* Oxford: Oxford University Press, [1959] 1983.

Ewbank, Michael B. "Of Idols, Icons, and Aquinas's *Esse:* Reflections on Jean-Luc Marion." *International Philosophical Quarterly* 42/2 (2002): 161–75.

Fabro, Cornelio. *Participation et causalité selon S. Thomas d'Aquin:* Préface de L. De Raeymaeker. Louvain: Publications universitaires de Louvain, 1961.

——. "The Transcendality of Ens-Esse and the Ground of Metaphysics." *International Philosophical Quarterly* 6 (1966): 389–427.

Finnis, John. *Aquinas: Moral, Political, and Legal Theory*. Oxford: Oxford University Press, 1998.

——. *Natural Law and Natural Rights*. Oxford: Oxford University Press, 1980.

Foot, Philippa. *Virtues and Vices and Other Essays in Moral Philosophy*. Oxford: Oxford University Press, 2003.

Fortin, Ernest L. "The New Rights Theory and the Natural Law." *Review of Politics*, 44 (1982): 590–612.

——. "St. Thomas Aquinas." In *History of Political Philosophy*, 3rd ed., ed. Leo Strauss and Joseph Cropsey, 248–75. Chicago: Rand-McNally, 1987.

French, Marilyn. *The Book as World*. Cambridge, Mass.: Harvard University Press, 1976.

Funkenstein, Amos. *Theology and the Scientific Imagination*. Princeton, N.J.: Princeton University Press, 1986.

Gadamer, Hans Georg. *The Idea of the Good in Platonic-Aristotelian Philosophy*. Trans. P. Christopher Smith. New Haven, Conn.: Yale University Press, 1986.

——. *Truth and Method*. Trans. Garrett Barden and John Cumming. New York: Seabury, 1975.

Galston, William. *Liberal Purposes: Goods, Virtues, and Diversity in the Liberal State*. Cambridge: Cambridge University Press, 1991.

Garcia, Laura. "Divine Freedom and Creation." *Philosophical Quarterly* 42 (1992): 191–213.

Gauthier, R. A. *Introduction historique au tome I de l'edition bilingue de la Summa contra Gentiles*. Paris: P. Lethielleux, 1961.

——. "Introduction" to *Somme Contre les Gentiles*. Paris: Editions Universitaires, 1993.

——. *La morale d' Aristote*. Paris: Presses Universitaires de France, 1958.

——. Préface to *Sententia libri de anima*, Leonine edition. Paris: J. Vrin, 1984.

Geach, Peter. *Mental Acts*. London: Routledge and Kegan Paul, 1957.

Geiger, Louis. "Abstraction et separation d'apres S. Thomas." *Revue des Sciences Philosophiques et Théologiques* 31 (1947): 3–40.

——. *La participation dans la philosophie de S. Thomas d'Aquin*. Paris: Vrin, 1942.

George, Robert P., ed. *Natural Law Theory: Contemporary Essays*. Oxford: Oxford University Press, 1994.

Gilson, Etienne. *Being and Some Philosophers*. Toronto: PIMS, 1949.

Girard, Rene. *A Theater of Envy: William Shakespeare*. South Bend, Ind.: St. Augustine's, 2004.

Goerner, E. A. "On Thomistic Natural Law: The Bad Man's View of Thomistic Natural Right." *Political Theory* 7 (1979): 101–22.

——. "Thomistic Natural Right: The Good Man's View of Thomistic Natural Law." *Political Theory* 11 (1983): 393–418.

Goldman, Alvin. "The Internalist Conception of Justification." In *Midwest Studies in Philosophy* 5 (1980): 27–73.

Greco, John. "Catholics vs. Calvinists on Religious Knowledge." *American Catholic Philosophical Quarterly* 71 (1997): 13–34.

Gutmann, Amy. *Democratic Education*. Princeton, N.J.: Princeton University Press, 1987.

Hadot, Pierre. *Philosophy as a Way of Life*. Malden, Mass.: Blackwell, 1995.

——. *What Is Ancient Philosophy?* Cambridge, Mass.: Belknap, 2002.

Haldane, John. "Reid, Scholasticism and Current Philosophy of Mind." In *The Philosophy of Thomas Reid*, ed. M. Dalgarno and E. Matthews. Dordrecht: Kluwer, 1989.

Hall, Pamela. *Narrative and the Natural Law.* Notre Dame, Ind.: University of Notre Dame Press, 1999.

Hankey, Wayne J. *God in Himself: Aquinas's Doctrine of God as Expounded in the Summa Theologiae.* Oxford: Oxford University Press, 1987.

Hauerwas, Stanley. "Murdochian Muddles: Can We Get Through Them if God Does Not Exist?" In *Iris Murdoch and the Search for Human Goodness,* ed. Maria Antonaccio and William Schweiker. Chicago: University of Chicago Press, 1996.

——. *Vision and Virtue.* Notre Dame, Ind.: University of Notre Dame Press, 1981.

Held, Virginia, ed. *Justice and Care: Essential Readings in Feminist Ethics.* Boulder, Colo.: Westview, 1995.

Hibbs, Thomas. "Aquinas, Virtue, and Recent Epistemology." *Review of Metaphysics* 52 (1999): 573–94.

——. *Dialectic and Narrative in Aquinas: An Interpretation of the Summa Contra Gentiles.* Notre Dame: University of Notre Dame Press, 1995.

——. "Kretzmann's Theism vs. Aquinas's Theism: Interpreting the *Summa contra Gentiles.*" *The Thomist* 62 (1998): 603–22.

——. "MacIntyre, Aquinas, and Politics." In *Review of Politics* 66 (2004): 357–83.

——. "Portraits of the Artist: Joyce, Nietzsche, and Aquinas." In *Beauty, Art, and the Polis,* ed. Alice Ramos, 117–37. Washington, D.C.: Catholic University of America Press, 2000.

——. *Virtue's Splendor: Wisdom, Prudence, and the Human Good.* New York: Fordham Press, 2001.

Hittinger, Russell. *A Critique of the New Natural Law Theory.* Notre Dame, Ind.: University of Notre Dame Press, 1987.

Hursthouse, Rosalind. *On Virtue Ethics.* Oxford: Oxford University Press, 2002.

Jaffa, Harry. *Thomism and Aristotelianism: A Study of the Commentary by Thomas Aquinas on the Nichomachean Ethics.* Chicago: University of Chicago Press, 1952.

Jenkins, John. "Expositions of the Text: Aquinas's Aristotelian Commentaries." *Medieval Philosophy and Theology* 5 (1996): 36–62.

——. *Knowledge and Faith in Thomas Aquinas.* Cambridge: Cambridge University Press, 1997.

Johnson, Mark. "Immateriality and the Domain of Thomistic Natural Philosophy." *Modern Schoolman* 67 (1990): 285–304.

Jordan, Mark. *The Alleged Aristotelianism of Thomas Aquinas,* Gilson Lecture, no. 15. Toronto: PIMS, 1992.

——. "The Evidence of the Transcendentals and the Place of Beauty in Thomas Aquinas." *International Philosophical Quarterly* 29 (1989): 393–406.

——. "The Names of God and the Being of Names." In *The Existence and Nature of God,* ed. Alfred Freddoso, 161–90. Notre Dame, Ind.: University of Notre Dame Press, 1983.

——. *Ordering Wisdom: The Hierarchy of Philosophical Discourses in Aquinas.* Notre Dame, Ind.: University of Notre Dame Press, 1986.

——. "The Protreptic Structure of the *Summa Contra Gentiles.*" *The Thomist* 50 (1986): 173–209.

Joyce, James. *Portrait of the Artist as a Young Man.* New York: Penguin Books, 1992.

——. *Ulysses.* New York: Random House, 1986.

Kearney, Richard. "Desire of God." In *God, the Gift, and Postmodernism,* ed. John

Caputo and Michael Scanlon, 112–45. Bloomington: Indiana University Press, 1999.

——. *The God Who May Be: A Hermeneutics of Religion*. Bloomington: Indiana University Press, 2001.

——. *Strangers, Gods, and Monsters: Interpreting Otherness*. New York: Routledge, 2003.

Kenner, Hugh. "The Cubist Portrait." In *Approaches to Joyce's Portrait*, ed. Staley and Benstock. Pittsburgh: University of Pittsburgh Press, 1976.

Kenny, Anthony. *Aquinas on Mind*. London: Routledge, 1993.

Kerr, Fergus. *After Aquinas: Versions of Thomism*. Malden, Mass.: Blackwell, 2002.

Koninck, Charles de. "Abstraction from Matter II." In *Laval théologique et philosophique* 13 (1957): 148–62, and 16 (1960): 53–69 and 169–88.

Kretzmann, Norman. *The Metaphysics of Creation: Aquinas's Natural Theology in Summa contra gentiles II*. Oxford: Oxford University Press, 1999.

——. *The Metaphysics of Theism: Aquinas's Natural Theology in Summa contra gentiles I*. Oxford: Clarendon, 1997.

Kretzmann, Norman, and Eleonore Stump. "Eternity, Awareness, and Action." *Faith and Philosophy* 9 (1992): 463–82.

——. "Eternity and God's Knowledge: A Reply to Shanley." *American Catholic Philosophical Quarterly* 72 (1998): 439–45.

Kupperman, Joel. *Character*. Oxford: Oxford University Press, 1991.

Lachterman, David. *The Ethics of Geometry: A Genealogy of Modernity*. New York: Routledge, 1989.

Lamb, Matthew. "Eternity and Time." In *Gladly to Learn and Gladly to Teach: Essays on Religion and Political Philosophy in Honor of Ernest L. Fortin, A.A.*, ed. Michael Foley and Douglas Kries, 195–214. New York: Lexington Books, 2002.

Lesher, James. "The Meaning of NOUS in the Posterior Analytics." *Phronesis* 18 (1973): 44–68.

Levering, Matthew. *Scripture and Metaphysics: Aquinas and the Renewal of Trinitarian Theology*. Malden, Mass.: Blackwell, 2004.

MacDonald, Scott. "Theory of Knowledge." In *The Cambridge Companion to Aquinas*, 160–95. Cambridge: Cambridge University Press, 1993.

MacIntyre, Alasdair. *After Virtue*. Notre Dame, Ind.: University of Notre Dame Press, 1981.

——. *Dependent Rational Animals*. Chicago: Open Court, 2001.

——. *Edith Stein: A Philosophical Prologue, 1913–1922*. Lanham, Md.: Rowman & Littlefield, 2006.

——. "The Intelligibility of Action." In *Rationality, Relativism, and the Human Sciences*, ed. Margolis, Krausz, and Burian. Dordrecht: Martinus Nijhoff, 1986.

——. "The Magic in the Pronoun 'My.'" *Ethics* 94 (1983): 113–25.

——. *Marxism and Christianity*. New York: Schocken Books, 1968.

——. "On Not Having the Last Word: Thoughts on Our Debts to Gadamer." In *Gadamer's Century*, ed. Malpas, Arnswald, and Kertscher. Cambridge: MIT Press, 2002.

——. "Sophrosune: How a Virtue Can Become Socially Disruptive." In *Midwest Studies in Philosophy*, Vol. 13, *Ethical Theory: Character and Virtue*, 1–11. Notre Dame, Ind.: University of Notre Dame Press, 1988.

——. *Three Rival Versions of Moral Enquiry*. Notre Dame, Ind.: University of Notre Dame Press, 1991.

Marion, Jean-Luc. *God Without Being*. Trans. Thomas Carlson. Chicago: University of Chicago Press, 1991.

——. *The Idol and Distance*. Trans. Thomas Carlson. New York: Fordham University Press, 2001.

——. "In the Name: How to Avoid Speaking of 'Negative Theology,'" In *God, the Gift, and Postmodernism*, ed. John Caputo and Michael Scanlon, 20–53. Bloomington: Indiana University Press, 1999.

——. "Saint Thomas d'Aquin et l'onto-théo-logie." *Revue Thomiste* 95 (1995): 31–66.

Maritain, Jacques. *Distinguish to Unite, or, The Three Degrees of Knowledge*. Translated under the supervision of Gerald Phelan. Notre Dame, Ind.: University of Notre Dame Press, 1995.

——. *A Preface to Metaphysics: Seven Lectures on Being*. New York: Sheed & Ward, 1946.

——. *The Rights of Man and Natural Law*. San Francisco: Ignatius, 1986.

Maurer, Armand. *About Beauty*. Houston, Tex.: Center for Thomistic Studies, 1983.

McAleer, G. J. *Ecstatic Morality and Sexual Politics*. New York: Fordham University Press, 2005.

McCool, Gerald. *From Unity to Pluralism: The Internal Evolution of Thomism*. New York: Fordham University Press, 1992.

McDowell, John. *Mind and World*. Cambridge, Mass.: Harvard University Press, 1994.

McInerny, Ralph. *Aquinas Against the Averroists: On There Being Only One Intellect*. West Lafayette, Ind.: Purdue University Press, 1993.

——. *Aquinas and Analogy*. Washington D.C.: Catholic University of America Press; reprint, 1998.

——. *Characters in Search of Their Author: The Gifford Lectures Glasgow 1999–2000*. Notre Dame, Ind.: University of Notre Dame Press, 2003.

——. *Ethica Thomistica*. Washington, D.C.: Catholic University of America Press, 1997.

——. "Ontology and Theology in Aristotle's Metaphysics." In *Being and Predication*. Washington, D.C.: Catholic University of America Press, 1986.

——. *The Question of Christian Ethics*. Washington, D.C.: Catholic University of America Press, 1998.

——. *Thomas Aquinas: Selected Writings*. New York: Penguin Classics, 1998.

——. "Thomas Reid and Common Sense." In an *American Catholic Philosophical Quarterly* volume devoted to Thomas Reid and ed. John Haldane, 74 (2000): 345–56.

Milbank, John. "Only Theology Overcomes Metaphysics." In *The Word Made Strange*, 42–43. Cambridge: Blackwell, 1997.

Morrow, Derek. "Aquinas, Marion, Analogy, and *Esse*: A Phenomenology of the Divine Names?" *International Philosophical Quarterly* 46 (2006): 25–42.

Murdoch, Iris. *Existentialists and Mystics: Writings on Philosophy and Literature*, ed. Peter Conradi. New York: Penguin Books, 1998.

—— *Metaphysics as a Guide to Morals*. New York: Penguin, 1992.

——. *Sovereignty of the Good*. New York: Schocken Books, 1971.

Narcisse, Gilbert. *Les raisons de Dieu: Argument de convenance et esthétique théologique selon saint Thomas d'Aquin et Hans Urs von Balthasar*. Fribourg: Editions Universitaires, 1997.

Nelson, Daniel Mark. *The Priority of Prudence*. University Park: Pennsylvania State University Press, 1992.

Newman, John Henry. *An Essay in Aid of a Grammar of Assent*. Notre Dame, Ind.: University of Notre Dame Press, 1979.

——. *The Idea of a University*. Notre Dame, Ind.: University of Notre Dame Press, 1982.

Nichols, Aidan. *Discovering Aquinas*. London: Darton, Longman and Todd, 2002.

Nietzsche, Friedrich. *Beyond Good and Evil*. Trans. Walter Kaufmann. New York: Vintage Books, 1966.

——. *The Birth of Tragedy*. Trans. Walter Kaufmann. New York: Random House, 1967.

——. *Will to Power*. Trans. Walter Kaufmann. New York: Vintage, 1968.

Noon, William. *Joyce and Aquinas*. New Haven, Conn.: Yale University Press, 1957.

Nussbam, Martha. *Upheavals of Thought: The Intelligence of Emotions*. Cambridge: Cambridge University Press, 2003.

Nussbam, Martha, and Hilary Putnam. "Changing Aristotle's Mind." In *Essays on Aristotle's De Anima*, ed. A. Rorty and M. Nussbaum, 27–56. Oxford: Clarendon, 1992.

O'Callaghan, John P. "The Problem of Language and Mental Representation in Aristotle and St. Thomas." *Review of Metaphysics* 50 (1997): 499–541.

——. *Thomistic Realism and the Linguistic Turn: Toward a More Perfect Form of Existence*. Notre Dame, Ind.: University of Notre Dame Press, 2003.

O'Meara, Thomas. "Virtues in the Theology of Thomas Aquinas." *Theological Studies* 58 (1997): 256–87.

O'Rourke, Fran. *Pseudo-Dionysius and the Metaphysics of Aquinas*. Leiden: E. J. Brill, 1992.

Owens, Joseph. "Aquinas as Aristotelian Commentator." In *St. Thomas Aquinas 1274–1974: Commemorative Studies*, 1:213–38. Toronto: PIMS, 1974.

Paglia, Camille. *Sexual Personae: Art and Decadence from Nefertiti to Emily Dickinson*. New York: Vintage, 1991.

Pascal, Blaise. *Pensées*. Trans. A. J. Krailsheimer. London: Penguin Books, 1966.

Pasnau, Robert. *Theories of Cognition in the Later Middle Ages*. Cambridge: Cambridge University Press, 1997.

Pieper, Josef. *Faith Hope Love*. San Francisco: Ignatius, 1997.

——. *The Four Cardinal Virtues*. Notre Dame, Ind.: University of Notre Dame Press, 1966.

——. *Hope and History*, five Salzburg lectures. Trans. David Kipp. San Francisco: Ignatius, 1994.

——. *Leisure, the Basis of Culture*. Trans. Alexander Dru with an introduction by T. S. Eliot. New York: Pantheon Books, 1964.

Pinckaers, Servais. *The Sources of Christian Ethics*. Trans. Mary Thomas Noble. Washington, D.C.: Catholic University of America Press, 1995.

Pippen, Robert. *Idealism as Modernism*. Cambridge: Cambridge University Press, 1997.

Plantinga, Alvin. *Warrant: The Current Debate*. Oxford: Oxford University Press: 1993.

——. *Warrant and Proper Function*. Oxford: Oxford University Press, 1993.

Putnam, Hilary. *Representation and Reality*. Cambridge: MIT Press, 1988.

Resnik, Irven, and Kenneth Kitchell. "Albert the Great on the 'Language' of Animals." *American Catholic Philosophical Quarterly* 70 (1996): 41–61.

Ricoeur, Paul. *Oneself as Another*. Trans: Kathleen Blamey. Chicago: University of Chicago Press, 1992.

Rorty, Amelie. "Virtues and their Vicissitudes." In *Essays on Aristotle's Ethics*, ed. Amelie Rorty. Berkeley: University of California Press, 1981.

Rosemann, Philipp. *Understanding Scholastic Thought with Foucault*. New York: St. Martin's, 1999.

Rosen, Stanley. *The Question of Being: A Reversal of Heidegger*. South Bend, Ind.: St. Augustine's, 2002.

——. *Metaphysics in Ordinary Language*. South Bend, Ind.: St. Augustine's, 2004.

——. "Thought and Touch: A Note on Aristotle's De Anima." *Phronesis* 6 (1961): 127–37.

Sallis, John. *Being and Logos: The Way of the Platonic Dialogue*. Bloomington: Indiana University Press, 1996.

Sandel, Michael. *Democracy's Discontent*. Cambridge, Mass.: Belknap, 1998.

——. *Liberalism and the Limits of Justice*. Cambridge: Cambridge University Press, 1982.

Schaefer, Jean-Marie. *Art of the Modern Age: Philosophy of Art from Kant to Heidegger*. Princeton, N.J.: Princeton University Press, 1992.

Scheffler, Samuel. *The Rejection of Consequentialism*. Oxford: Clarendon, 1994.

Schmitz, Kenneth. *The Gift: Creation*. Milwaukee, Wis.: Marquette University Press, 1982.

——. "The God of Love," *The Thomist* 57 (1993): 495–608.

Schneewind, Jerome. "The Misfortunes of Virtue." In *Virtue Ethics*, ed. Crisp and Slote, 178–200. Oxford: Oxford University Press, 1997.

Shanley, Brian. "Aquinas on God's Causal Knowledge: A Reply to Stump and Kretzmann." *American Catholic Philosophical Quarterly* 72 (1998): 447–57.

——. "Eternal Knowledge of the Temporal in Aquinas," *American Catholic Philosophical Quarterly* 71 (1997): 197–224.

——. "St. Thomas, Onto-Theology, and Marion," *The Thomist* 60 (1996): 617–25.

Shermann, Nancy. *Making a Necessity of Virtue: Aristotle and Kant on Virtue*. Cambridge: Cambridge University Press, 1997.

Simon, Yves. *Freedom of Choice*. New York: Fordham University Press, 1969.

——. *Philosophy of Democratic Government*. Chicago: University of Chicago Press, 1951.

——. *The Tradition of Natural Law*. New York: Fordham University Press, 1992.

——. *Work, Society, and Culture*. New York: Fordham University Press, 1971.

Sinopli, Richard. *The Foundation of American Citizenship: Liberalism, the Constitution, and Civic Virtue*. Oxford: Oxford University Press, 1997.

Skinner, Quentin. "The Republican Ideal of Political Liberty." In *Machiavelli and Republicanism*, ed. G. Bock, Q. Skinner, and M. Viroli. Cambridge: Cambridge University Press, 1990.

Slote, Michael. *From Morality to Virtue*. Oxford: Oxford University Press, 1992.

Smith, Nicholas, ed. *Reading Mind and World*. New York: Routledge, 2002.

Sokolowski, Robert. "Exorcising Concepts." *Review of Metaphysics* 40 (1987): 451–63.

——. *The God of Faith and Reason: Foundations of Christian Theology*. Washington, D.C.: Catholic University of America Press, 1995.

Solomon, David. "Internal Objections to Virtue Ethics." In *Ethical Theory: Character and Virtue, Midwest Studies in Philosophy* 13, 428–41. Notre Dame, Ind.: University of Notre Dame Press, 1988.

Statman, Daniel. "Introduction to Virtue Ethics." In *Virtue Ethics*, 2–41. Cambridge: Edinburgh University Press, 1997.

Stocker, William. "The Schizophrenia of Modern Ethical Theories." *Journal of Philosophy* 14 (1976): 453–66.

Stump, Eleonore. *Aquinas*. New York: Routledge, 2003.

——. "Aquinas on Justice." In *Proceedings of the American Catholic Philosophical Association* 71 (1997): 61–78.

Sultan, Stanley. *Eliot, Joyce, and Company*. Oxford: Oxford University Press, 1990.

Taylor, Charles. *Sources of the Self: The Making of the Modern Identity*. Cambridge, Mass.: Harvard University Press, 1992.

Thomas Aquinas. *Commentaria in octo libros Physicorum*. Turin, 1954.

——. *Expositio in Symbolum Apostolorum*. Turin, 1954.

——. *Expositio libri Perhermeneias*. Turin, 1955.

——. *Expositio libri Posteriorum Analyticorum*. Turin, 1955.

——. *Expositio super librum Boethii De Trinitate*. Leiden, 1955.

——. *In librum B. Dionysii De divinis nominibus expositio*. Turin, 1950.

——. *Principium Rigans Montes*. Turin, 1954.

——. *Quaestiones Disputatae De Malo*. Turin, 1953.

——. *Quaestiones Disputatae De Potentia*. Turin, 1953.

——. *Quaestiones Disputatae De Veritate*. Roma, 1970.

——. *Scriptum super Sententiis*. Parma, 1856.

——. *Sententia Libri De Anima*. Turin, 1959.

——. *Sententia Libri Ethicorum*. Rome, 1969.

——. *Sententia Libri Metaphysicorum*. Turin, 1950.

——. *Sententia Libri Politcorum*. Roma, 1971.

——. *Summa contra Gentiles*. Turin, 1961.

——. *Summa Theologiae*. Turin, 1948.

——. *Super Epistolam B. Pauli ad Hebraeos lectura*. Turin, 1953.

——. *Super I Epistolam B. Pauli ad Timotheum lectura*. Turin, 1953.

——. *Super Evangelium S. Ioannis lectura*. Turin, 1952.

Thompson, Walter Jay. "Aristotle: Philosophy and Politics, Theory and Practice." *Proceedings of the American Catholic Philosophical Association* 68 (1994): 109–24.

Thornton, Weldon. *The Antimodernism of Joyce's Portrait*. Syracuse, N.Y.: Syracuse University Press, 1994.

——. *Voices and Values in Joyce's Ulysses*. Gainesville: University Press of Florida, 2000.

Torrell, Jean-Pierre. *Saint Thomas Aquinas*, Vol. 1: *The Person and His Work*. Trans. Robert Royal. Washington, D.C.: Catholic University of America Press, 1996.

——. *Saint Thomas Aquinas*, Vol. 2: *Spiritual Master*. Trans. Robert Royal. Washington, D.C.: Catholic University of America Press, 2003.

Trianosky, G. V. "What Is Virtue Ethics All About?" *American Philosophical Quarterly* 27 (1990): 335–44.

Turner, Denys. *Faith, Reason and the Existence of God*. Cambridge: Cambridge University Press, 2005.

Velde, Rudi T. *Participation and Substantiality in Thomas Aquinas*. Leiden: E. J. Brill, 1995.

Voegelin, Eric. *Anamnesis: On the Theory of History and Politics*. Trans. M. J. Hanak, based on the abbreviated version originally trans. Gerhart Niemeyer. Edited with an intro. by David Walsh. Columbia: University of Missouri Press, 2002.

——. *The New Science of Politics*, Vol. 5 of *The Collected Works of Eric Voegelin*, ed. with an intro. by Manfred Henningsen. Columbia: University of Missouri Press, 2000.

Warner, Martin. *Philosophical Finesse: Studies in the Art of Rational Persuasion.* Oxford: Oxford University Press, 1989.

Westberg, Daniel. *Right Practical Reason: Aristotle, Action, and Prudence in Aquinas.* Oxford: Oxford University Press, 1994.

Wians, William. "Aristotle, Demonstration, and Teaching." *Ancient Philosophy* 9 (1989): 245–53.

Wilhelmsen, Frederick. "The 'I' and Aquinas." *Proceedings of the American Catholic Philosophical Association* (1977): 47–55.

——. *Man's Knowledge of Reality.* Englewood Cliffs, N.J.: Prentice-Hall, 1960.

Williams, Bernard. *Ethics and the Limits of Philosophy.* Cambridge, Mass.: Harvard University Press, 1985.

——. "Internal and External Reasons for Action." In *Moral Luck,* 101–13. Cambridge: Cambridge University Press, 1981.

——. *Truth and Truthfulness.* Princeton, N.J.: Princeton University Press, 2002.

Wippel, John. *Metaphysical Themes in Thomas Aquinas.* Washington, D.C.: Catholic University of America Press, 1995.

——. *The Metaphysical Thought of Thomas Aquinas.* Washington, D.C.: Catholic University of America Press, 2000.

Wolin, Sheldon. *Tocqueville Between Two Worlds.* Princeton, N.J.: Princeton University Press, 2001.

Wolterstorff, Nicholas. *John Locke and the Ethics of Belief.* Cambridge: Cambridge University Press, 1996.

——. *Thomas Reid and the Story of Epistemology.* Cambridge: Cambridge University Press, 2004.

Wright, N. T. *Jesus and the Victory of God.* Minneapolis, MN: Fortress Press, 1996.

Zagzebski, Linda. *Virtues of the Mind: An Inquiry into the Nature of Virtue and the Ethical Foundations of Knowledge.* Cambridge: Cambridge University Press, 1996.

INDEX

Thomas Hibbs is Dean of the Honors College and Distinguished Professor of Ethics and Culture at Baylor University. He is author of *Virtue's Splendor: Wisdom, Prudence, and the Human Good* and *Dialectic and Narrative in Aquinas: An Interpretation of the Summa Contra Gentiles*.

THE ETERNITY OF THE WORLD

In the Thought of Thomas Aquinas and his Contemporaries

EDITED BY

J.B.M. WISSINK

E.J. BRILL

LEIDEN · NEW YORK · KØBENHAVN · KÖLN
1990

ISSN 0169–8125
ISBN 90 04 09183 1

PRINTED IN THE NETHERLANDS BY E. J. BRILL

CONTENTS

INTRODUCTION

This volume contains the contributions to the symposium on the Eternity of the World, organized in December 1986 by the Thomas Aquinas Workgroup, in Utrecht, The Netherlands.

The Thomas Aquinas Workgroup is a group of theologians and philosophers, mainly from the different universities of The Netherlands, who are interested in Aquinas and his contribution to theology. Together they are involved in research on Aquinas, his sources and his reception in later centuries, right up to the 20th century. Since the revival of Thomism in the 19th century, strongly supported by the 1879 encyclical "Aeterni Patris" of Pope Leo XIII Aquinas' work has mainly been studied by Catholic philosophers and to a much smaller extent by theologians, and where theologians did study it, they were mainly concerned with its metaphysical parts as, for example, the famous quaestiones in the Summa Theologiae on the so-called five ways of demonstrating the existence of God.

One of the purposes of the research of the Thomas Aquinas Workgroup is to evaluate the thesis that Aquinas first of all has to be understood as a theologian who wants to understand what the Catholic faith tells him about the God of Jesus Christ, and that many of his works have to be read and interpreted from this point of view.

The members of the Workgroup are confronted with the fact that after the enormous revival of interest in Thomism in the late 19th and early 20th century, until about 1950, there has been an enormous decline of the interest in his work. Aquinas has virtually disappeared from the curricula of the philosophical and theological faculties of catholic universities and seminaries. The Workgroup seeks to know why this has happened. Has it something to do with the fact that Aquinas became the official "auctoritas" for Roman Catholic theology and philosophy at the end of the 19th century? And the question also has to be answered whether this official revival and the subsequent decline have been and will be good for theology. By its research on questions like these, the Thomas Aquinas Workgroup hopes to contribute to a rediscovery of the original Aquinas and his authentic thought.

As a part of its research programme the Workgroup organized a symposium in December 1986 on the reception of Aquinas in the thinking about the eternity of the world by theologians at the end of the 13th and the beginning of the 14th century. This question held and still holds the interest of philosophers and theologians, because of its relation with philosophical concepts such as eternity and infinity and the theological concept of creation. Thus this is a good question to bring together philosophers and theologians interested in Aquinas. Several contributions were studied and discussed, and they are now being made available to a wider public in this volume. F. de Grijs (a professor of theology at the Catholic Theological University Utrecht) defends the thesis that Aquinas' main interest in his De Aeternitate Mundi is not philosophical but theological; in support of this thesis he gives arguments concerning the form and the content of this work.

Professor J. Aertsen (Free University Amsterdam) opposes this thesis and tries to demonstrate Aquinas' philosophical purposes by comparing his De Aeternitate Mundi with his De Potentia and by study of Aquinas' concept of creation.

This volume continues with a survey, by P. van Veldhuijsen, of the history of the question of the Eternity of the World and an overview of the differences between Bonaventure and Aquinas on this subject, because those who disagree with Aquinas often claim to agree with Bonaventure.

M. Hoenen (Catholic University Nijmegen) writes on Aquinas' reception in the so called "Correctoria Literature' and makes clear that Aquinas' De Aeternitate Mundi does not play a role in it, though the discussion about Aquinas' position concerning the eternity of the world is vividly discussed.

Dr. J. Thijssen (Catholic University Nijmegen) deals with Aquinas' reception by Henry of Harclay and John of Alnwick, and points out the importance of the concept of infinity for one's ideas about the eternity of the world.

P. van Veldhuijsen (Free University Amsterdam) investigates Aquinas' reception by Richard of Middleton and emphasizes the importance of the concept "creatio ex nihilo" and shows Middleton's original interpretation of Aquinas' concept of "creatio ex nihilo", so that Thomas was in fact used as a supporter of Middleton's ideas about the Eternity of the World, which are nevertheless different from Aquinas's.

We hope that this volume will find its way to theologians and philosophers interested in Aquinas and we also hope to have created a kind of workbook for students in philosophy and theology, which may help them to form an impression of the medieval thought about an important subject in the history of theology and philosophy and of Aquinas' influence in this field.

I want to express my gratitude to J. van den Eijnden o.f.m., who did much work for the organisation of the symposium.

Utrecht, Catholic Theological
University April 1988

Workgroup Thomas Aquinas
Dr. J. WISSINK

THE THEOLOGICAL CHARACTER OF AQUINAS'
*DE AETERNITATE MUNDI**

F.J.A. DE GRIJS

1. *The Problem*

Text editions of the *De aeternitate mundi* as well as the related literature, unmistakably create the impression that this work belongs to the *Opuscula philosophica* of Saint Thomas Aquinas (Hoogveld, 1939, 39; Miehte & Bourke, 1980, 77–88). M.-.D. Chenu who strongly believes in the theological nature of Thomas' concern, thinking and aims, concludes his discussion of this opuscule by considering together Siger of Brabant and Thomas Aquinas and describing their opuscules which both bear the same name, as "deux belles pièces du patrimoine de la philosophie chrétienne" although he understood that Thomas was arguing against the so-called Augustinian theologians (Chenu, 1954, 289–290). In the meantime I. Brady has named John Peckham as the most probable addressee of Thomas' discussion, but Brady seems not to be impressed by the fact that such a difference of opinion has arisen between two "Magistri in sacra pagina" (Brady, 1974, 154).

One could argue that this is a point of little importance as it could easily become a rather fruitless dispute about competence in matters of religious thinking and conceptualizing. But if, on the other hand, the theological character of this work could be established, this probably would contribute to a better understanding of the opuscule and it would give some additional insight into Saint Thomas' "way of theology" (Corbin, 1974).

As far as I know, the late James Weisheipl has been the only scholar who in a recent study has drawn attention to the theological nature of *De aeternitate mundi* (Weisheipl, 1983). His view is based upon two arguments.

1. The work neither aims at a refutation of Aristotle or of radical Aristotelians among Aquinas' contemporaries, nor does it aim at a defence of Aristotelian argumentation against certain opponents. In such cases philosophical polemics would have been called for.

2. The subject matter of *De aeternitate mundi* is entirely theological, for it implies questions about the power of God and about the limits of human reason. Those problems "are the domain of theology as well as the church"

* I wish to thank Dr. H. Rikhof for his critical comments.

(Weisheipl, 1983, 258.270). Here Weisheipl refers to Lateranense IV (A.D. 1215): "Firmiter credimus et simpliciter confitemur quod unus solus est verus Deus aeternus . . . " (D.S. 800).

I agree with Weisheipl's view: the opuscule *De aeternitate mundi* is a theological work (albeit with many philosophical implications). I will explain my three reasons for this position briefly. They form in fact a further development of the second point of Weisheipl.

2. *Within the Catholic Faith*

From the very first lines, Thomas excludes every misunderstanding by mentioning that the discussion takes place within the "fides catholica". That is the prerequisite for any theological discourse: "Supposito secundum fidem catholicam quod mundus durationis initium habuit . . . " (Ae. 1–2). Now "fides catholica" has to be understood as the Church's rule of faith. By that "regula" holy Scripture is summarized or recapitulated, and so this rule is normative for the whole of Christian life and consequently for all inquiries and questions concerning the Christian faith (Fransen, 1961; Kelly, 1964, 52–54; 24–34).

In connection with this, one has to mention Thomas' explicit and repeatedly recurring concern about possible heretical opinions regarding the matter discussed ("error abominabilis", Ae. 9; "hereticum", Ae. 39.51.61.65; "erroneum", Ae. 70). In his *Summa theologiae* he has given a clarifying characterization of a heretic as someone who stubbornly ("pertinaciter") abandons one or another point of faith and explicitly refuses to follow the doctrine of the church in all matters of faith. The reason is that this doctrine of faith proceeds as the infallible and divine rule from the first Truth ("ex veritate prima"), manifested in holy Scripture (S.Th II.II.5.3.c).

A further indication of its theological nature is to be found in the language Aquinas uses. First of all in the creation-language, since creation for Aquinas always refers to the first article of faith. Although he is aware of arguments outside the Christian faith for the creation of the world (cf. In 2 Sent.d.1,q.1,a.2 sol.), his own concept of creation is first of all a scriptural one. Relevant expressions here are "factum" (Ae. 35.165.212.234.251); "ex nichilo" (Ae. 87.165.192); "creator" (Ae. 246.270.289); "conditor" (Ae. 270); "creatum a Deo" (Ae. 64.66.77.78.86); "creatura" (Ae. 164.181.192). It is also within this theological context that one has to understand Aquinas' use of "causa" in the doctrine of creation: "causa agens scilicet Deus" (Ae. 88); "Deus est causa" (Ae. 90); "deus causat per voluntatem" (Ae. 119). Often this is misunderstood as a quasi-physical or a metaphysical language and not recognized as a "formal feature" (Burrell, 1979, 15; 1986, 46) of theological creation language.

So if we are to discern the theological scope and texture of *De aeternitate mundi* as well as of the other works of Aquinas, we have to read all these terms and phrasings as being stamped and embossed by faith and not the other way round as if the "fides catholica" has been coined by these words.

Secondly we find indications in the use of other religious terms. In this opuscule for instance we find "omnipotentia" (Ae. 55.57.71.73); "peccata" (Ae. 76); "vestigium" (Ae. 226); "coaeternum" (Ae. 259.263.279.293); "immortalitas angelorum" (Ae. 285), "trinitas" (Ae. 293). Here also have to be mentioned the references to Saint Augustine (Ae. 54.214.242.293), Saint Anselm (Ae. 163), Saint John of Damascus (Ae. 257) and Hugh of St. Victor (Ae. 261).

One can find a last point of confirmation for the theological nature of this work in Thomas' mentioning of the "philosophi" in both the opening and the last lines of the work: " . . . non solum in fide, sed etiam apud philosophos" (Ae. 9–10); " . . . rationes . . . quas etiam philosophi tetigerunt . . . " (Ae. 297–298). As is well known (cf. Leclercq, 1961, 39– 67), in the 13th century, after a long and intriguing semantic history, the term "philosophi" designates the pagan authors of antiquity. Their speculations were developed within their own domain quite apart from holy Scripture and its faithful and believing explication, that is, quite apart from theology (Chenu, 1957, 376; Michaud-Quantin, 1970, 107). This suggests that Thomas had a rather sophisticated and well elaborated idea about the independent domain of philosophy (In 2 Sent. prol.; S.c.G. lib.2, cap.4; S.Th. I.8.c). Apparently he does not consider himself a philosopher, i.e. a scholar who contemplates created realities in their own nature and causes and qualities and who in that context also argues about certain issues of the christian faith as if from the outside, that is to say, reasoning from and not only by the natural "ratio".

3. *Thomas' Theological Way*

In *De aeternitate mundi* Aquinas does not focus his attention on created reality in its own nature. Nevertheless one cannot but notice that most of the time, grammatically speaking, "mundus" and its equivalents form the subject of his enunciations. For a long time this aspect confused me, till I perceived the tenor of Thomas' rather free quoting of Saint Augustine at the end of the opuscule. This led me to a somewhat different vision of the "fides catholica", because the holy Trinity is mentioned here in a rather special way: "Quia omnino incommutabilis est illa natura Trinitatis . . . " (Super Genes. ad litt., VIII, c.23; P.L. 34, 389). "Illa natura Trinitatis" is far from an obvious comment in this context, nor is it a hackneyed phrase. It has to be understood in connection with the *Definitio contra Albigenses et*

Catharos of the above mentioned 4th Lateran Council of 1215, and also with the condemnation of Joachim of Fiore by the same Council (D.S. 800.803–807). Going quickly through the 313 lines of the Leonina edition I have counted the word "deus" 38 times. For Aquinas what was intended by this word "deus" was crystal clear, namely "illa natura Trinitatis". And if I am right in this point, one could possibly see *De aeternitate mundi* as the outcome of a long and very special search for God.

In that case it has been a long path through a period of time, beginning in the *Scriptum*, proceeding via *Summa contra Gentiles*, *De potentia* and *Summa theologiae* going on to *Quodlibet* 3 and 12 and *Compendium theologiae*, and ending with *De aeternitate mundi* (Wippel, 1981; Weisheipl, 1983, 264). But that implies that the theological intentionality of Thomas' works is of real importance to questions of dating. In my opinion *De aeternitate mundi* has to be dated in the seventies of the 13th century. (Cf however R.L.T. 17, nr. 598 and R.L.T. 19, nr.78 concerning the opinions of Wippel and Weisheipl.) My most serious argument for this view lies in the following.

If my supposition is correct, the path is not only long in duration, but also special in kind, for it concerns a journey towards the knowledge of God. That brings to every section of the road the keen intention of the searching mind on God himself, the "natura Trinitatis", the "essentia divina". This is very special because we cannot possibly know what God is, but at the utmost what God is not. Therefore we cannot consider how God is, but rather how God is not (S.Th. I, qu.3, prol.). At every stage, in every haul, this focusing of attention has to be done in order to keep the mind's direction and orientation on the unknowable God open, and to prevent it from shifting to any creature however holy and sublime. A remarkable example of this special way of thinking is to be found in the first questions of *Summa theologiae* I.IIa pars. There St. Thomas is looking for men's ultimate "beatitudo". What is it that constitutes ultimate human happiness? It is not good fortune he is after, or bliss: the happiness searched for has to be the ultimate. In these questions, step by step, Aquinas writes off the one earthly reality after the other from worldly goods and wealth and prestige onwards power, health and beauty, lust and the joys of life on to the spiritual pleasures. All things considered, his conclusion is "quod impossible est beatitudinem esse in aliquo bono creato . . In solo igitur Deo beatitudo hominis consistit" (S.Th. I.II.2.8.c). And further: " . . . . in visione divinae essentiae" (S.Th. I.II.3.8.c), a witnessing in which God is fully being adhered to without ever being totally encompassed and fathomed (S.Th. I.II.4.3. ad 1; cf. I.12.7.c & ad 1). A similar process of thought takes place in the whole of Thomas' theology and finds a certain conclusion in *De aeternitate mundi*. In this opuscule he does not search for men's "beatitudo" but for God himself, for the "natura Trinitatis", the "essentia divina". And because we cannot know what God is, but only what he is not . . . first of all we have to consider how he is not . . . by removing from God everything that does not befit him . . . (S.Th. 1.3.prol.).

It is my contention that in the *De aeternitate mundi* the point under discussion is a more specific location or setting of "mundus" within the domain of men's knowledge of God. The problem is whether or not "mundus" can possibly display something about God. The "mundus" at issue is the same reality as is being explored in S.Th. I.II.2.8. and there indicated by "bonum creatum".

About "mundus" it is clear, firstly, that its "quid" is not God and, secondly, that its "quomodo" is not the "quomodo" of God. Now the question is whether "mundus" can show something about God even by the detour of its farthest removed possibilities.

When Thomas starts writing the *De aeternitate mundi* he had already "written off" many of history's and even of creation's realities, investigating a great number of non-divine objects and events and processes, wondering whether they could be a way to the knowledge of God. He had even considered the family of men, the church, the holy humanity of Christ. But in this work about the eternity of "mundus", he has arrived at all things gathered together, at all space and at all time. And it is precisely about all things that the "fides catholica" teaches that the triune God is their Creator. That is to say, in a unfathomable way by love and out of his freedom he has called heaven and earth into existence, the world and all that is upon it, "mundus". Thus when one speaks in terms of eternity about all that is, or about an eternal world meaning a cosmos with never ending duration, one can ask oneself: will there ever be such a length of duration that the duration itself becomes divine? or becomes God? Can a long or even a limitless duration become divine? Can God himself ever, in any real sense, be measurable by any duration? Only if a limitless duration of all things created is possible in itself, can one arrive at a true and faithful notion and a truthful understanding of "how God's eternity is not". This presupposes a somewhat special conception of analogy.

4. *Squared Analogy*

Only if an eternal world is in itself possible or non-contradictory, is true understanding possible of "how God's eternity is not". This requires a careful grammar of divinity (Burrell, 1986, 2). *De aeternitate mundi* suggests that Thomas, as in other works, gives a great deal of attention to language and linguistic usage. Forms of "dicere" occur 42 times and of "ponere" 26 times. Besides many other words relating to language and speech are found, such as "affirmatio" and "negatio", "vera" and "falsa", "expresse", "questio", "enuntiare", "inquit", "fatentur", "loquens", "mentio", "ineffabilis", "responsio", "obiciunt", "contradictio", etc., etc. In every three lines of *De aeternitate mundi* at least one reference of language occurs. Aquinas' search takes place via meticulous probings of what can be said and what has to be said when speaking about the eternity of the world in relation to God. He carefully investigates the workings of the "ratio" such as understanding and reasoning, and their "products" in the speculative reason: definition, proposition and syllogism (Schmidt, 1966,7; ref. to S.Th. I.II.90.1. ad 2), each of which forms a language-act. In this context as in the so-called "treatise on the One God" of the Prima Pars, the crux is Thomas' supposition for all language about God "ut omnem intellectum et virtutem excedat" (Ae. 72-73). That is the one formal characterization by which all talk about God has to be marked (cf. Rikhof, 1987). For plausible reasons Weisheipl (1983, 268–270) suspects that Thomas in his reading of Aristotle's *Libri Physicorum* has been affected by a deep theological insight. Reading certain passages he has his mind constantly going to the holy mysteries of the triune God in much the same way as a Christian reading psalm 22, or Isaiah 53 can hardly avoid remembering Jesus Christ. When he is in Paris for the second time, he reads Aristotle's *Physics*. Following Aristotle's line of thought, especially Lib.VIII, he becomes aware of the import of certain paraphrases of the "prima causa" as the "causa essendi". This term takes on a more and more decisive significance for him. Thomas saw Aristotle, proceeding from the eternity of the world, arguing for a "movens" who is "causa essendi" of the world (In Physicor., Lib.8, lect. 3, nr.996; and cf. lect.21, nr.1154). The central point here is that "esse" and "semper esse" do not exclude each other, whereas "causa essendi" cannot fall within the "esse causatum".

Before then Thomas had already discovered that in the language of cause and effect, one can also speak the truth about God, but only if one directly expresses what God is not and how God is not (Cf. S.Th. I.14.8.c; 19.4c). So when the analogous concept from Aristotle's *Physics*, "causa essendi", is referred to the "natura Trinitatis", this speech-act implies that an already analogous word is used analogously in a new way. Here analogy is being squared. Something like a linguistic dive is taking place. Suddenly the "natura Trinitatis" becomes the grammatical subject of the proposition. This has incalculable semantic consequences, because from then on "natura Trinitatis" qualifies all further things that are predicated of the subject. And this means that the language about God is being steered, directed, guided straight to what we do not know about God.

If I am right, speaking about a "aeternitas mundi" can imply a created reality of limitless duration, because no non-divine reality can possibly be withdrawn from the power and the freedom of God, while God's own triune being can never fall under any "causa essendi". So considered from the concept of God's omnipotence a "mundus aeternus" is not impossible.

Moreover one could ask whether in the language about God terms such as "duration", "beginning", "always" do not have to be reduced to the squared analogous language of being. Because in that case one can possibly make clear that, whatever is the meaning of "aeternus" when said of non divine reality, it still has to turn the somersault of "we cannot know what God is" and "we cannot consider how God is". Or, to put it differently, "aeternus" in itself does not give any other information than precisely about "what God is not".

What has been said about the meaning of "aeternus" applies also to the word "coaeternus" (Ae. 259.263.279.293). But in this case the role of the "fides catholica" is more distinct than it is in the case of "aeternus".

The "fides catholica", the source, light and context of Aquinas' theology, states the limits of theological language about what is the case, not of theological language about possibilities. About the possibility of an eternal world Thomas speaks freely in order to maintain the core of rightness and truth (cf. Corbin, 1980, p. 95–107) in speaking about God. About what is the case he confesses, according to the "fides catholica", "quod mundus durationis initium habuit" (Ae. 1–2). And this also happens to the word "coaeternus": "the fides catholica" states, as something that is the case, that it belongs exclusively to the language about the triune God. "Si quis dicit aut sentit ... creaturas deo coaeternos esse, anathema sit" (Anathemata against Origen as published in 543 AD at the Synod of Constantinople, can.8; D.S. 410). But in theological discussion questions can be asked about the meaning of this word and about its possible uses in theological language. Yet even with regard to this word "coaeternus", situated by the fides catholica, one has to maintain that it does not give any other knowledge about God than "how God is not".

5. *Conclusion*

There may have been more than one reason for Aquinas' treatise about the eternity of the world and for its sometimes passionate tone. I think that towards the end of a long and very special search for God his principal motive has been, to show his most fundamental presumption. It is this: even "mundus", even if it were limitless in duration, will never be the "natura Trinitatis", i.e. will never be God. Here lies his main reason for attaching such great importance to the possibility of an eternal world. He wants to make absolutely and unmistakably clear that the "natura Trinitatis" is not a creature, not even an eternal creature. This insight has far-reaching consequences for the understanding of Aquinas' considerations about God incarnate (S.Th. III. prol.) and about the indwelling of God through the holy Ghost in men (S.Th. I.43.3.c). Or is it the other way around? Is Thomas' discussion of the possibility of an eternal world one of some far-reaching theological consequences of his "assensus fidei"?

LITERATURE

(References to *De aeternitate mundi*: Ae., followed by the line numbers of the Leonina-edition.)

Brady, I., John Peckham and the background of Aquinas's *De Aeternitate mundi*, In: *Commemorrative Studies*, Vol. II, P.I.M.S., Toronto, 1974, 141–178.

Burrell, D.B., *Aquinas*, God and Action, London and Henley, 1979.

Burrell, D.B. *Knowing the Unknowable God: Ibn-Sina, Maimonides, Aquinas*, Notre Dame, Indiana, 1986.

Chenu, M.-D., *Introduction à l'étude de Saint Thomas d'Aquin*, Montréal, Paris, 2me édition, 1954.

Chenu, M.-D., *La théologie au douzième siècle*, Paris, 1957.

Corbin, M., *Le chemin de la théologie chez Thomas d'Aquin*, Paris, 1974.

Corbin, M., *L'inouï de Dieu*, Six études christologiques, Desclée de Brouwer, 1980.

D.S. = *Enchiridion Symbolorum Definitionum et Declarationum de Rebus Fidei et Morum*, ed. H. Denzinger, and A. Schönmetzer, Editio XXXIII, 1965. Fransen, P.., Kirchlicher Glauben, In: *Lexik. für Theol. und Kirche* 6 (1961) 301–302.

Hoogveld, J.H.E.J., *Inleiding tot leven en leer van S. Thomas van Aquino*, Nijmegen, Utrecht, 3rd ed., 1939.

Kelly, J.N.D., *The Athanasian Creed, Quicunque vult*, London, 1964.

Leclercq, J., *Études sur le vocabulaire monastique du Moyen Age*, Roma, 1961.

Michaud-Quantin, P., *Études sur le vocabulaire philosophique du Moyen Age*, Roma 1970.

Miehte, T.L., and Bourke, V.J., *Thomistic Bibliography*, 1940-1978, Westport, Conn., London, 1980.

R.L.T. = *Rassegna di Letteratura Tomistica*, red. Vansteenkiste, Cl.

Rikhof, H.W.M., Voorzichtig spreken over God, in: *De praktische Thomas*, Hilversum, 1987, pp. 57–73.

Schmidt, R.W., *The Domain of Logic According to Saint Thomas Aquinas*, The Hague, 1966.

Weisheipl, J., The Date and Context of Aquinas' *De aeternitate mundi* In: *Graceful Reason*, Essays in Ancient and Medieval Philosophy Presented to Joseph Owens, CSSR, ed. by Gerson, L.P., P.I.M.S., Toronto, 1983, 239–271.

Wippel, J.F., Did Thomas Aquinas Defend the Possibility of an Eternally Created World? (The *De aeternitate mundi* Revisited), In: *Journal of the History of Philosophy* 19(1981) 21–37.

THE ETERNITY OF THE WORLD: THE BELIEVING AND THE PHILOSOPHICAL THOMAS. SOME COMMENTS

J.A. AERTSEN

I

The eternity of the world is, so Albert the Great holds, a "very old question".[1] Yet in the thirteenth century, in connection with the reception of Aristotle, the discussion about this question acquired a particular intensity, since it became the point of crystallization of the relations between faith and reason, between the tradition of Christian thought and Greek philosophy. In the disputes about the eternity of the world it was Thomas Aquinas' position that especially gave rise to contradiction, even to "murmur". With scarcely concealed indignation William de la Mare, in his *Correctorium fratris Thomae*, speaks about Aquinas' view that non-eternity of the world cannot be demonstrated conclusively: such a view gives occasion to error (*occasio errandi*). Neither philosophically nor theologically (*nec philosophice nec theologice*) did Thomas resolve the arguments for the non-eternity of the world.[2]

I have been invited to give some comments on the papers of the seminar. In my afterthought I will confine myself to one aspect that seems to me essential for the general theme, namely, the character of Thomas' thought on the eternity of the world. Although Thomas was engaged in this topic at several places in his work, I focus on the treatise he explicitly devoted to this question, *De aeternitate mundi*. That choice is suggested by dr. de Grijs' contribution, for this treatise is central in it.

In his equally stimulating and provocative paper De Grijs argues that Thomas' writing is wrongly reckoned among the *Opuscula philosophica. De aeternitate mundi* has a theological character. De Grijs offers three reasons in support of this thesis. The first is that from the outset the discussion takes place within the "fides catholica". "That is the prerequisite for any theological discourse". Another indication lies in the language Aquinas uses, especially in the creation language, "since creation for Aquinas always refers to the first article of faith". The second reason is that Aquinas does not focus his attention on created reality in its own nature, but on God ('illa natura Trinitatis'). One could see *De aeternitate mundi* as the outcome of a long and very special search for God, a special search, for man cannot know what God is. Only if an eternal world is possible, is true understanding possible of "how God's eternity is not". The third reason for the theological character of *De aeternitate mundi* is that this treatise is marked by a careful grammar of divinity, as becomes apparent in Thomas' new use of a concept from Aristotle's Physics, the "causa essendi". De Grijs' conclusion is that Thomas' main reason for attaching such great importance to the possibility of an eternal world is that "he wants to make absolutely and unmistakably clear that the "natura Trinitatis" is not a creature, not even an eternal creature".

The thesis presented by De Grijs means a real challenge to philosophers – a genus to which I belong by profession. It has prompted me to review Thomas' intention in *De aeternitate mundi*. In the following sections I will discuss De Grijs' interpretation. As will appear, the relation between the believing and the philosophical Thomas is in question here.

II

Supposito secundum fidem catholicam quod mundus durationis initium habuit.

With this supposition Thomas commences his treatise *De aet. mundi* (1. 1-2 of the Leonine-edition). What does this beginning mean? At least this: with the supposition of faith Thomas opposes himself to the *philosophi*, a term which in his time refers to the "pagan" philosophers. That opposition is made explicit by Thomas elsewhere. "In the beginning God created heaven and earth": through this statement "the error" of the eternity of the world is excluded.[3] When Thomas, in his Commentary on the *Sententiae* (II,1,1,5) treats of the diverse opinions concerning the question: "Whether the world is eternal?, the first position he sets forth is "that of the philosophers, who said that not only God is eternal, but also other things". However differently from each other the philosophers elaborated this position, all their views are according to Thomas "false and heretical" (*falsae et haereticae*). Against the philosophers who maintain the aeternitas of the world, faith sets the *novitas* of the world.[4]

Does the beginning of *De aet. mundi* also mean that this treatise must be regarded (as De Grijs argues) not as a philosophical but as a theological work, since Thomas expressly places himself within the domain of faith? It seems to me that this inference does not follow simply. The supposition of faith is indeed a necessary prerequisite of such a conclusion, but not a sufficient one. Likewise, the content and the intention of the writing must be taken into consideration.

A concrete example may clarify this point. It is striking that the theologian Thomas spent so much time and energy commenting on Aristotle. In these commentaries he is confronted with the Philosopher's arguments for the eternity of motion and of heaven. Then Aquinas does not conceal his stance. Aristotle's view that motion has always existed is "contrary to our faith" (*In VIII Phys.*, lect. 2, 986). "We, however, do not say *secundum fidem catholicam* that heaven has always existed" (*In I De caelo*, lect. 6,64). Thomas explicitly takes the standpoint of faith, but his commentaries on Aristotle do not thereby lose their philosophical purport. On the contrary, until now they have been praised for their congenial understanding of the Greek philosopher.

Yet I am not insensitive to De Grijs' observations. It is not unfair to say that in Neoscholasticism a simple truth was sometimes forgotten, namely, that Thomas and the other great thinkers of the Middle Ages were theologians. That truth is something of a threat to the historian of medieval philosophy, for it appears to make him empty-handed. Such an embarrassment is described by the renowned historian of medieval philosophy, E. Gilson, in his intellectual autobiography *Le philosophe et la théologie*. On the basis of this inquiry into the sources of Descartes' thought he had came to the conviction, contrary to the generally accepted prejudice, that there exists a truly original philosophy in the Middle Ages. He gave expression to this insight in his studies *Le Thomisme* and *La philosophie de St. Bonaventure*. Gilson's newly acquired certainty of the existence of a "medieval philosophy" was, however, shaken by critics. The title of the latter work is incorrect, they objected. There does not exist a distinctive philosophy in Bonaventure, but only a theology. And Gilson was also deprived of the "philosophical Thomas", for the doctrine of Aquinas was shown not to be different in nature from that of Bonaventure. "There remained for me only theologies", Gilson writes.[5]

This experience induced him to a new reflection on the relation between theology and philosophy, which finally resulted in his notion of "Christian philosophy".[6] We do not enter into a discussion of this notion now, but what is of importance in our context is Gilson's observation on the nature of medieval theology. Many historians, theologians and philosophers are inclined to conceive the notion of theology so as to exclude the notion of philosophy. Rightly Gilson points out that this is an illusion with regard to the Middle Ages. It is the essence of the theology of this period to employ philosophy richly. "Because it draws on faith, it is a scholastic *theology*, but because of its distinctive use of philosophy, it is a *scholastic* theology".[7] That different philosophical premises can effect divergent options of theologians is acknowledged by Thomas himself in his Commentary on the Sentences. With reference to the question "Whether the firmament belongs to the nature of the lower bodies?" (II, dist. 14,q.1,a.2) he notes a diversity of opinions among the philosophers. Likewise the exegetes of Scripture disagreed on this matter, *secundum quod diversorum philosophorum sectatores fuerunt, a quibus in philosophicis eruditi sunt.* For Basil, Augustine and the majority of the *sancti* follow Plato's views in philosophical matters that do not touch faith (*in philosophicis quae ad fidem non spectant*), but others follow Aristotle's conceptions.

This "complex" situation, that is, the fact that a philosophical position is "implied" in the options of the theologians, can now also be established with respect to the subject of *De aet. mundi*. Immediately after having stated the supposition of faith that the world has a beginning of duration, Thomas goes on to say: *dubitatio mota est utrum potuerit semper fuisse* (1. 2–3). The relation of this "dubitatio" on the possibility of an eternally created world to the preceding supposition must be understood, in my opinion, in a manner rather different from the interpretation presented by De Grijs. The supposition of faith does not mean to define the theological character of the question and to determine the scope of the discussion accordingly. On the contrary, the supposition of faith is formulated in order to make clear that the question of *De aet. mundi* moves outside the domain of faith. Thomas wants to say something like this: however much I and my "adversaries" (1.5) may disagree on the outcome of the "dubitatio", the parting of the ways does not concern the supposition of the novelty of the world. In other words, the opening of *De aet. mundi* has the function of emphasizing that the "dubitatio" and the teaching of faith are of different orders.

This interpretation is strongly supported by a distinction Thomas introduces in the continuation of the treatise. There he explicitly distinguishes between the (lack of) truth of the question and its heretical character. Whether the possibility of an eternal creation be true or false, he writes, "it will not be heretical to maintain that God can bring about that something created by him should have always been". (1. 65–7). Thomas is able to make this distinction between "false" and "heretical", because the nature of the "dubitatio" is apparently such that it does not touch the doctrine of faith.

III

There remains however, the question of what Thomas' motive is for discussing a possibly eternal world. Why has this "dubitatio" been raised and what is its function? To get better insight into this question, it is first of all (1) necessary to indicate the main lines of the argument in *De aet. mundi*. Next (2) we will pay attention to a noteworthy but scarcely noticed correspondence with another text of Thomas. From the comparison between the two texts we can finally (3) draw some conclusions concerning the meaning of the "dubitatio" and the proper nature of Thomas' thought on the eternity of the world.

(1) The course of the argument in *De aet. mundi* is as follows:

(a) Thomas begins by explaining the "dubitatio" (3–16). Its purport is not to ask whether the world could have always been in the sense that it was not made by God. This would be an abominable error, even according to the philosophers. By "world" the *universitas creaturarum* (cf. S.th. I, 46,1 obj. 1) must be understood and it is concerning such a world that the question of whether it could have always been must be asked.

(b) Next (17–80) Thomas suggests three obstacles to the possibility of an eternally created world: the potency or power of God, the absence of any (eternally existing) passive potency, and the intrinsic contradiction between the concepts "to be created" and "to be eternal". The first two are dismissed rather quickly, for they present no real problem. But the third suggested obstacle, the contradiction of concepts, cannot be removed so easily. At this very point the gist of the "dubitatio" becomes fully apparent, for, in Thomas' view, the whole question comes down to the issue of the conceptual repugnance: *In hoc ergo tota consistit quaestio, utrum esse creatum a Deo secundum totam substantiam et non habere durationis principium, repugnent ad invicem, vel non* (77–80).

(c) Thomas shows in two phases that there does not exist any intrinsic contradiction. There is no mutual repugnance between the concepts "to be created" and "to be eternal" because an agent need not precede its effect in duration. Thomas adduces four arguments for this thesis (81–157).

(d) Second, there is no incompatibility between the two notes in question because, when it is said that the creature was made *ex nihilo*, it is not necessary that non-being precedes the creature in duration (157–210).

(e) If there were some contradiction, it is surprising that Augustine (in *De civitate Dei* X,31) did not perceive it (211–239), nor the greatest of the philosophers (240–254).

(f) Finally Thomas considers some objections against the possibility of an eternal world. If this were possible it is claimed, by an appeal to no less an authority than John Damascene, the creature would then be on a par with God in duration. Such co-eternity, however, does not follow, as is apparent from Boethius and Augustine (255–313).

This synopsis of *De aet. mundi* makes clear that it can hardly be maintained that Thomas focusses his attention on God, rather than on created reality. The kernel of the discussion consists in the question (*tota quaestio*) whether "to be created" and "to be eternal" involve a contradiction, as his adversaries contend. When the latter further claim (see point f) that an eternal creature would be equal to God in duration, Thomas rebuts this objection by referring, first, to an exposition of Boethius in his "Consolation of Philosophy" and, next, to a short statement of Augustine (*Quia omnino incommutabilis est illa natura Trinitatis, ob hoc ita eterna est ut ei aliquid coeternum esse non possit; Super Genes ad litt.* VIII, c.23). Augustine's statement gets a central place and decisive importance in the interpretation of De Grijs. My objection to it is that this quotation is detached from its place in *De aet. mundi* as a whole. It only forms part of a side line in the argument. Thomas' "principal motive" is certainly not to show that "natura Trinitatis" is not a creature, not even an eternal creature".

(2) Among the many texts in which Thomas speaks about the eternity of the world there is one which presents a striking correspondence with *De aet. mundi* in question and content. We are referring to *De potentia* 3,14.[8]

(a) The question discussed in *De pot* 3,14 is: *Utrum id quod est a Deo diversum in essentia, possit semper fuisse.* Here, too, the possibility of an eternal creation is being investigated. This very point marks the difference from the question raised in *De pot.* 3,17 which asks whether the world has always been (*Utrum mundus semper fuerit*). The subject of the question in 3,14 is not simply designated as "world", but as "that which differs in essence from God", in order to indicate the distinction from the question in the preceding article, dealing with the eternal generation of the Son (art. 13: *Utrum aliquod ens ab alio possit esse aeternum*). In other words: the essential difference between the world and the "natura Trinitatis" is already presupposed from the outset.

(b) The corpus articuli in *De pot.* 3,14 begins by distinguishing several meanings of "possible" and presents parallels with part (b) in our articulation of *De aet. mundi.* Something is said to be possible either by reason of some potency or by reason of no potency. In the former case it may be possible by reason of an active potency or by reason of a passive potency. In the latter case something is said to be possible absolutely, when the terms of a proposition are not incompatible with one another; whereas something is said to be impossible only when the proposition involves self-contradiction. Thomas then applies these distinctions to the statement in question: "that which differs in essence from God could have always been". This statement is not impossible in itself, for its terms do not involve a contradiction. "To be from another" is not repugnant to "to have been always" (cf. *De pot.* 3,13) except in cases where one thing proceeds from another by way of motion, something which does not occur in the procession of things from God, that is, in creation. The additional note "differing in essence" likewise introduces nothing that is incompatible with "to have always been". If "possible" is taken as referring to an active potency, it is clear that God does not lack the power to produce from eternity something that is different from himself. But if "possible" refers to a passive potency, then, presupposing the truth of the Catholic faith (*supposita catholicae fidei veritate*), one cannot say that something which differs in essence from God could have always been. For the Catholic faith supposes that everything (except God) has not existed at some time.

(c) The arguments *pro* adduced in *De pot.* 3,14 present parallels with part (c) of *De aet. mundi.* So the arguments 1 and 4/5 recur in the latter text. In the seventh argument an extensive quotation from Augustine's *De civitate Dei* (X,31) is given that also occurs in *De aet. mundi* (1.222–231). To be sure, a different emphasis can be noticed in the ways in which Thomas employs the same arguments in the two writings. In *De aet. mundi* he intends to show that "to be created" and to be eternal" are not imcompatible with one another, because an agent need not precede its effect in duration. In *De pot.* 3,14 his concern is to make clear that these arguments are not contrary to that which faith presupposes, because they start from the notion of "possible" either in reference to an active potency or taken absolutely.[9]

(d) The arguments *sed contra* in *De pot.* 3,14 combine the parts (d), (e) and (f) of the argumentation in *De aet. mundi.* In the first and second argument, where it is claimed that a creature cannot possibly be eternal since it would then be co-eternal with God, the same statements of Augustine, Boethius and John Damascene are quoted. In the reply to argument 7 which objects that the creature cannot be eternal because it is *ex nihilo,* Thomas gives an analysis of the phrase "out of nothing" identical to that in *De aet. mundi.*

(3) What findings result from the comparison between *De aet. mundi* and *De pot.* 3,14?

Firstly, we find remarkable similarities in the question posed, in the concentration on "possible" in the sense of no conceptual repugnance, in arguments and authorities quoted. On the basis of these correspondences it merits consideration whether the formulation at the beginning of *De aet. mundi*: "dubitatio mota est" in its use of the perfect tense ("has been raised") does not concretely refer to *De pot.* 3,14 (dating 1265–66). That would imply that Thomas' treatise must be dated earlier than is usually done. In any case, Weisheipl's reasons for a late date of *De aet. mundi,* which are endorsed by De Grijs, are unconvincing. Weisheipl is of the opinion that the possibility of an eternal creation became an object of serious consideration for Thomas not until he wrote his commentary on the *Physica.* For in this commentary, dating from his second period in Paris (ca. 1270), he would become aware of the fact that for Aristotle God is not only the cause of motion of the world, but also the *causa essendi.*[10] This reason, however, does not seem valid to me, since Thomas had already expressed the same insight in his earliest work, namely in *In II Sent.* 1,1,5 ad 1[2] (*Sicut dicit Commentator, Aristoteles numquam intendit quod Deus esset causa motus coeli tantum, sed etiam quod esset causa substantiae ejus, dans sibi esse*). From this text yet another fact appears: Thomas' insight that Aristotle's first cause is also the cause of being is based not on a "theological" reading but on the history of the exegesis of the Philosopher ("as the Commentator says").

Secondly, there are differences in the manners in which arguments are used in *De pot.* 3,14 and in *De aet. mundi.* This is connected with the distinct construction of the two texts. Whereas in *De pot.* 3,14 the supposition of faith that the world has a beginning of duration comes only at the end,[11] in *De aet. mundi* it is put first – in order that the nature of the "dubitatio" may immediately be clear to the adversaries.

Thirdly, closer inspection shows that the exposition in *De pot.* 3,14 contains some important additions to what is said in *De aet. mundi.* These additions concern the analysis which, in the two texts, plays a central part in the argumentation for the possibility of an eternal creation, namely, the semantical analysis of the phrase *ex nihilo.* In *De pot.* 3,14 (ad 7[2]) the thinker by whom Thomas was strongly influenced in this analysis, is mentioned by name: it is the Arabic philosopher Avicenna. In addition, Aquinas introduces here a distinction in the concept of creation, a distinction which, I believe, constitutes the distinctive element of Thomas' thought on the eternity of the world. In ad 7[2] he states: "The first creatures were produced not from something but from nothing. Not, however, from the notion (*ratio*) of this production itself but from the truth of faith is it necessary that the creatures were first non-existent and were later brought into being". The aspect of "beginning", so Thomas suggests, does not necessarily belong to the essence of creation. He formulates this distinction even more clearly in his reply to the 8th argument *sed contra*: "It belongs to the notion of creation to have a principle of origin (*principium originis*) but not of duration, unless creation is taken as faith takes it (*nisi accipiendo creationem ut accipit fides*)". Apparently it does not hold that for Aquinas "creation always refers to the first article of faith". It is against this background that the ultimate meaning of the "dubitatio" in *De aet. mundi* has to be understood. Thomas intends by means of the question as to the possibility of eternal creation to provide *a metaphysical* deepening of the concept of creation: the essence of creation does not lie exclusively in the aspect of duration, in the "novelty" of the world taught by faith.

IV

The distinction between a philosophical and a theological notion of creation must be gone into more extensively, because this duality is proper to Thomas. The distinction comes up at several places in his Commentary on the Sentences. In *In III Sent.* 11,1 Aquinas distinguishes between the manner in which faith speaks about creation (*secundum quod fides de creatione loquitur*) and the manner in which some philosophers considered creation (*secundum quod quidam philosophi posuerunt creationem*). In the same Commentary (III,25,1,2) Thomas treats of the articles of faith. Articles that belong to faith essentially cannot be demonstrated. Now some philosophers, like Avicenna, recognized on the basis of demonstration that God is the Creator of things. Hence it does not seem appropriate that the Symbolum includes an article on God as Creator. In his reply to this objection (ad 2), Thomas points out that the philosophi did not know that God is the Creator in the sense in which faith holds this (*sicut fides ponit*), namely that things were brought into being after they once were not. The philosophers conceived creation in another way (*secundum alium modum*). What does this philosophical understanding of creation involve?

The path towards the philosophical concept of creation proceeds, in Thomas, via the semantical analysis of the phrase *ex nihilo*. The significance of this analysis becomes obvious when we realize that for Thomas' colleague Bonaventure the notions "creation out of nothing" and "to be eternal" imply an evident contradiction (cf *In II Sent.* d.1,p.1,a.1,q.2). The temporal moment is contained in the notion of creation as such. In his view creation *necessarily* implies a beginning of duration. Hence the analysis of the phrase *ex nihilo* is crucial in Thomas' argumentation of *De aet. mundi*.

This analysis is found in *In I Sent.* 5,2,2 (*Utrum Filius sit ex nihilo*) for the first time. It is one thing, so Thomas contends, to say that something is "not out of something", another thing to say that something is "out of nothing". For in the former case the negation contained in the *nihil* includes the preposition "out of" ("*not out of something*"), in the latter case the preposition includes the negation ("*out of nothing*"). If it is said that "something is not out of something", the relation to a material substratum is denied; taken in that sense, it is justified to say that the Son is *ex nihilo*. It is different, however, so Thomas goes on, with the second mode of saying ("out of nothing"). In that case a relation to nothing is affirmed. Now the relation of a thing to nothing can be twofold, namely, an order of time and an order of nature. The temporal order implies that something has non-being prior to its having being. Consequently, this relation is not proper to that which is eternal. The order of nature occurs when something has an *esse dependens ab alio*. That which depends on another in virtue of its whole being has of itself only a non-being. And that which something is of itself is naturally prior to that which it is from another. Here Thomas adds a remark which deserves particular attention. For this remark is a clear anticipation of the later discussion on the possibility of an eternal world and it therefore indicates that Thomas already had this possibility in mind in the present exposition. "Thus", he says, "even if it be supposed that heaven has existed from eternity, yet it is true to maintain that heaven is out of nothing, as Avicenna proves". Thomas ends his treatment of the question by establishing that the Son does not have a relation to nothing in either of the ways explained. He has no temporal relation, since he is eternal; he has no order of nature, since his being is not dependent upon another.

In *In II Sent.* 1,1,2 Thomas applies this analysis of *ex nihilo* to the idea of *creatio*. It leads to the insight that the notion of "creation" has three features. The first mark is that "creation" presupposes nothing in the thing that is said to be created. In this regard "creation" differs from other changes, like "generation", since every becoming presupposes matter. The causality of the creator extends to all that is found in the thing: there is no preexisting substratum. For that reason, so Thomas argues in *Summa contra Gentiles* II,37, the consideration of such an origin is the task not of the philosopher of nature but of the metaphysician, for it is proper to the latter to consider being *as being*. In view of the opposition to natural generation it seems appropriate to define Thomas' first feature of the notion of "creation" as "origin of being" or "to be caused wholly".

The second characteristic of the idea of "creation" is that in the thing which is created non-being is prior to being. This priority must not be understood in a temporal sense but as a priority of nature. That is to say, if the created were left to itself, it would fall into non-being, since the created has being only from another. In his regard "creation" differs from the generation of the Son, because this being is not dependent on another but absolute. On the basis of this opposition the second feature of the notion of "creation" may be called "dependence in being" in accordance with the expression used by Thomas himself in this context.

At this juncture Thomas, as it were, takes stock. "If these two features suffice for the *ratio* of creation, then creation can be demonstrated; and in this way the philosophers have considered creation (*sic philosophi creationem posuerunt*)".

What has been explicitated so far is the truth of philosophical reason, which has thought of creation in a metaphysical manner. "If, however, we accept a third feature to be necessary for the essence of creation, namely, that the created thing has non-being prior to being, even in duration, ... then creation cannot be demonstrated. Nor is creation (in this sense) conceded by the philosophers, but is supposed by faith (*per fidem supponitur*)". Here the believing Thomas is speaking as he does at the beginning of *De aet. mundi*. Yet the order of the exposition in *In II Sent.* 1,1,2 makes clear that the third characteristic of the idea of creation, the "novelty of the world", does not exclude the two previous, metaphysical, features. The giving of being with the mark of novelty also implies a permanent dependence of being in the created thing (the second feature).

This finding is a renewed confirmation of our interpretation of Thomas' intention in *De aet. mundi*. The "dubitatio" is meant to clear the way for the other, philosophical features of "creation". In this way the aspect of "beginning" in the Christian concept of creation is deepened by a metaphysical reflection on "origin". The discussion of the philosophical Thomas on the possibility of an eternal creation makes a contribution to the proper understanding of creation.

NOTES

1. *De quindecim problematibus V*, in: *Opera Omnia* XVII/1 (Munster, 1975), p. 37.
2. See the contribution to this volume by M.J.F.M. Hoenen.
3. *In II Sent.* 1,1,6.
4. *In II Sent.* 1,1,5: ... a philosophis tenentibus aeternitatem mundi ... contra philosophos novitatem mundi.
5. E. Gilson, *Le philosophe et la théologie* (Paris, 1960), p. 106.
6. Cf. J.F.Wippel, *Metaphysical Themes in Thomas Aquinas* (Washington D.C., 1984, ch. 1: "Thomas Aquinas and the problem of Christian philosophy" (p. 1–33).
7. E. Gilson, *o.c.*, 109.
8. Dr. Peter van Veldhuijsen, who is preparing a doctoral thesis on "The question of the eternity of the world in Thomas Aquinas", must be credited for bringing this similarity to my notice.
9. Cf. *De potentia* 3,14 ad 8: Ratio illa non probat nisi quod esse factum, et esse semper, non habeant ad invicem repugnantiam secundum se considerata; unde procedit de possibili absolute.
10. J.A. Weisheipl, "The Date and Context of Aquinas' *De aeternitate mundi*", in: *Graceful Reason, Essays in Ancient and Medieval Philosophy presented to Joseph Owens* (Toronto, 1983), p. 267–71).
11. *De potentia* 3,14 (at the end of the corpus): Unde et dicitur a quibusdam quod hoc quidem est possibile ex parte Dei creantis, non autem ex parte essentiae a Deo procedentis, *per suppositionem contrarii, quam fides facit.*

THE QUESTION ON THE POSSIBILITY OF
AN ETERNALLY CREATED WORLD:
BONAVENTURA AND THOMAS AQUINAS

P. VAN VELDHUIJSEN

In hac celebri disputatione, an mundus potuerit esse ab aeterno, innumeri gravissimorum theologorum circumferuntur.

Dom. Banez[1]

Introduction

The quest for the origin of the world can mean one of two things: either one is seeking for a divine principle as first being that is cause of being or one is seeking for the first moment of the world's duration. Ancient wisdom about the origin of the universe, as known from the myths and cosmogonies of India, Babylonia, Israel, Iceland etc. always unites both possibilities. The world is seen as formed as a new creation at some point in the past by one god or more. However, it is not possible to identify the historic beginning of this universal human quest for the origin of things.

Eternal Creation and Antiquity

When Plato, in the beginning of the *Timaeus* (27C; 28B), and Aristotle, in *De caelo* 1,10 (279b4–5), raise the question, and they are most probably the first to do so, of whether the world is everlasting and eternal or had a beginning of duration, then the above mentioned double meaning vanishes and one can immediately fix the start of the philosophical and scientific quest concerning the past duration of the universe, – even if Albertus Magnus[2] has called this problem *a valde antiqua quaestio.*

Aristotle in *De caelo* 1,10–12; II,1 makes a forceful plea for the uncreatedness and imperishableness of the cosmos, by attacking the opposite position. In cap.10 (279b12) he asserts that all thinkers have attributed *genesis* to the universe. Therefore one can conclude that Aristotle considered himself as the first Greek thinker who taught and defended the uncreatedness or eternity of the world *a parte ante.*[3]

Of all the philosophers his master is the one who Aristotle especially, albeit anonymous, criticizes.[4] For in the *Timaeus* (28B7) Plato says about the world: "it has become (*gegonen*)".

With his critical confrontation Aristotle has inaugurated two disputes which have kept science busy until the present day. Firstly there is the philological discussion about the question of whether Plato literally meant by the *genesis* of the world a beginning of duration (as Aristotle imputed) or whether he wanted to express something else, namely eternal duration, by means of mythical or didactic language. Secondly there is the philosophical discussion about the question of the past duration of the world: did it have a beginning or has it always and ever been existent? Both questions were usually treated in antiquity as belonging together. But whether one is for, against, or by way of exception indifferent (e.g. Galenus) with respect to the eternity of the world, the emphasis is on the interpretation of the *Timaeus*, the bible of the ancient philosophers.[5]

The majority of the platonists interpret the statement "the world has become" in an eternalist sense. Plato's successors in the Old Academy developed contra Aristotle's exegesis the idea that the world is dependent on a highest cause which conserves it everlastingly in being without any notion of a durational beginning. In the course of history this metaphysical explanation on the basis of a cause (kat' aitian)[6] will determine not only the orthodox interpretation of the *Timaeus*, but will also form the core of every notion of eternal emanation or creation. However, in the 2nd century A.D. a group of platonists round Plutarch and Atticus comes to the fore, which rejects the above mentioned official exegesis and which from a philological standpoint, with a vast knowledge of Plato and with the required exactness breathes new life into Aristotle's literal interpretation. The world, according to those exegetes, is not everlasting but had a beginning of its existence, and this is the case because the world has "become" out of preexistent chaotic material, as Plato explains in the *Timaeus*.[7]

This heterodox exegesis was combatted extremely sharply by Porphyrius with much erudition and text-critical wit.[8] The notion of reality as eternally caused has achieved greater clarity by way of this vehement clash between platoniststs. For Porphyry wished to make clear through his attack that the divine demiurg does not need preexistent uncreated matter for his (eternal) work of creation.[9] The creation or causation of the world from eternity can therefore be called "from nothing"; for it does not presuppose anything which was already there, it only expresses absolute dependency of being. In the second place Porphyry wished to elucidate the barely intelligible notion of *creatio ab aeterno ex nihilo* by way of expressive, pictorial comparisons, such as the (eternal) sun which produces eternal light, or (eternal) light which throws an (eternal) shadow. Augustine[10] took over from Porphyry the metaphor of the eternal imprint caused by an eternal foot placed in dust, a comparison which became famous and much used in mediaeval discussions on eternal creation.[11]

Thus far the emphasis lies on the dependency of being of the world and not so much on the divine principle on which the world depends. Ammonius Hermiae put forward this divine aspect in particular with his remarkable interpretation of Aristotle's godhead, the first unmoved mover. According to the Alexandrian philosopher God is for Aristotle a demiurgical intellect, which is not only the final cause of the world but also the efficient or creative cause.[12] The question however is whether Ammonius conceived the eternal causation of the world by the universal godhead as "out of nothing". Possibly he thought of creation out of God, as out of the Good. Simplicius,[13] who knew the work of Ammonius well and relied heavily on it, says for example about the eternal creation of matter: "For matter and also privation, be they what they are, are themselves produced because of God and are brought about out of the Good".[14]

However that may be, the notion "eternal creation out of nothing" seen from the side of the creative cause as well as from the side of the created effect appears to be developed especially in Late Antiquity in the context of the concordant interpretation of Plato and Aristotle. The reception of this notion in the Latin Middle Ages passed via the Arab thinker Al-Farabi, the "second master" as he was called,[15] who himself expressly refers to Ammonius for his idea of eternal creation out of nothing.[16] However, it was Avicenna,[17] following his master Al-Farabi[18], who transmitted to mediaeval thought this notion of creation in a balanced way, i.e. doing justice to the position of *ex parte Dei* as well as *ex parte mundi*.

Eternal Creation and the Christian Middle Ages

The Christian world-view is a doctrine of salvation as to the deliverance from evil and sin in this world. Its doctrine is founded in history, as Hugh of St. Victor[19] says: "the foundation and the principle of sacred doctrine is history." This history of salvation has a beginning (creation and fall), a middle (incarnation and salvation) and an end (*dies irae* and the new creation). Even when one turns aside from the Christological connotations of this triptych of faith, it must be said that this beginning, middle and end as precise historic determinations co-determine salvation. In a certain sense it is therfore *communis opinio* amongst the Christian authors that the world has been created by God at a well-determined moment with a first beginning of duration, as *Genesis* 1,1 says: "In the beginning God created the heaven and the earth."

It will be clear that this thesis about the origin of things caused a sharp contrast with ancient thought, for although the latter knew in a certain sense creation out of nothing (see above), nonetheless there is an antithesis with the Christian conception because of its notion of *eternal* creation. Yet there have always been Christian thinkers until the very beginning of the 13th century, albeit only a small minority, who did advocate the idea of an eternally created world. Boethius[20] for example, Philoponus in his first period,[21] John Scotus Eriugena,[22] some platonists from the 12th century.[23] This important and intriguing interpretation however was repudiated as heterodox by the 4th Lateran council in 1215.[24] This council decided that the first beginning of duration of creation should be taught as a definite (and thus orthodox) article of faith: "The creator of all things, visible and invisible, spiritual and corporeal, who by his own omnipotent power, right from the beginning of time created from nothing both creations, the spiritual and corporeal. "After this judgement of the papal court every Christian teacher will teach that the world is not eternal *de facto* qua duration but had a beginning at a definite moment.[25]

Nevertheless the question was raised – and in this *a novum* presents itself in the history of the question *de aeternitate mundi* – whether the world *could have been* eternally created by God, even if he actually decided otherwise. This interest in the *possibility* of eternal creation rose then because in the 13th century the full reception of Aristotle and his commentators (Avicenna, Averroes, Maimonides) took place.[26] For the Christian authors this meant two things: *attraction* to a vast storehouse and encyclopedia of new scientific material in elucidation of various questions in the field of culture and nature. But it meant also *collision* with a world-view (a neo-platonic Aristotelianism), which sometimes stands diametrically opposed to the Christian world-view.

The question at issue can be formulated as follows: *Could God create the world form eternity?* According to Alanus of Lille[27] and Albert the Great[28] the wording of this question is ambiguous. Someone who raises it can simply render himself guilty of the fallacy of amphiboly, according to Alanus. When a word is ambiguous one speaks of homonymy and when a sentence is ambiguous one speaks of amphiboly.[29] Now the question just stated can have a double meaning: if you connect "could create" with "from eternity", you mean no more than that God's creative power is eternal. But no one will contest this, and so there is no problem or question at all, according to Albert. A question however arises if you connect "could create" with "the world from eternity". Then the sentence as a question is univocal.

But agreement in the answers to the question so formulated is very difficult to find, as Marsilius of Inghen[30] at the end of the 14th century remarks: "Utrum (mundus) potuerit produci coaeterne Deo, de hoc doctores nostri sunt diversi."

The following pages will pay attention to the positions of Thomas Aquinas and Bonaventure concerning the possibility of eternal creation from nothing. First I discuss the position of Bonaventure and second the position of Thomas Aquinas, as a critical reaction to his colleague in theology.

The Impossibility of Creation from Eternity: Bonaventure

The reason why Bonaventure emphasized so often the impossibility of an eternally created world lies, according to J.G. Bougerol,[31] in the starting-point of the "spéculation bonaventurienne", namely the idea of creation. The best way into a subject in Bonaventure's work is his *Commentary on the Sentences*, and so I restrict myself to this *magnum opus* for his thoughts on eternal creation. An exposition of the question of the eternity of the world in Bonaventure is usually confined to *In II Sent.* dist.1, pars 1, art.1, qu. 2: Utrum mundus productus sit ab aeterno, an ex tempore. But one has to start *ab ovo*, i.e. to look for Bonaventure's conception of creation in the preceding quaestio 1, where he asks: Utrum res habeant principium causale. The reason for this retrospection is that qu.1 already gives the answer, be it in an implicit way, to the problem of qu. 2. The structure of the answer to both questions (qu. 1–2), however, is given by Bonaventure even earlier in his *Commentary*. In the context of his study about God's power in Book I, dist. 42–44, he raises the very interesting question of whether God could have made the world older or sooner than he did *de facto* (art.1, qu. 4).[32]

Bonaventure begins his *respondeo* by making a distinction for a correct understanding of the question. He says this:

1. God could have created the world from eternity, although he produced it at the very first beginning of duration; in that case it would be older.

2. God produced the world in such a way that it had existed for a longer time; but yet it was finite.

The first position, according to Bonaventure, is absolutely impossible, because an older world that is eternally created implies a contradiction. The concept "to be made" implies a beginning, the concept "eternal" implies no beginning. But then there appears the consequence that a world with a first beginning should have no first beginning . . . Being created from eternity includes therefore a contradiction.[33] The second position thus remains to solve the question. Bonaventure summarizes here (the first position) qu.1: creation is *ex nihilo*, which means that the world had a first beginning, and qu. 2: creation is *ex nihilo*, which in the sense of creation "in the beginning" excludes the possibility of an eternally created world.

How then does Bonaventure explain this position and argument in a nutshell, when he speaks of creation *ex professo*, in Book II, dist.1, pars 1, art.1, qu. 1–2?

Quaestio 1 asks: utrum res habeant principium causale? which means: utrum res sint productae *omnino*, hoc est secundum principium materiale et formale, an tantum secundum *alterum* principiorum? The question is not whether there is a *principium productivum*, such a principle (God) is admitted by both theologians and philosophers, but whether this principle has caused the whole structure of reality (matter and form) or only a part of it.[34] Bonaventure's thesis is that God has made the esse of the world "from nothing", i.e. according to the whole of its formal and material constituents. The best argument, I think, by which he proves this assertion is arg. 6, the last of the proofs for the production of things according to both principles, form and matter. This argument, which is not contested after the solution (so Bonaventure takes it as a strict demonstration), runs as follows: Si res non est totaliter ab alio, aut hoc est ratione formae, aut ratione materiae. With respect to the form there will be no discussion, because nothing absolutely becomes without the production of forms. So the question concerns the *non ab alio ratione materiae*. According to Aristotle act precedes potency, i.e. passive or matter. Now, when the act (*forma* or *efficiens*) is *ab alio*, then matter is also *ab alio*. But matter is not *ab alio*, for it is and must be the principle for the becoming of all things; therefore it is a cause and does not have a cause for its own being.[35]

So far Bonaventure has followed the physics of Aristotle: the *genesis* of things requires an ungenerated subjectum, prime matter. Therefore nothing depends totally on anything else. Further he breaks through this philosophy of nature and raises the metaphysical question on the origin of prime matter. The first part of arg. 6 says that the form is *ab alio* in a relative way. In the second part Bonaventure uses this to ask for the *ab alio* of form and matter in an absolute, meta-Aristotelean way.

One can ask whether the form is *ex aliquo* or *ex nihilo*. If there is a reason for the *ex nihilo* of the form, then matter is also *ex nihilo* for the same reason. But if the form is *ex aliquo*, which *aliquid* is meant? The form is simple and so it is not caused by the essence of matter. But then the question arises: where does that something that is in matter come from? This "something" is certainly not from matter (matter then would be its cause; cf. the discussion on form). Therefore an infinite regress of causality follows, which is impossible.[36] Hence it is necessary to conclude that the essences of the forms are produced by the first Maker out of nothing. So the form of things is created by God ex nihilo. On the same line of reasoning then one can prove that matter is also out of nothing.

Bonaventure has, especially with this argument 6 pro, made clear his intentions on the meaning of creation: The whole being of the world according to its structural principles, matter and form, is not out of something apart from God, but it is totally from the creator, i.e. "out of nothing".

The question arises whether this metaphysical notion of ex nihilo strictly means the same as the theological notion of a very first beginning of creation. If this is the case, then the proof for the *ex nihilo* will be the proof for "in the beginning" (*Genesis* 1,1) with the conclusion that an eternally created world is impossible, because it implies a contradiction.

In the beginning of his compendium of theology, the *Breviloquium*, Bonaventure says that the *universitas machinae mundialis*[37] is brought into being by the first divine principle *ex tempore et de nihilo*. *Ex nihilo* excludes the idea that the material principle (and of course the formal principle too) of the world would be eternal and *ex tempore* excludes the false position of an eternal world *a parte ante*.[38] Bonaventure does not explicitly say that both concepts mean the same and include each other, so that there are two notions for one thing, but implicitly he does. Let me explain what might be his reason.

The truth, according to Bonaventure, about the production of the world, namely that it is created *ex nihilo* in the sense of "not out of something", could never be attained by the philosophers in their erring quest for the origin of the universe. This truth remained hidden for them.[39] But by the *faith in holy Scripture* it becomes absolutely clear what creation in its primary sense means, namely that the world is brought into being according to its totality and to its intrinsic principles.[40] It is certain that Bonaventure refers with the words "faith in holy Scripture" to *Genesis* 1,1: "in principio etc." *Ex nihilo* means *in principio*, i.e. at a very first and absolutely prime beginning. The *Breviloquium* II,2[41] says: creatio est de nihilo, ideo fuit in principio, ante omnem diem, tanquam omnium rerum et temporum fundamentum.

However, the second point is whether *ex nihilo* means necessarily and exclusively *in principio*. At the end of the *solutio* of quaestio 1 Bonaventure asserts that *Genesis* 1,1 is not in conflict with reason: ratio a fide non discordat. And he adds: sicut supra in opponendo ostensum est, i.e. on the basis of 6 arguments (of which we discussed arg. 6) it is demonstrated that the created world is brought into being *totaliter* (form and matter) and therefore *ex nihilo*.

Faith states that *Genesis* 1,1 expresses the notion of *creatio ex nihilo* (Scriptura quae dicit, omnia esse creata et secundum omne quod sunt in esse producta). That is why the demonstration for the *ex nihilo* of the world can be the same demonstration for the *in principio* of the world. Bonaventure therefore has shown in quaestio 1 what creation essentially and necessarily means, namely the production of the whole formal and material *machina mundialis* in an absolutely first instant: *creatio ex nihilo = creatio in initio/principio* (or as Bonaventure says: *creatio ex tempore*). With respect to the question of whether the world could be created from eternity one must conclude from

Bonaventure's solution of quaestio 1 that *creatio ab aeterno* is impossible: *ex nihilo* says *in principio* which excludes ab aeterno; therefore an eternal creation is a contradiction.

However, in quaesto 2 Bonaventure raises the question of an eternal world, and he does this as a further explication of his idea of creation ex nihilo. So he asks: Utrum mundus productus fuerit ex tempore, an ab aeterno.[42] The core of this question consists in the proof that an eternally created world implies an intrinsic contradiction and therefore must be impossible. The most ingenious and typically Bonaventurean argument is arg. 6 in oppos., which is endorsed and affirmed in the beginning of the solutio.[43] Let me concentrate then on this argument.

Arg. 6 in oppos.

Major: It is impossible for that which has being after non-being to have eternal being, because this implies a contradiction;

Minor: But the world has being after non-being;

Concl.: Therefore it is impossible that it be eternal.

In good scholastic fashion Bonaventure then tries to prove this syllogistic argument, i.e. to make its important components intelligible.

The major premiss is evident like a first principle, so there is no need for demonstration. But the minor premiss has to be proven, namely the statement that the world has being after non-being.

Major: Everything whose having of being is totally from another is produced by the latter out of nothing;

Minor: But the world has its being totally from God;

Concl.: Therefore the world is out of nothing.

Before Bonaventure proceeds with giving a proof of these two premisses, he explains the notion of "out of nothing". The world, he says, is not out of nothing *materialiter*, and so *originaliter*. Then he goes on to demonstrate the two premisses of the last syllogism.

Major: It is evident that everything which is totally produced by something differing in essence has being out of nothing. For what is totally produced is produced in its matter and form.

Minor: But matter does not have that out of which it would be produced because it is not out of God.

Concl.: Clearly, then, it is out of nothing.

The second premiss ("the world has its being totally from God") is, so Bonaventure says, evident from the discussion of an another question, and he refers to quaestio 1.[44]

So far Bonaventure has demonstrated that *creatio ab aeterno* implies a contradiction. Note that the core of his argument lies in the notion of *ex nihilo*, and this in the sense of *in principio*, as we have seen in the preceding discussion about quaestio 1.

It was said above that Bonaventure affirms this arg. 6 in the solution of the question, which means that the heart of the question on an eternally created world lies for him in the discussion about the precise meaning of creation, i.e. creation from nothing.

I answer, so Bonaventure starts his *solutio* and so I finish this section on his position, I answer this: It has to be said that to maintain that the world is eternal or eternally produced by claiming that all things have been produced out of nothing is entirely against truth and reason, as arg. 6 contra proves. It is so against reason that I do not believe that any philosopher, however slight his understanding, has maintained this. For such a position involves an evident contradiction.[45]

In the following I shall discuss the position of Thomas Aquinas, and I shall concentrate mainly on his concept of creation, for in this lies the principal difference with Bonaventure with regard to the question on the possibility of an eternally created world.

The Position of Thomas Aquinas

Thomas usually deals with the question of eternal creation in the context of his doctrine of creation. Since he has taken up the basic positions of his thought in the commentary on the *Sententiae* of Petrus Lombardus,[46] I am guided for what follows by this *Scriptum*. The treaty in book II, dist.1, qu.1, which can be called an exhaustive exposition of *Genesis* 1,1, has as one of the problems that recur in this text the question: "whether things were created from eternity", or otherwise: "whether the world is eternal"(art.5).[47]

Thomas is principally interested in the universal question of whether the created world as such, i.e. according to its essence, is or can be eternal. His interest in the question is not concerned with this or that creature (e.g. the human species), but with creation as created being. Nos autem intendimus universaliter, an aliqua creatura fuerit ab aeterno.[48] And with regard to the possibility of eternal creation, Thomas asks in the same universal way: Utrum quod est a Deo diversum in essentia (scil. created being), possit semper fuisse.[49]

When it can be proved that "eternal" or "not-eternal" can be necessarily predicated of "world" by way of a definition of "world", then the question *de aeternitate mundi* must be answered in an effective way. Such a demonstration should prove then that the world is necessarily eternal or necessarily not-eternal. But when it becomes evident that the essence of "world" does not necessarily involve "eternity" or "not-eternity", then it follows that the world is merely possibly eternal or not-eternal.

In the beginning of the solutio of the article on the eternity of the world (*Scriptum* II,1,1,5) Thomas says that there is a "triplex positio" with regard to the question at issue: the position of the philosophers (Aristotle according to Avicenna and Averroes), an anonymous position (Bonaventure is referred to) and the position of Thomas himself. Anyone who considers the texts of Thomas on the question will be struck by the fact that according to three of the above-mentioned four assertions he clarifies and arranges the labyrinth of arguments for and against. These three now appear to correspond with the three stated historical positions.

1. *The World is Necessarily Eternal*

The philosophers (Avicenna and Averroes) thought that the world existed form eternity in the sense of eternal creation. According to them this was also the opinion of Aristotle, the Philosopher.

This statement about the world can be proved by demonstrative arguments. Therefore the world is necessarily eternal.

Thomas' criticism of this view: the argumentation of the philosophers can not come to a necessary conclusion, because the will of God, which is the cause of things, accomplishes its effect not necessarily but freely. Neither is it possible to bring forward the authority of the Philosopher. According to Aristotle the question belongs to those problems that cannot be solved demonstratively but only dialectically.[50]

2. *The World is Necessarily Not-Eternal*

Bonaventure, as has been seen, teaches that creation necessarily implies an absolutely first beginning. Creation means that nothing *simpliciter* has preceded the first making of things by God. Creation is therefore "from nothing", which expresses nothing else than "in the beginning". Creation from eternity is thus intrinsically a contradiction.

Thomas' Criticism

An article of faith can not be proved demonstratively. But it is an article of faith that the world had a beginning to its duration. Ergo etc. The reason behind the first premiss is twofold: The principle of the demonstrative proof is the definition as the determination of the essence of the object under demonstration. The essence of world, namely the "from nothing" in the sense of dependence on being, says nothing about a first beginning of duration. Therefore the beginning of the world cannot be proved apodictically or demonstratively. Second: the creator of the world is a cause who acts by virtue of a free will. God's will, however, is impenetrable and only knowable via revelation. The beginning of creation is thus as an effect of divine ordinance a matter of faith and not of science.[51]

3. *The World is Possibly Eternal*

Thomas describes the third, his own position, as follows: "Tertia positio est dicentium quod omne quod est praeter Deum incepit esse; sed tamen Deus potuit ab aeterno res produxisse, ita quod mundum incepisse non possit demonstrari, sed per revelationem divinam esse habitum et creditum. (...) Et huic positioni consentio, quia non credo quod a nobis possit sumi ratio demonstrativa ad hoc.[52]

This *tertia positio* says the following. In fact the world was created with a beginning of its duration. However, this state of affairs cannot be demonstrated, for it relates wholly to a thesis of faith.

Nevertheless God could have made his creation from eternity.

How did Thomas arrive at this position of the possibility of an eternally created world?

Neither the philosophers nor the conservative theologians (Bonaventure and others) are able to give apodictic proofs for their positions. The level of argumentation is thus only probability. Now, when the question is confined to the "domain of probability" (*Topica* I,1), then the conclusions of one's arguments will not go any further than a dialectical or if the worst comes to the worst a sophistical syllogism![53]

Whoever has allowed Thomas to speak thus far will be ready to call him an agnostic or sceptic. This means that reason and science can neither prove that the world has had a beginning nor that it is eternal. However, seeking further will show that Thomas ultimately is not an agnostic. A fortiori he has even inaugurated a *novum* in the history of the question: the *possibility* of an eternally created world. In contradistinction to some early students and followers of Thomas (Thomas of Sutton, Jean Quidort) and some of his adversaries (Henry of Ghent, Richard of Middleton) the idea of the possibility of *creatio ab aeterno* is hardly seen as peculiar to Thomas' thinking about creation in the subsequent course of Aquinas exegesis until modern times.[54]

We have seen that Thomas rejects the assertations that the world is necessarily either eternal or not eternal, because this necessity is ungrounded and therefore illusory. Thus the assertion that the world is possibly eternal is logically left over. In the *Scriptum* II,1,1,art.2 Thomas expounds that creation taken in its philosophical sense can be proved demonstratively. But taken in its theological or religious sense ("In principio creavit Deus") creation cannot be strictly demonstrated. The concept of creation taken in its philosophical sense however says nothing about the duration of this creation i.e. it expresses not necessarily "being after not-being" in a durational sense, but only in a metaphysical sense: created being means dependency of being. From this we can conclude that creation in a philosophical sense might *possibly* have been from eternity. Thomas does not say this expressly in art. 2, but it is certainly implied in his text, as Richard of Middleton has sharp-wittedly shown.[55]

As art. 2 has developed a twofold concept of creation, so it can be said on account of this art. 5 has developed a twofold concept of the *duration* of creation, namely: creation from eternity as a possible (philosophical) position and creation "in the beginning" as the revealed, factual truth. In some of his writings Thomas has examined the philosophicum[56] of a possibly eternal world.

In *De potentia* 3,14 Thomas poses the question of whether it is possible for that which differs essentially from God to have existed always, or otherwise: can being which is created have eternal duration? To solve the problem Thomas points to the meaning of the central terms "can" and "possibility", and therefore he introduces two distinctions: the distinction of active and passive potency and the distinction of metaphorical and absolute possibility (art.14 *solution*). There is talk of active potency/power, as when we say that to a builder it is possible to build. Passive potency/power is meant, as when we say that it is possible for the wood to burn. Concerning the second distinction, Thomas only goes into the matter of absolute possibility. And he means by this that the terms of a proposition are in no way mutually contradictory (whereas we have the impossible when the terms exclude each other). For example, a square circle is a contradiction in terms and therefore impossible.[57]

Thomas thereupon applies these distinctions (with the exclusion of metaphorical possibility) to the question whether *creatio ab aeterno* is a possible position.

With regard to the logico-semantical side (absolute possibility), Thomas sees no problems, for, as he says, creation in the sense of dependency of being is not contradictory to eternal duration.[58] There is also no problem with regard to the active potency, namely God's potency or power to be able to create. If we refer the possibility for eternal creation to an active power, then God does not lack the power to produce from eternity an effect essentially different from himself.[59] But only on the ground of passive potency (or matter) should creation from eternity be impossible for God, because, as Thomas of Strasbourg[60] elucidates this passage in Aquinas, extra Deum nihil fuerit. When the world should be created from eternity by passive potency (or prime matter), then this *prima materia* should have been from eternity outside of God as uncreated, i.e. as not dependent for its being on the creator. But God can not have anything outside himself, for he has created *all* there is, even prime matter itself. Creation is *ex nihilo*, not out of a preexistent, eternal matter.[61] Therefore it is impossible that something is eternally created on the ground of passive potency. Thomas, however, only refers to the truth of catholic faith, that nothing which differs in essence from God can be created from eternity on the basis of passive potency. For the catholic faith, he says, supposes that all things other than God once (*aliquando*) did not exist. And on the basis of this statement from authority (e.g. *Genesis* 1,1) he gives the following argument. Now as it is impossible for a thing never to have existed, if it be granted that at some time it has been, so it is impossible for a thing to have been always, if it be granted that at some time it did not exist.[62] But (to finish Thomas' reasoning) creation from eternity on the ground of passive potency (which is eternally and uncreated, as we have seen) cannot be said not to have been. Therefore, such a creation is impossible.

Up to now Thomas has shown by philosophical reason that an eternally created being which differs in essence from its creator is possible, because there is no problem by referring to Gods' active potency to create such a being, nor is there any problem by referring to the concept of *creatio ab aeterno*, which implies no contradiction and is therefore intelligible (absolute possibility). But solely by faith he has shown that *creatio ab aeterno* is impossible on the ground of the third possibility, namely by passive potency. This last theological argument contra eternal creation can also be written in a philosophical way. Thomas does this in the seventh argument *sed contra* of *De pot.* 3,14: created being cannot be eternally made by God, because it is *ex nihilo*. And it must be *ex nihilo*, because it is impossible that created being were made from something (passive potency, prime matter) besides God which were not made by him.[63] For this impossibility see *De pot.* 3,5.

Creation, however, excludes something already preexistent besides the creator, such as an eternal *causa materialis*. On the contrary, creation concerns all there is, being as a whole with all its constituents. Therefore passive potency or matter is not outside God, but from him, or in other words *ex nihilo*.[64]

But if passive potency or prime matter is also *ex nihilo* and as a co-principle of the structure of being dependent in an absolute sense on the creator, then creation from eternity must be possible and intelligible. According to the seventh argument *sed contra* creation *ex nihilo*, as we have seen, means only this: creation cannot be eternal, because it is *ex nihilo*, i.e. made with a very first beginning of its duration. Impossibile autem est, quod fit ex nihilo, semper fuisse. Ergo impossibile est creaturam semper fuisse. To this argument, which is Bonaventure's main reason against creation from eternity, Thomas answers by bending his thoughts towards the semantics of "ex nihilo". He says that creation "from nothing" does not necessarily signify creation "in the beginning". First because "ex nihilo" may mean that the created thing is not made from something (e.g. from preexistent and eternal matter), so that the negation includes the preposition (*non ex aliquo*) and is not included by it, and thus denies the order implied by the preposition; while the preposition itself does not imply order to nothing.[65] *Creatio ex nihilo* in this sense of *creatio non ex aliquo* means only that there is nothing preexistent to creation, such as a primordial matter besides and outside the creator. Secondly: "ex nihilo" does not necessarily signify creation "in the beginning", because, if order to nothing is affirmed, and the preposition includes the negation (from nothing in the sense of after nothing[66]), then it still does not follow that once the creature was nothing. For one might say that nothing preceded the being of a thing not by duration but by nature. Since, to wit, were the creature left to itself it would have no being, and it has being solely from another (namely the creator). Because that which a thing is competent to have of itself is naturally prior to that which it is not adapted to have save from another.[67] *Creatio ex nihilo* in this second sense (*post nihilum*) means only conservation of being: the creature is nothing in itself but participates in being solely by the conserving hand of the creator, who is the fullness of being.

In short then, one can say that Thomas Aquinas has proven with his *quaestio disputata de potentia Dei* qu.3, art.14 that *creatio ab aeterno*, philosophically seen, is a possible and intelligible position.

NOTES

1. In Primam partem qu.46, art.2, in: *Scholastica commentaria in Primam partem Summae Theologiae S. Thomae Aquinatis*, Lugduni 1588, col.607A.
2. De 15 problematibus, in: *Opera omnia*, tom. XVII, pars I (ed. B. Geyer), Münster 1975, p. 37a.
3. Cf. E. Zeller, Die Lehre des Aristoteles von der Ewigkeit der Welt, in: *Vorträge und Abhandlungen*, Leipzig 1884, Bd III, p. 1 and note 1; Der Streit Theophrasts gegen Zeno über die Ewigkeit der Welt, in: *Kleine Schriften* (ed. O. Leuze), Berlin 1911, Bd I, p. 170; *Die Philosophie der Griechen*, Hildesheim⁵ 1963 (Leipzig⁴ 1921), Bd II, 2, p. 432. B. Effe, *Studien zur Kosmologie und Theologie der aristotelischen Schrift "Über die Philosophie"*, München 1970, p. 8 and note 9.
4. According to the ancient and modern commentators (Simplicius, Cornford) Plato is meant. Cf. Also Aristotle, *Physica* VIII, 1, 251a18).
5. Cf. M. Baltes, *Die Weltentstehung des platonischen Timaios nach den antiken Interpreten*, Leiden 1976 (2 vols).
6. *Baltes* I, p. 211 note 31, p. 84. There are two other explanations of the γέγονεν, viz. the methodical/didactical and the "physical" (p. 211–12, p. 82), but we are only interested in the metaphysical explanation, namely in connection with "eternal creation".

7. *Baltes* I, p. 38–69.
8. *Baltes* I, p. 136–63; see also p. 163–69.
9. W. Theiler, *Forschungen zum Neuplatonismus*, Berlin 1966, p. 176–77, cf. p. 42. Also H.-R. Schwyzer, Christlichkeit des Hierokles?, in: *Ammonios Sakkas, der Lehrer Plotins*, Opladen 1983, p. 88.
10. *De civitate dei* X, 31. Cf. *Baltes* I, p. 163–64.
11. In fact this metaphor is not quite to the point, for it is too static and discontinuous. Therfore some criticized it sharply, e.g. Richard of Middleton, *In II Sent.* dist.1, art.3, qu.4 ad2.
12. Cf. K. Verrycken, *God en wereld in de wijsbegeerte van Ioannes Philoponus*, Leuven 1985 (doctoral thesis), p. 132ff.
13. *In Arist. Phys.* 249, 16f. Cf. *Verrycken*, p. 408.
14. "Out of God" can nevertheless be conceived of as "out of nothing", namely in the sense that God is "nothing", as e.g. in Scotus Eriugena and Jacob Boehme.
15. The "first master" is of course Aristotle. Cf. M. Worms, *Die Lehre von der Anfangslosigkeit der Welt bei den mittelalterlichen arabischen Philosophen des Orients und ihre Bekämpfung durch die arabischen Theologen (Mutakallimun)*, Münster 1900, p. 19.
16. E. Behler, *Die Ewigkeit der Welt. Problemgeschichtliche Untersuchungen zu den Kontroversen um Weltanfang und Weltunendlichkeit in der arabischen und jüdischen Philosophie des Mittelalters*, München etc. 1965, p. 74.
17. Metaphysica tract. IX, cap.1–3, in: *Opera*, Venetiis 1508 (reprint Frankfurt/M 1961), fol. 101va–104rb.
18. *Behler*, p. 71–77, p. 128, p. 137.
19. *Didascalion* VI, 3. Cited in: M.-D. Chenu/O.H. Pesch, *Das werk des hl. Thomas von Aquin*, Graz etc. ²1982 (1960; Paris 1950), p. 269.
20. *De consolatione philosophiae* III, metrum 9 and V, prose 6; *De Hebdomadibus*. Cf. P. Courcelle, *Les lettres grecques en occident. De Macrobe à Cassiodore*, Paris 1943, p. 295–304; *La Consolation de Philosophie dans la tradition littéraire*, Paris 1967, p. 221–31. L. Obertello, *Severino Boezio*, Genova 1974, vol. I, p. 540–44, p. 670–72, p. 694–98; Eternità-perpetuità, in: *Severino Boezio. La Consolazione* della Filosofia. Gli opuscoli teologici, Milano 1979, p. 417–24.
21. *Verrycken*, p. 395f.
22. *Periphyseon* III, 5–10, ed. Sheldon/Bieler, Dublin 1981, p. 60–101.
23. R.C. Dales, Discussions on the eternity of the world during the first half of the 12th century, in: *Speculum. A Journal of Mediaeval Studies* 57(1982), p. 495–508.
24. H. Denzinger/A Schönmetzer, *Enchiridion symbolorum*, Barcione etc. 36(1976), p. 259 (nr.800).
25. It is noteworthy that Meister Eckhart in his exposition of the wording "in the beginning" says nothing about its durational or temporal meaning. See his Prologus generalis in opus tripartitum nr.14–21, in: *Prologi expositio libri Genesis. Liber parabolorum Genesis*, ed. K. Weiss Stuttgart 1964 (Die lateinischen Werke 1).
26. Cf. F. van Steenberghen, *La philosophie au XIIIe siècle*, Louvain. Paris 1966, p. 72–117.
27. Summa "*Quoniam homines etc.*" bk I, p. II, tract.2 nr.90, ed. P. Glorieux, in: *Archives d'Histoire Doctrinale et Littéraire du Moyen Age* 28 (1953), p. 233–34.
28. *In I Sent.* dist.44, art.1 sol., in: *Opera omnia*, ed. Borgnet, Parisiis 1893, vol. 26, p. 390a.
29. Cf. Aristotle, *De sophist. elench.* cap.4 (166a6f.).
30. *In II Sent.* dist.1, qu.1, art.2 sol., ed. Strasbourg 1501 (reprint Frankfurt/M 1966), fol. 206vb.
31. *Introduction à l'étude de S. Bonaventure*, Tournai 1961, p. 229.
32. *In I Sent.* dist.44, art.1, qu.4: Utrum Deus potuerit facere mundum antiquiorem, in: *Opera omnia*, ed. Quaracchi 1882f., tom.I, p. 787–89.
33. *Op. cit.*, p. 788a–b: Respondeo: Quod cum quaeritur, utrum Deus potuerit facere mundum antiquiorem, potest intelligi dupliciter: aut quod ipsum creaverit ab aeterno, cum produxerit ex tempore, et tunc esset antiquior, aut ita quod mundus durasset tempore longiori, tamen finito. Primum credo impossibile simpliciter, quoniam implicat in se contradictionem. Ex hoc enim, quod ponitur fieri, ponitur habere

principium. Ex hoc autem, quod ponitur aeternus, ponitur non habere principium. Unde idem est quaerere, utrum Deus potuerit ante mundum facere, quod mundus habendo principium non haberet principium; et hoc includit contradictionis utramque partem.

34. *Op. cit.*, tom.II, p. 14a: Cum constet secundum Sanctos et philosophos, quod omnes res mundanae habuerint principium productivum (. . .) – ideo hoc supposito, scilicet quod res habeant principium causale aliquo modo, est quaestio, utrum res sint productae omnino, hoc est secundum principium materiale et formale, an tantum secundum alterum principiorum.

35. *Op. cit.*, p. 15a (fund. 6): Si res non est totaliter ab alio, aut hoc est ratione formae, aut ratione materiae. Constat quod non formae, quia videmus, formas produci, et si formae non producerentur, omnino nihil produceretur. Si ratione materiae; sed contra: ut dicit Philosophus in Prima Philosophia, "actus est ante potentiam"; constat, quod non loquitur de potentia activa, sed passiva. Ergo cum actus rei sit ab alio, similiter et materia. Si tu dicas, quod intelligitur non de actu, qui est forma, sed efficiens, idem concluditur.–Et iterum, ego quaero, quare materia non sit ab alio. Si quia est principium, ex quo fiunt cetera, nec habet unde fiat.

36. *Op. cit.*, p. 15a–b (fund. 6 seq.): Tunc ego quaero de forma, utrum fiat ex aliquo, vel ex nihilo. Si ex nihilo, pari ratione et materia ex nihilo. Si ex aliquo, quaero, quid sit illud. Non essentia materiae; constat, quia forma simplex est. Ergo forma non fit ex materia, ita quod materia sit eius principium consitutivum. Nec fit ex materia, ita quod materia fiat forma: fit ergo ex aliquo, quod est in materia. Tunc ego quaero: de quo est illud? Et constat, quod non est ex materia, pari ratione. Ergo vel erit abire in infinitum in causando, vel necesse est ponere, essentias formarum a primo opifice productas ex nihilo. Ergo pari ratione et materiam. Note that Bonaventure tacitly presupposes the impossibility of an infinite regress of causality.

37. The expression "mundi machina" was probably used for the first time by Lucretius, *De rerum natura* V, 95 and was transmitted by Chalcidius in his commentary on the *Timaeus* (cap.147 and 299) to the Middle Ages. Since the 14th century the concept of "mundi machina" changed gradually from its organic character to the (early-) modern mechanistic meaning. Cf. M. Markowski, Die kosmologische Anschauungen des Prosdocimo de' Beldomandi, in: A. Maierù and A.P. Bagliani (eds), *Studi sul XIV Secolo in memoria di Anneliese Maier*, Roma 1981, p. 265.

38. *Breviloquium II*, cap. 1, in: *Opera omnia*, tom. V, p. 2190:(. . .) universitas machinae mundialis producta est in esse ex tempore et de nihilo ab uno principio primo, solo et summo. (. . .) Per hoc enim, quod dicitur ex tempore, excluditur error ponentium mundum aeternum. Per hoc, quod dicitur de nihilo, excluditur error ponentium aeternitatem circa principium materiale.

39. *In II Sent.* d.1, p.1, a.1, qu.1 sol., in *Opera omnia*, tom. II, p. 16a–b: Respondeo: Dicendum, quod haec veritas est: mundus in esse productus est, et non solum secundum se totum, sed etiam secundum sua intrinseca principia, quae non ex aliis, sed de nihilo sunt producta.–Haec autem veritas, etsi nunc cuilibet fideli sit aperta et lucida, latuit tamen prudentiam philosophicam, quae in huius quaestionis inquisitione longo tempore ambulavit per devia.

40. *Op. cit.*, p. 17a: Ubi autem deficit philosophorum peritia, subvenit nobis sacrosancta Scriptura, quae dicit, omnia esse creata et secundum omne quod sunt in esse producta. Et ratio etiam a fide non discordat, sicut supra in opponendo ostensum est (see *fundamenta*, p. 14b–15b).

41. *Op. cit.*, tom. V, p. 220a.

42. *In II Sent.* d.1, p.1, a.1, qu.2, in: *Opera omnia*, tom. II, p.19–24.

43. Bonaventure knew this argument, however, by his own tradition. See e.g. *Summa Halensis* I,1,2,4,1,4, sol. (ed. Quaracchi, p. 95b).

44. *In II Sent.* d.1, p.1, a.1, qu.2 fund.6, in: *Opera omnia*, tom. II, p. 22a: Ultima ratio ad hoc (viz. an eternally created world) est: Impossibile est, quod habet esse post non-esse habere esse aeternum, quoniam hic est implicatio contradictionis; sed mundus habet esse post non-esse; ergo impossibile est esse aeternum. Quod autem habet esse post

non-esse, probatur sic: Omne illud quod totaliter habet esse ab aliquo, producitur ab illo ex nihilo; sed mundus totaliter habet esse a Deo; ergo mundus ex nihilo. Sed non ex nihilo materialiter; ergo originaliter. Quod autem omne quod totaliter producitur ab aliquo differente per essentiam, habeat esse ex nihilo, patens est. Nam quod totaliter producitur, producitur secundum materiam et formam. Sed materia non habet ex quo producatur, quia non ex Deo; manifestum est igitur, quod ex nihilo. Minor autem, scilicet quod mundus a Deo totaliter producatur, patet ex alio problemate.

45. *Op. cit.*, sol., p. 22a–b: Respondeo: Dicendum, quod ponere, mundum aeternum esse sive aeternaliter productum, ponendo res omnes ex nihilo productas, omnino est contra veritatem et rationem, sicut ultima ratio probat. Et adeo contra rationem, ut nullum philosophorum quantumcumque parvi intellectus crediderim hoc posuisse. Hoc enim implicat in se manifestam contradictionem.

46. *M.-D. Chenu/O.M. Pesch*, p. 308.

47. Ed. P. Mandonnet, Parisiis 1929, tom. II, p. 27–41.

48. *Summa theol.* Ia, qu.46, art.2 ad 8, in: *Opera omnia*, ed. Leonina, Romae 1888f., tom. IV, p. 482b. Cf. William Peter de Godino, *Lectura Thomasina*, In II Sent. dist.1, qu.1: (. . .) nunc quaerimus, utrum creaturae unde creatura repugnat esse ab aeterno, cited in: L. Ullrich, *Fragen der Schöpfungslehre nach Jakob von Metz o.p. Eine vergleichende Untersuchung zu Sentenzenkommentaren aus der Dominikanerschule um 1300*, Leipzig 1966, p. 118 note 51.

49. *De potentia Dei* qu.3, art.14, in: *Quaestiones disputatae*, ed. Marietti, Romae 1965, p. 79–82. Cf. Joh. Duns Scotus, *Ordinatio* II, dist.1, art.3: Utrum sit possibile Deum producere aliquid "aliud a se" sine principio, in: *Opera omnia*, Civitas Vaticana 1973, vol. VII, p. 50–91.

50. *Summa theol.* Ia, qu.46, art.1 sol. (p. 479a); *In II Sent.* dist.1, qu.1, art.5 sol. (p. 33–34).

51. *Summa theol.* Ia, qu.46, art.2 sol. (p. 481b); Cf. *Quodlibetum III*, qu.14, art.31 *sed c.* sol., in: *Quaestiones quodlibetales*, ed. Marietti, Taurini. Romae 1927, p. 70b.

52. *In II Sent.* dist.1, qu.1, art.5 sol. (p. 33).

The sentence "Deus potuit res ab aeterno produxisse, ita quod" is omitted in the text of some editions, including the edition of Mandonnet; so also ed. Vivès. Mandonnet, however, notes that the Parma-edition (*Opera omnia*, Parmae 1856, vol. V, p. 392b) adds this sentence (p. 33 note 3). An important reason to insert the sentence is based on the fact that Thomas earlier in his *Scriptum* on the Sentences says: Utrum autem aliquod aeternum possit esse, quod non habeat principium durationis, quaeretur in principio secundi. (*In I Sent.* dist.8, qu.2, art.2 sol. (p. 204)). It is evident that he refers with this text to the question of an eternally created being in art.5 of Book I, dist.1, qu.1 (see also art. 2 sol.!).

All the editions read erroneously "potuit" in stead of "possit" in the sentence: "ita quod mundum incepisse non *possit* demonstrari".

53. *In II Sent.* dist.1, qu.1, art.5 sol. (p. 33): Dico ergo quod ad neutram partem quaestionis sunt demonstrationes, sed probabiles vel sophisticae utrumque.

With this text Thomas refers to the first and second position, not to his own solution, briefly described in the tertia positio.

54. A minority of exegetes has pointed to the thesis of the possibility of an eternally created world as typical for Thomas' position. See e.g.: A. Collell, El problema de la possibilitad de la creació ab aeterno, in: *Criterion* 3 (1927), p. 419–37.

F. Hendrickx, Das Problem der Aeternitas Mundi bei Thomas von Aquin, in: *Recherches de Théologie Ancienne et Médiévale* 34 (1967), p. 219–37. J.F. Wippel, Thomas Aquinas on the possibility of eternal creation, in: *Metaphysical themes in Thomas Aquinas*, Washington 1984, p. 191–214; first published in: *The Journal of the History of Philosophy* 19 (1981), p. 21–37.

It is noteworthy that Hendrickx' and Wippel's positions are diametrically opposed to each other. Hendrickx thinks that Thomas only in his youth defended the thesis of the possibility of an eternal world (he dates *De aeternitate mundi* before 1259) and that Aquinas later in his life more and more became philosophically convinced of the non-eternity of the world. Wippel, however, thinks that Thomas became more and more philosophically convinced of the possibility of an eternally created world until he arrived at full conviction in his *De aeternitate mundi*, which Wippel dates late in Thomas' life: ca 1270.

Whether you date *De aeternitate mundi* early (the minority of scholars) or late (the majority) in Thomas' life, this is not of any importance at all with regard to the thesis of Thomas that an eternally created world is philosophically seen a possible position, because, as I think, he always defended this thesis in the course of his career. The early dating of *De aeternitate mundi* has a strong basis, because, as Th. Bukowski has shown in his article An early dating for Aquinas' "De aeternitate mundi", in: *Gregorianum* 51 (1970), p. 277–303, - because the opposite position has no particular reasons to date or further substantiation of its dating. Bukowski then gives well-documented internal as well as external reasons for *his* dating. It can be added to his external reasons that the words "dubitatio mota est" (in: *Opera omnia*, ed. Leonina, Roma 1976, vol. 43, p. 85 rg.2–3) most probably refer to *De potentia Dei* qu.3, art.14: Utrum quod est a Deo diversum in essentia possit semper fuisse. This quaestio disputata must be dated 1265–66, see J.A. Weisheipl, *Friar Thomas d'Aguino*, Washington²1983 (1974), p. 363. But then, of course, must Bukowski's claim for dating *De aeternitate mundi* at or before 1259 be accomodated to a middle position between an early and a late dating, with an inclination towards the early dating.

55. *In II Sent.* dist.1, art.3, qu.4 sol., in: *Super IV libros Sententiarum. Quolibeta quaestiones*, Brixiae 1591 (reprint Frankfurt/M 1963), tom. II, p. 17b–18b.

56. Cf. F. Suárez, *De universo*, cap.2, in: *Opera omnia*, ed. Vivès, Parisiis 1861, vol.III, p. 9a: (. . .) an (mundus) potuerit esse ab aeterno, id enim philosophicum potius est, quam theologicum, quia nec ad fidei dogmata pertinet, nec cum illis necessariam connexionem habet.

57. *De potentia Dei* qu.3, art.14 sol. (p. 80b): Respondeo dicendum, quod secundum Philosophum possibile dicitur quandoque quidem secundum aliquam potentiam, quandoque, vero secundum nullam potentiam; secundum potentiam quidem vel activam vel passivam. Secundum activam quidem, ut si dicamus possibile esse aedificatori quod aedificet; secundum passivam vero, ut si dicamus, possibile esse ligno quod comburatur. Dicitur autem et quandoque aliquid possibile, non secundum aliquam potentiam, sed vel metaphorice, sicut in geometricis dicitur aliqua linea potentia rationalis, quod praetermittatur ad praesens, vel absolute, quando scilicet termini enuntiationis nullam ad invicem repugnantiam habent. E contrario vero impossibile, quando sibi invicem repugnant; ut simul esse affirmationem et negationem impossibile dicitur, non quia sit impossibile alicui agenti vel patienti, sed quia est secundum se impossibile, utpote sibi ipsi repugnans.

58. Cf. *In II Sent.* 1, 1, 2 sol.

59. *De potentia Dei* qu.3, art.14 sol. (p. 80b): Si ergo consideretur hoc enuntiabile, aliquid diversum in substantia existens a Deo fuisse semper, non potest dici impossibile secundum se, quasi sibi ipsi repugnans; hoc enim quod est esse ab alio, non repugnat ei quod est esse semper (. . .), nisi quando aliquid ab alio procedit per motum, quod non intervenit in processu rerum a Deo. Per hoc autem quod additur, diversum in substantia, similiter nulla repugnantia absolute loquendo datur intelligi ad id quod est semper fuisse. Si autem accipiamus possibile dictum secundum potentiam activam, tunc in Deo non deest potentia ab aeterno essentiam aliam a se producendi.

60. *In II Sent.* dist.1, qu.1, art.2 arg.1, in: *Commentaria in IV libros Sententiarum*, Venetiis 1564 (reprint Ridgewood, New Jersey 1965), fol. 127vb.

61. Cf. *De pot.* 3,5; *In II Sent.* 1,1,2; *Summa theol.* Ia, 44, 2. See for the problem of the origin of prime matter, *De pot.* 5,1–2.

62. *De pot.* 3,14 sol. (p. 80b): Si vero hoc ad potentiam passivam referatur, sic, supposita catholicae fidei veritate, dici non potest, quod aliquid a Deo procedens in essentia diversum, potuerit semper esse. Supponit enim fides catholica omne id quod est praeter Deum, aliquando non fuisse. Sicut autem impossibile est, quod ponitur aliquando fuisse, nunquam fuisse; ita impossibile est, quod ponitur aliquando non fuisse, semper fuisse.

63. *De pot.* 3,14 arg.7 sed contra (p. 80a): Si creatura est facta, aut ex nihilo, aut ex aliquo.

Sed non ex aliquo; quia vel ex aliquo quod est divina essentia, quod est impossibile; vel ex aliquo alio; quod si non esset factum, erit aliquid praeter Deum, non ab ipso creatum (. . .). Quod si est factum ex aliquo, aut procedetur in infinitum, quod est impossibile, aut devenietur ad aliquid quod est factum de nihilo. Impossibile autem est, quod fit ex nihilo, semper fuisse. Ergo impossibile est creaturam semper fuisse.

64. See note 61.

65. *De pot.* 3,14 ad 7 sed contra: (. . .) primae creaturae non sunt productae ex aliquo, sed ex nihilo. Non tamen oportet ex ipsa ratione productionis, sed ex veritate quam fides supponit, quod prius non fuerint, et postea in esse prodierint. Unus enim sensus praedictae locutionis esse potest, secundum Anselmum, ut dicatur creatura facta ex nihilo, quia non est facta ex aliquo, ut negatio includat praepositionem et non includatur ab ea, ut sic negatio ordinem ad aliquid, quem praepositio importat, neget; non autem praepositio importat ordinem ad nihil.

66. Cf. *In II Sent.* 1,1, 2 sol.

67. *De pot.* 3,14 ad 7 sed contra: Si vero ordo ad nihil remaneat affirmatus, praepositione negationem includente, nec adhuc oportet quod creatura aliquando fuerit nihil. Potest enim dici, sicut et Avicenna dicit, quod non esse praecedat esse rei, non duratione, sed natura; quia videlicet, si ipsa sibi relinqueretur, nihil esset; esse vero solum ab alio habet. Quod enim est natum alicui inesse ex se ipso, naturaliter prius competit ei, eo quod non est ei natum inesse nisi ab alio.

THE LITERARY RECEPTION OF THOMAS AQUINAS' VIEW ON THE PROVABILITY OF THE ETERNITY OF THE WORLD IN DE LA MARE'S CORRECTORIUM (1278–9) AND THE CORRECTORIA CORRUPTORII (1279–ca 1286)

M.J.F.M. HOENEN

I. *Introduction*

In 1278 or 1279, some years after the death of Thomas Aquinas, the Franciscan theologian William de la Mare composed a work that was to elicit a vehement reaction from Dominican theology. And not without reason, as Mare sharply opposed the views of Thomas, itemizing no less than 118 points of criticism.[1] The work was soon referred to as the *Correctorium Fratris Thomae*, under which name it has survived to our days.[2]

Mare's book met with considerable success, becoming the official response to the views of Thomas.[3] This may be gathered from such documents as the order issued by the Franciscan general chapter of Strasburg, admonishing its provincials not to copy Thomas's Summa unless a copy of Mare's corrections be included.[4]

Again, Dominicans were not indifferent to the attack on Aquinas. A growing number of Dominicans were beginning to look upon Thomas as the Teacher of their order. This may be clear from the notice issued in 1279 by the Dominican general chapter at Paris, sanctioning punishment of friars that spoke irreverently and indecently of Thomas, whose work (as was said) was such a credit to the order.[5] Furthermore, in 1286 it was decided by the same chapter that every Dominican should, to the best of his knowledge and ability speak up for the views of Thomas, as being at least a defendable position.[6] From these two facts we may learn that to many Dominican theologians William de la Mare was not merely criticizing Thomas Aquinas, but indeed Dominican theology as such. It is hardly surprising, then, that in the years after the Correctorium's publication no less than five Dominican responses were written, defending those views of Thomas that were attacked by William, and refuting, where necessary, William's own views.

The Dominican defenses have come to be known as the *Correctoria Corruptorii*. The "Corruptorium" in this generic title refers to the work of William of Mare, which – as the author of one of the replies put it – should more properly be called "Corruptorium Fratris Thommae" instead of "Correctorium".[7]

As a rule, the Dominican Correctoria have been handed down anonymously. Still, the question of their authorship has now largely been cleared up. Thus it is known that it was Richard of Knapwell who wrote what is probably the earliest Correctorium, the Correctorium "*Quare*" (like the other Correctoria called after its opening word or words).[8] Robert of Orford is held to be the author of the Correctorium "*Sciendum*".[9] The Correctorium "*Circa*" was written by John Quidort.[10] William of Macklesfield may have been the author of the Correctorium "*Quaestione*", but this is as yet a matter of dispute.[11] Finally, there is the *Apologeticum Veritatis Contra Corruptorii*, written by Robert of Bologna.[12] Generally speaking, the Correctoria Corruptorii originated between 1279 and ca. 1286.

These five works, together with William de la Mare's Correctorium Fratris Thomae, are of great importance to the history of the reception, more specifically the literary reception, of Thomas Aquinas' views. We would like to give four general considerations in support of this thesis. In the first place, being polemical writings, they neatly review those views of Thomas that were a subject of controversy at the end of the thirteenth century. Thus, it is possible to ascertain *which of Thomass's views* were seen as "new" and "uncommon" in those days. Secondly, as the Correctoria make frequent use of the work of Thomas, we may ascertain through them *which of Thomas's writings* were used and quoted in those days. Mare's Correctorium tells us something about which works of Thomas were studied by non-Dominicans, and about which writings were taken to be representative of his views outside his own order. Similarly, from the Dominican replies we may learn which writings were held to be of importance within the Dominican order itself, and which writings were preferentially quoted and referred to by Dominicans. In the third place, as the Correctoria make frequent use of Thomas's work, it is possible for us to ascertain through them *exactly what* was quoted from his writings, and *exactly how* this was set about. As a final consideration in support of the importance of the Correctoria, we point again to the fact that we are dealing with polemical writings. We may be sure that the authors studied Thomas as carefully and as exhaustingly as they could. A methodological advantage may be gained from this: not only the reference to particular works of Thomas will be telling, but also the absence of such reference. Thus for example as we shall see, nowhere in his Correctorium does Mare make reference to the third part of the Summa Theologiae and the opusculum De aeternitate Mundi. In almost every other kind of writing, be it a Quaestio Disputata or a Commentary on the Sentences, such curious omissions might be put down to coincidence or negligence. In the kind of work under consideration, however, this explanation is hardly convincing.

These remarks should suffice to introduce our study. It is now time to look in some detail at the use that was made of Thomas's texts in Mare's Correctorium and the Correctoria Corruptorii. First we shall look into Mare's Correctorium in general (section II, 1–3), ascertaining (1) against which of Thomas's works his criticism is directed; (2) in what way Thomas is quoted; and (3) what Mare's characterization is of Thomas's tenets. These sections will serve as background to the next section (II,4) in which the same questions will be posed specifically with regard to Thomas's view of the eternity of the world, as rendered in Mare's Correctorium. Finally (section III), we turn to the Correctoria Corruptorii, ascertaining *which of Thomas's works* are quoted with respect to this problem, and again, *how* they are quoted.

II. *William de la Mare's Correctorium*

Before going through the aforementioned questions, we would do well to pause briefly at the general construction of Mare's Correctorium. It consists of 118 articles, each dealing with a certain thesis taken from the work of Thomas.

The articles are ordered neither randomly nor thematically; rather, they systematically run through one writing after the other.

Each article opens with a reference to a certain place in the work of Thomas under consideration, and proceeds to quote the contentious opinion. For example, the sixth article begins as follows: "In the 46th quaestio (of the Summa Theologiae), in the body of the second article, Thomas says that it is an article of Faith, a subject not of knowledge but only of faith, that the world has a beginning..." Next, Thomas's arguments are given. Sometimes other contentious theses are added in the same article, along with Thomas's arguments. Having thus presented the opinion of Thomas, Mare points out *what* he thinks to be wrong with it, and finally shows *why* it is wrong.

1. *Which Works are Criticized?*

Which of Thomas's works are affected by Mare's criticism? They are seven, notably, the Summa Theologiae, the disputed questions De Veritate, De Anima, De Virtutibus, and De Potentia, the questions De Quolibet, and the Commentary on the Sentences. All these tracts, as can be noticed, are of a theological nature. William does not deal with Thomas's philosophical works, e.g., with his commentaries on Aristotle. There is not so much as a hint at these works.[13] The criticism, then, mainly concerns Thomas as a theologian – which is not to say that Mare does not on several occasions point out that Thomas's reasonings are philosophically speaking incorrect.[14]

A second point of interest is the striking absence of theses taken from the third part of the *Summa Theologiae*. William discusses and criticizes theses from the first part, from the first and second parts of the second part, but not from the third part, of which there is not even the faintest trace. Was the work unknown to Mare, then? For surely, had he known it, he might reasonably be expected to have quoted, discussed, or criticized theses from the third part, as well as from the other parts. The Summa's third part deals with, among other things, the relationship between the living and the dead body of Christ,[15] an issue on which Thomas holds to the unity of substantial form, and is criticized by Mare for being unable to maintain that the body of the living and the dead Christ is one and the same, as is stated by Faith.[16]

Thomas holds to the doctrine of the unity of substantial form, and is severely attacked for this by Mare. The doctrine is denounced by the Masters, so the latter says, because its consequences are contrary to Catholic Faith, contrary to philosophy, and contrary to the Holy Scripture.[17] We find this in Mare's discussion of the 76th question of the first part of the Summa. But there is more. The same rejection of Thomas's error recurs in the discussions of the 118th question of the same part of the Summa, of the 9th question of De Anima, of the 22nd question of De Potentia, and of the 6th question of the Quodlibet.[18]

In view of all this, it would hardly be reasonable to suggest that Mare, who seized upon every opportunity, on this as well as on other issues, to point out that Thomas is mistaken,[19] would not have discussed the third part of the Summa, had it been available to him. Now, it is certain that the Correctorium was written after 1277, probably in England, because Mare makes reference to the Paris condemnations of 1277, observing the order of condemned theses that was common in England.[20] These facts seem to suggest that (as Pelster has already hinted) at that time (1278 or 1279) the third part of the Summa had not yet been officially published,[21] or that it had not yet arrived at the place where Mare was writing his Correctorium (England), Knapwell, for that matter, author of the (first) Correctorium Corruptorii, written perhaps shortly after 1280, *does* make use of the Summa's third part, as do the other Correctoria.[22,23]

We may notice further that Mare's criticism of the Commentary on the Sentences is limited to theses taken from the first book; on the other three books there is nothing. Now, the Correctorium, as it has come down to us in the version of the Correctorium "Quare", concludes with nine theses from the first book of Thomas's Commentary on the Sentences. It is not unthinkable, then, that Mare in point of fact *did* criticize the remaining three books, but that this part of the Correctorium has been lost. Probable, however, this suggestion is not correct. Even the oldest manuscript of "Quare" reacts only on the nine theses extracted from the first book.[24] This is not to say, however, that the last three books of Thomas's Commentary on the Sentences were unknown to Mare. Criticizing a thesis taken from De Veritate on the issue of what befalls the soul in Hell, Mare makes reference – quite explicitly, and quoting literally – to the fourth book of the Commentary.[25] It is rather curious, though, that this place has not been dealt with in its own right. In his criticism of the 64th question of the first part of the Summa Theologiae, Mare shows Thomas's view to be alarmingly close to the eighth thesis condemned by Tempier in 1270, viz., that the soul, separated from the body after death, is not affected by the fire of Hell.[26] Why doesn't Mare repeat his criticism, we may ask, and why does he not single out for attention Thomas's remark in the Commentary on the Sentences? Furthermore, how is it that Mare does not mention theses taken from the second and the third book? As for the second book, he might readily have criticized Thomas's view on the eternity of the world, as he did with regard to the Summa and the questions De Quolibet.[27]

As for the third book, it may have given him yet another opportunity to criticize Thomas's Christology.[28] The Correctorium "Quare", to be sure, *does* make use of both the second and the fourth book of Thomas's Commentary on the Sentences.[29] Also the other Correctoria either make reference to or make use of these books.[30]

It is perhaps of interest to note here, that Knapwell, the author of the Correctorium "Quare", does not always seem to be entirely happy with Thomas's choice of words in the Commentary. As for the doctrine of angels, for example, he clearly prefers Thomas's wording in the Summa to that of the Commentary on the Sentences.[31] Incidentally, it may be pointed out that several other Dominican theologians also preferred the statement of Thomas's views in the Summa to those in his Commentary on the Sentences. A point in case is the author of the *Articuli in quibus frater Thomas melius in Summa quam in Scriptis*, a work from around 1280.[32]

Two last points should be made. In the first place, nowhere does William de la Mare submit to criticism theses from the Summa contra Gentiles, in spite of the fact that in this important work he would surely have found views to disagree with. Mare mentions it only once, not having in mind any place in particular, but referring rather to the overall design of the work. Mare is prompted by Thomas's opinion that one should not seek proof of what is solely a matter of Faith, in this case: that the world has been created in time.

According to Thomas, this would only expose us to the ridicule of the unbelievers, who might think that our Faith were grounded in deficient reasoning.[33] But if this is so, replies Mare, then why did Thomas bother to write the Summa contra Gentiles? Again, the Summa contra Gentiles is used by Knapwell, who mentions each of its four books. The other

Correctoria Corruptorii, too, either mention or make use of each of the four books.[34]

In the second place, in his criticism of the Quaestiones Disputatae Mare used a differently ordered collection than the one known to us today, and than the one used by Knapwell in his response. For example Mare speaks of question 220, where Knapwell, having the same article in mind, refers to it as Quaestio De Veritate 25 (=26) art.1.[35]

Apparently, Mare had a manuscript that numbered Thomas's articles consecutively.[36] In his version, the articles are called "questions". Knapwell, on the other hand, used a text in which different articles of Thomas are grouped together, these groups being called "questiones". In each of these groups the consecutive numbering of the articles starts anew, as is also customary in modern editions.[37]

2. *How Does Mare Quote Thomas?*

We have seen just now *which* of Thomas's works are quoted by Mare; now we shall turn to *how* and *what* is quoted from them. We shall start with the latter. From a quick survey we learn that the various articles of Mare's Correctorium quote either (1) from an article's body; or (2) from the responses to the arguments to the contrary; or (3) from both.[38]

Incidentally, however, (and this is interesting) Mare also gives (4) arguments from the "sed contra", presenting them as arguments of Thomas himself.[39]

How does Mare set about his quotations? As a rule, (1) he proceeds *verbatim*. Again, sometimes (2) he gives only a summary of Thomas's arguments. Sometimes, also, (3) he omits crucial qualifications, and sometimes the reader may even get the impression that (4) Thomas's views are misrepresented.[40] It is beyond the scope of the present paper, however, to verify the exact extent to which this impression is correct, which would take a meticulous and comprehensive study, for Mare will most certainly have read some parts of Thomas in the light of other parts, as is the right and plight of every reader, Mare's as well as ours. Now, notwithstanding the fact that Mare wrote a *Correctorium*, and even though he may really have been trying intentionally to misrepresent Thomas, we must still assume that he was sincerely seeking to peruse the content and significance of Thomas's teachings, even if some of his conclusions would strike us as somewhat curious (to say the least). Thus, from the thesis that individual and species coincide, in incorruptible beings, Mare concludes that Thomas advocated Averroes's theory of intellect.[41] The author of the Correctorium "Quare", however, does indeed seem to be under the impression that Mare

misrepresents Thomas's views. He complains more than once that he has
not been able to find the alleged quotations that Mare presents as the words
of Thomas. "I could not find this in Thomas, not in these words", the
author says with regard to an alleged quotation from the Summa.[42]
Similarly, with regard to a quotation from the disputed question De
Anima, where Thomas dealt with the question whether, according to the
philosophers, the celestial bodies are ensouled, Knapwell observes that
Mare is mistaken in making us believe that Thomas himself thought the
celestial bodies to be ensouled. According to Knapwell, Thomas did never
expressly say that they are; rather, he left the question open.[43]

But, of course, this is where the problem of interpreting Thomas's
position begins.[44]

3. *Mare's General Characterization of Thomas's Position*

Mare's writing is polemical; its intention is to show that Thomas's views are
susceptible to criticism in many points. Of course, this also affects the way
Mare characterizes Thomas's position. Most often he speaks of his
opinions' being "false", for example with regard to the view that beatitude
is essentially an act of intellect, not of will.[45] It is only very rarely that he
admits some aspect of an opinion expressed by Thomas to be correct, as
with the view that angels are by their nature incorruptible.[46] But apart
from the theses dubbed "false", many are described as being "erroneous",
or as "giving rise to errors".[47] What is meant by "errors"? According to
Mare, errors are theses or positions that are not just false, but that are more
specifically opposed to Faith, to Holy scripture, or to Tradition (i.e., to the
opinions of the Saints).[48] Thomas's work is said to contain not only views
that are merely false, but also views that are contrary to Faith, such as the
thesis that the angelic or human soul is not composed of matter and form.[49]
Furthermore, his work is said to contain theses that are contrary to Holy
Scripture, to the Gospel, to Saint Paul, and to Augustine.[50] Sometimes
even, Mare says, Thomas allegedly cites a sentence of Augustine, but the
quotation cannot be found there,[51] or he falsely cites the authority of one of
the Fathers in support of his own position.[52]

Again, sometimes Thomas runs counter to common opinion, sometimes
he contradicts himself, sometimes he starts from incorrect assumptions,
sometimes his reasonings do not hold, or his conclusions do not follow.[53]

Sometimes his position is at variance with experience, with the views of
Aristotle, or with those of the philosophers.[54] Again, sometimes Aristotle is
quoted on issues he should not have been quoted on, as on the question of
whether there could be another Earth apart from ours. According to Mare,
this is not a subject on which to appeal to Aristotle, who held the matter to

be impossible.[55] The appeal to Aristotle, therefore, is tantamount to denying God's omnipotence, hence to denying an article of Faith. Finally, Mare points out time and again that a number of Thomas's views (e.g., those concerning angels) come under theses condemned in 1241, in 1270, or in 1277.[56] In fine, Thomas's views are not only called suspect from a theological point of view, but also suspect from a philosophical perspective.

In the next section, a closer look at Mare's criticism of Thomas's view on the provability of the eternity of the world will illustrate both kinds of criticism, thereby giving some insight into the general attitude towards Thomas in the Franciscan camp.

4. Thomas's View on the Provability of the Eternity of the World, as Rendered in the Correctorium Fratris Thomae

4.1. Which works are cited by Mare?

Thomas's position on this issue is discussed twice by Mare, first in articles 6 and 7, discussing theses from the Summa Theologiae (here the 46th question, art.2, of the first part is quoted), next in article 109, discussing theses from the questions De Quolibet (quoting the 3rd Quodlibet, q14 art.2).[57] Thomas's position in these two works can briefly be sketched as follows. Reason cannot demonstrate the necessity of a beginning of the world, any more than it can demonstrate the articles of Faith (e.g., that God is one and three), because Creation depends only on God's free will. God's free will, however, can be manifested through revelation. Therefore, the fact that the world had a beginning is credible, but not demonstrable. Furthermore, Creation is not successive change from not-being to being. Hence, the idea of Creation does not logically imply a beginning in time or a maker who antecedes the thing made. Special attention should be given to one of the objections in the Summa Theologiae, trying to prove that the world has a beginning in time.[58] The argument runs as follows. If the world (and consequently the huma race) did not have a beginning in time, there would be an infinite number of immortal souls actually existing. However, there cannot be an actually infinite number of things. Therefore we know, not only be revelation, but also by reason that the world had a beginning in time. To this objection, Thomas responds first by listing the solutions that have been given by those who hold the world to be eternal. Next, he remarks that the objection could be answered by claiming that the world is eternal, at least with respect to some creatures, such as angels, though not man. It is clear from Thomas's Commentary on the Sentences and his small tract De Aeternitate Mundi[59] that Thomas considers this objection difficult to cope with. As we shall see in section 4.3., this very argument is used by Mare against Thomas.

4.2. Which of Thomas's views are called false and dangerous by Mare, and how are they presented?

In the sixth article of Mare's Correctorium, the quotations from Thomas are almost *verbatim*. Thomas's article from the Summa Theologiae is summarized in a single sentence. Next, Mare quotes from the "sed contra", where Thomas (1) has quoted some authorities, arguing that articles of Faith cannot be proved. Curiously, the arguments from the "sed contra" are introduced by Mare with the words "quod probat (scl. Thomas) primo . . . "[60] Next, almost the entire body is quoted, where Thomas has indicated (2) why the world cannot be proved not to be eternal, and (3) that the non-eternity of the world is a matter only of Faith, not of proof. Again, form the body of the article Mare quotes (4) that proofs should not be sought for matters that are entirely of Faith, lest one should give the infidels occasion for ridicule and mockery. In the seventh article of his Correctorium, Mare quotes from the Summa Theologiae Thomas's discussion (5) of the view that a cause need not always precede its effect in time.

As for this last quotation, it is interesting to pause briefly at the variants occuring in the various known manuscripts of the Correctorium. One Ms briefly summarizes the matter as follows: "In his response to the first arguments, Thomas seems to be saying that Creation is co-eternal with God."[61] This sheds significant light on the way Thomas's teaching was then thought of. A similar attitude may be found in other manuscripts. Where Thomas wrote that "(Some philosophers) hold it to be not necessary (. . .) that God should exist before the world does", the manuscripts either omit the "(Some philosophers) hold that", or put "(Thomas) holds that" in its place.[62] As goes without saying, this upsets the meaning of Thomas's words. In point of fact, Thomas did no more than explicate the opinion of certain philosophers with regard to a quotation from Augustine. The Correctorium's wording, however, makes it look as of Thomas was giving his own opinion.

Finally, in his seventh article Mare gives from the Summa Theologiae Thomas's exposition of (6) how to vitiate the argument that the eternity of the world implies the existence of infinitely many souls.[63]

In the 109th article, a large part of the body from the question from the Quodlibet is quoted *verbatim*. Mare cites the place where Thomas has said (7) that the non-eternity of the world cannot be proved (because it is dependent only on God's will), and (8) that no proof should be sought for articles of Faith. These arguments correspond with two of the above arguments, and bring nothing new. Mare, however, seizes the opportunity (as he does so often) to criticize Thomas anew on these points.

4.3. *Mare's characterization of Thomas's views . . .*

It would be beyond the scope of this paper to enter deeply into the substance of Mare's criticism. However, to give the reader an impression of the truly vigorous opposition Thomas's teaching met with, let us briefly gather here the various verdicts Mare passed on the theses mentioned above. There will be instances of almost every kind of judgement used in Mare's work to characterize Thomas's views.

Thus, the first thesis (1), that articles of Faith cannot be proved, is called false, contrary to Scripture, contrary to the Saints, and contrary to the doctors; it is also said to nourish doubt and infirmity of Faith.[64] The second and the third thesis, (2) that the non eternity of the world cannot be proved, and (3) that the non-eternity of the world is solely a matter of Faith, are also called false. For as a matter of fact, according to Mare, the world *can* be proved to be not eternal, not by a demonstration *propter quid*, but by a *deductio ad impossible*. If the world were eternal, Mare says, then two impossible consequences would follow, viz., (a) that an infinite number of immortal souls would actually exist, which is impossible as there cannot simultaneously be infinitely many things, and (b) infinitely many days would have passed, which is impossible as what is infinite cannot be traversed. Since the consequences are impossible, the premise (that the world is eternal) must be false.[65] To be sure, Thomas tried to vitiate these two problems. But Mare swears to God that Thomas did not give a viable solution, neither real nor apparent, neither philosophically nor theologically.[66] Furthermore, Thomas is accused of inconsistency in trying to defend those who take the world to be eternal (*vide* (6) above). The problem of the infinite number of souls (a) he tries to solve by assuming that man could have been created at a later time. Here, Mare says, Thomas seeks to defend the view of Aristotle. At the same time, however, Mare adds, he contradicts the view of Aristotle, because Aristotle took all species, including the human species, to be eternal.[67] The fourth thesis, (4) that no proof should be sought of matters of Faith, is called false, contrary to Scripture, and contrary to the Saints. Mare also points out that Thomas is contradicting himself; did he not himself undertake to defend Faith by means of reason against the infidels in his Summa contra Gentiles? Again, Thomas's opinion is called unreasonable: Whenever a demonstrative proof is possible (and Mare thinks this is possible here), one should not rest at giving merely probable or sophistic arguments, but rather give the proof itself.[68]

In the discussion of the question from the De Quolibet, Thomas's thesis (7), that the world cannot be proved to be eternal, is said to afford opportunity for the error of believing that the world is, or could have been, eternal.[69] And of maxim (8), that no proof should be sought for matters of Faith, it is said that it is harmful rather than conducive to Faith.[70]

Finally, with regard to Thomas's statement (5), that a cause need not always precede its effect in time, Mare reproaches Thomas for implying that the world could have existed from eternity. Quite strikingly, Mare sees danger even in the suggestion of a mere possibility: the idea that the world could have existed from eternity is just false, and very close to the error of those who hold it to be really eternal.[71]

From Mare's judgements we may conclude that in addition to the doctrine of the unity of substantial form, and to the doctrine of angels, it may well have been Thomas's view on the provability of the eternity of the world that was most objectionable to Mare, philosophically, but especially theologically.

III. *The Correctoria Corruptorii*

As this paper cannot be more than a first step towards an investigation into the literary reception of Thomas's view of the eternity of the world, no attempt will be made here to compile and order the mass of implicit quotations from Thomas in the Correctoria. Nor shall we try to ascertain how the various authors have interpreted and assimilated his opinions on this issue.[72] All we want to do here is to sketch some broad outlines. However, as may presently become clear, this will suffice to give us a fair enough impression of how the various authors have variously handled Thomas's thought.

Our procedure will be as follows. As each of the Correctoria takes as its starting-point the text of the Correctorium of William de la Mare, responding to its criticism of one thesis after the other, the theses numbered (1)–(8) above may serve as a suitable key to our reading of the Correctoria. For convenience sake, we shall divide these theses into four groups, (A)–(D). Thus we shall go through the what and how of quotations from Thomas in the Correctoria with regard to the following issues: (A) whether matters of Faith can be proved (cf. thesis (1) above);[73] (B) whether the world can be proved not to exist from eternity (cf. (2), (3), (6) and (7) above); and (C) whether or not one should seek to prove matters of Faith (cf. thesis (4) and (8) above). Finally, (D) we shall consider at how the authors dealt with Thomas's saying that a cause need not always precede its effect in time (cf. (5) above).

(A) Can Matters of Faith be Proved?

A marked difference among the Correctoria is the fact that some of them mention the name of Thomas only occasionally, no more than sporadically making reference to his works, whereas others do so much more frequently, most notably the Correctorium "Quare", and to a lesser degree the "Sciendum". Thus with regard to the provability of matters of Faith, the Correctorium "Quaestione" and the "Apologeticum" do not refer to any particular work of Thomas, nor do they explicitly attribute any particular opinion to him. To be sure, it is unquestionable that they *did* make use of Thomas's works. Thus, the wording of the Correctorium "Quaestione" betrays the fact that its author has consulted the Summa contra Gentiles, the Summa Theologiae, and De Veritate. Quotations from these works, however, have been assimilated into the text in such a way that the reader is never under the impression of being given a quotation, not even in the case of longer passages.[74] The "Apologeticum", on the other hand, is somewhat more explicit in giving Thomas's opinions. Thomas's view is presented here as the opinion of "quorundam qui dicunt".[75] In this tract, the opinion of Thomas is contrasted not only with that of Mare, but also with the views of two other "aliqui", one being Henry of Ghent, the other being Richard of Middletown.[76] In the other Correctoria William de la Mare figures as the sole opponent.

In the Correctorium "Quare" the Summa contra Gentiles is mentioned; from its wording it is clear that the third and fourth chapter of the first book are being referred to.[77] In these chapters Thomas had argued that there are things about God that can be proved (e.g. that he is one), but also things that cannot be proved (the articles of Faith). These chapters are among the *loci classici* with regard to Thomas's view of the relationship between Faith and Reason. Again, the Correctorium "Sciendum" refers to the Summa Theologiae, giving the well-known fragment from the second article of the second question of the first book, where it is said that whatever can be known by reason does not belong to Faith, but rather precedes Faith. Let us pause briefly at the exact way in which the author of the Correctorium "Sciendum" has rendered the passage. Did he treat Thomas fairly, or did he perhaps overstep his mark? Among the things that we can know about God, but that are not articles of Faith because they can be proved by natural reason, the autor includes not only the fact that there is but one God, but also the fact that He is omnipotent.[78] Yet, the latter point does not reflect Thomas's view. Elsewhere, Thomas unambiguously states God's omnipotence to be an article of Faith, as it cannot be proved![79] The Correctorium's "slip of the pen" is rather common though: other Thomists (e.g., Thomas of Sutton) also thought that Thomas taught that God's omnipontence can be proved.[80]

The "Quare" also makes use (without mentioning it) of the beginning of the second part of the Summa, where Thomas dealt with issues concerning the object of Faith.[81] In the Correctorium "Quaestione", the entire passage is cited almost *verbatim*, again without mentioning either source or author.[82]

A final point of interest here concerns the explicit references to or literal quotations from passages in the work of Thomas, prompted by Mare's quoting Richard of St. Victor's well-known saying, "that there is no lack of necessary arguments in explaining Faith".[83] The Correctorium "Sciendum" refers to the Summa (I q 32 a 1 ad 2) and to the Commentary on the Sentences (I d 3 q 4 ad 3), where Thomas has given his interpretation of Richard's *dictum*. The author of the Correctorium "Quaestione" seizes the opportunity to give Thomas's interpretation almost *verbatim*, again, however, without mentioning his source.[84]

(B) *Is it Impossible to Prove that the World does Not Exist from Eternity?*

On the issue of the provability of the eternity of the world, the Correctorium "Quaere" refers to the Summa contra Gentiles. Here as well as elsewhere, so the author tells us, we learn that the arguments of those who believe that the world can be proved to be not eternal, do not hold.[85] He goes on to criticize Mare for wrongly insinuating that Thomas shared the view of those who hold the world to be eternal (cf. thesis (6) above). "Thomas never held this position. On the contrary, he showed their arguments to be defective".[86] Such is also the response of the Correctorium "Quaestione"; reference is here to the Commentary on the Sentences, to the Summa contra Gentiles, and to Thomas's Commentary on the Physics. This last reference is quite interesting, as "Quaestione" is the only Correctorium that makes reference here to Thomas's Commentary on the Physics. Moreover, it is pointed out in both tracts that Thomas's refutation of the argument of the infinite number of souls does not involve anything suspect, as Mare had suggested. The authors draw attention to the fact that Thomas merely wanted to show how the argument might be countered.[87] A further point of interest is the way the Correctorium "Quaestione" responds to the two arguments of Mare that were supposed to show that the world can be proved not to exist from eternity. Without mentioning either the work or the name of Thomas, the author presents these arguments by means of literal quotations from the objections in the work of Thomas. Both the first argument (the eternity of the world allegedly implies the existence of infinitely many souls), and the second argument (it would similarly imply that an infinite number of days would have passed), are given in the wording of the Summa Theologiae (I q 46 a 2 obj 6, obj 8) and the Commentary on the Sentences (II d 1 q 1 a 5 obj 3). (Note that the phrasing of the second argument is identical in the Summa and in the Commentary). Special attention should be given to the author's response to the second argument, which consists of two literal quotations. The response starts out with the first part of Thomas's answer to the objection in his Commentary on the Sentences, then goes on with a quotation from Thomas's answer to the objection in the Summa, and concludes with the last part of the response in the Commentary on the Sentences.[88] Could this be an indication, perhaps, that the author of the Correctorium "Quaestione" used some special compilation of quotations from Thomas? In the "Apologeticum" the solution of the first argument is quoted from the same place in the Commentary on the Sentences. Here, however, the source is mentioned, and Thomas's response is quoted in one piece, without the admixture of other quotations.[89] Furthermore, it is interesting to note that on the issue of the provability of the eternity of the world there is only one Correctorium, viz., the "Circa", which makes reference to Thomas's small tract De Aeternitate Mundi. Neither Mare nor his other respondents mention it. It seems, then, that this tract did not figure in the discussion between the Dominican and the Franciscan way, notwithstanding the fact that it was probably designed and written against the Franciscan persuasion.[90]

Finally, we want to draw attention to two curiosities. In the first place, as we have seen above, Mare had sworn to God that Thomas did not solve the problem of the infinite number of souls and of the infinite number of days. The Correctorium "Quare" dismisses the oath as a straight-out *testimonium paupertatis*, not worthy of any further discussion.[91] The author of the Correctorium "Quaestione", however, sets out to expose in more detail the utter ridiculousness of Mare's oath. Though it may be proper to swear an oath in criminal court or in the cause of engaging in matrimonial bonds, it has no place in an enquiry into the truth that proceeds by way of a disputation.[92]

It is quite conceivable that, once more, the author was anxious to give the opinion of Thomas, expressed elsewhere and in a different context. For as Thomas had said, "it is ridiculous to resort to an oath when trying to confirm one's case in a scientific disputation".[93]

In the second place, Mare reproached Thomas for being inconsistent in his alleged defence of Aristotle (vide thesis (6) above), referring to the tract De Vegitabilibus (which he attributed to Aristotle). The author of the

Correctorium "Quaestione" observes on this occasion that the work was translated from the Arabic, and hence will most probably depart from the original Greek, as is the case in several other translations.[94] On other occasions, too, he expresses his concern with the unreliability of some Arabic translations from the Greek.[95] The author of the "Quaestione", then, displays a distinct sense of textual criticism.

(C) Should One Seek Proof of Matters of Faith?

Thomas's statement that proof should not be sought for articles of Faith is explained in the Correctoria with reference to the Summa contra Gentiles. "Quare" and "Sciendum" refer to and quote from the ninth chapter of the first book, where Thomas set forth the general procedure of the Summa. Their object is to refute Mare's accusation of self-contradiction in Thomas. "Quare" gives an extensive literal quotation; "Sciendum" confines itself to some well-chosen characteristic phrases.[96] Furthermore, "Sciendum" refers to the fourth chapter of the first book, where Thomas says that some divine truths, viz. the articles of Faith, cannot be proved, whereas others can (e.g., the fact that God exists). Again, "Sciendum" confines itself to some characteristic wording.[97] The Correctorium "Quaestione" refers to and quotes *verbatim* from chapters 5 and 6 of the first book in order to show that Thomas was not of the opinion that an attempt should never be made to make matters of Faith reasonable. On this point, "Sciendum" refers to the Summa Theologiae (I q 1 a 8), where the manner of demonstration in theology is discussed.[98]

(D) Does a Cause Always Precede its Effect in Time?

In response to the accusation that Thomas's view of the eternity of the world comes very close to the error of those who hold the world to exist from eternity, the Correctorium "Quare" gives the entire passage on which Mare's criticism is based (STheol I q 46 a 2 ad 1), "so as better to understand what Mare wants to refute". The Correctorium gives the exact wording of Thomas's fragment, without the curious omission we find in Mare's text. "Thomas does not go beyond Augustine here". The author of the Correctorium writes. He tells us that Thomas is merely explaining what the philosophers, whose opinions were rendered by Augustine, meant by claiming that the world was eternal. Neither Augustine nor Thomas can justly be accused of sharing the views of these philosophers.[99] As the Correctorium "Quaestione" puts it, it is pointless to attack Thomas for his choice of examples, "for no example goes on all fours".[100]

The response to Mare's criticism of the quaestio De Quolibet occurs only in "Quare"[101] and "Sciendum".[102] It is absent in the other Correctoria. On the issues (7) and (8), "Quare" refers the reader "to what has been said above", as does the Correctorium "Sciendum". The latter, however, also briefly discusses Mare's comment on (7) and (8), though without referring to Thomas.

We shall end this chapter with a brief survey of the works referred to or used in the Correctoria to refute Mare's arguments in support of the view that the world can in point of fact be proved to be created in time. The core of Mare's arguments can be summarized as follows. In the first place, all that has been made has originated in time because the process of being made and the outcome of the process cannot exist at the same time. Hence, the world (which has also been made) must have originated in time and cannot exist from eternity. Secondly, originating "ex nihilo" implies "esse post non esse". Therefore, there is always a moment of non-being that precedes the being of the world. Hence, the world does not exist from eternity.[103] In its response the Correctorium "Quare" draws upon the first part of the Summa Theologiae (I q 45 a 2 ad 2), in which Thomas explains the difference between "creatio" and "mutatio". Creation, so it is said, is not a change, except merely according to our way of understanding. The same text is quoted in the Correctorium "Quaestione", but more extensively and truer to the original wording, although some sentences are left out and replaced with others. Again, "Quaestione" cites the discussion in the Summa Theologiae of whether "creation" means "to make something out of nothing (I q 45 a 1 ad 3), and also quotes a large passage from De Potentia (q 3 a 1 ad 7). However, neither these sources nor the name of Thomas are mentioned.[104] "Sciendum" refers to the questions De Quolibet and to De Potentia (q 3 a 1 ad 11), from which it quotes literally.[105] The purpose of these quotations is to elucidate the meaning of "creation" and especially of "creation ex nihilo". Following Thomas, the authors hold that for something to be created ex nihilo does not mean that it has been created in time, contrary to what Mare held.

We shall conclude our investigation here in posing a final question. Of what concern is all this to the history of the literary reception of Thomas's thought? What methodological conclusion is to be gained from the above? Our study has been focused on the Correctoria, because – as has been argued above – they admit of the assumption that not only the presence of a reference or quotation is telling, but also its absence. Hardly any other kind of work has this methodological advantage with respect to the history of the literary reception of Thomas's thought. Thus for example the fact that only one Correctorium makes reference to the De Aeternitate Mundi (and then only in passing), is highly significant for our subject. The Correctoria's design excludes the possibility of a mere coincidence; we may be almost certain that De Aeternitate Mundi had no prominent part to play in the period 1279–1286. *Mutatis mutandis*, the same goes for the other opuscula. At the focus of attention were the Summa Theologiae and the Summa contra Gentiles.

Methodologically speaking, these observations on the use or absence of certain works are highly significant. They (help to) make it possible to draw up a list of the works and loci that were more or less commonly used in elucidating Thomas's views. In its turn, such a list may serve as a valuable heuristic principle. For consider a third author, whose references depart from the standard list; the fact that he quotes different loci, or different works, now gains significance. Without the list, however, (which can of course cover only a limited number of problem areas) this fact would have remained obscure and insignificant. A tentative first list is given below as an Appendix.

Moreover, a note should be made on the manner of quotation from Thomas by Dominican writers. Time and again, the authors of the Correctoria give *verbatim* quotations from Thomas's work without informing the reader of this fact. In itself, there is nothing very peculiar to this. But sometimes the case is such that the reader would almost think (were he not to know better) that the author is speaking for himself. And this latter case *is* remarkable, because on other occasions these same authors *do* refer to particular places in the work of Thomas, sometimes even most explicitly, or at least not without saying that they are giving Thomas's view.

Equally worthy of attention in this connection is the fact that sometimes quotations from various works of Thomas are interlaced, a literal quotation from work A being inserted into a literal quotation from work B. We have already seen an example of this. Should we conclude, perhaps, that quotations were sometimes taken from earlier compilations of Thomas's works?[106]

Or did the authors rather make their own compilations in order to ameliorate or elucidate their response to Mare?

Finally, which kind(s) of remarks from Thomas's work did Mare comment on? The question is important: was it only the views that Thomas put forward as being his own, or also the opinions of others for example of Aristotle, presented by Thomas without explicitly refuting them? As we have seen, Mare's censorship was not confined to Thomas's own opinions, but also included those views, rendered by Thomas and considered dangerous by Mare, that Thomas had not explicitly refuted (e.g., the opinion of those who hold the world to exist from eternity), as well as those of which Thomas merely says that they do not pertain to the doctrine of Faith (e.g., as to the question whether the celestial bodies are ensouled). From this we may learn that a thirteenth century censor not only attended to the opinions an author presented as being his own, but also to whatever other opinions were to be found in a work that were dangerous, but left unrefuted. A case in point are the condemnations of 1277. Among the condemned theses there are various reactions against certain views that are mentioned, but neither endorsed nor refuted, in the work of Siger of Brabant. Although Siger had explicitly stated that these views are contrary to Faith,[107] the censors of 1277 were apparently not satisfied with this comment. On the methodological plane, we may learn from this not to condemn a critic of Thomas too easily for having misread or misunderstood him, when calls dangerous a view that is described by Thomas, but never explicitly defended by him. Was the critic perhaps less concerned with Thomas than with Truth?

APPENDIX

Thomas's thesis	The CORRECTORIA CORRUPTORII	Loci used by the CORRECTORIA CORRUPTORII in proof of Thomas's thesis (literal quotations are in italics)

Abbreviations used:

De Aeter Mundi = De Aeternitate Mundi
De Pot = Quaestiones Disputatae de Potentia
De Ver = Quaestiones Disputatae De Veritate
Phys = Expositio in Octo Libros Physicorum Aristotelis
Quaest Disp = Quaestiones Disputatae
ScG = Summa contra Gentiles
Sent = Commentarium in Quatuor Libros Sententiarum
STheol = Summa Theologiae

(A)

1. Matters of Faith cannot be proved	QUARE	De Ver q 14 a 9 c; ScG I c 3; STheol I q 1 a 2 c; ScG I c 4; De Ver q 14 a 9 ad 3um.
	SCIENDUM	STheol II,II q 1 a 4 c; STheol II,II q 2 a 9 ad 2um; *STheol I q 2 a 2 ad 1um*; STheol II,II q 1 a 5 c; *STheol I q 32 a 1 ad 2um*; *I Sent d 3 q 4 ad 3um*.
	CIRCA	*ScG I c 4.*
	QUAESTIONE	ScG I c 3; ScG I c 4; STheol I q 1 a 8 c; STheol I q 2 a 2 ad 1um; ScG I c 4; De Ver q 14 a 9 ad 8um; STheol I q 32 a 1 ad 2um.
	APOLOGETICUM	—

(B)

2. The world cannot be proved to exist from eternity	**3. It is a matter of Faith that the world is not eternal**	QUARE	*ScG II c 31* (= 38); *ScG II cc 34–36* (= 35 – 37).
		SCIENDUM	—
		CIRCA	*II Sent d 1 q 1 a 5; STheol q 46 a 2; Quaest Disp; De Aeter Mundi.*
		QUAESTIONE	STheol II,II q 1 a 4 c; STheol II,II q 89 a 1 c; II Sent d 1 q 1 a 5 obi 3 – STheol I q 46 a 2 obi 6; STheol I q 46 a 2 obi 8; II Sent d 1 q 1 a 5 ad 3um; STheol I q 46 a 2 ad 6um; II Sent d 1 q 1 a 5 ad 3um; STheol I q 61 a 3 c; *ScG; Sent; Phys.*
		APOLOGETICUM	II Sent d 1 q 1 a 5 ad 3um.

(C)

4. One should not seek to prove matters of Faith	QUARE	*ScG I c 9.*
	SCIENDUM	*STheol I q 1 a 8*; *ScG I c 9*; *ScG I c 4.*
	CIRCA	—
	QUAESTIONE	*ScG I c 8*; ScG I c 5; *ScG.*
	APOLOGETICUM	—

(D)

5. Causes do not always precede their effects in time 6. Various ways are open to philosophers for rebutting the argument that the eternity of the world would imply the existence of an infinite number of souls	QUARE	*STheol I q 45 a 2 ad 2um.*
	SCIENDUM	*De Pot q 3 a 1 ad 1um*; *De Quolibet q 18.*
	CIRCA	—
	QUAESTIONE	STheol I q 45 a 2 ad 2um; STheol I q 45 a 3 c; STheol I q 45 a 1 ad 3um; De Pot q 3 a 1 ad 7um.
	APOLOGETICUM	—

NOTES

1. We have two works of William de la Mare in which he opposes the views of Thomas. The first is the well-known Correctorium that prompted the Dominicans' vehement reaction. The work dates from between March 1277 and August 1279 (see Glorieux 1928 p. 72, Creytens 1942 p. 325, and Callus 1954 (1)), and is composed of 118 articles. It has been edited in the edition of the Correctorium Corruptorii "Quare" (Quare 1927). Mare's second work was written some time after, between 1279 and 1284 (see Creytens 1942 p. 327). It is a new, enlarged edition of the first work, composed of 138 articles. Unlike the first work, the latter did not figure in the

discussion between Dominicans and Franciscans. Mare's second edition does not respond to the Dominican responses to his first work (which were perhaps as yet unknown to him), nor do the Dominicans respond to this second edition (see Creytens 1942 p. 328). Three articles of this second edition have been edited in Hissette 1984. The small work that was long taken to be Mare's Ur-Correctorium' (see Pelster 1931 and Pelster 1947 (2)), edited by Pelster in 1956 (see Pelster 1956), is not a first draft of the (first) Correctorium, but really a summary of the second by some unknown later author (see Callus 1954 (2) and Hissette 1984). Biographical and bibliographical data on William de la Mare can be found in Pelster 1955.

2. Cf. the remark of Henry of Ghent in his Quodlibet 13 q 14 (written in 1289)" ... in tractatu quodam quem scholares appellant Correctorium ... " (ed. cit., fol 543v). Mare's work was also known by other names. In a quaestio disputata of 1280–1281, P.I. Olivi o.f.m. calls it the "Correctiones Thomae" (see Heynck 1967 p. 14). The Franciscan general chapter, in 1282, speaks of "Declarations" (see nt 4 below). Other titles that were used included "Articuli reprobati" and "Articuli fratris Guillelmi de Mara" (see Ehrle 1913 p. 272).

3. See Roensch 1964 p. 15.

4. See Archivum Franciscanum Historicum, 26 (1933), p. 139, quoted in Roensch 1964 p. 25: "Item minister generalis imponit ministris provincialibus, quod non permittant multiplicari Summam fratris Thome nisi apud lectores rationabiliter intelligentes, et hoc nonnisi cum declarationibus fratris Wilhelmi de Mara ..."

5. See acta capitulorum generalium ordinis praedicatorum, ed. Reichert, Vol. I, Rome 1898, p. 204, quoted in Roensch 1964 p. 25: "Cum venerabilis vir memorie recolende fr. Thomas de Aquino, sua conversacione laudabili et scriptis suis multum honoraverit ordinem, nec sit aliquatenus tolerandum, quod de ipso vel scriptis eius aliqui irreverenter et indecenter loquantur, eciam aliter sencientes, iniungimus prioribus provincialibus et conventualibus et eorum vicariis ac visitatoribus universis, quod si quos invenerint excedentes in predictis, punire acriter non postponant."

6. See Acta capitulorum generalium ordinis praedicatorum, ed Reichert, Vol. I, Rome 1898, p. 204, quoted in Roensch 1964 p. 26: "Districtius iniungimus et mandamus, ut fratres omnes et singuli, prout sciunt et possunt, efficacem dent operam ad doctrinam venerabilis magistri Fratris Thome de Aquino recolende memorie promovendam et saltem ut est opinio defendenda ... "

7. Apologeticum 1943 p. 9.

8. See Glorieux in Quare 1927 p. xliv–lv, Bataillon 1953 p. 1257–1258, and Hödl 1966 p. 93. Both Glorieux and Hödl are of the opinion that the work was written before 1286; Hödl even considers the possibility of a terminus ad quem close to 1280. Pelster 1947 (1) p. 458.461, however, has argued that the work was written between 1286 and 1292 by Thomas of Sutton, a view that is refuted by Hödl 1966 p. 88sqq.

9. Pelster 1952 p. 424sqq, Hödl 1966 p. 98. In the earliest part of our century the authorship was much disputed. See the references in Sciendum 1956 p. 12sq. It was attributed to William of Macklesfield by Glorieux (see Sciendum 1956 p. 12sqq), a view that was challenged by Hödl op. cit. p. 97sq. Pelster op. cit. holds the work to be written shortly after 1288, whereas Bataillon (1953) dates it to between 1279 and 1288. Hödl gives 1286 as its terminus ad quem (op. cit.)

10. The authorship is unanimously accepted in the secondary literature on the subject, cf. Muller in Circa 1941 p. xxixsqq., Pelster 1952 p. 427, and Hödl 1966 p. 99. The question of its date, however, is still rather controversial. Muller dates it to between 1282 and 1284 in Circa 1941 p. xxxvi. Pelster 1952 p. 437 takes the work to be written after 1286, possibly shortly before 1300. Hödl op. cit. gives 1286 as terminus ad quem.

11. In the preface to his edition (Quaestione 1954 p. xxix), Muller comes to the conclusion that the author must have been an English Dominican theologian; as to the author's name, however, there can be no certainty, though Muller argues that, it may have been William of Macklesfield. See also Callus 1954 (1), and Hödl 1966 p. 111. Hödl op. cit. p. 109 gives 1286 as the terminus ad quem of this Correctorium.

12. Muller, Apologeticum 1943 p. xxiv. Muller (*op. cit.* p. xxvsq) conjectures that the work originated between the last part of 1286 and 1299.

13. Though the Correctoria Corruptorii, unlike Mare's Correctorium, do refer to Thomas's philosophical works, these references are very rare. Especially his shorter works, such as De Ente et Essentia and De Unitate Intellectus, are hardly ever mentioned at all in the Correctoria, and are completely absent in Mare's Correctorium. De Aeternitate Mundi is mentioned in only one of the five Correctoria Corruptorii with regard to the problem of the eternity of the world, viz. in "Circa" (Circa 1941 p. 44), and does not occur in Mare's Correctorium. This is all the more remarkable if Van Steenberghen is correct in holding the work to be written against Bonaventure, or against other Franciscan theologians (Van Steenberghen 1966 p. 463), or if it was directed against Pecham, as Brady argues (Brady 1974). According to Van Steenberghen, Mare's Correctorium should be seen as the "codification" of the neo-Augustinism that was "inspired" (as Van Steenberghen puts it) by Bonaventura, and "founded" by Pecham. See Van Steenberghen 1966 p. 470. The view that De Aeternitate Mundi was written against Bonaventure or Pecham, however, is challenged by Weisheipl. According to him, Thomas's De Aeternitate is not against any one person or determination, but against the common position of Parisian masters, see Weisheipl 1983 p. 230–1.

14. See for example *op. cit.* p. 85, 103, 119, 129, 192 and 382, where certain views of Thomas are said to be "contra philosophiam" or "contra philosophos". In spite of the fact that Mare's criticism is largely directed against Thomas as a theologian, and although the Correctoria hardly use any but Thomas's theological works, Pelster regrets that (as he sees it) the Correctoria's discussion has almost exclusively been confined to philosophical issues, or to issues that concern the use of certain philosophies in theology. See Pelster 1947 (3) p. 415. He probably has in mind the extensive discussions of questions like that of the unity of substantial form, or of the doctrine of angels. There can be no doubt, however, that Mare's concern is with the theological implications of Thomas's views, as is also noticed by Pelster 1947(2) p. 235.

15. STheol III, q 50.

16. *Op. cit.* p. 129: "Fides ponit quod unum illud corpus numero quod Filius Dei de Virgine sumpsit, quod Virgo peperit et quod pependit in cruce, unum et idem fuit numero . . . Si autem illius corporis Christi non fuisset alia forma substantialis quam intellectiva, postquam fuit separata, remansit prima materia sola vel alia forma substantialis fuit introducta. Ex quibus sequitur quod non fuit idem corpus . . . "

17. Ib. "Haec positio de unitate formae substantialis reprobatur a magistris, primo, quia ex ipsa plura sequuntur contraria fidei catholicae; secundo, quia contradicit philosophiae, tertio, quia repugnat Sacrae Scripturae." To get an impression of the philosophical and theological problems that, according to some thirteenth century theologians, are involved in this position, we refer to a letter of Robert Kilwardby to Peter of Conflans OP, bishop of Corinth. Peter has asked Kilwardby, archbishop of Canterbury, for some explanation with regard to the condemnations of 1277. In his answer to Peter, Kilwardby sets out what he takes to be the problems that beset the theory in question. See Ehrle 1889 p. 624sqq; also Birkenmayer 1922 p. 60sqq, who also gives the letter's final part, which is lacking in Ehrle's edition. The letter is discussed in Sharp 1934, especially pp. 313sqq. Callus 1955 p. 19sqq gives a discussion and an evaluation of some letters of Pecham on the subject. Like Kilwardby and Mare, Pecham is radically opposed to the doctrine of the unity of substantial form. See also Zavalloni 1951 pp. 213–221, Roensch 1964 pp. 170sqq and Jordan 1982 for a discussion of the views of these theologians.

18. *Op. cit.* pp. 197, 223, 372, 390 and 396.

19. E.g., Thomas's view that angels are only specifically distinct, not numerically, is discussed three times by Mare, *op. cit.* pp. 60, 122 and 365. Thomas's view of the eternity of the world is discussed twice (see below, part II, section 4.1).

20. E.G., *op. cit.* pp. 95 and 96. Paris thesis nr.71 is called 6 (= 7.7 in the Collectio

Errorum of Du Plessis d'Argentré); nr.76 is called 11 (=7.12), and nr.78 is called 13 (=7.14). This is also done by the writer of the Correctorium "Quare". See *op. cit.* pp. 99 and 100. Nr.71 is called 6 (=7.7), nr.78 is called 13 (=7.14). The order that is observed by both Mare and Knapwell is that of the Collectio Errorum in Anglia et Parisiis Condemnatorum, which originated in England (see CUP p. 556, Pelster 1955 p. 79), and was published (with a difference of 1 nr) in Du Plessis d'Argentré's Collectio Judiciorum de Novis Erroribus (du Plessis 1724 p. 188sqq).

21. See, Pelster 1947 (2) p. 229. In support of this thesis, he refers to the Paris University tax list of books (CUP I p. 646), dated to between 1275 and 1286 by Denifle, on which the work (written at Naples, 1272-3) does not occur.

22. E.g., *op. cit.* p. 135sq and p. 148sq.

23. Sciendum, *op. cit.* pp. 36 and 144; Quaestione, *op. cit.* p. 146, and Apologeticum, *op. cit.* p. 182.

24. See the description of Ms "O" (Vat. Ottob. Lat. 184) in Quare 1927 p. xxviiisq. Also the Mss that contain only Mare's Correctorium, without the Dominican response (e.g., Vat. Lat. 813), give only theses taken from the first book. See Creytens 1942 p. 49, which corrects the manuscript's description by Ehrle 1913 p. 275 on this point. In the short work Pelster mistook for Mare's "UR-Correctorium" (Pelster 1931 p. 398–402, and 1947 (2) p. 222), no theses from the Commentary on the Sentences are discussed, as is also the case with the tract Creytens calls the Correctorium's second edition (Creytens 1942 p. 319sq).

25. *Op. cit.* p. 336, "In IV suo super Sententias, distinctione 21 (=44) in solutione principali ultimae quaestionis ita dicit: "Ille ignis inquantum est instrumentum divinae iustitiae habet ut spiritum quodam modo retineat alligatum et in hoc veraciter ille ignis spiritui est nocivus; et sic anima ignem sibi noxium videns ab igne turbatur" (Cf, Thomas, IV Sent. d 44q 3 a 3 solutio iii c).

26. *Op. cit.* p. 110sq, where Mare quotes (and contends) the opinion of Thomas, viz., that (Cf. STheol I q 64 ad 1) "Locus non est poenalis angelo aut animae, quasi afficiens alterando naturam; sed quasi afficiens voluntatem contristando, dum angelus vel anima apprehendit se esse in loco non convenienti suae voluntati". According to Mare, this view implies that the soul is not really punished in Hell. Thus, the position of Thomas in point of fact comes under a thesis condemned by the bishop of Paris. Ib.: "Praedicta positio plane innuit quod daemones et animae non puniantur in inferno nisi intellectualiter, vel imaginarie vel phantastice, non vere . . .

Unde haec positio videtur favere errori alias condemnato Parisiis a Domino Stephano, Parisiensi episcopo, qui est quod anima separata post mortem non affligitur nec patitur ab igne corporeo". Mare seems to refer here to the eighth thesis of Tempier's condemnations of 1270, "Quod anima post mortem separata non patitur ab igne corporeo" (see CUP I p. 487 nr.8), and not (as Glorieux claims, l.c.) to the 19th thesis of 1277, "Quod anima separata nullo modo patitur ab igne" (see CUP I p. 544 nr. 19). Mare's criticism on Thomas's view in the Commentary on the Sentences is the same as that on his view in the Summa (see *op. cit.* p. 338sq).

27. As we shall see, Mare's criticism on this point is quite strong.

28. Especially III Sent d 22, where Thomas deals with questions that touch on the above problem. Whether Mare would really have had the opportunity to return to the problem of the unity of substantial form with respect to Thomas's Commentary on the Sentences (which is an early work), is hard to tell. Some modern writers claim that the theory can already be found in Thomas's earliest works (e.g., Callus 1955 p. 27). Others, however, are more reluctant, holding that the theory is not yet explicit in the Commentary on the Sentences (e.g., Krizovljan 1961 p. 136, with references to the literature on this subject). The question whether Mare would have been able to find (objection to) Thomas's theory of the unity of substantial form in the Commentary on the Sentences, has therefore no straightforward answer.

29. *Op. cit.* pp. 186 (bk 2 d 11 q 2 a 3, on the doctrine of angels), 244 (bk 4 d 26 q 2 a 2, on matrimony), 262 (bk 4 d 19 q 2 a 3, on the "correctio fraterna"), and 345 (bk 4 d 44 q 3 a 2, on the way the soul can be affected by the fire of Hell).

30. Sciendum, *op. cit.* p. 101: bk 2 and bk 4; Quaestione, *op. cit.* p. 38sq bk 2 (see below), and Circa, *op. cit.* p. 44 bk 2 (see below) and p. 135 bk 4.

31. *Op. cit.* p. 186. Having set out Thomas's view of the Summa and of the Commentary on the Sentences, respectively, Knapwell continues: "Sed primum quod hic dicit Thomas in prima parte . . . magis intelligo".

32. See Gauthier 1952.

33. *Op. cit.* p. 33.

34. E.g., Quare, *op. cit.* p. 35sq bk 1 (see below, section III); p. 38 bk 2; p. 334 bk 3; p. 364 bk 4. Sciendum, *op. cit.* p. 52 bk 1 (see below, section III; p. 340 bk 2; p. 214 bk 3; p. 141 bk 4. Quaestione, *op. cit.* p. 40 bk 1 (see below, section III); p. 38 bk 2 (see below, section III); p. 5 bk 3; p. 9 bk 4.

35. *Op. cit.* p. 348sq.

36. This can easily be checked by means of the consecutive numbering in the Marietti edition of the Quaestiones Disputatae. It holds for each but the last of the nine theses quoted from De Veritate by Mare. De Veritate q 28 a 3 is referred to as quaestio 234 (other Mss read 24 and 224), which should be quaestio 239. At the questions from De Anima, Mare's numbering starts anew, and from then on runs parallel to the modern numbering. Furthermore, the consecutive numbering of the questions from De Virtutibus is continued in that of the questions from De Veritate. Also, the questions from De Potentia are numbered consecutively. Incidentally, we remark that one should give due consideration to adjustments made by copyists, in the course of checking references.

37. According to some authors, this would be evidence of the English origin of the Correctorium. See Pelster 1955 p. 79.

38. E.g., (1) *op. cit.* p. 1 (ad STheol I q 12 a 2): "in responsione principali dicit . . . "; (2) *op. cit.* p. 12 (ad STheol I q 14 a 11): "in responsione primi argumenti dicit . . . ", and (3) *op. cit.* p. 87 (ad STheol I q 55 a 3): "in responsione principali dicit . . . et infra in solutione tertii argumenti dicit . . . "

39. E.g., *op. cit.* p. 118; see also, below notes 51 and 60.

40. Examples of (1) and (2) can be found at the very beginning of the Correctorium, in the first article, *op. cit.* p. 1sq (ad STheol I q 12 a 2). Mare opens with a summary of Thomas's article by means of literal quotations (= 1). He continues, "Et hoc videtur insinuare quatuor rationibus. Prima quam insinuat, licet non expresse, est talis . . . ", whereupon a summary (= 2) is given of one of the points made by Thomas. The text proceeds, "Secunda ratio est . . . ", followed by a literal quotation (= 1). Next, there is "Tertio ratio . . . ", followed again by a literal quotation. Mare even copies Thomas's remark "ut supra ostensum est", which is of course quite meaningless in his own text. He concludes with a "Quarta ratio . . . ", followed again by a literal quotation. See also op. cit. p. 209. An example of (3) will be given below. See part II, section 4.2. Case nr. (4) occurs now and then in Mare's interpretation of the positions of Thomas, which is given after the theses have been formulated. See, e.g., note 63 and 67. In these interpretations, too, we can find summaries of the positions of Thomas, occasionally quoting literally from his works.

41. *Op. cit.* p. 45 (ad STheol I q 47 a 2, "Quod in rebus incorruptibilibus non est nisi unum individuum unius speciei . . . ") "Hoc reputamus erroneum quia cum anima intellectiva sit incorruptibilis, tunc non essent plures animae intellectivae numero differentes sed tantum una, qui fuit error Averrois super iii. De Anima, qui error est multipliciter contra fidem". Mare draws this same conclusion from STheol I q 76 a 2 ad 1, (*op. cit.* p. 125).

42. The question at issue is whether Thomas said in STheol 1.II q 88 a 2 that (1) "ratio est proprium principium mali actus", and in Mare's reading, that (2) "ibidem loquitur (Thomas) de ratione divisa contra voluntatem", *op. cit.* p. 241. Knapwell responds, "Non potui invenire illud sub his verbis".

43. *Op. cit.* p. 371, "Positio illa quod coeli sunt animati a Thoma nec hic nec alibi affirmatur; ipse enim sub dubio sine assertione eam derelinquit". The reference is to De Anima q un a 8 ad 3.

44. Notice, however, Thomas's remark in the Summa contra Gentiles II c 70: "Hoc autem quod dictum est de animatione caeli, non diximus quasi asserendo secundum fidei doctrinam, ad quam nihil pertinet sive sic sive aliter dicatur".

45. See, e.g., *op. cit.* pp. 1, 64, 85, 87, 103, 122, 161, 170, 174, 183, 190, 109, 210, 230, 237, 246, 252, 260, 268, 275, 298, 303, 362, 379, 390, 393 and 398. In all these cases, Mare says that "quod dicit hic patet esse falsum", or "hoc videtur falsum", or "haec positio videtur essa falsa". The example mentioned above (ad STheol I.II q 3 a 4) can be found in *op. cit.* p. 209.

46. *Op. cit.* p. 67 (ad STheol I q 50 a 5) and *op. cit.* p. 227.

47. E.g., *op. cit.* pp. 45, 69, 71, 110, 125, 223,336,380,381 and 394, where it is said that "hoc videtur erroneum", and pp. 170, 324, 348, 426sq, where it is said that "hoc praebet occasionem errandi". An instance of the latter case is Thomas's view that the human intellect is unable to have knowledge of singularia (STheol I q 14 a 11 ad 1), *op. cit.* p. 13.

48. According to Mare, then, not all that is false is also an error, which is evident from such remarks as, "Non dicimus quod sit error, sed putamus quod sit falsum" (ad STheol I q 108 a 3 ad 3), *op. cit.* p. 190, or "Haec positio non solum videtur nobis falsa, sed erronea" (ad STheol I.II q 17 a 1), *op. cit* p. 233 "Errores" are views that are contrary to Faith, see *op. cit.* pp. 18 and 223 ("Erroneum propter multa contraria fidei"), contrary to the Scripture and to the tradition, *op. cit.* pp. 170, 336sq ("Haec sunt . . . dicta quae videntur erronea, quia sunt contra Evangelium et contra doctrina Sanctorum").

49. *Op. cit.* p. 49 (ad STheol I q 50 a 2) and p. 376 (ad De Anima q 14). Other theses that are held to be contrary to Faith can be found at *op. cit.* pp. 129, 192, 363 and 376.

50. Respectively, *op. cit.* pp. 129 (that there is only one substantial form in man); 336; 243, 110, 119, 227, 253, 268, 278, 329, 382 and 419.

51. *Op. cit.* p. 120, "Quod adducit de Augustino non inveni, licet diligenter quaesierim. Si tamen hoc dicit (Augustine), dicere intendit quod . . . " At issue is a quotation from the "sed contra" of STheol I q 75 a 5, "Augustinus probat in 7. super Gen. ad Litt. quod anima non est facta nec ex materia corporali, nec ex materia spirituali (PL 34, 358sq)." Mare first gives the brief contents of this article, then introduces the quotation (from the "sed contra") with the words "quod probat (Thomas) primo per Augustinum . . . " We see again that the theses criticized by Mare are sometimes taken from the "sed contra" (see above). However, Knapwell elegantly pays Mare back, see *op. cit.* p. 368: "Quad dicunt de puncto centrali, nec ubi dicunt nec alibi, ad istam materiam ab Augustino inveni applicatum".

52. *Op. cit.* p. 339, "Auctoritates vero quas adducit (Thomas) in confirmationem sui dicti, male adductae sunt, sicut patet per inspectionem originaliu..ı'".

53. Respectively, *op. cit.* pp. 348; 3; 19; 46, 248, 26, 325, 380; 192.

54. Respectively, *op. cit.* pp. 85, 279, 103, 382, 103, 104, 159, 427.

55. *Op. cit.* p. 48 (ad STheol I q 47 a 3).

56. E.g., *op. cit.* pp. 60 (CUP nr.81), 72 (CUP nr.218), 95 (CUP nr.71 and 76), 107 (CUP nr.71) and 395 (CUP nr.204). Sometimes he refers to the condemnation of 1241, see *op. cit.* p. 394 (CUP p. 170 nr.4) and p. 92 (CUP l.c. nr.9), sometimes to that of 1270 (see note 26 above).

57. These articles bear the titles "Quod mundum incepisse non potest demonstrari" (art. 6, *op. cit.* p. 30), "Quod non sequitur si Deus est causa activa mundi quod sit prior mundi duratione" (art. 7, *op. cit.* p. 40) and "Quod demonstrative non potest probari mundum non esse aeternum" (art 109, *op. cit.* p. 410). In his discussion of the questions from the De Quodlibet Mare used a manuscript with a consecutive numbering of the articles in Quodlibet I and II, but with a new numbering of those in Quodlibet III. At *op. cit.* p. 31, Mare refers to the Quaestiones Disputatae, quaestio 54 (?), by means of a literal quotation. From the quotation it is clear, however, that he had in mind the question from the Quaestiones De Quolibet mentioned above. Furthermore, one Ms adds a reference to De Potentia a 17, betraying the fact that the copyist (like Mare, see above, part II section 1) used a manuscript of Thomas's

Quaestiones Disputatae that had a consecutive numbering: De Potentia a 17 = De Potentia q 3 a 4.

58. STheol I q 46 a 2 ob 8.

59. See, II Sent d 1 q 1 a 5 ad 6um (*ed. cit.* p. 395) and De Aeternitate Mundi (*ed. cit.* p. 89).

60. The same procedure, arguments from the "sed contra" being presented by Mare as if they were Thomas's own, is followed at oc. p. 118 (see note 39 above), and at *op. cit.* p. 91.

61. *Op. cit.* p. 40 Ms "V" (= Vat. Lat. 825): ". . . in responsione primi argumenti videtur dicere quod creatio sit coaeterna Deo".

62. Thomas STheol I q 46 a 2 ad 1 reads, "Unde dicunt (philosophi quidam) quod non sequitur ex necessitate, si Deus est causa activa mundi, quod sit prior mundo duratione . . . " Some Mss collated by Glorieux (Quare 1927) read "Unde non sequitur ex necessitate . . . " Ms Merton 267, transcribed by Muller (Quaestione 1954), reads (p. 42) "unde dicit quod non sequitur ex necessitate . . . "

63. (6) is not included under the "verba Thomae", but is cited in Mare's judgement of Thomas's position.

64. *Op. cit.* p. 31, "Dicimus quod falsum est, et contra Sacram Scripturam, et contra sanctos, et contra doctores; insuper est occasio haesitandi et non firmiter credendi".

65. These two arguments can also be found in Bonaventure, Sent II d 1 p 1 a 1 q 2 c and e (*ed. cit.* p. 14) and in Matthew of Aquasparta, Quaestiones Disputatae de Productione Rerum, q 9 (*ed. cit.* p. 210).

66. *Op. cit.* p. 32 "Ambas istas rationes, scl de transitu infinitorum et infinitate animarum, ipse ponit in obiciendo pro novitate mundi, et conatur eas dissolvere; et veritatem infinitam quae Deus est, invoco, teste conscientia mea, quod nec vere nec apparenter, nec philosophice nec theologice eas dissolverit".

67. *Op. cit.* p. 33, "Et sic conatur defendere opinionem ponentium aeternitatem mundi et eam negare. Dicit enim Philosophus cuius opinionem ipse defendit, libro De Vegetabilibus . . . " Mare, then, takes Thomas to be defending the view of Aristotle. The argument that man could have been created latter is presented by Mare (*op. cit.* p. 33) as an argument of Thomas himself: "Post istas falsitates absurdissimas (viz., the arguments some philosophers, according to Thomas, might have put forward) ipse ponit suam dicens quod posset aliquis dicere quod mundus fuit aeternus . . . non autem homo". It is rather questionable, though, whether Thomas would have endorsed this view himself. His precise words are "Unde posset dicere aliquis . . . ", using a carefully chosen irrealis.

68. IB.

69. *Op. cit.* p. 411, "Quod demonstrative probari non possit mundum non esse aeternum, videtur esse occasio errandi ad credendum quod fuerit vel esse potuerit aeternus".

70. IB.

71. *Op. cit.* p. 40, "Videtur nimis expresse aliqua dicere ex quibus sequitur quod creatio mundi potuit esse aeterna . . . et hoc est dicere quod possibile fuit mundi creationem esse Deo coaeternam; et hoc est simpliciter falsum et valde propinquum erroni ponentium mundum esse aeternum".

72. For this, the reader is referred to Jordan 1982.

73. See above, part II, section 4.2.

74. "Quaestione" *op. cit.* pp. 33sqq. A single example may suffice to show how this Correctorium treats quotations from Thomas, assimilating them in its text without notification. In Thomas's Summa contra Gentiles I c 3 we read, "Est autem in his quae de Deo confitemur duplex veritatis modus. Quaedam namque vera sunt de Deo quae omnem facultatem humanae rationis excedunt, ut Deum esse trinum et unum. Quaedam vero sunt ad quae etiam ratio naturalis pertingere potest, sicut est Deum esse, Deum esse unum, et alia huiusmodi; quae etiam philosophi demonstrative de Deo probaverunt, ducti naturalis lumine rationis". The Correctorium "Quaestione" begins its response to *op. cit.* p. 33: "Ad horum igitur solutionem sciendum est quod in his quae de Deo confitemur, duplex veritatis modus invenitur. Quaedam enim sunt

ad quae ratio naturalis pertingere potest, sicut Deum esse et unum esse et similia, quae philosophi de Deo demonstrative probaverunt, praecipue Plato et Aristoteles. Alia sunt vera de Deo quae omnem facultatem humanae rationis excedunt, sicut Deum esse trinum et unum et alia huiusmodi quae sunt articuli fidei". The Correctorium closely follows the text of Thomas's Summa contra Gentiles, but without so much as mentioning it.

75. "Apologeticum" *op. cit.* p. 51.
76. "Apologeticum" *op. cit.* p. 51.
77. "Quare" *op. cit* pp. 35 and 36.
78. "Sciendum" *op. cit.* p. 50 "... dicendum, quod sicut habetur Prima Parte, quaestione (2) ad primum argumentum, quia Deum esse non est articulus fidei, eo quod per naturalem rationem est homini notum sicut et Deum esse unum et omnipotentem ... " Thomas's text (STheol I q 2 a 2 ad 1) reads: "Dicendum quod Deum esse, et alia huiusmodi quae per rationem naturalem nota possunt esse de Deo ... non sunt articuli fidei ... " See also ScG 1 c 3 (see note 74 above).
79. E.g., De Veritate q 14 a 9 ad 8 "Unitas divinae essentiae talis qualis ponitur a fidelibus, scl. cum omnipotentia et omnium providentia et aliis huiusmodi, quae probari non possunt, articulum constituit".
80. Thomas of Sutton, Contra Quodlibet p. 91sqq, where he tries to prove God's omnipotence "ratione necessaria" (in response to the 7th question of Duns Scotus's Quaestiones Quodlibetales), using extensive quotations from Thomas Aquinas.
81. "Quare" *op. cit.* p. 49.
82. "Quaestione" *op. cit.* p. 37.
83. Richard of St. Victor, De Trinitate I, 4 ed. Ribaillier p. 89.
84. "Sciendum" *op. cit.* p. 51; "Quaestione" *op. cit.* p. 36.
85. "Quare" *op. cit.* p. 37. "Omnes enim rationes quae ad hoc (quod novitas mundi demonstrari potest) possunt adduci, nullo supposito quod ad fidem aliquo modo pertinet, possunt impediri prout docet frater Thomas, libro Contra Gentiles II c 31 (= 38) et alibi".
86. "Quare" *op. cit.* p. 37, "Nec conatur fidei zelator defendere opinionem ponentium aeternitatem mundi; immo destruit eam efficacius quam nunquam isti facerent, et efficacissime omnes eorum rationes quas quidam demonstrativas reputabant, sophisticas immo nullas omnino ostendendo, hic et alibi, libro II Contra Gentiles cc 34, 35 et 36 (= 35, 36 and 37) par totum".
87. "Quare" *op. cit.* p. 37, "Doctor veritatis nullam dicit falsitatem dicendo quod posset fingi quod mundus esset aeternus quoad aliquas sui partes, licet homo non esset ab aeterno, sed solum tangit quamdam viam per quam aliqui evaderent illam rationem de infinitate animarum." "Quaestione" *op. cit.* p. 39, "Ista responsio non est absurda falsitas, sed est possibilis positio, cuius contrarium sola fide tenemus".
88. "Quaestione" *op. cit.* p. 38.
89. "Apologeticum" *op. cit.* p. 92.
90. See note 13 above. Brady dates De Aeternitate Mundi to between January 1269 to April/May 1271, see Brady 1974 p. 146. Weisheipl dates it in 1271, see Weisheipl 1983 p. 270. Why this tract is ignored by Mare, and by all but one of his respondents, is as yet unclear to us.
91. "Quare" *op. cit.* p. 37, "Iuramentum vero eorumdem ut argumentum infirmum nimis praetereamus".
92. "Quaestione" *op. cit.* p. 37, "Et quia adversarii iurant invocando infinitam veritatem quae Deus est in conscientia sua quod doctor egregius non solvit quasdam rationes quibus videtur posse demonstrari mundum incipisse, primo quidem dicendum est quod iuramentum in purgandis criminibus et in causa matrimoniali et similibus, ubi de veritate dicenda iuratur, locum habent, non autem in inquisitione veritatis quam fit per disputationem. Nunc autem non causas ventilamus, sed veritates disputative inquirimus".
93. STheol II.II q 89 a 1 c.
94. "Quaestione" *op. cit.* p. 40, "Illa etiam translatio cum sit de arabico, suspecta est de

falsitate, nam in aliis libris invenitur multum discrepare a graeca veritate ...".

95. See, e.g. "Quaestione" *op. cit.* p. 73, "Obscure autem et truncate loquitur (Commentator), quia translatio illa quam exponit est corrupta vitio translatoris".

96. "Quare" *op. cit.* p. 38sq; "Sciendum" *op. cit.* p. 52.

97. "Sciendum" ib.

98. "Quaestione" *op. cit.* p. 40, "Non autem dicit doctor noster quod non sunt rationes quales haberi possunt adducendae ad declarandum quae sunt fidei, immo in libro suo Contra Gentiles dicit ...". "Sciendum" *op. cit.* p. 52, "Frater Thomas Prima Parte q 8 (= I q 1 a 8) docet similiter qualiter theologia est argumentativa".

99. "Quare" *op. cit.* p. 44, "Haec sunt verba fratris Thomae ex integro in quibus patet quod nihil addit supra beatum Augustinum, X De Civitate Dei, nisi quod in fine explanat modum illum vix intelligibilem per quem ponebant illi philosophi mundi aeternitatem. Pro quo nec Augustinus nec ipse, qui eius dictum declarat, est arguendus". The same procedure is also used elsewhere by Knapwell. E.g., at *op. cit.* p. 228 he gives the complete text of a passage from the Summa, only part of which had been rendered by Mare, thus showing Mare to be mistaken in accusing Thomas of going against Bernard's De Diligendo Deo. "Si responsio fratris Thomae ad argumentum illud 5um (STheol I.II q 4 a 5 ad 5) ex integro accipiatur, quod nihil faciunt contra ipsum istae auctoritates praeallegatae declaratur. Ait enim (Thomas) sic ..."

100. "Quaestione" *op. cit.* p. 48.

101. "Quare" *op. cit.* p. 412

102. "Sciendum" *op. cit.* p. 335sq.

103. *op. cit.* p. 43–4. The same arguments can be found in Matthew of Aquasparta, Quaestiones disputatae de productione rerum q 9 (*ed. cit.* p. 214–217). The second argument is also to be found in Bonaventure, Sent II d 1 p 1 a 1 q 2 f (*ed. cit.* p. 15).

104. "Quare" *op. cit.* p. 44; "Quaestione" *op. cit.* p. 45sq.

105. "Sciendum" *op. cit.* p. 56

106. Cf. Grabmann 1936 pp. 424–484.

107. Cf. Hissette 1977, especially p. 327.

BIBLIOGRAPHY

The correctoria

Le Correctorium Corruptorii "Circa" de Jean Quidort de Paris, ed. J.P. Muller, *Studia Anselmiana fasc. XII/XIII*, Rome 1941 (Circa 1941).

Le Correctorium Corruptorii "Quare", ed. P. Glorieux, *Les Premières Polémiques Thomistes I, Bibliothèque Thomiste IX*, Le Saulchoir Kain 1927. (Quare 1927).

Le Correctorium Corruptorii "Quaestione", Texte anonyme du ms. Merton 267, ed. J.P. Muller, *Studia Anselmiana fasc. 35*, Rome 1954 (Quaestione 1954).

Le Correctorium Corruptorii "Sciendum", ed. P. Glorieux, *Les Premières Polémiques Thomistes II, Bibliothèque Thomiste XXXI*, Paris 1956. (Sciendum 1956).

Rambert de "Primadizzi de Bologne, Apologeticum Veritates contra Corruptorium, ed. J.P. Muller, *Studi e Testi 108*, Vatican City 1943 (Apologeticum 1943)

OTHER WORKS

Bataillon, L.J. Reviews 2506–2511, in: "*Bulletin Thomiste*" 8(1947–1953), 1251–1259. (Bataillon 1953).

Birkenmaier, A. Vermischte Untersuchungen zur Geschichte der Mittelalterlichen Philosophie, *Beiträge zur Geschichte der Philosophie des Mittelalters, Texte und Untersuchungen, Bd XX*, Heft 5, Münster 1922. (Birkenmayer 1922).

S. Bonaventure, Liber II Sententiarum. *Opera Theologica Selecta II*, Florence 1938.

Brady, I, John Pecham and the Background of Aquinas's De Aeternitate Mundi, in: *St.*

Thomas Aquinas 1274–1974 Commemorative Studies, ed. A.A. Maurer e.a., Toronto 1974 (Brady 1974).

Callus, D.A. Review of J.P. Muller, Le Correctorium Corruptorii "Quaestione", in: *"Bulletin Thomiste"* 9 (*1954–1956*), 643–655. (Callus 1954 (1)).

Callus, D.A. Review of Declarationes Magistri Guilelmi de la Mare o.f.m. ed. F. Pelster, in: *"Bulletin Thomiste"* 9 (*1954-1956*), 944–948. (Callus 1954(2))

Callus, D.A., *The Condemnation of St. Thomas at Oxford*, Blackfriars 1955. (Callus 1955)

Creytens, R. Autour de la Litterature des Correctoires, in: *"Archivum Fratrum Praedicatorum"* 12 (*1942*), 313–330. (Creytens 1942)

Chartularium Universitatis Parisiensis, Vol. I, edd. H. Denifle and A. Chatelain, Paris 1889. (CUP)

Ehrle, F. Beiträge zur Geschichte der mittelalterlichen Scholastik.

Ein Schreiben des Erzbischofs von Canterbury Robert Kilwardby zur Rechtfertigung seiner Lehrverurtheilung vom 18. März 1277, in: *"Archiv für literatur und Kirchengeschichte"*, 5 (*1889*), 603–635. (Ehrle 1889)

Ehrle, F, Der Kampf um die Lehre des Hl. Thomas von Aquin in den ersten fünfzig Tahren nach Seinem Tod, in: *Zeitschrift für Katholische Theologie"*, 37 (1913), 206–318. (Ehrle 1913)

Gauthier, R.-A, Les "Articuli in quibus frater Thomas melius in Summa quam in Scriptis", in: *Recherches de Théologie Ancienne et Médiévale"*, 19 (*1952*), 271–326 (Gauthier 1952)

Glorieux, P., La Litterature des Correctoires. Simples Notes, in: *"Revue Thomiste"*, 33(1928), 69–97 (Glorieux 1928)

Glorieux, P, "Non in marginibus positis", in: *"Recherches de Théologie Ancienne et Médiévale,"* 15 (1948), 182–184. (Glorieux 1956)

Grabmann, M, Hilfsmittel des Thomasstudiums aus alter Zeit (Abbreviationes, Concordantiae, Tabulae), in: *Mittelalterliches Geistesleben, Abhandlungen zur Geschichte der Scholastik und Mystik, Bd. II*, München 1936, 424–484. (Grabmann 1936)

Henry of Ghent, *Quodlibeta Magistri Henrici Goethals a Gandavo*, Paris 1518, reprint Louvain 1961. (Quodlibeta)

Heynck, V. Zur Datierung des "Correctorium fratris Thomae" Wilhelms de la Mare. Ein unbeachtetes Zeugnis des Petrus Johannis Olivi, in: *"Franziskanische Studien"*, 49 (1967), 1–21. (Heynck 1967)

Hissette, R. Enquête sur les 219 articles condamnés à Paris le 7 Mars 1277, *Philosophes Médiévaux, Tome XXII*, Louvain-Paris 1977. (Hissette 1977)

Hissette, R. Trois Articles de la seconde Redaction du "Correctorium" de Guillaume de la Mare, in: *Recherches de Théologie Ancienne et Médiévale 51 (*1984*)*, 230–241. (Hissette 1984).

Hödl, L. Geistesgeschichtliche und literarkritische Erhebungen zum Korrektorienstreits (1277–1287), in: *"Recherches de Théologie Ancienne et Médiévale"*, 33 (*1966*), 81–114. (Hödl 1966)

John of Paris (Quidort) OP, Commentaire sur les Sentences. Reportation, Livre 1, ed. J.P. Muller, *Studia Anselmiana, Fasc. 48*, Rome 1961. (John of Paris 1961).

Jordan, M.D. The Controversy of the "Correctoria" and the Limits of Metaphysiscs, in: *Speculum 57 (*1982*)*, 192–314. (Jordan 1982).

Krizovljan, H.A. Primordia Scholae Franciscanae et Thomismus, in: *"Collectanea Franciscana"*. 31 (1961), 133–175. (Krizovljan 1961)

Matthew of Aquasparta, Quaestiones Disputatae de Productione Rerum et de Providentia, ed. G. Gal, *Bibliotheca Franciscana Scholastica Medii Aevi XVII* Quaracchi Florence 1956.

Pelster, F. Les "Declarationes et les Questiones de Guillaume de la Mare, in: *"Recherches de Théologie Ancienne et Médiévale"*, 3 (1931), 397–411. (Pelster 1931)

Pelster, F. Thomas von Sutton und das Correctorium "Quare detraxisti", in: *Mélanges Auguste Pelzer, Études d'histoire littéraire et doctrinale de la Scholastique Médiévale offertes à Monseigneur A. Pelzer, Louvain 1947*, 441–466. Pelster 1947 (1)

Pelster, F, Das Ur-Correctorium Wilhelms de la Mare. Eine theologische Zensur zu Lehren der Hl. Thomas, in: *"Gregorianum"*, 28 (1947), 220–235. (Pelster 1947 (2))

Pelster, F, Review of Rambert de 'Primadizzi de Bologne, Apologeticum Veritatis contra Corruptorium, ed. J.P. Muller, in: *"Gregorianum"*, 28 (1947), 413–415. (Pelster 1947(3)).

Pelster, F, Zur Datierung der Correctoria und der Schriften des Johannes von Paris OP, in: *"Divus Thomas" (Freiburg)*, *30 (1952)*, 417–438. (Pelster 1952)

Pelster, F, Einige ergänzende Angaben zum Leben und zu den Schriften des Wilhelms de la Mare o.f.m., in: *"Franziskanische Studien"*, *37 (1955)*, 75–80. (Pelster 1955).

Pelster, F, Declarationes Magistri Guilelmi de la Mare o.f.m. de variis sententiis s. Thomae Aquinatis, ed. F. Pelster, *Opuscula et Textus, Ser. Schol. XXI*, Münster 1956, (Pelster 1956)

du Plessis d'Argentré, C, *Collectio Judiciorum de Novis Erroribus, Vol. I, Paris 1724*. (du Plessis 1724)

Richard de Saint-Victor, De Trinitate, Texte critique avec introduction, notes et tables, publié par J. Ribaillier, *Textes Philosophiques du Moyen Age, Vol. VI*, Paris 1958.

Roensch, F.J. *Early Thomistic School*, Dubuque Iowa, 1964. (Roensch 1964)

Sharp, D.E., The 1277 Condemnation of Kilwardby, in: *"The New Scholasticism"*, 8 (1934), 306–318. (Sharp 1934) van Steenberghen, F, La Philosophie aux XIIIe Siècle, *Philosophes Médiévaux Tome IX*, Louvain-Paris 1966. (Van Steenberghen 1966)

Thomas Aquinas, *Commentum in Quatuor Libros Sententiarum*, ed. Parmae, Parma 1856. (Sent)

Thomas Aquinas, *De Aeternitate Mundi*, ed. Leonian, Rome 1976.

Thomas Aquinas, *Quaestiones Disputatae*, Vol. I et II, ed. Marietti, Turin-Rome 1953.

Thomas Aquinas, *Summa contra Gentiles*, ed. Leonina, Rome 1918, (ScG)

Thomas Aquinas, *Summa Theologiae*, ed. Leonina, Rome 1888 (STheol)

Thomas of Sutton, *Contra Quodlibet Iohannis Duns Scoti*, ed. J. Schneider, *Bayerische Akademie der Wissenschaften, Veröffentlichungen der Kommission für die Herausgabe ungedruckter Texte aus der mittelalterlichen Geisteswelt Bd 7*, München 1978. (Contra Quodlibet)

Weisheipl, J.A. The Date and Context of Aquinas' "De Aeternitate Mundi", in: *Graceful Reason, Essays in Ancient and Medieval Philosophy Presented to Joseph Owens CSSR*, ed. L.P. Gerson, Toronto 1983. (Weisheipl 1983).

R. Zavalloni, *Richard de Mediavilla et la controverse sur la pluralité des formes*, Louvain 1951. (Zavalloni 1951).

RICHARD OF MIDDLETON CONTRA THOMAS AQUINAS ON THE QUESTION WHETHER THE CREATED WORLD COULD HAVE BEEN ETERNALLY PRODUCED BY GOD

P. VAN VELDHUIJSEN

Preface

In book III of his *Commentary on the Sentences* Bonaventure says that the question of the creation of the world is among the most exalted and noble problems to discuss.[1] That is perhaps the principal reason why Bonaventure, considering the question of an eternally created world, lays so much stress on the precise meaning of creation, namely that it is *ex nihilo* in the sense of "not out of something" and simultaneously "in the beginning". Therefore *creatio ab aeterno* is impossible. Thomas Aquinas however is likewise much concerned to achieve a good understanding of the notion of creation when he searches for the intelligibility of *creatio ab aeterno*. So both thinkers stand diametrically opposed to each other with respect to the problem of the possibility of an eternally created world. In the following I shall try to expose this controversy on the basis of the position of Richard of Middleton, who while strictly in line with his master Bonaventure has nevertheless developed original criticism on Thomas Aquinas.[2] His critique is of methodological as well as of substantive importance, for, as we shall see, Richard turns his opponent's text against itself and secondly he gives an interpretation of Thomas on eternal creation and conservation that is essential for a clear understanding of Thomas' position.

Richardus de Mediavilla was a Franciscan theologian, who became known by the honorary-title of *doctor solidus*. He was born ca 1249 in England or, according to some, in France. He died in Reims on the 30th of March 1302. Richard probably studied at Paris under Pietro Falco, William de la Mare and Matthheus de Aequasparta. From 1284–87 he was *magister regens* of the Franciscan house of studies. In general his thinking is in line with Augustine, but in particular he is a student of Bonaventure, i.e. a student of the second generation, after John Peckam and Aequasparta. Richard's main work is his commentary on the *Sentences* of Petrus Lombardus, which is accessible in print together with two *Quodlibeta* books in the edition of Brixiae 1591.[3] For further information on Richard's life, work and writings I refer to the erudite and solid study of E. Hocedez.[4]

Richard of Middleton and Creatio Ab Aeterno

The question of whether the world could have been created eternally is treated by Richard in his *Scriptum super secundum Sententiarum*, distinctio 1 in the context of a study of creation, creaturae emanatio, sive eius exitus in esse, de quo determinatur in prima parte huius secundi.[5] The 5 articles are concerned first about the *quidditas* of creation (art.1) and thereafter about the *comparatio* of creation and conservation (art.2), creation and the world (art.3), creation and the divine cause (art.4) and creation and the divine end (art.5) Each article is again divided into questions. When the comparison of creation and the world comes up for discussion the last of the questions raised is: utrum possibile fuit machinam mundialem ab aeterno creari (qu.4) The problem posed and its solution had already been analysed and prepared, explicitly in art. 3, qu.1 and implicitly in qu.2. Accordingly I will first pay attention to both these questions.

Quaestio 1: Utrum machina mundialis sit facta (p. 13b–14a).

The conclusion of this question fits in with the thesis, quod ista machina mundialis, et omnis res alia, a Deo facta est. Its proof is as follows. Richard draws up four assertions with the help of the terms "eternal" and "made":

a. The world is eternal and not made
b. The world is not eternal and not made
c. The world is eternal and made
d. The world is not eternal and made

He then shows that the world must be made by proving that the assertions a. and b. are impossible.

Ad.a. Something that is eternal and not made has necessarily esse per se. Well then, such a being is not dependent on anything else; such an independent being is likewise the highest; and something that is the highest, is God. Therefore, if the world is eternal and were not made, then it would be God, which is impossible.[6]

Ad.b. Something that is not eternal has a beginning of being. Well then, each being that begins to be is made. Therefore it is impossible that something that is not eternal is also not made.

Conclusion: The world is made.

Concerning assertions c. and d., Richard says that he does not need them, because his only intention is to prove that the world is made. Probably Richard has mentioned these two first to complete the position, negation and connection of the terms "eternal" and "made", and secondly, which is more important, to refer to question 4 on the (im)possibility of an eternally created world.

Summarizing:

Only God is eternal and not made. Not eternal or having a beginning means to be made, which holds for everything that is not God, for example the *machina mundialis*. Therefore, and this conclusion will be put in the centre of qu.4, the world cannot possibly be simultaneously eternal and made. Assertion d. at last is Richard's own position: The world is made (qu.1) and not eternal (qu.4).

Quaestio 2: Utrum mundialis machina sit de nihilo facta.

Richard here gives an implicit argument against the possibility of *creatio ab aeterno* before he argues it *ex professo* in qu.4. He asserts in the solution of qu.2. that the world is created *ex nihilo*, since God is not only the cause of particular being but also of universal being in general. Therefore he is the cause of everything that belongs to the essence of the world. This essence implies the form but also the matter of things; that is why God has produced matter too. Conclusion: Matter therefore is not made from anything else.[7]

Thus matter is *ex nihilo*. And the same thing holds good for the world.[8] Richard conceives the *non de aliquo* or *ex nihilo* of the world merely in the sense of "having a temporal beginning" or "not eternal". This becomes evident in the solution of qu.4, where it is said that being created means *accipere esse non de aliquo*. And this acquisition of being *ex nihilo* does not say that *non de aliquo* is the same as *ab aliquo* (then creation would be eternal and the same as conservation), but that *non de aliquo* necessarily and primarily expresses a nunc, namely the very first now of the created world: creari est primo habere esse nunc ab alio non de aliquo.[9] Because this "nunc" is in contradistinction with "eternal duration", it follows that the world could not have been eternal. Thus in qu.4 Richard explicates his conception of "ex nihilo" and makes it evident that the answer to qu.2. was already a rejection of the possibility of *creatio ab aeterno*.

The two arguments from qu.1 (being made eternally is contradictory, and so forth) and qu.2 (*ex nihilo* implies necessarily a first beginning, and so forth), which anticipate the refutation of an eternal world qu.4, have been brought to the fore here because they turn up again in more elaborated form in qu.4 where they take up the whole doctrinal part of the solution.

Both arguments however derive from Bonaventure, but the elaboration is typically Richard's contribution. Now what is his position to the point?

Quaestio 4: Utrum possibile fuit machinam mundialem ab aeterno creari.

Richard investigates in this question the possibility of an eternally created world, not so much the position that the world *de facto* is eternal. As usual he begins by setting forth the arguments *pro* and *contra*. The eight arguments *pro*[10] are traditional as to origin and method of statement, except arg.4, which has a certain originality. Thus I will concentrate on this argument.

Arg.4 pro: Richard cites in support of the major premiss the well-known dictum of Aristotle's *Topica I*, 11 (104b5–17): Philosophus primo topicorum dicit, quod sunt problemata de quibus rationem non habemus cum sint magna, ut utrum mundus sit aeternus, vel non. The minor accepts this lack of an apodictic demonstration: Sed si non fuisset possible mundum esse ab aeterno, haberemus necessariam rationem ad probandum ipsum ab aeterno non fuisse. Conclusion: *creatio ab aeterno* is possible.[11] Richard's solution of this argument is equally ingenious: The argumentation *per auctoritatem Philosophi* does not do justice to the text of Aristotle, for he explains his comments about the lack of *rationes*. Immediately after this statement Aristotle says that it is difficult for both parties (for and against an eternal world) to give a necessary demonstration. According to Richard, Aristotle means by this that the question is not impossible to solve, but that a solution is hard and difficult.[12] Apart from the question that rises herewith, namely how Richard interprets the position of Aristotle, he himself thought (as will be clear henceforth) that the non-eternity of the world can be strictly and necessarily demonstrated. So for him the "difficile" of the *problema magnum* was not insurmountable!

With the help of seven arguments *contra*, of which the conclusions will be endorsed in the solutio, Richard will show that *creatio ab aeterno* is impossible and that therefore its opposite must be necessary. I discuss arg. 6 in detail, because it is the most interesting (perhaps a discovery of Richard's own). The rest is traditional, although their wording (see also the arguments *pro*) is somewhat different from usual.

Arg.1 proves that God has to create at a well-fixed first *instans;* arg.2–5 and 7 prove that an eternal world includes infinities, which is impossible.

Arg.6 contra: By way of circumstantial argumentation Richard shows here that *creatio ab aeterno* is impossible, because it would be then necessary for the creator that he must create, which is not possible; and so forth. Nothing impossible follows upon a realized possibility, according to Aristotle in *Anal. priora* I,13 (32a18–20). Thus, if *creatio ab aeterno* had been effected by God, then there would follow an impossibility, namely that God had to create necessarily. It was proved however in Book I[13] that this is not possible. Therefore creation from eternity is impossible.[14] Henceforth Richard proves the minor (the major, taken from Aristotle, he regards as evident), namely that creation from eternity is a necessary creative act. For this he states three arguments:

a. If God had created the world from eternity he would not have been able not to create the world from eternity (i.e. he would have had to create the world from eternity; PvV), for according to Aristotle in *De interpr.* cap. 9 (19a23) everything that is, is necessary, when it is.

b. *Before* God's supposed creation of the world from eternity, it was not possible for him not to create the world from eternity, for before the eternal there is nothing.

c. *After* God's supposed creation of the world from eternity, it would not have been possible for him not to create the world from eternity, for it cannot be brought about, according to Augustine in *contra Faustum* 26, 5, that what was made should not be made.

Therefore it is clear, says Richard, that the position of an eternally created world which means "necessarily created" is impossible.[15]

In the *solutio* Richard endorses and confirms the argument contra the possibility of eternal creation, as he himself says: Respondeo, quod sicut bene probant rationes adductae ad hanc partem (scil. the argumentation *contra*), non fuit possibile machinam mundialem ab aeterno creari.[16] The conclusion henceforth consists of a doctrinal part, a historical part and an *auctoritas*-part. All these three parts remind us of Thomas Aquinas and his position to the point. But what evidence is there here that Richard critically receives Thomas? What is his method, which works of Thomas has he especially in view and how does he interpret his opponent before he refutes him?

The solution of quaestio 4:
1. The doctrinal part: thesis and argumentation.
Richard begins the first part with the statement that it was impossible for the world to be created from eternity. In support of this statement he gives two reasons, which already show something of Thomas Aquinas.

The first argument is as follows:

The being of what has been created is not numerically identical with the being of the creator. This difference qua being implies necessarily that the being of what has been created is new. Since newness and eternity mutually exclude each other, creation from eternity is intrinsically contradictory, and thus impossible.[17]

The term "new" or "newness" means nothing else than "in the beginning" or "with a very first beginning".

Richard alludes with his statement about the difference of being between creator and creation to Thomas's treaty *De potentia* qu.3, art. 14, where the question is: Whether it is possible for that which differs from God essentially to have always existed? Honed down to the *ex nihilo*-argument Thomas says in his answer to arg.7 sed contra that *creatio ex nihilo* not only means creation "in the beginning", which is the implication of arg.7 sed contra, but that "*ex nihilo*" also means dependency of being and conservation of being. Thus Thomas implicitly says that *creatio ex nihilo* does not necessarily mean creation "in the beginning", but can also mean creation from eternity, in the sense of dependency and conservation of being. That which differs essentially from God can therefore be created from eternity. The same argument can be found in Thomas's treaty *De aeternitate mundi*.[18]

Richard however thinks that this equivocal meaning of "*ex nihilo*", which expresses the *esse post non esse* of creation, is *inexact* and erroneous. The second argument makes this criticism clear: The difference of being between God and creation implies, according to the first *ratio*, that the created world once was new. The second *ratio* will show that this *novitas* of the world is included in the notion of creation as such. *Creari* is to receive being but not from something. This "non de aliquo", "not from something" can be conceived in two ways. Primo: "not from something" is the same as "not from something but by someone". Secundo: "not from something" is to receive being at a well determined first beginning by someone, but not from something.

Richard rejects the first meaning, namely that *ex nihilo* should signify the same as "not from something" in the sense of absolute dependency of being on a first origin without any notion of a first beginning. The reason for his rejection is this: As long as created being exists, it is dependent qua being on someone, namely the creator. If creation is from nothing only in the sense of dependent qua being, then it would be created eternally as long as it stays in being. But this is erroneous, because otherwise creation and conservation would be the same, which Richard has refuted before in art.2, qu.1.[19]

Richard has also here Thomas in view, but now his *Scriptum super Sententiis* II, dist.1, qu.1, rat.2. Although Richard's second reason uses the same *ex nihilo*-argument as his first reason, the context is different. The first reason was concerned with the difference of being between creator and creation, the second reason is concerned with the very notion of creation.

Thomas begins the solution of art.2 about the question on creation by saying and showing that creation can be demonstrated by reason, and that it is not only a matter of faith.[20] Henceforth he exposes what belongs to the essence (*ratio*) of creation. In particular there are two things which can both be deduced under the same denominator "*ex nihilo*":

1. *Creatio ex nihilo* presupposes nothing in the thing that is said to be created. Hence in this regard creation differs from other changes as generation or alteration. But the causality of that which brings about creation extends to all that is in the thing. Creation is said to be out of nothing precisely because there is nothing that precedes creation as something not created, such as preexistent matter.[21] Creation in this sense

can thus be called absolute dependency of being, because the whole being of the creature is dependent on the first creative principle. But this dependency must be taken in a restricted, narrow and even negative sense: the creature is *not* out of something. Or, as Thomas[22] elsewhere says, "*ex nihilo*" in the sense that the negation includes the preposition ("fit *ex nihilo*, idest non fit ex aliquo") denies relationship to a material cause.

2. *Creatio ex nihilo* can also be understood according to a second meaning, namely that in the thing which is said to be created, non-being is prior to being. This stems not from a priority of time or of duration, but rather from a priority of nature, such that, if the created thing were left to itself, non-being would result, since the created thing has being only from the pouring in of a superior cause.[23]

Creation in this sense can thus be called also absolute dependency of being, because the whole being of the creature is dependent on the permanent influx of *esse;* without this inflow it is nothing. This dependency, however, must be taken in the broad and positive sense of conservation of being.[24]

Now, when these two meanings of creation *ex nihilo* are to be compared with the first meaning of the "non de aliquo" of Richard's second argument, it is very probable that Richard has Thomas in view. This will be clear when he gives an interpretation of the two meanings of "*ex nihilo*" as exposed above.

The given interpretation of "*ex nihilo*" by Thomas says nothing about the *duration* of the created thing, and that means, according to Richard, that *creatio ex nihilo* might have been from eternity. But, so he says, this is an erroneous conclusion, for then one would confuse *conservatio* and *creatio*.[25] *Conservatio*, i.e. conservation of being lasts as long as the created thing exists. But, *creatio* implies necessarily a very first beginning of duration. Therefore it is excluded that dependency of being might possibly have been from eternity. And the same applies of course to conservation of being. Richard has seen clearly that Thomas, even in the solution of art.2, where he seemingly speaks only about creation as such, implicitly proposes the possibility of creation from eternity by way of the meanings of "*ex nihilo*".

However, Richard has not yet come to the heart of his criticism, but he has prepared it forcibly. He concludes, after the twofold reasoning for this thesis, that creation is by someone, namely God, and that it is not from something and thus "in the beginning".[26]

2. The historico-critical part: the core of the solutio

The anonymous opponent (very probably Thomas Aquinas) is allowed here to measure himself with Richard, naturally to go to the wall. Once more the concept of "*ex nihilo*" is at the centre of the discussion about the problem of creation from eternity. The assertion that the created thing is by God and not from something, can have three meanings, Richard says:

a. the created thing has received its being by someone, the creator, but not from something else;

b. the created thing is conserved in its received being, which is not from something else, by the creator;

c. the created thing is, as long as it is, by someone, God, but not from something else.[27]

Richard comments that the created thing according to the first two meanings is from or by God and not from something else which is preexistent. Thus he repeats what he said earlier: the dependency of being in the restricted, negative sense and the dependency of being in the broad sense of conservation of being are according to his opponent strictly speaking the same.[28]

What matters now is the third meaning, where it is said that the created thing is, as long as it is, by God, and not from something else. But does the concept "as long as the created thing is" not have a double meaning, so Richard seems to ask. The meaning of "as long" can be both "from eternity" and "from/with a very first beginning".[29] This interpretation of Richard has once again reference to Thomas' treaty on creation in *In II Sent.*1,1,art.2. In this article Thomas develops a twofold notion of creation, a philosophical and a strictly Christian. Up to now Richard (and in his track my exposition) has brought to the fore the first, namely philosophical notion: *creatio ex nihilo*, as the philosophers understand and prove it, has two characteristics: dependency of being in the narrow sense of totally from God and not from something else (1) and dependency of being in the broad sense of conservation or influx of being (2). About these two meanings of *creatio ex nihilo* Richard has said that they do not exclude *creatio ab aeterno* but rather make it possible, – a subtle interpretation of Thomas' text.

After his twofold explanation of the philosophical creation *ex nihilo* Thomas, however, proceeds by saying that there is another, third meaning of *ex nihilo*, namely when creation is conceived in the way that faith but not philosophy takes it. Then the created thing must have being after non-being in the sense of duration, since it begins to exist after nothingness. So creation cannot be demonstrated, nor is it conceded by the philosophers.[30] In short, the third meaning of creation *ex nihilo* is according to the Christian faith, that the created thing has had a very first beginning; this is Thomas' position. Richard reminds of this threefold interpretation of creation *ex nihilo*, when he sets forth the above-mentioned three meanings of creation from nothing. But, as was said, the third one he puts into words with a double meaning, which it does not have in Thomas' text.

Richard does this to make clear that creation, in particular the *duration* of creation, found in Thomas has an ambiguous meaning. The third meaning, once more, is in Richard's words, that the created thing is, as long as it is, by someone but not from something. That is, whether the created thing is *ab aeterno* or *in principio*, it is always dependent on being (in both senses). So he reads Thomas' exposition along these lines, that the philosophical meaning of dependency of being (in both senses) also forms part of creation *ex nihilo* as faith understands it. This interpretation is correct, for the only difference between the philosophical and Christian notion of creation, according to Thomas, is the difference qua *duration*: creation in accordance with faith implies necessarily a very first beginning, but also dependency of being; creation in accordance with philosophy, however, is indifferent to a well-determined meaning of its duration *a parte ante*, – so it can imply both a first beginning and an eternal duration. Thus, according to Thomas' text creation *ab aeterno* is not impossible, philosophically, but an intelligible position.

And then Richard sets to with his critique! The question is: does dependency of being in both senses mean the same in creation *ab aeterno* and creation *ab initio*? Or is dependency of being necessarily different in creation *ab initio* from what it is in creation *ab aeterno*? Richard criticizes Thomas by making use, so he says, of his opponent's acuteness. That is, the exposed triptych of *creatio ex nihilo*, which he calls an acute argument, is converted by Richard to his own advantage. *Sed haec cavillatio magis facit pro mea opinione, quam pro contraria.* The method which he follows here is that he puts in the centre the concept "to make" (*facere*), and he does so because both he and his opponent conceive creation as a work which is made. But, so Richard exacerbates his conception, "*facere*" implies necessarily a very first beginning, since the being of the world could not precede its being made. Therefore, whichever meaning of "*facere*" is taken, be it in the sense of *creatio ab initio*, be it in the sense of *creatio ab aeterno*, it is always necessary to presuppose an absolutely first beginning. Then *creatio ab aeterno* must be excluded as impossible. Richard assumes here that "creatio ab aeterno' is a pseudocencept, using it only to confute his opponent better. It is a pseudo- or quasi-concept, because *creatio* as "being made" could not be made in the past *ad infinitum* but would have to presuppose that there was once an absolutely first now.[31]

The reversal which Richard achieves can thus be exposed. Creation *ex nihilo* is conceived by him only in the sense of being produced "in the beginning", i.e. acquisition of being from a very first beginning by the creator and without any preceding substrate. In this manner the third meaning of Thomas's conception of creation *ex nihilo*, namely that faith ascribes to the world a first beginning, comes with the first meaning, namely that of dependency of being in the narrow sense ("creation is not from something else"). According to Richard, acquisition of being is identical with this sense of dependency of being. That is why the identity between dependency of being in the narrow sense and dependency of being in the sense of conservation of being, as found in Thomas, is dropped and makes way for the difference between both. Then, however, *creatio ab aeterno* is no longer possible

3. The authority part: affirmation of Richard's own thesis by way of an especially chosen authority

According to Joh. Damascenus in his *De fide orthodoxa* I, 8 the created world is the work of God, which exists by his will. It is not coeternal with the creator, for what is brought forth out of non-being to being is not such that it is co-eternal with him who has no beginning but is for ever and always. So creation from eternity is impossible.[32] The reason why Richard has chosen this authority is most probably polemical, against Thomas, who advances the same authority and the same text to support his thesis that creation from eternity is not impossible, as he does in *De aet. mundi* and *De pot.* 3,14.[33] Thomas thinks that the possible eternity of the created thing is not necessarily the same eternity of God, but another one; *aeternitas Dei* is not identical with *perpetuitas mundi*. That is why the created thing can be in a certain sense co-eternal with its creator.[34]

Finally and succinctly, what is Richard's specific critical view?

1. Richard levels his criticism at the very heart of the problem: the *ex nihilo* argument.

2. He singles out for his contest Thomas's *In II Sent.*1,1,2, a text which till then had never been used to clear up Thomas's position on the possibility of an eternally created world.

3. Richard's method is a gradual construction of a critique: first an allusion to his opponent and after that the start of the main critique without touching, however, the heart of the *ex nihilo*-problem. Then he comes to the core, whereby the opponent at first appears to have a point but is eventually totally turned upside down to support the thesis of his critic.

NOTES

1. *In III Sent.* 24, 2, 3 ad 4 (ed. Quaracchi, vol. III, p. 524b).
2. See for the controversy between Bonaventure and Aquinas my article "The question on the possibility of an eternally created world. Bonaventure and Thomas Aquinas" in this volume.
3. Richardus de Mediavilla, *Super quatuor libros Sententiarum Petri Lombardi quaestiones subtilissimae*, Brixiae 1591 (reprint Frankfurt/M 1963. Together with *Quolibeta quaestiones octuaginta*.
4. *Richard de Middleton. Sa vie, ses œuvres, sa doctrine*, Louvain. Paris, 1925. See also the

article of D.E. Sharp, "Richard of Middleton", in: Idem, *Franciscan philosophy at Oxford*, London 1930 (reprint Farnsborough 1966), p. 211–76.

5. *In II Sent.* prologus (ed. Brixiae, vol. II, p. 1a).

6. Cf. *In I Sent.* dist.1, art.1, qu.1 (ed. Brixiae, vol. I, p. 28a–29b).

7. As a second reason for the *non de aliquo alio* of matter, Richard gives this one: quia per eam intelligimus infimum in entibus. He means probably this: there must be something ultimate as a substratum to account for generation and alteration in the world.

8. *In II Sent.* dist.1, art.3, qu.2 sol. (ed. Brixiae, vol. II, p. 14b–15a): Dico ergo ad quaestionem, quod ista machina mundialis facta est de nihilo. Deus enim non tantum est causa mundialis machinae, vel cuiuscunque alterius creaturae sub ratione qua est hoc ens, utpote sub ratione qua est huius speciei vel illius, sed etiam sub ratione qua ens; ergo est causa omnis rei pertinentis ad essentiam sui effectus. Cum ergo materia pertineat ad essentiam machinae mundialis, Deus est causa illius. Et constat quod non potest dici quod de aliquo alio sit creata, quia per eam intelligimus infimum in entibus. Restat ergo quod mundialis machina facta est a Deo, non tantum modo quantum ad formam, sed etiam quantum ad materiam; ex quo sequitur quod facta est non de aliquo.

9. *Ibidem*, qu.4 sol. (p. 18a).

10. The arguments 1–5 come to the conclusion of the possibility of an eternally created world, but 6–8 go further, for they conclude that the world must be eternally created by God.

11. *In II Sent.* dist.1, art.3, qu.4 arg.4 (ed. Brixiae, vol. II, p. 16b). The argument can also be used, formally seen, to prove that the world is possibly eternal.

12. *Ibidem*, qu.4 ad 4 (p. 18b): Ad quartum quod arguebatur per auctoritatem Philosophi, dicendum quod verbum suum glosat vel contemperat. Quia postquam dixit quod de illis rationem non habemus, cum sint magna, statim subiungit sic difficile arbitrantes esse quare assignare; in quo videtur significare, quod habere ad hoc rationem, non est impossibile, sed difficile.

13. Cf. *In I Sent.* dist.44, art.1, qu.6 and dist.45, art.2, qu.3 (ed. Brixiae, vol.I, p. 394–95a; 403–404a).

14. *In II Sent.* dist.1, art.3, qu.4 arg.6 sed contra (ed. Brixiae, vol. II, p. 17b): (...) secundum Philosophum primo priorum possibile est, quo posito in esse, nullum sequitur impossibile. Sed si Deus creasset mundum ab aeterno ex hoc secutum fuisset impossibile, scilicet quod Deus de necessitate mundum creasset. Probatum est enim in libro primo, quod Deus non potuit creare mundum de necessitate, nec de necessitate naturae nec de necessitate voluntatis. Restat ergo, quod mundum ab aeterno creari fuit impossibile.

15. *Ibidem* (sequel): Quod autem Deus mundum de necessitate creasset, si ipsum ab aeterno creasset, patet sic, quia non potuisset ipsum non creare *quando* creabat, quia secundum Philosophum libro primo perihermen. Omne quod est, quando est, necesse est. Nec potest dici, quod potuisset ipsum non creare *antequam* creasset, quia ante aeternum nihil. Nec potuisset ipsum non creasse, postquam creasset, quia non potest facere, quod illud, quod factum est, non fuerit factum secundum Augustinum vigesimosexto lib. contra Faustum. Et ita patet, quod si mundum ab aeterno creasset, ipsum de necessitate creasset, quod est impossibile. (My italics)

This strong argument was raised for the first time by Henry of Ghent against Aquinas' position of the possibility of an eternally created world, see his *Quodlibet* I, qu.7–8, in: Henricus de Gandavo, *Opera omnia*, vol. V, ed. R. Macken, Leuven.Leiden 1979, p. 40 line 9–42 line 57; cf. my article "Hendrik van Gent contra Thomas van Aquino. Over de mogelijkheid van een eeuwig geschapen wereld", in: *Stoicheia* 2 (1987), p. 3–26.

Aquinas' position was defended against Henry (and others as Richard of Middleton) e.g. by Jean de Paris (Quidort), *In II Sent.* dist. 1, qu. 4 arg. 4/ad 4, in: *Commentaire sur les Sentences* (reportation), ed. J.-P. Muller, Romae 1964, p. 25 line 38–41/p. 28 line 132–50. Jakob von Metz, *In II Sent.* dist.1, qu.1, cf. L. Ullrich, *Fragen der Schöpfungslehre nach Jakob von Metz*, Leipzig 1966, p. 107–108.

16. *In II Sent.* dist.1, art.3, qu.4 sol. (ed. Brixiae, vol. II, 0. 17b).

17. *Ibidem* (p 17b–18a): Respondeo, quod (. . .) non fuit possibile machinam mundialem ab aeterno creari. Cuius ratio est, quia machina mundialis non potuit accipere esse creari accipiendo idem esse in numero cum esse creantis. Sed accipere esse ab aliquo diversum ab esse dantis est accipere esse novum. Ergo machina mundialis non potuit a Deo creari, nisi accipiendo ab ipso esse novum. Sed accipere esse novum et ipsum (scil. esse novum; PvV) accipere ab aeterno repugnantia sunt. Novitas enim repugnat aeternae durationi. Et ideo non fuit possibile machinam mundialem ab aeterno creari.

18. With respect to the text of *De potentia* 3, 14, see my article in this volume. Cf. *De aeternitate mundi,* in: Thomas Aquinas, *Opera omnia,* ed. Leonina, Roma 1976, vol.43, p. 87–88 lines 158–210.

19. *In II Sent.* dist.1, art.3, qu.4 sol. (sequel) (ed. Brixiae, vol. II, p. 18a): Praeterea haec videtur includi in significato (ed. Brixiae reads 'signato'; PvV) creationis, quia creari est accipere esse non de aliquo. Hoc autem aut significat idem quod habere esse non de aliquo ab aliquo, aut nunc primo habere esse ab alio non de aliquo. Non primo modo, ut videtur, quia cum creatura quamdiu est, sit ab alio, si non de aliquo, semper crearetur quamdiu est, quod falsum est. Tunc enim nihil aliud esset ipsum conservari, quam ipsam creari, quod ante improbatum est (cf. *Ibidem,* art.2, qu.1 (p. 8b–10a).

20. *In II Sent.* dist.1, qu.1, art.2 sol. (ed. Mandonnet, Parisiis 1929, vol. II, p. 17–18): Respondeo quod creationem esse non tantum fides tenet, sed etiam ratio demonstrat. Constat enim quod omne quod est in aliquo genere imperfectum, oritur ab eo in quo primo et perfecte reperitur natura generis (. . .). Cum autem quaelibet res, et quidquid est in re, aliquo modo esse participet, et admixtum sit imperfectioni, oportet quod omnis res, secundum totum id quod in ea est, a primo et perfecto ente oriatur. Hoc autem creare dicimus, scilicet producere rem in esse secundum totam suam substantiam. Unde necessarium est a primo principio omnia per creationem procedere.
Cf. *De potentia* qu.3, art. 5 sol., secunda ratio; and conclusion in fine: Sic ergo ratione demonstratur et fide tenetur quod omnia sint a Deo creata.

21. *Ibidem* (sequel): Sciendum est autem quod ad rationem creationis pertinent duo.
Primum est ut nihil praesupponat in re quae creari dicitur. Unde in hoc ab aliis mutationibus differt, quia generatio praesupponit materiam quae non generatur, sed per generationem completur in actum formae transmutata; in reliquis vero mutationibus praesupponitur subjectum, quod est ens completum. Unde causalitas generantis vel alterantis non sic se extendit ad omne illud quod in re invenitur, sed ad formam, quae de potentia in actum educitur. Sed causalitas creantis se extendit ad omne id quod est in re. Et ideo creatio ex nihilo dicitur esse, quia nihil est quod creationi praeexistat, quasi non creatum.

22. Cf. *Summa theol.* Ia, 45, 1 ad 3; *De potentia* qu.3, art.1 ad 7.

23. *In II Sent.* dist.1, qu.1, art.2sol. (sequel): Secundum est ut in re quae creari dicitur prius sit non esse quam esse. Non quidem prioritate temporis vel durationis ut prius non fuerit et postmodum sit, set prioritate naturae, ita quod res creata si sibi relinquatur, consequatur non esse, cum esse non habeat nisi ex influentia causae superioris.
Cf. the very interesting text *In I Sent.* dist.5, qu.2, art.2: Utrum Filius sit ex nihilo.

24. The suggestion that creation in this sense of dependency of being is realiter identical with conservation needs, of course, a penetrating study.

25. *In II Sent.* dist.1, art.3, qu.4 sol. (sequel) (ed. Brixiae, vol. II, p. 18a): (. . .) videtur, quia cum creatura quamdiu est, sit ab alio, si non de aliquo, semper crearetur quamdiu est, quod falsum est. Tunc enim nihil aliud esset ipsum conservari, quam ipsam creari.

26. *Ibidem* (sequel): Restat ergo, quod creari est primo habere esse nunc ab alio (scil. a Deo; PvV) non de aliquo. Sed rem habere esse nunc primo ipsam includit non esse ab aeterno.
Richard concludes the first part of his solutio with these words:
Si ergo Deus potuisset machinam mundialem ab aeterno creasse, potuisset facere contradictoria simul esse, quod falsum est, ut in primo libro probatum est (cf. *In I Sent.* dist.42, art.1, qu.4 (ed. Brixiae, vol. I, p. 374a–75b).

27. *Ibidem* (sequel): Huic tamen rationi (see text note 26) respondere conantur tenentes opinionem contrariam (scil. that the world was possibly created from eternity). Dicentes, quod creaturam esse ab alio non de aliquo tripliciter potest intelligi, scilicet aut quia habet esse, quod accepit ab alio non de aliquo. Aut quia ab alio conservatur in esse accepto, non de aliquo. Aut quia quamdiu est, fit ab alio non de aliquo.

28. *Ibidem* (sequel): Duobus primis modis creatura est ab alio, scilicet a Deo non de aliquo. Et sic esse ab alio non de aliquo non est idem quod accipere esse ab alio non de aliquo.

29. *Ibidem* (sequel): Sed esse ab alio non de aliquo modo tertio est idem quod accipere esse non de aliquo. Et illo modo creatura non est ab alio, non de aliquo, quamdiu est. Creatura enim non semper fit a Deo.

30. *In II Sent.* dist.1, qu.1, art.2 sol. (ed. Mandonnet, p. 18): Si autem accipiamus tertium (scil. a third notion; PvV) oportere ad rationem creationis, ut scilicet etiam duratione res creata prius non esse quam esse habeat, ut dicatur esse ex nihilo, quia est tempore post nihil, sic creatio demonstrari non potest, nec a philosophis conceditur, sed per fidem supponitur.

31. *In II Sent.* dist.1, art.3, qu.4 sol. (sequel) (ed. Brixiae, vol. II, p. 18a): Sed haec cavillatio magis facit pro mea opinione, quam pro contraria. Omne enim quod factum est, et non est in continuo fieri, in aliquo instanti incepit fieri vel factum est. Cum ergo mundus factus sit, et non sit in continuo fieri, nec ista duo simul esse possent, ut etiam ponentes praedictam cavillationem concedunt, sequitur quod mundus incepit fieri in aliquo instanti, aut factus est, nec aliter produci potuit. Sed quocunque istorum dato, sequitur quod mundus ab aeterno esse non potuit, quia cum fieri terminetur ad esse. Esse non potuit praecedere suum fieri, quod etiam factum est in aliquo instanti ante, quod aliud non fuit.

32. *Ibidem* (sequel) (ed. Brixiae, p. 18a–b): Ad conclusionem etiam principalem potest adduci auctoritas Damasceni libro primo, cap. quarto, sic dicentis: Creatio est Dei voluntate opus existens, non coaeterna est cum Deo, quia non aptum natum est, quod ex non ente ad esse deducitur, coaeternum esse ei qui sine principio est et semper est. Ergo secundum ipsum contra naturam creaturae, unde creatura est, est esse ab aeterno. Sed Deus non potest dare creaturae illud, quod repugnat creaturae, inquantum creatura est. Et ita patet, quod non fuit possibile mundum ab aeterno creari. Sicut non fuit possibile ipsum esse creaturam et non creaturam simul.

33. *De potentia* qu.3, art.14 sed contra[2]: Damascenus dicit (. . .) quod ex non ente ad esse deducitur non est aptum natum esse coaeternum ei quod sine principio et semper est. *De aeternitate mundi* in fine (ed. Leonina, p. 89 lines 257–60).

34. Cf. *De potentia* qu.3, art.14 ad sed contra[2]; *De aeternitate mundi* in fine (p. 89 lines 265–77).

THE RESPONSE TO THOMAS AQUINAS IN THE EARLY FOURTEENTH CENTURY: ETERNITY AND INFINITY IN THE WORKS OF HENRY OF HARCLAY, THOMAS OF WILTON AND WILLIAM OF ALNWICK O.F.M.

J.M.M.H. THIJSSEN

During the last ten years, Thomas Aquinas' views on the eternity of the world have received relatively much attention, not least because they have given rise to disagreement among medievalists. In this connection we may call to mind controversies about the date and context of Aquinas' *De aeternitate mundi*, about the question whether he did, in fact, defend the possibility of eternal creation, about the cogency of his position with regard to the indemonstrability of the temporal beginning of the world, and about Maimonides' influence on his interpretation of Aristotle's views about the eternity of the world.[1]

Considerably less attention has been given to the *influence* of Aquinas' thought on this subject. We have some studies on the reception of Aquinas' arguments in connection with the eternity of the world among 13th century thinkers, but the reception of his thought on this point in the 14th century is still largely *terra incognita*.[2] In this study an attempt will be made to map a part, however small, of this unknown country.

For this purpose I shall here discuss the influence Thomas Aquinas exerted on the ideas of the Oxford theologian Henry of Harclay (d. 1317) in his *Quaestio "utrum mundus potuit fuisse ab aeterno"*.[3] From the outset it should be clear that Henry mainly responds negatively to Aquinas' views, but he nevertheless *responds*, and in this sense one can speak of an Aquinas reception.[4]

Beyond the obvious advantage that Harclay explicitly refers to Thomas Aquinas, he is also for some other reasons an interesting objective for this investigation.

At the time Harclay was writing, the Dominican (Thomistic) and Franciscan schools that embodied the great doctrinal controversies were already breaking down in Oxford.[5] Something of this development is reflected in the independent stance he takes vis-à-vis certain positions of Aquinas. As will be confirmed below, Harclay was certainly no representative of the institutionalised Franciscan reaction against Aquinas.

A further advantage to be gained from the study of Aquinas' influence on Harclay is that it will bring us to the crux of the discussion of the world's eternity: the notion of the infinite.

The analysis of the infinite, although in itself a mathematical subject, profited greatly from its theological setting provided in the debate over the world's eternity, but also provided in the debates over God's infinity and over God's knowledge of the infinite.[6] It was especially in this kind of theological context that Aristotle's central definition of "infinite" as "that which cannot be gone through" underwent some interesting revisions, and it is especially from these texts that one may gather the pervasiveness of mathematics throughout later medieval philosophy and theology.[7]

This pervasiveness, by the way, finds a surprising modern parallel in the correspondence undertaken by Georg Cantor (1845–1918), the creator of transfinite set theory, with certain Neo-Thomist theologians working in the spirit of Pope Leo XIII's encyclical *Aeterni Patris*.[8] From this correspondance it becomes apparent that the Neo-Thomist response to Cantor's transfinite set theory was positive. Neo-Thomist theologians of the late 19th century found that Cantor's theory might be reconciled with Catholic understanding of the nature of infinity.[9]

In the later middle ages, however, the interaction between mathematics and theology more often than not revealed itself in the form of a clash, or to put in in the words of Luther "there is no part of philosophy that is so hostile towards theology than mathematics".[10] The stance taken with regard to the possible eternity of the world was guided by the notion of the infinite.[11] As we will see below, something of this clash between theology and mathematics also surfaces in the *Quaestio* of Harclay on the possible eternity of the world.

After having indicated in this way the broader context of the reception of Aquinas' views with regard to the world's eternity, let us now turn to the *Wirkungsgeschichte* itself of his thought. Aquinas' influence on Harclay is confined to two topics. First of all Harclay responds to Aquinas' notion of the infinite that is involved in an eternal past world. Secondly, he responds to Aquinas' interpretation of Aristotle's teaching with regard to the world's eternity.

In connection with this last topic, I shall treat the response to the writings of Aquinas by two other English theologians who, in a broad sense belonged to the intellectual milieu of Harclay: William of Alnwick o.f.m. (d. 1333) and Thomas of Wilton (fl. 1314–1320). The texts selected to be studied here, are Wilton's *Quaestio* "*An ista simul stent, quod motus sit aeternaliter a Deo productus et cum hoc quod Deus sic producit mundum libere, quod potuit ipsum non produxisse*", and Alnwick's *Quaestio* "*Utrum asserere mundum fuisse ab aeterno fuerit de intentione Aristotelis*".[12] As will be shown below, their response to the opinions of Aquinas will turn out to have been a response to the text of Harclay.

1.0 *Infinity and eternity*

The substance of Harclay's reaction to Aquinas is located in a *Quaestio* that treats the possible past eternity of the world (*utrum mundum potuit fuisse ab aeterno*). In this *Quaestio* Henry distinguishes three conceivable positions (*opiniones*): (1) the world had existed from eternity and could not not have existed; (2) the world did not exist from eternity but could have; (3) the world could not have existed from eternity and consequently did not.[13]

On the basis of these three opinions, Harclay's *Quaestio* can be divided into three sections. The first section, which takes up the first opinion, is largely devoted to the interpretation of Aristotle's views on the world's eternity (pp. 231–240 of the edition). According to Harclay, Aristotle taught the world's eternity.

In the second section (p. 242), the briefest of the *Quaestio*, Harclay supports his own opinion: the world and motion could have existed from eternity, since none of the arguments that "demonstrate" the impossibility of the eternity of the world and motion are conclusive and since God in his divine omnipotence could have made the world eternal, for an eternal world does not involve a contradiction.[14]

Section 3 is the most substantial part of Harclay's *Quaestio*. Here, in a part that precedes section 2, he presents the arguments of other thinkers that are supposed to demonstrate that the world could not have existed from eternity (pp. 240–242). After having presented his own opinion (section 2, p. 242), Harclay continues the second part of section 3 with a refutation of these "demonstrative" arguments (pp. 242–255). Most of these arguments concern infinity.

As a matter of fact, Harclay devotes more efforts to understanding the infinite that is involved in an eternal world, than to the problem of the possibility of a past (or future) eternal world as such. The theory of the infinite that Harclay develops here, was frequently criticized as running contrary to the more usual (Aristotelian) position with respect to infinity.[15]

While developing his dissident analysis of the infinite, Harclay explicitly takes notice of certain arguments of Thomas Aquinas. In the first place he criticizes Aquinas' stance with regard to the problem that an eternal world entails the traversal of an infinity. Secondly, Harclay responds to Aquinas' position with regard to unequal infinites.

Both issues were introduced into the debate on the *aeternitas mundi* by Bonaventure. At the time Harclay was writing (beginning of the 14th century), they had become commonplace among thinkers who occupied themselves with the problem of the world's eternity.[16]

In what follows, I shall first discuss Harclay's criticism of Aquinas' position with regard to the traversal of an infinity, and secondly his response to Aquinas' view on unequal infinites.

1.1. *The traversal of an infinite series*

In order to gain a better understanding of Aquinas' and Harclay's arguments, it will be useful to first give a brief outline of Bonaventure's position in this matter.

Bonaventure maintains the opinion that the world could not have existed from eternity and consequently did not, because the notion of an eternal world entails an intrinsic contradiction.[17] Most of his arguments in support of this position amount to showing that an eternal world implies a number of contradictions with regard to the infinite.

One of his inconsistency arguments is based upon the contention that the infinite cannot be traversed: *impossibile est infinita pertransiri*. An eternal world, however, entails an infinite series of past events, or, as Bonaventure puts it, an infinite number of revolutions. So the present could never have been reached.

In the same argument Bonaventure anticipates a possible evasion: those who assert that the infinite series of past events have not been traversed because there is no first event, or that the infinite series of past events could be traversed in an infinite time, must answer the question whether some event preceded the present by an infinite time, or whether none did. If none did, all past events are separated from the present by a finite distance, and therefore the series of past events would have a beginning. If, however, some past event is infinitely distant from today, then what about the one that immediately followed it, and the one that immediately followed upon that one, etc. In this case, one past event would not be further distant from another -for they are all infinitely distant- and they would consequently all be simultaneous.[18] The infinite series of past events cannot be traversed, not even in an infinite time, and so we must conclude that the world has had a beginning.

Let us now turn to Aquinas' argumentation. His version of the "traversal" argument is limited in comparison to Bonaventure's. Aquinas does not go into the possible evasions of the postulate *"impossibile est infinita pertransiri"* that are anticipated upon by Bonaventure.[19]

According to this version of the "traversal" argument an eternal world implies the traversal of infinitely many days or revolutions of the Sun. However, an infinity cannot be traversed, so the world could not have existed from eternity.[20]

In his reply to this argument, Aquinas makes the same two assumptions as Bonaventure: (1) an eternal world entails that the present day has been preceded by an infinite number of days, and (2) the infinite cannot be traversed. However, he does not confirm Bonaventure's conclusion, made on the basis of these two assumptions, that the world could not have existed from eternity.[21] The reason is, that Aquinas denies that an eternal world entails the traversal of an infinity.

According to Aquinas, the infinite number of past days *ab aeterno* can be taken successively, and in this way can be traversed, because any designated past day is separated from the present day by a *finite* number of intermediate days. Suppose that all the past days of an eternal world would have been taken simultaneously, then, according to Aquinas, there would be no question of a traversal. A traversal is always from one terminus to another, but, since the world did not have a beginning in the past, a first terminus is lacking.[22]

Aquinas' argumentation may be summarized as follows. If the world is eternal (*a parte ante*), the past days can be taken all simultaneously, or in succession. If the past days are taken simultaneously, there is no traversal, because a beginning is lacking. If the past days are taken successively, there is a beginning, e.g. because a certain day of the infinitely numerous past days has been designated as such, and thus a traversal of a (finite) stretch: the intermediary between the present day and the designated day from the past.

Put in modern terms, the point of controversy between Bonaventure and Thomas Aquinas is, whether an infinite series of past days contains any day separated from the present day by an infinite number of intermediate days, or not.[23] According to Bonaventure an actually infinite past means, that some past days are separated from the present day by an infinite number of intermediate days. On the basis of the principle that an infinity cannot be traversed, we are confronted with the absurd conclusion that the present day could not have existed.

From Aquinas' remarks on the other hand, it becomes apparent that he is of the opinion that it is quite possible for there to be an infinite number of days that have really occured such, that each of these days is separated from the present day by a *finite* number of intermediate days. Underlying his opinion is the assumption that the infinite number of days is a successive infinity.[24]

Aquinas contents himself here with refuting an argumentation against the eternity of the world, but he does not explicitly assert the possibility of an eternally created world.[25]

Let us now turn to Harclay's criticism of Aquinas. Harclay addresses Aquinas' argument as a stupid evasion (*rudis fuga*).[26] According to Harclay an eternal world does entail the traversal of an infinity: *totum tempus infinitum est pertransitum*.[27] However, it is a traversal that only has one terminus: the present day. The reason is, that the infinite cannot have two termini.[28] The present day acts as beginning of an eternal world *a parte post*, or as end of an eternal world *a parte ante*.[29]

The infinitely numerous past days form a set that is open at one end and closed at the other (the present day being the closure). The set is infinite, because before each past day there was another day, and after each future day there will be another day.

As we have seen, Aquinas held the view that the "infinity" traversed during the world's eternity, really is a finite stretch. Harclay, on the other hand, maintains that an eternal world involves the traversal of an infinity, but a traversal that only has one terminus.

It is of some interest to note here that Harclay's criticism of Aquinas does not fit in the tradition of the *Correctoria* literature. The *Correctorium* (*Fratris Thomae*) of William de la Mare o.f.m. (1297) which was intended to present a correction of the controversial matter from the works of Thomas Aquinas, and which was officially adopted for use by the Friars Minor, only casually mentions that Aquinas did not succeed in solving the argument that an eternal world entails the traversal of an infinity.[30]

Bonaventure, Thomas Aquinas and Henry of Harclay represent three different stances with regard to the traversal of an infinite set. Aquinas tries to argue that an eternal world does not really involve the traversal of an infinite set. He is rebuked for this by Harclay. Both Harclay and Bonaventure agree that an eternal world entails the traversal of an infinity. Bonaventure, on this ground, denies the possibility of an eternal world. Harclay, on the other hand, indicates in what way the traversal of an infinite past (or future), and whence an eternal world, is possible.

1.2. *Unequal infinites*

As has already been noted above, the second point where Harclay mentions the views of Thomas Aquinas, concerns the paradox of unequal infinites.

The paradox was invoked to reject the possibility of an eternal world. During the actual infinite time, the argument commonly read, that would have elapsed since eternity, the number of revolutions of the moon would be unequal to the number of revolutions of the sun; but at the same time, both numbers being infinite, they would also be equal.

The problem at heart here is the problem of the existence of parts of infinites being equal to the whole infinites of which they are parts.[31] For the infinite number of revolutions of the Sun relates as a part to the infinite number of revolutions of the Moon, but they relate as wholes in as far as

they are both infinite. The argument rests on the assumption that all
infinites are equal: infinite equals infinite.

Another argument, frequently employed, which is based upon this
assumption, involves the problem of adding to the infinite. The argument
reads as follows. An eternal world is not possible, for this would mean that
the infinite can be added to, or, in other words, that something can be
greater than the infinite. For instance the infinite past time where the day
of tomorrow will be added to, will be greater than the infinite past time
until today.[32] Harclay's solution of these arguments amounts to a straightforward rejection of the assumption that infinites are equinumerate. He
simply claims that the infinite can be added to and that infinites can be
unequal: the infinite number of revolutions of the moon is greater than the
infinite number of revolutions of the sun.[33]

In order to substantiate his claim of the existence of unequal infinites,
Harclay appeals to the opinion of Aquinas that there can exist *proportionalitas*
(but not *proportio*) between the finite and the infinite.[34] Before turning to
Harclay's argumentation it will be useful to have a closer look at this
opinion of Thomas Aquinas.

As Harclay already indicates, Aquinas' dictum is taken from the *Quaestio*
"whether God knows other things than himself" which occurs in *De veritate*
(q.2 art.3).[35] In one of the arguments of this *Quaestio* (arg.4) the view is
defended that God, by knowing his divine essence cannot know the
creatures, because the divine essence is not proportional (*proportionata*) to
a creature. The reason is that the divine essence exceeds a creature in
infinity and there does not exist a *proportio* between an infinity and
a finity.[36]

In his reply to this argument, Aquinas distinguishes between two senses
of proportionality: *proportio* and *proportionalitas*. He agrees that there does
not exist a proportionality between an infinity and a finite thing in the
sense of *proportio*. However, there does exist proportionality in the sense of
proportionalitas.

From the example Aquinas provides in his text, it is clear that he uses
proportio in its common medieval sense, that is "ratio".[37] According to
Aquinas there exists no ratio of the infinite to the finite.[38]

Proportionalitas, on the other hand, can best be translated as "proportion", as can be gathered from Aquinas' definition and the accompanying
example. Aquinas defines *proportionalitas* as *similitudo proportionum*, that is, as
an equality of ratios.[39] Put in other words, *proportionalitas* is a *similis habitudo
aliquorum duorum ad alia duo*: the ratio of 6 to 3 is the same as the ratio of 8
to 4.[40]

According to Aquinas, nothing prevents the existence of proportionality
between finite and infinite quantities in this last sense of proportionality for

in the same way as one finite quantity equals another finite quantity, in the same way one infinite quantity equals another one.[41]

Unlike the example cited a few lines above, Thomas here only compares equalities, that is ratios of 1 to 1. Apparently comparing infinite quantities means to Thomas comparing equalities.

Let us now see in what way Harclay "applies" Aquinas' argument. At first sight, Harclay takes up Aquinas' *dictum* about the proportionality of an infinite quantity to a finite quantity: *finiti ad infinitum potest esse proporcionalitas, etsi non proporcio.*[42]

However, in the example that serves to clarify the notion of *proportionalitas*, Harclay introduces a completely new element. The proportionality (*proportionalitas*) of the finite to the infinite means, according to Harclay, that the *proportio* of one finite quantity to another finite quantity equals the *proportio* of one infinite quantity to another infinite quantity. In other words, the ratio of eight to four equals the ratio of infinite octuples to infinite quadruples. So, one infinite quantity is greater than another one.[43]

The new element introduced here is the existence of a ratio (*proportio*) other than the ratio of 1 to 1, and hence of an unequality, of one infinite quantity to another infinite quantity. Where Aquinas only compares *equal* finites to *equal* infinites, Harclay also wishes to include other ratios.[44]

Harclay's example is implied by the definition of *proportionalitas* as the equality of the ratio of a to b, to the ratio of c to d. It is nowhere stipulated that this ratio should be a ratio of 1 to 1, as Aquinas tacitly assumes. Harclay's manoevre is prompted by his notion of the infinite, which admits the existence of unequal infinites. In contradistinction to Harclay, Aquinas is of the opinion that all infinites are equal.

Harclay was well aware of the fact that the Euclidean axiom that every whole is greater than its part impeded his acceptance of unequal infinites. However, his attempt to devise a new part-whole axiom that could account for infinites related as equals and unequals, as both wholes and parts, unfortunately failed.[45]

Nevertheless, he made such an attempt and, as North subtly points out, in retrospect we now value more the attempts made to resolve the paradox than those of men who wished to use it to refute an eternal world, or who acknowledged that the concepts of equality and inequality were not applicable to infinites.[46]

Given Harclay's assumption that one infinite can be unequal to another infinite, the argument against the possible existence of an eternal world no longer poses a problem: if the world had existed from eternity, the infinite number of past revolutions of the Moon would indeed be greater than the infinite number of revolutions of the Sun.[47]

2.0 *The medieval interpretation of Aristotle's teaching on the world's eternity*

After having examined Harclay's discussion with Aquinas on the notion of the infinite that is involved in an eternal world, I will now turn to the second topic that receives Harclay's attention: Aquinas' interpretation of Aristotle' teaching with regard to the world's eternity. Two other actors who played a part in this aspect of the reception of Aquinas' thought will also be discussed here: the 14th century theologians Thomas of Wilton and William of Alnwick o.f.m., both of English origin.

I propose to examine first of all Harclay's references to Thomas Aquinas and then, following a presentation of Wilton's and Alnwick's references, I will attempt to show that these go back to Harclay's text.

In the beginning of his *Quaestio* (section 1, p 231) Harclay examines whether it was the intention of Aristotle to prove that the world had existed from eternity. Harclay himself is of the opinion that Aristotle did teach the world's eternity.[48]

He opens, however, with a reference to the view of Thomas Aquinas, according to whom Aristotle did not teach the world's eternity as a demonstrated truth.[49] In support of this contention, Harclay cites some texts of Aquinas, and then informs the reader that actually it was Maimonides from whom Aquinas took his own interpretation of Aristotle. Harclay's claim that Aquinas copied Maimonides is substantiated by some citations of Maimonides' *Guide of the Perplexed*.[50] Harclay furthermore claims that Aquinas' view that the question of the world's eternity or novelty is not susceptible to demonstrative proof, also stems from Maimonides.[51]

The fact that Harclay correctly identifies here Maimonides as the source of Aquinas' view that Aristotle did not teach the world's eternity, and that none of the arguments seeking to prove its *aeternitas* or *novitas* do so with demonstrative force, will not concern us here.[52] What interests us here is the fact that Thomas of Wilton and William of Alnwick remark upon Aquinas' use of Maimonides in a similar fashion as Harclay did, albeit that in their texts any malicious undertones are absent. Let us briefly examine the relevant passages.

Wilton, in a *quaestio de quolibet* on the world's eternity states that it is a point of controversy whether the arguments that Aristotle employed to defend the world's eternity, are demonstrative or probable.[53] He then proceeds with citing Maimonides' opinion that Aristotle did not demonstrate the world's eternity, neither its novelty.[54] As Wilton sees it, the very same position was taken up by Thomas Aquinas:"*Istam autem opinionem tenet frater Thomas per omnia.*"[55] Like Harclay, Wilton makes a connection between the views of Aquinas and Maimonides on this point.

The same is true for William of Alnwick. In a *Quaestio* that forms part of his *Determinationes* and that is especially devoted to the interpretation of Aristotle's stance with regard to the world's eternity, Alnwick states that both Maimonides and Thomas Aquinas judged that the question whether the created world could have been *ab aeterno*, could not be decided by demonstrative arguments.[56]

The striking resemblances presented here, tempt one to conjecture that Wilton and Alnwick borrowed their remarks on Aquinas' interpretation of Aristotle from Henry of Harclay. A hypothesis, indeed, that will not only be corroborated below by further textual evidence, but that also fits in the general historical picture of Harclay and his near contemporary intellectual milieu.

For already Pelster, in his fundamental article on Harclay, drew attention to manuscript evidence from which it could be gathered that Wilton and Alnwick were especially concerned with Harclay's views on infinity and continuity. Their criticism received a more thorough invest-igation in studies by Maier and Murdoch.[58] Furthermore, Maier showed in an elaborate study on William of Alnwick, that in his *Determinationes* he attacks the views of Thomas of Wilton.[59]

The general picture that emerges from these studies is that Wilton was familiar with the views of Harclay, and Alnwick was familiar with the views of both Harclay and Wilton, although explicit references are often absent.

More in particular, Wilton in his *Quaestio* "*An ista simul stent, quod motus sit aeternaliter a Deo productus et cum hoc quod Deus sic producit mundum libere, quod potuit ipsum non produxisse*" shows familiarity with Harclay's *Quaestio* "*Utrum mundus potuit fuisse ab aeterno*", and Alnwick in his *Quaestio* "*Utrum asserere mundum fuisse ab aeterno fuerit de intentione Aristotelis*" appears to be familiar with Harclay's and Wilton's *Quaestiones*.

If we focus again on these three texts, it is not hard to come across passages that reflect this interdependence. In the first place all three texts agree in quite a number of arguments that all amount to proving that Aristotle did in fact teach the world's eternity. One example is a long quotation from Grosseteste's *Hexaëmeron* concerning the interpretation of Aristotle's stance with regard to the world's eternity.[60] A second example concerns an argument where Plato's view regarding the world's eternity is confronted with that of Aristotle.[61] Although this argument is also taken from Grosseteste's *Hexaëmeron*, there are other textual parallels where the hypothesis of one common source, viz. the *Hexaëmeron*, underlying our three texts, fails.[62] These parallels can only be explained by a direct mutual dependence of the texts of Harclay, Wilton and Alnwick.

Alnwick's direct dependence on Wilton is revealed in a long argument

which runs almost *verbatim* the same in both texts and which does not occur
in Harclay's text.[63] For reasons of chronology, a dependence the other way
around must be ruled out: Alnwick's *Disputationes* are dated later than
Wilton's *Quaestio*.[64]

Alnwick's dependence on Harclay's text is most obviously displayed in
a passage where Alnwick presents a series of arguments from and references
to various works of Aristotle. Step by step all these arguments and
quotations from Aristotle are taken from Harclay's text.[65]

Wilton's dependence on Harclay's text, finally, comes to the open in
a passage where Wilton discusses the notion of infinity. In this passage
Wilton cites and afterwards refutes an argument which in the margin of the
manuscript is described as *"opinio magistri Herkeley"*. The fact that this
argument indeed literally occurs in Harclay's *Quaestio*, makes it very likely
that Wilton had Harclay's text at his disposal.[66]

The evidence gathered here, strongly suggests that Wilton had Harclay's
Quaestio at his disposal, and that Alnwick was familiar with both Harclay's
and Wilton's *Quaestiones*.

Where does all this leave us now? If the foregoing hypothesis is correct,
namely that Wilton and Alnwick have borrowed from Harclay's text, this
would mean that they might as well have been borrowing the references to
Aquinas' interpretation of Aristotle's teaching on the world's eternity. And
this in turn means that Wilton's and Alnwick's remarks on Thomas
Aquinas say more about the impact of Harclay's thought, than they do
about the response to Aquinas' thought.[67]

Conclusion

We are now left with the task of evaluating Harclay's response to Thomas
Aquinas. There is no doubt that Harclay approaches the views of Aquinas
negatively, but the important question is whether Harclay's attacks on
Aquinas are part of a general hostile attitude towards him (or the
Dominicans), or whether they should be explained in a different way.[68]

The evidence collected here does not give reason to suppose that Harclay
represents any anti-Thomistic school, and certainly not that he was
a representative of the Franciscan school.[69] His criticism of Aquinas is too
nonconformist for that, and this nonconformism, or even dissent, touches
precisely the heart of Harclay's response to Aquinas. For in all those
instances where Harclay dissociates himself from Aquinas, he has to make
his own philosophical point.

This approach also surfaces very clearly in Harclay's discussion of other
topics where Aquinas' views are criticized, such as his views on the unity of
substantial form, on the immortality of the intellectual soul, and on divine
prescience and predestination.[70]

Harclay's polemic against Aquinas is not different from standard procedures in 14th century commentaries on the *Sentences*. Thomas Aquinas serves as a "try-your-strenght machine" that enables Harclay to develop his own ideas.[71]

Maurer's judgement that Harclay's "vigourous anti-Thomism" is attributable to a mentality of conservatism and Christian orthodoxy, seems to miss this point.[72] Although Maurer's judgement may be true for Harclay's discussion of the plurality of substantial forms, it certainly is not true for this discussion of the traversal of an infinity and of the paradox of unequal infinities.

From both discussions it is evident that Harclay employs a dissident concept of the infinite, and this exactly is the reason why he criticizes Thomas Aquinas: his criticism is guided by genuine philosophical committments, and his polemics against Aquinas reflect one of the more original minds at work in a debate that was overshadowed by conventional notions and arguments.[73]

NOTES

1. Without pretending to present an exhaustive bibliography, we may refer to Craig (1977); Dales (1982); Dunphy (1983); Van Steenberghen (1978); Weisheipl (1983); Wippel (1981); Zimmermann (1976).
2. Among the studies devoted to the response to Aquinas on this point in the 13th century, mention should be made of Brady (1972), (1974); Bukowski (1979); Dales (1982) and Weisheipl (1983).
3. The text is edited in Dales (1984).
4. Pelster (1924), 352–353 was one of the first to notice that Harclay explicitly refers to works of Thomas Aquinas, mostly in order to challenge his views. Maier (1947) in (1964), 51, Murdoch (1981) 236 n. 41 and Dales (1984), 228–229 also draw attention to Harclay's references. However, none of these authors has systematically discussed them.
5. Cf. Catto (1984), esp. 496–513, where he discusses, among other things, the influence of the teaching of Thomas Aquinas on Oxford theology at the end of the 13th and the beginning of the 14th centuries.
6. Cf. Murdoch (1982), 566 and North (1987), 245–247. Cf. also Maier (1947) on the 14th century discussion on the existence of an actual infinite. Note that Maier's article is almost exclusively based upon a study of *theological* texts, which deal with the possible eternality of the world.
7. For other examples cf. Murdoch (1969).
8. Cf. Dauben (1977), and also (1979), 140–148.
9. Cf. Dauben (1977), 96–108 and (1979), 144–148. This interest of Catholic theologians in Cantor's theory particulary bore upon the discussion of God's infinity and not upon the discussion of the world's eternity.
10. The *dictum* "Mathematica est inimicisima omnino theologiae, quia nulla est pars philosophiae, quae tam pugnat contra theologiam" of Luther is cited in Hägglund (1955), 11. For the sake of completeness, it should be mentioned that Luther makes his remark in connection with the theological discussion of the Trinity.
11. Cf. Maier (1947), in (1964), 48 n.21 and 52–53.
12. The text of Wilton was edited by Senko (1964), that of Alnwick by Prezioso (1962). Although Prezioso (1962), 17–19 did notice Alnwick's references to Thomas Aquinas,

he did not discuss them thoroughly. The same is true for Alnwick's references to Thomas in another *Quaestio*, that were noticed by Maier (1947), in (1964), 58. To the best of my knowledge, Wilton's references to Thomas have remained unnoticed.

13. Henry of Harclay, *op. cit.*, 231: "Hic sunt 3 opiniones: una quod mundus fuit ab eterno, nec potuit non fuisse; 2a quod non fuit, potuit tamen fuisse; 3a quod non potuit fuisse, et per consequens non fuit". A different tripartition of conceivable positions can be found in the commentary on the *Sentences* of Giles of Rome: (1) one might assert that eternity of the world is possible; (2) one might maintain that it is not possible to demonstrate the impossibility of the eternity of the world; (3) one might claim only that the impossibility of the eternity of the world has not yet been demonstrated. Cf. Wippel (1981), 22–23.

14. Henry of Harclay, *op. cit.*, p. 242: "2a opinio est quam teneo ad presens: quod mundus et motus poterunt fuisse ab aeterno, non propter aliam racionem nisi quia, ut videtur michi, raciones in oppositum non concludunt necessario, potencie autem divine attribuendum est totum quod scitur non includere contradiccionem vel quod non scitur includere contradiccionem".

15. Harclay was one of the few medieval defenders of the existence of an actual infinite. His theory of the infinite is discussed in Maier (1947), 47–55, Murdoch (1981) and Dales (1984b).

16. Cf. Murdoch (1982), 569–570. The arguments are to be found in Bonaventura, *Commentarius in quattuor libros Sententiarum Petri Lombardi*, II dist.1 pars 1 art.1, q.2, (1938), 12–17.

17. Bonaventura, *op. cit.*: "Respondeo: Dicendum quod ponere mundum aeternum esse sive aeternaliter productum, ponendo res omnes ex nihilo productas, omnino est contra veritatem et rationem, sicut ultima ratio probat; et adeo contra rationem, ut nullum philosophorum quantumcumque parvi intellectus crediderim hoc posuisse. Hoc enim implicat in se manifestam contradictionem".

18. Bonaventura, *op. cit.*: "Tertia propositio est ista. Impossibile est infinita pertransiri; sed si mundus non coepit, infinitae revolutiones fuerunt: ergo impossibile est illas pertransire: ergo impossibile fuit devenire usque ad hanc. Si tu dicas quod non sunt pertransita, quia nulla fuit prima, vel quod etiam bene possunt pertransiri in tempore infinito; per hoc non evades. Quaeram enim a te, utrum aliqua revolutio praecesserit hodiernam in infinitum, an nulla. Si nulla: ergo omnes finite distant ab hac, ergo sunt omnes finitae, ergo habent principium. Si aliqua in infinitum distat, quaero de revolutione, quae immediate sequitur illam, utrum distet in infinitum. Si non: ergo nec illa distat, quoniam finita distantia est inter utramque. Si vero distat in infinitum, similiter quaero de tertia et de quarta et sic in infinitum; ergo non magis distat ab hac una quam ab alia: ergo una non est ante aliam: ergo omnes sunt simul".

19. Van Steenberghen (1978), 168 has pointed out that "le parallelisme entre l'objection de S. Bonaventure et celle que refute S. Thomas est très partiel". It may well be the case that Thomas did not have specifically Bonaventure in mind when developing his argument, but more generally Aristotle's dictum "impossibile est infinita pertransire". Cf. *Anal. Post.* I.22 82 b 38–39 and *De caelo* I.4 272 a 3.

20. I shall here give Aquinas' argument, the way it occurs in the *Summa contra gentiles*. According to Dales, the editor of Harclay's *Quaestio*, this is the text of Aquinas to which Harclay refers. However, the same argument also occurs in the *Summa theologiae* I.46, 2 and in the *Scriptum super libros Sententiarum* II, d.1 q.1 a.5. Harclay does not explicitly mention the text he is referring to. Thomas Aquinas, *Summa contra gentiles* II, 38 arg.4: "Adhuc. Quia infinita non est transire. Si autem mundus semper fuisset, essent iam infinita pertransita: quia quod praeteritum est, pertransitum est; sunt autem infiniti dies vel circulationes solis praeteritae, si mundus semper fuit".

21. For this reason Van Steenberghen (1978), 169 reproaches Thomas with "une singulière logique". No matter how one judges Aquinas' stance, one cannot accuse him of being illogical here.

22. Thomas Aquinas, *op. cit.*,: "Quod etiam tertio ponitur, non est cogens. Nam infinitum, etsi non sit simul in actu, potest tamen esse in successione: quia sic quodlibet infinitum

acceptum finitum est. Quaelibet igitur circulatio praecedentium transiri potuit: quia finita fuit. In omnibus autem simul, si mundus semper fuisset, non esset accipere primam. Et ita nec transitum, qui semper exiget duo extrema".

23. Cf. Smith (1987) for a lucid exposition of the controversy about infinity and the eternal past in contemporary philosophical literature.

24. The positions of Bonaventure and Aquinas have found contemporary defenders in Van Steenberghen (1978) and Zimmermann (1976) respectively. Although it is not my purpose here to examine who is correct in his argumentation, I personally think, contrary to what Van Steenberghen believes, that Thomas did escape Bonaventure's dilemma. Smith (1987), 65 and 72 explains with the help of set theory in what way the members of an infinite set can have a finite distance from one another.

25. Cf. also Wippel (1981), esp. 25–26.

26. Henry of Harclay, *op. cit.*, 244–245: "Ad 5, cum arguitur quod infinitum tempus esset pertransitum, respondet frater Thomas, tenens hanc opinionem quod non est pertransitum ... Ideo non pertransita nisi quantum ad aliquam partem signatam cuius sunt termini. Sed ista responsio nichil valet ... Unde non est nisi rudis fuga, et nichil ad rem". The same qualification is used by William of Alnwick in the *Quaestio* "utrum possibile fuerit entia successiva, ut motum et tempus, fuisse ab aeterno", which forms part of his *Determinationes* (unedited). Cf. Maier (1947), in (1964), 58.

27. Henry of Harclay, *op. cit.*, 245. As has already been noted, Dales identifies this reference as a reference to the *Summa contra gentiles*. Harclay could, however, also have had in mind passages from the *Summa theologiae* or the *Commentary on the Sentences*. Cf. footnote 19.

28. Henry of Harclay, *op. cit.*, 245: "Et racio est quia infinitum non potest habere utrumque terminum, licet posset habere alterum terminorum".

29. Henry of Harclay, *op. cit.*, 245: "Unde si mundus fuisset ab aeterno, non habuisset principium a parte ante, bene tamen haberet terminum a parte post. Sic modo si inciperet in eternum duraturus, haberet principium, sed nunquam finem.

30. The *Correctorium* of William de la Mare was soon followed by a Dominican response in the form of *correctoria coruptorii*, at least three of which were compiled in Oxford. Cf. Roensch (1964), esp. 15–19 and 28–57 and Catto (1984), 499–504. The text of de la Mare's *Correctorium* with regard to the "traversal" argument will here be cited in the version printed together with its Dominican refutation in the *Correctorium coruptorii* "*Quaestione*", ascribed to William of Macclesfield OP. Cf. "*Quaestione*" (1954), 30–32: "Item, ... dicit quod mundum incipisse est de articulis fidei sive credibile non scibile ... In ista positione tria falsa continentur ... Secundum est quod inceptio sive novitas mundi demonstrative probari non potest. Dicimus quod falsum est, quia quamvis inceptio vel novitas mundi non possit demonstrari demonstratione potissima dicente propter quid, potest tamen demonstrari deducendo ad impossibile, de infinitate animarum, si mundus fuit aeternus, et quod infinita sunt pertransita. Ambas istas rationes de transitu infinitorum et infinitate animarum ipse (scil. Thomas Aquinas) ponit in obiciendo pro novitate mundi et conatur eas dissolvere. Sed virtutem infinitam invoco testem, quae Deus est, in conscientia mea, quod nec vere nec apparenter, nec philosophice nec theologice eas dissolvit".

31. Cf. also Murdoch (1981), 235–236 and North (1987), 252–253.

32. Henry of Harclay, *op. cit.*, 241: "6a: quia sequeretur quod infinito possit fieri addicio, quia toti tempori infinito pertransito additur dies crastina, et sic infinito esset aliquid maius".

33. Henry of Harclay, *op. cit.*, 246: "Ad propositum ergo, cum addicio ista fuit ab eterno tempore infinito, quod uni revolucioni solis addite sunt 12 revoluciones lune, sequitur quod nunc sit maior numerus revolucionum lune quam solis ..."

34. Henry of Harclay, *op. cit.*, 247: "Preterea, iste doctor frater Thomas, sic respondens, concedit alibi quod finiti ad infinitum potest esse proporcionalitas, etsi non proporcio".

35. Henry of Harclay, *op. cit.*, 247: "Unde in libro suo quem vocat De veritate in questionibus de sciencia dei, questio prima: "Utrum deus cognoscit alia a se",

respondendo ad 4m argumentum, concedit quod proporcionalia sunt finita et infinita".

36. Thomas Aquinas, *De veritate*, q.2 art.3 arg.4: "Praeterea, medium per quod res cognoscitur debet esse propotionatum ei quod per ipsum cognoscitur; sed essentia divina non est proportionata ipsi creaturae cum in infinitum ipsam excedat, infiniti autem ad finitum nulla sit proportio; ergo Deus cognoscendo essentiam suam non potest cognoscere creaturam".

37. Cf. Sylla (1984) for a survey of the transformation that took place in the terminology of *proportio*.

38. Aquinas' opinion goes back to Aristotle's *dictum* that "finiti ad infinitum nulla est proportio". Cf. *De caelo*, I.6 274 a 7–8.

39. The definition of *proportionalitas* goes back to Book V of Euclid's *Elements* as Harclay rightly adds to his reference to Thomas. Cf. note 42 with regard to this citation from Euclid.

40. Thomas Aquinas, *De veritate, loc. cit.*: "Ad quartum dicendum quod aliquid dicitur proportionatum alteri dupliciter: uno modo quia inter ea attenditur proportio, sicut dicimus quatuor proportionari duobus quia se habet in dupla proportione ad duo; alio modo per modum proportionalitatis, ut si dicamus sex et octo esse proportionata quia sicut sex est duplum ad tria ita octo ad quatuor: est enim proportionalitas similitudo proportionum. Et quia in omni proportione attenditur habitudo ad invicem eorum quae proportionata dicuntur secundum aliquem determinatum excessum unius super alterum, ideo impossibile est infinitum aliquod proportionari finito per modum proportionis; sed in his quae proportionata dicuntur per modum proportionalitatis non attenditur habitudo eorum ad invicem sed similis habitudo aliquorum duorum ad alia duo . . . "

41. Thomas Aquinas, *op. cit.*: " . . . et sic nihil prohibet esse proportionatum infinitum finito quia sicut quoddam finitum est aequale cuidam finito ita infinitum est aequale alteri infinito".

42. Cf. note 39. For the definition of *proportionalitas* as the equality of ratios (*similitudo proportionum*) Harclay refers the reader to Book V of Euclid's *Elements*. Although some Greek manuscripts do contain this definition, Heath (1956), II, 119 considers it to be an interpolation. Be this as it may, the whole Latin Euclid tradition does present the definition *proportionalitas est similitudo proportionum* in Book V in between the definitions 3 and 4. Cf. Cunningham (1972).

43. Henry of Harclay, *op. cit.*, 247: "Igitur qualem proporcionem habet unum finitum ad alium finitum, talem habere potest unum infinitum ad aliud infinitum. Sicut igitur 8 sunt in dupla proporcione ad 4, sic infiniti octonarii sunt in dupla proporcione ad infinitos quaternarios. Igitur unum infinitum est maius alio.

44. Also in his *Quaestio* on the possible *future* eternity of the world (utrum mundus potuit durare in eternum a parte post), Harclay asserts that one "infinite number can stand to another infinite number in any numeral or non-numeral ratio". Cf. Murdoch (1981), 240.

45. Cf. Murdoch (1981), 239–240.

46. Cf. North (1987), 252–253. Here, in a nutshell we have a summary of the three different ways thinkers coped with the paradox of unequal infinites. Cf. also Murdoch (1982b), 168–170.

47. An even stronger expression of Harclay's conviction that infinites can be unequal is provided in the following passage. Cf. Henry of Harclay, *op.cit.*, 251: "Respondeo igitur ad consimilia argumenta, et concedo quod plures essent revoluciones lune quam solis, et similiter quod si mundus fuisset ab eterno, quod duracio solis prolixior esset duracione totali infinita omnium hominum, et quod unum infinitum unius racionis potest esse maius alio infinito eiusdem racionis, sicut una linea alia si utraque esset infinita, et una multitudo alia multitudine, licet utraque sit infinita.

48. Henry of Harclay, *op. cit.*, 234: "Contra hoc. Quod (Dales edition here reads "Contra hoc quod . . .") de intencione Aristotilis fuit ponere eternitatem mundi probatur sine condicione, non solum in 8 Physicorum, sed in 12 Metaphysice . . ." The section

continues until p. 237 with an enumeration of arguments that prove that Aristotle did defend the world's eternity,

49. Henry of Harclay, *op. cit.*,231: " De prima opinione (scilicet quod mundus fuit ab aeterno) est dubium an fuerit de intencione Aristotilis. Dicit enim frater Thomas quod non fuit proprie intencio eius ostendere nec affirmare eternitatem, quod probat auctoritate, signo, et persuasione." Note, however, that Aquinas in his *De aeternitate mundi* became convinced, contrary to his earlier view and to Maimonides, that Aristotle really thought that he had demonstrated the world's eternity. Cf. Weisheipl (1983), 270. This makes it unlikely that Harclay used, or perhaps even knew, *De aeternitate mundi*.

50. Henry of Harclay, *op. cit.*, 232–233: "Ex hiis igitur concludit quod non fuit intencio Aristotilis asserere mundi eternitatem. Ista opinio originem habuit a Raby Moyse libro *De duce neutrorum* id est *dubitancium*. Dicit enim ... (p. 233) ... Patet igitur manifeste quod frater Thomas habet opinionem istam totaliter ab alio."

51. Henry of Harclay, *op. cit.*, 233: "Preterea, idem frater Thomas dicit quod ad neutram partem sunt demonstraciones .... Hoc eciam dictum accipit a Raby Moyse, qui dicit ... "

52. For Aquinas' use of Maimonides in this matter cf. Dunphy (1983), esp. 373–374, and further Dales (1982), 316 and (1984), 228.

53. Thomas of Wilton, *Quaestio de quolibet "An ista simul stent, quod motus sit aeternaliter a Deo productus et cum hoc quod Deus sic producit mundum libere, quod potuit ipsum non produxisse"*, (1964), 157 1.39–43: "Postmodum probat Philosophus idem, quod motus semper esset, utendo eadem ratione, qua utebatur ad probandum, quod motus semper fuit. Et licet certum sit, quod haec sit sententia Aristotelis, tamen utrum ipse huic conclusioni firmiter tamquam conclusioni demonstratae adhaeserit, vel solummodo istas rationes adduxerit tamquam rationes probabiles, probabiliores rationibus alterius partis, in hoc est controversia."

54. Thomas of Wilton. *op. cit.*, 157–158:"Rabbi Moyses enim in superlecta in secundo libro suo *De duce neutrorum* vel *dubium*, capitulum 60, dicit, quod Aristoteles non inducit demonstrationem super antiquitatem mundi, et quod bene scit, quod nec habuit demonstrationem ad hoc probandum ... (p. 158) ... Dicit etiam Rabbi Moyses capitulo 17o, quod rationes, quas faciunt alii ad probandum novitatem mundi, non reputat demonstrationes."

55. Cf. Thomas of Wilton, *op. cit.*, p. 158, following the passage cited in the foregoing footnote.

56. William of Alnwick, Quaestio *"Utrum asserere mundum fuisse ab aeterno fuerit de intentione Aristotelis"*, (1962), 39–40: "In solvendo istam quaestionem sic procedam: primo ponam opinionem dicentium quod non fuerit de intentione Aristotelis per rationem necessariam et demonstrativam, asserere mundi aeternitatem, nec alicuius quod est in mundo ... Quantum ad primum est opinio Thomae et Rabbi Moysis iudaei, quod Aristoteles non intendebat demonstrare, nec demonstrative asserere mundum, aut motum aut tempus fuisse ab aeterno, non quod huic conclusioni adhaesit tamquam conclusioni demonstratae, sed quod intendebat solum rationes probabiliores inducere, quam alii ponentes mundi novitatem ... (p. 40) ... Hanc opinionem, ut videtur, sensit Thomas ex dictis Rabbi Moysis iudaei in libro *De duce neutrorum*, id est *dubiorum* ... "

57. Cf. Pelster (1924), 328–329.

58. Cf. Maier (1947) in (1964), 55–59 and (1960) in (1964), 313–315 and Murdoch (1974), 26–27; (1981), 221, 240, 258 and (1982), 571–572.

59. Cf. Maier (1949) in (1964).

60. Robert Grosseteste, *Hexaëmeron*, I c.8, 2 (1982), 58 1.25–59 1.6: "Sunt tamen quidam moderni, vanius istis philosophantes, immo demencius istis desipientes, qui dicunt maxime Aristotilem non sensisse mundum carere temporis inicio, sed eum in hoc articulo catholice sensisse, et temporis et mundi inicium posuisse; quos arguit manifeste ipsa litera Aristotilis, et media inducta ad eius conclusionem, et ultima libri sui conclusio quam intendit probare de motore primo per motus perpetuitatem.

Expositores quoque omnes eiusdem loci Aristotiles, tam greci quam arabes, dictum
locum de perpetuitate motus et temporis et mundi, id est eorum duracione ex parte
utraque in infinitum, concorditer exponunt" and further *op. cit.* I c.8, 4, (1982), 61
1.2–11: "Hec adduximus contra quosdam modernos, qui nituntur contra ipsum
Aristotilem et suos expositores et sacros et simul expositores de Aristotile heretico facere
catholicum, mira cecitate et presumpcione putantes se limpidius intelligere et verius
interpretari Aristotilem ex litera latina corrupta quam philosophos, tam gentiles quam
catholicos, qui eius literam incorruptam originalem grecam plenissime noverunt. Non
igitur se decipiant et frustra desudent ut Aristotilem faciant catholicum, ne inutiliter
tempus suum et vires ingenii consumant, et Aristotilem catholicum constituendo, se
ipsos hereticos faciant". The quotation can be found in Henry of Harclay *op. cit.*
236–237 and William of Alnwick, *op. cit.*, 49. Alnwick also cites the same phrase that
Harclay uses to connect these two quotations from Grosseteste: "Et statim adducit
auctoritates praedictas sanctorum pro se et postea concludit sic: "Haec adduximus . . . "
Wilton, *op. cit.*, 159 1.39–46 only cites the second part of the passage taken from
Grosseteste (= p. 61 1.2–11). Maier (1947) in (1964), 58 n.42 and (1949) in (1964), 24
already pointed out this citation. She did not notice, however, that Wiltons's citation
only partially corresponds to the one of Harclay and Alnwick.

61. Cf. Robert Grosseteste, *op. cit.* 1 c.9, 2, p. 63 1.17–33 which recurs in Henry of Harclay,
    op. cit. , 238–239, Thomas of Wilton, *op. cit.* , 165 1.10–20 and William of Alnwick, *op.
    cit.*, 33.

62. Grosseteste's place in medieval discussions of the world's eternity is investigated in
    Dales (1986). The article, however, is not specifically about Grosseteste's influence on
    Harclay, Alnwick or Wilton.

63. Compare William of Alnwick, *op. cit.*, 42–42 to Thomas of Wilton, *op. cit.*, 158 1.21–46.

64. Maier (1964), 279 dates Wilton's *Quodlibet* around 1315, whereas Alnwick's *Disputa-
    tiones* are dated around 1322. Cf. Maier (1949) in (1964), 1.

65. Compare Henry of Harclay, *op. cit.*, 234–235 to William of Alnwick *op. cit.*, 44–45. It is
    striking to observe that in a number of instances where Alnwick borrows from Harclay,
    his text, as edited by Prezioso, does not exactly agree with the critical edition of
    Harclay's text, but with the variant reading of manuscript B (= Vatican Borghese 171,
    fols. 22v–24v). Perhaps superfluously, it should be mentioned that Alnwick's
    borrowings from Harclay's text do not occur in Wilton's text.

66. Thomas of Wilton, *op. cit.*, 172: "Ad sextum respondet unus doctor subtilis dicens, quod
    necesse est concedere concedenti aeternitatem motus corporum caelestium, quod
    plures fuerunt revolutiones solis quam lunae ex ea parte etiam, qua utraeque
    revolutiones sunt infinitae. Similiter dicit quod duratio solis ex parte praeteriti
    prolixior est duratione totali infinita omnium hominum praeteritorum et quod
    infinitum eiusdem rationis potest esse maius infinito eiusdem rationis, ut in lineis, si
    essent infinitae. Dicet etiam: non esset dubium, si quantitas aliqua esset vel esse posset
    infinita, quin in ea esset totum et pars excedens et excessum. Et per hoc solvit ad
    inconvenientia, quae deducuntur ex aeternitate motus vel temporis, scilicet quod pars
    sit aequalis vel maior toto". This passage occurs in Henry of Harclay, *op. cit.*, 251.

67. Alnwick's qualification of an argument of Thomas Aquinas as "*rudis fuga*", in another
    (unedited) *Quaestio*, points in the same direction, for he uses exactly the same words as
    Harclay. See note 26.

68. Pelster, who already remarked upon Harclay's attacks on Aquinas, suggests that
    perhaps Harclay's difficulties with the Dominicans as a university administrator,
    played a role in his hostile attitude. Cf. Pelster (1924), 314–316 and 352–353.

69. Pelster (1924), 353 also doubted that Harclay in his criticism of Thomas belonged to
    a certain "school".

70. Cf. Henninger (1980) and Maurer (1957), (1966) and (1974).

71. Harclay's theory of the infinite certainly confirms this observation. With regard to the
    problem of the world's eternity, however, the situation is more delicate. Dales (1984),
    223 claims that Harclay maintains the view of Aquinas: the existence of an eternal
    world is possible. From the careful study of Wippel (1981), however, it is clear that

Aquinas in no text prior to his *De aeternitate mundi* maintains positively and without qualification that an eternal world is possible. So, on this point too Harclay's and Aquinas' views seem to diverge.

72. Maurer, (1974), 128.

73. Dales (1984b), 301 also remarks upon Harclay's creative approach to his sources. He underestimates, however, Harclay's influence. For a more appreciative judgement cf. Murdoch (1981), 221–222, who points out that Harclay's view are mentioned (and refuted) not only by Wilton and Alnwick, but also by such important thinkers as Adam Wodeham, Crathorn, Michael of Massa and Thomas Bradwardine.

LIST OF WORKS CITED

A) *Medieval Works*

Bonaventura, *Commentarius in quattuor libros Sententiarum Petri Lombardi*; Editio minor; Opera theologica selecta. Quaracchi, 1938.

Le Correctorium coruptorii "Questione"; ed. J-P. Muller. Roma, 1954.

Henry of Harclay, *Quaestio "Utrum mundus potuit fuisse ab aeterno"*; ed. R.C. Dales, *Archives d'histoire doctrinale et littéraire du moyen âge*, 50, 223–255.

Robert Grosseteste, *Hexaëmeron*; ed. by R.C. Dales and S. Gieben o.f.m. Cap. London, 1982 (Auctores Britannici Medii Aevi VI).

Thomas Aquinas, *De veritate*; ed. R.M. Spiazzi *et al.* Roma, 1964.

Summa contra Gentiles; ed. Leonine vols. 13–15. Citta del Vaticano, 1934.

Thomas of Wilton, *Quaestio"An ista simul stent, quod motus sit aeternaliter a Deo productus et cum hoc quod Deus sic producit mundum libere, quod potuit ipsum non produxisse"*; ed. W. Senko, *Studia Mediewistyczne*, 5, 1964, 156–190.

William of Alnwick, o.f.m., *L'eternità Aristotelica del mondo in una "Quaestio" inedita di Guglielmo Alnwick (d. 1333)*; ed. F.A. Prezioso. Padova, 1962.

B) *Contemporary Works*

Brady, I (1972). The Questions of Master William of Baglione o.f.m. *De aeternitate mundi* (Paris 1266–67), *Antonianum*, 42, 368–375.

—— (1974). John Peckham and the Background of Aquinas's *De aeternitate mundi*, in *St. Thomas Aquinas 1274–1974*; ed. A.A. Maurer, vol. 2. Toronto.

Bukowski, T (1979). J. Peckham, T. Aquinas et al., on the Eternity of the World, *Recherches de Théologie ancienne et médiévale*, 46, 216–221.

Catto, J.I. (1984), Theology and Theologians 1220–1320, in *The History of the University of Oxford*, vol. 1. Oxford.

Craig, W.L. (1977). The Cosmological Argument and the Possibility of Infinite Temporal Regression, *Archiv für Geschichte der Philosophie*, 59, 261–279.

Cunningham, T.J. (1972). *Book V of Euclid's Elements in the twelfth century. The arabic-latin traditions*. Ph.D. thesis Univ. of Wisconsin.

Dales, R.C. (1982). Maimonides and Boethius of Dacia on the Eternity of the World, *The New Scholasticism*, 56, 306–319.

—— (1984). See Henry of Harclay.

—— (1984b). Henry of Harclay on the Infinite, *Journal of the History of Ideas*, 45, 295–301.

—— (1986). Robert Grosseteste's Place in Medieval Discussions of the Eternity of the world, *Speculum*, 61, 544–563.

Dauben, J.W. (1977). Georg Cantor and Pope Leo XIII: Mathematics, Theology and the Infinite, *Journal of the History of Ideas*, 38, 85–109.

—— (1979). *Georg Cantor. His Mathematics and Philosophy of the Infinite*. Cambridge, Mass.

Dunphy, W. (1983). Maimonides and Aquinas on Creation. A Critique of their Historians, in *Graceful Reason*; ed. by L.P. Gerson. Toronto.

Hägglund, B. (1955). *Theologie und Philosophie bei Luther und in der Occamistischen Tradition.* Lund.

Heath, T.L. (1956). *The thirteen books of Euclid's Elements*; translated . . . by Sir. T.L. Heath. 3 vols. New York.

Henninger, M.C. (1980). Henry of Harclay's Questions on Divine Prescience and Predestination, *Franciscan Studies*, 40, 167–244.

Maier, A. (1947). Diskussionen über das aktuell Unendliche in der ersten Hälfte des 14. Jahrhundert, in Maier (1964), 41–85.

—— (1949). Wilhelm von Alnwicks Bologneser Quaestionen gegen den Averroismus (1323), in Maier (1964), 1–40.

—— (1960). Der anonyme Sententiarus des Borgh. 346, in Maier (1964), 307–334.

—— (1964). *Ausgehendes Mittelalter.* Vol. 1. Roma.

Maurer, A.A. (1957). Henry of Harclay's Questions on Immortality, *Mediaeval Studies*, 19, 79–107.

—— (1966). St. Thomas and Henry of Harclay on Created Nature, in *La filosofia della natura nel mediaevo.* Milano.

—— (1974). Henry of Harclay's Disputed Question on the Plurality of Forms, in *Essays in honour of A.C. Pegis*; ed. J.R. O'Donnell. Toronto.

Murdoch, J.E. (1969). *Mathesis in Philosophiam Scholasticam Introducta.* The Rise and Development of the Application of Mathematics in Fourteenth Century Philosophy and Theology, in *Arts Liberaux et Philosophie au Moyen Age.* Montreal.

—— (1974). Naissance et développement de l'atomisme au bas moyen âge latin, in *La science de la nature: théories et pratiques.* Montreal.

—— (1981). Henry of Harclay and the Infinite, in *Studi sul XIV secolo in memoria di Anneliese Maier*; ed. A. Maieru e A. Paravicini Bagliani. Roma.

—— (1982). Infinity and Continuity, in *The Cambridge History of Later Medieval Philosophy*; ed. by N. Kretzmann, A. Kenny, J. Pinborg. Cambridge.

—— (1982b). William of Ockham and the Logic of Infinity and Continuity, in *Infinity and Continuity in Ancient and Medieval Thought*; ed. N. Kretzmann. Ithaca, N.Y.

North, J.D. (1987). Eternity and Infinity in Late Medieval Thought, in *L'Infinito nella Scienza*; ed. G. Toraldo di Francia. Roma.

Pelster, F. (1924). Heinrich von Harclay, Kanzler von Oxford und seine Quästionen, in *Miscellanea Francesco Ehrle.* Vol. I. Roma.

Preziozo, F.A. (1962) see William of Alnwick.

Roensch, F.J. (1964). *Early Thomistic School.* Dubuque, Iowa.

Smith, Q. (1987). Infinity and the Past, *Philosophy of Science*, 54, 63–75.

Van Steenberghen, F. (1978). Le mythe d'un monde éternel, *Revue Philosophique de Louvain*, 76, 157–179.

Sylla, E. (1984). Compounding ratios. Bradwardine, Oresme, and the first edition of Newton's *Principia*, in *Transformation and Tradition in the Sciences*; ed. by E. Mendelsohn. Cambridge.

Weisheipl, J.A. (1983). The Date and Context of Aquinas' *De aeternitate mundi*, in *Graceful Reason*; ed. L.A. Gerson. Toronto.

Wippel, J.F. (1981). Did Thomas Aquinas Defend the Possibility of an Eternally Created World? (The *De aeternitate Mundi* Revisited), *Journal of the History Philosophy*, 19, 21–39.

Zimmermann, A. (1976). "Mundus est aeternus". Zur Auslegung dieser These bei Bonaventura und Thomas von Aquin, in *Die Auseinandersetzungen an der Pariser Universität im XIII. Jahrhundert*; ed. A. Zimmermann. Berlin.